Why Do You Need This New Edition?

6 good reasons why you should buy this
new edition of *The Curious Writer*!

1. New readings: 24 new readings include visual selections, student sample papers, and professional essays on topics such as social media, digital culture, gaming, and sustainability. Notable new readings include Buzz Bissinger's provocative proposal, "Why College Football Should Be Banned"; Edward Tufte's famous argument, "Why PowerPoint is Evil"; and a new cluster of readings on Facebook and depression.

2. New visuals: All-new *Prose+* readings in every project chapter feature visual models like graphic novels, photo essays, infographics, and slide presentations.

3. New projects: New assignments for every project chapter provide options to extend your writing into visual and digital projects. These new features encourage you to see how each assignment can be re-imagined as a project that includes visual, graphic, and even audio elements.

4. New digital learning options: MyLab media icons in each chapter direct you to online content including video tutorials, animations, and activities. These online learning experiences help you explore chapter content and master the learning objectives for each chapter.

5. New learning objectives: Every chapter opens with a set of learning objectives so you can predict what skills and strategies you'll be learning in the chapter. Marginal annotations connect discussions in the text to each chapter-opening objective and are supported by end-of-chapter "Using What You Have Learned" summaries to help you apply what you've learned in your own writing.

6. New student sample papers: Great new sample papers by real students, including a personal essay on military service in Iraq, a reflection on reality TV, a review of the film *Young Adult,* and more, demonstrate how peers have implemented different writing strategies in their own compositions.

PEARSON

THE CURIOUS WRITER

THE CURIOUS WRITER

Brief Fourth Edition

Bruce Ballenger

Boise State University

PEARSON

Boston   Columbus   Indianapolis   New York   San Francisco   Upper Saddle River
Amsterdam   Cape Town   Dubai   London   Madrid   Milan   Munich   Paris   Montréal   Toronto
Delhi   Mexico City   São Paulo   Sydney   Hong Kong   Seoul   Singapore   Taipei   Tokyo

Senior Acquisitions Editor: Lauren A. Finn
Senior Development Editor: Michael Greer
Editorial Assistant: Shannon Kobran
Senior Supplements Editor: Donna Campion
Senior Media Producer: Stefanie Snajder
Senior Marketing Manager: Sandra McGuire
Production Manager: Eric Jorgensen
Project Coordination, Text Design, and Composition: Integra
Electronic Page Makeup: Integra
Cover Design: John Callahan
Cover Image: Exactostock/SuperStock
Photo Research: Integra
Image Manager: Jorgensen Fernandez
Senior Manufacturing Buyer: Dennis J. Para
Printer and Binder: RRD-Crawfordsville
Cover Printer: Lehigh/Phoenix Color/Hagerstown

This title is restricted to sales and distribution in North America only.

For permission to use copyrighted material, grateful acknowledgment is made to the copyright holders on pp. CR-1 to CR-4, which are hereby made part of this copyright page.

Library of Congress Cataloging-in-Publication Data
Ballenger, Bruce P.
    The curious writer/Bruce Ballenger.—4th ed.
      p. cm.
    Includes bibliographical references and index.
    ISBN 978-0-205-23577-3—ISBN 978-0-205-87665-5 (Brief ed.)—ISBN 978-0-205-87664-8
(Concise ed.)
    1. English language—Rhetoric—Handbooks, manuals, etc.   2. Interdisciplinary approach in
education—Handbooks, manuals, etc.   3. Academic writing—Handbooks, manuals, etc.   I. Title.
    PE1408.B37 2012
    808'.042—dc23
                                                                    2012028008

Copyright © 2014, 2011, 2008, 2005 by Pearson Education.

Full (Hardcover) Edition
13-Digit ISBN: 978-0-205-23577-3
10-Digit ISBN: 0-205-23577-8

2 3 4 5 6 7 8 9 10—DOC—15 14 13

Brief (Softcover) Edition
13-Digit ISBN: 978-0-205-87665-5
10-Digit ISBN: 0-205-87665-X

Concise (Softcover) Edition
13-Digit ISBN: 978-0-205-87664-8
10-Digit ISBN: 0-205-87664-1

PEARSON

Contents

Part 2 INQUIRY PROJECTS   69

Chapter 3 Writing a Personal Essay   71

Chapter 5 Writing a Review   155

Part 4 RE-INQUIRING 531

Preface

I have a friend, a painter, who teaches art at my university, and his introductory courses teach the sub-skills of painting, things like how to use a brush, mix paints, and understand color theory. Common sense suggests that such fundamentals are the starting place for any creative activity, including writing. But college writers walk into our classes with a lifetime of language use. They already know a lot about making meaning with words, more than they think they know. Yet there is much to teach, and perhaps the most powerful thing is that writing isn't just for getting down what you know but discovering what you think. I've learned to never underestimate the power of this, and that's why discovery is the beating heart of this book.

What's New in This Edition?

This fourth edition represents a substantial revision. Building on suggestions from teachers using the third edition, I have made revisions throughout with the overall aim of improving the book's teachability and appeal for students, including:

- **NEW multimodal assignment options** for every project chapter provide options to encourage students to see how each assignment can be re-imagined as a project that includes visual, graphic, and even audio elements. The fourth edition provides new support for these multimodal projects by including technical tips on designing web pages, using audio software, and publishing online.

- **NEW *Prose+* readings** in every project chapter feature visual models such as infographics, slide presentations, photo essays, graphic novels, and other visual genres.

- **NEW expanded treatment of how to craft an inquiry question:** Recognizing that the success of any inquiry project depends on the quality of the questions behind it, the fourth edition explains how questions of "fact" can evolve into questions that require judgment. Every assignment is framed by the inquiry questions relevant to the genre, which gives each project a clear purpose.

- **NEW readings selections:** 24 new readings appear in the fourth edition, including visual and multimodal selections, student sample papers, and professional essays on topics including social media, digital culture, gaming, and sustainability. Notable new readings include Roger Ebert's review of *A Christmas Story*; Buzz Bissinger's provocative proposal, "Why College Football Should Be Banned"; Edward Tufte's famous argument,

"Why PowerPoint is Evil"; a new short story by Gish Gen, "Who's Irish?"; and a new cluster of readings on Facebook and depression in Chapter 10, Writing a Research Essay.

- **NEW focus on learning outcomes:** Every chapter in the fourth edition opens with a series of Learning Objectives tied to the inquiry-based approach of the book and grounded in the principles of the WPA outcomes for first-year composition. These learning objectives are highlighted by annotations in the margins that help connect discussions in the text to each objective and are supported by "Using What You Have Learned" summaries at the end of each chapter, helping students apply strategies in their own writing.

- **NEW digital learning options:** MyLab media icons in each chapter direct students to online content including video tutorials, animations, and activities. These online learning experiences help students explore and engage with chapter content and master the learning objectives for each chapter.

Inquiry in the Writing Classroom

Most of us already teach inquiry, although not all may realize it. For instance, our writing classes invite students to be active participants in making knowledge in the classroom through peer review workshops. When we ask students to fastwrite or brainstorm, we encourage them to suspend judgment and openly explore their feelings or ideas. And when we ask students to see a draft as a first look at a topic, and revision as a means of discovering what they may not have noticed, we teach a process that makes discovery its purpose. Indeed, most composition classrooms create a "culture of inquirers" rather than passive recipients of what their teachers know.

Historically, composition teachers have struggled to decide what besides reading and writing skills students can export to their other classes and, later, into their lives. Often we vaguely refer to "critical-thinking" skills. *The Curious Writer* offers a comprehensive approach for teaching inquiry.

For inquiry-based courses on any subject, there are five key actions I believe instructors should take:

1. Create an atmosphere of mutual inquiry. Students are used to seeing their teachers as experts who know everything that students need to learn. But in an inquiry-based classroom instructors are learners too. They ask questions not because they already know the answers but because there might be answers they haven't considered.

2. Emphasize questions before answers. The idea that student writers begin with an inflexible thesis or a firm position on a topic before they engage in the process of writing and thinking is anathema to inquiry-based learning. Questions, not preconceived answers, lead to new discoveries.

3. Encourage a willingness to suspend judgment. Student culture at most schools works against this. Papers get written at the last minute, multiple deadlines in multiple classes compete for students' time, and multiple-choice

tests or lecture courses imply that there is one true answer and the teacher knows it. To suspend judgment demands that we trust the process that will lead us to new insights. This requires both faith in the process and the time to engage in it. The composition course, with its emphasis on process, is uniquely suited to nurture such faith.

4. Introduce a strategy of inquiry. It's not enough to simply announce that we're teaching an inquiry-based class. We have to introduce students to the strategy of inquiry we'll be using. In the sciences, the experimental method provides a foundation for investigations. What guidance will we give our students in the composition course? *The Curious Writer* features a strategy that is genuinely multidisciplinary, borrowing from science, social science, and the humanities.

5. Present inquiry in a rhetorical context. An essay, a research project, an experiment, any kind of investigation is always pursued with particular purposes and audiences in mind. In an inquiry-based class, the situation in which the inquiry project is taking place is always considered.

You'll find all of these elements of inquiry-based learning integrated in *The Curious Writer*. For example, each assignment in Part 2, "Inquiry Projects," leads students toward writing subjects that offer the most potential for learning. Rather than write about what they already know, students are always encouraged to choose a topic that they want to find out more about. In addition, the discussion questions that follow the student and professional essays are crafted to do more than simply test their comprehension of the piece or reduce it to a single theme. In many cases, questions are open ended and can lead students in many directions as they analyze a reading. *The Curious Writer* maintains a voice and persona throughout the book that suggests that I am working along with the students as a writer and a thinker, which is exactly the experience of mutual inquiry I try to create in my classes. Finally, *The Curious Writer* is organized around a strategy of inquiry that is present in every assignment and nearly every exercise. Introduced in Part 1, "The Spirit of Inquiry," I call on the model often in every subsequent chapter. The inquiry strategy is the thematic core of the book.

The Inquiry Strategy of *The Curious Writer*

A strategy of inquiry is simply a process of discovery. In the sciences, this process is systematic and often quite formal. The model I use in this book borrows from science in some ways through its insistence on continually looking closely at the "data" (sensory details, facts, evidence, textual passages, and so on) and using it to shape or test the writer's ideas about a subject. But the heart of the model is the alternating movement between two modes of thinking—creative and critical—in a dialectical process. One way of describing this is shifting back and forth between suspending judgment and making judgments (see Figure A).

This inquiry strategy works with both reading and writing, but in Chapter 2, "Reading as Inquiry," I offer four categories of questions—those that explore, explain, evaluate, and reflect—that I think will help guide students in reading most texts more strategically. These types of questions will be most evident in the follow-up questions to the many readings throughout *The Curious Writer*.

Finally, a strategy of inquiry is useful only if it makes sense to students; I've tried very hard, particularly in the first section of the book, to make the model comprehensible.

Other Features

Because the inquiry-based approach is central to *The Curious Writer*, it's crucial for students to work through the first two chapters in Part 1, "The Spirit of Inquiry." Part 2—the largest—focuses on "inquiry projects." The range of assignments in this part should satisfy the needs of most composition instructors. If your university is lucky enough to have a two-semester sequence, *The Curious Writer* includes assignments suitable for both courses, including personal, argument, and research essays. Also included is the ethnographic essay, a form that engages students in field research; *The Curious Writer* is the first major text to include ethnography.

The book's focus on genres of writing also makes it appealing for advanced composition courses. For example, assignments such as the profile, review, and proposal help students see how to apply what they've learned to distinct rhetorical situations and help them to understand how those situations shape the genres.

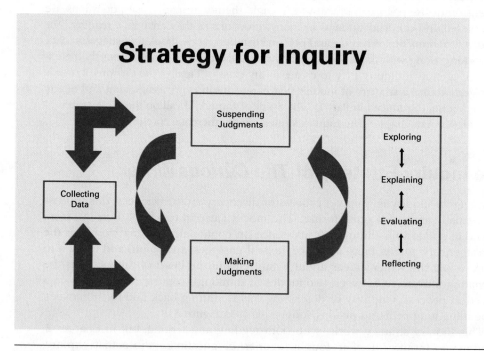

Figure A   In nearly every assignment in *The Curious Writer*, students will use this strategy of inquiry.

In recent years, I've become interested in reading strategies, a topic that I never mentioned as a novice teacher. There was simply so much to say about the writing process that I didn't think reading was a topic that should get much airtime. Yet, as in writing, students bring many prior beliefs and assumptions about reading into our classrooms, and because reading is always an important part of teaching writing, I've come around to talking more about it. *The Curious Writer* reflects this. Chapter 2, "Reading as Inquiry," is devoted to the topic. I've also expanded the discussion to reading images. This emphasis on visual rhetoric echoes the latest developments in composition in response to the growth of the Web and the growing visual literacy of our students.

Finally, the approach of *The Curious Writer* grows in part from my own scholarship on research writing, particularly the criticism that research is too often isolated in the writing course. Students understandably get the idea that research is reserved only for the research paper if they're asked to do it only when they're assigned a research project. This book makes research a part of every assignment, from the personal essay to the proposal, emphasizing that it is a useful source of information, not a separate genre.

This is the third textbook I've written with the "curious" moniker. Because all are inquiry-based, the word is a natural choice. And although I'm very interested in encouraging my students to be curious researchers, readers, and writers, I also hope to remind my colleagues who use the books that we should be curious, too. We should model for our students our own passion for inquiring into the world. We should also celebrate what we can learn from our students, and not just about writing, or the many topics they might choose to write about. I'm curious every time I walk into the writing classroom what my students will teach me about myself. That's a lifetime inquiry project for all of us, as teachers and as people.

Approaches to Teaching with the Book

The Instructor's Manual, written by my colleague Michelle Payne, will give you detailed suggestions about ways to teach *The Curious Writer*. Here are a few additional suggestions drawn with a much broader stroke.

I organized the book to span, if necessary, a two-semester composition course, though it can easily be adapted to one semester. Typically, in a two-semester sequence the first course focuses on the writing process, exposition, critical analysis, writing to learn, and so on. The second semester often focuses on argument and research. A single-semester composition course tries to combine them all. Fortunately, *The Curious Writer* is extremely flexible, with ample material to keep students busy for one or two semesters.

Sequence

Whether you use this book for one course or two, it's wise to introduce *The Curious Writer* to students by first working through Part 1, "The Spirit of Inquiry," because this section lays the foundation for all that follows. The many exercises in these chapters will help students experience firsthand what we mean by inquiry. Part 2, "Inquiry Projects," is the heart of the book. I've organized chapters in an order that roughly follows typical composition courses, beginning with genres that draw heavily on students' personal experiences and observations and then moving them outward toward other sources of information and encounters with other people's experiences and ideas. In a one-semester course, for example, you might begin with the personal essay, and then move to the profile, followed by the review, and then the argument or research essay. This builds nicely by challenging students to work with more sources of information and leads to a more sophisticated understanding of persuasion and rhetoric. A two-semester course has the luxury of more assignments, of course, allowing you to potentially use most of the inquiry projects in Part 2.

Certain assignments clump together. For example, while arguably all writing is persuasive, the following genres are most explicitly so: proposal, review, argument, critical essay, and often the research essay. A course that focuses on argument might emphasize these assignments. A research-oriented course might exploit the wealth of material with a strong emphasis on outside sources, including the proposal, review, argument, research essay, and ethnography. A single-semester composition course that attempts coverage of critical thinking and writing as well as research and argument might move from personal essay to profile, and then cover persuasion through the review or critical essay, move on to the argument, and finish with the ethnographic and research essays.

Integrating the Research and Revision Sections

An unusual feature of the book is its treatment of research skills and revision. Research is an element of every assignment, but it receives special attention in Part 3, "Inquiring Deeper," in which students are introduced not only to the research essay but to research strategies and skills. I hope you will find that this section, particularly Chapter 11, "Research Techniques," is immediately relevant because students will be encouraged to consider research angles in every assignment they tackle. Consider assigning this chapter early in your course, particularly the sections on developing a working and focused knowledge of a subject.

Similarly, revision is an element of every assignment. That's hardly a novel idea, but what is unusual is that *The Curious Writer* devotes an entire section of the book—Part 4, "Re-Inquiring"—to revision. Like the section on research, the chapters on revision are relevant to students from their very first assignment. The first half of Chapter 13, "Revision Strategies," is a useful introduction to what it means to revise, and you might assign this material early on in your course. The chapter also features specific revision strategies that your students will use in every assignment.

Chapter 14, "The Writer's Workshop," can also be assigned at any time and in sections. Consider having your students read the first half of that chapter—an introduction to peer review—before the first class workshops. The second half of the chapter focuses on methods of responding, specific workshop formats that are most helpful for drafts at different stages in the writing process. Ask students who are responsible for presenting their work to read about the method of response they'll use in their workshop as preparation for it.

Using the Exercises

Learning follows experience, and the exercises in *The Curious Writer* are intended to help students make sense of the ideas in the text. I often plan the exercises as an in-class activity, and then assign the relevant reading to follow up that experience. Sometimes the discussion following these in-class exercises is so rich that some of the assigned reading becomes unnecessary. The students get it without having to hear it again from the author. More often, though, the reading helps students deepen their understanding of what they've done and how they can apply it to their own work.

However, assigning all of the exercises isn't necessary. Don't mistake their abundance in the book as an indication that you must march your students in lockstep through every activity, or they won't learn what they need to. *The Curious Writer* is more flexible than that. Use the exercises and activities that seem to emphasize key points that you think are important. Skip those you don't have time for or that don't seem necessary. If you're like me, you also have a few rabbits of your own in your hat—exercises and activities that may work better with the text than the ones I suggest.

For Instructors

The following resources are available to qualified adopters of Pearson English textbooks.

The Instructor's Resource Manual

ISBN 0-205-87740-0/978-0-205-87740-9
This manual includes several sample syllabi, as well as a helpful introduction that will offer general teaching strategies and ideas for teaching writing as a form of inquiry. It also gives a detailed overview of each chapter and its goals, ideas for discussion starters, handouts and overheads, and a large number of additional writing activities that teachers can use in their classrooms to supplement the textbook.

PowerPoint Presentation

A downloadable set of PowerPoint slides can be used by instructors who want to use presentable visuals to accompany chapter readings and discussions. These slides, designed by Michelle Payne (who also developed the *Instructor's Manual*), illustrate each learning objective and key idea in the text in visual form. Each slide includes instructors' notes.

Online Resources
for Instructors and Students

Pearson MyLabs

The Pearson English MyLabs empower students to improve their skills in writing, grammar, research, and documentation with market-leading instruction, multimedia tutorials, exercises, and assessment tools. Students can use the MyLabs on their own, benefiting from self-paced diagnostics and extra practice in content knowledge and writing skills. Instructors can use MyLabs in ways that best complement their courses and teaching styles. They can work more efficiently and more closely with students by creating their own assignments and using time-saving administrative and assessment tools. The marginal icons found in this book link students to enhanced online resources and assessments through the Pearson eText, which is also available in an iPad version. To learn more, visit www.pearsonhighered.com/englishmylabs or ask your Pearson representative.

Pearson eText

An interactive online version of *The Curious Writer* is available as an eText, bringing together the many resources of the MyLab with the instructional content of this successful book to create an enhanced learning experience for students. Marginal icons in the Pearson eText link to a wealth of online resources:

 Video tutorials illustrate key concepts, offering tips and guidance on critical reading, evaluating sources, avoiding plagiarism, and many other topics.

 Audio podcasts discuss common questions about grammar, usage, punctuation, and mechanics.

 Sample documents illustrate the range of writing students do in composition classes, their other courses, the workplace, and the community.

 Additional exercises help students assess their understanding of concepts before applying them in their own writing.

CourseSmart eTextbook

Students can subscribe to *The Curious Writer* at CourseSmart.com. The format of the eText allows students to search the text, bookmark passages, save their own notes, and print reading assignments that incorporate lecture notes.

Android and iPad eTextbooks

Android and iPad versions of the eText provide the complete text and the electronic resources described above.

Acknowledgments

Making such a large and complex book as this one is a team effort. From the first edition of *The Curious Writer*, I've been lucky to have an extraordinarily gifted group of Pearson people working with me. Some of these I'll never know because they work off stage on production and design. But among those with whom I worked directly, there are several collaborators who deserve special thanks. Randee Falk was development editor for much of this edition. She was demanding and brilliant, an editor who made me work harder than any I've ever had. The result is a much, much better book. Toward the end of the project, Randee passed the editorial baton to Michael Greer, a talented and congenial collaborator who is one of the best development editors in the business. On the production side, I got to work with my old friend Sarah Burkhart. Her keen eye for the details, combined with her wit and charm, make Sarah a joy to work with. Lauren Finn, senior acquisitions editor at Pearson, was instrumental in helping me focus on how to improve the new edition. Finally, thanks, as always, to Joe Opiela, Senior Vice President, for the support and encouragement that have made all the *Curious* books possible.

My students are also key collaborators, though they often don't know it. For their assistance in the fourth edition, I'd like to thank the following students: Andrea Oyarzabal, Becca Ballenger, Julia Ballenger, Seth Marlin, Micaela Fisher, Bernice Olivas, Briana Duquette, Julie Bird, Gordon Seirup, Kersti Harter, Margaret Parker, and Amy-Garrett Brown.

Reviewers of books like these can be crucial to their development. I was lucky enough to have some excellent reviewers for each edition, including the following folks who guided me on the first edition:

Jeffrey T. Andelora, Mesa Community College; Ken Autrey, Francis Marion University; Sandra Barnhill, South Plains College; Patrick Bizzaro, East Carolina University; Sara M. Blake, El Camino College; Pamela S. Bledsoe, Surry Community College; Libby Bradford Roeger, Shawnee Community College; Sharon Buzzard, Quincy College; Maria A. Clayton, Middle Tennessee State University; Dr. Keith Coplin, Colby Community College; Rachelle Darabi, Indiana University/Purdue University–Fort Wayne; Virginia B. Earnest, Holmes Community College–Ridgeland; Terry Engebretsen, Idaho State University; Shari Hammond, Southwest Virginia Community College; Anneliese Homan, State Fair Community College; David C. Judkins, University of Houston; Robert Lamm, Arkansas State University; James C. McDonald, University of Louisiana–Lafayette; Rhonda McDonnell, Arizona State University; Bryan Moore, Arkansas State University; John D. Moore, Eastern Illinois University; Margaret P. Morgan, University of North Carolina–Charlotte; Dr. Peter E. Morgan, University of West Georgia; Brigid Murphy, Pima Community College; Robin L. Murray, Eastern Illinois University; Dorothy J. Patterson, Oakwood College; Steven R. Price, Mississippi College; Mark Reynolds, Jefferson Davis Community College; David H. Roberts, Samford University; Elaine J. Roberts, Judson College; Robert A. Schwegler, University of Rhode Island; Dr. Bonita Selting, University of Central Arkansas; Vicki Stieha, Northern Kentucky University; Elizabeth A. Stolarek, Ferris State University; Lisa Tyler, Sinclair Community College; Marjorie Van Cleef, Housatonic Community College; Worth H. Weller,

Indiana University Purdue University–Fort Wayne; Ann R. Wolven, Lincoln Trail College; and Richard T. Young, Blackburn College.

Reviewers for the second edition included Melissa Batai, Triton College; Jennifer Black, McLennan Community College; Mark Browning, Johnson County Community College; Jo Ann Buck, Guilford Technical Community College; Jason DePolo, North Carolina A&T State University; John Christopher Ervin, University of South Dakota; Greg Giberson, Salisbury University; Nels P. Highberg, University of Hartford; William Klein, University of Missouri–St. Louis; Mary C. Leahy, College of DuPage; Lynn Lewis, University of Oklahoma; Steve Luebke, University of Wisconsin–River Falls; Michael Lueker, Our Lady of the Lake University; Jacqueline L. McGrath, College of DuPage; Betty Porter, Indiana Wesleyan University; Kristie Rowe, Wright State University; Kathleen J. Ryan, University of Montana; and Heath Scott, Thomas Nelson Community College.

Reviewers for the third edition included Angela Cardinale Bartlett, Chaffey College; Jennifer Black, McLennan Community College; James C. Bower, Walla Walla Community College; Susan Butterworth, Salem State College; Donna Craine, Front Range Community College; Brock Dethier, Utah State University; Rosemarie Dombrowski, Arizona State University (DPC); Kevin Ferns, Woodland Community College; Michael Hammond, University of San Francisco; Vicki M. Hester, St. Mary's University; Charlotte Hogg, Texas Christian University; Shelly Horvath, University of Indianapolis; Dawn Hubbell-Staeble, Bowling Green State University; Tom Moriarty, Salisbury University; Jason E. Murray, University of South Dakota; Amy Ratto Parks, University of Montana; Susan Pesznecker, Clackamas Community College; Lynn Raymond, UNC Charlotte; Mark A. Smith, Lock Haven University of Pennsylvania; Ruthe Thompson, Southwest Minnesota State University; BJ Zamora, Cleveland Community College.

And for this latest, fourth edition, reviewers include Susan Achziger, Community College of Aurora; Ellen Barker, Nicholls State University; Shanti Bruce, Nova Southeastern University; Carol Burnell, Clackamas Community College; Donna Craine, Front Range Community College; Daniel Gonzalez, University of New Orleans; Gwendolyn N. Hale, Savannah State University; Charlotte Hogg, Texas Christian University; Chad Jorgensen, Metropolitan Community College; Lilia Joy, Henderson Community College; Rosemary Mack, Baton Rouge Community College; Kara M. Manning, The University of Southern Mississippi; Amanda McGuire Rzicznek, Bowling Green State University; James J. McKeown, Jr., McLennan Community College; Eileen Medeiros, Johnson & Wales University; Betty Porter, Indiana Wesleyan University; Amy Ratto Parks, University of Montana; Teryl Sands, Arizona State University; and Marian Thomas, Boise State University.

Finally, I want to thank my daughters, Rebecca and Julia, who allow themselves to be characters in all of my books. They are both actors, and like good theater people, they are more than willing to play their parts in these texts, no matter what role I assign. I'm especially grateful to Karen, my wife, who has endured multiple editions of these books and their hold on my attention, which has often come at her expense. She's the beacon I follow through this blizzard of words, always guiding me home.

BRUCE BALLENGER

THE CURIOUS
WRITER

1

THE SPIRIT
OF INQUIRY

Writing as inquiry is an invitation to wonder and discover again.

Writing as Inquiry

1

Learning Objectives

In this chapter, you'll learn to

1.1 Reflect on and revise your beliefs about yourself as a writer.

1.2 Understand what kinds of questions will sustain inquiry into any subject.

1.3 Practice a method of writing and thinking that will help you generate ideas.

1.4 Apply rhetorical knowledge to make choices in specific writing situations.

Yesterday in class, Tina wrote an essay about whether adultery is forgivable. She isn't married but has good friends who are, a couple she said everyone thought had the "perfect" marriage. The woman's husband, apparently, had an affair. Tina, who was in a pretty tight relationship with her boyfriend, had strong feelings about cheating on a partner. It ticked her off. "If it happened to me," she wrote, "I would have dumped him." Tina's essay could easily have become a rant about infidelity—a blunt, perhaps shrill argument about adultery's immorality or the depravity of two-timing men. It wasn't. Instead, she wondered about the relationship between friendship and love in marriage. She wondered about what kind of communication between spouses might short-circuit cheating. She wondered how attitudes towards sex differ between men and women. Many of these questions were explored by Michel de Montaigne, a sixteenth-century writer we were studying in that class, and Tina began to wrap his thinking around hers as she struggled to make sense of how she felt about what happened to her friends.

Tina was engaged in an act of inquiry.

Her motive was to *find out* what she thought rather than prove what she already knew. And writing was the way Tina chose to think it through.

Many of us admit that we really don't like to write, particularly when forced to do it. Or we clearly prefer certain kinds of writing and dislike others: "I just like to write funny stories," or "I like writing for myself and not for other people," or "I hate writing research papers." I can understand this, because for years I felt much the same way. I saw virtually no similarities between a note to a friend and the paper I wrote for my philosophy class in college. Words had power in one context but seemed flimsy and vacant in another. One kind of writing was fairly easy; the other was like sweating blood. How could my experiences as a writer be so fundamentally different? In other words, what's the secret of writing well in a range of writing contexts *and* enjoying it more in all contexts? Here's what I had to learn:

1. You don't have to know what you think before you're ready to write. Writing can be a way of *discovering* what you think.
2. A key to writing well is understanding the *process* of doing it.

They're not particularly novel ideas, but both were a revelation to me when I finally figured them out late in my career as a student, and they changed for good the way I wrote. These two insights—that writing is a means of discovery and that reflecting on how we write can help us write—are guiding principles of this book. I won't guarantee that after they read *The Curious Writer* haters of writing will come to love it or that lovers of writing won't find writing to be hard work. But I hope that by the end of the book you'll experience the pleasure of discovery in different writing situations, and that you'll understand your writing process well enough to adapt it to the demands of whatever situation you encounter.

Motives for Writing

Why write? To start, I'd propose two motives, one obvious and the other less so:

reasons for writing →

1. To share ideas or information—*to communicate.*
2. To think—*to discover.*

These two motives for writing—to *communicate* with others and to *discover* what the writer thinks and feels—are equally important. And both may ultimately relate to what I call our *spirit of inquiry,* which is born of our deeper sense of wonder and curiosity or even confusion and doubt, our desire to touch other people, our urge to solve problems. The spirit of inquiry is a kind of perspective toward the world that invites questions, accepts uncertainty, and makes each of us feel some responsibility for what we say. This inquiring spirit should be familiar to you. It's the feeling you had when you discovered that the sun and a simple magnifying glass could be used to burn a hole in an oak leaf. It's wondering what a teacher meant when he said that World War II was a "good" war and Vietnam was a "bad" war. It's the questions that haunted you yesterday as you listened to a good friend describe her struggles with anorexia. The inquiring spirit even drives your quest to find a smartphone, an effort that inspires you to read about the technology and visit consumerreports.org. Inquiry was Tina's motive when she decided to turn her academic essay on adultery away from a shrill argument based on what she already believed into a more thoughtful exploration of why people cheat.

Beliefs About Writing and Writing Development

Most of us have been taught about writing since the first grade. We usually enter college with beliefs not only about what makes a good paper and what "rules" of writing to follow, but also about how we can develop as writers. As I mentioned earlier, I've learned a lot about writing since my first years in college, and a big part of that learning involved unraveling some of my prior beliefs about writing. In fact, I'd say that my development as a writer initially had more to do with *unlearning* some of what I already knew than it did with discovering new ways to write. But you have to make your beliefs explicit if you're going to make decisions about which are helpful and which aren't. So take a moment to find out what your beliefs are and to think about whether they actually make sense.

1.1 Reflect on and revise your beliefs about yourself as a writer.

Exercise 1.1

This I Believe (and This I Don't)

STEP ONE: From the following list, identify *the one belief* about writing that you agree with most strongly and *one* that you're convinced isn't true.

1. Writing proficiency begins with learning the basics and then building on them, working from words to sentences to paragraphs to compositions.

2. The best way to develop as a writer is to imitate the writing of the people you want to write like.

3. People are born writers like people are born good at math. Either you can do it or you can't.

4. The best way to develop as a writer is to develop good reading skills.

5. Practice is the key to a writer's development. The more a writer writes, the more he or she will improve.

6. Developing writers need to learn the modes of writing (argument, exposition, description, narration) and the genres (essays, research papers, position papers, and so on).

7. Developing writers should start with simple writing tasks, such as telling stories, and move to harder writing tasks, such as writing a research paper.

8. The most important thing that influences a writer's growth is believing that he or she can improve.

9. The key to becoming a better writer is finding your voice.

STEP TWO: Look over the following journal prompts (for more on journals, see the "Inquiring into the Details: Journals" box). Then spend five minutes writing in your journal about *why* you agree with the one belief and disagree with the other. This is an open-ended "fastwrite." You should write fast and without stopping, letting your thoughts flow in whatever direction they go. In your fastwrite, you can respond to any or all of the prompts to whatever extent you want.

> **Rules for Fastwriting**
> 1. There are no rules.
> 2. Don't try to write badly, but give yourself permission to do so.
> 3. To the extent you can, think through writing rather than before it.
> 4. Keep your pen moving.
> 5. If you run out of things to say, write about how weird it is to run out of things to say until new thoughts arrive.
> 6. Silence your internal critic to suspend judgment.
> 7. Don't censor yourself.

Journal Prompts

- *What* do you mean, exactly, when you say you agree or disagree with the belief? Can you explain more fully why you think the belief is true or false?

- *When* did you start agreeing or disagreeing with the belief? Can you remember a particular moment or experience as a student learning to write that this agreement or disagreement connects to?

- *Who* was most influential in convincing you of the truth or falsity of the belief?

One Student's Response

Bernice's Journal

EXERCISE 1.1
STEP TWO

I used to be a firm believer in the idea of born writers—it was a genetic thing. People were gifted with the gold pen genes, or they weren't. Writing as a process involved a muse, inspiration, and luck. Things uncontrollable by the writer. Then I started writing, mostly for my 101 class, and I started to feel powerful when I put words on paper. In control. The idea of my voice, my words, just being on the page and other people reading it and maybe liking it was a rush. I was always the girl who specialized in the art of being unnoticed, unseen, blending in. My Comp 101 prof. liked my writing and pushed really hard to work on my basics, to think about my process, to prewrite and revise. I started to see a clear distinction between how to write and what to write. How is all mixed up with the process, with discipline, with practice and perseverance....The how isn't something you are born with; its something you develop, something you practice, a skill you hone....Becoming a good writer takes learning how to write, figuring out a process that works for you, and then letting your voice be heard on the page.

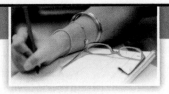

Inquiring into the Details

Journals

Here are five things that make a journal especially useful for writers:

- Whether print or digital, the journal must be a place where you're able to largely ignore your internal critic, a place where you feel comfortable *writing badly*.

- Use it *throughout the writing process*. Journals can be indispensible for invention whenever you need more information, not just at the beginning. They can also be a place where you talk to yourself about how to solve a writing problem.

- Write both *specifically and abstractly*. Sometimes you'll be trying to be as concrete as possible, generating details, collecting facts, exploring particular experiences. Other times, use the journal to think in more-abstract language, thinking through ideas, reflecting on process, analyzing claims.

- *Don't make any rules* about your journal. These usually begin with a thought like "I'll only write in my journal when…." Write in your journal whenever you find it useful, and in any way that you find useful, especially if it keeps you writing.

- *Experiment*. Your journal will be different from my journal, which will be different from the journal of the woman sitting next to you in class. The only way to make a journal genuinely useful is to keep trying ways to make it useful.

Unlearning Unhelpful Beliefs

You won't be surprised when I say that I have a lot of theories about writing development; after all, I'm supposedly the expert. But we are *all* writing theorists, with beliefs that grow out of our successes and failures as students who write. Because you don't think much about them, these beliefs often shape your response to writing instruction without your even knowing it. For example, I've had a number of students who believe that people are born writers. This belief, of course, would make any kind of writing class a waste of time, because writing ability would be a matter of genetics.

A much more common belief is that learning to write is a process of building on basics, beginning with words and then working up to sentences, paragraphs, and perhaps whole compositions. This belief was very common when I was taught writing. I remember slogging my way through Warriner's *English Grammar and Composition* in the seventh and eighth grade, dutifully working through chapter after chapter.

Today, along with a lot of experts on writing instruction, I don't think that this foundational approach to writing development is very effective. While I can still diagram a sentence, for example, that's never a skill I call on when I'm composing.

And yet building on the basics seems like common sense, doesn't it? This brings up an important point: Unlearning involves rejecting common sense *if* it conflicts

Unlearning involves rejecting common sense if it conflicts with what actually works.

with what actually works. Throughout this book, I hope you'll constantly test your beliefs about writing against the experiences you're having with it. Pay attention to what seems to work for you and what doesn't. Mostly, I'd like you at least initially to play what one writing instructor calls the *believing game*. Ask yourself, *What do I have to gain as a writer if I try believing this is true?* For example, even if you've believed for much of your life that you should never write anything in school that doesn't follow an outline, you might discover that abandoning this "rule" sometimes helps you to use writing to *discover* what you think.

The Beliefs of This Book

Allatonceness. One of the metaphors I very much like about writing development is offered by writing theorist Ann E. Berthoff. She said learning to write is like learning to ride a bike. You don't start by practicing handlebar skills, move on to pedaling practice, and then finally learn balancing techniques. You get on the bike and fall off, get up, and try again, doing all of those separate things at once. At some point, you don't fall and you pedal off down the street. Berthoff said writing is a process that involves *allatonceness* (all-at-once-ness) and it's simply not helpful to try to practice the subskills separately. This book shares the belief in the allatonceness of writing development.

Believing You Can Learn to Write Well. Various other beliefs about writing development—the importance of critical thinking, the connection between reading and writing, the power of voice and fluency, and the need to listen to voices other than your own—also help to guide this book. One belief, though, undergirds them all: *The most important thing that influences a writer's growth is believing that he or she can learn to write well.* Faith in your ability to become a better writer is key. From it grows the motivation to learn how to write well.

belief, a very good one . . .

Faith isn't easy to come by. I didn't have it as a writer through most of my school career, because I assumed that being placed in the English class for underachievers meant that writing was simply another thing, like track and math, that I was mediocre at. For a long time, I was a captive to this attitude. But then, in college I wrote a paper I cared about; writing started to matter, because I discovered something I really wanted to say and say well. This was the beginning of my belief in myself—and of my becoming a better writer. Belief requires motivation, and one powerful motivator is to approach a writing assignment as an opportunity to learn something—that is, with what I have called the spirit of inquiry.

Habits of Mind

When I first started teaching writing, I noticed a strange thing in my classes. What students learned about writing through the early assignments in the class didn't seem to transfer to later assignments, particularly research papers. What was I doing wrong? I wondered. Among other things, what I failed to make clear to my students was that certain "habits of mind" (or *dispositions*, as one writer terms them) could be consistently useful to them, in writing papers in my course and in any course involving academic inquiry—habits related to seeing writing as a process of discovery. We'll look at several closely related habits here; later in this chapter, you'll see how they play a role in the writing process.

Starting with Questions, Not Answers

A lot of people think that writing is about recording what you already know, which accounts for those who choose familiar topics to write on when given the choice. "I think I'll write about _____," the thinking goes, "because I know that topic really well and already have an idea what I can say." Writers who write about what they know usually start with answers rather than questions. In some writing situations this makes a lot of sense, because you're being asked specifically to prove that you know something. I'm thinking of an essay exam, for instance. But more often writing in a university is about inquiry, not reporting information. It's about discovery. It's about finding the questions that ultimately lead to interesting answers.

1.2
Understand what kinds of questions will sustain inquiry into any subject.

Making the Familiar Strange. Starting with questions rather than answers changes everything. *It means finding new ways to see what you've seen before.* Take this for example:

What is it? An iPhone, of course. Not much more to say, right? But imagine that your purpose wasn't to simply provide the quickest answer possible to the simple factual question *What is it?* Consider instead starting with questions that might inspire you to think about the iPhone in ways you haven't before; for example,

- *What does it mean* that iPhone owners spend twice as much time playing games as other smartphone users?
- *What should be done* about the environmental impacts of iPhone production in China?

Both these questions lead you to potentially new information and new ways of seeing that familiar phone in your pocket. They promise that you'll discover something you didn't know before.

Questions open up the inquiry process, while quick answers close it down. When you discover what you think, you don't cook up a thesis before you start—you discover the thesis as you explore. But to work, the inquiry process demands something of us that most of us aren't used to: suspending judgment.

Suspending Judgment

We jerk our knee when physicians tap the patellar tendon. If everything is working, we do it reflexively. We're often just as reflexive in our responses to the world:

- "What do you think of American politicians?"
  "They're all corrupt."

- "Is it possible to reconcile economic growth with the preservation of natural resources?"
  "No."

- "Isn't this an interesting stone?"
  "It's just a rock."

It's okay to write badly. Resist the tendency to judge too soon and too harshly.

We make these judgments out of habit. But this habit is in fact a way of seeing, based on this premise: Some things are really pretty simple, more or less black-and-white, good or bad, boring or interesting. Academic inquiry works from another, very different premise: The world is really a wonderfully complex place, and *if we look closely and long enough*, and ask the right questions, we are likely to be surprised at what we see. A condition of inquiry is that you *don't* rush to judgment; you tolerate uncertainty while you explore your subject. Academic inquiry requires that you see your preconceptions as hypotheses that can be tested, not established truths. It is, in short, associated with a habit of *suspending* judgment.

Being Willing to Write Badly

In a writing course such as this one, the challenge of suspending judgment begins with how you approach your own writing. What's one of the most common problems I see in student writers? Poor grammar? Lack of organization? A missing thesis? Nope. *It's the tendency to judge too soon and too harshly.* A great majority of my students—including really smart, capable writers—have powerful internal critics, or, as the novelist Gail Godwin once called them, "Watchers at the Gates." This is the voice you may hear when you're starting to write a paper, the one that has you crossing out that first sentence or that first paragraph over and over until you "get it perfect."

The only way to overcome this problem is to suspend judgment. In doing so, you essentially tell your Watchers this: *It's okay to write badly.* Godwin once suggested that writers should confront their internal critics by writing them a letter.

Dear Watcher,

Ever since the eighth grade, when I had Mrs. O'Neal for English, I've been seeing red. This is the color of every correction and every comment ("awk") you've made in the margins on my school writing. Now, years later, I just imagine you, ready to pick away at my prose every time I sit down to write. This time will be different...

It might help to write your internal critic a letter like this. Rein in that self-critical part of yourself, and you'll find that writing can be a tool for *invention*—a way to generate material—and that you can *think through writing* rather than waiting around for the thoughts to come. You need your internal critic. But you need it to work with you, not against you. Later in this chapter, I'll show you how to accomplish this.

Searching for Surprise

Starting with questions, making the familiar strange, suspending judgment, and writing badly—all are related to searching for surprise. In fact, one of the key benefits of writing badly is *surprise*. This was a revelation for me. I was convinced that you never pick up the pen unless you know what you want to say. Once I realized I could write badly and use writing not to *record* what I already knew, but to *discover* what I thought, this way of writing promised a feast of surprises that made me hunger to put words on the page. If you're skeptical that your own writing can surprise you, try the following exercise.

1.3 Practice a method of writing and thinking that will help you generate ideas.

> ### Conditions That Make "Bad" Writing Possible
> 1. Willingness to suspend judgment
> 2. Ability to write fast enough to outrun your internal critic
> 3. Belief that confusion, uncertainty, and ambiguity help thought rather than hinder it
> 4. Interest in writing about "risky" subjects, or those about which you don't know what you want to say until you say it

Exercise 1.2

A Roomful of Details

STEP ONE: Spend ten minutes brainstorming a list of details based on the following prompt. Write down whatever comes into your mind, no matter how silly. Be specific and don't censor yourself.

Watch the Animation on **Brainstorming** in your MyLab

> Try to remember a room you spent a lot of time in as a child. It may be your bedroom in the back of the house at the edge of the field, or the kitchen where your grandmother kneaded bread or made thick, red pasta sauce. Put yourself back in that room. Now look around you. What do you see? What do you hear? What do you smell?

> ### Brainstorming
> - Anything goes.
> - Don't censor yourself.
> - Write everything down.
> - Be playful but stay focused.

STEP TWO: Examine your list. If things went well, you will have a fairly long list of details. As you review the list, identify the one detail that surprises you the most, a detail that seems somehow to carry an unexpected charge. This might be something that seems connected to a feeling or a story. You might be drawn to a detail that confuses you a little. Whatever its particular appeal, circle it.

Watch
the Animation on
Freewriting
in your MyLab

STEP THREE: Use the circled detail as a prompt for a seven-minute fastwrite. Begin by focusing on the detail: What does it make you think of? And then what? And then? Alternatively, begin by simply describing the detail more fully: What does it look like? Where did it come from? What stories are attached to it? How does it make you feel? Avoid writing in generalities. Write about specifics—that is, particular times, places, moments, and people. Write fast, and chase after the words to see where they want to go. Give yourself permission to write badly.

You may experience at least three kinds of surprise after completing a fastwriting exercise such as the one above:

1. Surprise about *how much* writing you did in such a short time

2. Surprise about discovering a topic you didn't expect to find

3. Surprise about discovering a *new way of understanding or seeing a familiar topic*

One Student's Response

Bernice's Journal

EXERCISE 1.2
STEP THREE

DETAIL: STAINLESS STEEL COUNTERS

When I was five or six my father and I made cookies for the first time. I don't remember what prompted him to bake cookies, he liked to cook but he didn't very well so he didn't like to use cook books. I remember sitting on the cold stainless steel, the big red and white cook book splayed over my lap. I was reading it out loud to my dad. The kitchen was warm but everything gleamed; it was industrial and functional. It was the only room in our house that still looked like it belonged to the "Old Pioneer School." My dad and uncles had renovated every other room into bedrooms, playrooms, family rooms. The place was huge but cozy, it was home. I remember reading off ingredients until I got to the sugar. It called for 3/4 cup and I didn't understand the fraction. I thought it meant three or four cups. We poured so much sugar into the bowl. The cookies were terrible. Hard and glassy, too sweet and brittle. It wasn't until years later that I understood that my dad didn't understand the measurement either. He was persistent though. We pulled down every cook book in the house until we found one that described the measuring cups and what they meant. We started all over and our second batch was perfect. My dad is one of the smartest people I know, inventive, imaginative but he only has a rudimentary educa- tion. He can read and write enough to get by, he's gifted with numbers, but I can't help looking back and wondering what he could have been, what he could have done for the world if just one person had taken him by the hand and showed him what he showed me. If just one person had told him not to give up, to keep trying, that in the end it will be worth all the work, I wonder who he could have been if one person had seen his curiosity and imagination and fostered it instead of seeing his muscles and capable hands and putting him to work. If just one person had told him that his mind was the greatest tool he possessed. If just one person baked cookies with him.

The kind of surprises you encounter doing this sort of writing may not always be profound. They may not even provide you with obvious essay topics. With any luck, though, by hunting for surprises in your own work, you will begin to experience the pleasure of writing *to learn*. That's no small thing, particularly if you've always believed that writers should have it all figured out before they pick up the pen.

Writing Situations and Rhetorical Choices

The following isn't good writing, is it?

> im happy to be back w/u guys it was a too long of a weekend- dancing friday then? u hailey and i runnin tomorrow- sounds fun 2 me

Actually, the answer is, of course, that it depends.

Writing occurs in a writing situation, and different writing situations are associ- ated with different types of writing and forms of communication—different genres and media. Think of how many writing situations we encounter these days and how many types of writing we do. For example, besides writing part of this textbook chapter, I wrote e-mails to an editor and a student, freewrote in my journal, drafted some text for a web page, sent a text to my daughter, and posted a comment on Facebook.

In each case, the writing situation demanded something different from me. In each, however, I had to make appropriate *rhetorical* choices—choices related to the following four considerations:

- **Purpose for writing:** What is the text trying to do?
- **Audience:** For whom is it intended?
- **Subject:** What is it about?
- **Genre/Medium:** What type of writing—what form of communication— would work best in view of my purpose, audience, and subject? What are its strengths and limitations, and what are its conventions?

1.4

Apply rhetorical knowledge to make choices in specific writing situations.

[handwritten note: ✱ what your writing depends on how you write.]

That is, to write effectively, I had to think about why I was writing, to whom I was writing, what I was writing about, and what type of text I was writing. The effectiveness of my writing depended on my making appropriate choices in light of these considerations. And the rhetorical choices that we make in a writing situation are wide ranging; they include not only big choices (What's the best genre for accomplishing my purpose with this audience?), but also many smaller choices (Is it okay to say "ur" instead of "you're"?).

Now let's go back to the text message, written by my daughter to a friend.

Watch
the Video on
Purpose
in your MyLab

Explore
the Interactive
Exercise on
**The Rhetoric
of Audience**
in your MyLab

Rhetorical Consideration	The Text Message
Purpose	Expressive and informational purposes: to reinforce intimacy; to plan
Audience	A close friend, with considerable shared knowledge
Subject	Personal details related to knowledge of a shared experience
Genre/ Medium	Text message; limited to 160 characters, with a shorthand shared by users

Based on this analysis, my daughter's text message is clearly good writing after all. It uses the conventions of the genre/medium to fulfill its purpose—reinforce intimacy and make a Friday-night plan—for the audience the writer had in mind. My daughter used her *rhetorical knowledge* to make choices that resulted in an effective piece of writing. Of course she would think it was weird to call her understanding of how to write a text message "rhetorical knowledge." But that's exactly what it is. She just doesn't think about it that way.

But what happens when you *do* think about it?

1. You become more skillful at composing in writing situations with which you are familiar.

2. You can learn to master unfamiliar writing situations much more quickly.

You have more rhetorical knowledge than you think. After all, you've been writing and speaking all your life. But when you start becoming aware of this knowledge, it becomes more powerful, and you become a better writer. Throughout *The Curious Writer*, I'll encourage you to think rhetorically.

In the next few years of college, you'll be encountering unfamiliar writing situations, so learning to reflect on how each involves *rhetorical choices* will make you a much better communicator. (By the way, we also use this rhetorical knowledge to analyze how well someone else communicates, which is the focus of Chapter 2.) Learning to write well, then, isn't simply learning how to craft transitions, organize information, and follow grammatical rules—it's also learning to recognize that each writing situation asks you for something different. For example, in college writing situations, the basic rhetorical considerations, as in Figure 1.1, "Thinking rhetorically," may be expanded with questions such as these:

questions to consider

- What is the purpose of the assignment? To interpret or analyze? Synthesize or summarize? Argue or explore?

- What is the subject, and what does that imply about my approach? Are there certain ways of writing about topics in history, psychology, or literature that differ from writing about topics in biology, social science, or business?

- Am I writing for an expert audience or a general audience? For my instructor or my peers?

- What is the form or genre for this assignment, and what are its conventions? What kind of evidence should I use? How is it organized?

You won't always have control over all of these choices. In college, you'll get writing assignments that may supply you with a purpose: "Write an essay that compares the energy efficiency of solar panels with that of a conventional coal power plant." Sometimes the form isn't up to you: "Write a five-page argument paper." But even when you have such constraints, you still have a lot of rhetorical choices to make—things like: "Should I use the first person? What evidence do I need, and where should it come from?"

Each genre and medium imposes its own conditions on the writer. For example, my daughter's text message can't be more than 160 characters, and that

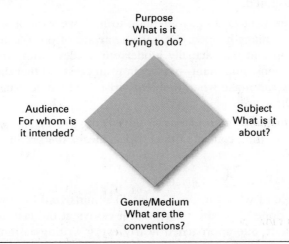

Purpose
What is it
trying to do?

Audience
For whom is
it intended?

Subject
What is it
about?

Genre/Medium
What are the
conventions?

Figure 1.1 **Thinking rhetorically.** Rhetorical choices involve four considerations: purpose, subject, audience, and genre/medium. Each consideration is associated with questions. For genre/medium, these include conditions and conventions regarding what you can say and especially how you say it. While all considerations have always been important in rhetorical thinking, genre and medium are especially critical to consider now that you may have alternatives to writing traditional term papers, including PowerPoints, podcasts, video, visuals, and a host of other multimodal approaches.

Explore
the Interactive
Exercise on
**The Rhetorical
Situation**
in your MyLab

limitation inspired, among other things, a shorthand for composing that uses characters sparingly. Considering genre and medium is especially important now that the forms of communication have expanded radically, even in academia. You may write not just a term paper. You might do a PowerPoint, make a poster, build a web page, collaborate on a wiki, or produce a podcast.

Thinking about rhetorical contexts increases the chance that you'll make good choices when you solve problems as a writer, particularly in revision. Much like riding Berthoff's bike, in composing, writers usually think about purpose, audience, subject, and genre/medium all at once, drawing on their experience with similar writing situations.

A First Reflection on Your Writing Process

There is a process for doing almost anything—fixing a broken washing machine, learning how to play tennis, studying for the SAT, and, of course, writing. Why, then, do some English teachers seem to make such a big deal out of the writing process? Here's why:

- First, the process of writing, like any process that we do frequently, is not something that we think about.

- As a consequence, when we write, we tend to focus just on *what* and not on *how*, just on the product and not on the process. And then, when problems arise, we don't see many options for solving them—we get stuck and we get frustrated.

- If, however, we start to pay attention to how we write in a variety of situations, two things happen: We become aware of our old habits that don't always help and may actually hinder our success with writing. Second— and this is most important—we begin to understand that there are actually *choices* we can make when problems arise, and we become aware of what some of those are.

- In short, *the more we understand the writing process, the more control we get over it*. Getting control of the process means the product gets better.[1]

A Case Study

Here's an example of what I mean. Chauntain summarized her process this way: "Do one and be done." She always wrote her essays at the last minute and only wrote a single draft. She approached nearly every writing assignment the same way: Start with a thesis, and then develop five topic sentences that support the

---

[1]There is considerable research in learning theory that confirms these conclusions; in particular, so-called *metacognitive thinking*—the awareness of how you do things—increases the transfer of relevant knowledge from one situation to another. In other words, what you learn about how to do something in one situation gets more easily activated in another.

Inquiring into the Details

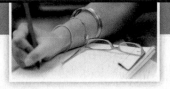

Organizing Your Computer Files

Avoid lots of headaches later on by working out a convention for naming files at the beginning of your course. One method might be the following:

- Genre (i.e., essay, exercise, letter, response, and so on)
- Title of document
- Version number
- Date

Using the underscore key, separate each element when naming your document. For example, *essay_importanceofwritingbadly_v2_2012-December-12*. A file name like this takes a little more time to compose, but it ultimately saves time by helping you locate documents more easily.

thesis, with three supporting details under each. This structure was a container into which she poured all her prose. Chauntain deliberated over every sentence, trying to make each one perfect, and as a result, she spent considerable time staring off into space searching for the right word or phrase. It was agony. The papers were almost always dull—she thought so too—and just as often she struggled to reach the required page length. Chauntain had no idea of any other way to write a school essay. As a matter of fact, she thought it was really the *only* way. So when she got an assignment in her economics class to write an essay in which she was to use economic principles to analyze a question that arose from a personal observation, Chauntain was bewildered. How should she start? Could she rely on her old standby structure—thesis, topic sentences, supporting details? She felt stuck.

Because she failed to see that she had choices related to both process and this particular writing situation, she also had no clue what those choices were. That's why we study process. It helps us solve problems such as these. And it must begin with a self-study of your own habits as a writer, identifying not just how you tend to do things, but the patterns of problems that might arise when you do them.

Thinking About Your Process

You will reflect on your writing and reading processes again and again throughout this book, so that by the end you may be able to tell the story of your processes and how you are changing them to produce better writing more efficiently. The reflective letter in your portfolio (see Appendix A) might be where you finally share that story in full. Now is a good time to begin telling yourself that story.

Watch
the Animation on
The Writing Process
in your MyLab

Inquiring into the Details

Portfolios

Why are portfolios—end-of-the-semester submissions of student work—so popular?

- They work from the assumption that you should perform better at the end of the semester because that's when you know the most.
- They create a powerful opportunity for student writers to reflect on what they've done and what they've learned.
- They provide students with some control over how to present what they've learned.
- Electronic portfolios, especially, allow students to incorporate multimodal genres—podcasts, PowerPoints, video, and so on.
- They promote revision. Because final evaluation of writing is often tentative until it is submitted in the portfolio at the end of the course, it can be considered work in progress until then.

What do you remember about your own journey as a writer both inside and outside of school? One of my earliest, most pleasant memories of writing is listening to the sound of the clacking of my father's old Royal typewriter in the room down the hall as I was going to sleep. I imagine him there now, in the small study that we called the "blue room," enveloped in a cloud of pipe smoke. It is likely that he was writing advertising copy back then, or perhaps a script for a commercial in which my mother, an actress, would appear. I loved the idea of writing then. The steady hammering of typewriter keys sounded effortless yet at the same time solid, significant. This all changed, I think, in the eighth grade when it seemed that writing was much more about following rules than tapping along to a lively dance of words.

Spend some time telling your own story about how your relationship to writing evolved.

When you get a writing assignment, your habit may be to compose carefully. This assignment, in contrast, is all about invention—about generating ideas.

Exercise 1.3

Literacy Narrative Collage

In your journal, create a collage of moments, memories, and reflections related to your experience with writing. *For each prompt, write fast for about four minutes. Keep your pen or fingers on the keyboard moving, and give yourself permission to write badly.* After you've responded to one prompt, skip a line and move on to the next one. Set aside about twenty minutes for this generating activity.

1. What is your earliest memory of writing? Tell the story.

2. We usually divide our experiences as writers into private writing and school writing, or writing we do by choice and writing we are required to do for a grade. Let's focus on school writing. Tell the story of a teacher, a class, an essay, an exam, or a moment that you consider a *turning point* in your understanding of yourself as a writer or your understanding of school writing.

3. Writing is part of the fabric of everyday life in the United States, and this is truer than ever with Internet communication. Describe the roles that writing plays in a typical day for you. How have these daily roles of writing changed in your lifetime so far?

4. What is the most successful (or least successful) thing you've ever written in or out of school? Tell the story.

Congratulations. You've made a mess. But I hope this collage of your experiences as a writer is an interesting mess, one that brought some little surprises. As you look at these four fragments of fastwriting, you might begin to sense a pattern. Is there a certain idea about yourself as a writer that seems to emerge in these various contexts? It's more likely that one, or perhaps two, of the prompts really took off for you, presenting trails you'd like to continue following. Or maybe nothing happened. For now, set your journal aside. You may return to this material if your instructor invites you to draft a longer narrative about your writing experiences, or you might find a place for some of this writing in your portfolio.

Now that you've spent some time telling a story of your background as a writer, use the following survey to pin down some of your habits and experiences related to school writing. The questions in the survey can help you develop a profile of your writing process and help you identify problems you might want to address by altering your process.

Exercise 1.4

What Is Your Process?

STEP ONE: Complete the Self-Evaluation Survey.

Self-Evaluation Survey

1. When you're given a school writing assignment, do you wait until the last minute to finish it?

   Always———Often———Sometimes———Rarely———Never

2. How often have you had the experience of learning something you didn't expect through writing about it?

    Very often———Fairly often———Sometimes———Rarely———Never

3. Do you generally plan out what you're going to write before you write it?

    Always———Often———Sometimes———Rarely———Never

4. *Prewriting* describes activities that some writers engage in before they begin a first draft. Prewriting might include such invention activities as freewriting or fastwriting, making lists, brainstorming or mapping, collecting information, browsing the web, talking to someone about the essay topic, reading up on it, or jotting down ideas in a notebook or journal. How much prewriting do you tend to do for the following types of assignments? Circle the appropriate answer.

    ■ A personal narrative:

    A great deal———Some———Very little———None———Haven't
    written one

    ■ A critical essay about a short story, novel, or poem:

    A great deal———Some———Very little———None———Haven't
    written one

    ■ A research paper:

    A great deal———Some———Very little———None———Haven't
    written one

    ■ An essay exam:

    A great deal———Some———Very little———None———Haven't
    written one

5. At what point(s) in writing an academic paper do you often find yourself getting stuck? Check all that apply.
    ❏ Getting started
    ❏ In the middle
    ❏ Finishing
    ❏ I never/rarely get stuck (go on to question 9)
    ❏ Other: _____

6. If you usually have problems getting started on a paper, which of the following do you often find hardest to do? Check all that apply. (If you don't have trouble getting started, go on to question 7.)
    ❏ Deciding on a topic
    ❏ Writing an introduction
    ❏ Finding a good place to write
    ❏ Figuring out exactly what I'm supposed to do for the assignment
    ❏ Finding a purpose or focus for the paper

❑ Finding the right tone

❑ Other: _____

7. If you usually get stuck in the middle of a paper, which of the following cause(s) the most problems? Check all that apply. (If writing in the middle of a paper isn't a problem for you, go on to question 8.)

❑ Keeping focused on the topic

❑ Finding enough information to meet page-length requirements

❑ Following my plan for how I want to write the paper

❑ Bringing in other research or points of view

❑ Organizing all my information

❑ Trying to avoid plagiarism

❑ Worrying about whether the paper meets the requirements of the assignment

❑ Worrying that the paper just isn't any good

❑ Messing with citations

❑ Other: _____

8. If you have difficulty finishing a paper, which of the following difficulties are typical for you? Check all that apply. (If finishing isn't a problem for you, go on to question 9.)

❑ Composing a last paragraph or conclusion

❑ Worrying that the paper doesn't meet the requirements of the assignment

❑ Worrying that the paper just isn't any good

❑ Trying to keep focused on the main idea or thesis

❑ Trying to avoid repeating myself

❑ Realizing I don't have enough information

❑ Dealing with the bibliography or citations

❑ Other: _____

9. Rank the following list of approaches to revision so that it reflects the strategies you use *most often to least often* when rewriting academic papers. Rank the items 1–6, with the strategy you use most often as a 1 and least often as a 6.

_____ I just tidy things up—editing sentences, checking spelling, looking for grammatical errors, fixing formatting, and performing other proofreading activities.

_____ I look for ways to reorganize existing information in the draft to make it more effective.

_____ I try to fill holes by adding more information.

_____ I do more research.

_____ I change the focus or even the main idea, rewriting sections, adding or removing information, and changing the order of things.

_____ I rarely do any revision.

10.   Finally, do you tend to impose a lot of conditions on when, where, or how you think you write most effectively? (For example, do you need a certain pen, do you always have to write on a computer, do you need to be in certain kinds of places, must it be quiet or noisy, do you write best under pressure?) Or can you write under a range of circumstances, with few or no conditions? Circle one.

Lots of conditions———Some———A few———No conditions

If you impose conditions on when, where, or how you write, list some of those conditions here:

1.

2.

3.

STEP TWO: In small groups, discuss the results of the survey. Begin by picking someone to tally the answers to each question. Post these on the board, a large sheet of paper, or a spreadsheet, so they can then be added up for the class. Analyze the results for your group. In particular, discuss the following questions:

- Are there patterns in the responses? Do most group members seem to answer certain questions in similar or different ways? Are there interesting contradictions?
- Based on these results, what "typical" habits or challenges do writers in your class seem to share?
- What struck you most?

Problem Solving in Your Writing Process

If you took the survey, you probably uncovered some problems with your writing process. The great news for those of us who struggle with certain aspects of writing—and who doesn't?—is that you can do something about it. As you identify the obstacles to doing better work, you can change the way you approach writing tasks. For instance, consider some of the more common problems students struggle with and some ideas about how *The Curious Writer* can help you with them.

Writing Problem	Possible Cause	A Solution
Consistently writes short. Often can't meet page requirements for assignments.	Writer works from scarcity. Begins the draft with too little information on the topic.	Focus on invention. Generate more material *before* you begin the draft, through research, fastwriting, etc. (see "Inquiring into the Details: Invention Strategies" on p. 25).
Dislikes revision, especially if it involves more than "tidying" things up.	Writer spends a great deal of time writing the first draft and trying to make it "perfect." Gets overcommitted to the initial approach to topic.	Write a fast draft and then do deeper revision. Attack the draft physically (see Revision Strategy 13.18 in Chapter 13).
Writer's block.	Internal critic is too harsh too early in the writing process. Often involves anxiety about audience.	Find a place where you can write badly without it feeling like a performance. A journal or notebook often works (see "Journals" on p. 7).
Dislikes open-ended assignments. Would rather be told what to write about.	Writer may be unused to valuing own thinking. Little experience with assignments in which writer must discover own purpose.	Use your own curiosity and questions to drive the process. Craft questions that are useful guides for exploration and promise discovery and learning (see "Starting with Questions, Not Answers" in this chapter).
Struggles with focus. Able to write a lot but can't seem to stay on topic.	Writer doesn't exploit key opportunities to look at writing critically, to evaluate and judge what she has generated.	Effectively combine invention with evaluation, generating with judging, by using a process that makes room for both as you write (see "The Nature of the Writing Process" below).

👁
┌ Watch ┐
the Video on
Overcoming
Writer's Block
in your MyLab

The Nature of the Writing Process

Earlier you saw Chauntain's writing process. Here was my writing process when I was in school:

1. Get the assignment. Find out when it is due and how long it is supposed to be.
2. Wait until the night before it is due and get started.
3. Stare off into space.
4. Eat ice cream.
5. Write a sketchy outline.

6. Write a sentence; then cross it out.

7. Stare off into space.

8. Write another sentence, and then squeeze out a few more.

9. Think about Lori Jo Flink, and then stare off into space.

10. Write a paragraph. Feel relief and disgust.

Suspending judgment feels freer, exploratory... Making judgments shifts the writer into an analytical mode.

I would get the work done eventually, but the process was agonizing and the product mediocre. What did I conclude from this back then? That I wasn't good at writing, which was no big surprise because I pretty much hated it. Something happened to me to change that view, of course, because you hold my book in your hands. I came to understand the problems in my writing process: I looked on writing as a straight march forward from beginning to end, one where I had to wait for something to come into my head and then try to get it down. At all costs, I avoided things like new ideas or other ways of seeing a topic—anything that might get in the way of the drive to the conclusion. If I thought about anything, it was trying to find the "perfect" way of saying things or worrying about whether I was faithfully following a certain structure. I rarely learned anything from my writing. I certainly never expected I should.

The Writing Process as Recursive and Flexible

But this straight march isn't the way experienced writers work at all. The writing process isn't a linear trajectory, but a looping, recursive process—one that encourages *thinking*, not simply recording the thoughts that you already have. Writing doesn't involve a series of steps that you must follow in every situation; on the contrary:

- The writing process is *recursive*, a much messier zigzag between collecting information and focusing on it, exploring things and thinking about them, writing and rewriting, reviewing and rearranging, and so on. For example, invention strategies are useful at many points in the writing process.

- The process is *flexible* and always influenced by the writing situation. For instance, experienced writers have a keen sense of audience, and they use this to cue their choices about a change in tone or whether an example might help clarify a point. These are exactly the kinds of adjustments you make in social situations all the time.

A System for Using Writing to Think

What do I mean when I say the writing process encourages thinking? Usually, when we imagine someone who is "deep in thought," we see them staring off into space with a furrowed brow, chin nested in one hand. They are not writing. They may be thinking about what they're *going* to write, but in the meantime the cursor is parked

Inquiring into the Details

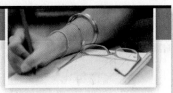

Invention Strategies

Invention is a term from rhetoric that means the act of generating ideas. While we typically think of *rhetoric* as something vaguely dishonest and often associated with politics, it's actually a several-thousand-year-old body of knowledge about speaking and writing well. Invention is a key element in rhetoric. It can occur at any time during the writing process, not just at the beginning in the "prewriting" stage. Some useful invention strategies include:

- **Fastwriting:** The emphasis is on speed, not correctness. Don't compose, don't think about what you want to say before you say it. Instead, let the writing lead, helping you discover what you think.

- **Listing:** Fast lists can help you generate lots of information quickly. They are often in code, with words and phrases that have meaning only for you. Let your lists grow in waves—think of two or three items and then pause until the next few items rush in.

- **Clustering:** This nonlinear method of generating information, also called *mapping*, relies on *webs* and often free association of ideas or information. Begin with a core word, phrase, or concept at the center of a page, and build branches off it. Follow each branch until it dies out, return to the core, and build another. (For an example, see p. 91.)

- **Questioning:** Questions are to ideas what knives are to onions. They help you cut through to the less obvious insights and perspectives, revealing layers of possible meanings, interpretations, and ways of understanding. Asking questions complicates things but rewards you with new discoveries.

- **Conversing:** Conversing is fastwriting with the mouth. When we talk, especially to someone we trust, we work out what we think and feel about things. We listen to what we say, but we also invite a response, which leads us to new insights.

- **Researching:** This is a kind of conversation, too. We listen and respond to other voices that have said something, or will say something if asked, about topics that interest us. Reading and interviewing are not simply things you do when you write a research paper, but activities to use whenever you have questions you can't answer on your own.

- **Observing:** When we look closely at anything, we see what we didn't notice at first. Careful observation of people, objects, experiments, images, and so on generates specific information that leads to informed judgments.

Watch
the Video on
**Prewriting
and Invention
Strategies**
in your MyLab

Watch
the Animation on
Clustering
in your MyLab

on the computer screen or the pen rests on the desk. Thinking like this is good—I do it all the time. But imagine if you also make thought external by following your thinking on paper or screen and not just in your head. Here is some of what happens:

- You have a record of what you've thought that you can return to again and again.
- As you *see* what you've just said, you discover something else to say.
- Because the process of thinking through writing is slower than thinking in your head, you think differently.
- Because externalizing thought takes mental effort, you are more immersed in thought, creating what one theorist called a state of "flow."

As I've already mentioned, thinking through writing is most productive when you suspend judgment, reining in your internal critic. You may actually do some pretty good thinking with some pretty bad writing.

Using writing as a way of thinking is even more powerful if there is a *system* for doing it that reliably produces insight. One method, which we could call a *dialectical system*, exploits two different kinds of thinking—one creative and the other critical, one wide open and the other more closed. So far in this chapter, we've focused on the creative side, the generating activities I've called "writing badly," which restrain your internal critic. But you need that critical side. You need it to make sense of things, to evaluate what's significant and what's not, to help you figure out what you might be trying to say. If you use both kinds of thinking, "dialectically" moving back and forth from one to the other, then you're using a method that is at the heart of the process you'll use throughout *The Curious Writer*.[2] Try the next exercise to see how this might work for you.

Exercise 1.5

Two Kinds of Thinking

Let's return to the subject you began writing about in Exercise 1.3—your experiences as a writer—but focus on something that was probably part of your response to the third prompt in that exercise: your experience with writing technology.

Using Creative Thinking

STEP ONE: What are your earliest memories of using a computer for writing? In your journal or on the computer, begin by telling the story and then let the writing lead from there. Keep your pen or the cursor moving, and allow yourself to write badly.

---

[2]For Greek philosophers such as Plato, *dialectic* was a way of arriving at truth through back-and-forth conversation between two people who were open to changing their minds. Similarly, the process of writing and thinking I propose here is a back and forth between two parts of yourself—each receptive to the other—in an effort to discover your own "truths," ideas, and insights.

STEP TWO: Brainstorm a list of words or phrases that you associate with the word *literate* or *literacy*.

Reread what you just wrote in steps 1 and 2, underlining things that surprise you or that seem significant or interesting to you. Skip a line and move on to step 3.

Using Critical Thinking

STEP THREE: Choose one of the following sentence frames as a starting point. Complete the sentence and then develop it as a paragraph. This time, compose each sentence while thinking about what you want to say before you say it and trying to say it as well as you can.

> What I understand now about my experiences with writing on computers that I didn't understand when I started out is _____.
>
> When they think about writing with computers, most people think _____, but my experience was _____.
>
> The most important thing I had to discover before I considered myself "computer literate" was _____.

Reflecting

If you're like most people, then the parts of this exercise where you creatively generated material felt different than the part where you judged as you wrote. But *how* were they different? How would you distinguish between the experience of generating and judging? Talk about this or write about it in your journal.

A Writing Process That Harnesses Two Currents of Thought

The two parts of Exercise 1.5 involving creative and critical thinking were designed to show you the difference between the two and also to simulate the shift between them, the shift from suspending judgments to making judgments—something I referred to as "dialectical" thinking. In the first two steps, you spent some time fastwriting without much critical interference, trying to generate some information from your own experience. In the third step, which began with "seed" sentences that forced you into a more reflective, analytical mode, you were encouraged to look for patterns of meaning in what you generated.

As you probably noticed, these two distinct ways of thinking each have advantages for the writer:

- *Suspending judgment* feels freer, is exploratory, and may spark emotion.
- *Making judgments* shifts the writer into an analytical mode, one that might lower the temperature, allowing writers to see their initial explorations with less feeling and more understanding.

suspending / making judgements.

Thus, creative thinking creates the conditions for discovery—new insights or ways of seeing—while critical thinking helps writers refine their discoveries and focus on the most significant of them.

The Sea and the Mountain. Here's another way to conceptualize creative and critical thinking (see Figure 1.2):

- When you write creatively, you plunge into the sea of information. You don't swim in one direction, but eagerly explore in all directions, including the depths.

- When you write critically, you emerge from the water to find a vantage point—a mountain—from which to see where you've swum. From the mountain, you are able to see patterns that aren't visible from the water. You are able to make judgments about what you encountered there: What's significant? What isn't? Why?

The key is not to stay on the mountain. Instead, you take the patterns you saw and the judgments you made and plunge back into the sea, this time with a stronger

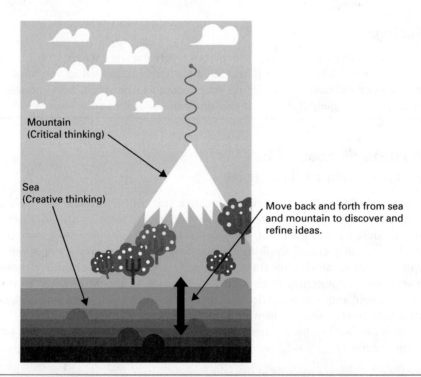

Mountain
(Critical thinking)

Sea
(Creative thinking)

Move back and forth from sea and mountain to discover and refine ideas.

Figure 1.2   Generating insight using critical and creative thinking. Thinking to inquire is like the movement back and forth from the sea of information to the mountain of reflection. In one you explore, and on the other you evaluate. Insight develops when you continually move back and forth; as you refine your ideas, when in the sea, you swim in ever smaller circles with a stronger sense of purpose.

sense of purpose. You're clearer about what you want to know and where you need to swim to find it. This back and forth between mountain and sea continues until you've discovered what you want to say. In fact, you made just this sort of movement in Exercise 1.2 and then in Exercise 1.5 when you moved from generating to judging. It is a process of induction and deduction, working upwards from specifics to infer ideas, and then taking those ideas and testing them against specifics.

Figure 1.3 lists yet other ways in which you can visualize the movement between creative and critical thinking. In narrative writing, for instance, creative thinking helps you generate information about *what happened*, while critical thinking may lead you to insights about *what happens*. Likewise, in research writing, investigators often move back and forth between their *observations of* things and their *ideas about* them.

As you work through the book, you'll find it easier to shift between contrasting modes of thought—from collecting to focusing, from generating to judging, from showing to telling, from exploring to reflecting, from believing to doubting, from playing to evaluating. In short, you'll become better able to balance creative and critical thinking. You'll know when it's useful to open up the process of thinking to explore and when it's necessary to work at making sense of what you've discovered.

Answering the *So What?* Question. An important function on the critical thinking side is to make sure you can answer the one question you must answer when writing for an audience:

So what?

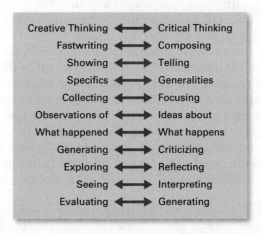

Creative Thinking	◄─►	Critical Thinking
Fastwriting	◄─►	Composing
Showing	◄─►	Telling
Specifics	◄─►	Generalities
Collecting	◄─►	Focusing
Observations of	◄─►	Ideas about
What happened	◄─►	What happens
Generating	◄─►	Criticizing
Exploring	◄─►	Reflecting
Seeing	◄─►	Interpreting
Evaluating	◄─►	Generating

Figure 1.3 Alternating currents of thought. When writers alternate between creative and critical thinking, they move back and forth between two opposing modes of thought—the creative and the critical. One seems playful and the other judgmental; one feels open ended and the other more closed. Activities such as fastwriting and brainstorming promote one mode of thought, and careful composing and reflection promote the other.

So what? can be a pretty harsh question, and I find that some students tend to ask it too soon in the writing process, before they've fully explored their topic. A danger is that this can lead to a feeling of frustration. You may, for example, have found yourself high and dry if you've tried to reflect on possible meanings of a moment you've written about for only eight minutes. Another danger is that the writer is tempted to seize on the first convenient idea or thesis that comes along. This abruptly ends the process of inquiry before the writer has had a chance to explore.

When you can't come up with an answer to *So what?* the solution is usually to generate more information.

A Writing Process Driven by Questions

Watch
the Animation on
Questioning
in your MyLab

The inquiry approach is grounded in the idea that the writing process depends, more than anything else, on finding good questions to address.

I recently visited teachers in Laredo, Texas, and I told them that with a good question even the most boring topic can become interesting. I would prove it, I said, and picked up a lemon that was sitting on a table and asked everyone, in turn, to ask a question about the lemon or about lemons. Twenty minutes later, we generated sixty questions. In the process, we began to wonder how the scent of lemons came to be associated with cleanliness. We wondered why lemons appeared so often in wartime British literature. We wondered why the lime and not the lemon is celebrated in local Hispanic culture. We wondered a lot of interesting things that we never expected to wonder about, because a lemon is ordinary. Questions can make the familiar world we inhabit yield to wonder.

The point is this: *There are no boring topics—just wrong questions.*

But what are good inquiry questions? Obviously, for a question to be good, you have to be interested in it. Furthermore, others must also have a stake in the answer, because you'll be sharing what you learn.

Usually, when we investigate something we don't know much about, we start by asking informational questions. Say you're interested in the Disney Corporation's sustainability projects. You first need to know what those are. You might search online and read about Disney's commitment to recycling or to energy efficiency. This is basic background information—facts about what has already been said about a topic. But in college writing, you're usually not writing a report or a summary of what's known about a topic. Just explaining what Disney is doing to reduce emissions isn't enough. You have to *do* something with that information. This involves that critical mind that we talked about earlier, one that asks you to make judgments.

Different types of questions lead to different kinds of judgments. And it's landing on the appropriate type of question for your project that will launch you into meaningful inquiry. These question types include the following:

- *Value questions:* Is it good or bad? Useful or useless?

- *Relationship questions:* Are they similar or dissimilar? Is there a cause and effect? What's the connection?

[handwritten margin note:] questions that make you think about and make diff judgements.

- *Policy questions:* What should be done?
- *Interpretation questions:* What might it mean?
- *Hypothesis questions:* What is the best explanation?
- *Claim questions:* Are the assertions valid? What is most persuasive?

You can apply these kinds of questions to nearly any topic, depending what interests you about it. For example, in Figure 1.4 I tried to imagine how someone exploring Disney's sustainability programs might use each of these question types. With a little factual background, it isn't hard to start framing possible inquiry questions that can really steer your project in different—and possibly interesting—directions.

A good question not only lights your way into a subject, but may also illuminate what form you could use to share your discoveries. Certain kinds of writing—reviews, critical essays, personal essays, and so on—are often associated with certain types of questions, as you can see in Figure 1.4. In Part 2 of *The Curious Writer*, which features a range of inquiry projects from the personal essay to the research essay, you'll see how certain questions naturally guide you towards certain kinds of writing.

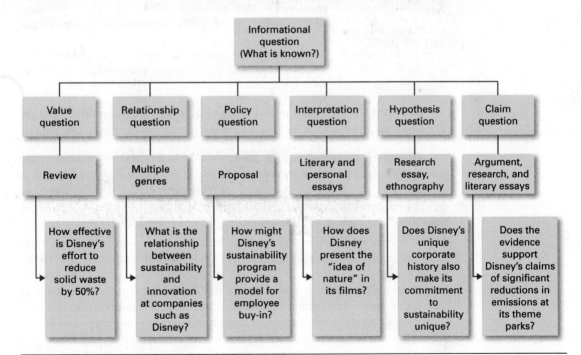

Figure 1.4 Categories of inquiry questions. The inquiry process often begins with informational questions: What is already known about this? As writers learn more about their topics, they refine their questions so that they are more likely to lead to analysis or argument rather than mere report. Some of these questions are associated with certain kinds of writing that are covered in this book.

Questioning, Generating, and Judging: A Strategy for Inquiry

If you combine the power of good questions with the back-and-forth process of writing creatively and critically, you have a strategy of inquiry that you can use for every assignment in this book:

- Typically, you begin exploring a subject, sometimes generating some initial thoughts through fastwriting, listing, or other invention methods.

- Like landscape shots in photography, subjects cover a huge amount of ground. You need to narrow your subject and eventually arrive at a yet narrower topic, or some *part* of the landscape to look at more closely.

    As an example, take popular music. That's a huge subject. But as you write and read about it a little, you may begin to see that you're most interested in the blues, and especially in its influence on American popular music. This last might seem promising as a general topic.

- With a tentative topic in hand, you are searching for a few inquiry questions about your topic that both interest you and will sustain your project. These are the questions that will help you focus your topic, that will guide your research, and that may eventually become the heart of an essay draft on your topic.

    For example, beginning with the topic of the influence of the blues on pop music, you might arrive at an inquiry question something like this relationship question:

    > What is the relationship between Mississippi delta blues and the music of white performers such as Elvis who were popular in the fifties and sixties?

    An inquiry question may be no more than a temporary guide on your journey. As you continue to write, you may find another, better question around which to build your project. But beginning with a good question will get and keep you on the right track—something you'll find enormously helpful as you collect information.

- As you collect information, some of the best insights you get about what the answers to your questions might be will come from the alternating currents of thought—generating and judging, suspending judgment and making judgments—that energize your writing and thinking processes. In practical terms, this means combining open-ended methods such as fastwriting to explore what you think with more focused methods such as summarizing that will help you evaluate what you discover.

Most of all, this inquiry strategy uses questions to direct your attention to what's relevant and what's not. Imagine that an inquiry question is a flint that gives off sparks when it strikes potentially meaningful information, whether that information comes from personal experiences or research. These sparks are the things that will light your way to discoveries about your topic.

The inquiry strategy I'm proposing should work with nearly any topic. Let's try one in Exercise 1.6.

Exercise 1.6

A Mini Inquiry Project: Cell Phone Culture

The alternating currents of thought—generating and judging, exploring and evaluating, opening up and focusing, mountain and sea—can be put to work in any situation where you want to figure out what you think. Writing is a key part of the system. In this exercise, I'll guide you to think one way and then another. Later, you may find you do this on your own without thinking about it. But for now, let me guide you.

More than 90 percent of us now have cell phones, and according to one study, about a third of people aged eighteen to twenty-nine say that they "couldn't live without" them. Cell phones make us feel safer, and of course they're an enormous convenience. But they've also introduced new annoyances into modern life, like the "halfalogue," the distracting experience of being subjected to one half of a stranger's conversation with someone on their cell phone. It's a technology that is fundamentally changing our culture—our sense of community and connection, our identities, the way we spend our time. But how? Try exploring that question for yourself, to see if you can discover what *you* find interesting about the topic.

Invention: Generating

STEP ONE: Let's first take a dip in the sea of information. Recent research on "cell phone addiction" suggests that, as with Internet addiction, "overuse" of the technology can result in anxiety, depression, irritability, and antisocial behavior. This research also suggests that college students are particularly vulnerable to cell phone addiction. One survey to determine whether someone is cell phone addicted asks some of the following questions:

- Do you feel preoccupied about possible calls or messages on your mobile phone, and do you think about it when your cell is off?
- How often do you anticipate your next use of the cell phone?
- How often do you become angry and/or start to shout if someone interrupts you when you're talking on a cell phone?
- Do you use a cell to escape from your problems?

Start by exploring your reaction to this list in a fastwrite in your journal, print or digital. Write for at least three minutes, but write longer if you can. What do you make of the whole idea of "cell phone addiction"? What does this make you think about? And then what? And then?

Judging

STEP TWO: Reread your fastwrite, underlining anything that you find interesting, surprising, or possibly significant. Pay particular attention to anything that might have surprised you. Then thoughtfully finish the following sentence.

> *One interesting question that this raises for me is: _____ ?*

Generating

STEP THREE: Focus on the question you came up with in step 2. Return to the sea and write about specific *observations, stories, people, situations, or scenes* that come to mind when you consider the question you posed. Don't hesitate to explore other questions as they arise as well. Let the writing lead. Write fast for *at least* another three minutes without stopping.

Judging

STEP FOUR: Review what you just wrote, then thoughtfully complete the following sentence, and then follow that first sentence for as long as you can compose here, rather than fastwriting, thinking about what you're going to say before you say it.

> *So far, one thing I seem to be saying is that we . . .*

Finding a Question

STEP FIVE: You haven't generated much writing on cell phone culture yet, but if you've written for ten minutes or so, you should have enough information to take a stab at writing a tentative inquiry question. Using the question categories in Figure 1.4, try to draft a question about cell phones, cell phone culture, cell phone addiction, or any other topic suggested by your writing. Remember, the question should be one of the following:

- A value question: Is it any good?
- A policy question: What should be done?
- A hypothesis question: What is the best explanation?
- A relationship question: What is the relationship between _____ and _____?
- An interpretation question: What might it mean?
- A claim question: What does the evidence seem to support?

Reflecting on the Process

STEP SIX: In your journal, or on an online discussion board, answer the following questions about what you've just done.

1. What, if anything, do I understand now that I didn't before?

2. What most surprised me?

3. What's the most important thing I take from this?

Reflective Inquiry About Your Writing

I should be a really good guitar player. I've played since I was eleven. I'm okay. But among my other problems was a lousy sense of rhythm—at least until recently, when I began playing with my friend Richard, who can play skillfully in all the ways I can't. How did I solve the rhythm problem by playing with Richard? What exactly did I learn to do that helped me adjust my strum so I could provide passably good backup to Richard's leads?

To get better at a process, we need to ask questions about it. And to answer these questions, we have to have three things:

1. Some knowledge of how the process is done or how it might be done

2. The language to define the problem

3. Some ideas about possible solutions

Since the beginning of this chapter, I've argued that taking the time to reflect on your knowledge and think about writing, and paying attention to how you use this knowledge and thinking as you write, is well worth the effort. It will speed up your learning, help you to adapt more easily in a range of writing situations, and make writing less frustrating when things go wrong. Experts call this "reflective inquiry," and they observe that experienced professionals in many fields often do this kind of thinking. In a way, reflective inquiry is thinking *about* thinking. It isn't easy. But it is also one of the most important ways in which we *transfer* what we know from one situation to another. Reflective thinking is key to making the most of your learning in this writing course.

You've tried your hand at reflective inquiry in several exercises so far, including the previous one on "cell phone culture." Let's get a little more practice with it before we move on.

Exercise 1.7

Scenes of Writing

Think about the writing and thinking you've done about yourself as a writer in this chapter. Review your notes from all of the exercises you tried that asked you to reflect on that (Exercise 1.1, your beliefs about writing; Exercise 1.3, your literacy collage; and Exercise 1.4, the survey on your writing process). Now imagine the kind of writer *you would like to be*.

Scene 1

A month ago, you got a writing assignment in your philosophy course: a twelve-page paper that explores some aspect of Plato's dialogues. It's the night before the paper is due. Describe the scene. What are you doing? Where? What's happening? What are you thinking? If you can, make use of the various types of writing that can convey scene: description, narration, dialogue.

Scene 2

Rewrite scene 1. This time, script it as you *wish* it would look.

Finally, imagine that each scene is the opening of a film. What would they be titled?

Reflective Inquiry

Think about the terms we've used in this chapter to talk about the writing process—terms such as these:

- *Prewriting*
- *Revision*
- *Focusing*
- *Critical and creative thinking*
- *Invention*
- *Reflection*
- *Exploration*
- *Inquiry questions*
- *Habits of mind*
- *Suspending judgment*
- *Genre*
- *Alternating currents of thought*
- *Writing situation*
- *Rhetorical choices*

Draft a 200- to 250-word essay or discussion-board post about your own writing process—past, present, or future—that uses as much of the terminology of the writing process as you find relevant and useful to your essay or post.

Using What You Have Learned

Remember the learning goals at the beginning of the chapter?

1. **Reflect on and revise your beliefs about yourself as a writer.** In this chapter, you started to tell yourself the story of yourself as a writer. Like any good story, you tell it for a reason: What does it tell you about the kind of writer you think you've been? Is that the writer who will work for you now as you deal with a wider range of writing situations in college and out of college? The great thing is that if your beliefs about yourself are holding you back, you can change them. And you will as you work your way through this book. Reflect continuously on what you do as a writer that works for you (and on what you do that doesn't). This isn't just an academic exercise; it is knowledge that you can put to work for you to help solve writing problems.

2. **Understand what kinds of questions will sustain inquiry into any subject.** Academic inquiry is driven by questions that will keep you thinking. But what kinds of questions will sustain your investigation of a subject over time? In this chapter, you learned how you can start with an informational question—What is known about a topic?—and refine that into a question that will help you discover what you want to say. You'll see later how these questions often lead to certain kinds of writing. The ability to understand what kinds of questions will guide your writing and thinking is something that you can draw on in nearly every college class.

3. **Practice a method of writing and thinking that will help you generate ideas.** Throughout *The Curious Writer*, you'll use the technique you were introduced to here: using your creative mind to explore and generate material, and your critical mind to narrow down and evaluate what you've generated. As you get more practice with this method, you'll find that you may not even think about it, as you shift naturally from withholding judgment to making judgments. If this works for you, you'll find that it's a powerful way to use writing to discover what you think in nearly any writing situation when you're trying to figure that out.

4. **Apply rhetorical knowledge to make choices in specific writing situations.** In this book, *rhetoric* is never a bad word. You learned here that the term doesn't describe someone who blows smoke in an attempt to deceive, but rather represents a way of thinking about how to communicate effectively. Rhetoric is a system for analyzing writing situations by looking at purpose, audience, and genre, so that you can see more clearly what your choices are when you're composing any kind of text. You already have considerable rhetorical understanding. Anyone with any skill in social situations does. But as you become more conscious of rhetorical analysis, you'll discover how fundamental it is to speaking and writing well.

Watch
the Video on
Analyzing Rhetorical
Situations
in your MyLab

Complete
Additional Exercises
and Practice on
Chapter I
in your MyLab

Reading to inquire opens a conversation with a text in which the words on the page are only part of the dialogue between the author and the reader.

Reading as Inquiry

Learning Objectives

In this chapter, you'll learn to

2.1 Apply reading purposes relevant to reading in college.

2.2 Examine your existing beliefs about reading and how they might be obstacles to reading effectively.

2.3 Recognize reading situations and the choices about approaches to reading they imply.

2.4 Understand the special demands of reading to write and practice doing it.

2.5 Understand some conventions of academic writing and recognize them in texts.

You've been reading all of your life. Why read a chapter on the subject, especially in a book about writing? Well, I'm going to argue that reading in college is different than much of the reading you've done in school up until now. To start with, the *kinds* of reading, or *genres*, you'll encounter will range widely from poems to journal articles with pretty-dense academic prose. You'll also be reading subjects about which you may have very little prior knowledge. It's hard to overstate what a difference this makes in your ability to understand what you read and use it in your writing. The graphic on this page is a sort of symbolic representation of this difference. When readers know a lot about a subject, they have mental categories and hierarchies for that subject—slots into which the new information they read is organized—which makes it easier for them to retrieve and use the information later in their writing. In contrast, when readers don't know much about

the subject of their reading—and that's often the case in undergraduate inquiry-based projects—they don't know what to make of what they're reading. We can picture their mental process as a scrambled struggle to simply understand the text. Going on to actually *use* the information in their writing will be an entirely different, and much bigger, problem. You probably know these situations, and they don't feel good. You're bored or frustrated with what you're reading. You can't focus. All you want to do is watch *Jersey Shore* on TV, and you actually hate that program.

An obvious solution to this problem is to develop some knowledge about a topic so you can read with more understanding. But there are other strategies, too, that can help you read—and use—difficult texts in unfamiliar genres, and I'll introduce you to them in this chapter. They include the following:

- *Be clear about your goals in reading a text.*
- *Use questions to drive the process.* In reading to inquire, I think there are four types of questions that can direct your attention as you read: exploring, explaining, evaluating, and reflecting questions.
- *See a text in its rhetorical context.* In other words, you can work more effectively with any kind of reading if you can see the kind of work its author *intended* it to do.
- *Understand that reading is a process.* The more you reflect on how you do it, including in different situations, the more control you get over the process.
- *Write as you read.* You can apply creative and critical thinking to generating insight about texts, too, through something such as a double-entry journal (described further on in this chapter).
- *Understand the features of academic discourse.* Knowing what to look out for will help you understand what you're reading.

⊙
┌ **Watch** ┐
the Video on
**Previewing
a Text**
in your MyLab

Purposes for Academic Reading

2.1

Apply reading
purposes relevant
to reading in
college.

Why read? We pick up a book for pleasure, read a news website for information, and so on. But I'd like to be more specific. What are the purposes for reading in college? First imagine some typical contexts for academic reading. You might, for example,

- Read a textbook to acquire knowledge about a subject. You may be required to demonstrate what you've learned on a test or in a paper.
- Read a textbook (such as this one?) that is a guide to a process. You use it to help you *do* something—write, perform an experiment, design a website.
- Read a journal article or short story closely, to analyze the arguments of the article or interpret the meaning of the story.
- Read material you have found online, to see how you might use information in your own writing or to prepare a presentation.

Each of these reading situations involves multiple purposes, and in each case one or two purposes is especially important. Although reading is a cognitively complex thing, I'd propose that the purposes of academic reading boil down to four—to *explore*, *explain*, *evaluate*, and *reflect*.

Reading with the spirit of inquiry turns books, essays, and articles into one side of a dialogue that you're having with an author.

Imagine that each purpose involves asking a text different kinds of questions. We don't typically start reading with questions in mind. I know when I was an undergraduate, the question I usually had when I was reading a textbook was (aside from "When will I be done so I can go play the guitar?") "Will this be on the test?" On my really deep thinking days, I might read an assigned article in, say, my environmental studies class and wonder, "Do I agree or disagree with this?" These are reasonable questions. But they aren't very good guides for reading well. The research on reading says that the best readers have conscious goals when they read. These can expressed as questions. Here, then, are some general questions that can express the different purposes. Notice that you can ask these questions about both the text and parts of the text.

Purpose	Some Examples of Readers' Questions
Explore	Why could I learn from this? What does this make me think?
Explain	What do I understand this to be saying?
Evaluate	Is this persuasive? How do I interpret this?
Reflect	How is this put together? What do I notice about how I'm thinking about this?

Watch
the Video on
**Asking Questions
About a Text**
in your MyLab

Each of these questions will lead you to read the same text in a different way. In using the purposes and questions, keep in mind that we often have more than one main purpose for reading a text. For example, when we read a biology textbook to learn things about cell structure for a test in two weeks, we will read it to explore *and* explain. When we have to analyze a website as a source for an academic paper, we have to make a judgment about whether it has persuasive content (evaluate) *and* think about how it's designed to be persuasive (reflect).

But to demonstrate how each of these purposes might change the way you read a text, we'll try to apply each of them separately in the following exercise.

Exercise 2.1

Using the Four Purposes for Academic Reading

Every year, the *Chronicle of Higher Education* publishes data about last year's college undergraduates. Here's a table (Figure 2.1) from that report that describes students' employment levels outside of school. Read the table using the four purposes for reading—exploring, explaining, evaluating, and reflecting—one at a time.

Percentage of college students age 16 to 24 who were employed, by hours worked per week, October 2009				
	Full-time students		Part-time students	
	Worked 20 or more hours	Worked less than 20 hours	Worked 20 or more hours	Worked less than 20 hours
All undergraduates	23%	16%	62%	11%
Female	25%	18%	64%	12%
Male	21%	13%	59%	10%
Hispanic	27%	10%	60%	12%
White	24%	19%	63%	13%
Black	20%	9%	64%	n/a
Asian	12%*	9%	n/a	n/a
By type of Institution attended:				
Public 2-year	28%	16%	59%	11%
Public 4-year	24%	15%	63%	13%
Private 4-year	13%	20%	80%	n/a
* Large margin of error				
Note: The designation "n/a" means no figures were provided because statistical standards were not met. For that reason, no figures were provided for American Indians or Pacific Islanders.				
Source: Census Bureau				

Figure 2.1   Employment patterns for college undergraduates

Explore

STEP ONE: First just figure out what you make of this information. Tables, like fiction, tell a story that is implied. What are some of the stories this table seems to be telling? Make a list of these in your journal. Some inferences are probably obvious. For example, part-time students clearly work more than full-time students. No surprise there. Work towards teasing out some of the less obvious implications, especially those that you find surprising. When you're done, look at your list of inferences. What questions do these raise? For example, private college students who are full-time clearly worked less than full-time students enrolled in public schools. And yet, if they attend part-time, students enrolled at private colleges work *far more than* part-time students at public institutions. Why? What might explain this?

Explain

STEP TWO: Turn your list from step 1 into a fat paragraph that summarizes what you think are the story lines in this table. What are the things it seems to be saying?

Evaluate

STEP THREE: Based on your reading of the data in the table, make a one-sentence assertion about what you think is *the most significant finding*. Write this down in your journal.

Reflect

STEP FOUR: Statistical tables are inevitably selective on what data to include. They also group information into categories that make the data easier to understand but may obscure other important results. In this table, students' employment was categorized by students who work more or less than 20 hours. Does this seem sensible to you? Make a case for or against using that distinction.

In class, or on the online discussion board, talk about your experience with reading for each of these four purposes.

- Which step of the exercise was hardest for you?
- With which of these purposes do you typically read texts in school? Which are new to you?
- How did each reading purpose change the focus of your reading?

We always have a purpose for reading something. We rarely think about this purpose. In this section, I've tried to convince you that you'll read much more skillfully and efficiently—particularly in college—when you do consider *why* you're reading something. The advantages of this awareness are huge: You'll know what to look for in a text that's relevant to the task. You'll know what questions to ask yourself to evaluate what you're reading. And you'll know what you might use from a text in your own writing. There's another thing that will help, too. Reading, like writing, is something you've done much of your life, and you've developed habits and beliefs that govern how you approach reading. These can help you or they can hurt you. But you can't determine that until you know what they are.

Watch
the Video on
Reading and Writing
in your MyLab

Beliefs About Reading

2.2

Examine your existing beliefs about reading and how they might be obstacles to reading effectively.

You have theories about reading much like you have theories about writing—including beliefs about what makes a "good" reader and about yourself as a reader. They're not beliefs you're aware of, probably, but they profoundly affect how you read everything you read. Through an exercise that gets you thinking a little about your own literacy history, let's start to tease some of these beliefs out into the open so you can get a look at them.

Exercise 2.2

Watch
the Video of a poet
talking about
Reading and Writing
in your MyLab

A Reader's Memoir

Generating

STEP ONE: There is considerable evidence that attitudes about reading are heavily influenced by how reading is viewed at home. Were there books around when you were growing up? Did you parents encourage you to read? Did they read? Fastwrite for five minutes about your memories of reading as a child in your home. Describe what you remember, and try to be as specific as possible.

Judging

STEP TWO: Speculate about the beliefs these early experiences with reading might have encouraged. In your journal, compose an answer to this inquiry question: *What is the relationship between my early reading experiences at home and my current beliefs about reading?*

Generating

STEP THREE: Now think about your reading experiences in school up until now. Fastwrite for five minutes, telling stories about your experiences with particular books or teachers, especially those that might have influenced the way you think of reading and of yourself as a reader.

Judging

STEP FOUR: As before, try to summarize how these experiences in school might have influenced how you view yourself as a reader now. Answer this question: *What is the relationship between my experiences reading in school and my current beliefs about reading and myself as a reader?*

One Common Belief That Is an Obstacle

I hope that Exercise 2.2 revealed some of the beliefs that shape how you feel about reading. When I wrote about my memories of reading at home, I realized that I had been lucky to grow up in a family that celebrated reading but that I had preferred to "read" television instead of a book. I can see now how this made me a reluctant reader who lacked confidence in his reading ability. When I wrote about my memories of academic reading, I immediately remembered—with revulsion—tanking on the reading portion of the SAT, and I realized that for years I'd thought the only purpose of reading in school was to say back what it said in a test or a paper.

My belief about school reading is a common one, and for good reason. Most reading instruction seems to focus on comprehension—you know, the SAT- or ACT-inspired kind of situation in which you are asked to read something and then explain what it means. This often becomes an exercise in recall and vocabulary, an analytical challenge in only the most general way. Essentially, you train yourself to distinguish between specifics and generalities and to loosely follow the author's reasoning. In English classes, sometimes we are asked to perform a similar exercise with stories or poems—what is the theme, or what does it mean?

> Only by understanding how we read in certain situations can we acquire more control over what we get out of the reading experience.

Instruction and assignments such as these encourage students to see reading as an archaeological expedition where they must dig for hidden meaning. The "right" answers to the questions are in the text, like a buried bone; you just have to find them. The trouble with this approach is the belief that it tends to foster, which is that *all meaning resides in the text and the reader's job is merely to find it.* This belief limits the reader's interaction with the text. If meaning is fixed within the text, embedded like a bone in antediluvian mud, then all the reader has to do is dig. Digging isn't a bad thing, but reading can be so much more than laboring at the shovel and sifting through dirt.

Reading Situations and Rhetorical Choices

This chapter began with a list of typical reading situations you might encounter as an undergraduate. You read a textbook to acquire information for a test. You mine an article for material to put in a paper or analyze a short story to interpret its theme, and so on. In each of these situations, you're going to make choices about *how* you read that text. Usually, these choices are governed by habit. This is the way you *always* read a textbook or a short story.

2.3 Recognize reading situations and the choices about approaches to reading they imply.

I'm going to try to convince you to make these choices differently. First, they should be conscious choices. For example, earlier we talked about purpose-directed reading. To read by asking questions based on your purpose is to make conscious choices.

Recall from Chapter 1 that to write effectively in a writing situation, you need to make appropriate rhetorical choices and that one of the considerations these are based on is your writing purpose. Similarly, in a reading situation, to read effectively you make choices based in part on your reading purpose.

When you're reading for a writing assignment, your purpose for reading basically has already been determined. For example, you might get an assignment like this in an English class:

- *Closely read and **explicate** the poem by Mary Oliver.*

Or perhaps you get an assignment like this in a marketing class:

- *Find and read company websites for mission statements and **explain** how companies distinguish between goals and objectives.*

In each of these situations, what you need to do is to start by *reading the assignment rhetorically*, to make sure you understand your purpose for reading. The main clue is usually the verb: *explicate, explain, argue, summarize, interpret, analyze,* and so on. These verbs tell you what you are supposed to do with what you read.

Frequently, however, you will have much less direction than this on what to do with your reading. Sometimes reading is just a part of a larger project, presentation, or paper, and *you* have to figure out what to do with every text you encounter. In these cases, you will need to figure out your purpose along with three other considerations that affect the choices you make about how to read something. These considerations, which I'll call *frames for reading*, are similar to those that come into play in rhetorical choices for writing.

Four Frames for Reading

- **Your purpose:** Why are you reading this text? (To explore, explain, evaluate, and/or reflect?)

- **Your knowledge of the genre/medium:** What do you know about this kind of text, and what do you therefore expect? What is it trying to do, and for whom is it likely written?

- **Your knowledge of the subject:** What do you already know about the subject of the reading? What biases might you have about it?

- **Self-perception:** How good do you think you are at reading a text in this genre and on this subject?

These considerations inevitably affect our reading. For example, a few years ago, when I was a novice at the shorthand of text messaging, I was painfully aware that I lacked genre knowledge. What do those abbreviations mean? When one of my daughters sent me a message, my first concern was decoding some of it. As I gained familiarity with the form, the problem of genre knowledge faded and I could focus more immediately on *why* they were telling me what they were telling me. They were asking for money? They wanted me to back off on the boyfriend? Experienced readers are aware of these frames and deliberately look at a text through them in order to make their reading more efficient.

Reading Scenarios

Consider a couple of scenarios involving academic reading and how an experienced writer might apply the four frames for reading.

Scenario #1. You're assigned two chapters in your college physics textbook for an exam. You don't know physics, much less college physics. Based on your feelings about reading textbooks and your inexperience with the subject, you're not feeling good about the time you'll spend reading for the assignment.

Faced with this situation, an experienced reader might apply the four frames as follows:

1. *Purpose.* I'm reading this to be able to explain what I know for an exam. I better pay attention to key concepts and terms when I read it and make sure I can explain them to myself. I think I'll write a summary in my

notebook of the key ideas—and a running list of terms and definitions—as I read. This is gonna slow me up but in the end will be worth it.

2. *Genre/medium knowledge.* I know that textbooks for intro courses are intended for readers with low subject knowledge, but even so it might be a struggle for me to understand and remember terms. Textbooks usually have cues about what's important—I'll pay particular attention to terms that are emphasized by length of treatment and visual cues such as italics and headings.

3. *Subject knowledge.* I don't know much about physics, so I can't skip around when I read this. I'll need to work through the text from the beginning and not move on to a new section until I think I understand the last one.

4. *Self-perception.* I stink at science and don't much like reading textbooks. Because I know I'm going to get frustrated, I'll allow some time to get through this—maybe reading over a few days rather than in one sitting.

Scenario #2. You're writing a research essay for your composition class on the impact of climate change in Australia, a place that one observer noted was a kind of "miner's canary" on the issue—in other words, likely to be among the first to experience problems and provide a warning sign for what is to come for the rest of the world. The question you're asking is whether chronic water shortages in the Outback are really climate related. Along with other material, you've found a great article in *Rolling Stone Magazine* that seems really on topic.

Here's how an experienced reader might approach reading the article:

1. *Purpose.* No one is telling me why I should read this article. I've got to figure that out. The *Rolling Stone* piece might be the most strongly stated thing I've read so far that argues that climate change is responsible for Australia's environmental problems. I'm going to read it to find some of those passages. Maybe I can use them in my paper. I'm also going to pay particular attention to the evidence provided on water shortages.

2. *Genre/medium knowledge.* This is *Rolling Stone,* not an academic article. It won't provide the quality of evidence that a journal article would. I also know that because of the magazine's youthful audience and its focus on popular music, *Rolling Stone* might be prone to overstating things a bit for dramatic effect. I'm going to read a little more critically.

3. *Subject knowledge.* I know a fair amount about the climate-change issue, and because I feel really strongly about it, I'm going to try to read this article critically, as a doubter more than a believer (see "Inquiring into the Details: Reading Perspectives"). What is the writer ignoring? Does he address counterarguments?

4. *Self-perception.* This article should be easy for me to read and understand.

Inquiring into the Details

Reading Perspectives

One of the best ways to read strategically is to consciously *shift* our perspective while we read. Like changing lenses on a camera or changing the angle, distance, or time of day to photograph something, this shift in reading perspective illuminates different aspects of a text. Here are some of the perspectives you might take:

- **Believing:** What the author says is probably true. Which ideas can I relate to? What information should I use? What seems especially sound about the argument?

- **Doubting:** What are the text's weaknesses? What ideas don't jibe with my own experience? What are the gaps in the information or the argument? What isn't believable about this?

- **Updating:** What does this add to what I already know about the subject?

- **Hunting and gathering:** What can I collect from the text that I might be able to use?

- **Interpreting:** What might be the meaning of this?

- **Pleasure seeking:** I just want to enjoy the text and be entertained by it.

- **Connecting:** How does this information relate to my own experiences? What is its relationship to other things I've read? Does it verify, extend, or contradict what other authors have said?

- **Reflecting:** How was this written? What makes it particularly effective or ineffective?

- **Resisting:** This doesn't interest me. Why do I have to read it? Isn't *Survivor* on television right now?

Exercise 2.3

Reading a Life

Here's a scenario for you to consider, one that involves reading a different kind of text—a photograph. I'd like you to apply the four frames for reading to this photograph, much the way I applied them in the previous two scenarios.

First, some background. One of the many ways we all make inferences about people is by paying attention to the details of their lives. What things do they value? What is their behavior in significant social situations? What groups do they belong to? While we may do this informally all the time, academics and writers do it, too—for example, when they study members of social or cultural groups or when they plan to write a profile of someone. One academic version of this is called *ethnography*, something you may learn about in Chapter 9. It relies on

very close observation of people in the places that their groups typically inhabit. Photographs can be an important source of data for such inquiries.

The photograph above, "Ruth's Vanity (on the day she died)," potentially tells us a lot about who Ruth was, through the things on her vanity and the dresser that is visible in the mirror above the vanity. I'd like you to think about how to read this photograph, by applying the four frames for reading: purpose, genre/medium knowledge, subject knowledge, and self-perception. Explain, as I did in the previous scenarios, how each frame might influence *how* you might read this photograph: Number each frame, and then write a brief paragraph explaining how the frame influences how you will read the photograph to make inferences about Mrs. Smith. Your instructor may ask you to do this in your journal, submit it as a short response, or post it to the online discussion board.

Reading situations, like writing situations, can really differ, and each asks something different from you. There is no one "right" way to read well, or to write well, in most situations. Instead, there are choices. These choices are rhetorical; in every reading situation, you need to think about your purpose in reading the text, about the text itself—its subject, its genre/medium, and the author's likely purpose and audience—and about your self-perception in relation to the text's subject and genre/medium. You need to think about what these frames together imply about how you *might* approach the text. It's not a science. There's no formula to follow. Mostly, you simply want to be a *flexible* reader and writer, one who can read a situation well enough to make decisions about how to approach it. This becomes possible when you pay attention to your process.

A Process for Reading to Write

2.4

Understand the special demands of reading to write and practice doing it.

The process of reading to write is going to be different than, say, that of reading for pleasure. For example, lately I'm reading books about the Chicago mobster Al Capone. My motives are both learning and pleasure, but I really don't plan on writing anything about Capone, so I'm not as active a reader as I am when I'm reading something for, say, an essay I'm writing or a book I'm researching. I spend considerably less time taking notes, marking passages, mining the bibliography, and doing other things like that. I'm less worried about *what I can do* with what I'm reading.

Not long ago, I was working on an essay in which I was exploring why certain landscapes—usually the ones we know best from our childhoods—often get under our skins even if we no longer live in those places. My reading for this project led me to all kinds of sources—articles in anthropology, history, and literary works. This reading was enjoyable, but it was also work. In the back of my mind, I was always asking, *Does this relate to the questions I'm interested in?* It was a reading process that was much more directed by my purposes—by my desire to use what I was reading in my own writing.

Questions for the Process of Reading to Write

So far we've explored the various ways we might approach academic reading situations in general. We've explored questions like these: What are typical situations? How might frames such as purpose or genre knowledge influence what we do? Now let's look specifically at processes for those reading situations—typical in college—in which you have to write about what you read, especially when this involves inquiry into a topic.

What Do I Want to Know? Inquiry is driven by questions, not answers. What do you want to know? In Chapter 1 (see "A Writing Process Driven by Questions" on pp. 30–31), I explained that inquiry into most topics about which you know little often begins with informational questions: What is known about the impact

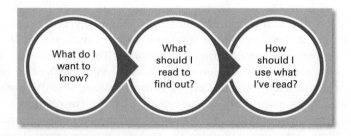

Figure 2.2 Reading to write is one of the most goal-oriented types of reading. First, you are guided by your research question: What do you want to know? If you know this, you know what to look for and how to use it in your own work.

of climate change in the Australian Outback? Why are reality shows so popular? In the beginning of an inquiry project, this larger goal—to develop some background knowledge—provides some guidance for how you read, but the reins will be pretty loose. You're likely to wander around a lot. That's okay as a start, but the reading and writing processes need the discipline of good questions that will keep you focused.

Consider some writing I did about theories of dog training. This writing actually originated with the behavior of our golden retriever: Ada was being bad—jumping on people, barking, and generally being a pest. Ada's behavior launched some research on websites, in books, and even in academic articles. At first, I just wanted to know what the schools of thought were on getting Ada in line—a question of fact. Before long, I knew enough to come up with much better questions, more specific and more directive, which changed not only what I was reading, but also how I read it. From the question "What are theories of dog training?" I ended up asking "What is the relationship between the use of shock collars and dog aggression and submission?"

Obviously, the second question is a much better guide to what I should read and what I should ignore. That one step of focusing the reading process on a narrower question, taken at an appropriate point, can then make a huge difference in the efficiency of the process.

What Should I Read to Find Out? Should I buy a new iPhone? Who cares? Well, I care. But because this is a question in which only I have a stake, I'm likely to read all kinds of things to help me answer the question. I won't be picky. But suppose my question were less personal and more academic, or less concerned with just me and instead addressed to a larger audience—for example, "Do people's emotional attachments to their iPhones have any of the qualities of clinical addiction?" With this question, I'll be a lot more picky about what I read. I'll look in the usual places—some quality websites—but I'll also check out some books on addictive behavior and search scholarly articles, probably in psychology, to see if anyone has studied users' emotional bonds to cell phones.

In other words, *what* you read (the kinds of texts you focus on) is determined not just by the question you're asking but the context in which you're asking it—the rhetorical choices related to your writing: Who are you writing for and why? What kinds of information will that audience find most persuasive? Are there certain kinds of evidence they would expect you to offer?

What Do I Do with What I've Read? There are lots of reading situations in which this question is answered by someone else:

> *Based on your reading about painters in the Italian Renaissance, explain in 250 words how an artist such as Caravaggio chose his subject matter.*

In this case, you know why you're reading and what you need to do with what you've read—explain a particular point. But in many reading situations, especially those that are inquiry based, you'll have considerable freedom to determine not only your own purposes for your reading, but also, more specifically, how you might use some of it in your paper or presentation. For example, are you reading a book chapter to find an explanation for a particular idea? Are you analyzing a statistical table to find evidence that supports a point you're trying to make?

In either type of reading situation, to actually do something with what you've read, you first have to know what you think about what you've read. How can you possibly make a decision about whether to quote an author or summarize some-one's ideas or select this fact or another if you don't know what *you* make of what the text is saying? If you don't know much about the Italian Renaissance, let alone Caravaggio, then at the very least you'll need to try to *understand* as much as you can from your reading about both.

We've already talked about how reading isn't a monologue. "Blah, blah, blah," says a text, and you mindlessly write, "The text says, 'blah, blah, blah.'" That's a monologue, not a conversation. You're not talking with—or back to—what you're reading; you're parroting what you've read. In the next section, I'll propose a method for encouraging conversations with what you read that will help you to discover what you think.

Having a Dialogue with What You Read

⊙
Watch
the Video on
Reading Actively
in your MyLab

A typical process for reading to write:

1. Google some keywords on a topic.
2. Go to the first link that seems promising and click on it.
3. If the site seems relevant, read it once quickly online. Bookmark or print.
4. Go read something else and repeat the process.
5. Hope that you'll remember what you've read when you have to write on the topic.

Another standard version of the process:

1. Get a reading assignment.
2. Read it once, maybe twice. Highlight a few things.
3. Compose something quickly about what you've read for the assignment, looking for a slot to put what you highlighted.

These are passive readings. While they're fine for some reading tasks, they don't work well when you have to write about what you read in a paper or for a presentation.

Imagine an alternative scenario: An assigned reading, a book, or an article is open in front of you, but so is your notebook. Your pen is poised to mark up the text—underlining, making marginal notes, adding question marks next to confusing passages and checks next to those you think are important (see Figure 2.3). When you're finished with your first reading, you go back and focus on what you marked. On the left-hand page of your notebook, you write down quoted passages that seem

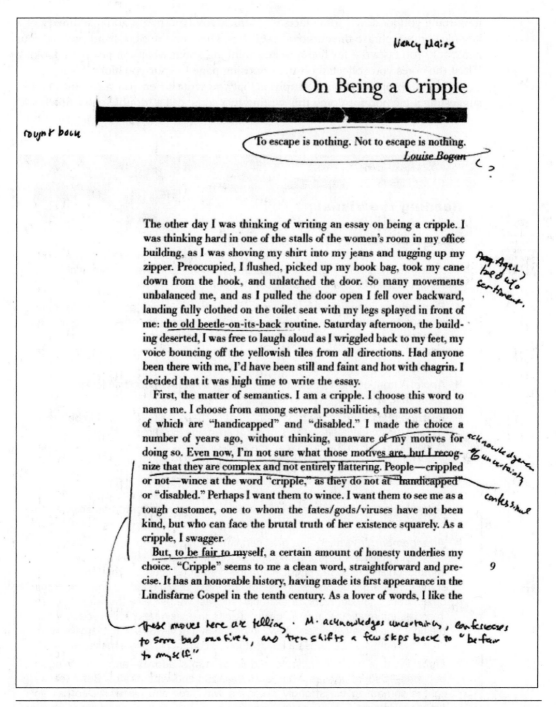

Nancy Mairs

On Being a Cripple

roun r baiu

To escape is nothing. Not to escape is nothing.
Louise Bogan

The other day I was thinking of writing an essay on being a cripple. I was thinking hard in one of the stalls of the women's room in my office building, as I was shoving my shirt into my jeans and tugging up my zipper. Preoccupied, I flushed, picked up my book bag, took my cane down from the hook, and unlatched the door. So many movements unbalanced me, and as I pulled the door open I fell over backward, landing fully clothed on the toilet seat with my legs splayed in front of me: the old beetle-on-its-back routine. Saturday afternoon, the building deserted, I was free to laugh aloud as I wriggled back to my feet, my voice bouncing off the yellowish tiles from all directions. Had anyone been there with me, I'd have been still and faint and hot with chagrin. I decided that it was high time to write the essay.

First, the matter of semantics. I am a cripple. I choose this word to name me. I choose from among several possibilities, the most common of which are "handicapped" and "disabled." I made the choice a number of years ago, without thinking, unaware of my motives for doing so. Even now, I'm not sure what those motives are, but I recognize that they are complex and not entirely flattering. People—crippled or not—wince at the word "cripple," as they do not at "handicapped" or "disabled." Perhaps I want them to wince. I want them to see me as a tough customer, one to whom the fates/gods/viruses have not been kind, but who can face the brutal truth of her existence squarely. As a cripple, I swagger.

But, to be fair to myself, a certain amount of honesty underlies my choice. "Cripple" seems to me a clean word, straightforward and precise. It has an honorable history, having made its first appearance in the Lindisfarne Gospel in the tenth century. As a lover of words, I like the

marginal annotations:
Play Agent, bored w/ to sentiment.

acknowledges uncertainty

confessional

9

these moves here are telling. M. acknowledges uncertainty, confesses to some bad motives, and then shifts a few steps back to "be fair to myself."

Figure 2.3   When you read to write, you should leave your tracks everywhere on a text—underlining, asking questions, making comments. This is the beginning of a dialogue between you and an author.

important; you jot down some facts that struck you. You might add a summary of a key idea or paraphrase the author's assertions. Then, on the right-hand page of your notebook, you fastwrite for five minutes, thinking about what you just read, looking left at the notes you collected on the opposing page to spur you along.

What I'm proposing, quite simply, is that you write when you read. But I'm also suggesting a method for doing this writing that some call a "double-entry notebook"

Watch the Video on **Reading Visuals Critically** in your MyLab

Inquiring into the Details

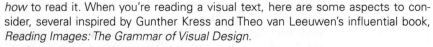

Reading the Visual

As you know by now, it helps enormously when reading a new text to have some knowledge of *how* to read it. When you're reading a visual text, here are some aspects to consider, several inspired by Gunther Kress and Theo van Leeuwen's influential book, *Reading Images: The Grammar of Visual Design*.

- ■ **Framing:** As in writing, what the photographer, advertiser, painter, or designer chooses to include in an image and what she chooses to leave out profoundly affect the story, idea, or feeling that an image communicates. Framing might also establish a viewer's distance from the action. An up-close-and-personal image suggests intimacy, while a long shot has the opposite effect.

- ■ **Angle:** A front-on view of a subject creates a different effect than looking up, or down, at it.

- ■ **Relationships:** One of the most important of these is the relationship between you and the image itself. Is the subject of an image looking directly at the viewer or looking away? In the first case, the subject seems to make some kind of demand, and in the second, perhaps an invitation to simply be an onlooker.

- ■ **Color:** Designers know that color affects mood. Not surprisingly, for example, red is a color that communicates feelings of passion and energy. White suggests "purity" and innocence. Yellow is sunny and joyous. For further analysis on color and emotion in visuals, search the web on the subject.

- ■ **Arrangement:** In writing, we give certain information emphasis by where we place it in a sentence, in a paragraph, or in the composition as a whole. Visual information also uses the physical arrangement of objects for emphasis, making some things larger or smaller, in the foreground or background, to one side or the other. Kress and Leeuwen, for example, suggest we perceive the left side of an image as information that is a "given," things that viewers readily accept, while the right side is perceived as "new," information that viewers aren't familiar with. Thus, the right side becomes a key feature for communicating a message.

- ■ **Light:** What is most illuminated and what is in shadows—and everything in between—also influences what is emphasized and what is not. But because light is something we strongly associate with time and place, it also has an emotional impact.

or "dialogue journal." If you're using a notebook, you use the left-hand page to collect important ideas, facts, quotations, or arguments from what you've read, and then you use the right-hand page to think about them through writing. You can use this method with any kind of text, including visual texts. See how the double-entry journal technique works for you to analyze an image. (You can find some ideas about analyzing images in "Inquiring into the Details: Reading the Visual.")

Exercise 2.4

Double-Entry Journaling with a Visual Text

Advertisements make arguments. They are carefully designed to combine text and images to persuade a particular audience to *do* something: buy a product, join an organization, vote for a referendum, make a donation. You know this, of course. But most of us are generally unaware of the methods of visual arguments. We don't think much about how they use visual language to direct our gaze and touch our emotions. To read an advertisement with these things in mind involves *rhetorical analysis*. Up until now, we've looked at analyzing the rhetorical situations we find ourselves in as readers. Now we'll turn our attention to analyzing texts. What is the intended audience of an ad? What are the appeals designed specifically for that audience? How does the ad use emotion? How was it composed to emphasize certain ideas or feelings?

> Watch
> the Video on
> Evaluating a Text
> for Claims, Reasons,
> and Evidence
> in your MyLab

In Chapter 7, on writing arguments, we'll look at this kind of rhetorical analysis more closely, but for now, take a close look at the following ad for a male fragrance and practice using the double-entry journal technique to analyze the ad's argument.

STEP ONE: Here are the questions for your reading of the ad:

- What specifically are the appeals in the advertisement, and to whom are they directed?
- What specific evidence in the ad would you point to as examples of those appeals?
- Do you think they are persuasive for the intended audience? Why or why not?

Following the instructions below, use two blank opposing pages in your journal to explore these questions.

STEP TWO: On the left-hand page, collect some information from the ad. Make a list of everything you look at in the ad, *in the order you look at it*. What do you see first? Then what? Then what? Be as specific as you can. When you've got a satisfactory list, circle those items that you think are particularly effective.

STEP THREE: On the right-hand page, explore your thinking about what you've collected. Begin a fastwrite by explaining to yourself why you think the items you circled on the other side of the page were effective. For whom? What kind of

audience response might they get? How would these visual arguments convince a man to buy a "fragrance"?

STEP FOUR: Go back to the questions in step 1. How would you answer them?

STEP FIVE: Reflect in writing, in class, or on your class's online discussion board about your experience using the double-entry journal to analyze the ad.

- What worked? What didn't?
- How might you apply the double-entry journal to other reading situations?
- What did the method encourage you to do in the exercise that you don't usually do when you read?

Techniques for Keeping a Double-Entry Journal You're going to discover ways to make a reading journal work best for you. But if the journal is going to help you have *conversations* with what you read, I think there are some essential elements.

Watch
the Animation on
Keeping a Journal
in your MyLab

1. **You must focus on what the author or text actually says.** That's the beauty of the left-facing page of a double-entry journal. Because it contains passages, facts, ideas, and claims from your reading, you're working with what the text said, not what you vaguely remember that it said.

2. **Try to suspend judgment.** When we feel strongly about what we're reading, it's human to decide right away whether we agree or disagree with an author or come to a quick conclusion about what a text says and what it means. But you can use writing—and especially the open-ended, exploratory process of fastwriting—to really think things through before you come to conclusions.

3. **Use questions.** Sometimes, as in Exercise 2.4, the questions are provided to direct your reading. More often, you read to discover the questions that interest you about a topic. These will fuel bursts of writing that lead you towards having something to say about what you read.

4. **Read to write and write to read.** This is fundamental. No matter what technique you use to help you use what you read in your writing, you should always write *as you read* and, if possible, immediately after.

The double-entry journal method I'm proposing here typically involves a notebook and a pen, but if you prefer to work on a tablet or laptop, you can accomplish much the same thing with a two-column Word or Pages document. If you use a notebook, imagine that the spiral binding that divides opposing pages is a kind of table. On the left sits a text and an author; on the right sits you. You're having a conversation across that imaginary table. What do you talk about?

First, you have to try to understand what a text is saying. That's what the left-hand page is for—to try to collect information and ideas from what you're reading that you think are central to understanding the reading. On the right-hand page of your journal, you respond to, think and ask questions about, and explore what you've collected on the opposite page.

Here's one approach for organizing a conversation with a text using the double-entry approach.

Exercise 2.5

Reading Creatively, Reading Critically

Now that you've seen how the double-entry journal can help analyze an image, let's try it with a more familiar kind of text. I published the essay "The Importance of Writing Badly" some years ago, but I think it still expresses several of the main

Listen
to the Audio on
Critical Reading
in your MyLab

ideas behind this book. I'd like you to read the piece critically, though, using the double-entry journal method I've described in the previous section.

As before, you'll use opposing pages of your journal.

Watch
the Animation on
Critical Reading
in your MyLab

STEP ONE: Read the essay once through, marking it up. (Make a copy if you don't want to write in your book.) Read it a second time and, on the left-hand page of your notebook, carefully *copy* lines or passages from the essay that

- Connected with your own experience and observations
- Raised questions for you
- Puzzled you
- You thought seemed to be key points
- You disagreed or agreed with or you think about differently
- You found surprising or unexpected

The Importance of Writing Badly
Bruce Ballenger

1   I was grading papers in the waiting room of my doctor's office the other day, and he said, "It must be pretty eye-opening reading that stuff. Can you believe those students had four years of high school and still can't write?"

2   I've heard that before. I hear it almost every time I tell a stranger that I teach writing at a university.

3   I also hear it from colleagues brandishing red pens who hover over their students' papers like Huey helicopters waiting to flush the enemy from the tall grass, waiting for a comma splice or a vague pronoun reference or a misspelled word to break cover.

4   And I heard it this morning from the commentator on my public radio station who publishes snickering books about how students abuse the sacred language.

5   I have another problem: getting my students to write badly.

6   Most of us have lurking in our past some high priest of good grammar whose angry scribbling occupied the margins of our papers. Mine was Mrs. O'Neill, an eighth-grade teacher with a good heart but no patience for the bad sentence. Her favorite comment on my writing was "awk," which now sounds to me like the grunt of a large bird, but back then meant "awkward." She didn't think much of my sentences.

7   I find some people who reminisce fondly about their own Mrs. O'Neill, usually an English teacher who terrorized them into worshipping the error-free sentence. In some cases that terror paid off when it was finally transformed into an appreciation for the music a well-made sentence can make.

8   But it didn't work that way with me. I was driven into silence, losing faith that I could ever pick up the pen without breaking the rules or drawing another "awk" from

a doubting reader. For years I wrote only when forced to, and when I did it was never good enough.

Many of my students come to me similarly voiceless, dreading the first writing assignment because they mistakenly believe that how they say it matters more than discovering what they have to say.

9

The night before the essay is due they pace their rooms like expectant fathers, waiting to deliver the perfect beginning. They wait and they wait and they wait. It's no wonder the waiting often turns to hating what they have written when they finally get it down. Many pledge to steer clear of English classes, or any class that demands much writing.

10

My doctor would say my students' failure to make words march down the page with military precision is another example of a failed education system. The criticism sometimes takes on political overtones. On my campus, for example, the right-wing student newspaper demanded that an entire semester of Freshman English be devoted to teaching students the rules of punctuation.

11

There is, I think, a hint of elitism among those who are so quick to decry the sorry state of the sentence in the hands of student writers. A colleague of mine, an Ivy League graduate, is among the self-appointed grammar police, complaining often about the dumb mistakes his students make in their papers. I don't remember him ever talking about what his students are trying to say in those papers. I have a feeling he's really not that interested.

12

Concise, clear writing matters, of course, and I have a responsibility to demand it from students. But first I am far more interested in encouraging thinking than error-free sentences. That's where bad writing comes in.

13

When I give my students permission to write badly, to suspend their compulsive need to find the "perfect way of saying it," often something miraculous happens: Words that used to trickle forth come gushing to the page. The students quickly find their voices again, and even more important, they are surprised by what they have to say. They can worry later about fixing awkward sentences. First, they need to make a mess.

14

It's harder to write badly than you might think. Haunted by their Mrs. O'Neill, some students can't overlook the sloppiness of their sentences or their lack of eloquence, and quickly stall out and stop writing. When the writing stops, so does the thinking.

15

The greatest reward in allowing students to write badly is that they learn that language can lead them to meaning, that words can be a means for finding out what they didn't know they knew. It usually happens when the words rush to the page, however awkwardly.

16

I don't mean to excuse bad grammar. But I cringe at conservative educational reformers who believe writing instruction should return to primarily teaching how to punctuate a sentence and use *Roget's Thesaurus*. If policing student papers for mistakes means alienating young writers from the language we expect them to master, then the exercise is self-defeating.

17

It is more important to allow students to first experience how language can be a vehicle for discovering how they see the world. And what matters in this journey—at least initially—is not what kind of car you're driving, but where you end up.

18

Page #	Notes from Reading	Exploratory Response
	■ Direct quotations ■ Summaries of key ideas ■ Paraphrases of assertions, claims ■ Facts, specific observations, data ■ Premises and reasons ■ Interesting examples or case studies	Focused fastwrite on material in left-hand column or page. ■ What's relevant to the question? ■ What questions does it raise? ■ What do I think and feel about this? ■ How does it change the way I think about the subject? ■ What surprised me? ■ What's the most important thing I take away from the reading? ■ How does it connect to what I've heard, seen, or read before?

Figure 2.4 An approach to keeping a double-entry journal. Note that you should keep track of page numbers (if any) in the reading from which you collected information and put in the left-hand column or page. Particularly when doing research, you should begin by jotting down key bibliographic information about each source.

STEP TWO: Now use the right-hand page of your notebook to think further about what you wrote down on the left-hand page. Use the questions in Figure 2.4 as prompts for a focused fastwrite. Write for five or six minutes without stopping.

STEP THREE: Reread what you've written. Again, on the right-hand page of your notebook, write your half of the imaginary dialogue below with someone who is asking you about the idea of "bad writing."

Q: I don't understand how bad writing can help anyone write better. Can you explain it to me?

A:

Q: Okay, but is it an idea that makes sense to you?

A:

Q: What exactly (i.e., quotation) does Ballenger say that makes you feel that way?

A:

STEP FOUR: Finish the exercise by reflecting in your journal for five minutes on what, if anything, you noticed about using the double-entry journal to have a "conversation" with a text. In particular:

■ How did it change the way you usually read an article such as this one?

■ How might you adapt it for other situations in which you have to read to write?

■ What worked well? What didn't?

■ Do you think the method encouraged you to think more deeply about what you read?

One Student's Response

Briana's Journal

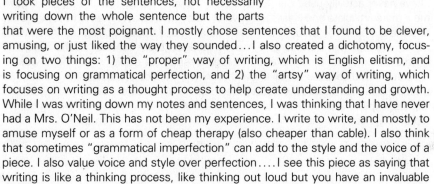

EXERCISE 2.5
STEP TWO

I took pieces of the sentences, not necessarily writing down the whole sentence but the parts that were the most poignant. I mostly chose sentences that I found to be clever, amusing, or just liked the way they sounded...I also created a dichotomy, focusing on two things: 1) the "proper" way of writing, which is English elitism, and is focusing on grammatical perfection, and 2) the "artsy" way of writing, which focuses on writing as a thought process to help create understanding and growth. While I was writing down my notes and sentences, I was thinking that I have never had a Mrs. O'Neil. This has not been my experience. I write to write, and mostly to amuse myself or as a form of cheap therapy (also cheaper than cable). I also think that sometimes "grammatical imperfection" can add to the style and the voice of a piece. I also value voice and style over perfection....I see this piece as saying that writing is like a thinking process, like thinking out loud but you have an invaluable record of your thoughts. I also get that you need to write and write a lot. The more the better; it gives you more to work with. I also think that it helps you write better and enjoy it because you are getting a lot of experience. It's not so much about how you wrote it as it is about what you write about.

STEP THREE

Q: I don't understand how bad writing can help anyone write better. Can you explain it to me?
A: What you have to say is just as important as how you write it. Writing is a way of thinking, sort of like thinking out loud—a way of thinking through things and reflecting more deeply on things. It feels awesome to write with reckless abandon and show no concern for punctuation or grammar. It helps you think unhindered, to find out how you truly think and feel. Thoughts and feelings have little concern for these things. Looking back at your thoughts that you have written you can see your thoughts. Then you can look at how you have written. Being observant and introspective of your own writing will help you develop better writing skills.

Q: Okay, but is it an idea that makes sense to you?
A: Definitely, I prefer to write badly. I believe that it's a better expression of my actual thoughts, flaws and all. When I write on my computer my spellcheck goes crazy with "fragment sentences." But who cares? That's what I want to say and that is how it comes out and how it sounds in its natural state. I don't change it. Give me all your green squiggly underlinings, Windows Vista. It has been driven into so many students that we have to write perfectly—use correct punctuation, no vague pronouns, correct verb tense, good sentence syntax, and structure. I think that writing should be more than that. I think that it should be more of a form of expression.

One Student's Response *(continued)*

Q: What exactly (i.e., quotation) does Ballenger say that makes you feel that way?

A: "Many of my students come to me similarly voiceless, . . . because they mistakenly believe that how they say it matters more than discovering what they have to say."

I have never actually used the "double-entry" journal method before. I think it gave me a more articulate and clear idea of what I thought and how I came to think that. It became a map of my thought process. I usually have trouble pulling my thoughts in my writing together, but this gave me my thoughts more concisely. I also liked that I had a record of my thoughts and that regardless of the quality of writing, it was an accurate record because we all know that memory is not all that reliable. I think that method would be good when you have to opine on a subject at length. I liked the explore, explain, evaluate, and reflect structure because when you are writing off the top of your head it is easy to lose focus. So this helps keep you on track.

Wrestling with Academic Discourse: Reading from the Outside In

The one thing that most influences your ability to understand and use what you read is prior knowledge. If you're reading about a topic you know little about— say, the biology of the Palouse worm, a creepy, disturbingly large creature that lives deep underground in northern Idaho—then you will work harder than if you read about a topic you know a lot about. In college, unfortunately, much of what you read will be about subjects that are new to you. This means, quite simply, that you may struggle. You'll get frustrated. In your worst moments, you might want to throw an assigned reading out the window. I did that once.

But here's the good news: The more you learn about a topic, the more competent you'll feel. And it isn't just topic knowledge that will make you feel this way. It's also learning to understand the *discourse* of a particular discipline. You learn how to read, for instance, the discourse of biologists who write about worms, or the discourse social workers use to write to each other about poverty. There are all kinds of *discourse communities*, or groups of people who share certain ways of thinking, asking questions, and communicating—not just scholarly ones. Electricians share certain ways of communicating with each other. So do surfers.

It might seem that reading specialized discourses such as these is just about deciphering jargon. It's actually about much more than that. Academic discourse, for example, includes not just the language insiders use, but also

- The kinds of questions participants typically ask that guide research in the field
- Preferred methods for answering questions

- The kinds of evidence a discourse community considers persuasive
- Conventions for reporting discoveries

Maybe the best way to introduce the idea of academic discourse is to show you two excerpts from different publications on the same topic: the appeal and effects of watching reality television. One is from the *Internet Journal of Criminology* and the other from a popular book on the reality television phenomenon.

Exercise 2.6

Reading Reality TV

Reflective, rhetorically aware readers will immediately notice significant differences between the excerpts. Some are obvious. For example, there are citations in excerpt 1 but not in excerpt 2. The first has a more formal style than the second. You probably know that the journal excerpt (excerpt 1) is more *authoritative* than the web excerpt, particularly if you are reading them for a college paper. But do you know why? Read the excerpts closely, thinking about the differences.

EXCERPT 1

There has been a considerable interest in how real reality television shows are as well as how such programming creates and reinforces gender and racial stereotypes (Cavender and Bond-Maupin 1993; Eschhotz et al. 2002; Estep and Macdonald 1983; Oliver 1994; Prosise and Johnson 2004).[1] Many researchers focus on crime-based reality television because this type of television programming blurs the line between entertainment and fact. Televised police offers are theoretically sent on real-life calls to interact with actual criminals. More than two decades ago, Sheley and Ashkins (1981) documented that the officer and perpetuator most likely depicted on police television dramas was far from reality (see too Oliver 1994; Oliver and Armstrong 1998). Oliver (1994), in a content analysis of reality-based police shows, found that white characters on these shows were more likely to be portrayed as police officers than perpetrators of crimes, whereas black and Hispanic characters were more likely to be shown as criminals than police officers. If viewers appreciated that this was Hollywood entertainment albeit docudrama, such images might not be so troublesome. However, as Prosise and Johnson (2004) write, most people report that their knowledge of crime, as well as their understanding of law enforcement generally, comes through the media rather than from direct experience (see too Oliver and Armstrong 1998).

---

[1]Monk-Turner, Elizabeth, Homer Martinez, Jason Holbrook, and Nathan Harvey. 2007. "Are Reality TV Crime Shows Continuing to Perpetuate Crime Myths?" *The Internet Journal of Criminology* (n.d.). Web. Retrieved 1 Sept. 2011.

EXCERPT 2

Reality TV: An Insider's Guide to TV's Hottest Market[2]

For all of Reality's faults, I still liken critics who blanketly bash it while favoring sitcoms and dramas to wine snobs who can't just enjoy an orange soda now and then. Good Reality TV rivals the best traditionally scripted television for entertainment value, and its positive impact on popular culture cab be felt just as deeply, if not more so, than its negative....

Consider the number of people emboldened by shows like *The Biggest Loser* to make positive changes in their lives. The popular Reveille series for NBC started a national movement to get in shape that echoed across America, making heroes (and moguls) of personal trainers Bob Harper and Jillian Michaels. While the show has been taken to task by critics for its wall-to-wall product placement, one can hardly argue that any other show in recent history has done so much measureable good for viewers.

Generating

STEP ONE: Explore your reaction to each excerpt. Which *are you* most inclined to believe? Why? What exactly is it about the less persuasive excerpt that makes it unconvincing? How do your own feelings about beliefs about reality TV figure into your reaction? Fastwrite for three minutes, thinking through writing about your reasons for believing one excerpt more than the other.

Judging

STEP TWO: Focus your analysis on the persuasiveness of each excerpt by summarizing what you discovered in the fastwrite. Make a list of at least three reasons why, if you were writing a college essay on the influence of reality TV on fans, you might prefer one excerpt over another.

STEP THREE: In excerpt 1, what do you notice about the author's relationship with others who have written on the topic of reality TV? How would you contrast that with the same relationship in excerpt 2? Jot down a few ideas.

STEP FOUR: You probably noticed that the second excerpt uses the first person, while the first doesn't. Much, though not all, academic discourse avoids the first person. This isn't a rule. It's a convention, a feature of this kind of writing that people typically use because it serves some rhetorical purpose. What purpose might it serve in excerpt 1? List a few ideas about this.

STEP FIVE: Because the excerpts are so brief, you don't have much to work with. But can you speculate on what kind of evidence might be sufficient to support

---

[2]Devold, Troy. 2011. *Reality TV: An Insider's Guide to TV's Hottest Market*. Studio City, CA: Michael Weise Productions, 22. Print.

an assertion when someone writes an essay on a commercial website and what might be necessary in the field of criminology?

STEP SIX: Try to pull some of this together in a short paper or discussion-board post. Using examples from the excerpt, write about 200 words in response to the following two questions:

What are some characteristics distinguishing between the discourse of criminology and the discourse of popular writing on crime? How might these differences influence how you read and use each as a college writer and a reader writing a paper on reality TV?

Features of Academic Discourse

There isn't a single academic discourse. There are *discourses.* Academic discourse varies from discipline to discipline. Why? Though all academic disciplines—from those in the humanities to those in the natural sciences—are dedicated to creating new knowledge, they each look at different aspects of the world. Some, say, look at language. Others observe natural phenomena. A few, like math, work with often highly abstract concepts or ideas. Because the materials for discovery differ, the methods of discovery do, too. These differences naturally lead to unique ways of describing things and reporting them. Before long, you have different discourse communities.

2.5 Understand some conventions of academic writing and recognize them in texts.

Despite all these differences, it is possible to make some observations about academic discourse that apply across discourse communities. As you become more experienced reading in various fields, you will begin to recognize some of these basic patterns, and this will help immensely with your academic reading.

1. **Billboards.** Academic writers announce, usually somewhere near the beginning of an article, what they are going to do.

2. **Reviews.** Like the first excerpt in the previous exercise, academic texts often include a review of what others have already said on a topic. This is also near the beginning.

3. **Hedges.** Contrary to the popular assumption that academic texts usually deal in certainty, much academic writing qualifies assertions. They signal caution by using words such as *appear to be, tend,* or *suggest.*

4. **Signposts.** Most academic subjects are complicated neighborhoods, and scholarly writing offers plenty of explicit direction about turns in an argument (e.g., *however*), presentation of reasons (e.g., *because*), and evidence (e.g., *for example*).

5. **Questions.** Academic writing is about inquiry and discovery, and these arise from questions to explore or problems to solve. Identifying the question or the problem that an academic article proposes to address is key to understanding what it's about; knowing the question driving the research also makes the path authors took to a study's conclusions much more obvious.

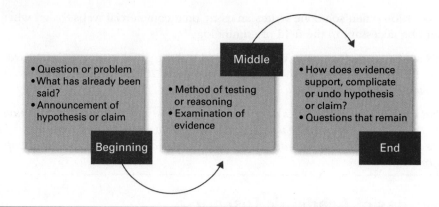

Figure 2.5   How academic articles are organized. Scholarly articles have a beginning, middle, and end, like stories do. Beginnings "billboard" the research question and review the literature. In the middle, writers tell what happened in their own investigation of the question, and in the end, they analyze the significance of what they've found.

These five conventions are some handholds that you can seize as you wrestle your way through much academic discourse. Figure 2.5 may also help you understand how scholarly articles typically organize their content.

I distinctly remember the first time I had to read articles in biology, my undergraduate major. I was lost. I felt stupid. And I vowed to avoid scholarly books and articles if at all possible. In the Internet age, this kind of avoidance can seem even more possible. But the truth is that, even if more possible, it's not a good idea. Popular writing on the web can help you to develop a working knowledge of your topic—and this will help you begin to understand the scholarship—but it is the academic sources that will always lead you in the deepest, richest understandings of the things that interest you. Now is the time to learn how to break through the initial reaction to academic prose—"This is so boring!"—and enter the messy, exciting marketplace where knowledge is made. That, after all, is the business of the university, and, as a curious writer and reader, you're invited to become a part of it.

Using What You Have Learned

Reflect on the learning goals introduced at the beginning of the chapter.

1. **Examine your existing beliefs about reading and how they might be obstacles to reading effectively.** You began to explore this when you wrote about your past experiences with texts, beginning with the attitudes about reading that you inherited from home and school. As you become a more experienced reader in college, your beliefs about your own competence should *evolve* along with your understanding of how different kinds of texts work. In the days ahead, think about this. Are you thinking about reading any differently than when you began the course?

2. **Apply reading purposes relevant to reading in college.** In other classes, you'll be asked to do a lot of reading. Often enough, you'll know why you're doing it. You have to memorize information from a textbook for a test. You've got to summarize findings from a research article. On the other hand, your purpose for much of the reading you do will be decided by you. You're re-searching a paper or a presentation, for instance, and you collect all kinds of texts. How do you want to *use* them? To explore, explain, evaluate, or reflect? What "frames" will you use to make that decision?

3. **Recognize reading situations and the choices about approaches to read-ing that they imply.** In Chapter 1, you learned that writers are guided by their rhetorical awareness. Why am I writing, and for whom? Are there certain kinds of writing that will work best in this situation? Readers are rhetorically aware, too, in much the same way. Just as there is no "right" way to write in all situations, there is no "right" way to read whenever you have a read-ing assignment. Hopefully, you will see that each situation implies certain choices. Think about what they are and you'll read much more strategically.

4. **Understand the special demands of reading to write, and practice doing it.** We've spent time in this chapter thinking about the process of reading in a very particular situation: when you have to write about what you read. This is much more active reading, and the best way to jumpstart your engagement with a text is *to write* while you read and after. Always have a pen in your hand. We think in dialogue with a text. It is from this conversation that we collaborate with a text to discover our own ideas about something. Throughout *The Curious Writer*, I'll encourage you to keep up this dialogue, using some form of the double-entry journal and through questions.

5. **Understand some conventions of academic writing and recognize them in texts.** In this chapter, you learned about *academic discourse*, a weighty-sounding term that describes the range of conventions that scholarly communities use to ask questions, choose methods, and report on discoveries. Whatever major you end up in, you'll be required to learn some of the conventions of academic discourse in your field. Don't let anyone tell you that academic discourse is just one thing—it varies from scholarly community to scholarly community—but we have explored general features of much academic writing, things such as how many scholarly articles are organized. I hope that the practice you've had here of looking for some of these conventions makes you alert to them as you continue to take courses in other fields. It's invaluable rhetorical knowledge that will help you immensely as you write papers for other classes.

Complete Additional Exercises and Practice on Chapter 2 in your MyLab

2

INQUIRY PROJECTS

Writing a personal essay can be like seeing an old picture of yourself. This publicity photograph of my mother (an actress), my older brother, and me in the 1950s returns me to that world—a time when fathers were often missing from the picture.

Writing a Personal Essay

3

Learning Objectives

In this chapter, you'll learn to

3.1 Use personal experiences and observations to drive inquiry.

3.2 Apply the exploratory thinking of personal essays to academic writing.

3.3 Identify the characteristics of personal essays in different forms.

3.4 Use invention strategies to discover and develop a personal essay topic.

3.5 Apply revision strategies that are effective for shaping narratives.

Writing About Experience and Observations

Most us were taught and still believe that we need to know what we are going to write before we actually pick up the pen or sit in front of the computer. My student Lynn was typical.

"I think I'll write about my experience organizing the street fair," she told me the other day. "That would be a good topic for a personal essay, right?"

"Do you think so?" I said.

"Well, yes, because I already know a lot about it. I'll have a lot to write about."

"Okay, but is there anything about this experience that you want to understand better?" I said. "Anything about it that *makes you curious*?"

"Curious? It was just a street fair," she said.

"Sure, but is there something about what happened that makes you want to look at the experience again? Is there a chance that you might learn something about yourself, or about street fairs, or about the community, or about people, or…?"

Lynn was clearly sorry she asked. What I should have said was much more to the point: The best personal essay topics are those that are an itch you need to scratch. These tend not to be topics you have already figured out. While the topics can be familiar to you, the results of your inquiry are usually much better if you don't yet know what you think about your topics and you're interested to learn more about them. The best topics ask to be written about because they make you wonder *Why did I do that? What does that mean? Why did that happen? How did I really feel? What do I really think?*

Unlike most other forms of inquiry, the personal essay invites an initial display of confusion or uncertainty from writers regarding their subjects. In other words, the personal essay can be, and often is, a vehicle for writers to work through their thinking and feeling on a subject, directly in front of their readers.

> The personal essay is a vehicle for writers to work through their thinking and feeling on a subject, directly in front of their readers.

As a form, the *personal* essay places the writer at center stage. This doesn't mean that once she's there, her responsibility is to pour out her secrets, share her pain, or confess her sins. Some essays do have these confessional qualities, but more often they do not. Yet a personal essayist, no matter the subject of the essay, is still *exposed*. There is no hiding behind the pronoun *one*, as in "one might think" or "one often feels," no lurking in the shadows of the passive voice: "An argument will be made that…" The personal essay is first-person territory.

In this sense, the personal essay is much like a photographic self-portrait. Like a picture, a good personal essay tells the truth, or it tells *a* truth about the writer/subject, and it often captures the writer at a particular moment in time. This explains why the experience of taking a self-portrait, or confronting an old picture of oneself taken by someone else, can create the same feeling of exposure that writing a personal essay often does.

But it does more. When we gaze at ourselves in a photograph, we often see it as yanked from a larger story about ourselves, a story that threads its way through our lives and gives us ideas about who we were and who we are. This is what the personal essay demands of us: We must somehow present ourselves truthfully and measure our past against the present. In other words, when we hold a photograph of ourselves, we know more than the person we see there knew, and as writers of the personal essay, we must share that knowledge and understanding with readers.

Though the personal essay may be an exploration of a past experience, it needn't always be about memories. A personal essay can instead focus on some aspect of writers' present lives, just as long as it raises questions that interest them. Why is it so irritating to overhear certain cell phone conversations? Why do I have an obsession with zombie-killing apps? What does it feel like to be an international student in Idaho? All of these kinds of questions might lead to a personal essay, and the challenge of writing about the present is the same as writing about the past: What do I understand about this now that I didn't understand when I started writing about it?

Motives for Writing a Personal Essay

3.1
Use personal experiences and observations to drive inquiry.

Essai was a term coined by the sixteenth-century French nobleman Michel de Montaigne, a man who endured plague epidemics, the bloody civil war between French Catholics and Protestants, and his own bouts of ill health. His tumultuous and uncertain times, when old social orders and intellectual traditions were under assault, proved to be ideal ferment for the essay. The French verb *essaier* means "to attempt" or "to try," and the essay became an opportunity for Montaigne to work out his thoughts about war, the education of children, the evils of doctors, and the importance of pleasure. The personal essay tradition inspired by Montaigne is probably unlike what you are familiar with from school. The school essay is often formulaic—a five-paragraph theme or thesis-example paper—while the personal essay is an open-ended form that allows for uncertainty and inconclusiveness. It is more about the process of coming to know than presenting *what* you know. The personal essay attempts *to find out* rather than *to prove*.

It is an ideal form of inquiry if your purpose is exploratory and if you're particularly interested in working out the possible relationships between your subject and yourself. Because the personal essay is openly subjective, the writer can't hide. The intruding *I* confronts the writer with the same questions over and over again: *Why does this matter to me? What do I make of it? How does this change the way I think of myself and the way I see the world?* Because of this, one of the principal dangers of the personal essay is that it can become narcissistic; it can go on and on about what the writer thinks and feels, and the reader can be left with that nagging question—*So what?* The personal essayist must always find some way to hitch the particulars of his or her experience to something larger—an idea, a theme, or even a feeling that readers might share.

On the other hand, one of the prime rhetorical advantages of the personal essay is its subjectivity. Because it is written with openness and honesty, the essay can be a very intimate form, inviting the reader to share in the writer's often concealed world. The *ethos* of personal essayists, or their credibility (see the rhetorical triangle in Chapter 7, p. 241), revolves around the sense that they are ordinary people writing about ordinary things. In the personal essay, we often get to see the face sweating under the mask. Honesty is one of the essay's primary virtues, and because the form allows for uncertainty and confusion, the writer doesn't need to pretend that he has *the* answer or that he knows more than he lets on about his subject.

The Personal Essay and Academic Writing

In some ways, the personal essay might seem like a dramatic departure from the kind of academic writing you've done in other classes. Openly subjective and sometimes tentative in its conclusions, the personal essay is a relatively open form that is not predictably structured like much academic writing. Additionally, the tone of the personal essay is conversational, even intimate, rather than impersonal and removed. So, if your sociology or economics professor will never ask for a personal essay, why bother to write one in your composition class?

3.2
Apply the exploratory thinking of personal essays to academic writing.

It's a fair question. While the pleasures of personal essay writing can be reason alone to write these essays, there are also other important reasons, related to your academic work:

- Because of your connection to the subject matter, the personal essay, more than any other form, gives you an opportunity to use exploration as a method of inquiry, and to practice those habits of mind that are so important to academic inquiry: suspending judgment, tolerating ambiguity, and using questions to challenge easy assumptions.

- For this same reason, the essay is especially conducive to the kind of thinking typical of academic inquiry: a movement back and forth between critical and creative thinking. In many ways, the personal essay is *inductive* like scientific thinking; it looks closely at the data of experience and attempts to infer from that information theories about the way things are.

- The essay emphasizes the *process* of coming to know about yourself and your subject, exposing your reasoning and the ways you use knowledge to get at the truth of things. Reflecting on these things can tell you a lot about how you think.

Finally, the personal essay and academic writing are actually not that far apart. We often assume that "academic" is supposed to be "objective," that self and subject should never mix. "Never use I" is supposedly the rule, and never, ever talk about yourself in an academic paper. These *are* common conventions, especially in the sciences. One reason for this is that the appearance of objectivity gives research more authority. Another is that in many disciplines attention generally needs to be on the data and not the author.

And yet a surprising number of academic articles make use of the first person, and not just in the humanities, where you might expect a more subjective perspective. The first person—and a more personal approach to scholarship—is evident in many disciplines, including literary criticism, business, anthropology, education, nursing, and even geology. This first-person writing often tells a story, sometimes through a case study, a narrative of the writer's experiences, or an account of his or her intellectual journey.

In any case, don't let the relative rarity of the first person in scholarship fool you into not seeing that there's something personal in even the most formal academic writing. It's *always* personal. What we choose to write about, the questions that interest us, and our particular ways of seeing are always at work, even in academic prose. True, the sciences use methods to minimize the researcher's biases. But it's impossible to eliminate them. Whenever anyone—scientist or humanist—uses language to communicate discoveries, they enter a social marketplace where words have meanings that are negotiated with others. For writers—any kind of writers—language is a social currency.

The essay, more than any other form, gives you an opportunity to use exploration as a method of inquiry.

But most important, much of what you are asked to write in college is about what *you* think. Not what your instructor thinks, or what the textbook author thinks, or what someone said in a journal. All of these things provide you with something to think about. You decide what you want to say. One of the great things about the personal essay is that it insists on flushing writers out into the open. You can't hide in the wings, concealed in the shadow of other people's opinions or someone else's findings. What *you* think is what the essay is all about.

Features of the Form

Feature	Conventions of the Personal Essay
Inquiry questions	What does it mean to me? What do I understand about this now that I didn't then?
Motives	Self-discovery is often the motive behind writing a personal essay—the essay is in first person, and the essayist is center stage.
Subject matter	Essayists often write about quite ordinary things; they find drama in everyday life, past or present. Personal essays can be about taking a walk, breaking up on Facebook, the housefly on your beer glass. In some ways, the real subject of a personal essay is the writer herself and how she makes sense of her world.
Structure	Essays often tell stories, but, unlike fiction, they both show *and* tell, using both narrative and exposition, sometimes alternating between the two. When about the past, there are two narrators in the essay—the "then-narrator" and "now-narrator." One describes what happened and the other what the narrator makes *now* of what happened. The thesis may come near the end rather than at the beginning. And the essay isn't necessarily chronological.
Sources of information	Like any essay, the personal essay might use all four sources of information—memory, observation, reading, and interview. But it is likely to lean most heavily on memory and observation.
Language	Personal essays work in two registers—the more general language of reflection and the very specific detail of experience and observation. This specific language is often sensory: What did it look like exactly? What did you hear? How did it feel?

Prose+

Josh Neufeld's "A Matter of Perspective" is a kind of personal essay. The theme—the idea that we have moments in our lives when we feel very, very small—speaks not only to Josh's experience, but our own. A graphic essay such as this one exploits image and text in combination, amplifying the power of each.

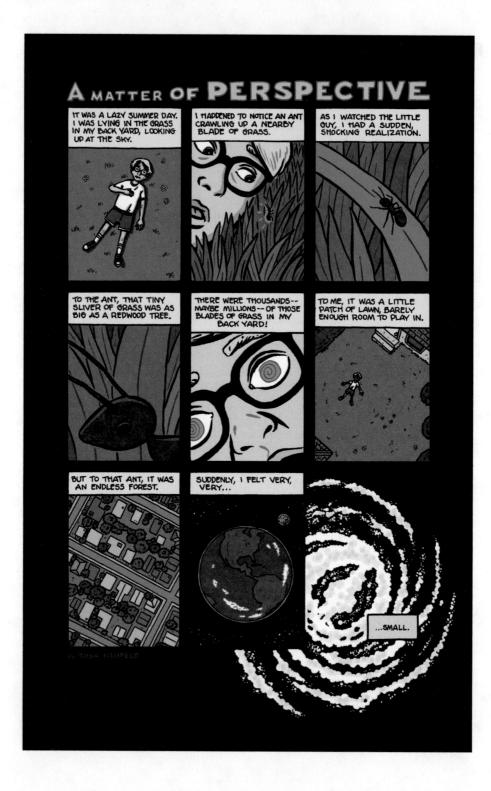

READINGS

▶ Personal Essay 1

Try this exercise: Think about things, ordinary objects, that you have held onto all these years because you simply can't throw them away. They *mean* something to you. They are reminders of another time, or a turning point in your life, or a particular moment of joy, or sadness, or perhaps fear. Consider a few of mine: a green plaster Buddha, handmade; a glow-in-the-dark crucifix; an old pair of 7 × 50 Nikon binoculars; a 1969 Martin D 28 guitar; a brown-handled flathead screwdriver with a touch of red nail polish on the handle; a homemade lamp made from a wooden wallpaper roller; a red dog's collar. While they are meaningless to you, naturally, to me each of these objects carry a charge; they remind me of a story, a moment, a feeling. The personal essay makes space for writers to explore the meanings of such ordinary things.

Taking Things Seriously: 75 Objects with Unexpected Meanings, the book from which the following short essay was taken, is a gallery of objects—a bottle of dirt, a Velveeta Cheese box, a bear lamp, a pair of shells, and more—that are displayed along with the meditations on their significance by the writers who have carefully kept them as reminders on a shelf, in a closet, by their beside. Laura Zazulak's short essay focuses on a doll that she snatched from a neighbor's trash can. Just telling a story about what happened is not enough in an essay. The essay must have something to say to someone else. As you read Zazulak's brief piece, consider what that might be.

Every Morning for Five Years

Laura Zazulak

Every morning for five years, I was not so welcomingly greeted by my middle-aged, developmentally disabled neighbor across the street. Scotty never smiled and seemed to hate everyone. He never left the perimeter of his mother's lawn and apparently didn't know how to do anything but rake, shovel, take out the trash, and yell in a high-pitched voice. I'd pull out of my driveway and see him there, wearing a neon orange hunting cap, raking absolutely nothing at the same spot that he'd raked the day before. I'd think to myself, "Don't make eye contact!" But I always did. He'd stare at me and neither of us would blink.

1

Near the end of my fifth year on the street, Scotty stopped coming out of his house. At first, I was thankful. But as time passed, I began to worry. Then one Saturday morning in the middle of January I noticed that his window was wide open. Later that day, a police car showed up. Maybe Scotty and his mother got into one of their screaming

2

(continued)

(continued)

matches again? Then a funeral-home van pulled up and they brought out Scotty's body. Although it came as a surprise to me to discover that he knew how miserable his life was, he had killed himself.

3   The next day Scotty's uncle came over and began furiously carting things off to the dump. He left behind a garbage can in the driveway piled with all of Scotty's earthly possessions. I noticed two little pink feet sticking up into the air.

4   After dark, I crept across the street to the garbage can, armed with a travel-sized bottle of hand sanitizer. I looked left, then right. I dashed forward, tugged at the feet, and then ran as fast as I could back into my own backyard with my prize. Only then did I look at what I'd rescued. I would like you to meet Mabel.

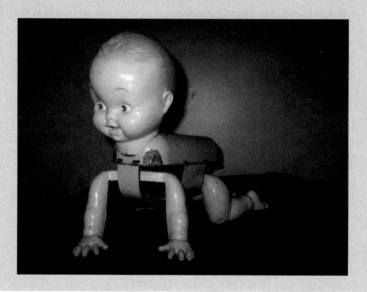

Inquiring into the Essay

Throughout *The Curious Writer*, I'll invite you to respond to readings, using questions related to the four motives for reading discussed in Chapter 2. The following questions, therefore, encourage you to explore (*What do I think about this?*), explain (*What do I understand that this is saying?*), evaluate (*What's my judgment about this?*), and reflect to discover (*How does this work?* or *How am I thinking about it?*) and shape what you think about the reading. In Chapter 2, I encouraged you to write while you read and after. Try that now using the double-entry journal technique (see pp. 55–60). As soon as you finish your first reading of "Every Morning for Five Years," open up your journal and on the right-hand page fastwrite your response to the explore and explain questions above. Write for at least three minutes. Then go back to Zazulak's essay and on the left-hand page jot down sentences or passages from it that you think are important to your understanding of it. Build your responses to the questions that follow from these first thoughts about what you just read.

1. **Explore.** All of the essays in the book *Taking Things Seriously*, from which the piece you just read was taken, have this to say: It is remarkable how much meaning we can invest in the ordinary when we take the time to notice. This is an idea you can explore on your own. Brainstorm a list of objects that might have "unexpected significance" for you. Choose one and fastwrite about it for four minutes. Then skip a line, choose another, and write for another four minutes. If this is interesting to you, repeat this over a few days and create a collage of brief stories that four or five objects inspired. Are there any themes that seem to run through all of them? Do they speak to each other in any way?

2. **Explain.** Explain how, read together, the photograph and the essay work together to create meanings that might not be apparent if they were read separately.

3. **Evaluate.** Personal essays like "Every Morning for Five Years" *imply* their meaning rather than state it explicitly. In that way, an essay like this one is more like a short story. Make an argument for your own understanding of the meaning of Zazulak's essay, and use passages from the piece to support your claim.

4. **Reflect.** One of the features of the personal essay is two narrators: the "now-narrator" and the "then-narrator." One looks back on experience from the present, applying knowledge that the "then-narrator" did not have. From this comes fresh insight. But these two narrators aren't always obvious. Can you see them in this essay?

▶ Personal Essay 2

America is a nation of immigrants, whose stories often haunt their children. Judith Ortiz Cofer moved from Puerto Rico as a child with her family in the mid-1950s to a barrio in Paterson, New Jersey. There she became both part of and witness to a familiar narrative, that of the outsider who finds herself wedged between two worlds, two cultures, and two longings: the desire to return "home" and the desire to feel at home in the new place. While this is a story most immigrants know well, it is also a deeply personal one, shaded by particular places, prejudices, and patterns.

In "One More Lesson," Cofer describes both of the places that competed for her sense of self—the Puerto Rico of her childhood, where she spent time as a child while her Navy father was away at sea, and an apartment in New Jersey, where she would go when he returned.

One More Lesson

Judith Ortiz Cofer

1   I remember Christmas on the Island by the way it felt on my skin. The temperature dropped into the ideal seventies and even lower after midnight when some of the more devout Catholics—mostly older women—got up to go to church, *misa del gallo* they called it; mass at the hour when the rooster crowed for Christ. They would drape shawls over their heads and shoulders and move slowly toward town. The birth of Our Savior was a serious affair in our *pueblo*.

2   At Mamá's house, food was the focal point of *Navidad*. There were banana leaves brought in bunches by the boys, spread on the table, where the women would pour coconut candy steaming hot, and the leaves would wilt around the sticky lumps, adding an extra tang of flavor to the already irresistible treat. Someone had to watch the candy while it cooled, or it would begin to disappear as the children risked life and limb for a stolen piece of heaven. The banana leaves were also used to wrap the traditional food of holidays in Puerto Rico: *pasteles*, the meat pies made from grated yucca and plantain and stuffed with spiced meats.

3   Every afternoon during the week before Christmas Day, we would come home from school to find the women sitting around in the parlor with bowls on their laps, grating pieces of coconut, yuccas, plantains, cheeses—all the ingredients that would make up our Christmas Eve feast. The smells that filled Mamá's house at that time have come to mean anticipation and a sensual joy during a time in my life, the last days of my early childhood, when I could still absorb joy through my pores— *when I had not yet learned that light is followed by darkness, that all of creation is based on that simple concept, and maturity is a discovery of that natural law.*

4   It was in those days that the Americans sent baskets of fruit to our barrio—apples, oranges, grapes flown in from the States. And at night, if you dared to walk up to the hill where the mango tree stood in the dark, you could see a wonderful sight: a Christmas tree, a real pine, decorated with lights of many colors. It was the blurry outline of this tree you saw, for it was inside a screened-in-porch, but we had heard a thorough description of it from the boy who delivered the fruit, a nephew of Mamá's, as it had turned out. Only, I was not impressed, since just the previous year we had put up a tree ourselves in our apartment in Paterson.

5   Packages arrived for us in the mail from our father. I got dolls dressed in the national costumes of Spain, Italy, and Greece (at first we could not decide which of the Greek dolls was the male, since they both wore skirts); my brother got picture books; and my mother, jewelry that she would not wear, because it was too much like showing off and might attract the Evil Eye.

6   Evil Eye or not, the three of us were the envy of the pueblo. Everything about us set us apart, and I put away my dolls quickly when I discovered that my playmates would not be getting any gifts until *Los Reyes*—the Day of the Three Kings, when Christ received His gifts—and that even then it was more likely that the gifts they

found under their beds would be practical things like clothes. Still, it was fun to find fresh grass for the camels the night the Kings were expected, tie it in bundles with string, and put it under our beds along with a bowl of fresh water.

The year went by fast after Christmas, and in the spring we received a telegram from Father. His ship had arrived in Brooklyn Yard. He gave us a date for our trip back to the States. I remember Mother's frantic packing, and the trips to Mayagüez for new clothes; the inspections of my brother's and my bodies for cuts, scrapes, mosquito bites, and other "damage" she would have to explain to Father. And I remember begging Mamá to tell me stories in the afternoons, although it was not summer yet and the trips to the mango tree had not begun. In looking back I realize that Mamá's stories were what I packed—my winter store.   7

Father had succeeded in finding an apartment outside Paterson's "vertical barrio," the tenement Puerto Ricans called *El Building*. He had talked a Jewish candy store owner into renting us the apartment above his establishment, which he and his wife had just vacated after buying a house in West Paterson, an affluent suburb. Mr. Schultz was a nice man whose melancholy face I was familiar with from trips I had made often with my father to his store for cigarettes. Apparently, my father had convinced him and his brother, a look-alike of Mr. Schultz who helped in the store, that we were not the usual Puerto Rican family. My father's fair skin, his ultra-correct English, and his Navy uniform were a good argument. Later it occurred to me that my father had been displaying me as a model child when he took me to that store with him. I was always dressed as if for church and held firmly by the hand. I imagine he did the same with my brother. As for my mother, her Latin beauty, her thick black hair that hung to her waist, her voluptuous body which even the winter clothes could not disguise, would have been nothing but a hindrance to my father's plans. But everyone knew that a Puerto Rican woman is her husband's satellite; she reflects both his light and his dark sides. If my father was respectable, then his family would be respectable. We got the apartment on Park Avenue.   8

Unlike El Building, where we had lived on our first trip to Paterson, our new home was truly in exile. There were Puerto Ricans by the hundreds only one block away, but we heard no Spanish, no loud music, no mothers yelling at children, nor the familiar *¡Ay Bendito!,* that catch-all phrase of our people. Mother lapsed into silence herself, suffering from *La Tristeza,* the sadness that only place induces and only place cures. But Father relished silence, and we were taught that silence was something to be cultivated and practiced.   9

Since our apartment was situated directly above where the Schultzes worked all day, our father instructed us to remove our shoes at the door and walk in our socks. We were going to prove how respectable we were by being the opposite of what our ethnic group was known to be—we would be quiet and inconspicuous.   10

I was escorted each day to school by my nervous mother. It was a long walk in the cooling air of fall in Paterson and we had to pass by El Building where the children poured out of the front door of the dilapidated tenement still answering their   11

(continued)

(continued)

mothers in a mixture of Spanish and English: "Sí, Mami, I'll come straight home from school." At the corner we were halted by the crossing guard, a strict woman who only gestured her instructions, never spoke directly to the children, and only ordered us to "halt" or "cross" while holding her white-gloved hand up at face level or swinging her arm sharply across her chest if the light was green.

12   The school building was not a welcoming sight for someone used to the bright colors and airiness of tropical architecture. The building looked functional. It could have been a prison, an asylum, or just what it was: an urban school for the children of immigrants, built to withstand waves of change, generation by generation. Its red brick sides rose to four solid stories. The black steel fire escapes snaked up its back like an exposed vertebra. A chain-link fence surrounded its concrete playground. Members of the elite safety patrol, older kids, sixth graders mainly, stood at each of its entrances, wearing their fluorescent white belts that criss-crossed their chests and their metal badges. No one was allowed in the building until the bell rang, not even on rainy or bitter-cold days. Only the safety-patrol stayed warm.

13   My mother stood in front of the main entrance with me and a growing crowd of noisy children. She looked like one of us, being no taller than the sixth-grade girls. She held my hand so tightly that my fingers cramped. When the bell rang, she walked me into the building and kissed my cheek. Apparently my father had done all the paperwork for my enrollment, because the next thing I remember was being led to my third-grade classroom by a black girl who had emerged from the principal's office.

14   Though I had learned some English at home during my first years in Paterson, I had let it recede deep into my memory while learning Spanish in Puerto Rico. Once again I was the child in the cloud of silence, the one who had to be spoken to in sign language as if she were a deaf-mute. Some of the children even raised their voices when they spoke to me, as if I had trouble hearing. Since it was a large troublesome class composed mainly of black and Puerto Rican children, with a few working-class Italian children interspersed, the teacher paid little attention to me. I re-learned the language quickly by the immersion method. I remember one day, soon after I joined the rowdy class when our regular teacher was absent and Mrs. D., the sixth-grade teacher from across the hall, attempted to monitor both classes. She scribbled something on the chalkboard and went to her own room. I felt a pressing need to use the bathroom and asked Julio, the Puerto Rican boy who sat behind me, what I had to do to be excused. He said that Mrs. D. had written on the board that we could be excused by simply writing our names under the sign. I got up from my desk and started for the front of the room when I was struck on the head hard with a book. Startled and hurt, I turned around expecting to find one of the bad boys in my class, but it was Mrs. D. I faced. I remember her angry face, her fingers on my arms pulling me back to my desk, and her voice saying incomprehensible things to me in a hissing tone. Someone finally explained to her that I was new, that I did not speak English. I also remember how suddenly her face changed from anger to anxiety. But I did not forgive her for hitting

me with that hard-cover spelling book. Yes, I would recognize that book even now. It was not until years later that I stopped hating that teacher for not understanding that I had been betrayed by a classmate, and by my inability to read her warning on the board. *I instinctively understood then that language is the only weapon a child has against the absolute power of adults.*

I quickly built up my arsenal of words by becoming an insatiable reader of books.   15

Inquiring into the Essay

Here's another chance to use writing to think about what you've just read. Try the double-entry technique that I suggested in Chapter 2. On a right-hand notebook page (or top of a Word document), finish your first reading of Cofer's essay with a fastwrite that explores and explains your reaction to and understanding of what you just read. Then on the left-hand page (or below your initial fastwrite in a Word document) collect some sentences or passages from the essay that seem relevant to your first thoughts.

1.   **Explore.** In the 1950s and 1960s, many saw America as a "melting pot." The idea was that although we may have many different immigrant backgrounds, we should strive toward some common "Americanism." For some this is still a powerful idea, but for others the melting pot metaphor reflects cultural dominance and even prejudice, a demand that differences be ignored and erased rather than celebrated. In your journal, write about your own feelings on this controversy. Tell the story of a friend, a relative, a neighbor who was an outsider. Tell about your own experience. What did it mean to assimilate, and at what cost?

2.   **Explain.** Explain what you understand Cofer to mean in the second-to-last sentence of the essay: *I instinctively understood then that language is the only weapon a child has against the absolute power of adults.* To arrive at this explanation, consider exploring your thinking first. Fastwrite for one full minute without stopping, beginning with "The first thing I think when I read this is…And then I think…And then…"

3.   **Evaluate.** What might this essay be asserting about cultural assimilation in America during the 1950s and 1960s? Would such an assertion still be relevant?

4.   **Reflect.** One of the most common reasons students cite for liking a story is that "they could relate to it." Usually, this seems to mean that the author's and reader's experience coincide somehow: "I've felt like that" or "That happened to me, too." Does this mean that an American reader from the Chicago suburbs won't ever "relate to" a story by a child-soldier in Uganda? And can an Anglo reader of Cofer's essay genuinely "relate to" her experience as an American of Puerto Rican descent? Reflect on what it means to "relate to" something you read by talking about your experience reading Cofer's essay.

Seeing the Form

Photo Essays

In 1997, Brooklyn photographer Lauren Fleishman was living in France when she met the love of her life. When the affair ended, she composed a photo essay about the relationship, with the poignant title "You Would Have Loved Him, Too." She assembled 29 images, including shots of handwritten notes from her former lover, into a visual personal essay. One of her photographs for that series is included here. Fleishman is a professional photographer, but people create photo essays all the time on sites such as Flickr. Though the authors may not be consciously composing essays, these photographic series often do what personal essays do, but without words: They tell a story.

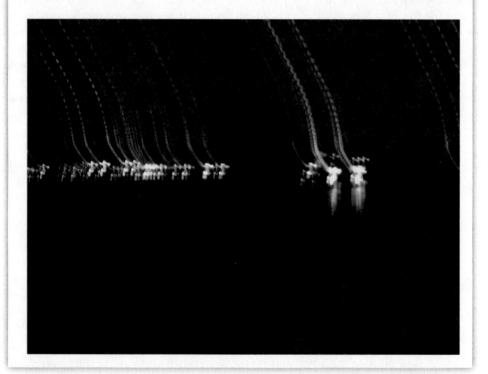

THE WRITING PROCESS

Inquiry Project **Writing a Personal Essay**

👁
⌐ **Watch** ⌐
the Animation on
Writing Memoirs
in your MyLab

Here are some approaches to writing a personal essay as an inquiry project—a traditional essay and some multimodal methods. Your instructor will give you further guidance on the details of the assignment.

Inquiry questions: What does it mean to me? What do I understand about this now that I didn't understand then?

Write a personal essay on a topic that you find confusing or that raises interesting questions for you. Topics need not be personal, but they should arise from your own experiences and observations. The essay should offer a central insight about what you've come to understand about yourself and/or the topic. In other words, you will "essay" into a part of your life, past or present, exploring the significance of some memories, experiences, or observations. Your motive is personal discovery—reaching that new insight.

Your essay should do all the following (see also p. 75 for typical features of the personal essay):

- Do more than tell a story. There must be a *purpose* behind telling the story that speaks in some way to someone else. It should, ultimately, answer the *So what?* question.

- Include some reflection to explain or speculate about what you understand *now* about something that you didn't understand *then*. Your essay should have both a then-narrator and a now-narrator, one who remembers what happened and the other who sees what happened with the understanding you have now.

- Be richly detailed. Seize opportunities to *show* what you mean rather than simply explain it.

Prose+

Write your essay as a radio essay/podcast, and digitally record yourself reading the piece, using Audacity, GarageBand, or other audio software. (See p. 143 for more information on using Audacity.) This essay should be no longer than 2 to 3 minutes. The incorporation of music is optional. Keep the following in mind:

- This is a conversational medium. Write the piece like you talk.

- Be concise. Don't waste any words.

- The point (S.O.F.T.—say one fricking thing) of your essay should be clearly stated.

- Emphasize story, and avoid long stretches of exposition.

Write your essay to then publish on the web using Blogger, Wordpress, or other blogging software. You can use the site throughout the semester to post personal essays on other topics, and use this experience in a final paper to explore some aspect of the theme "The Public and the Personal." Some tips for writing a personal essay in this form include:

- Craft a good title for your essay so search engines and RSS readers will notice your piece.
- People who read unfamiliar blogs will often merely glance at them first. Write your essay to get your readers' attention and make it easily "scannable." Use subheadings, images, boxes, and so on.
- Write with voice. Your essay should have a strong persona that you can imagine using in almost any blog you write.

Write a personal essay modeled after "Every Morning for Five Years" (p. 77–78). Begin with a digital photograph of an object that is meaningful to you, and then explore its significance.

Writing Beyond the Classroom

Essaying "This I Believe"

The essay genre, which has been around for about five hundred years, is a vibrant and increasingly common form of writing on the radio and online audio. Why? One reason might be that the intimacy of the essay—the sense of a writer speaking directly to a reader without the masks we often wear when we write—seems particularly powerful when we hear

A public dialogue about belief—one essay at a time.

this i believe®

Writing Beyond the Classroom (*continued*)

the voice of writing embodied in speech. Certainly, the ease with which we can "publish" essays as podcasts accounts for the explosion of online essayists.

This I Believe, a program heard on public radio (thisibelieve.org), is typical of radio programs that actively seek to broadcast student essays (which are subsequently published as podcasts). The program was begun in the 1950s by famed journalist Edward R. Murrow, who invited radio listeners and public figures to submit very brief (350–500 word) essays that stated some core belief that guided their "daily lives." As revived by the nonprofit organization This I Believe, the program is enormously popular and features work from people from all walks of life, including college students who may have written a "This I Believe" essay in their writing courses.

The program's website offers this advice to essayists:

1. Find a way to succinctly and clearly state your belief.
2. If possible, anchor it to stories.
3. Write in your own voice.
4. "Be positive," and avoid lecturing the listener.

What Are You Going to Write About?

With the personal essay, nearly anything goes. Essayists write about everything from their struggles with eating disorders, adjusting to life after military service, or dealing with the loss of a sibling to what we typically consider utterly commonplace things: a walk, negotiating use of an armrest with a fellow airplane passenger, a fondness for weird hats. Whatever you write about, what matters most is that you've chosen the topic because you aren't quite sure what you want to think about it. Write about what confuses you, what puzzles you, or what raises itchy questions.

3.4 Use invention strategies to discover and develop a personal essay topic.

The process for discovering a topic (see Figure 3.1) begins simply with what I call opening up, or generating lots of material. Open the warehouse of memory and walk around, or open your eyes and look around you *now*. Just collect some things, without judging their value for this project. Next, narrow things down. Make some judgments. Decide on an experience or observation that raises the most interesting questions—about how you feel or what it means. Now try out this topic by generating more material that focuses on it. Finally, make some judgments about what (if anything) all this writing has helped you to understand about yourself or the topic. These insights help you to clarify what your essay might really be about. The essayist Vivian Gornick writes that personal essays have both a *situation* and a *story*. The situation is what happened—the doctor told you when you were twelve that your leg was broken. The story is what you understand *now* about the significance of that situation. Maybe that time of walking on crutches gave you insight into a kind of suffering that you otherwise wouldn't have known, and this inspired the empathy you feel now for a disabled friend.

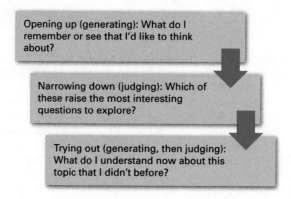

Figure 3.1 A process for discovering a personal essay topic

Generate material about possible situations to write about, narrow them down, and then focus on trying to discover the larger story you might be trying to tell.

Opening Up

Watch
the Animation on
Writing Reflections
in your MyLab

Even if you've already got an idea for a personal essay topic, spend some time exploring the possibilities before you make a commitment. It doesn't really take much time, and there's a decent chance that you'll discover a great topic for your essay you never would have thought of otherwise.

The journal prompts that follow will get you going. What you're after is to stumble on an interesting topic. Actually, it's more like stumbling through the *door* to an interesting topic—a door that gives you a look at what you might fruitfully explore with more-focused writing. Try several prompts, looking for a topic that might, after some writing, raise questions such as these:

- *Am I uncertain about what this might mean?*
- *Is this topic more complicated than it seemed at first?*
- *Might I understand these events differently now than I did then?*

Listing Prompts. Lists can be rich sources of topic ideas. Let them grow freely, and when you're ready, use an item as the focus of another list or an episode of fastwriting. The following prompts should get you started thinking about both your experiences and your observations.

1. Make a list of experiences you've had that you can't forget. Reach into all parts and times of your life.

2. Make a list of things that bug you. Think about everyday things like people with Apple computer fetishes or friends who send text messages in the middle of a serious conversation.

When they work, writing prompts open a door to promising topics. More-focused writing later will help you to explore the room and generate the information that may lead to a sketch or draft.

Fastwriting Prompts. Early on, fastwriting can help you settle on a narrower topic, *if* you allow yourself to write "badly." Then use a more focused fastwrite, trying to generate information and ideas within the loose boundaries of your chosen topic.

1. Choose an item from a list you've created to use as a prompt. Just start fastwriting about the item; perhaps start with a story, a scene, a situation, a description. Follow the writing to see where it leads.

One Student's Response

Lauren's Journal: Lists of Things That Bug Me

People who write in library books

Dead batteries

Goatheads in bicycle tires

Bad instructions

Spitting

Bad beer

Profane football fans

Global warming deniers

2. Most of us quietly harbor dreams—we hope to be a professional dancer, a good father, an activist, a marketing executive, an Olympic luger, or a novelist. Begin a fastwrite in which you explore your dreams. When the writing stalls, ask yourself questions: *Where did this dream come from? Do I still believe in it? In what moments did it seem within reach? In what moments did it fade?* Plunge into those moments.

3. What was the most confusing time in your life? Choose a moment or scene that stands out in your memory of that time, and, writing in the present tense, describe what you see, hear, and do. After five minutes, skip a line and choose another moment. Then another. Make a collage.

4. What do you consider "turning points" in your life, times when you could see the end of one thing and the beginning of something else? Fastwrite about one of these for seven minutes.

Visual Prompts. Images trigger ideas, and so can more-visual ways of thinking. Let's try both. Boxes, lines, arrows, charts, and even sketches can help us see more of the landscape of a subject, especially connections between fragments of information that aren't as obvious in prose. The clustering or mapping method is useful to many writers early in the writing process as they try to discover a topic. (See the "Inquiring into the Details" box on p. 92 for more details on how to create a cluster.) Figure 3.2 shows my cluster from the first prompt listed here.

1. What objects would you most regret losing in a house fire? Choose a most-treasured object as the core for a cluster. Build a web of associations from it, returning to the detail in the core whenever a strand dies out.

2. Find a photograph from your past, perhaps like the one from mine that opens this chapter. Fastwrite about what you see in the picture, what you don't see, and a story that it inspires.

3. Draw a long line on a piece of paper in your journal. This is your life. Divide the line into segments that seem to describe what feels like distinct times in your life. These don't have to correspond to familiar age categories such as adolescence or childhood; they could correspond to periods in your life you associate with a place, a relationship, a dilemma, a job, a personal challenge, and so on. In any case, make the segments chronological. Examine your timeline, and, as a fastwrite prompt, put two of these periods in your life together. Explore what they had in common, particularly how the earlier period might have shaped the later one. See Figure 3.3 for a sample timeline.

4. Get on Google Earth. Find the town or city where you were born or lived as a young child. Zoom in on your neighborhood. Fastwrite about what this makes you remember. Alternatively, find the house you live in now. Using the "street view" feature, "walk" down the street, stopping at the homes of interesting neighbors that you know or have observed. With the image on the screen, fastwrite in your journal, telling yourself stories about the people in your neighborhood.

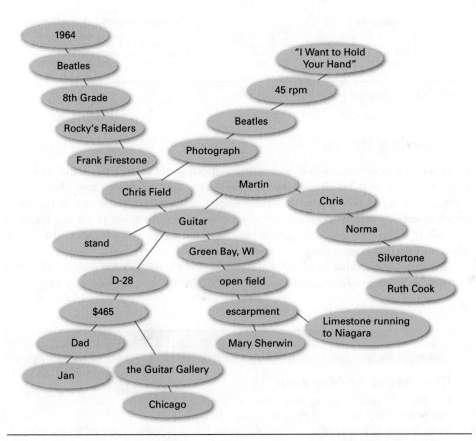

Figure 3.2   A cluster built around the one object I would most regret losing in a house fire: my Martin guitar

Research Prompts. Things we hear, see, or read can be powerful prompts for personal essays. It's tempting to believe that personal essays are always about the past, but just as often essayists are firmly rooted in the present, commenting and pondering on the confusions of contemporary life. In that sense, personal essayists are researchers, always on the lookout for material. Train your eye with one or more of the following prompts.

1. Put this at the top of a journal page: "Things People Do." Now go outside and find a place to observe people. Write down a list of everything you see people doing. Choose one action you find interesting and fastwrite about it. Is it weird? Why?

2. Look up the definition of "infatuation." Write it down on the top of a journal page, and then write for five minutes about your experience and observations of infatuations with people, things, places, ideas.

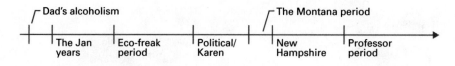

Figure 3.3   A sample timeline from my own life

Narrowing Down

Okay, you've generated some bad writing about your experiences and observations. Can any of it be shaped into a personal essay? Are there any clues about a topic you could develop with more-focused fastwriting? These are particularly tough questions when writing a personal essay, because most of us are inclined to think that the only one who could possibly care about what happened to us or what we observe is ourselves (or maybe Mom).

Don't make the mistake of judging the material too soon or too harshly. Personal essayists write successfully about any topic—often including quite ordinary things—so

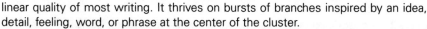

Clustering or Mapping

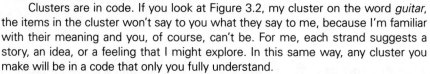

A method of visual thinking and invention, clustering (or mapping), is a refreshing alternative to the linear quality of most writing. It thrives on bursts of branches inspired by an idea, detail, feeling, word, or phrase at the center of the cluster.

Clusters are in code. If you look at Figure 3.2, my cluster on the word *guitar*, the items in the cluster won't say to you what they say to me, because I'm familiar with their meaning and you, of course, can't be. For me, each strand suggests a story, an idea, or a feeling that I might explore. In this same way, any cluster you make will be in a code that only you fully understand.

How do you cluster?

1. Begin with a blank page in your journal. Choose a core word, phrase, name, idea, detail, or question; write it in the middle of the page and circle it.

2. Relax and focus on the core word or phrase, and when you feel moved to do so, build a strand of associations from the core, circling and connecting each item. Write other details, names, dates, place names, phrases, and so on—whatever comes to mind.

3. When a strand dies out, return to the core and begin another. Keep clustering until the page looks like a web of associations. Doodle, darkening lines and circles, if that helps you relax and focus.

4. When you feel the urge to write, stop clustering and use one of the strands as a prompt for journal work.

don't give up on a promising topic this early in the game. But first, how do you decide what's promising?

What's Promising Material and What Isn't? The signs of a promising personal essay topic include the following:

- **Abundance.** What subject generated the most writing? Do you sense that there is much more to write about?

- **Surprise.** Did you see or say something you didn't expect about a topic?

- **Confusion.** What subject raises questions you're not sure you can answer easily?

In the personal essay, this last item—confusion and uncertainty—may yield the most-fertile topics. All of the questions listed at the beginning of "Opening Up," on page 88, are related in some way to a feeling that some experience or observation—even if it's familiar to you—has yet to yield all of its possible meanings.

Questions About Purpose and Audience. Who cares about my middling career as a high school cross-country runner? Who cares that I grew to love that gritty neighborhood in Hartford? Who cares that I find high school reunions weird? When we write about ourselves, we can't help but wonder why anyone, other than ourselves, *would* care. Maybe they won't. But if you discover something about your life that helps you to understand it better—even in a small way—you will begin to find an audience. After all, we are interested in understanding our own, often ordinary lives, and perhaps we can learn something from you.

To find an audience for a personal essay, you have to discover something to say about your experiences and observations that speak to others—a theme that you could express in a "we statement."

Obviously, why you're writing and for whom will profoundly influence your approach. That's a fundamental principle of rhetoric, one that you applied when you jotted that note to your teacher explaining the late assignment or texted your friend about your new bicycle. Although it is useful to consider your purpose and audience early on, make sure you don't let purpose and audience considerations squeeze off your writing. You always want to be open to the unexpected places your writing might lead you, especially in the early stages of the process. Being too vigilant about what readers think can discourage you from welcoming the messy accidents that can make for helpful discoveries.

Trying Out

Recently, I began working on a personal essay about my experiences going to high school reunions. I went to my fortieth last fall. As I generated "bad writing" on the subject of high school reunions, I kept returning to the same question: If I find these reunions generally weird and unsatisfying, why do I keep going? Using this inquiry question, I tried out my topic with the focused fastwrite that follows:

> *Last fall, I went to my 40th high school reunion...I had been to the 10th and the 20th, both of which required travel, once from the East coast and once from the West. I have no idea why I went to the effort...I didn't like high school...and I don't have many friends left in the Chicago suburb where I grew up. Why does anyone go to a high school reunion? I wonder if I've gone because...like it or not...high school is part of the narrative of our growing up that is at once mysterious and utterly familiar. I can remember everything...my failure to make the swim team that my brother was a star on...breaking the mercury barometer in physics class with my elbow while cleaning chalk erasers at the window...the sexual thrill of sitting on a bench next to Suzie Durment at a football game and feeling her thigh press close to mine. And yet I can't explain so much of high school...It just doesn't make sense. Why would I run cross country for four years and absolutely hate every minute of it?...How could I so thoroughly mishandle the kindness and affection of Jan Dawe, my first serious girlfriend?...And why all those years did I still pine for Lori Jo Flink, a girl from the 7th grade?...I guess that's one reason I go to my high school reunion...To enjoy the melancholy of seeing Lori Jo again and to relish the bittersweet taste of rejection....She always comes...Yet when I did see her this time it wasn't the same. We had a very brief conversation..."I looked you up on the Internet," she said, and was promptly swept to the dance floor by Larry Piacenza...She looked me up on the Internet...This should have given me a thrill but it didn't...Why not?...These days I've been stripping the siding off so many old narratives about myself, stories that I've mistaken for walls that bear weight...Perhaps I tossed Lori Jo on that pile of discarded lumber...along with the desire to attend another high school reunion. As I'm counting the gifts of middle age, I gladly add this one.*

What I hope you notice in my focused writing on reunions is how I keep using questions to tease out meaning, starting with a question I've never really asked myself before: Why do I go to high school reunions? Why would anyone? These inquiry questions pulled me out of the sea of experience and onto the mountain of reflection (highlighted passages), where I begin to see a possible answer: I go to reunions to revive old stories about myself that may no longer matter. In the personal essay, judging involves *reflection*. What do we make of what happened then that we didn't quite see until now? What might our observations of the world around us now *say* about that world and, maybe more important, about ourselves?

Questions for Reflection. In Chapter 1, I talked about thinking with writing as a movement back and forth between the creative and critical minds. In a way, personal essays and other narrative genres make this movement of the mind visible. In the essays you read earlier in the chapter, you may have noticed that some of the pieces seem to subtly shift from situation to story, from narrative to exposition, memory to reflection. This movement often has to do with time. You remember that something happened, recently or long ago. You describe what you remember, traveling back in time. But you aren't really a time traveler. You write from the present, and it is the present that allows you to understand what you couldn't have understood in the past. This is the source of reflection in the personal essay.

One way of thinking about this is in terms of the then-narrator and the now-narrator. The two narrators collaborate to make meaning. But it is the now-narrator who provides the judgment. Now that you've tried out your topic, put yourself in the now-narrator's perspective, answering questions such as these:

- What do you understand now about this topic that you didn't fully understand when you began writing about it? Start some writing with this phrase: "As I look back on this now, I realize that..."

- What seems to be the most important thing you're trying to say so far?

- How has your thinking changed about your topic? Finish this seed sentence as many times as you can in your notebook: *Once I thought* _____, *and now I think* _____.

Writing the Sketch

Throughout *The Curious Writer*, I'll encourage you to write what I call "sketches." As the name implies, this is a first look at something roughly drawn. It is a pretty rough draft of your piece, perhaps no more than about 300 words, with a tentative title. Though it may be sketchy, your sketch should be reader-based prose. You want someone else to understand what it's about. Don't assume they know what you know. When you need to, explain things.

Watch
the Video on
**Writing Personal
Narratives**
in your MyLab

A sketch is a good starting point for a personal essay in any mode. If you're working on a radio essay, for example, the sketch will be much the same as one that you write for a conventional essay. It's simply a very early script.

Choose your most promising material, and tell the story. If it's drawn from memory, incorporate both what happened then and what you make of it now. If it's built on observations, make sure they are detailed, anchored to particular times and places, and in some way significant.

You may or may not answer the "So what?" question in your sketch, though you should try. Don't muscle the material too much to conform to what you already think; let the writing help you figure out what you think.

To summarize, then, in a sketch try to do the following:

- Have a tentative title.
- Keep it relatively short.
- Write it fast.
- Don't muscle it to conform to a preconceived idea.
- Write to be read, with an audience in mind.
- Make it specific instead of general.

▶ Student Sketch

Amanda Stewart's sketch, "Earning a Sense of Place," faintly bears the outlines of what might be a great personal essay. When they succeed, sketches are suggestive; it is what they're not quite saying that yields promise. On the surface, "Earning a Sense of Place" could seem simply a piece about Amanda's passion for skiing. So what? And yet, there are lines here that point to larger ideas and unanswered questions. For example, Amanda writes that the "mental reel" of her swishing down a mountain on skis is "the image that sustains me when things are hard, and when I want to stop doing what is right and start doing what is easy." Why is it that such a mental image can be sustaining in hard times? How well does this work? The end of the sketch is even more suggestive. This really might be a piece about trying to find a "sense of place" that doesn't rely on such images; in a sense, the sketch seems to be trying to say that joy on the mountain isn't enough.

The pleasure of writing and reading a sketch is looking for what it might teach you, learning what you didn't know you knew.

I've highlighted portions of the text to illustrate a revision exercise that follows Amanda's essay.

Earning a Sense of Place
Amanda Stewart

1   The strings to my earflaps stream behind me, mixing with my hair as a rooster-tail flowing behind my neck. Little ice crystals cling to the bottom of my braid and sparkle in the sunlight. The pompom on top of my hat bobs up and down as I arc out, turning cleanly across the snow. I suck in the air, biting with cold as it hits my hot lungs, and breathe deep as I push down the run.

2   This is what I see when I picture who I want to be. It's the image that sustains me when things are hard, and when I want to stop doing what is right and start doing what is easy. I have made so many terrible decisions in the past that I know how far astray they lead me; I don't want that. I want the girl in the mental reel in her quilted magenta jacket and huge smile. She's what I grasp at when I need help getting through the day.

3   She's an amalgam of moments from the past mixed with my hopes for the future. I love to ski, and have since my parents strapped little plastic skis onto my galoshes when I was a year and a half old. From that day I flopped around our snow-covered yard, I've been in love with skiing. It's the only time I feel truly comfortable. Day to day I often feel so awkward. I wonder if my hair is right, or if my clothes fit. Last night, my roommate had a boy over, and as he sat on the couch talking to me, all I felt was discomfort and awkwardness. I didn't know what to say, felt judged, felt out of place. I never feel that way on skis. Even floundering in heavy, deep snow, or after a fall that has packed my goggles with snow

and ripped the mittens off my hands I know exactly what to do. I'm a snow mermaid, only comfortable in my medium. I often wish I could trade in my walking legs for something like a tail that is more truly me.

My dad's coffee cup at home says, "I only work so I can ski," and for him, it's true. Sometimes I feel like I only push through my daily life so I can get to the next mountain and zip up my pants and go. I don't want to live like that though: it's too much time looking forward to something, and not enough looking at what I'm living in. I need to appreciate my life as it is, snowy cold or sunny warm. That sense of place I have on skis can probably be earned here on the flat expanses of campus just as easily as I got it pushing myself down the bunny slopes so long ago. I just have to earn it.

4

Moving from Sketch to Draft

Here's the journey with the assignment you've taken so far:

Watch
the Animation on
**Writing Narration
Essays**
in your MyLab

1. You've generated some "bad writing," openly exploring possibilities for personal essay topics while suspending judgment.

2. You landed on a tentative topic.

3. You tried out this topic through more writing, some of it still "bad."

4. Your critical mind took over as you began to judge what you have so far. What questions does this material raise for you? What might it *mean?* With judgment comes a growing concern for audience. Why would they care about this?

5. You tried out the topic in a sketch. It's written with an audience in mind.

At the heart of the process I'm describing is a movement from "writer-based" to "reader-based" prose. This movement occurs with any type of writing, but it's particularly tricky with the personal essay. When you're writing about yourself, there is always this: *Who cares?*

The movement from sketch to draft must address this question. But how?

Evaluating Your Own Sketch. One way to assess whether your sketch might be meaningful to someone other than you is to look for the balance between narrative and reflection, or the then-narrator and the now-narrator. Try this:

- Take two highlighters, each a different color.
- Go through your sketch from beginning to end, using one color to highlight text that's story-telling, what happened or what you saw, and then use the other color to highlight text that is explanatory, more-general commentary about what happened or what you saw. What's the pattern of color?

There are several possibilities here:

1. **One color dominates.** Your sketch is mostly narrative or mostly summary, all then-narrator or all now-narrator. A personal essay that is mostly narrative

usually fails to address the "So what?" question. It seems to tell a story without a purpose. On the other hand, a personal essay that is all explanation fails to engage readers in the writer's *experiences*. It's all telling and no showing. Personal essays must both show *and* tell.

2. **One color dominates except at the end.** Typically, there is all narrative until the very end, when the writer briefly reflects, much like the formula for a fable, with its moral at the end. This can seem predictable to readers. But you can work with it in revision by taking the reflection at the end and using it to reconceive the essay *from the very beginning*. Can you take the ending and use the insight to organize your thinking in a revision?

3. **The colors alternate.** Sometimes this is the most interesting type of personal essay, because the two narrators are in genuine collaboration, trying to figure out what happened and what it *means*.

In my markup of Amanda's sketch (pp. 96–97), you can see how there is some shifting in the pattern of color. But exposition dominates. Her revision might need more story, more *showing* readers what happened that has made her think the things she now thinks.

If our personal experiences and observations are to mean anything to someone else, then they must, at the very least, both show and tell. They should, through details, descriptions, and scenes, invite an audience into the sea of our experiences. But they must also be clear about the *reason* behind the invitation—about what we have come to understand and want our audience to understand. In revising your sketch, focus on these two concerns above all.

Reflecting on What You Learned. In Chapter 1, I introduced the dialectical method of thinking through writing that moves back and forth between creative thinking and critical thinking, generating and judging. Highlighting the two narrators in your sketch is a way to actually see yourself thinking that way *in your own writing*—or not, depending on the patterns of color you see. Make a journal entry about this. In your sketch, which of the two narrators is more active, and why do you think that's so? In a revision of this sketch, how might you address any imbalance between the two? Where could the now-narrator tell more, or where could the then-narrator show more?

Developing

In the last section, you focused on using a sketch to identify the *purposes* of telling someone else about your memories, experiences, or observations. For example, in the sample sketch, Amanda seems to be telling us about her love for skiing because it suggests a longing that most of us feel: to transfer the confidence we feel in one part of our lives to every part. The key to developing your draft is to arrive at a fuller understanding of what your purpose is in telling your own stories *and then rebuild your essay around that insight from the beginning.*

In other words, as you begin your revision, focus on exploring the answer to these questions:

- What might this essay be saying, not only about me, but more generally about people who find themselves in similar situations?

- What questions does it raise that might be interesting, not only to me, but also to others who may not know me?

Fastwrite in your journal about these questions for as long as you can. One word of caution, though, and I can't stress it enough: YOU DO NOT NEED TO BE PROFOUND. Most of us aren't philosophers or really deep thinkers. We are ordinary people who are just trying to make sense of our lives and work towards those little insights that make us understand things a little better.

As you get a grip on the purpose behind your essay, you can focus your efforts on developing those parts of the narrative that are relevant. What scenes, anecdotes, details, observations, facts, stories, and so on might focus your attention—and later your readers' attention—on what you're trying to say about the topic?

For this, try some of the following strategies:

- *Explode a moment.* Choose a scene or moment in the story or stories you're telling that seems particularly important to the meaning of the essay. Reenter that moment and fastwrite for a full seven minutes, using all your senses and as much detail as you can muster.

- *Make lists.* Brainstorm a list of details, facts, or specifics about a moment or scene that was part of an experience or about an observation. Then list other experiences or observations that seem connected to this one (see "Cluster" below).

- *Research.* Do some quick-and-dirty research that might bring in other voices or more information that will deepen your consideration of the topic.

- *Cluster (or fastwrite).* Try to move beyond narrating a single experience or observation and discover others that might help you see important patterns. For example, let's say your sketch is about your experience working with the poor in Chile. Have you had other encounters with extreme poverty (or extreme wealth)? Can you describe them? What do they reveal about your feelings or attitudes about poverty or your reactions to what happened in Chile?

Drafting

Some of my students get annoyed at all the "stuff" I encourage them to do before they begin a first draft of a personal essay. In some cases, all the journal work isn't necessary; the writer very quickly gets a strong sense of direction and feels ready to begin composing. But from the beginning, I've encouraged you to gravitate toward topics that you find confusing, and with that kind of material, exploratory writing is time well spent. Remember, too, that journal writing counts as writing.

It not only offers the pleasures of surprise, but can ultimately make the drafting process more efficient by generating material that you won't have to conjure up during those long, painful periods of staring at the computer screen, wondering what to say next.

As you begin drafting, keep in mind what you've learned from your writing so far. For example:

- What is the most important question that is behind your exploration of the topic?
- What do you understand now that you didn't understand fully when you started writing about it?
- How can you show *and* explain how you came to this understanding?
- Have you already written a strong first line for the draft? Can you find it somewhere in all your journal writing?

Draft with your reader in mind. As you draft, ask yourself,

What does the reader most need to know to understand my thinking and feelings about this topic? What should I show about what happened, to give the reader a clear sense of what happened?

Methods of Development. Narrative is an especially useful method of development for personal essays. How might you use it to develop your subject?

Narrative. Narrative can work in a personal essay in at least three ways. You can use it to:

1. Tell an extended story of what happened.
2. Tell one or more anecdotes, or brief stories, that somehow address the question behind your interest in the topic.
3. Tell the story of your thinking as you've come to understand something you didn't understand before.

Often, a single essay uses narrative in all three types of ways.

Consider beginning your draft with the anecdote or the part of the story you want to tell that best frames the question, dilemma, or idea that is the focus of your essay (see "Inquiring into the Details: More Than One Way to Tell a Story"). If you're writing about the needless destruction of a childhood haunt by developers, then consider opening with the way the place looked *after* the bulldozers were done with it—description related to the end of your narrative.

Time in writing is nothing like real time. You can ignore chronology, if it serves your purpose. You can write pages about something that happened in seven minutes or cover twenty years in a paragraph. The key is to tell your story or stories in ways that emphasize what's important.

Using Evidence. How do you make your essay convincing, and even moving, to an audience? It's all in the details. Like most stories, the personal essay thrives on particularity: What exactly did it look like? What exactly did she say? What exactly did it sound and smell like at that moment? Evidence that gives a personal essay authority are details that make a reader believe the writer can be trusted to observe keenly and to remember accurately. All of the professional essays in this chapter are rich in detail. There is the neighbor with the "neon orange hunting cap" who rakes the same spot every day in Laura Zazulak's "Every Morning for Five Years," and the wilting banana leaves that curl around the coconut candy in Judith Ortiz Cofer's "One More Lesson." This focus on the particular—what it *exactly* looked like, smelled like, felt like, sounded like—makes an essay come alive for both writer and reader.

As you draft your essay, remember the subtle power of details. Tell, but always show, too.

Inquiring into the Details

More Than One Way to Tell a Story

This is my daughter Julia telling a story:

"And she was like..."

"And then I was like..."

"And then she was like..."

When we think about organizing experiences—something that personal essays try to do—we immediately think of narrative, and then, naturally, we think of the most common narrative structure: chronology. This is Julia's method of oral storytelling, as it is for most of us.

Yet in essay writing, strict chronology—this happened and then this and then this—may not be the best way to tell a story. Once locked into a strictly chronological narrative, you may feel compelled to tell the *whole* story. While chronological storytelling might be a good way to remember what happened as you explore your experiences in your journal or in early drafts, what you need to do in your essay is to tell those *parts* of the story (or stories) that are relevant to the question you're exploring or the thing you're trying to say.

Structure in the personal essay, as in all writing, must be a servant to purpose. Simply put, purpose is how you might answer a potential reader who wants to know this: *So what?* Why should I read this? Organize a narrative essay with the *So what?* question in mind. That may mean that you start a narrative essay in the part of the story that illuminates the question you're exploring, the idea you're trying to understand. Typically, this won't be the beginning of the story ("The alarm clock went off at 6 AM, and I was groggy from sleep"); it may be the middle or even the end.

Judith Ortiz Cofer, for example, opens her story about her struggles as a young Puerto Rican immigrant to the United States in the 1950s with an anecdote about her memories of Christmas on the island. The Christmas anecdote frames the narrative's controlling idea: that in life "light is followed by darkness" and that

> **One Student's Response** (*continued*)
>
> this is an immutable fact. The most important part of organizing a personal narrative is not how you tell what happened. It is what you *now* think about the significance of what happened. It is this shift from past to present—from what you remember and what you understand about it now that you didn't then—that is the most important structure of all.

Workshopping

If your draft is subject to peer review, see Chapter 14 for details on how to organize workshop groups and decide on how your group can help you. To help you decide, use the guidance, starting on p. 578, in Chapter 14. Each workshop type is described more fully in that chapter.

Sharing a personal essay with peers might present some special challenges. After all, in this kind of essay, you're really putting yourself out there. You're honestly talking about yourself, and about *your* experiences and observations. If your essay is a podcast or radio piece, you'll be sharing not only your writing but also your voice, and my students tell me that in a spoken essay, it's nearly impossible to lie. It's a kind of writing that, as E. B. White once said, should not indulge "in deceit or in concealment," for the writer "will be found out in no time."

Under these circumstances, it's hard not to feel a least a little vulnerable when sharing personal essay. (If this is a real source of anxiety, talk to your instructor.) But you will find that exactly *because* the personal essay is personal, your peers will be enthusiastic readers of your work. The key is to channel that enthusiasm towards a response that will help you revise.

At this stage in writing the personal essay—the first full draft—what you may need most are responses that address the things you've worked on most in your sketch: Does the draft clearly answer the "So what?" question (purpose)? Is it clear what the one main thing is that the essay is trying to say (meaning)? All other revision concerns are subordinate to these questions. Why? Because without a clear purpose and clear sense, it's impossible to make any judgments about content.

Annie Dillard, a writer of many nonfiction books and essays, once said that she believed that the biggest challenge in writing comes down to this basic question: *What to put in and what to leave out.* In a narrative essay such as the one you're working on, you might conclude that the answer to the question is equally simple: You tell the "whole" story. Yet the truth is that you never do, even in telling a story to friends. We shape and shade a story depending on our motive for telling it. The same is true in prose. Your purpose and what you are trying to say are the two things that determine what belongs in a story and what doesn't. So this is where you should begin.

Questions for Readers. The following grid, which focuses on these two key concerns, can help you to guide your peers' response to your first draft.

Questions for Peer Reviewers	
1. Purpose	What would you say this essay is about? Do you have a clear sense of *why* I'm writing about this topic?
2. Meaning	Most essays need to say one fricking thing (S.O.F.T.). What would you say is the point of this draft? What is the main thing I seem to be saying about this topic?

Reflecting on the Workshop. After the workshop session, do a follow-up entry in your notebook that summarizes what you heard, what made sense and what didn't, and how you plan to approach the next draft. Your instructor may ask you to share this information in a cover letter submitted with the revision.

Revising

Revision is a continual process—not a last step. You've been revising—"reseeing" your subject—from the first messy fastwriting in your journal. But the things that get your attention vary depending on where you are in the writing process. With your draft in hand, revision becomes your focus through what I'll call "shaping and tightening your draft."

3.5
Apply revision strategies that are effective for shaping narratives.

Chapter 13 contains strategies that can help you revise any inquiry project, and the "Guide to Revision Strategies" on page 105 can help you locate these strategies. There are also certain things to think about that are especially useful for shaping a personal essay.

Shaping. In your draft, you made a tentative commitment to your topic, hoping that you could shape it into something that might have meaning for someone other than you. Fundamentally, you've been trying to figure out *what you're trying to say* and then rebuild your essay so that this is both clear and convincing. In a personal essay, you might also want it to be moving.

Shaping focuses on larger concerns first: purpose and meaning—the very largest concerns, which you've looked at if you workshopped your draft—and the next-to-largest concerns of information and organization. It starts with knowing what your essay is about—your inquiry question and maybe your theme—and then revising to make every element of the draft focused on that question or idea.

What to Cut and What to Add. Ryan wrote a personal essay about the epic battles he had with his brother growing up. He realized writing it that, while they didn't exactly hate each other, they certainly behaved like they did back then. The purpose of Ryan's essay was to explore a question: *Why were these sibling rivalries so intense, and how do they shape the brothers' relationships today?* As he reflects on what he wrote and understands what he wanted to convey, Ryan can make the decisions that Dillard says revision demands: what to cut and what to add. Ryan will cut the part that focuses on his father, because it does little to help readers see the brothers' rivalry. He will add more about the chess game in which they finally came to blows. A key to revising a personal essay, then, is this:

Given my essay's purpose and meaning, what should I cut and what should I add?

- What information—scenes, descriptions, observations, explanations—is no longer relevant to the purpose and meaning?

- What information is missing that should be added to help readers understand and, in a small way, experience, so that they will appreciate my point?

The Question of Time. Revising a narrative essay also involves the question of time. Consider this in two ways:

1. Where will information come from to develop your story—from the past or from the present? The then-narrator is master of the past. What happened? And then what? The now-narrator is charged with commenting from the present. What do I make of what happened from where I sit now? Personal essays that tell stories need information from both past and present.

2. How does time organize the information in the draft? Do you tell your story chronologically? Is that the best way to structure the essay? What might happen, for example, if you begin in the middle of the story, or even at the end? Will that better dramatize the question or dilemma that you're exploring?

Research. I'm not talking about extensive research, but about quick searches for background information, relevant facts, and maybe even something on what other writers or experts have said. Here's an example. I was writing an essay in which I recalled a total solar eclipse that happened in August 1964. Did it really? A quick web search confirmed it, but I also got information about exactly how long it lasted, and this information helped strengthen the scene I was writing. Say you're writing an essay about iPhone infatuation. Why not look up a definition of "infatuation" and then do some quick research on how students use their iPhones in a typical day?

Other Questions for Revision. Make sure you address the following questions as you revise:

- Does the draft begin in a way that gives your readers a sense of where the essay is going? Is your purpose clear? (This is especially important for podcast essays.)

- Is there too much explaining? Narrative essays are usually built on the backbone of story—anecdote, scene, description. This is how we help the audience appreciate, in some small way, the experiences that have inspired the insights we want to share. Personal essays *do* need to tell, but they must also *show*.

- By the end of your essay, does the reader appreciate the significance of the story you're telling? Have you said what you need to say about how, though it's your experience, the meaning you discover might apply to others as well?

Polishing. When you are satisfied with the shape of your draft, focus on paragraphs, sentences, and words. Are your paragraphs coherent? How do you manage transitions? Are your sentences fluent and concise? Are there any errors in spelling or syntax? The section of Chapter 13 called "Problems with Clarity and Style" can help you focus on these issues.

Before you finish your draft, work through the following checklist:

✓ Every paragraph is about one thing.

✓ The transitions between paragraphs aren't abrupt.

✓ The length of sentences varies in each paragraph.

✓ Each sentence is concise. There are no unnecessary words or phrases.

✓ You've checked grammar, particularly for verb agreement, run-on sentences, unclear pronouns, and misused words (*there/their*, *where/were*, and so on). (See the Handbook at the end of the book for help with these grammar issues.)

✓ You've run your spellchecker and proofed your paper for misspelled words.

Chapter 13 has strategies to help you solve all kinds of revision problems, large and small. Use the "Guide to Revision Strategies" below to know where to look in that chapter to both shape and polish your draft.

Guide to Revision Strategies

Watch the Animation on **How to Edit** in your MyLab

Problems in the Draft (Chapter 13)	Page Number
Unclear purpose	538
▪ Not sure what the essay is about? Fails to answer the *So what?* question?	
Unclear thesis, theme, or main idea	543
▪ Not sure what you're trying to say?	
Lack of information or development	551
▪ Needs more details; more showing and less telling?	
Disorganized	555
▪ Doesn't move logically or smoothly from paragraph to paragraph?	
Unclear or awkward at the level of sentences and paragraphs	564
▪ Seems choppy or hard to follow at the level of sentences or paragraphs?	

▶ Student Essay

Military veterans often bring their rich, complicated experiences into my writing classes, and because what they've seen and done often raises questions they can't easily answer, they learn to love the personal essay. Seth Marlin served in Iraq. In the essay "Smoke of Empire," he remembers that during his first night in the country, there was a stench he didn't recognize. It turns out this was the smell of things—often perfectly good things—burning. The refuse of war. This memory inspires a meditation on war, waste, and empire.

The piece was written for the radio, and Seth produced an audio essay using Audacity software that blended his voice reading of "Smoke of Empire" with music that gave the essay even more power. As you read Seth's essay, keep in mind that he wrote it with the idea that his audience would hear it a single time. Consider as you read it how that changes his approach to the writing. You can also listen to the essay at bruceballenger.com.

Smoke of Empire
Seth Marlin

1   When I was in Iraq, we used to have this rotating detail. Call it "*Hajji*-watch." Bring in local guys, pay them ten bucks to move sandbags, haul trash. Post a couple soldiers with rifles in case anyone gets froggy. Locals try to sell you stuff, turn them down. They ask for soap, shampoo, toothpaste, say you don't have any. That's the order they drill into you: *Do Not Buy, Sell, or Give Items to Local Nationals.*

2   Locals were poor. Dirt poor. Steal the gloves out of your pocket if they thought they'd get some use. Who could blame them? One guy I saw stole a bedroll once; another, maybe fifteen, jacked a soccer-ball, said it was for his little brother. Our squad-leader said it was contraband, said the ball would be waiting for him when he came back next week, soon as he got a memorandum from the base-commander.

3   That kid never got his ball, you kidding me? Lot of poor guys with families; that line stretched two miles up the road back into town. He'd have been lucky to get in at all. I doubt he ever got that ball back; most likely, it just went to the burn-pit.

* * *

4   Fun fact: Wars generate waste. The Department of Defense estimates that its wars each generate ten pounds of garbage per service member per day. At over 150,000 service members deployed, that's a lot of trash. Unfortunately, the locals tend not to cotton to your leaving messes all over their soil; thus, in the name of diplomacy, the invaders have to clean up after themselves. On places like Joint Base Balad, all that refuse goes to one place: the burn-pit.

Picture a base, fifteen miles across, set in a swath of palm-dotted farmland. Now picture on part of that a landscape of hills, valleys, and craters—all of it garbage, all bigger than a dozen football fields. Now picture that on fire. Through the haze, you might see the figures who manage all that incoming drek—orange-turbaned Sikhs wearing blue jumpsuits, some of them wearing goggles and surgical masks if they're lucky. These pits are typically run by private contractors; OSHA guidelines mean little to nothing here. Your tax dollars at work.

My first night in Iraq, I remember looking west from my trailer and being surprised to see a sunset of blazing orange. It was at least two hours after dusk, and the stars were out, at least a couple anyway. Then I realized that *that wasn't sunlight I was seeing—* that it was *flames*. Those weren't clouds I was seeing, but rather smoke. I didn't know what all that was yet, only that it took up half the northern sky. But oh, I learned. The first thing I learned about was the smell, like burning oak-leaves mixed with scorched plastic and warping aluminum. Wood, fabric, paper, metal—if it burned, they burnt it. If not, they threw something on it until it did. On a clear day it threw smoke a half-mile high; on the cold days during the rainy season, October through March, the flames got tamped down by the constant downpour. Made the world smell like a half-smoked cigarette, all wet soot and chemicals. Made you gag passing through it on your way to the motor pool. During the summer months the ashes blew into the town just north of us, a little two-rut burg called Yethrib. Turned the air gray, sent hot embers raining down on the farmers' fields. Sitting in a tower on a weeklong rotation of guard-duty, I remember watching one day as some hundred-odd acres of sunflower, sorghum, and lentils went up in flames. An entire season's crops destroyed, in a part of the country where the median income was two dollars a day.

* * *

I remember convoying home from bridge-sites late at night; I used to peer over the steering-wheel and look for the banded floodlights, the blood-red haze of smoke. Waste never sleeps. On a bulletin-board in my platoon's Ops office, I remember they'd posted a memo signed by two Air-Force lieutenants-colonel. The memo cited the effects of long-term exposure to the smoke, expressed outrage at the lack of incinerators, ordered the memo posted in every company headquarters, every permanent file of every soldier in service on that base. I'm sure that memo's still in my record somewhere; then again, the VA does have a tendency to lose things.

I saw a lot of strange, scary, moving things during my time deployed. Sunrises over the Tigris, Sumerian ruins, farmers praying in their fields at dawn. But the image that sticks with me is the burn-pit. Why? Maybe because the sight of all that waste, made tangible, left some mark on me, like tracking mud on floors as a guest, uninvited. War is consumption, I've realized. Conspicuous consumption. It's embarrassing, really: this is the democracy we bring to a foreign nation, consumption and waste. Look at all we've got. Fast-food, electronics, medicine. You can't have any, and we're going to burn it all right in front of you.

(continued)

5

6

7

8

(continued)

9   You know, the last night I was writing this I pulled up Google Earth, pinned down where I was posted. Our old motor-pool was taken down, bulldozed over; our old living-areas and trailers had been carted away. Even the burn-pit was silent, but it still sits there, like a grease-stain you can see from the air. Big sign in English: "NO DUMPING," it says, while behind it sits a mountain of blackened, twisted steel. The Balad pit may sit quiet now, but I'll bet even money those fires are still going elsewhere.

10   All day. Every day. The smoke of consumption, of Empire.

Evaluating the Essay

Discuss or write about your response to Seth Marlin's essay, using some or all of the following questions.

1. What do you understand this essay to be saying about war, empire, and waste? Where does it say it most clearly or memorably?

2. Throughout this chapter, I've promoted the idea that personal essays have two narrators—the now-narrator and the then-narrator. Are they both present in "Smoke of Empire"? Where?

3. What is the main thing you might take away from reading this piece and apply when you write or revise your own personal essay?

4. This piece was written to be heard rather than read, and the writer assumed that it would be heard only once. Imagine this rhetorical situation: You're in the car listening to the radio driving to campus and you hear Seth reading "Smoke of Empire." Because he's not in the car with you, you don't have to be polite. You don't even know him. You can change the station if what you hear doesn't interest you. What special demands does this situation make on *how* a personal essay is written? How might it affect the writing and organization of a piece?

Using What You Have Learned

Let's revisit the list of things at the beginning of this chapter that I hoped you'd learn.

1. **Use personal experiences and observations to drive inquiry.** Even before you read this chapter, you've told stories about yourself—we all do all the time—but it rarely occurs to us that these stories can be a source of insight even in some academic situations. The questions that drive our inquiry into

how we understand our lives are no less important than the questions that inspire us to explore other subjects. In fact, Montaigne, the first essayist, believed that self-knowledge is the most important knowing of all.

2. **Apply the exploratory thinking of personal essays to academic writing.** Next time you get a writing assignment in another class, start the work by "essaying" the topic—by developing a quick list of questions and responding to them. One great template for exploring almost any topic is a relationship question: What is the relationship between _____ and _____? For example, "What is the relationship between tutoring programs for college athletes and academic success?" Rather than trying to come up with a quick answer, spend some time fastwriting to find out what *you* think based on what you've read, heard, experienced, or observed. What you discover might lead to a thesis later.

3. **Identify the characteristics of personal essays in different forms.** Personal essays lend themselves to different forms, and if you know what a personal essay looks like, you can write yours in one of these different forms. Some of the most vibrant examples of the genre are podcasts, radio essays, or photographic essays. With the availability of free software for digitally recording your voice, publishing an essay online is easier than ever. The blog is also an extremely popular new form of the personal essay. Though these media can work with almost any form of writing, they seem to lend themselves especially to autobiographical work. There's something about hearing the writer's voice in a podcast or the easy intimacy of the blog that encourages personal essays.

4. **Use invention strategies to discover and develop a personal essay topic.** When I suggest using invention strategies, I mean this in two ways. First, you can use techniques such as fastwriting and clustering to discover a topic for personal writing. But perhaps more important, you can use such invention techniques to generate *insight*—not just an idea about something to write about, but discoveries about what you think about that topic.

5. **Apply revision strategies that are effective for shaping narratives.** The story—whether it's a recollection of what happened or our experience observing what is happening—is one of the most basic ways we all organize information: This happened, and then this, and then this…Yet chronology isn't always the best way to organize information from experience in writing, and, more important, story isn't just about what happened. It's also a "narrative of thought," or the story of what we now make of what happened. Even if you never write another personal essay, you can use narrative to tell the story of what you first thought about a subject and what you came to understand.

Complete
Additional Exercises
and Practice on
Chapter 3
in your MyLab

"If you want to write about mankind, write about a man," advises author E. B. White. The profile is a form that accomplishes this by giving an idea, a feeling, or an issue a human face.

Writing a Profile

Learning Objectives

In this chapter, you'll learn to

4.1 Use a profile of a person as a way to focus on an idea, a personality trait, or a situation.

4.2 Identify some of the academic applications of profiles.

4.3 Identify the characteristics of profiles in different forms.

4.4 Use invention strategies, including interviews, to discover and develop a profile of someone.

4.5 Apply revision strategies that are effective for shaping profiles.

Writing About People

Researching a book on the culture of the New England lobster-fishing industry, I wandered into the lighthouse keeper's house in Pemaquid Point, Maine. The lighthouse, built in 1827, was automated—like all but one lighthouse on the East Coast—but the empty keeper's house had been turned into a tiny fishing museum. I found my way there one late spring day, stepped inside, and was greeted by Abby Boynton, sitting on a folding chair, working on needlepoint. I had come to look at historical objects related to lobster fishing, but instead I encountered Abby, an elderly widow whose husband, a local lobsterman, had died of cancer several years before.

I liked Abby immediately, and as she led me to the back of the museum to show me a picture book that documented a few days of her husband's work at the traps offshore from New Harbor, Maine, I began to think that she was opening a door I hadn't considered: What was it like to live with a man who made his living hauling lobster traps? I had researched the science, gone out in boats, and interviewed lobstermen. But what about their wives (or, in rare cases, husbands) who, as Abby told me that day, are charged with "keeping dinner warm" while waiting? And what about that waiting? What was it like?

These are the seeds of a profile. You see someone interesting, and you're drawn to that person's unique story, and at the same time you sense that he or she might also stand in for a larger idea or group: What does it mean to wait every day for a boat to come in? Who are these people who do the waiting?

There may be no better way of dramatizing the impact of a problem or the significance of an idea than showing how it presents itself in the life of one person.

This accidental interview with the lobsterman's wife led to a brief vignette, much like the one you'll see later in this chapter of a man who owns a lobster museum. Had I developed it further, I would have talked to Abby Boynton again. I might have included statistics about the divorce rate among Maine fishing families, or information about the economic pressures on families during a bad fishing season—all the factors that might easily make it hard for a marriage to survive. The result would have been a profile that would put a face on the idea that lobster fishing is difficult, but for many a good life.

Motives for Writing a Profile

4.1
Use a profile of a person as a way to focus on an idea, a personality trait, or a situation.

E. B. White, author of the children's classics *Charlotte's Web* and *Stuart Little* and many essays for the *New Yorker* magazine, once offered this advice: "If you want to write about mankind, write about a man." The profile is the form that accomplishes this most directly. Through Abby Boynton we can see something about other lobstermen's wives and families—and about human beings in general. There may be no better way of dramatizing the impact of a problem, the importance of a question, or the significance of an idea than showing how it presents itself in the life of one person.

Although when we think of profiles we often think of the celebrity profile—a form we see in slick magazines such as *People*, on websites such as TMZ, and in segments on *Entertainment Tonight*—profiles of "ordinary" people like Mrs. Boynton are more relevant and revealing to most of us. They are lives we recognize—lives that are no less complex and interesting than those of the rich and famous. In fact, we may even write profiles as part of preserving our family history (see "Writing Beyond the Classroom: Digital Profiles," on pages 134–135).

The most important motive behind composing a profile—whether it's a conventional written essay, a photo essay, an "infographic" (see the "Prose+" profile of Steve Jobs), or any other mode—is that the subject is *interesting*. What makes someone interesting? That's pretty subjective, of course. But generally, interesting people can stand in for larger groups to which they belong—lobstering families, fast-order chefs, nannies, international students, world-class bicyclists—and have stories to tell about their experiences. As an inquiry project, a profile is driven by a question: If I look closely at this one person, might I gain insight about *people*, and particularly about people like him or her?

4.2
Identify some of the academic applications of profiles.

The Profile and Academic Writing

The profile is closely related to the case study, a common academic form, especially in the social sciences. The case study, like the profile, takes a close look at the life of a person who is interesting and in some way representative of a group, in order to arrive at a fuller picture of that group. For example, later in the chapter you may read "Learning About Work from Joe Cool," an extended case study of a guy who worked at Kroger, a grocery store. Originally published in the *Journal of Management Inquiry*, "Joe Cool" was part of a larger article that asked, "What is the meaning of work?" Often, as with "Joe Cool," the profile or case study attempts to document the impacts of some topic that affects people's lives. For example, suppose you're interested in examining the success of your university's commitment to ethnic and racial diversity, a principle the administration has

> The profile relies on interviews and observation, particularly those revealing details that say something about the character or feelings of the person profiled.

publicly embraced. One way to approach the topic is through a profile or case study of an international student. What has been her experience on campus? Which campus programs have proved useful? What programs are needed? The voice of your profile subject and the details of her experience would help dramatize an otherwise abstract policy debate, and the story she tells could offer a foundation from which to explore the issue.

Profiles might also be an element of an ethnography, a method used in anthropology and other academic disciplines (see Chapter 9). Through fieldwork, ethnographers attempt to document the customs, rituals, and behaviors of cultural groups in the locations where members live, work, or play. This often involves interviewing and describing individuals. For example, an ethnographer interested in the superhero phenomenon (ordinary people who dress up in costumes and actually try to fight crime) might describe the interactions of budding superheroes in online discussion boards and profile a particularly interesting participant.

More than any other form of inquiry, the profile relies on interviews. This is not only for information, so that the voice of the writer's subject can come through, but also for observation, because the right details can say a lot about the character or feelings of the person profiled. The way one man stands with his feet apart and arms folded on his chest to emphasize his biceps can show his arrogance, the way a woman carefully knots the scarf around her neck can show her fastidiousness, and so on. Interview skills are a key method of collecting information in communications and the social sciences, and writers who want to practice these skills will find the profile a useful challenge.

Features of the Form

Feature	Conventions of the Profile
Inquiry questions	Does this one person's story tell us anything about the perspectives of others who belong to a group and about people in general? What does this person's story say about social situations, trends, or problems?

4.3
Identify the characteristics of profiles in different forms.

(continued)

Feature	Conventions of the Profile
Motives	Profiles put a "face" on groups and on issues, problems, or questions, and in doing so, dramatize them. Whether they're anecdotes or case studies in a larger work or fully developed portraits of someone, profiles are in the service of ideas. They aren't simply objective pictures of someone, but an effort to *use* a portrait to say something.
Subject matter	You can profile anyone, of course, but not anyone makes a good profile. The best profile subjects are both unique *and* typical. Their very individual attitudes and experiences might set them apart, but they also stand in as representative of others. They are also accessible, willing, and interesting to talk to.
Structure	*Why this person?* Profiles must start by answering that question—or providing a strong hint. From there, a profile might be structured as a story (e.g., a day in the life, significant events, the story of the interview).
	Anecdote is a building block of a profile.
	Other typical elements are background (subject's name, place, reputation, social relationships), quotations or dialogue, scenes, description of the subject, and commentary from the writer.
	Point of view is a key decision. Will the writer be part of the story or stay in the background?
Sources of information	The profile depends most on interview and observation. The more you can talk to your profile subject, the better; and if you can see your subject in action, then you have the material for scene, an element that brings a profile to life.
	You might also interview people who know your profile subject, to get a fuller picture of who he or she is.
	Information might also come from research—taped interviews, archived articles, letters, e-mails.
Language	Scene, anecdote, and description—all key to "seeing" a person—require writing with sensory detail. This language is very specific and often exact. What *exactly* did she look like? What did she say? Background information is similarly concrete: date of birth, age, hometown, job, favorite books.

Prose+

1955 Jobs was born in San Francisco and was adopted by the family of Paul and Clara Jobs of Mountain View, California.

1972 Jobs enrolled at Reed College in Portland, Oregon.

> " If I had never dropped in on that single calligraphy course in college, the Mac would have never had multiple typefaces or proportionally spaced fonts. "

1974 Jobs returned to California and began attending meetings of the Homebrew Computer Club with Steve Wozniak. He took a job as a technician at Atari, with the primary intent of saving money for a spiritual retreat to India.

His Work 1976

WHEN JOBS WAS JUST 21, HE AND WOZNIAK STARTED APPLE COMPUTERS.
The duo started in the Jobs's family garage, after Jobs sold his Volkswagen bus and Wozniak sold his beloved scientific calculator.

In an age of information overload, a new generation of visual storytellers is helping us make sense of things by organizing data graphically. Their "infographics"—compositions of images, graphics, text, and color—are increasingly used in journalism to help explain complex stories.

This infographic, "Farewell to a Genius," applies the method to the profile. It is a fascinating example of how even the complicated biography of Steve Jobs, a story that might otherwise take thousands of words, can be told graphically in many fewer, and no less powerfully. What better tribute for a man who helped usher in the information age than a profile that merges text, images, colors, and graphics?

READINGS

▶ Profile 1

While working on my book about lobster fishing in New England, I happened into the Mt. Desert Oceanarium, a museum dedicated to protecting Maine's coastal environment. The founder and director was an energetic former Episcopal priest named David Mills. When he discovered I was a writer, David volunteered to be my guide, introducing me to local fishermen and showing me around town. Within minutes of meeting him, I knew I wanted to write about David Wells, though I had no idea what I might want to say about him. It turned out that my profile, "Museum Missionary," says as much about the interviewer as about his subject.

If the writer doesn't step into a profile directly by offering commentary or appearing in scenes, profiles can appear to be completely objective and readers' gaze remains focused on the profile subject. But sometimes the writer enters the frame, and inescapably his or her presence in the picture—asking questions, offering comments, and sharing observations—shifts the focus. Profiles such as these—and "Museum Missionary" is one of them—read in some ways like a personal essay. There's nothing wrong with this *if* the writer doesn't crowd out the profile subject, who is usually the person readers most want to see.

I'm happy to report that David Mills is still director of the Mt. Desert Oceanarium in Maine, and he's still wowing visitors with frightfully large lobsters, the fodder for delicious nightmares.

Museum Missionary

Bruce Ballenger

1 David Mills, surrounded by children, held a small lobster aloft and asked if anyone wanted to touch it. Index fingers sprouted everywhere. "Just don't knock him," he said. "We don't want to give him a headache." I stood at the back of the Lobster Room, an exhibit area in the Mount Desert Oceanarium, and watched while Mills instructed children and their parents in the ways of the lobster and the lobsterman. Twenty of us were there, crowded into that little room, and though I had been to such talks before, I was enchanted.

2 Mills reached into the Touch Tank and pulled out a berried female lobster, carrying a mass of eggs under her tail. The kids gasped. "There's a passage in the Bible where the Lord said to be fruitful and multiply. This lobster sure be fruitful," he said. The adults laughed.

3 "How many of you have ever eaten an eight- to twelve- pound lobster?" No one raised their hands. "Well, that's good. When I do find people who have I ask them whether they'll ever eat another, and nine times out of ten they say they won't have

a second one. They just don't taste very good." Mills went on to argue the merits of Maine's maximum-size law, the only lobstering state that has one, which prohibits taking lobsters larger than five inches in carapace length.

"There are two reasons not to buy big lobsters," he said. "They make more babies, and they don't taste good."

4

Mills, a former Episcopal priest, found a new ministry in 1972 when he started the Mount Desert Oceanarium: preaching to kids and their parents about marine life off the northern New England coast and the need to protect it. "We'd been coming up here on vacation, and my wife has some family in Bangor. We love scuba diving and developed an interest in oceanography. I had hoped my kids would take it up. But if you've done any counseling, you learn that sometimes the desires you have for your kids are really your own."

5

"I had been an inner-city pastor," he continued. "I marched in Selma, that sort of thing, but didn't really change any lives. I was one of the ministers who didn't really know the Lord. When I prayed I did all the talking. But one day the Lord said go to Maine and start that museum."

6

Sixteen years ago, Mills and his wife heeded that call and moved into an old waterfront building in Southwest Harbor that once served as a chandlery for schooners. It was heavily timbered, able to stand up to twenty tons of seawater aquaria and to tourist foot traffic. Contributions from local fishermen soon filled his saltwater tanks with the local marine life. Despite the years he's put into the Oceanarium, David Mills still zips around the place with missionary zeal, pointing out the holes in the floor where rigging rope was once sold, explaining the eyes on a sea scallop, examining a strange-looking starfish. But he seems most taken by lobsters.

7

On one wall of the Lobster Room hang the wooden pot buoys used by four generations of the Spurlings, a local lobstering family. Mills handed me a Maine Lobsterman's Association hat and told me he'd take me down to the wharf to talk to Ted Spurling.

8

We found him in a back room of the Southwest Lobster Company, standing near bait barrels that bulged with salted herring and mackerel, talking to several other fishermen. Ted Spurling is a small man, with a reserve that seemed to deepen every time I lifted my note pad. "Don't know that there's much I can tell you," he said quietly, when David Mills introduced us. We talked awkwardly for a time, while David rushed about trying to find more people for me to interview, and I realized then how odd it must seem to a man like Ted Spurling that I should be writing about how he makes a living.

9

"I felt kind of bad for Ted," David told me in the car later. "It's hard to have someone firing questions at you."

10

"What should I have done differently?" I asked.

11

"Well, I think it's better to just go with the flow."

12

I knew he was right, and it reminded me once again how difficult it is for someone "from away" to easily walk into a lobsterman's life and expect to understand

13

(continued)

(continued)

much about it. I wonder if in some ways the working fishermen are as much victims of the public passion for lobsters as they are beneficiaries. Those of us who don't work the water sentimentalize their lives, or at least have a nosy curiosity about it. Hangerson at the waterfront wharves often find lobstermen sullen, partly because they have work to do.

14   "You know, years ago a fisherman was classed with those people who used to go around and clean outhouses," seventy-year-old lobsterman Willie Morrison told me one evening, as we sat talking on his front porch in Rye, New Hampshire. "As a matter of fact, when someone would ask what your father does, you'd say he was a farmer. You'd never say he was a fisherman. After World War II, all of a sudden for crying out loud, the lobsterman was something special. People were constantly coming up to you and asking all sorts of questions. It was a pain."

15   Some lobstermen like Morrison find all the attention a bother. Others may even find it a bit alienating, especially when the popular notion of what their lives are like is often so much at variance with its realities. It is a feeling they may share with cowboys and writers and actors—anyone whose livelihood is the subject of popular myth.

16   I didn't ask Ted Spurling about this feeling. I was too busy taking notes, thinking up questions, trying to pry my way into the secrets of his work. I was so eager to find insights about the lobstermen's culture that I had stopped really listening to this quiet man, who happened to be a lobsterman.

17   Years ago, David Mills had learned something about listening, and it led him to open a museum. In his own kind way, he passed the advice on to me.

Inquiring into the Essay

1. **Explore.** In your journal, brainstorm a list of people you've known whom you can't forget. Let this list grow in waves for about four minutes. Choose one person you'd like to focus on. Put his or her name in the center of a blank journal page and quickly build a cluster (see page 92 for more on this technique), building branches outward from the name, listing moments, words, other names, dates, places, things, and other details you associate with the person you chose. When a branch dies out, start another. Each branch is a potential beginning to a profile on your subject. Draft a lead paragraph for a possible profile that, like "Museum Missionary," begins with a scene.

2. **Explain.** Explain the ways in which "Museum Missionary" exemplifies the profile essay as it's described in the "Features of the Form" section (pp. 113–114).

3. **Evaluate.** Like most other types of essays, a profile is organized around one main thing the writer is trying to say. In a sense, a profile is making an argument—you need to see this person *this* way—and offering evidence to convince you that the profile's perspective is believable. I was trying to argue in "Museum Missionary" that David Mills was a person who found an

unusual channel for his religious faith: in praise of lobsters and lobstering. Evaluate the evidence in the profile that you think supports this thesis. What do you think is the *best* evidence? Does this say anything about the types of evidence that are most persuasive in a profile? Explain what you think "Museum Missionary" is trying to say. Where does it say it most clearly, at least for you?

4. **Reflect.** If you want to write about somebody else, one of the decisions you've got to make is whether to talk about yourself. What kind of presence, if any, will you have in your essay? Will you mention that you're asking questions? Will you comment on the answers? Or will you stay out of it completely, working behind the scenes? In "Museum Missionary," I decide to step in. Reflect on what this adds to—and takes away from—this profile and any profile.

▶ Profile 2

The memory of 9/11 is seared into the brain of most Americans, and perhaps New Yorkers most of all. Many were eyewitnesses, and too many suffered the loss of people they knew or loved. But with the passing of time, at least for those of us not directly touched by the tragedy, the memory loses some of its edge. Ian Frazier's profile of Salvatore Siano, a retired New Jersey bus driver, demonstrates E. B. White's dictum that if you want to write about humankind, you should write about a person. This is the power of the profile—to put a face on something that is abstract and to show, through one person, why it matters. In "Passengers," written on the tenth anniversary of 9/11, Frazier finds in Siano a way of writing about 9/11 that transforms it from a public tragedy into a personal loss. His profile helps us recalibrate our response to the attack, looking behind the public symbols and the speeches to see, once again, the many ways 9/11 continues to change people's lives.

Passengers
Ian Frazier

Before Salvatore Siano, known as Sal, retired, last December, he had driven a   1
bus for the DeCamp bus company, of Montclair, New Jersey, for forty-two years. DeCamp has eight or ten routes, but Sal mostly drove the No. 66 and the No. 33, which wind among West Caldwell and Bloomfield and Clifton and Nutley before joining Route 3 and heading for the Lincoln Tunnel. Unlike some bus drivers and

(continued)

(continued)

former bus drivers, Sal himself is not buslike but slim and quick, with light-gray hair and eyebrows, and a thin, mobile face. In a region where the most efficient way to commute is by train, the bus can be cozier, more personal. When he drove, Sal reconfigured his bus as his living room, lining the dashboard with toy ducks, chatting over his shoulder with passengers, and sometimes keeping snowballs handy to throw at policemen through the open door. He used to caution children, "I am not a role model!" His travel-guide monologues upon arrival at the Port Authority Bus Terminal—"Welcome to sunny Aruba! Don't forget your sunblock! Cha-cha-cha!"—won him minor fame.

2   On the morning of September 11, 2001, Sal was driving a No. 66 bus that began its run at eight-twenty-five. As he headed for the city on Route 3, he saw the smoke rising from downtown. By the time he reached the tunnel, it had been closed, and Sal had received a call from another driver telling him about the first plane. Wedged in heavy traffic, Sal managed to back the bus onto an entrance ramp, turn around, and retrace his route, dropping the passengers at their stops and returning their tickets or cash fares along the way. Six hundred and seventy-nine New Jerseyans, many from towns that Sal drove through, died in the attacks. Afterward, Sal stopped joking around on the bus. When asked why, he grew sad and dispirited, and said that he was too emotionally caught up in the tragedy. Eventually, he began to joke again.

3   Among his passengers, Sal had many fans. Once, when he pulled up to the Bellevue Plaza stop, in Upper Montclair—this was years ago, before September 11th—he saw such a crowd that he thought he would have to order another bus. But then everyone yelled, "Surprise!" They had been waiting there to give him a party. He had great affection for his riders, and considered ninety-nine percent of them to be wonderful people. He never asked anyone's name or occupation, but he learned a lot about his regulars anyway. He believed that he had a skill for picking out the ones who would succeed and, as an example, cites a boy named John Miller, then a Montclair high-school student, who became a well-known journalist and one of the only Americans to interview Osama bin Laden.

4   Sal lives by himself in a garden apartment in Clifton. In his retirement, he sometimes works for an auto shop, driving to pick up parts. Afternoons, he goes to Brookdale Park, in Montclair, and spends a couple of hours playing tennis or reading the newspapers. Recently, one of his fan-passengers—who can recall many drab morning walks that were improved by the sight of Sal waving to him from the driver's seat of a passing No. 66—stopped by the park to say hello. Sal was sitting in his car, taking shelter from the rain. A gloomy, apocalyptic quality of the light, maybe caused by the approaching hurricane, led to thoughts about the upcoming anniversary of September 11th. Sal said, "The other day, I was remembering this one passenger from Upper Montclair who always got on at the Norwood Avenue stop, by the public library. After the attacks, I read in the paper—someone must have told me his name—that this man had passed away. He was such a pleasant human being. A man about my height,

wore glasses. I had seen him just the week before. The obituary in the *Times* said this man volunteered to work in homeless shelters, and sometimes slept in them to experience what they were like." (Here Sal began to cry.) "When I read that, I knew that my instincts about him had been right. I remember him whenever I go by Norwood and the library."

The passenger's name was Howard L. Kestenbaum. Along with the names of nearly three thousand other people who died that day, his is inscribed on a granite wall at the edge of the memorial garden in Eagle Rock Reservation, a county park in nearby West Orange, at the top of a ridge with a clear view of lower Manhattan. "He had a wife and daughter, and they are special people, too," Sal continued. "I still see them around Montclair on a regular basis. Whenever I do, I embrace them and give them a kiss on the cheek." 5

Inquiring into the Essay

1. **Explore.** In "Passengers," Frazier writes that Salvatore Siano, "unlike some bus drivers and former bus drivers," was "not buslike but slim and quick, with light-gray hair and eyebrows, and a thin, mobile, face." A physical description of the person you're writing about is often an element of a profile, and it's hard to do. Practice it by writing a one-sentence description of three people you know (or can see): parents, siblings, spouse, friend, classmate. What distinguishes a good physical description from one that's not so good?

2. **Explain.** "Passengers" exemplifies the idea that showing readers a problem through the experiences of one person affected by it is more powerful than just generally explaining the problem. If you think there's truth to this, can you explain why it might be so? How is Salvatore's unique experience (after all, we're not bus drivers and likely don't live in New Jersey) a better way of understanding the 9/11 attack than explanations about its effect on people?

3. **Evaluate.** Compare and contrast the different choices the writers of "Museum Missionary" (pp. 116–118) and "Passengers" made about their own presence in their stories. One is part of the narrative, and the other stays out of it. It's hard to say which is a better approach in a profile, but what might be some factors that influence this decision? How will you decide in the profile you will write?

4. **Reflect.** What are the ethics of writing about someone? After all, a profile essay isn't fiction; you're not inventing a character, you're making a character out of a real person. What ethical obligations, if any, do you have to the person you profile?

▶ Profile 3

Joe Cool, a.k.a. Lonnie Beasley, worked in the produce department at Kroger, and he was the emcee of overstock. "Hey folks," he said on the store PA, "this is Joe Cool and my manager's jumpin' all over me 'cause I done stacked too many beans out there.... So, please—come on over and buy some of these beans so I can get my manager off my back." The following profile of Beasley was originally published in the *Journal of Management Inquiry*. It is a work of academic scholarship, even if it doesn't read like one.

Many academic fields have turned to case studies and even personal narratives, because those kinds of alternative scholarship offer knowledge that cannot otherwise be obtained. For example, one business scholar who reviewed "Learning About Work from Joe Cool" wrote that "this story represents a more holistic view of work...than is usually the case in studies of organizational behavior." Another wrote that this profile is "powerful in reminding us that the analysis of work is ultimately etched in the life experiences of workers." The chance to look into the life of someone like Beasley, these scholars argue, provides knowledge that traditional quantitative research does not.

Learning About Work from Joe Cool

Gib Akin

1   The announcement over the supermarket PA system cut through the anonymous burble of shopping talk: "Hey folks, this is Joe Cool and my manager's jumpin' all over me 'cause I done stacked too many beans out here. Old Joe won't be COOOOL no more if he don't get these things movin'. So, please—come on over and buy some of these beans so I can get my manager off my back. And while you're here we've got a great buy on California navel oranges."

2   Here's Joe Cool himself: slim, angular, small turned-up nose on a face that is slightly dished, older than what you would expect from the name. But that's part of what makes him cool, acting so youthful, even at 55, and sporting an intensely white beard. The hair is striking in its contrasting black, and is parted in the middle, with a wing-like sweep back over each temple, plastered flat. It gives him an old fashioned look, like your jolly barkeep from the 1890s. A name tag on his denim apron makes it official that he really is Joe Cool. He's constant motion and constant talk, moving produce, keeping the customers, especially women customers, happy.

3   Lonnie Beasley became Joe Cool in the Kroger produce department, first only behind the scenes and then out front with the customers. He started produce work in 1971 and by 1975 his coworkers had begun to corroborate the Joe Cool persona. They gave him a pair of sunglasses to emulate the Peanuts cartoon showing Snoopy

as Joe Cool. Stickers of the cartoon character began appearing on his locker, as well as near the water fountain and the time clock. The back room was becoming Joe Cool's domain. The work there was physically demanding, and all were amazed at Lonnie's youthful strength and endurance—lifting, unloading trucks, and stacking and moving large four-wheeled carts of produce.

But the idea that Lonnie was cool came mainly from his constant joking, talking, and relentlessly youthful attitude. "He would say anything." The mostly younger coworkers liked it that someone older could be like them, always fooling around, not serious, "a nut." But he also retained his seniority, and was paternal as well. He helped everybody. Susan Marsh remembers that "he always made me feel like a daughter he hadn't seen in quite a while." (She didn't know the circumstances that give her simile its keenness.)

And, he rode a motorcycle to work, the crash helmet worn for protection also creating his nineteenth-century hairdo. He didn't ride a mean machine as an aging outlaw biker, but a friendly, playful one as the fresh-air kid. That was really cool. He had a sly affection for the slightly wild image of a motorcyclist, even though he claimed he started riding motorcycles because of the good gas mileage.

When the store moved to a new location, a system of weighing and pricing produce in the section rather than at the register was started, and Lonnie was given the "out front" job as scale man. That's when grocery shoppers got to meet Joe Cool. Donald Linke, who also worked in produce and like Lonnie had come from the other store, now made an "official" name tag that read JOE COOL.

From his new job out front, Lonnie also became the idol of the airwaves. When he got on the PA system to announce some special promotion, people in the store would be quiet so they could hear what Joe Cool was going to say. On one Fourth of July holiday, the store manager, in response to running out the year before, had over-stocked hamburger and hot dog rolls. As the day wore on and there were mountains of unsold buns remaining, Lonnie gave the play-by-play: "Folks, the manager has gone crazy, flipped his lid, gone bananas. He's giving away rolls, two for the price of one." And ten minutes later, "He's getting worse, now the poor fool has gone completely over the edge. He's giving four for the price of one. Y'all better get over here and stop this before we have to carry him off." As people arrived, Lonnie would load their baskets and whisk them off. What to do with all the buns? Nobody worried; it was Joe Cool.

Someone said to the manager, "Do you hear what that guy is saying about you?"

"Don't bother me none. Them rolls are moving aren't they?"

Lonnie was especially attentive to the ladies. He claimed that his beard had turned white as a result of all the smooching he had done (wink, touch your shoulder). Women shoppers always knew that both they and their vegetables were beautiful. Having been raised on a farm and always having his own garden even when living in town, Lonnie knew about produce and would help women pick the best vegetables and then advise on preparation.

(continued)

(continued)

11   Attention to women was also about kids. Kids loved Joe Cool and would have their mothers take them to see him.

12   The grocery store job was a second one, even though for most of the time it was a 40-hour-a-week commitment, a full-time job in its own right. Lonnie had always been a two-job man. "I guess working is just my thing." He had worked as a salesman at Sears and drove a Yellow cab as a second job. He sold life insurance as a first job and sold tires at the B. F. Goodrich store as a second. In 1971, he joined the University of Virginia police department working the graveyard shift and soon after began working days at the supermarket.

13   The police job had a lot of the same opportunities to help people. Lonnie claimed only 30 percent was crime fighting, and 70 percent was helping people and doing PR. And especially with University police, you got to deal with better people. Still, the people in produce were an antidote to some of the unfixable unhappiness he saw as a police officer.

14   Coworkers at the store would wonder how, and why, he would do it. "How much sleep you get?"

15   "Three or four hours."

16   "You call that living?"

17   "Depends on your aim."

18   Lonnie had two aims in work. One was simple, conventional, economic, and easy to talk about. Lonnie described himself as a depression baby, born in 1931. His parents separated when he was five, and his mother carried him back to the country where her people were. They never had anything but always worked to pay their way. You didn't want to owe anything or anybody. And what you did was work.

19   He had always wanted to go back to the country, and the work earnings eventually allowed the purchase of a house and seven acres—not really a farm, but a place that could be lived on farm-like. In an open, ramshackle barn, is stored his second motorcycle, a blue 500cc Yamaha that replaced the Honda 350 he started with in 1976. They look faded and scrawny next to his current ride, a huge Honda Gold Wing with a sidecar. There's also a little-used RV. Three old cars live on the acreage, only three of many projects in various states of completion.

20   Depression babies, who never had anything, don't throw things away. Lonnie and Nancy's house was full of things collected deliberately or just impossible to part with. And they all had stories connected with them. Lonnie told the stories while Nancy listened. She sometimes interjected to show physical traces of the story, a photo, a card, a toy, a piece of clothing. (There was quite a collection of icons of the Snoopy Joe Cool character, modeled in banks, T-shirts, soap, a radio.) In retrieving one thing, something else always surfaced, and that kicked off another story. It wasn't having the things themselves, it was that they provided a kind of archaeology, the shards in which their life was encoded, an aid to the remembering and telling that make things real.

The accumulation has now attained some sort of critical mass so that there is not the same need to work so much. (Nancy, who Lonnie always calls "Mamma" or "doll," has never worked.) Part of the fullness has been achieved by inheriting some money, primarily from Nancy's side of the family. The farmers who were her kin may have lived poorly, but in the end their land had substantial cash value, which helped Lonnie and Nancy finally have something.   21

The other aim of Lonnie's work was less conventional and harder to tell.   22

Lonnie and Nancy referred to their son, James Irvin, as the achievement of their life. He was born in 1954, two years after they were married. At the age of two, James Irvin was taken sick with encephalitis and spent the rest of his life in need of special care. He died in a hospital in Lynchburg, 60 miles away from his family, in 1976. While he was alive, Lonnie, always devoted to helping people, couldn't really help as he would have liked.   23

During the time when James Irvin was alive and after his death, work was a form of therapy. "Cheaper than a psychiatrist," Lonnie claimed. It was a way to keep busy, a way to keep from worrying himself into the hospital.   24

Nancy quietly did most of the direct care giving, while Lonnie, feeling more and more distressed, took a second job and spent more time working. A friend admonished Nancy that Lonnie was running away and not helping. But Nancy, uncharacteristically, stood up strong, defending that Lonnie was doing his part by working to pay the bills, doing what he could do in his own way for James Irvin.   25

When his son died, Lonnie cried, but he kept on working.   26

Lonnie also couldn't help his daughter as he would have liked. Born seven years after James Irvin and named Nancy like her mother, she always knew her dad was cool. What was really cool was being delivered to school by taxi, a regular treat when Lonnie worked a second job as a driver for Yellow Cab. She recalled motorcycle trips to visit relatives in the Tidewater and that her dad would do anything to help someone in need, including her and her stricken brother.   27

The younger Nancy was married before finishing high school. Her dad didn't exactly approve ("I may be Joe Cool, but I'm a square"). He remained supportive of her, nevertheless. Nancy and her husband had a daughter, but soon separated, and Nancy went to California—a place that for Lonnie was mysterious and dangerous, a place that changed people and made his daughter into someone he didn't know. He worried that she was drawn to men who were bad for her. But he was still there for her, even helping her move back to California after some time back at home. When she left with "her fellah" (Lonnie still can't say the name of the man he so disliked), Nancy's daughter Amber stayed with her grandparents.   28

Later, Lonnie and Nancy sued for custody of Amber, who was living with them. At the time, the younger Nancy was angry that her parents were trying to take her daughter away. She now sees it differently, that Lonnie had to make this arrangement to be able to get Amber into school and to be able to provide medical care. Her reframing keeps alive the father she knows as helping people, as being supportive of her even if not approving.   29

(continued)

(continued)

30   When the younger Nancy's "fellah" was killed in an accident, Lonnie paid for the funeral and helped Nancy get resettled. And Nancy, exactly as her father would have done, managed the pain and confusion by going to work. Employed as a receptionist at a psychiatric hospital, she was back at her job the next day. When a fellow employee, surprised that she was working so soon after the loss, asked what she was doing there, she replied, "To keep from going crazy. And if I do go crazy here you can just put me in one of the rooms down the hall." Work as therapy seemed to be an idea with genetic connections.

31   Lonnie doesn't like to talk about these times. It's as if he doesn't know how, that there is no understandable face to put on it, no way to make anyone happy. It's not like what he could do at work.

32   There is less pain now, and there are fewer bills to pay. Lonnie wants to spend time with Amber. And with the two Nancys. Be at home more. Lonnie is so social at work you might expect him in retirement to want to be around other people. He's a self-declared "people person," but that doesn't mean just being social: it means being personal. Sociability covers much of the pain that comes from not being able to help, to make someone else happy. There's less of that now, so there isn't as much need for work as therapy.

33   When an early leave plan was offered by the grocery company in late 1986, Joe Cool could retire. He still worked the graveyard shift as a university police officer, but spent more time at home with Amber and Nancy, his wife of 41 years and a "right cute chick" he still likes to do things for.

34   On a recent Sunday, as Lonnie, Amber, and the two Nancys were strolling the local shopping mall, they were approached by a young mother. "Aren't you Joe Cool? I want you to say hello to my son."

Inquiring into the Essay

1. **Explore.** Academic reviews of this essay suggest that this kind of scholarship offers us knowledge of subjects that traditional academic research does not. In your notebook, explore that idea. Take three minutes to make a fast list in response to this question: *What does knowing Joe Cool through this profile tell me about the nature of some workers and workplaces?*

2. **Explain.** Choose one (or more) of the segments in this essay—the sections separated by a line of space—and explain its purpose. What particular knowledge about workers or workplaces does the segment seem to offer? Why was it included?

3. **Evaluate.** Evaluate the effectiveness of "Joe Cool" as research. Do you agree that this kind of research—informal case studies that read like stories— make a valuable contribution to our knowledge of a subject? What are the shortcomings of this approach compared to, say, a statistical study?

4.   **Reflect.** Reflect on what you would do if you were Gib Akin, the author of this story, charged with writing a profile of Joe Cool. What parts of the process would you enjoy? What parts would you find hard? As you consider writing your own profile of somebody, what do you worry about most?

Seeing the Form

"Sun Boy" by William Soule

Visual anthropology uses images as a way to study culture. Photographs such as this one, a portrait of a Kiowa man taken by the well-known Plains photographer William Soule, would presumably be a great subject for study of the tribe in the late 1800s. But can a photographic profile be trusted as historical evidence? We like to imagine that photographs are documentary, objective reports of reality. But pictures are taken by photographers, who are influenced by their own sense of what's real. Culture profoundly influences beliefs, and when this photograph was taken, attitudes about Native American people among whites included the idea that they were "noble savages," or simply "savages." Portraits of Indian women often presented them as "maidens" or Indian "princesses." With these cultural biases in mind, how would you critically "read" this profile of Sun? What does this tell you about critically reading all kinds of profiles?

THE WRITING PROCESS

Inquiry Project **Writing a Profile**

Watch
the Animation on
Writing a Profile
in your MyLab

Inquiry questions: Does this one person's story tell us anything about the perspectives of others who belong to a group and about people in general? What does this person's story say about social situations, trends, or problems?

Write a profile of someone who strikes you as interesting. Consider four possible "frames" for your inquiry into this person: group, ideas about, event, or quality (see pp. 132–133).

Your essay should do all the following (see also pp. 113–114 for typical features of the profile essay):

- Use one of the four frames to focus your profile.
- Be organized around a theme. What one main thing are you trying to say about or through your profile subject?
- Include several revealing anecdotes about your profile subject.
- Include a physical description of the person you're writing about.
- Incorporate the voice of your subject through interesting and telling quotes.

Prose+

- Add Images to your profile essay by taking photographs of your subject or incorporate relevant images that your subject provides. Alternatively, consider a photographic essay of your subject. This might be a collage of photographs of the person, organized around some theme.
- Create an audio profile. Digitally record your interviews with your profile subject using your laptop microphone—or an external mic—and audio soltware (see "Inquiring into the Details: Using Audacity to Record and Edit Audio," on pages 143–144). Choose the best material from the interviews and write narration around it, creating two tracks (or three if you add music).
- Audio archives abound online that provide great material for profiles of people who were involved in historical events like World War II and 9/11. For example, the Library of Congress's Veterans History Project (http://www.loc.gov/vets/) is a remarkable archive of voices, video, photographs, and documents of veterans who served in America's major conflicts, from World War I through the recent conflicts in the Middle East.

Who Are You Going to Write About?

One of the great profile writers, John McPhee, wrote recently that promising subjects for profiles "are everywhere. They just go by in a ceaseless stream." But McPhee also observed that the great majority of people he chose to write about were those who knew something about a topic he had long been interested in. Begin there. What have you wondered about for a while, and is there a person who might teach you more about it?

A challenge with any writing project in college is time. This is especially true for assignments, such as this one, that depend on someone besides you. Therefore, you'll want to choose someone to write about who is accessible, willing, and with whom you might spend some time. (Profiles that use online materials such as the Library of Congress Veterans History Project, which I mentioned earlier, don't involve interview scheduling problems, but you also have less control over the material. Someone else asked the questions.)

In the three sections that follow—"Opening Up," "Narrowing Down," and "Trying Out"—you can use writing to help you get ideas about who you might profile. You'll use a series of prompts to generate a range of possibilities, which you'll then narrow down to a possible profile subject. Next, you'll try out this subject, in your journal or on your computer, and judge what you have.

Opening Up

As McPhee suggests, subjects for profiles are "everywhere." Let's start by looking everywhere for possibilities.

4.4

Use invention strategies, including interviews, to discover and develop a profile of someone.

Listing Prompts. Quick lists are great triggers for ideas. Try these:

1. To select a topic within which you'd like to find someone to profile, generate each of these lists in thirty seconds.

   ■ List types of people—categories such as "musicians" or "car mechanics"— that interest you or with whom you have had contact.

   ■ List local issues, controversies, or problems that you feel something about.

   ■ List jobs that interest you.

2. Spend two minutes making a fast list of people you think of when asked this question: *Who have you known who you can't forget?*

Fastwriting Prompts. Fastwriting is a great way to loosen up your creative side and at the same time generate raw material. Here are a few prompts to get you writing:

1. Choose the name of someone you know who you might want to profile. Use the "seed sentences" below to launch two separate fastwrites on your subject, each lasting at least three minutes (unless you can't stop writing).

   ■ *When I first think of _____, I think of _____.*

   ■ *The one word I would use to describe _____ would be _____.*

- _____ had a strange habit.
- *Typically,* _____ *would* _____.
- _____ *is best known for* _____.
- *The one thing that most people fail to notice about* _____ *is* _____.
- *When I first met* _____, *I noticed* _____.
- _____ *said, "* _____."

2. Think about three people you observed or spent time with who do something that you admire. Maybe they're a police officer, a fly fisher, and a great chef. Start with one name and fastwrite for about four minutes, describing this person and what happened the last time you saw him or her. For this exercise, focus on description. Write as if you are behind a camera, describing in words what you see. Skip a line and do the same thing for each of the two others. Which of these snapshots seems most compelling to you?

Visual Prompts. Visual prompts can be images or they can be visual methods of thinking, such as clusters, charts, drawings and diagrams.

1. Put the name of a possible profile subject in the center of a cluster. Build a web of associations for five minutes, and then begin fastwriting when you feel the urge.

2. Go through your digital photographs for ideas about profile subjects; this might be especially useful for reminding yourself of family and friends who might be good subjects.

Research Prompts. It is impossible to write a profile without conducting research of some sort, if not in the library or online, then in the field with one's subject. Doing some research up front, then, can be a useful way to find a subject to write about.

1. Return to the list of local issues you generated in the "Listing Prompts" section. Choose an issue in the community or on campus. Check the community and campus newspapers to discover who has been active as an advocate on the issue, or who has been impacted by it. Is any one person suitable for a profile?

2. Discuss your topic with your friends or people in your class. Who do they know who would be good as a profile subject?

3. If you have a career interest, a profile of a working member of the profession can be compelling. Call or e-mail the state professional association for suggestions about how to find an interview subject, or ask friends and family for suggestions.

4. Search online for audio archives and transcripts such as the Library of Congress Veterans History Project or interviews with people who witnessed or survived the 9/11 attacks.

One Student's Response

Bruce's Journal

RESEARCH ON LIST OF ISSUES

Issue	Interview Subjects
Recall	Margaret the storekeeper, Mayor Coles
Owyhee's wilderness	Congressperson, Simpson, Pat Ford
Migrant workers	Miguel Gomez, Rep. Bieter
Foothills preservation	Jack Coulter, Mayor, Nancy Maynard

Narrowing Down

You've got several ideas for profile subjects. How do you narrow them down to one?

What's Promising Material and What Isn't? Consider the following criteria:

Watch the Animation on **Understanding an Assignment** in your MyLab

- **Assignment.** Which subjects best fit the requirements of the assignment?
- **Accessibility.** The greatest subject in the world is no good to you if he is inaccessible.
- **Unfamiliarity.** A stranger is often a better choice of subject than a family member or friend. The challenges of setting up an interview with a stranger might seem a little daunting. However, you are more likely to learn something interesting from a stranger; you are far less likely to have a preconceived idea about your subject, so your profile is more likely to be based on the ideas you *discover*; and you'll learn more about the interviewing process—not only about gathering and recording information, but also about collaboration and organization.
- **Background.** Writers often look for information that may already exist: perhaps an article or two, a diary, a cigar box full of old pictures. Might you have access to such information on a possible subject?
- **Typicality.** Is the subject representative in some way of an aspect of a topic you'd like to investigate?
- **Extremity.** On the other hand, you may look for a subject who represents not the norm in a category of experience, but an extreme.
- **Spontaneity.** Less-experienced subjects, the kind you are most likely to profile, often have appeal because they *aren't* practiced at talking about themselves. There can be a freshness and even naïveté about what they say and how they say it that makes a profile particularly compelling.
- **Quotability.** Sometimes you simply can't know how quotable a subject might be until the interview. But if you do know beforehand that someone speaks in an interesting way, you may have a great profile subject.

- **Willingness.** This shouldn't be a problem. A few people may resist being interviewed, but most people love to talk about themselves. An interview gives a subject a willing listener; how often do we enjoy the undivided attention of someone who is vitally interested in what we have to say about ourselves?

Questions About Audience and Purpose. I'll admit that I read celebrity profiles in *People* in the waiting room at my doctor's office. Such magazines and their websites are successful because they've found a huge audience for features on Paris Hilton or Lindsay Lohan. The appeal of the celebrity profile to many of us is hard to explain (that would be a good essay topic, in fact), but because you're

> The profile can, like good fiction, provide insight into the complexities of the human mind and soul.

likely to be writing about someone who is not famous at all, you've got a rhetorical challenge. Why would anyone be interested in your profile of your neighbor who invents things in her garage? They won't unless the purpose of your profile is clear. The possible "frames" discussed in the next section can help you to discover this purpose.

The readers of profiles also respond to stories. So anecdotes are important, and when you interview, a key question will be *Can you tell me the story behind that?*

If you're ready to choose a tentative profile subject, try it out using some of the following strategies.

Trying Out

Like any inquiry project, a profile is an attempt to find patterns in the information you collect. The more data you have to work with, the easier it will be for you to see these patterns. This means making sure your interviews are long enough to give you enough data. It also means having a sense, before your interviews, of what patterns you might look for.

Possible Frames. One way to think about patterns to look for is to see this in terms of looking for a suitable frame for your portrait. Each frame represents a different purpose for a profile:

- **Group.** Sometimes we can understand a little about a group of people by examining one person who belongs to it. One nurse is, in some ways, like other nurses. A woman who stayed home in rural Illinois while her husband fought in the war stands in for military spouses whose partners are overseas.

- **Ideas about.** Profiles can also be in the service of ideas about something. Subjects might exemplify something you want to say about an issue, a problem, a place. The frame for your profile of a cowboy can be the idea that the mythology of the American West is still strong.

- **Event.** Your subject might have been a participant in a public event—national or even international (9/11, the invasion of Iraq), or just local (the founding of a homeless shelter). These events become the frame for your profile.

■ **Quality.** In each of these first three frames, the profile makes a point about something more general than the subject. But your frame can also be your dominant impression of your subject. What strikes you most about their personality? Perhaps they are intensely competitive, or painfully shy. Maybe they're dreamers or bullies. This possible frame probably won't strike you until you interview your subject.

Questions for Reflection. We see people and we see through them. A guy on the street in layered clothing and a wool hat pulled over his ears pushes a shopping cart full of stuff. We see him as we drive by, but we also see the problem of homelessness. We can only know if the man is homeless if we ask him, of course, which is why the profile, like many other forms of writing, requires evidence. But here's the problem: Do our assumptions about someone—the judgments we make in the absence of evidence—trip us up even as we're talking with a profile subject? How do you deal with those assumptions so that you are seeing someone on their own terms, at least as much as is humanly possible?

Interviewing

You're ready to start talking with an interview subject. How should you approach that encounter? That doesn't seem like a complicated question. You arrange a time and place to talk, collect as much material as you can, and go write your profile. But should you talk to him more than once? Should you talk to others who know him? Should you spend *time* with your subject, watching them do what they do?

👁
⌐ Watch ¬
the Animation on
Conducting
Interviews
in your MyLab

Interview Approaches. For his more lengthy profiles of an environmentalist, a birch-bark canoe maker, a long-distance truck driver, and many others, John McPhee describes his method as something like this[1]:

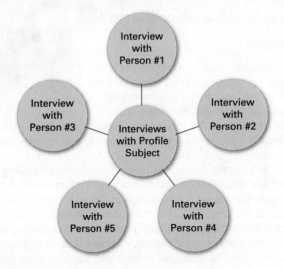

---

[1]McPhee, John. "Progression." *The New Yorker* (Nov. 14, 2011): 36–42.

At the center are interviews with the subject of the profile, the person that McPhee will talk to the most. The surrounding circles represent interviews with *people who know* the subject. Obviously, this is a much more time-consuming approach. But what an extraordinarily rich portrait it promises! Alternatively, your profile might be based on a much more limited model: interviewing only the person you're going to write about. Experienced interviewers will tell you that a single conversation with your subject is usually not enough. The first interview gives you the seeds of the story, and subsequent interviews allow you to harvest the material you need to make it work. Which approach you're going to take is the first decision you need to make about interviewing once you've chosen your subject.

Interview Techniques. His interview subjects sometimes see John McPhee as "thick-witted." At times McPhee seems to ask the same questions over and over, and he frequently seems to possess only the most basic information about his subjects. According to William Howarth, when McPhee "conducts an interview he tries to be as blank as his notebook pages, totally devoid of preconceptions." His theory is that unless his interview subjects "feel superior or equal to their interviewer," they won't talk as freely or at length. McPhee never uses a tape recorder, but jots down spare notes in a notebook; these are the telling details and facts that reveal his subject's character.

You can find more information about interviewing techniques in Chapter 11, "Research with Living Sources," but the tips here should help you start developing a plan for your interviews.

Writing Beyond the Classroom

Digital Profiles

Susan was a graduate student of mine who is working on a memoir about growing up on a farm in the desolate desert country of southern Idaho. Though her plan was to publish her book, Susan's project is typical of the kind of family history projects that have inspired millions to unravel genealogies, interview aging grandparents, and revisit the places where family roots run deep.

Interviews with living family members can yield compelling profiles, and the family members become characters in a longer story we can discover about ourselves. For example, Susan's Uncle Al, her father's brother, was not only an invaluable source of information, but he also became a memorable presence in her story, with a richer portrait than any photograph or painting could offer.

There are many genealogical resources online (just try googling "researching family history"), but the audio recordings you make of your family members

Writing Beyond the Classroom (*continued*)

create profiles that wouldn't otherwise exist. It's easier than ever. Digital recording is easily edited on your computer using free audio editing software such as Audacity (for more on this program, see "Inquiring into the Details: Using Audacity to Record and Edit Audio," on pages 143–144). You can trim and move audio clips from your interview into a more coherent profile, and even add voiceovers or music. Your audio files can be easily converted to MP3 format, which can be played on MP3 players and computers and sent to your relatives in Kansas. These family profiles can also be combined with visuals using a program such as Microsoft's Photo Story, another free download, and this can help you tell an even more powerful story about someone who matters in your family.

Microsoft Photo Story, a free download, can be used to tell a story with photos.

Making Contact. Asking a family member or friend to be an interview subject is easy, but how do you ask a stranger? You start by introducing yourself and straightforwardly describing the profile assignment, including your feeling that the subject would be a great focus for your piece. You must be prepared to answer the almost inevitable follow-up question: "Well, gee, I'm flattered. But what is it about me that you find interesting?" Here's where McPhee's elementary knowledge is crucial: Although you need to know only a very little about your interview subject, you must know enough to say, for instance, that you're aware of his role in a bit of history or his involvement in a local issue, or recognize him as being knowledge-able about a topic you find of interest.

What you want from this initial contact is *time*. The conventional interview—when you sit across from your informant asking questions and writing down answers—can be very useful, but it may be more productive if you can spend time *doing* something with your profile subject that relates to the reason you've chosen him or her. For example, if you are profiling a conservative activist, spend an hour watching him work the telephone, lining up people for the meeting at city hall. Your interview with a homeless woman could take place during lunch at the local shelter. *Seeing* your subject in a meaningful situation, which is what academic ethnographers do, can generate far more information than the conventional interview. Give some thought to what the best situations might be.

What do you do if your subject doesn't want to be interviewed? In that unlikely event, you're permitted to ask why. If your reassurances aren't sufficient to change the person's mind, then you need to find another subject.

Conducting the Interview. Should you prepare questions? Sure, but be prepared to ignore them. Interviews rarely go as planned, and if they do, they are often disappointing. An interview is a *conversation*, and these are best when they head in unexpected directions.

Certain generic questions can reveal things about a subject's character. These are *open-ended questions* that often lead in surprising and interesting directions. As I said before, one of the most important questions you can ask prompts a subject to tell a story: *What happened? . . . And then what happened?* Other questions that often yield useful information include the following:

- In all your experience with _____, what has most surprised you?
- What has been the most difficult aspect of your work?
- If you had the chance to change something about how you approached _____, what would it be?
- Can you remember a significant moment in your work on _____? Is there an experience with _____ that stands out in your mind?
- What do you think is the most common misconception about _____? Why?
- What are significant trends in _____?
- Who or what has most influenced you? Who are your heroes?
- If you had to summarize the most important thing you've learned about _____, what would you say? What is the most important thing that people should know or understand?

Inquiring into the Details

Recording Interviews

Here are some tips on recording your interviews digitally:

- **You can use your MP3 player.** If you have the music player—and don't have a digital recorder—then you can buy an adapter that turns your MP3 player into a digital recorder. It's cheap, too. One manufacturer sells the adapter for less than $20.

- **You can record phone conversations.** A $20 adapter will also allow you to record phone conversations, but legally you must ask your subject's permission to do so. Covert recordings are very uncool. You can also use Skype to record phone conversations.

- **You can use software to transcribe recordings.** Several free programs like Audacity are available online that will help you control the playback speed so you can more easily type what you're hearing and will allow you to label and reorganize interview clips.

- **Take notes.** A combination of old (well, really old) technology, such as handwritten notes, with the new technology, such as digital recording, makes it more likely that your interview will yield the best material. Your notes—even if sketchy—provide an outline of what you've recorded and help you to find that great quote or essential piece of information more easily.

Note taking during an interview is a challenge. I'd recommend digitally recording your interviews as well as taking notes. For more information on how to combine the two, see "Inquiring into the Details: Recording Interviews." Your notes should include any facts, details, phrases, mannerisms, or even personal reactions you have during the interview.

While my students have used the double-entry journal effectively as a note-taking format for profiles, putting the observed information and quotations on the left page and personal responses on the right, I'm keen on those pocket-sized memo books. They're incredibly unobtrusive and easy to carry, and they force you to be spare. I especially like the ease with which I can take the memo book out and put it away, at times using it to signal to my subject that I'm more—or less—interested in something he's saying.

Listening and Watching. The art of interviewing relies, more than anything else, on the craft of listening. Few of us are good listeners, which is why profile writing can be so hard. First you must control your anxiety about getting things down, asking the next question, and making your subject relaxed.

When is a conversation good? When it generates the kind of information that will help you write the profile, including the following:

- **Stories.** Interesting anecdotes help you build a narrative backbone to your essay.

- **Memorable quotations.** A typical interview produces only a handful of these, so don't desperately write down everything a subject says. A digital recorder often helps moderate the anxiety that you'll miss something, allowing you to concentrate on writing down quotes that are nicely put or distinctive, particularly those that reveal something about your subject's character.

- **Background information.** This can be in the form of stories, but might also be basic but essential information such as your subject's age, place of birth, and history of involvement in relevant jobs or issues.

- **Feeling.** A good conversation is an honest one in which the subject is willing to let the mask slip to reveal the face sweating underneath. Be alert to those moments of feeling when your subject seems to be revealing herself—what *really* matters to her, what might be hard, where she finds joy.

▶ Interview Notes

Below are interview notes (she did not record) that Margaret Parker took in preparation for writing a profile of someone who is a beginning medical student. As you read her notes, imagine the kinds of questions she had to ask to produce this kind of specific information about her subject, JD. Note the care Parker takes to get the facts straight, as well as her work to create a story through scenes and characterizations.

Your interview notes are the main source of information for your profile. If they're skimpy—brief or vague—you can't possibly write a profile that brings your subject to life.

Selected Interview Notes: "Medical Student"

Margaret Parker

Notice how careful the writer is to collect specific details—exact times, descriptions, and so on.

"Oh my God JD you look so...together!"

Day begins at 3:30 a.m. and ends at 8:30. Every fifth day "On-Call," goes to bed around nine in the student call room, divided by a sheet, sleeps in scrubs and sweatshirt and thick socks because it's freezing, around midnight a trauma comes in and have to do surgery. Then back to work the next day at 5:00 a.m., start with rounds and quizzed at 6:30 by residents.

110 hr/week is average . . . 120 hrs one week because she had call three times.

Operating Room (OR) environment—everything is sterile, only see eyes of people, must keep hands between waist and shoulders at all times, if not, the OR nurses scream at you and you have to go leave and rescrub, shames, OR nurses like Nazis, her first week she was screamed at constantly, you just don't realize how hard it is to keep hands in place and the terror of getting yelled at. Just trying to please and doing really menial tasks like holding retractors or skin and muscle back so that the surgeon can do his thing, back spasms, very exhausting for five or eight hours, terrified to move. Med students are everybody's peon, the OR nurses are the worst . . .

The Worst Day

Supposed to be there at 5:00 for rounds, and meet with residents at 6:30 for the residents, her alarms didn't go off and the clock read 5:45. It takes forty-five minutes to drive from her apartment to Olympia Fields hospital, arrives at 6:27, "peeing my pants," Kelley—a short mall rat junior high looking girl, starts screaming at all of them, she asks JD a question and she doesn't know it, she walks away and the team is angry with JD. She scrubs in for the surgery, a cholecystectomy of a 16 yr. old girl, expected to last two hours, hands drop below the waist slightly and the OR nurse screams "I don't believe this crap, Student, you better go rescrub," the attending with open contempt in his eyes, the resident satisfied smirk barely detectable below the mask, holds the camera in the stomach for hours, the surgery starts to go badly, it is apparent it will take much longer than two hours, drags into its fourth hour, struggle to keep still, back spasms, "Wrong Goddamn direction!", everybody in shock, the camera is still in the girl's stomach, nobody moves to do anything, then he gets a hold of himself and resumes, it goes on, terrified, trying not to shake, part of her wants to walk out, screw him, she didn't sign up for this, paying 30 grand a year to be shaken and terrorized by psychopaths, but she stays, five hours the surgery is over, "God walks out," Kelly comes up and says, "Oh my God JD, don't worry about it, he's a jerk," and for a second these words are gratefully received, felt like an abused woman wanted to get in a car wreck so she wouldn't have to go, cried the whole way home, calculating the hours till she has to go back.

In her notes, the writer integrates quotations within the overall narrative. She organizes her notes by roughly following the story she wants to tell. This often isn't possible because you don't yet know the story when you interview.

The Team

Ryan—top of his class, wanted to do surgery but after the first week decided on Family UP practice or ER, counseled each other every day, go and hide and bitch

Keith "Special K"—disorder, you name it he's got it, OCD, super book smart but no social skills, disappears for hours, she tried to follow him but he lost her, then her friend Bernie called and swore that he saw him on campus, a good 45 minutes away, "Where the f—k is Keith," SD had to take over his surgeries because certain

Here the writer breaks with the narrative to get down descriptions of other characters.

(continued)

An extended quotation. These help the reader really hear your subject's voice, and they can be quite revealing. They're also hard to get without a tape recorder or excellent note-taking skills.

(continued)

nurses wouldn't work with him, he touched his head and was generally unresponsive to their abuse, yet they wouldn't tell him, "SD tell him to put on his scrubs, tell him to go away," every night nightmares

Kelly—"so bipolar," seems like your chatty mall rat friend but then she turns into a demon

Trauma was better, the people were nicer, she was more valued, did useful things like chest compressions, took patient histories so they read her notes, Wendy Marshall the head honcho—British, teacher in every aspect, 'Pump-firing away of questions...'

"I have always wanted to be a doctor, and I couldn't really explain why. It was kind of a joke during my medical school interviews, because they always ask you, why do you want to be a doctor? And I'd reply with the generic, I wanna help people. But I guess now I think that I really like talking to people, and maybe in medicine I can help them. I think talking is the most important way to help sick people, not the real medicine that they teach you in school. People have such absolute faith in their doctor, and I love that feeling, that people confide in me."

Writing the Sketch

Whether you're working on a written essay or a multimodal project such as a podcast, a sketch is a great way to try out your angle on the profile. But it will flop if you don't have much information. The sketch is a brief treatment of a promising subject, written with readers in mind. More than anything you've done so far, this will help you to test your profile idea to see if it is worth developing into a draft. For your profile sketch, your instructor will tell you which of the following elements you should incorporate:

- At least two potentially revealing anecdotes about your profile subject
- At least two strong quotations from your subject
- A title
- A paragraph of background information, including your informant's age, a physical description, and perhaps relevant job or personal history
- A strong lead (perhaps one of the anecdotes)

Moving from Sketch to Draft

In its roughest form, a profile sketch might look something like this:

1. Here's who I'm writing about.
2. Here's something she did.

3. And here's something she said.

4. And here's something else she did.

5. And another thing she said.

6. Here's why I'm writing about this person.

This isn't a bad start. But your goal in revising your sketch into a draft is to find the "frame"—the idea, event, group, or dominant impression related to your subject—and rebuild the draft around it *from the beginning*. If this frame isn't apparent to you at this point, it's probably because you don't have enough material yet.

Evaluating Your Sketch. To see if you've got a possible frame for your profile, ask yourself these questions:

1. **Frame.** What exactly am I trying to show—or might I show in the next draft—about my subject's connection to an idea, an event, or a group? Or is the sketch focusing on a quality of my subject—a personality trait or belief?

2. **Theme.** If someone were to ask this question—"What do you want readers of your profile to understand most about your subject?"—what would I say?

3. **Information.** If I've tentatively decided on the frame and theme for the profile, what questions should I ask in my next interview to develop them further?

Reflecting on What You've Learned. Before you begin composing the next draft, make a journal entry that explores your thinking about the sketch and everything you heard. Begin an entry with the prompt *Based on what I've learned so far about my profile subject, the main thing I seem to be trying to show is* _____.

Developing

Like most writing projects, developing your profile involves research: conducting more interviews and collecting relevant secondary sources (articles about your subject, information from their web pages, background research on a relevant event, etc.).

Research, Interviews, and Reinterviews. Now that you're closing in on a frame for your profile, you can focus on getting the information you need to develop the portrait you hinted at in your sketch. Interview your profile subject again. In addition, you might consider other sources of information:

- Interview people who know your profile subject (the John McPhee approach mentioned earlier).

- Do background research on your profile subject. Find out more about what she does or where she does it. Find out how she fits into a larger context. If you're writing about a nurse-midwife, find out how many are working in the state and what their licensing requirements are.

- If your subject is a public figure, do library or web research for background.

- Research the idea, issue, or event, if any, that provides the context for your profile. This is especially useful for profile frames that focus on events and ideas.

The quotes and information you gather can be used in your profile, usually with attribution.

Establishing the Frame. Your opening paragraph or two—often called "leads" in journalism—should help readers understand the frame (or purpose) you're planning to build around your subject. For example, look at the following "lead" from "Museum Missionary," one of the readings earlier in the chapter:

> *David Mills, surrounded by children, held a small lobster aloft and asked if any- one wanted to touch it....I stood in the back of the Lobster Room, an exhibit in the Mt. Desert Oceanarium, and waited while Mills instructed children in the ways of lobster and lobstermen....Mills reached into the touch tank and pulled out a ber- ried female lobster, carrying a mass of eggs under her tail... "there's a passage in the Bible where the Lord said to be fruitful and multiply. This lobster sure be fruit- ful," he said.* ("Museum Missionary")

A lead establishes, usually within a couple of paragraphs in a short essay, the frame the writer is taking on the profile subject. For example, the opening above establishes the quality of David Mills that will be the focus of the profile: He is a man who brings missionary zeal to the wonders of the lowly lobster.

Revise your sketch so that the frame you're tentatively using becomes clear within the first two paragraphs. Use the title, too, to help with this (e.g., the title of the profile of David Mills is "Museum Missionary"). Try either or both of these revision techniques to clarify the frame:

Watch the Animation on **Writing a Title** in your MyLab

- **Title tsunami.** In your notebook, spend two minutes brainstorming as many titles as you can for your profile. Play with descriptive titles, one-word titles, titles from great quotations. Try multiple variations of the same title. Make a long list and don't censor yourself, riding each wave of ideas until it dies. Choose a title for your draft that points to the frame you want to use.

- **Multiple leads.** Instead of just writing one opening, write three, starting the draft in three different places, with three different anecdotes, scenes, or descriptions. Choose the one that points the draft in the way you want it to go. (See Chapter 13, Revision Strategy 13.17, "Multiple Leads.")

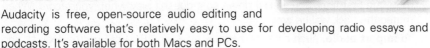

Inquiring into the Details

Using Audacity to Record and Edit Audio

Audacity is free, open-source audio editing and recording software that's relatively easy to use for developing radio essays and podcasts. It's available for both Macs and PCs.

- **To download a copy,** point your browser to audacity.sourceforge.net and find the version for your operating system.

- **After installing,** there's a tricky step. Without any add-ins, the program typically saves files in two formats: .aup or .wav. Both are much less convenient than using the familiar mp3 format, which yields much smaller files. To export your audio from Audacity as an mp3 file, you need to install an add-in aptly named a "lame encoder." Click on the "downloads" tab on the Audacity web page for a link to an external site that has the encoder. Download the file for your operating system, and install it someplace where you can find it later. Audacity will ask you for it when you save your first mp3.

- **Before you record,** make sure Audacity recognizes your recording device. Click on "Preferences" and "Audio i/o." If you're using a laptop or desktop with an internal microphone, this will usually be "built-in audio."

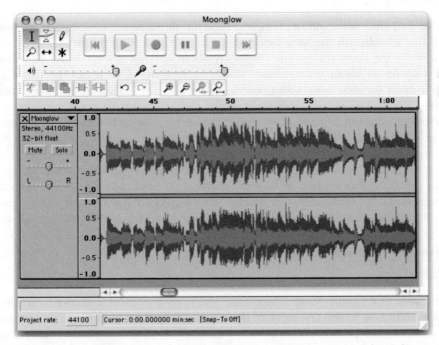

Audacity is free audio editing software that can be used to edit interviews for profiles.

Inquiring into the Details (*continued*)

- **To record,** press the red button on the toolbar.

- **To record a second track,** such as music or ambient sound, make sure you mute the first track you've laid down so it doesn't play when you record. When muted the track will be gray.

- **To import audio,** such as a music track, click on "Project" on the toolbar, and then "Import audio." Music must be in mp3 format.

- **To delete,** simply highlight the selection and click on the scissors icon.

- **To fade in and fade out,** use the "envelope tool." With the tool enabled, insert a series of dots in the waveform, and use these to contract or expand the track.

- **To move tracks around,** use the "time-shift tool." You'll find that in the upper left corner. You might want to magnify the track to be more precise.

- **To combine multiple tracks,** use "Quick mix." Holding the shift key, click on the information box at the far left of every track. When you do this, the track will become gray. Then click on "Project" in the toolbar and "Quick Mix." All of the tracks will be combined into one.

Drafting

You've collected more information and thought about possible openings for your draft that establish in the very beginning why you're writing the profile. Why this person? Of the many things one might say about someone, what is the one thing you want to say about your subject? Choose a lead that establishes the frame for your subject (quality, idea about, event, or group), and follow it and see where it goes. Remember as you draft your profile that you want to present the person you're writing about to readers in a way that makes him or her memorable. Think about which of the following methods of organizing the material might help you accomplish this.

Keep in mind, too, that as your subject is likely a stranger to your readers, you must introduce him or her in writing: name, age, physical description, relevant background (e.g., birthplace, job, quirks). And, especially if you're putting yourself into the profile, make sure that the voice of your subject is an integral part of it.

Methods of Development. You can pursue various strategies to structure your profile.

Narrative. The profile form often relies on narrative. Most commonly, a piece uses narrative by telling the story of the writer's encounter with his or her subject. For example, the profile of David Mills (see pp. 116–118) is organized around the writer's visit one day to Mill's Maine Lobster Museum. The account includes the writer's reactions to what the subject was saying and doing. Often, profile writers make this kind of narrative a first-person account—my day with my subject. However, consider whether a first-person point of view interrupts the narrative too much and interferes with the reader's view of the profile subject. After all, the writer isn't the main subject of the profile. Don't get in the way of the picture you're trying to create.

Known to Unknown. If your profile subject is a public figure and your motive is to reveal a less well-known aspect of your subject's life or work, beginning the essay with information that first seems to confirm public perceptions but then promises to challenge them—in other words, moving from what's known to what's less known—can be an effective way to structure the profile. This method of development is quite common for celebrity profiles.

Using Evidence. The most authoritative information in a profile is the voice of your subject. It is also the information that will be most heavily scrutinized by the subject herself: "Did I really say that?" Readers of the profile often believe that the subject's voice is the most authentic information because it is less mediated by the writer, an assumption that isn't always accurate. After all, unless quotations were recorded, interviewers must rely on their note-taking skill. Even with a recorded transcription, writers commonly tidy up bad grammar and remove irrelevant utterances such as "uh" and "um."

Profile writers must also establish their authority by giving readers a sense that they are keen and careful observers; they do this by carefully using not just quotation, but also detail, description, and research.

Workshopping

If your draft is subject to peer review (see Chapter 14 for details on how to organize workshop groups), think carefully about the kind of responses you need from readers at this point in the process. In a workshop of a profile essay, you're introducing your peers to a stranger. You have to give them some reasons to be interested in the person you profile, and particularly in an audio profile, those reasons need to be clear right away.

One of the essential questions of revision seems simple: what to put in and what to take out. But how do you decide? There's an equally simple answer: You must know your purpose and what you're trying to say. That knowledge guides the saw and the shovel; it helps you decide what to cut away, what new information to dig for, and where it might be added. You can talk about a lot of things in a workshop, but I think you should always begin with purpose and meaning.

Reflecting on the Workshop. After your workshop, annotate your draft with ideas about how you might revise it based on peer comments. You can do this by hand or by using the "review" feature of your word processing program. Your instructor may ask you to hand this in.

Questions for Peer Reviewers	
1. Purpose	What seems to be the "frame" for this profile: quality, event, idea, or group? Why does the writer seem to think this person is interesting? When in the draft do you know that? Is it early enough?
2. Meaning	What's the S.O.F.T.? ■ If the profile is focused on a quality of its subject, what is it? ■ If the profile is seeing through a subject to say something about an idea, what's the idea? ■ If it's focused on how the subject represents a larger group, what is it saying about that group? ■ If the profile is using its subject to illuminate a public event, what is it saying about that event?

Revising

4.5

Apply revision strategies that are effective for shaping profiles.

Revision is a continual process, not a last step. You've been revising—"reseeing" your subject—from the first messy fastwriting in your journal. But the things that get your attention vary depending on where you are in the writing process. With your draft in hand, revision becomes your focus through what I'll call shaping and tightening your draft.

Chapter 13 contains strategies that can help you revise any inquiry project, and the "Guide to Revision Strategies" on page 148 can help you locate these strategies. There are also certain things to think about that are especially useful for shaping a profile essay.

Shaping. If you wrote a sketch and a draft of your profile, you're essentially working on the third draft. If all is going well, you've clarified the purpose and meaning of the piece. Now you want to redesign it around both.

Analyzing the Information. After purpose and meaning, shaping focuses on information and organization. It involves, among other things, arranging and rearranging information so that it is organized around the main idea, question, or theme. One way to think about the structure of your profile is to see the information you've collected in categories. In a profile, these typically include the following:

Anecdote   Background   Description

Scene   Dialogue/Quote   Commentary

When shaping a profile, you'll be working with information that falls into types such as these and that you'll have to arrange in an effective order. There is no formula for this. But consider the readings earlier in the chapter. For example, "Museum Missionary" (pp. 116–118) is organized something like this:

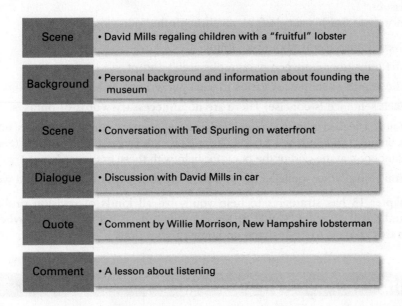

Scene	• David Mills regaling children with a "fruitful" lobster
Background	• Personal background and information about founding the museum
Scene	• Conversation with Ted Spurling on waterfront
Dialogue	• Discussion with David Mills in car
Quote	• Comment by Willie Morrison, New Hampshire lobsterman
Comment	• A lesson about listening

This essay uses information categories typical of a profile. Like many profiles, it begins with a scene that helps to dramatically establish the focus of the piece. Remember that whatever information type you choose to open your profile, your opening needs to help readers understand why you're writing about your subject.

One way to play around with the structure of your profile is to use the "Frankenstein Draft" (Revision Strategy 13.18 in Chapter 13). Cut up your draft with scissors into pieces that fall into the categories mentioned here—anecdote, scene, background, etc.—and then play with the order. Worry about transitions later.

Other Questions for Revision. Profiles typically have some of the following problems, most of which can be addressed by selecting appropriate revision strategies, or by repeating some of the earlier steps in this chapter.

- The frame for the profile needs refining or clarifying.
- There isn't enough material for the frame to work. Do you need to do another interview?
- The profile subject is obscured by the writer's intrusions into the text, or too much telling and not enough showing. Add more scenes, anecdotes, or descriptions?

Polishing. Shaping focuses on things such as purpose, meaning, and design. No less important is looking more closely at paragraphs, sentences, and words. Are your paragraphs coherent? How do you manage transitions? Are your sentences fluent and concise? Are there any errors in spelling or syntax? The section of Chapter 13 called "Problems with Clarity and Style" (p. 564) can help you focus on these issues.

Before you finish your draft, work through the following checklist:

✓ Every paragraph is about one thing.

✓ The transitions between paragraphs aren't abrupt.

✓ The length of sentences varies in each paragraph.

✓ Each sentence is concise. There are no unnecessary words or phrases.

✓ You've checked grammar, particularly verb agreement, run-on sentences, unclear pronouns, and misused words (*there/their*, *where/were*, and so on). (See the Handbook at the end of the book for help with these grammar issues.)

✓ You've run your spellchecker and proofed your paper for misspelled words.

Chapter 13 has strategies to help you solve all kinds of revision problems, large and small. Use the "Guide to Revision Strategies" below to know where to look in that chapter to both shape and tighten your draft.

Watch
the Animation on
Transitions
in your MyLab

Guide to Revision Strategies

Problems in the Draft (Chapter 13)	**Page Number**
Unclear purpose	538
■ Not sure what the essay is about? Fails to answer the *So what?* question?	
Unclear thesis, theme, or main idea	543
■ Not sure what you're trying to say?	
Lack of information or development	551
■ Needs more details; more showing and less telling?	
Disorganized	555
■ Doesn't move logically or smoothly from paragraph to paragraph?	
Unclear or awkward at the level of sentences and paragraphs	564
■ Seems choppy or hard to follow at the level of sentences or paragraphs?	

▶ **Student Essay**

Micaela Fisher took the city bus one day—the Number 6 Orchard—and she encountered a bus driver much like the one profiled earlier in Ian Frazier's "Passengers"—a man who endears himself to commuters through his large heart and quirky character. To write her profile of Oscar, Micaela rode the bus with him again and took copious notes that allowed her to write the profile through one extended scene. It's beautifully written. But it's also a wonderful example of how a profile can use a subject to express an idea about other things. In this case, Micaela comes to understand how Oscar's tale of a California man who lost millions—as unbelievable as it seemed—is just another of the many stories we all tell, large and small, that melt away every hour, immediately after they are told by one stranger to another. Does this make them any less important?

Number 6 Orchard

Micaela Fisher

The You-Are-Here arrow my bike is leaning against points at "Zone 1."   1

"Is there a bus coming shortly?" asks a kid in a black coat.   2

"I don't know," I say. "I would like to know, too." My hands are numb and there are   3
what the weatherman called "trace amounts of snow" in the air, though none adhered to any surface. The bus does come. Number 6 Orchard; maybe it will take me to climates where the trees have green leaves and ripening fruit.

A young man waves to the bus driver from outside, and then he veers toward the bus   4
and boards. "I'm back," he says. The bus driver doesn't quite remember him.

"It's been a while," the young man says helpfully. The bus driver asks, "What's your   5
name again?" and the young man says, "Oh, it doesn't matter. Names don't matter." The bus driver nods. "Oh, you're back," he says.

The bus heaves out into traffic, like an iceberg calving and rolling toward 16th,   6
toward Main. The two well-dressed ladies say, "You'll tell us where to get off close to the hotel, won't you?" The bus driver says, "Yeah, sure, sure, like I said." He tells them, as the brakes creak, "Now. And then walk over the bridge, and your hotel is right there." A woman with grey hair blown back like a cartoon character tells them, "Just walk over the bridge, and you'll be right there." They thank her, and the bus driver. The river under the bridge has glassy edges of ice, like my bus window has icy edges around its glass.

We turn left onto Orchard Street, no apples or peaches or cherries to be seen.   7
A young man in a green hoodie and glasses gets on. He says, "Cesar, man, it's been a long time."

(continued)

(continued)

8   "Yeah, a long time," says the bus driver. The young man stands on the white line, the line that passengers are prohibited from crossing while the bus is in motion. He looks polite, well raised. Cesar asks, "Still reading the Bible?"

9   "Yeah, yeah, all the time," the green hoodied kid says. Cesar says, "That's what your mom tell me."

10   "Yeah, my mom," the young man says. "She's still working at Micron, she's in a different department now."

11   "And she like it? She's less stressful now?"

12   "I do think she likes it. She seems a lot less stressed." Neither says anything more, and after a couple of minutes, Cesar hands the kid a card. "This is my phone number," he says. "Call me." The young man in the green hoodie nods, and as he is sliding the card into his billfold, his cell phone rings. "Speaking of which," he says, and then answers the phone.

13   "Hello, Mama," he says. He explains that since Dick's car broke down, he just caught the bus. "Oh, I'll make it work, Mama," he says, "I'll make it work if I have to ride the bus the entire way out there. Don't start getting stressed. You have a good night. I love you." He pulls the yellow cable, Cesar stops the bus, and the young man says goodbye to Cesar and steps past the white line and into the thin winter air.

14   We turn right onto Curtis Road.

15   A woman carrying three grocery bags boards, calling, "Hi, Cesar!" as she slides her electronic bus pass through the ticket counter. A block later a young man climbs on and sits across from the woman. He has on a blue and orange BSU t-shirt and a blue and orange BSU jacket. He is edgy and glances around as he eats from his blue bag of chips, but he doesn't look at the woman with the grocery bags when she says, "Hi, John. How are you?" He simply answers too loudly, "Fine."

16   "Well, that's better than not fine," she says, "right?"

17   "True," the young man says too loudly.

18   "Cesar, dear," the woman calls a few minutes later, "can you let me off at the daycare?"

19   "I need off at the Seven-Eleven," the blue and orange man says quickly, and then he says it again more loudly, "I need off at the Seven-Eleven." The woman says, "He'll take you up to the church, John," but John gets upset and says, "I don't get off at Overland anymore. I don't get off at Overland anymore!"

20   "Why don't you?" asks Cesar from up front.

21   "Because I got chased by a dog last Thursday," John says, and adds loudly, "I don't like this bus change." But he gets off at the 7-11. The bus lurches three rights and then a left that puts us back on Curtis.

22   I've been the only passenger for several blocks before the bus driver's curiosity gets the better of him. "Have you take the wrong bus?" his mouth in the mirror asks.

23   "No, I'm just riding around today," I say. "I've never taken the bus before. I would like to get to know the routes."

"How do you get around usually then?" he asks. I say I ride my bike usually, I live in   24
the north end. "Number Fourteen," he says nodding. "Hyde Park." I understand and nod too.

"Have you been driving buses for a while?" I ask the bus driver.   25

"Thirteen years," he says.   26

I say, "Do you get bored riding in circles?"   27

"Sometimes yes, sometimes I do," the bus driver says. "Before, I have a job driving in   28
California. And before that, I was accountant. And this job is so much better, has so much
more interest."

We are on the I-184 ramp, above the city. White mountains form in M's of landscape   29
on the driver's side, far enough away that I can't make out the buses of skiers rounding
switchbacks and more switchbacks to the top. My snowboarding class starts in a few weeks.

"Do you go to school?" the bus driver asks me.   30

"Yeah," I say. "BSU. I'm studying English. Writing."   31

"You write books?" he asks, more attentive now.   32

"Maybe someday," I say smiling to the mirror. He says, "I am looking for a person who   33
write—I know someone who say I can write a story of his life, but I need a person who is
really a writer." I say, Oh, and he continues with the life story, glancing back and forth
between the road and the mirror.

"I worked in California for a man who have millions," he says. "The man he has a son,   34
and the son was airline pilot, made a lot of money. One day the son had an accident, he
crashed and was in coma for three years."

"Three years," I say. "And he woke up?"   35

"Yes, for three years he was in coma, and one day, he wake up, he just wake up from   36
his coma. But while he was in coma, his mother, who is millionaire too, she took all the
money from the insurance, I think was twenty-three million or something. A lot of money,
she took it and spend it on houses, and traveling, and everything she want. She has three
houses. And when the young man wake up, she bought him YMCA pass and bus pass, you
know, little things. Well, there was this teacher, too, and the teacher had a problem with
her legs, she couldn't walk from the time she was girl in school and other children in class
take her wheelchair. Well, she want to grow up and be a teacher, and so she is teacher
now in a wheelchair. And she goes to this YMCA every day to do exercises for her legs, and
here comes this young man. They liked each other, and the man tell his mother, 'I want to
get married to this teacher.' His mother say, 'You can't get married,' because, you know,
he have lost, he has some problem with his mental, and his mind is not like it used to be.
Well, they get married anyway. And they take his mom to court for all the money she steal
from him, and they in fact win. And you know they have this little girl now? I saw them
last week when I was in California, I was in Costco with my brother and hear, 'Cesar!' and
there that young man is pushing the teacher in a wheelchair, and she have this little girl
on her lap. And you know, it's beautiful this marriage, because what the girl can't do because she can't walk—and they spend a lot of money for doctors, because they have a lot
of money now—the man, he can do that for her. And what the man can't do because his

(continued)

(continued)

mind is not so strong, the teacher, she do that for him, because she is real smart woman. And I tell them, 'I want to make a book and a movie of your life, and I will give you half the money,' and he tell me, 'Cesar, you take this paper that say you can write all my life, and don't you worry about the money, because I have all the money I need right now.' And so I am looking for a writer."

37   The bus driver gets up and walks over so that he is standing in front of me. I have been in coma listening. The story is amazing, I tell him. I say three years in a coma, and I shake my head. I tell him good luck, that is definitely a story worth writing. I gather my hat and gloves and backpack and step off the bus to unhook my bike for a cold ride home.

38   A week later I sit at home and type phrases into a search engine: "three years in a coma," "plane crash," "california," "son of a millionaire." I stop soon with nothing found; there's no way. Names matter in search engines.

39   It is not my story to write, and likely it won't ever be written. Most bus drivers never produce art the size of books or screenplays, though they may dream of it when the interest of all-day one-hour circles lags, though they may tell every passenger on the bus those dreams. And the passengers have their own stories, and together with the bus driver they create even more—scenes and conversations forgotten even as they form. Tiny moments like snowflakes that melt as soon as they touch a surface. It's no great loss most of the time. No one cares whether young men without names chat with bus drivers they call Cesar; no one would remember what is said or unsaid. And if someone cared, who could write the stories of a day, of a single hour? Even the most beautiful stories melt as soon as they are spoken, from thin air returning to thin air.

Evaluating the Essay

1.   In your own words, what do you understand "Number 6 Orchard" to be saying in the last paragraph?

2.   Analyze how Micaela uses the categories of information typical of a profile: anecdote, scene, description, background, and comment.

3.   What is the one thing that you might take away from this reading and apply to your own writing?

Using What You Have Learned

Let's revisit the list of things at the beginning of this chapter that I hoped you'd learn about this form of writing.

1. **Use a profile of a person as a way to focus on an idea, a personality trait, or a situation.** Think of any problem that you really care about—the degradation of the oceans, tax policies, the treatment of wild horses—and you can probably think of a way to put a "face" on that problem to make it compelling for someone else. The power of the profile is that it not only appeals to our interest in the lives of other people, but it makes their situations more compelling, too. In future writing projects, think about when a profile—or simply an anecdote about someone—can help you make a case that a problem needs attention.

2. **Identify some of the academic applications of profiles.** Profiles can be entertaining, but they can also be serious academic work. The case study is a version of the profile that is qualitative research—looking closely at an individual in a social setting to study their circumstances. This use of observation skills—sometimes called "deep description"—is invaluable in fieldwork in a range of disciplines.

3. **Identify the characteristics of profiles in different forms.** Now when you think of a profile, you might think of a portrait of someone who might be drawn not only from interviews but also from archival research. You might also imagine a profile that combines images and texts or even uses images alone in a revealing sequence.

4. **Use invention strategies, including interviews, to discover and develop a profile of someone.** You can apply some of the techniques for generating ideas about profile subjects to any project that might benefit from a case study, anecdote, or individual example. In particular, use the idea of frame to brainstorm: Might a portrait of someone help reveal aspects of a situation, an idea, a quality, or a social type?

5. **Apply revision strategies that are effective for shaping profiles.** Revision of a profile builds on your rewriting skills by encouraging you to organize several stories around a main idea and to use these to say something about someone. This revision requires that you manipulate more kinds of information, too, and because much of it comes from observation and interview—and not out of your head—you confront a fundamental problem of rewriting: the need to write from abundance. You have to be able to throw stuff away.

Complete
Additional Exercises
and Practice on
Chapter 4
in your MyLab

One challenge of evaluating something is keeping an open mind, sometimes despite our initial feelings about it.

Writing a Review 5

Learning Objectives

In this chapter, you'll learn to

5.1 Use reasons and evidence to support a judgment about something's value.

5.2 Identify the criteria behind a judgment and determine their relevance.

5.3 Identify the characteristics of different forms of the review, including academic applications.

5.4 Use invention and focusing strategies to discover and develop a review essay.

5.5 Apply revision strategies that are effective for shaping reviews.

Writing That Evaluates

One of the occasions when I feel fairly stupid is after watching a movie with my wife, Karen. She always wants to know what I think. I don't have much of a problem arriving at a gut reaction—I loved the movie *Amelie*, for example, but I have a hard time saying why.

Essentially, Karen is asking me to evaluate a film, to make a judgment about its quality. This is something we do all the time. Buying a pair of jeans involves evaluating the reputation of the manufacturer, the quality of the denim, the particular design, and especially the way the jeans look on us when we wear them. I think most of us like to think these decisions are quite rational. But, in fact, many of our evaluations have a lot more to do with emotion than logic. We *really do* buy that pair of jeans because an ad suggests that we'll look sexy or attractive in them.

One challenge of evaluating something is keeping an open mind, sometimes *despite* our initial feelings about it. Because evaluation often begins in emotion and in what are essentially subjective value judgments, a tension always exists between our *desire* to prove our point and our *willingness* to consider other points of view. That emotion figures into our judgments of things isn't a bad thing. It's a human thing. And emotion can lead us to insight and understanding. We just need to be aware of the role of emotion, so we can suspend judgment long enough to get a more balanced look.

Evaluation involves four things:

1. *Judgment(s)*. Something is good or bad, useful or not useful, relevant or not relevant, convincing or not convincing, worth doing or not worth doing—or perhaps somewhere in between.

2. *Reasons*. We have reasons for deciding that something is good or bad or somewhere in between and for all our other judgments. Our reasons usually are based on our criteria and evidence.

3. *Criteria*. These form the basis for deciding that something is good or bad, useful or not useful, and so on. The more we know about something—cars, movies, or whatever—the more elaborate and sophisticated our criteria become.

4. *Evidence*. The evidence (specific details, observations, or facts about the thing itself) in support of our reasons is what makes our judgment—and evaluation—persuasive.

When we evaluate something, most of us have no problem expressing a judgment—"Amazon's new Kindle Fire is disappointing"—or offering up some reason—"Its web browser is too slow"—and evidence for it. We may have a tougher time expressing the criteria behind our judgment (see Figure 5.1). Our criteria often involve our implicit beliefs—beliefs we are not even aware of—about what makes a thing "good" and about the standard against which something is being judged.

When you write a review, your evaluation of something, you may not always state these criteria, but you should always be aware of them. As part of suspending judgment and taking a balanced look, you should examine the beliefs on which your criteria are based and think about whether these are sound. A review is an evaluation for an audience. So you will also want to ask yourself: Are my criteria based on widely held beliefs? If not, do I need to defend my criteria?

Motives for Writing a Review

5.1

Use reasons and evidence to support a judgment about something's value.

Once you start thinking about evaluative writing, you'll find it everywhere—the book reviews in the Sunday *Times*, the music reviews in *Spin*, the analysis of websites on Web Sites That Suck. It's probably the most common form of workplace writing, too, for everything from assessing the performance of an employee to evaluating a plan to preserve historic buildings. One motive for reviews is to help people make informed decisions.

In inquiry-based projects, especially, you may be reviewing something about which you simply haven't made a judgment yet. You may not even have a gut reaction. Reviews usually begin from a question that we often ask about things: How good is it? They are an attempt to answer that question by basing whatever judgment

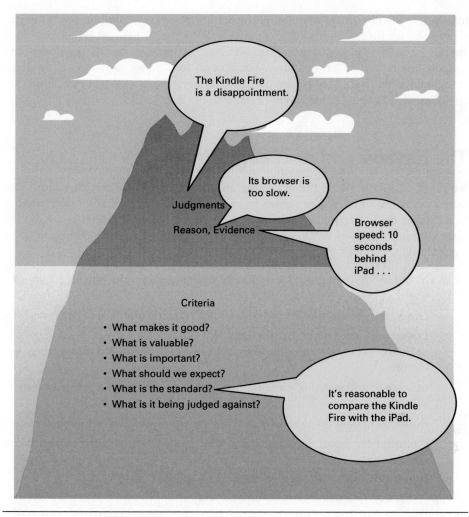

Figure 5.1 **Evaluation.** Like an iceberg, much of what goes into our evaluation of something may be submerged. We make judgments and might even give some reasons and evidence. But we're often not aware of the criteria behind our judgments, let alone of the beliefs on which these criteria are based—beliefs about what is good, valuable, important, or the standard. So we also need to look at our criteria and the beliefs they rest on to see if they're sound.

5.2
Identify the criteria behind a judgment and determine their relevance.

you come to on criteria you've thought about and on evidence you've found. You don't simply say, "That smartphone isn't any good." Instead, you say "that smartphone is disappointing… and here's why." Like any inquiry-based project, a review gives you a chance to explore.

Your gut reaction to something's value might satisfy a friend, but it won't satisfy an audience that needs to be *persuaded* that your judgment is sensible. Imagine, for instance,

Evaluative writing is an enormously practical form, relevant in all sorts of situations in and out of school.

that you're in charge of writing performance reviews of employees. The employees won't be satisfied with evaluations that state in general terms how they should improve. They will want reasons and, especially, specific evidence and suggestions based on criteria they can accept. In a sense, a review is an argument, and a motive for a review is like a motive for any argument: You want someone else to see it your way.

The Review and Academic Writing

We don't usually think of the review as an academic form, although you may be asked to review a film you're shown in an English class or perhaps a performance in a theater class. But reviews are a form of evaluative writing that is among the most common types of writing in all kinds of college classrooms. Here are some examples:

- In English, you might do a rhetorical evaluation of a document, a film, or a story.
- Courses in music, theater, and dance might include a review of performances.
- Courses in art history or photography might call for you to review one or more artworks (see the box "Seeing the Form: Choosing the Best Picture").
- In science and social science classes, you may evaluate the methodology of studies.
- Business writing often involves reviewing proposals or marketing plans.
- Philosophers make arguments, but they also evaluate whether arguments are effective.
- In composition, you'll review the writing of your peers.

Seeing the Form

Choosing the Best Picture

When documentary photographer Dorothea Lange encountered Florence Thompson and her family camped by a frozen pea field, she took multiple pictures. One—and only one—of them became famous. Titled "Migrant Mother," it is considered an indelible image of the Depression. If you were charged with evaluating the six shots that Lange took of Thompson and her family, seen here, which would you choose as the best shot? What reasons would you have for making this judgment?

Seeing the Form (*continued*)

Five photographs Dorothea Lange took of Florence Thompson.

5.3

Identify the characteristics of different forms of the review, including academic applications.

Watch
the Animation on
Writing a Review
in your MyLab

Features of the Form

Feature	Conventions of the Review Essay
Inquiry questions	How good is it? What is its value?
Motives	Your basic motive is to make a judgment about something that you may or may not be familiar with, and then, using reasonable criteria and evidence, convince others that your judgment is sensible.
Subject matter	Reviews aren't just about books, films, and performances. Nearly anything is fair game: consumer products, web pages, cars, apps, policies, restaurants, ski areas, college dorms, vacation destinations, and so on. The key is that you evaluate something that interests you but also might matter to someone else.
Structure	Many reviews have the following elements: • *Description*. What does it look like? What are some other key characteristics? • *Back story*. What is the background? What do readers need to know about if they don't know as much as you do? • *Judgments*. What do you think? These don't have to lead to some grand thesis—it was good or bad—but can be a series of assessments given over the course of the review. • *Reasons, evidence*. What are the reasons behind your judgments? And what evidence do you have to support these reasons? • *Criteria*. What is the basis for your reasons? Criteria may be stated explicitly or implied. • *Relevant comparisons*. What category does it belong to? What else is it like, and why is it better or worse?
Sources of information	The raw material of any review is specific evidence drawn from your experience and research on the subject. What specifically influenced your judgment? What did you see? What did you hear? How did it work? What did they say? What were the results? What are the facts? How does it compare? Many review topics (e.g., film, plays, cars, clothes, books) will be most informed by your direct experience with your subject. But research can help any review. You can read about it or ask people what they think of it.

Feature	Conventions of the Review Essay
Language	The review can be tricky, especially if you're an expert on the thing you're reviewing. Be careful of "insider" language—terms, definitions, and so on that people unfamiliar with your topic may not know. Frequently, the "voice" of the reviewer, especially a particular way of saying things, is especially strong. For example, think about successful music or movie reviewers. Often, the persona they project through their writing voice is part of their appeal: sometimes cranky or even snarky, sometimes humorous, frequently clever.

Prose+: Beyond Words

An online review such as this on the Kindle Fire, an excerpt from the full site, is a powerful combination of text, links, images, and video. The reviewer exploits video to demonstrate some of the features of the device. The text of the review, along with comparison charts, images, and links, is largely supportive of the video content. Notice that criteria for this evaluation of the Kindle are based in part on the idea of Apple's iPad as a standard for comparison.

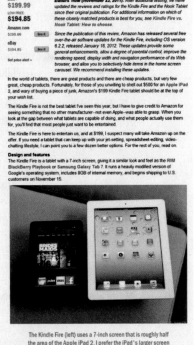

The Kindle Fire (left) uses a 7-inch screen that is roughly half the area of the Apple iPad 2. I prefer the iPad's larger screen for Web browsing, reading magazines, and watching videos, but I also like the idea of saving $300.

READINGS

▶ **Review 1**

One test of a great film is one's willingness to see it again and again, with each viewing yielding some new pleasure. However, holiday films seem like a special category. We see them every year at least in part because of ritual; we watch a movie at Christmastime because we always watch that movie at Christmastime. For a lot of people, *A Christmas Story* (1983) is one of those cinematic rituals. The film tells the story of Ralphie, who more than anything wants a Daisy Red Ryder BB gun for Christmas. Unfortunately, everyone in Ralphie's universe is convinced that if he possesses such a weapon, he will surely "shoot his eye out."

What distinguishes *A Christmas Story* from other popular holiday films, according to the critic Roger Ebert, is that the film possesses "many small but perfect moments" that remind us of "a world that no longer exists in America." In other words, this isn't simply a Christmas film. It's a great film by any measure.

Roger Ebert is perhaps the dean of American movie critics. He is a longtime columnist for the *Chicago Sun Times*, and his website is a popular resource for all things related to film.

A Christmas Story

Roger Ebert

1   One of the details that "A Christmas Story" gets right is the threat of having your mouth washed out with Lifebouy soap. Not any soap. Lifebouy. Never Ivory or Palmolive. Lifebouy, which apparently contained an ingredient able to nullify bad language. The only other soap ever mentioned for this task was Lava, but that was the nuclear weapon of mouth-washing soaps, so powerful it was used for words we still didn't even know.

2   There are many small but perfect moments in "A Christmas Story," and one of the best comes after the Lifebouy is finally removed from Ralphie's mouth and he is sent off to bed. His mother studies the bar, thinks for a moment, and then sticks it in her own mouth, just to see what it tastes like. Moments like that are why some people watch "A Christmas Story" every holiday season. There is a real knowledge of human nature beneath the comedy.

3   The movie is based on the memoirs of Jean Shepherd, the humorist whose radio programs and books remembered growing up in Indiana in the 1940s. It is Shepherd's voice on the soundtrack, remembering one Christmas season in particular, and the young hero's passionate desire to get a Daisy Red Ryder 200-shot Carbine Action BB Gun for Christmas—the one with the compass in the stock, "as cool and deadly a piece of weaponry as I had ever laid eyes on."

In a memorable scene from *A Christmas Story,* Ralphie observes firsthand what happens when a warm tongue meets cold metal.

I owned such a weapon. I recall everything about it at this moment with a tactile memory so vivid I could have just put it down to write these words. How you stuffed newspapers into the carton it came in to use it for target practice. How the BBs came in a cardboard tube with a slide-off top. How they rattled when you poured them into the gun. And of course how everybody warned that you would shoot your eye out.   4

Ralphie's life is made a misery by that danger. He finds that nobody in northern Indiana (not his mother, not his teacher, not even Santa Claus) is able to even *think* about a BB gun without using the words "shoot your eye out." At one point in the movie, in a revenge daydream, he knocks on his parents' door with dark glasses, a blind man's cane and a beggar's tin cup. They are shocked, and ask him tearfully what caused his blindness, and he replies coolly, "Soap poisoning."   5

The movie is not only about Christmas and BB guns, but also about childhood, and one detail after another rings true. The school bully, who, when he runs out of victims, beats up on his own loyal sidekick. The little brother who has outgrown his snowsuit, which is so tight that he walks around looking like the Michelin man; when he falls down he can't get up. The aunt who always thinks Ralphie is a 4-year-old girl, and sends him a pink bunny suit. Other problems of life belong to that long-ago age   6

(continued)

(continued)

and not this one: clinkers in the basement coal furnace, for example, or the blowout of a tire. Everybody knows what a flat tire is, but many now alive have never experienced a genuine, terrifying loud instantaneous *blowout*.

7   "A Christmas Story" was released in the Christmas season of 1983, and did modest business at first (people don't often go to movies with specific holiday themes). It got warm reviews and two Genie Awards (the Canadian Oscars) for Bob Clark's direction and for the screenplay. And then it moved onto home video and has been a stealth hit season after season, finding a loyal audience. "Bams," for example, one of the critics at the hip Three Black Chicks movie review Web site, confesses she loves it: "How does one describe, in short form, the smiles and shrieks of laughter one has experienced over more than 15 years of seeing the same great movie over and over, without sounding like a babbling, fanboyish fool who talks too much?"

8   The movie is set in Indiana but was filmed mostly around Toronto, with some downtown shots from Cleveland, by Clark, whose other big hits were "Porky's" and "Baby Geniuses." It is pitch-perfect, telling the story through the enthusiastic and single-minded vision of its hero Ralphie, and finding in young Peter Billingsley a sly combination of innocence and calculation.

9   Ralphie's parents, Mr. and Mrs. Parker, are played by Darren McGavin and Melinda Dillon, and they exude warmth, zest and love: They are about the nicest parents I can remember in a non-smarmy movie. Notice the scene where Mrs. Parker gets her younger son, Randy, to eat his food by pretending he is "mommy's little piggie." Watch the delight in their laughter together. And the enthusiasm with which the Old Man (as he is always called) attacks the (unseen) basement furnace, battles with the evil neighbor dogs and promises to change a tire in "four minutes flat—time me!" And the lovely closing moment as the parents tenderly put their arms around each other on Christmas night.

10   Some of the movie's sequences stand as classic. The whole business, for example, of the Old Man winning the "major award" of a garish lamp in the shape of a woman's leg (watch Mrs. Parker hiding her giggles in the background as he tries to glue it together after it is "accidentally" broken). Or the visit by Ralphie and Randy to a department store Santa Claus, whose helpers spin the terrified kids around to bang them down on Santa's lap, and afterward kick them down a slide to floor level. Or the sequence where a kid is not merely dared but Triple-Dog-Dared to stick his tongue onto a frozen lamp post, and the fire department has to be called. And the deep disillusionment with which Ralphie finally gets his Little Orphan Annie Secret Decoder Ring in the mail, and Annie's secret message turns out to be nothing but a crummy commercial.

11   There is also the matter of Scut Farcas (Zack Ward), the bully, who Ralphie assures us has yellow eyes. Every school has a kid like this, who picks on smaller kids but is a coward at heart. He makes Ralphie's life a misery. How Farcus gets his comeuppance makes for a deeply satisfying scene, and notice the perfect tact with which Ralphie's mom handles the situation. (Do you agree with me that Dad already knows the whole story when he sits down at the kitchen table?)

In a poignant way, "A Christmas Story" records a world that no longer quite exists   12
in America. Kids are no longer left unattended in the line for Santa. The innocence
of kids' radio programs has been replaced by slick, ironic children's programming on
TV. The new Daisy BB guns have a muzzle velocity higher than that of some police
revolvers, and are not to be sold to anyone under 16. Nobody knows who Red Ryder
was, let alone that his sidekick was Little Beaver.

So much has been forgotten. There is a moment when the Old Man needs an   13
answer for the contest he is entering. The theme of the contest is "Characters in
American Literature," and the question is: "What was the name of the Lone Ranger's
nephew's horse?"

Victor, of course. Everybody knows that.   14

Inquiring into the Essay

1. **Explore.** Think about the holiday film that you'd like to see every year.
   Fastwrite for five minutes about the film and your memories of watching
   it. After the fastwrite, answer this question: What makes this a "good" film?
   Or think about some other film that you'd like to see every year and do the
   fastwrite and answer the question.

2. **Explain.** Underline or highlight sentences or passages in which Ebert is
   telling readers how and why *A Christmas Story* is a great movie. Then summarize in your own words what Ebert is saying about the film, incorporating
   several words or phrases from the material you underlined or highlighted.

3. **Evaluate.** Ebert uses various kinds of evidence to support his judgment
   that this is a great movie because of its "small but perfect moments" that
   get all the details of childhood in America right. He uses personal evidence,
   evidence from others, and of course lots of evidence from the movie. Find
   examples of these different kinds of evidence, and assess how effective they
   are in supporting the reasons Ebert gives for his judgment of the movie.

4. **Reflect.** In evaluative writing, judgments can be as small as brief comments
   or as big as thesis statements. Is there a thesis statement somewhere in
   Ebert's review of *A Christmas Story*? If so, where is it? If not, is this a problem? Does every piece of persuasive writing need a thesis?

▶ Review 2

Few popular rock bands are as controversial as the Canadian group Nickelback.
Though they are hugely successful, selling something like 50 million albums,
Nickelback also regularly gets torched by critics who complain that the group's
music is formulaic. In the review that follows, music critic Melinda Newman begs
to differ. Writing for her blog on the website Hitfix, Newman calls Nickelback's

album *Here and Now* a worthy effort with songs that "are tightly-coiled bullet blasts with little bloat for the most part."

Mind-bending phrases like that are common in much writing about contemporary rock music, part of a style that was inspired by the reviews in *Rolling Stone* magazine. Although *Rolling Stone* remains the best-known source of commentary on the popular music scene, online sites such as Hitfix, Music Reviewer, and Spin are popular sources for music reviews, and bloggers such as Melinda Newman, who once wrote for *Billboard* magazine, dominate the discussion of new music. One site, Metacritic, keeps score of the critical reception new releases receive. The "metascore" for *Here and Now*? Fifty-one percent, based on nine reviews—apparently a flunking grade. This will not deter the group's fans, however, one of whom explained that the "awesome" record gets "hate just because it's by Nickelback."

Nickelback's
Here and Now
Melinda Newman

1   Nickelback seems to hold a special place in critics' hearts. Seldom has a band drawn such slings and arrows. It's as if every time one of their fans buys a Nickelback album— and they've bought more than 50 million of them—a critic's puppy gets kicked and evil edges one step closer to winning.

2   Please. That's such wasted energy. There's always been a space for acts that folks in the flyover states love and that snobs on the coasts hate (I can say that since I'm originally from North Carolina). Or to put it in political language, even though they are from Canada, Nickelback is about as red state a band as ever existed.

3   On "Here and Now," out today, Chad Kroeger and the boys do nothing to endear themselves to any of their haters, including those 50,000+ people who signed a petition protesting the band's halftime performance during Thanksgiving's Detroit Lions/ Green Bay Packers game.

4   Instead, the meat-and-pototoes rockers have stuck with a tried-and-true formula of well-crafted songs that celebrate their common-man status (despite their presumably millionaire savings accounts) and love for pliant strippers, a certain leafy plant, and all forms of alcohol.

5   Nickelback is back to producing themselves, but the lessons learned from working with uber-producer Mutt Lange on 2008's "Dark Horse" remain: Even if there's little here that possesses the potential stickiness of 2005's mega-smash "Photograph," the songs on "Here and Now" are tightly-coiled bullet blasts with little bloat for the most part starting with opening slab "This Means War." Ryan Peake's gunfire guitar work and Kroeger's screaming chorus give notice that they

aren't going down without a fight. It's a rallying cry that permeates much of the rest of the album.

The first two singles, released simultaneously—the party-til-you-puke-or-pass-out anthem "Bottoms Up" and the strumming, acoustic "When We Stand Together," which addresses world hunger among other societal ills—demonstrate the inherent paradox in Nickelback. 6

What undoubtedly confuses folks is that Nickelback can go from these Neanderthal anthems about women who will "lick my pistol clean" on "Midnight Queen" and that reduce men to their absolute basest urges and women to cartoon playthings to songs that uplift and inspire, such as "Lullaby" which is a soothing love letter to someone who is contemplating suicide. Guess what? You're thinking too hard about it. Trust me, the members of Nickelback hasn't [sic] spent a minute contemplating why they can have hits with such seemingly disparate songs as "Rockstar" and "If Everyone Cared." They're too busy spending their money on the next lap dance or buying a new Maserati. 7

What's a little harder to reconcile is their ability to totally objectify women and compare them to cars and turn around and write love songs that resonate with equal validity. The best of the trio of love tunes on "Here and Now" is "Don't Ever Let It End," a song, that quite frankly, is so sweet that the Kroeger who's singing on "This Means War" would punch out the wimpy Kroeger who's singing this love ode and push him into a locker. Despite that, it's a punchy pop song that has a great melody and lovely harmonies. 8

If you're looking for innovation, Nickelback's music has always been the wrong place and when the band tries to experiment, the results are spotty at best, such as on "Everything I Wanna Do," a mess of a song that mashes up metal, rock, weird pastiches of electronica, and distorted vocals. I bet it was a blast to create in the studio, but it should have stayed off the record. Same with the fuzzy stomp of "Kiss It Goodbye," which attempts to reinforce Nickelback's outsider status. 9

Inquiring into the Essay

1. **Explore.** In her review of Nickelback's *Here and Now*, Melinda Newman makes certain claims, implicitly or explicitly. Here are a few of them:

   a. Critics of the group, and there are many of them, judge Nickelback unfairly.

   b. Sticking to a "tried-and-true formula" for making music isn't a bad thing.

   c. Contradictory messages in music—e.g., misogynistic lyrics and empathetic lyrics—aren't a problem.

   In your journal, explore your own thinking about these claims.

2. **Explain.** Define what you believe are the qualities of "good" music. What are your criteria for evaluating music?

3. **Evaluate.** Using the definition you drafted above, what is your judgment about Nickelback? If you're unfamiliar with the group, rely on what Newman

says in the review and your experience listening to a few of their songs on the web.

4. **Reflect.** Presumably, Newman's Nickelback review will be read by some people who are inclined to dislike the group's music. Reflect on the rhetoric of the review. Does Newman aim to persuade that audience? If so, how does she go about it?

▶ Review 3

The video gaming industry hauls in something like $10 billion a year, so it's no surprise that more writers than ever are penning reviews of the latest releases. These reviews, if they're any good, balance technical information about the game with attention to the experience of playing it. It is a well-described gaming experience, not arcane detail, that will appeal to most readers. That's why Seth Schiesel's review of "Grand Theft Auto IV," a hugely popular video game released in 2008, is such a great example of how to write a review that might make even non–video game players interested in giving it a try.

Even when he doesn't make them explicit, the criteria Schiesel uses to determine the qualities of a good game aren't hard to find. One criterion he clearly uses is what we often look for in film and literature: "fully realized characters." When you

Niko Bellic (top center) is the main character of the video game "Grand Theft Auto IV," a game that Seth Schiesel calls "violent, intelligent, profane, endearing, obnoxious, sly, richly textured and thoroughly compelling."

think about it, this is a pretty extraordinary accomplishment in a video game. After all, characters in a game such as "Grand Theft Auto IV" must consistently service the action, making things (usually violent things) happen, and this wouldn't seem to provide the time or the situations to develop character. But according to Schiesel, protagonist Niko Bellic is "one of the most fully realized characters video games have yet produced."

Seth Schiesel sidesteps the ethics of producing games such as "Grand Theft Auto IV," which makes efficient killing a key to advancement. But this is a review, not a public argument on the virtues of gaming, and his readers likely aren't interested in such ethical questions. They just want to know whether the game is any good. As you read "Grand Theft Auto Takes on New York," consider what exactly Schiesel sees as being a good video game. On what other criteria does he base his judgment?

Grand Theft Auto Takes on New York
Seth Schiesel

I was rolling through the neon deluge of a place very like Times Square the other night in my Landstalker sport utility vehicle, listening to David Bowie's "Fascination" on the radio. The glittery urban landscape was almost enough to make me forget about the warehouse of cocaine dealers I was headed uptown to rip off. 1

Soon I would get bored, though, and carjack a luxury sedan. I'd meet my Rasta buddy Little Jacob, then check out a late show by Ricky Gervais at a comedy club around the corner. Afterward I'd head north to confront the dealers, at least if I could elude the cops. I heard their sirens before I saw them and peeled out, tires squealing. 2

It was just another night on the streets of Liberty City, the exhilarating, lusciously dystopian rendition of New York City in 2008 that propels Grand Theft Auto IV, the ambitious new video game to be released on Tuesday for the Xbox 360 and PlayStation 3 systems. 3

Published by Rockstar Games, Grand Theft Auto IV is a violent, intelligent, profane, endearing, obnoxious, sly, richly textured and thoroughly compelling work of cultural satire disguised as fun. It calls to mind a rollicking R-rated version of Mad magazine featuring Dave Chappelle and Quentin Tarantino, and sets a new standard for what is possible in interactive arts. It is by far the best game of the series, which made its debut in 1997 and has since sold more than 70 million copies. Grand Theft Auto IV will retail for $60. 4

Niko Bellic is the player-controlled protagonist this time, and he is one of the most fully realized characters video games have yet produced. A veteran of the Balkan wars and a former human trafficker in the Adriatic, he arrives in Liberty City's rendition of Brighton Beach at the start of the game to move in with his affable if naïve cousin Roman. Niko expects to find fortune and, just maybe, track down someone 5

(continued)

(continued)

who betrayed him long ago. Over the course of the story line he discovers that revenge is not always what one expects.

6   Besides the nuanced Niko the game is populated by a winsome procession of grifters, hustlers, drug peddlers and other gloriously unrepentant lowlifes, each a caricature less politically correct than the last.

7   Hardly a demographic escapes skewering. In addition to various Italian and Irish crime families, there are venal Russian gangsters, black crack slingers, argyle-sporting Jamaican potheads, Puerto Rican hoodlums, a corrupt police commissioner, a steroid-addled Brooklyn knucklehead named Brucie Kibbutz and a former Eastern European soldier who has become a twee Upper West Side metrosexual.

8   Breathing life into Niko and the other characters is a pungent script by Dan Houser and Rupert Humphries that reveals a mastery of street patois to rival Elmore Leonard's. The point of the main plot is to guide Niko through the city's criminal underworld. Gang leaders and thugs set missions for him to complete, and his success moves the story along toward a conclusion that seems as dark as its beginning. But the real star of the game is the city itself. It looks like New York. It sounds like New York. It feels like New York. Liberty City has been so meticulously created it almost even smells like New York. From Brooklyn (called Broker), through Queens (Dukes), the Bronx (Bohan), Manhattan (Algonquin) and an urban slice of New Jersey (Alderney), the game's streets and alleys ooze a stylized yet unmistakable authenticity. (Staten Island is left out however.)

9   The game does not try to represent anything close to every street in the city, but the overall proportions, textures, geography, sights and sounds are spot-on. The major landmarks are present, often rendered in surprising detail, from the Cyclone at Coney Island to the Domino Sugar factory and Grand Army Plaza in Brooklyn and on up through the detritus of the 1964–65 World's Fair in Queens. Central Park, the Empire State Building, various museums, the Statue of Liberty and Times Square are all present and accounted for. There is no Yankee Stadium, but there is a professional baseball team known, with the deliciousness typical of the game's winks and nods, as the Swingers.

10   At least as impressive as the city's virtual topography is the range of the game's audio and music production, delivered through an entire dial's worth of radio stations available in almost any of the dozens of different cars, trucks and motorcycles a player can steal. From the jazz channel (billed as "music from when America was cool") through the salsa, alt-rock, jazz, metal and multiple reggae and hip-hop stations, Lazlow Jones, Ivan Pavlovich and the rest of Rockstar's audio team demonstrate a musical erudition beyond anything heard before in a video game. The biggest problem with the game's extensive subway system is that there's no music underground. (Too bad there are no iPods to nab.)

11   The game's roster of radio hosts runs from Karl Lagerfeld to Iggy Pop and DJ Green Lantern. It is not faint praise to point out that at times, simply driving around the city listening to the radio—seguing from "Moanin'" by Art Blakey and the Jazz Messengers to the Isley Brothers' "Footsteps in the Dark" to "The Crack House" by Fat Joe featuring Lil Wayne—can be as enjoyable as anything the game has to offer.

Grand Theft Auto IV is such a simultaneously adoring and insightful take on   12
modern America that it almost had to come from somewhere else. The game's main
production studio is in Edinburgh, and Rockstar's leaders, the brothers Dan and Sam
Houser, are British expatriates who moved to New York to indulge their fascination
with urban American culture. Their success places them firmly among the distinguished cast of Britons from Mick Jagger and Keith Richards through Tina Brown who
have flourished by identifying key elements of American culture, repackaging them
for mass consumption and selling them back at a markup.

It all adds up to a new level of depth for an interactive entertainment experi-   13
ence. I've spent almost 60 hours practically sequestered in a (real world) Manhattan
hotel room in recent weeks playing through Grand Theft Auto IV's main story
line and the game still says I have found only 64 percent of its content. I won't ever
reach 100 percent, not least because I won't hunt down all 200 of the target pigeons
(known as flying rats here) that the designers have hidden around the city.

But like millions of other players I will happily spend untold hours cruising   14
Liberty City's bridges and byways, hitting the clubs, grooving to the radio and running
from the cops. Even when the real New York City is right outside.

Inquiring into the Essay

1. **Explore.** This review doesn't address the ethical questions raised by a game
   that celebrates "gloriously unrepentant lowlifes" including potheads, gangsters, and "crack slingers." "Grand Theft Auto IV" may be no worse than other
   violent video games, and unless you've played it, criticism or praise of this
   particular game is unfair. But in a four-minute fastwrite, explore your own
   feelings about violent video games. In his review, Schiesel argues that "Grand
   Theft Auto IV" is cultural satire. Would that make a difference? Can games
   such as this one serve a larger, even useful purpose?

2. **Explain.** In your own words, state what Seth Schiesel seems to see as the
   qualities of a good video game.

3. **Evaluate.** How rhetorically effective is this review for different readers? Assess
   what parts would work—or wouldn't—for the following categories of readers:

   a. People who have never played a video game in their lives but might
      consider it.

   b. People who are avid and experienced gamers.

   c. People who, when asked, usually consider playing video games "a waste
      of time."

4. **Reflect.** Video game reviews are but one of a growing number of review
   subgenres, which include reviews of movies, books, blogs, websites, best
   and worst dressed, and so on. Consider the subgenres of reviews you read
   or might read. What exactly would you be looking for in a "good" review?

THE WRITING PROCESS

Inquiry Project **Writing a Review Essay**

Inquiry questions: How good is it? What is its value?

Write a review essay on any subject—a performance, a book, a website, a consumer product, a film, whatever. Just make sure your review has the following qualities (see also pages 160–161 for typical features of the review essay):

- The essay is focused on an specific example of a larger category. (For instance, the film *Maltese Falcon* is an example of forties film noir, *The Curious Writer* is an example of a composition textbook, and Lady Gaga's song "Born This Way" is an example of politically themed contemporary rock music.)

- The writer's judgments are clearly stated and are supported with reasons and evidence.

- The evaluation seems balanced and fair. The criteria for judging the value of the subject seem sound.

Prose+

Watch
the Animation on
**Graphics and
Visuals**
in your MyLab

Write and publish your review for an online audience. There are review sites for nearly anything, from the very focused (e.g., birding binoculars) to the quite broad (music, film, TV, *and* video games). For example,

- For a book review, consider publishing on the Amazon or Barnes & Noble site, or on a site such as Goodreads or LibraryThing.
- For music, check out the website Music-Critic.
- For music, movies, TV, apps, or video games, look to sites such as Metacritic.
- For consumer products, there is Eopinions.

Turn your review into a video project. If you're writing about a consumer product, for example, demonstrate in a short film how it works and how it should work better. (There are a gazillion examples of this on YouTube.) If you're reviewing a movie or television show, put together a short film that incorporates clips, if available online, with your voiceover commentary. Make sure you allow time to learn how to use the basics of your video editing software.

Add images to your essay. You might, for example, take a series of photographs to demonstrate how something works or to highlight key features.

What Are You Going to Write About?

Imagine all the things about which you might ask, "How good is it?" From smart-phones to theater performances, movies to college websites, books to dog-training programs—the possibilities are endless. You don't have to start with an opinion about your review subject—and it's better if you don't—but it should be something that interests you.

Get started thinking about what you're going to write about by opening up the possibilities with the following prompts, most of which involve generating ideas. Later, you'll narrow things down to a promising topic and try it out.

5.4
Use invention and focusing strategies to discover and develop a review essay.

Opening Up

Suspend judgment to explore a range of possible review essay topics.

Listing Prompts. Lists can be rich sources of triggering topics. Let them grow freely, and when you're ready, use an item as the focus of another list or an episode of fastwriting. The following prompts should get you started.

1. Fold a piece a paper into four equal columns. You'll be making four different brainstormed lists. In the first column, write "Things I Want." Spend two minutes making a quick list of everything you wish you had but don't: a new computer, a classical guitar, a decent boyfriend, and so on.

2. In the next column, write "The Jury Is Still Out." In this column, make a fast list of things in your life that so far are hard to judge: the quality of the school you attend, this textbook, your opinion about the films you saw last month, how well Susie cuts your hair, and so on.

3. In the third column, write "My Media." Devote a fast list to particular films, TV shows, books, websites, or musicians you like or dislike; jot down whatever you watch, listen to, or read regularly.

4. Finally, make a list of "Things of Questionable Quality." Try to be specific.

Fastwriting Prompts. Remember, fastwriting is a great way to stimulate creative thinking. Turn off your critical side and let yourself write "badly."

1. Choose an item from any of the four preceding lists as a prompt for a seven-minute fastwrite. Explore your experience with the subject, or how your opinions about it have evolved.

2. Begin with the following prompt, and follow it for five minutes in a fastwrite: *Among the things I have a hard time judging is* _____. If the writing stalls, shift subjects by writing, *And another thing I can't judge is* _____.

Visual Prompts. Sometimes the best way to generate material is to see what we think represented in something other than sentences. Boxes, lines, webs, clusters, arrows, charts, and even sketches can help us see more of the landscape of a subject, especially connections that aren't as obvious in prose.

1. On a blank page in your journal, cluster the name of an artist, musician, film, book, author, performance, band, building, academic course or major, restaurant, university bookstore, tablet, computer, food store, or pizza joint. Cluster the name of anything about which you have some sort of feeling, positive or negative. Build a web of associations: feelings, details, observations, names, moments, facts, opinions, and so on. Look for a single strand in your essay that might be the beginning of a review.

2. Draw a sketch of what you think is an *ideal version* of something you need or use often: a computer, a classroom, a telephone, a wallet or handbag, and so on. If you could design such a thing, what would it look like? Use this as a way of evaluating what is currently available and how it might be improved.

Research Prompts. Explore what other critics are saying, look around, or collaborate.

1. Do an Internet or library search for reviews on one of your favorite films, books, sports teams, artists, and so on. Do you agree with the evaluations? If not, consider writing a review of your own that challenges the critics.

2. Take a walk. Look for things to evaluate that you see as you wander on and off campus—downtown architecture, the quality of local parks, paintings in the art museum, neighborhoods, coffee shops. You'll be amazed at how much is begging for a thoughtful judgment.

3. Here's an entertaining generating activity: Plan a weekend of movie watching with a few friends. Ask each of them to suggest two or three favorite films, then obtain a slew of them, and when you're thoroughly spent watching the films, discuss which might be most interesting to review.

Narrowing Down

Now that you've opened up possibilities for review topics, there are choices to make. Which do you want to write about?

What's Promising Material and What Isn't? My favorite coffee shop in my hometown of Boise, Idaho, is a place called the Flying M. It's a funky place with an odd assortment of furniture, overstuffed couches, worn armchairs, and wobbly tables. On the walls, there's work from local artists, mostly unknowns with talent and unusual taste. There are other coffee places in town, including the ubiquitous Starbucks and another more local chain called Moxie Java. I don't find much difference in the coffee at any of these places, and they're all rather pleasant. What makes me prefer the Flying M?

I've never really thought about it. That's one of the reasons I liked the idea of reviewing my favorite local coffeehouse when the Flying M appeared on one of my lists. The best inquiry-based projects begin when you're not quite sure what you think and want to explore a topic to find out.

- *Is there anything in your lists and fastwrites that you might have an initial judgment about but really haven't considered fully?*

- *As you consider potential subjects for your review, do some clearly offer the possibility of comparison with other similar things in that category?*

- *Do any of your potential subjects offer the possibility of primary research, or research that might involve direct observation?* Can you listen to the music, attend the performance, read the novel, examine the building, visit the website, look at the painting?

- *Does a topic lend itself to demonstration through visuals or video?* Can you download clips, film a demonstration, take pictures, create an infographic?

Questions About Audience and Purpose. When people read reviews, they either are actively *seeking information* (they are considering buying the tablet or attending the dance performance) or are *looking for reinforcement* (reasons why what they've already decided to do makes sense). I bought a Ford Escape recently, and now I read every review I see on the car, hoping to feel good about my decision. These two audiences have very different dispositions. The information-seekers are more critical readers than those who seek reinforcement. But what they both share is a stake in the topic under review. They're *interested*. As you consider a review topic, ask yourself whether it's easy to imagine an audience who would care, one way or another, about a judgment about the usefulness or value of the thing.

Trying Out

Let's work with your tentative topic, doing some more-focused work, culminating in a sketch, or a first try at writing it up for an audience.

Focusing the Category. First, let's try focusing your topic in the context of a category. Can you see how your topic fits into broader and narrower categories? An inverted pyramid is a nice model for this:

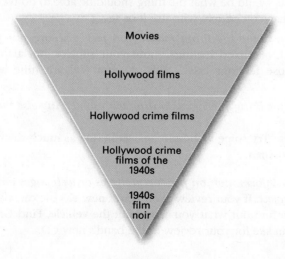

Movies

Hollywood films

Hollywood crime films

Hollywood crime films of the 1940s

1940s film noir

Suppose you love the 1940s film classic *The Maltese Falcon*, and you'd like to explore why it's so good. You can evaluate the film as an example of movies generally, but that makes little sense because the category's too broad. However, suppose you list progressively narrower subcategories of film to which *The Maltese Falcon* might belong. You might end up evaluating the film as an example of 1940s film noir. Why is this useful?

1. *It gives you a way of seeing appropriate comparisons.* You're comparing *The Maltese Falcon* not to all Hollywood movies—there are, after all, so many different kinds—but to other 1940s Hollywood crime films that belong to the film noir genre.

2. *It helps you focus on appropriate criteria.* Just as it would be weird to compare *The Maltese Falcon* with *A Christmas Story* because they are such different types of films, it would be hard to arrive at criteria for such an evaluation. What makes a 1940s crime film "good" will be very different than what makes a family comedy "good."

Try creating an inverted pyramid on your subject, looking for a category that is narrow enough to make comparisons and criteria more appropriate.

Fastwriting. Through a focused fastwrite, explore your initial feelings and experiences, if any, about your subject. Use one of the following prompts to launch this exploration. If the writing stalls, try another prompt to keep you going for five to seven minutes.

- *Write about your first experience with your subject.* This might be, for example, the first time you remember visiting the restaurant, or hearing the performer, or seeing the photographs. Focus on scenes, moments, situations, and people.

- *Write about what you think might be important qualities of your subject.* Ideally, this would be what the thing should be able to do well or what effects it should have on people who use it or see it.

- *Write about how the thing makes you feel.* Explore not just your initial good, bad, or mixed feelings about your subject, but also the place from where those feelings arise. Why do you feel anything at all about this thing?

- *Compare the thing you're evaluating with something else that's similar.*

Web Research. Try some web searches, gathering as much relevant background information as you can.

- *Search for information on product websites or web pages devoted specifically to your subject.* If your review is on Ford's new electric car, visit the company's website to find out what you can about the vehicle. Find Green Day's home page or fan site for your review of the band's new CD.

- *Search for existing reviews or other evaluations on your subject.* One way to do this is to google using the keyword "review" or "reviews" (or "how to evaluate") along with your subject. For example, "laptop reviews" will produce dozens of sites that rank and evaluate the machines. Similarly, there are countless reviews on the web of specific performers, performances, CDs, consumer products, and so on.

Interviews. If possible, interview people about what they think. You may do this formally by developing a survey, or informally by simply asking people what they like or dislike about the thing you're evaluating. Also consider whether you might interview someone who's an expert on your subject. For example, if you're evaluating a website, ask people in the technical communications program what they think about it, or what criteria they might use if they were reviewing something similar.

Experiencing Your Subject. This may be the most useful activity of all. Visit the coffeehouses, examine the website, listen to the music, attend the performance, read the book, view the painting, visit the building, look at the architecture, watch the movie. As you do this, gather your impressions and collect information. Take notes. Take pictures. Shoot video.

Thinking About Criteria

You hate something. You love something. You have mixed feelings about it. All of these judgments arise from your criteria, your assumptions about the qualities that make such a thing good. And thinking about your criteria can help you know what to look for.

Refining Criteria for Better Evidence. Consider a process of evaluation something like the one in Figure 5.2.

You see a website and think, "This is really ugly." You look more closely and conclude, "I think there's too much text." You could stop there, of course, but you want to provide a more thorough evaluation. A natural next step, then, would be to consider the criterion behind your reason and judgment. You could simply say, "Good websites don't use too much text," but that doesn't advance your evaluation any further because the criterion is too general and vague. After a little research into what this criterion's really about, you arrive at this: "Good sites break text into readable chunks." Sites that don't have readable chunks give the visual appearance of too much text. What's a "readable chunk"? Turns out it is around 80 characters per line. Now you can take another look at your ugly website with a criterion that really helps you support your judgment with better evidence.

This implies a couple things about good criteria in evaluation:

1. The more specific your criterion for evaluation, the better.
2. Identifying criteria is a powerful tool for finding better evidence to support your judgment.

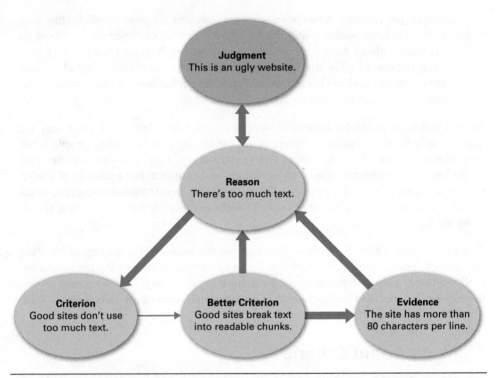

Figure 5.2   A process for refining criteria and using criteria to generate better evidence

The more you know about something, the more specific your criteria are likely to be. For example, I asked my daughter Becca, a dancer, what criteria she would use to judge a modern performance (see the box). I'm unschooled in dance, so I don't understand all of her criteria, but I'm certain I could use some of them next time I see a modern performance, to evaluate what I see.

Considering Criteria and Rhetorical Context. We often don't think about our criteria and whether they're valid; we treat them as self-evident and may assume that our audience would agree with them. But careful reviewers at the very least

---

Becca's Criteria

A good modern dance performance has...

1. Interesting features—props, comedy, or music
2. Something improvised
3. Visible expressions of the dancers' enjoyment
4. Interesting variation
5. Good balance in choreography between repetition and randomness
6. Beginning, middle, and end seamlessly joined

consider the criteria that shape their reactions and decide whether they're fair and sensible. (If you're finding your criteria hard to tease out, or want to know what criteria others might have, try getting some help; see "Inquiring into the Details: Collaborating on Criteria.")

In thinking about criteria, you need to think about rhetorical context: audience and purpose. As you saw in Chapter 1, the qualities of "good" writing really depend on the situation: purpose, audience, genre. A main purpose of a review is to give readers potentially useful information. So, if you're evaluating a new type of downhill skis, you'd need to think about skis for whom. An advanced skier fond of deep powder will have different expectations of her skis' performance than will an intermediate skier like me, who falls on his face off groomed runs. For this reason, in thinking about criteria that might guide your evaluation of the thing you're reviewing, you'll find it useful to

First, identify your audience:

- *Who will be using the thing (going to the performance, etc.)?*

Then, take another look at your criteria:

- *Are the criteria that you are thinking in terms of appropriate for your audience?*

Inquiring into the Details

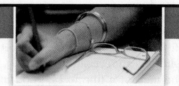

Collaborating on Criteria

What makes it "good"? Being clear on your criteria can help you discover what you think and, once you do, explain your reasons. Asking others for their opinions can help. Consider the following strategy:

1. Write the category of the thing you're reviewing—a modern dance performance, coffeehouses, a hip-hop CD, a science fiction novel, or whatever—on the top of a piece of newsprint or paper.

2. Post your newsprint on the wall of your classroom.

3. For twenty minutes, everyone in class rotates around the room to each newsprint, trying to answer the following question about the category listed there: In your judgment, what makes a particularly good _____ (dance performance, coffeehouse,...)?

4. Briefly list your criteria for judging each category on the newsprint, or elaborate on criteria that are already there. In other words, in your mind, what makes a good _____?

5. If you don't know that much about the category, make a reasonable guess about a basis for judging it.

Writing the Sketch

A sketch, as the name implies, is a kind of verbal drawing of your topic—an early draft—to see if you should develop it further. While you write a sketch with readers in mind, it is hardly polished. You are "essaying" the topic to try it out, and you may not know yet what you think or what you want to say. Your review sketch, however, should include the following:

- A tentative title.
- An effort to help readers understand why they might have a stake in the thing you're evaluating. What's significant about this particular CD, book, performance, place, or product?
- A tentative answer to the inquiry question "How good is it?"
- A few clear reasons for your judgment that are tied to specific evidence from the thing itself.

▶ Student Sketch

Here are some common criteria for a good film:

1. There is someone in the film who we come to like, despite their flaws.
2. Characters change. They learn from mistakes.
3. The story ends with some resolution of the conflict.

According to Laura Burns, whose sketch of the Charlize Theron film *Young Adult* follows, that movie doesn't meet any of the three criteria. And yet, she argues, *Young Adult* is a great film. Obviously, Laura is saying that criteria most of us assume must be met for a film to be good in fact don't have to be met. Because she challenges our assumptions, Laura needs to be particularly persuasive in her review. How does she do in this first attempt?

Recipe for a Great Film: Unlikeable People, Poor Choices, and Little Redemption

Laura Burns

1   Charlize Theron is arguably the most traditionally beautiful woman in film. High, smooth cheekbones, long, thin legs, a delicate nose set at the center of a perfectly proportioned face. This considered, it's remarkable how ugly she can get.

2   *Young Adult* is a movie about unlikeable people making poor life choices which they don't learn from. Theron plays Mavis Gary, an ex-prom queen from Mercury, Minnesota, making her

living as a ghostwriter of a teen series in what the Mercurians call the "Mine-apple." From the first sequence of the film, we can tell that Mavis is a mess. She gets wasted, slumps around her apartment in sweats, and guzzles Diet Coke in a way that almost gave me heartburn. Upon receiving a birth announcement email from her now-married ex-prom king, the aptly named Buddy (Patrick Wilson), Mavis decides to pop an old mixtape into her dirty Mini Cooper and win him back.

This is, essentially, the entire plot of *Young Adult*. Mavis' trip back to Mercury is a kind of *anti*-hero's journey. On her first night in town, getting wasted in a local dive, she meets her "guide," Matt (the wonderful Patton Oswalt), a former classmate who remains crippled from an assault during high school. Through the course of the film, as she reunites with her parents (Jill Eikenberry & Richard Bekins), insinuates herself into Buddy and his wife Beth's (Elizabeth Reaser) lives, and gets plastered on Matt's home-brewed bourbon, rather than moving towards revelation, Mavis seems to retreat further and further into her past.

Unlike *Juno*, writer Diablo Cody's most well-known film, *Young Adult* rejects preciousness in favor of obscenity. It's difficult to make a film about terrible people enjoyable, but Cody injects just enough silliness to keep us from feeling too badly. Director Jason Reitman rightly focuses on Mavis, and both Theron and Oswalt are brave enough to let us into their characters' grossness and un-likeability. Smartly, Cody refuses to manufacture empathy for her characters, leaving us to boldly accept the ugliness of these people fully.

I don't doubt that *Young Adult* will displease many movie-goers who are used to redemptive stories and characters who are "good at heart." Cody refuses to indulge that expectation. When Mavis dresses to go out (which is often), Theron's extraordinary beauty is obvious. Yet we're never allowed to shake that Mavis is truly ugly at her core—an effective subversion of expectation that is the exemplar of this memorable performance. This isn't a feel-good film, and thank goodness. If Cody and Reitman had tried, I think we might leave the theater feeling worse.

Moving from Sketch to Draft

A sketch is an audition. It's a brief performance for an audience that may or may not work out well. In a review, what do you look for in your own performance? To start with, you've got to still care, of course. This should be a topic you still want to write about. But what else?

Evaluating Your Sketch. Start with a summary of what you think the sketch is saying by finishing the following sentence.

Because of ___(reason 1)___ and ___(reason 2)___, I think that ___(thing you're evaluating)___ is ___(judgment of value)___, and the strongest evidence for this is _____ and _____.

Example: Because of its unusually hefty neck and its thick solid rosewood body, the Martin 0-28VS acoustic guitar has a bright sound that belies its small size, and the strongest evidence for this is how great it sounds with light fingerpicking and its long sustains.

If you can finish the sentence to your satisfaction, your audition was successful. You know, more or less, where you might be going. (Don't be surprised if you change your mind as you revise.) However, you might have encountered some problems. Maybe you haven't yet arrived at a judgment. Or perhaps you can't come up with two compelling reasons for the judgment you do have. In any case, these are the things you should focus on as you develop your review:

- *Clarify your judgment.* What is the one thing you're trying to say (S.O.F.T.) about the thing you're reviewing?

- *Explain your reasons.* What is behind your evaluation? And are the criteria that these reasons are based on sensible?

- *Provide the back story.* What is it, where did it come from, how does it compare, why is it important, what is the history?

- *Gather evidence.* How will you prove that your reasons are persuasive? What specifically can you point to?

Reflecting on What You've Learned. To get some perspective on what you've learned so far about the thing you're reviewing, fastwrite in your journal or on the computer using the following prompt:

When I first started exploring this, I thought _____, and now I'm beginning to think _____.

Developing

Before you revise your sketch into a draft, generate more material through writing and research. This is almost always necessary.

Talking It Through. Generate more material by having a conversation with me about your topic. Imagine I'm sitting across the table from you, asking you the following questions about the thing you're reviewing. Respond in your journal to each question, in order, fastwriting a response for at least a few minutes. If the writing takes off in response to any one question, run with it. The order of the questions may prove to be a useful organizing principle for your draft, so write as much as you can in the exercise.

Bruce	You
To start with, why are you reviewing this? To whom might it matter and under what circumstances?	

Bruce	You
Can you describe it? What does it look like? What is the story behind it? Would you compare it to anything else I might know about?	
Okay, so what do you most want me to know about it? What is it you're saying, exactly?	
Interesting. Why do you say this?	
Surely, not everyone thinks this. What do people who disagree with you say? How would you respond to that?	

Consider the following research strategies for developing your draft.

Re-Experience. Probably the single most useful thing you can do to prepare for the next draft is to collect more observations of your subject. Why? You're much more focused now on what you think, what criteria most influence that judgment, and what particular evidence you were lacking in the sketch that will make your review more convincing. You might also consider documenting your research not only with notes but multimedia as well. Could you take pictures to demonstrate a feature or show how the thing you're reviewing is used? Might you include screenshots of the relevant websites? Download images of the thing being used?

Interview. If you haven't already done so, collect the comments, opinions, and observations of others about the subject of your review. If you reviewed a concert or other event, find others to interview who also attended. If you reviewed a film, get some friends to watch the movie with you and jot down their reactions afterward. If it would be helpful to collect data on how people feel, consider designing a brief survey.

  Also consider interviewing someone who is an expert on the thing you're reviewing.

Read. Go to the library and go online and search for information about your subject. Try finding:

- *Information about how it's made or designed.*
- *Other reviews on your topic.*
- *Information on relevant people, companies, traditions, local developments— any background that will help readers see the thing you're reviewing in a larger context.*

Drafting

When you've got enough information, start your draft, beginning at the beginning.

Finding an Opening. Seth Schiesel's review of the fourth version of the video game "Grand Theft Auto" (see pp. 169–171) begins this way:

> I was rolling through the neon deluge of a place very like Times Square the other night in my Landstalker sport utility vehicle, listening to David Bowie's "Fascination" on the radio. The glittery urban landscape was almost enough to make me forget the warehouse of cocaine dealers I was headed uptown to rip off.

It isn't simply the punchy language (e.g., "neon deluge," "rip off") that makes this lead paragraph compelling. The paragraph does three things that good beginnings should do:

1. Raises questions the reader might want to learn the answers to.
2. Creates a relationship between reader and writer.
3. Gets right to the subject without unnecessary scaffolding.

While we know from the title of the piece that this is about a video game, Schiesel's opening makes us wonder about what exactly is going on here, who this guy is, and what he is talking about. It immediately immerses us in the *experience* of playing the game.

Here are some other approaches to a strong lead for a review:

- Begin with a common misconception about your subject and promise to challenge it.
- Begin with an anecdote that reveals what you like or dislike.
- Help readers realize the relevance of your subject by showing how it's used, what it says, or why it's needed in a familiar situation.
- Provide interesting background that your readers may not know.

Methods of Development. What are some ways to organize your review?

Narrative. If you're reviewing a performance or any other kind of experience that has a discrete beginning and end, then telling a story about what you saw, felt, and thought is a natural move. Another way to use narrative is to tell the story of your thinking about your subject—an approach that lends itself to a delayed thesis essay, where your judgment comes late in the review.

Comparison/Contrast. Comparison with other items in the same category—say, other science fiction films, electric cars, or laptops—is a common and useful element in reviews. If comparison is especially important to your review, you might structure your essay around it.

Question to Answer. One of the most straightforward methods of structuring a review is to simply begin by raising the question *What makes _____ good?* This way, you make your criteria for evaluation explicit. From there, the next move is obvious: How well does the thing you're evaluating measure up?

Using Evidence. As you compose your draft, keep in mind that the most important evidence in a review is probably your own observations of the thing. These should be specific, and most likely they will draw on *primary research* you conducted by attending the concert, listening to the CD, or visiting the coffeehouse. As illustrated in Figure 5.2, thinking about your criteria can be a tool for finding strong evidence. You may also use evidence from secondary sources: For example, what did another critic say or observe?

Workshopping

If your draft is subject to peer review, see Chapter 14 for details on how to organize workshop groups and decide on how your group can help you. To help you decide, use the guidance, starting on p. 578, in Chapter 14. Each workshop type is described more fully in that chapter.

Watch
the Animation on
Discussing
in your MyLab

When you workshop a review, you're sharing your evaluation of something your peers may have no experience with. Maybe they've never seen the movie, tried the coffee, visited the restaurant, or listened to the music. This has rhetorical implications you should consider as you prepare to discuss your draft:

1. *Context.* Do you provide enough background on the thing you're evaluating: who they are, how it works, why it's significant, what it does, etc.?

2. *Comparisons.* Even if none of your readers have, say, ridden the road bike you're reviewing, most have ridden a bicycle of some kind. Did you establish common ground with readers by exploiting any overlaps between their experience and your review topic?

3. *Definitions.* You can't assume that your peers are familiar with insider jargon. Did you define terms and explain features and so on that readers may not know?

In workshopping the first draft of your review, your initial focus should be on what peers make of the purpose and meaning of your essay. Above all else, knowing what you're trying to do and say in an essay will help you decide what to cut and what to add in revision. It's the most powerful knowledge you can have for rewriting. This grid can help you frame the questions for your workshop group.

Questions for Peer Reviewers	
1. Purpose	Why is this being reviewed? Who has a stake in whether it's good or not?
2. Meaning	In your own words, what exactly is my judgment? In your words, what are my main reasons for this judgment? Are they persuasive? Why or why not?

If you're reviewing something that your peers may be familiar with—and perhaps have strong feelings about—you might consider a workshop for your draft that encourages participants to debate your conclusions, both supporting your judgments and challenging them (see box).

Option for Review Essay Workshop

1. Divide each workshop group into two teams—believers and doubters.
2. Believers are responsible for presenting to doubters why the writer's review is convincing and fair.
3. Doubters challenge the writer's judgments and respond to the believers' claims.
4. The writer observes this conversation without participating.
5. After five minutes, believers and doubters drop their roles and discuss suggestions for revision with the writer.

Reflecting on the Draft. Immediately after your workshop session, fastwrite in your journal (paper or computer) on what you learned about writing an effective review *from reading your peers' drafts.* How might you apply these things to your revision?

Revising

5.5

Apply revision strategies that are effective for shaping reviews.

Revision is a continual process—not a last step. You've been revising—"reseeing" your subject—from the first messy fastwriting in your journal. But the things that get your attention vary depending on where you are in the writing process. With your draft in hand, revision becomes your focus through what I'll call "shaping and tightening your draft."

Chapter 13 contains strategies that can help you revise any inquiry project, and the "Guide to Revision Strategies" on page 188 can help you locate these strategies. There are also certain things to think about that are expecially useful for shaping a profile essay.

Shaping. You've clarified the purpose and meaning of the piece. Now you want to redesign it around both.

Analyzing the Information. Shaping involves, among other things, arranging and rearranging information so that it is more effectively organized around your main idea. One way to think about the structure of your review is to look at its information in terms of the elements that reviews typically include:

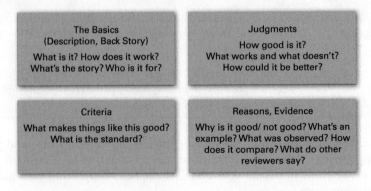

The Basics
(Description, Back Story)
What is it? How does it work?
What's the story? Who is it for?

Judgments
How good is it?
What works and what doesn't?
How could it be better?

Criteria
What makes things like this good?
What is the standard?

Reasons, Evidence
Why is it good/ not good? What's an example? What was observed? How does it compare? What do other reviewers say?

By analyzing your draft in this way, you can look at whether you've included enough information for each element. While there's no formula for ordering this information, consider the structure of your draft rhetorically. If your audience is familiar with the thing you're reviewing, then "the basics" need less emphasis; obviously, the opposite is true if your audience has little knowledge. In either case, the basics are usually early in the draft. Similarly, audiences who are familiar with your topic (e.g., they've seen the movie or used the device) may share your assumptions about criteria already. You can spend less time explaining them. Others who are unfamiliar with your topic need to learn the criteria you're using, so give these more emphasis. Judgments can appear anywhere in the draft, not just as a thesis in your first paragraph.

To imagine organizing strategies, you can try the "Frankenstein Draft" (Revision Strategy 13.18 in Chapter 13): Cut up your draft with scissors into the different elements mentioned here, and then play with the order. What seems to be most effective? Worry about transitions later.

Other Questions for Revision. Because a review's a form of argument, start by asking yourself, "Is my evaluation clear, and will it be persuasive to readers?" For example, here's a paragraph from Jesse's review of the film *Crank*:

> *Crank* (2006), written and directed by Mark Neveldin and Brian Taylor, is a fast-paced, dark, action comedy. This is not your typical "good guy saves the day" action film though. With a lot of profanity, wild antics and defiance of the law, it is very edgy. It really reminds me of a Grand Theft Auto Vice City. The star of the show even steals a cop's motorcycle and rides it around the city recklessly. But don't be quick to judge this film only by its novel gamer appeal. This movie also had good theatrical performances.

Jesse's evaluation is clear: The film *Crank* is good. And he explains why: strong performances and an "edgy" feel similar to that of the video game "Grand Theft Auto." One way to "re-see" an evaluation is to plunge under its surface to see the criteria and assumptions underneath. Jesse works from an assumption that a film that has the feel and look of a familiar video game is a good thing. But why? To make his evaluation more compelling to readers, when Jesse revises, he should probably explain that assumption.

Consider starting your rewrite by thinking about the criteria and assumptions behind the judgments you make. Which need to be explicitly addressed because an audience might not agree with them?

Polishing. Shaping focuses on things such as purpose, meaning, and overall design and structure. No less important is polishing—looking more closely at paragraphs, sentences, and words. Are your paragraphs coherent? How do you manage transitions? Are your sentences fluent and concise? Are there any errors in spelling or syntax? The section of Chapter 13 called "Problems with Clarity and Style," on page 564, can help you focus on these issues.

Before you finish your draft, work through the following checklist:

✓ Every paragraph is about one thing.

✓ The transitions between paragraphs aren't abrupt.

✓ The length of sentences varies in each paragraph.

✓ Each sentence is concise. There are no unnecessary words and phrases.

✓ You've checked grammar, particularly verb agreement, run-on sentences, unclear pronouns, and misused words (*there/their, where/were,* and so on). (See the Handbook at the end of the book for help with these grammar issues.)

✓ You've run your spellchecker and proofed your paper for misspelled words.

Chapter 13 has strategies to help you solve all kinds of revision problems, large and small. Use the "Guide to Revision Strategies" below to know where to look in that chapter to both shape and tighten your draft.

Watch
the Animation on
**Revising and Editing
Your Essay**
in your MyLab

Guide to Revision Strategies

Problems in the Draft (Chapter 13)	Page Number
Unclear purpose	538
■ Not sure what the essay is about? Fails to answer the *So what?* question?	
Unclear thesis, theme, or main idea	543
■ Not sure what you're trying to say? Judgment isn't clear?	
Lack of information or development	551
■ Needs more details; more evidence supporting the reasons?	
■ Criteria need work?	
Disorganized	555
■ Doesn't move logically or smoothly from paragraph to paragraph?	
Unclear or awkward at the level of sentences and paragraphs	564
■ Seems choppy or hard to follow at the level of sentences or paragraphs?	

▶ Student Essay

Earlier in the chapter, you saw Laura Burns's sketch, a review of the Charlize Theron film *Young Adult*. Here you can see Laura's next draft, in which she's revised her essay into a web page. This is the first web page she's created, and she did it with Microsoft Word; the program has more than enough tools for the novice designer. Laura followed much of the advice in "Inquiring into the Details: Design Tips for Basic Web Pages" (Chapter 6, p. 224), including limiting the character length of each line, working with standard fonts, and keeping things simple. The result is pleasing. It's also more information rich, with links to another review, the film's trailer, and information about the screenwriter. Most important, though, is that it's Laura's writing here that makes the review successful, not the design tricks. Her positive evaluation of the film is nicely captured by the title she chose and the punchy prose that follows it. Like a lot of reviews, "How Not to Feel Good and Feel Good About It" depends on a strong writing voice, and Laura's celebration of "unlikeable people making poor life choices from which they don't learn a thing" is easy to listen to, even if you don't agree with it.

How to Not Feel Good and Feel Good About It

A Review of *Young Adult*
Laura Burns

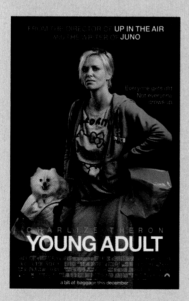

1 Charlize Theron is certainly one of the most beautiful women in film. High, smooth cheekbones, long, thin legs, and a delicate nose set at the center of a perfectly proportioned face. This considered, it's remarkable how ugly she can get.

2 <u>Young Adult</u> is a movie about unlikeable people making poor life choices from which they don't learn a thing. Theron plays Mavis Gary, an ex-prom queen from Mercury, Minnesota, making her living in the "Mini-apple" (as the Mercurians call Minneapolis) as the ghostwriter of a formerly popular teen book series. From the first sequence of the film, we can tell that Mavis is a mess. She gets wasted, slumps around her apartment in sweats, and guzzles Diet Coke in a way that almost gave me heartburn. Upon receiving a birth announcement email from her now-married ex-prom king beau, the aptly named Buddy (the similarly beautiful Patrick Wilson),

(continued)

(continued)

Mavis decides to pop an old mix tape into her dirty Mini Cooper and go home to Mercury to win him back.

3　　This is, essentially, the entire plot of *Young Adult*. Mavis' trip back to Mercury is a kind of *anti-hero's* journey. On her first night in town, getting wasted in a local dive, she meets her guide, Matt (the wonderful Patton Oswalt), a former classmate who remains crippled from a high school assault by jocks who mistakenly thought he was gay. Through the course of the film, as she reunites with her parents (Jill Eikenberry & Richard Bekins), insinuates herself into the lives of Buddy and his wife Beth (Elizabeth Reaser), and gets plastered on Matt's home-brewed bourbon, rather than moving towards revelation, Mavis seems to retreat further and further into her past.

Young Adult is writer Diablo Cody's most mature work yet.

4　　Unlike writer <u>Diablo Cody</u>'s most well-known and Oscar-winning screenplay *Juno, Young Adult* rejects preciousness in favor of obscenity. It's difficult to make a film about terrible people enjoyable, but Cody injects just enough silliness to keep us from feeling too badly. Director Jason Reitman (who also paired with Cody on *Juno*) wisely keeps us focused on Mavis through every moment, from the night out to the morning after, and both Theron and Oswalt are brave enough to let us into their characters' grimy inner selves. Smartly, Cody refuses to manufacture empathy for her characters, leaving us to boldly accept the ugliness of these people fully.

5　　I don't doubt that *Young Adult* will displease many movie-goers who are used to redemptive stories and characters who, as *Salon* put it are "<u>good at heart.</u>" Cody refuses to indulge that expectation. When Mavis dresses to go out and drink (which is often), Theron's extraordinary physical beauty is obvious. Yet we're never allowed to shake that Mavis is truly ugly at her core—an effective subversion of expectation that is the reason this memorable performance works. This isn't a feel-good film, and thank goodness. If Cody and Reitman had tried, I think we might leave the theater feeling worse.

Evaluating the Essay

1. Laura "re-mixes" her sketch into a web page. What's your evaluation of that move? Do you find it an effective revision of her review, and what criteria are you using to make that judgment?

2. As I've already mentioned, reviews often thrive on the persona—and the voice—of the reviewer. I think Laura has a strong persona in this review. The question is, how is persona communicated in a piece such as this one? What exactly would you point to in her review that reflects an individual voice and character?

3. Describe the structure of Laura's review. Diagram it using the elements of a review: description, back story, judgment, reasons, evidence, and criteria.

Using What You Have Learned

Let's revisit the list from the beginning of this chapter of things I hoped you'd learn about this form of writing.

1. **Use reasons and evidence to support a judgment about something's value.** Even if you never write another review (and I'm guessing you probably will because evaluative writing is so common), your experience with this project introduces you to the basics of argument. In the next two chapters, you'll see how judgments (or claims), reasons, and evidence figure into all kinds of persuasive writing. Of course, it's not news that judgments are supported by reasons and evidence, but now you can think about these things more systematically and, as a result, have tools to analyze not only your own arguments but the arguments of others.

2. **Identify the criteria behind a judgment and determine their relevance.** Remember the iceberg metaphor in the beginning of the chapter? Above water were judgments, reasons, and evidence—the most visible elements of an argument—but the great unseen mass below the surface is criteria. In a review, these are assumptions we make about what makes something "good," and they are often unexamined. In Chapter 7, "Writing an Argument," you'll see that assumptions can make or break an argument. Knowing to look for assumptions will give you a strong footing when analyzing any argument.

3. **Identify the characteristics of different forms of the review, including academic applications.** Reviews aren't just about books and films. They are a method of evaluating virtually anything. Whenever you are asked to evaluate something—a professor, a proposal, a methodology, even an argument—you can apply the skills you practiced here.

4. **Use invention and focusing strategies to discover and develop a review essay.** One of the biggest challenges in academic writing (and much other writing) is focusing your topic. In this chapter, you practiced a skill you can apply in nearly any paper you write: how to see your topic *in context*, recognizing its place in an ever-larger scheme of things (remember the inverted pyramid?). Use this to imagine how any topic can be divided and subdivided, for finding a frame that is appropriate for your purpose.

5. **Apply revision strategies that are effective for shaping reviews.** In Chapter 4, you applied revision strategies that helped you build an essay around an idea by seeing it through a person. In this chapter, you did something similar, except instead of a profile, you wrote about a thing. What's different, however, is that your review used a wider range of evidence, and this required you to cast a wider net for information as you revised. This is a skill that you'll build on in the next assignments, as you write more and more with outside sources.

Complete
Additional Exercises
and Practice on
Chapter 5
in your MyLab

Researching and thinking about solutions can be a bit like following a horse race: You might favor one solution until another one suddenly races up from behind as you learn more.

Writing a Proposal

6

Learning Objectives

In this chapter, you'll learn to

6.1 Describe a problem of consequence, framing it narrowly enough to explore convincing solutions.

6.2 Identify the wide range of rhetorical situations that might call for a proposal argument.

6.3 Argue effectively for both the seriousness of the problem and the proposed solutions, using strong evidence.

6.4 Use appropriate invention strategies to discover and develop a proposal topic.

6.5 Apply revision strategies that are effective for a proposal.

Writing About Problems and Solutions

Several students sit around the table in my office. We're talking about problems each of us would love to solve. "I've got a short story due at three this afternoon and I've only written three pages," says Lana. Everyone nods sympathetically. "I'd really like to feel better about work," confides Amy, who works as a chef at a local restaurant. "Most days I just don't want to go." Margaret is a history major, familiar with the making and unmaking of nations and other grand narratives of colonialism, war, and social change. Her problem, however, is a bit more local. "I can't get my boyfriend to clean up the apartment," she says.

"What about you?" they ask me.

"The problem I most want to solve today is how to avoid getting scalded in the shower when someone in my house flushes the toilet," I say, getting into the spirit of things.

This conversation had not gone quite the way I expected. I know these students are socially engaged, politically aware, and academically gifted people. When I asked about problems that need solutions, I expected that they might mention local issues such as housing developments that threaten the foothills, the difficulty that nontraditional students have adjusting to the university, or budget cuts that threaten the availability of courses next semester. If they had been thinking on a larger scale—say, nationally or even internationally—perhaps the conversation would have turned to the federal deficit or the conflict in Darfur. Of course, I hadn't asked them to suggest social or economic problems. I had simply asked them what problems most vexed them at the moment.

I should not have been surprised that these would be boredom with work, too little time, and a messy boyfriend. These problems are quite real, and they demand attention, *now*. One was easy to solve. Lana would carve out extra time in the afternoon to finish her story—"I already know what I need to do," she said. But the other two problems—disenchantment with work and a boyfriend who's a slob—Amy and Margaret actually saw not so much as problems to solve as realities they had to live with. In fact, all the students admitted that they rarely look at the world from the perspective of problem solving—the perspective that's at the heart of a proposal.

"What if you did?" I asked.

"Then I guess I'd ask myself if there was an opportunity to learn something," said Amy.

Problems of Consequence

6.1

Describe a problem of consequence, framing it narrowly enough to explore convincing solutions.

problems w/ consequence.

While not all problems are equally solvable, the process of seeking and proposing solutions can be rewarding if you see, as Amy did, the opportunity to learn. There's another motivation, too: If the problem is shared by others, whatever you discover may interest them. Part of the challenge is recognizing problems *of consequence*. What makes a problem consequential?

1. It potentially affects a number of people.
2. The solution may not be simple.
3. There may be multiple solutions and people disagree about which is best.

My problem with getting scalded in the shower if somebody flushes a toilet is clearly not consequential; all I need to do is go to Ace Hardware and buy a device for the showerhead. But what about Margaret's problem with her boyfriend? Is that a problem of consequence? Undoubtedly there are lots of people with messy mates, the solution is not at all obvious (just ask Margaret), and there are likely multiple ways of dealing with the problem.

If a problem is consequential, it's more likely that someone else will have said something about it. Like many other forms of inquiry, problem solving usually requires some research. After all, if we already knew the solution, we wouldn't have the problem. An important consideration, then, is whether others have said something about the problem that might help you think about the best ways to solve it. On a quick search of the web and several library databases, Margaret found some material that she thought could serve as background for an essay that looks at the problem of a messy mate and proposes some solutions. While Margaret may not succeed in getting her boyfriend to pick up his socks, she will probably learn a few things about how to deal with the problem.

> While not all problems are equally solvable, the process of seeking and proposing solutions can be rewarding if you see the opportunity to learn.

Problems of Manageable Scale

What about the sorts of larger-scale problems my students didn't mention that day? Here we're obviously talking about problems of consequence. The problems of world hunger, war, environmental destruction, poverty and lack of economic development, and human rights violations are problems that matter to us all. These are also among the most complex problems to solve. I'm always delighted when writers in my classes are passionate about these issues, and they certainly can be great topics for writing. But narrowing the topic to something manageable is a crucial first step.

Obviously, you're not going to have anything meaningful to say about solving world hunger in a five-page essay (see Figure 6.1). But it might be possible to write a focused essay about the troubles over food production in Zimbabwe, once one of Africa's top agricultural producers. Even better, narrow the topic further and investigate U.S. aid policies that are failing to help feed hungry Zimbabwean children. Your interest in hunger can also easily lead to topics with a local angle—say, the reluctance of some hungry families in your community to use food stamps because of a local supermarket's policies. By focusing on the narrower problem, you can often reveal aspects of the larger problem much more powerfully while developing a solution that's more implementable.

In other words, when you are choosing a problem to explore for a proposal, the *manageable scale* of a problem is as important as its consequentiality.

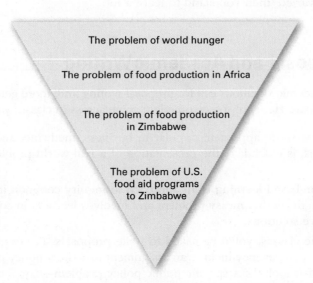

Figure 6.1 Narrowing the focus of the problem. Most of us want to find solutions to the big problems of the world, but big problems such as world hunger are complicated and do not readily yield to simple solutions. Unless you are writing a book-length proposal, it is better to narrow the focus of the problem to which you will propose solutions.

Motives for Writing a Proposal

Quite simply, people write proposals to try to argue convincingly to others that a problem is worth tackling and a proposed solution is a good way to tackle it. Your motives for writing a proposal will probably include the following:

- *You* care *about the problem.* Whether it's something in your personal life (avoiding procrastination, having a more obedient dog, or finding a way to use less water in the garden) or a public issue (protecting bicyclists from traffic, increasing neighborhood police protection, or battling adolescent obesity) you should feel that the problem deserves your attention.

- *You hope to change something.* Writing a proposal is a way of overcoming powerlessness. Maybe you feel helpless about the daily deluge of scammers and junk messages in your e-mail. You can just complain about it. I do. But you can also research a proposal that might help you—and the many others affected by the problem—to avoid the Nigerian scammers who want to "give" you $8.5 million if you just send them a copy of your passport and $1,750.

- *You hope to learn something.* A proposal is like all other inquiry projects: You choose a topic because you're motivated to discover things you don't know. This motive alone isn't sufficient, of course. Others must be affected by the problem and have a stake in considering your solution. But if the problem is sufficiently complex and the solutions varied, then you stand to learn a lot.

Writing a proposal is a way of overcoming powerlessness.

The Proposal and Academic Writing

6.2
Identify the wide range of rhetorical situations that might call for a proposal argument.

Numerous academic situations call for proposal writing and, more generally, writing to solve problems. Here are some you might come across in classes you take:

- The case-study approach, popular in business, medicine, and some social sciences, is essentially the presentation of a real-world problem for you to solve.

- Problem-based learning is an approach to inquiry common in the sciences that begins with a messy problem and involves learners in coming up with tentative solutions.

- In some classes, you'll be asked to write proposals. For example, political science courses may include an assignment to write a policy proposal or an essay that looks at a specific public policy problem—say, the organization of the city government or the state's role in wolf management (a big issue here in Idaho)—and suggests some possible solutions. In a marketing class, you might be asked to draft a proposal for dealing with a particular management problem.

Academics in many disciplines write research proposals. These identify a question and then propose a plan for studying it (see "Inquiring into the Details: Writing a Research Proposal"). The research question may relate to a problem—air pollution inversions in the valley, energy inefficiencies in buildings, and so on—or simply to a topic that could be useful to study—use of iPads in the classroom or the effects of birth order. To get grants for their research, academics usually need to submit proposals.

Inquiring into the Details

Read the Interactive Research Proposal in your MyLab

Writing a Research Proposal

A research proposal is a kind of action plan that explains your research question, what you expect might be the answer, how your investigation contributes to what has already been said on the topic, and how you will proceed.

While the format varies, most research proposals aim to persuade readers that (1) the project is reasonable given the investigator's time and resources, (2) the research question or problem is significant, and (3) the researcher has a good plan for getting the job done.

The following elements are typically included in a research proposal:

- ■ **Title:** Short and descriptive.
- ■ **Abstract:** A brief statement of what you intend to do, including your research question and hypothesis, if you've got one.
- ■ **Background or context:** Why is the project worth doing? What problem does it solve, or how does it advance our understanding of the subject? This key section establishes where your question fits into the ongoing conversation about your topic, in your class, in the academic literature, or both. You also want to demonstrate that you've done your homework—you've got a handle on the relevant literature on your topic and understand how you might build on it.
- ■ **Methodology or research design:** How will you try to answer your research question? How will you limit your focus? What information will you need to gather, and how will you do it?
- ■ **Results:** This isn't a common section for proposals in the humanities, but it certainly is in the sciences. How will you analyze the data you collect?
- ■ **References or works cited:** Almost all research proposals, because they review relevant literature, include a bibliography. Sometimes you may be asked to annotate it (see Appendix B, "The Annotated Bibliography").

Because the research proposal is a persuasive document, craft it to keep your reader engaged; find a good balance between generalities and detail, avoid jargon, and demonstrate your curiosity and eagerness to pursue your question.

Read
the
Interactive
Proposal
in your MyLab

Features of the Form

Feature	Conventions of the Proposal
Inquiry questions	What is the problem? What should be done?
Motives	You hope to change a problem related to something that matters to you and others, and there is the promise that you will learn something about the problem and possible solutions.
Subject matter	Proposals suggest a best plan of action on any problem of consequence. Proposals could address large problems (the homeless problem in town) or small ones (a boyfriend who doesn't take dirty dishes seriously), as long as others have a stake in solving the problem. Research proposals suggest a plan for studying a problem or other question.
Structure	Proposals typically address both the problem and the solution, in that order, but may emphasize one or the other. When an audience largely agrees that the problem is significant, a proposal might focus on the solution. When there is disagreement about the significance of the problem, a proposal might focus on why the problem needs attention. Other elements of a proposal include: • *Causes and effects.* These can help establish why the problem needs attention and why the proposed solution will deal with the problem. • *Justifications.* Typically proposals that argue for certain solutions over others offer clear reasons why the proposed solutions are the best ones. • *Evidence.* Evidence from research and experience makes a case for the problem and for the solutions. • *Other perspectives.* If you're writing about a problem of consequence, then other people have said something about it and probably have proposed various solutions. • *Visual rhetoric.* Often, problems and/or solutions can be illustrated with pictures, tables, and graphs; headings and bulleted lists can also be useful.
Sources of information	Writers who have experience with a problem should tap that experience in a proposal. However, if they're not experts, then personal experience alone may not be persuasive evidence. Proposals usually depend on information from research—reading or interviews—on what people who *are* experts on the problem say about it.

Feature	Conventions of the Proposal
Language	Proposals are a form of argument. As with other arguments, the language you use depends largely on the rhetorical situation. Formal proposals intended for an expert audience, such as research or marketing proposals, take a formal tone. Others—for example, a proposal that's a letter to the editor or a blog entry—are much more casual and even personal.

Prose+

Alexandra Muresan's infographic "CO_2 Paper Pie Chart" highlights the sources of the world's carbon dioxide emissions related to individuals and the ways to reduce these emissions. Notice that both the problems and solutions are integrated into a single paper pie chart. When unfolded as a *C*, the chart shows the sources of emissions in each paper fold. When unfolded as an *O*, it gives suggestions for reducing emissions. Muresan's paper pie chart is an elegant visual proposal. It not only beautifully presents the problem of CO_2 emissions, but also literally puts the solution to the problem into a user's hand.

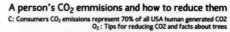

A person's CO_2 emmisions and how to reduce them
C: Consumers CO_2 emissions represent 70% of all USA human generated CO2
O_2: Tips for reducing CO2 and facts about trees

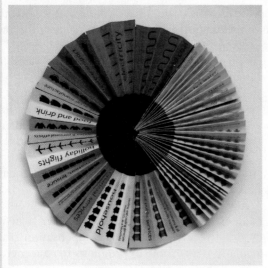

the pollution

the solution

Data Sources: http://www.cutco2.org/ http://www.erasecarbonfootprint.com/ http://www.eoearth.org/

Designed by Alexandra Muresan www.ixycreativity.ro

READINGS

▶ Proposal 1

I teach at a university with a football team that is frequently ranked in the top ten nationally. Our stadium's blue turf is more famous than any one of our academic programs, prompting the university's marketing folks to coin the slogan "Beyond the Blue." In other words, we just want you to know that there is actually teaching and research going on here, not just football. And yet, the games are fun, and the athletic program is the strongest link the university has to the community. The sale of sports paraphernalia—hats, t-shirts, bobble-heads, and dog collars emblazoned with the school colors—funds student scholarships. Is college football really a problem? Buzz Bissinger thinks so. He notes that these are often hugely expensive programs that hemorrhage money in a time of endless tuition hikes. The solution: Ban college football.

Why College Football Should Be Banned

Buzz Bissinger

1   In more than 20 years I've spent studying the issue, I have yet to hear a convincing argument that college football has anything do with what is presumably the primary purpose of higher education: academics.

2   That's because college football has no academic purpose. Which is why it needs to be banned. A radical solution, yes. But necessary in today's times.

3   Football only provides the thickest layer of distraction in an atmosphere in which colleges and universities these days are all about distraction, nursing an obsession with the social well-being of students as opposed to the obsession that they are there for the vital and single purpose of learning as much as they can to compete in the brutal realities of the global economy.

4   Who truly benefits from college football? Alumni who absurdly judge the quality of their alma mater based on the quality of the football team. Coaches such as Nick Saban of the University of Alabama and Bob Stoops of the University of Oklahoma who make obscene millions. The players themselves don't benefit, exploited by a system in which they don't receive a dime of compensation. The average student doesn't benefit, particularly when football programs remain sacrosanct while tuition costs show no signs of abating as many governors are slashing budgets to the bone.

If the vast majority of major college football programs made money, the argument to ban football might be a more precarious one. But too many of them don't—to the detriment of academic budgets at all too many schools. According to the NCAA, 43 percent of the 120 schools in the Football Bowl Subdivision lost money on their programs. This is the tier of schools that includes such examples as that great titan of football excellence, the University of Alabama at Birmingham Blazers, who went 3-and-9 last season. The athletic department in 2008–2009 took in over $13 million in university funds and student fees, largely because the football program cost so much, *The Wall Street Journal* reported. New Mexico State University's athletic department needed a 70% subsidy in 2009–2010, largely because Aggie football hasn't gotten to a bowl game in 51 years. Outside of Las Cruces, where New Mexico State is located, how many people even know that the school has a football program? None, except maybe for some savvy contestants on "Jeopardy." What purpose does it serve on a university campus? None.

The most recent example is the University of Maryland. The president there, Wallace D. Loh, late last year announced that eight varsity programs would be cut in order to produce a leaner athletic budget, a kindly way of saying that the school would rather save struggling football and basketball programs than keep varsity sports such as track and swimming, in which the vast majority of participants graduate.

Part of the Maryland football problem: a $50.8 million modernization of its stadium in which too many luxury suites remain unsold. Another problem: The school reportedly paid $2 million to buy out head coach Ralph Friedgen at the end of the 2010 season, even though he led his team to a 9-and-4 season and was named Atlantic Coast Conference Coach of the Year. Then, the school reportedly spent another $2 million to hire Randy Edsall from the University of Connecticut, who promptly produced a record of 2-and-10 last season.

In an interview with the *Baltimore Sun* in March, Mr. Loh said that the athletic department was covering deficits, in large part caused by attendance drops in football and basketball, by drawing upon reserves that eventually dwindled to zero. Hence cutting the eight sports.

This is just the tip of the iceberg. There are the medical dangers of football in general caused by head trauma over repetitive hits. There is the false concept of the football student-athlete that the NCAA endlessly tries to sell, when any major college player will tell you that the demands of the game, a year-round commitment, makes the student half of the equation secondary and superfluous. There are the scandals that have beset programs in the desperate pursuit of winning—the University of Southern California, Ohio State University, University of Miami, and Penn State University among others.

(continued)

(continued)

10   I can't help but wonder how a student at the University of Oregon will cope when in-state tuition has recently gone up by 9% and the state legislature passed an 11% decrease in funding to the Oregon system overall for 2011 and 2012. Yet thanks to the largess of Nike founder Phil Knight, an academic center costing $41.7 million, twice as expensive in square footage as the toniest condos in Portland, has been built for the University of Oregon football team.

11   Always important to feed those Ducks.

12   I actually like football a great deal. I am not some anti-sports prude. It has a place in our society, but not on college campuses. If you want to establish a minor league system that the National Football League pays for—which they should, given that they are the greatest beneficiaries of college football—that is fine.

13   Call me the Grinch. But I would much prefer students going to college to learn and be prepared for the rigors of the new economic order, rather than dumping fees on them to subsidize football programs that, far from enhancing the academic mission instead make a mockery of it.

Inquiring into the Essay

1. **Explore.** Here's a sampling of assertions from Bizzinger's essay:

    ■ "College football has no academic purpose."

    ■ The beneficiaries of college football aren't the students, the athletes, or the school but coaches who pull in salaries in the millions.

    ■ The vast sums invested in coaches, stadiums, and training facilities often end up being a drain on universities' budgets. This is especially objectionable in an age of tuition increases.

    Choose one of these assertions (or another from the essay you'd like to write about) and fastwrite for five minutes, exploring your own thinking about the claim. If you can, write about what you observe on your own campus.

2. **Explain.** Follow up on your fastwrite in the last step by composing a summary of your own thinking about Bissinger's proposal to ban college football.

3. **Evaluate.** One of Bissinger's key claims is that college football programs often lose big money, and as evidence he cites the NCAA, which reported that 43 percent of the schools in the Football Bowl Subdivision were in the red. Using your own research, evaluate that claim.

4. **Reflect.** A proposal is an argument: There is a problem, here are some solutions, and this is evidence that makes them credible. It's never that simple, of course. For one thing, you have to secure audience agreement

that there is a problem in the first place, and if your audience agrees, then there are many possible solutions. Why yours? Finally, some evidence is better than other evidence, and there is the issue of what you *don't* say. Is there a counter-argument? Is there inconvenient evidence you ignore? With all this in mind, how would you evaluate Bissinger's proposal that college football should be banned?

▶ Proposal 2

A lot of people can't imagine a proposal without PowerPoint (or Keynote for Mac users). It's a remarkably versatile program that exploits the potential of visual rhetoric. You can combine images with text, animation, and even audio. Presentation slides challenge the user to think about what ideas to emphasize and which visual arrangements might dramatize them to an audience. Depending on how you order the slides, you can tell a different story. Maybe because of all these possibilities, PowerPoint presentations can be boring. There may be too much text, the animation can be obnoxious, or the images might be distracting. Worse still, the presenter uses presentation slides like a script rather than a technique for focusing emphasis on key points. Watching someone's back while he or she reads PowerPoint text is an invitation to nod off.

The following PowerPoint proposal, "Green Dining," describes how the dining services at University of California–Santa Cruz are trying to solve the problem of energy inefficiency in the kitchen. This proposal doesn't dramatize the problem. It doesn't really need to, because most everyone agrees that wasting energy in dining halls (or any other campus building, for that matter) is a problem. This slide presentation focuses on some solutions, and it works well because the proposal has modest ambitions. It addresses one very specific aspect of the campus dining operation: dishwashing. Even better, there is concrete evidence that one solution is already making a difference in energy use. After documenting this success, "Green Dining" goes on to present other measures that should have a similar impact.

Notice how much can be accomplished with simple images, minimal text, and logical arrangement.

Monterey Bay Green Business Certification

3

- An official recognition awarded by the *Monterey Bay Area Green Business Program*
- Businesses must take extensive measures to conserve resources prevent pollution, and minimize waste.

Savings Opportunities

4

- A typical dishwashing operation can use **over 2/3** of all water consumed at an establishment

- Often **1/2** of that water use is consumed by **pre-rinse spray nozzles**

- And that water is heated with energy

Smart Rinse Spray Nozzles

5

Low-flow "Smart-rinse" nozzles are one upgrade that can save hot water when rinsing and help businesses achieve Green Business Certification.

Spray Nozzle Specs

6

- Fisher "Ultra Spray"
- 1.15 GPM @ 60 PSI
- 1-hole clearance
- Easy-use, "knife spray" action that allows food to be easily removed
- Cost: roughly $50/unit

Benefits

7

- Saves water
- Saves energy
- Saves money
- Cleans faster
- Less splash back
- Covers larger surface area

Success at UC Santa Cruz

8

5 "low-flow" nozzles were installed in various locations: • Crown/Merrill Dining • College 8/9 Dining • Owl's Nest Café • Terra Fresca Cafe	Nozzles were supplied and installed FOR FREE through the "Smart Rinse Program," a program of Ecology Action, a local Santa Cruz non-profit

Quantifiable Savings

9

Energy Saving Estimates

Total # of Nozzles	Hours used per day	Gallons saved per day	Therms saved per day	Annual Dollar Savings
5	65	3229	16.23	$8,175

Current Dining Projects

10

T8 Lighting retrofit

- 5 major dining halls
- Upgrade 32 watts → 28 Watts
- 1248 Lamps counted
- Roughly 5 KW saved

11 Future Dining Project	12 Project Benefits
Variable control exhaust hoods • Controls for commercial kitchen ventilation exhaust hoods • Reduce energy costs by up to 70% during slow cooking periods	• Massive energy savings • Improved indoor air quality • Optimum kitchen comfort • Improved fire safety • 1–4 year payback • \$1,500–\$10,00 in annual savings

13
Questions?

Inquiring into the Essay

1. **Explore.** Finish the following sentences in your journal, and follow each for a minute if you can. Write quickly.

    a. As far as I'm concerned, PowerPoint is _____.

    b. The best slide presentations _____.

    c. The worst slide presentations _____.

    d. When I do PowerPoint (or Keynote), the main thing I think about is _____.

    e. A lot of times, people do PowerPoint when they should _____.

2. **Explain.** Using some of the ideas you generated in the first question, craft a definition of an effective PowerPoint proposal, identifying specifically what qualities it should have.

3. **Evaluate.** Use your definition in the previous question to evaluate "Green Dining." Is it persuasive?

4. **Reflect.** The preceding series of questions, if used consecutively, constitutes a method for thinking through writing about what you've read, working toward a more thoughtful evaluation. Reflect on how that process worked for you. Did you end up getting better ideas about what you think because you took time to do the prewriting?

▶ **Proposal 3**

Some people experience what psychologists call "learned helplessness." Like Eeyore in *Winnie the Pooh*, they feel that there is nothing they can do about the problems that confront them. "Why bother?" they say. "What difference will it make?" And yet, it's hard not to feel a little like Eeyore in the face of climate change. It's such a big problem, and what can the little guy do? Michael Pollan, quoting Wendell Berry, argues in the following essay that this is the "cheap-energy mind" talking, the one that encourages us to believe that we're hopelessly dependent on other people and their grand technologies to get what we need. The climate problem *is* huge, but in "Why Bother?" Pollan has a simple solution: Grow a vegetable garden, even a tiny one. What is so intriguing to me about his essay is not just the simplicity of the solution it offers, but that Pollan manages to make it persuasive. See if you agree.

Why Bother?

Michael Pollan

1   Why bother? That really is the big question facing us as individuals hoping to do something about climate change, and it's not an easy one to answer. I don't know about you, but for me the most upsetting moment in *An Inconvenient Truth* came long after Al Gore scared the hell out of me, constructing an utterly convincing case that the very survival of life on earth as we know it is threatened by climate change. No, the really dark moment came during the closing credits, when we are asked to…change our light bulbs. That's when it got really depressing. The immense disproportion between the magnitude of the problem Gore had described and the puniness of what he was asking us to do about it was enough to sink your heart.

2   But the drop-in-the-bucket issue is not the only problem lurking behind the "why bother" question. Let's say I do bother, big time. I turn my life upside-down, start biking to work, plant a big garden, turn down the thermostat so low I need the Jimmy Carter signature cardigan, forsake the clothes dryer for a laundry line across the yard, trade in the station wagon for a hybrid, get off the beef, go completely local. I could theoretically do all that, but what would be the point when I know full well that halfway around the world there lives my evil twin, some carbon-footprint *doppelgänger* in Shanghai or Chongqing who has just bought his first car (Chinese car ownership is where ours was back in 1918), is eager to swallow every bite of meat I forswear and who's positively itching to replace every last pound of CO_2 I'm struggling no longer to emit. So what exactly would I have to show for all my trouble?

A sense of personal virtue, you might suggest, somewhat sheepishly. But what good is that when virtue itself is quickly becoming a term of derision? And not just on the editorial pages of the *Wall Street Journal* or on the lips of the (former) vice president, who famously dismissed energy conservation as a "sign of personal virtue." No, even in the pages of the *New York Times* and the *New Yorker,* it seems the epithet "virtuous," when applied to an act of personal environmental responsibility, may be used only ironically. Tell me: How did it come to pass that virtue—a quality that for most of history has generally been deemed, well, a virtue—became a mark of liberal softheadedness? How peculiar, that doing the right thing by the environment—buying the hybrid, eating like a locavore—should now set you up for the Ed Begley Jr. treatment.

And even if in the face of this derision I decide I am going to bother, there arises the whole vexed question of getting it right. Is eating local or walking to work really going to reduce my carbon footprint? According to one analysis, if walking to work increases your appetite and you consume more meat or milk as a result, walking might actually emit more carbon than driving. A handful of studies have recently suggested that in certain cases under certain conditions, produce from places as far away as New Zealand might account for less carbon than comparable domestic products. True, at least one of these studies was co-written by a representative of agribusiness interests in (surprise!) New Zealand, but even so, they make you wonder. If determining the carbon footprint of food is really this complicated, and I've got to consider not only "food miles" but also whether the food came by ship or truck and how lushly the grass grows in New Zealand, then maybe on second thought I'll just buy the imported chops at Costco, at least until the experts get their footprints sorted out.

There are so many stories we can tell ourselves to justify doing nothing, but perhaps the most insidious is that, whatever we do manage to do, it will be too little too late. Climate change is upon us, and it has arrived well ahead of schedule. Scientists' projections that seemed dire a decade ago turn out to have been unduly optimistic: the warming and the melting is occurring much faster than the models predicted. Now truly terrifying feedback loops threaten to boost the rate of change exponentially, as the shift from white ice to blue water in the Arctic absorbs more sunlight and warming soils everywhere become more biologically active, causing them to release their vast stores of carbon into the air. Have you looked into the eyes of a climate scientist recently? They look really scared.

So do you still want to talk about planting gardens?

I do....

For us to wait for legislation or technology to solve the problem of how we're living our lives suggests we're not really serious about changing—something our politicians cannot fail to notice. They will not move until we do. Indeed, to look to leaders and experts, to laws and money and grand schemes, to save us from our

(continued)

(continued)

predicament represents precisely the sort of thinking—passive, delegated, dependent for solutions on specialists—that helped get us into this mess in the first place. It's hard to believe that the same sort of thinking could now get us out of it.

9   Thirty years ago, Wendell Berry, the Kentucky farmer and writer, put forward a blunt analysis of precisely this mentality. He argued that the environmental crisis of the 1970s—an era innocent of climate change; what we would give to have back *that* environmental crisis!—was at its heart a crisis of character and would have to be addressed first at that level: at home, as it were. He was impatient with people who wrote checks to environmental organizations while thoughtlessly squandering fossil fuel in their everyday lives—the 1970s equivalent of people buying carbon offsets to atone for their Tahoes and Durangos. Nothing was likely to change until we healed the "split between what we think and what we do." For Berry, the "why bother" question came down to a moral imperative: "Once our personal connection to what is wrong becomes clear, then we have to choose: we can go on as before, recognizing our dishonesty and living with it the best we can, or we can begin the effort to change the way we think and live."

10   For Berry, the deep problem standing behind all the other problems of industrial civilization is "specialization," which he regards as the "disease of the modern character." Our society assigns us a tiny number of roles: we're producers (of one thing) at work, consumers of a great many other things the rest of the time, and then once a year or so we vote as citizens. Virtually all of our needs and desires we delegate to specialists of one kind or another—our meals to agribusiness, health to the doctor, education to the teacher, entertainment to the media, care for the environment to the environmentalist, political action to the politician....

11   Here's the point: Cheap energy, which gives us climate change, fosters precisely the mentality that makes dealing with climate change in our own lives seem impossibly difficult. Specialists ourselves, we can no longer imagine anyone but an expert, or anything but a new technology or law, solving our problems. Al Gore asks us to change the light bulbs because he probably can't imagine us doing anything much more challenging, like, say, growing some portion of our own food. We can't imagine it, either, which is probably why we prefer to cross our fingers and talk about the promise of ethanol and nuclear power—new liquids and electrons to power the same old cars and houses and lives.

12   The "cheap-energy mind," as Wendell Berry called it, is the mind that asks, "Why bother?" because it is helpless to imagine—much less attempt—a different sort of life, one less divided, less reliant. Since the cheap-energy mind translates everything into money, its proxy, it prefers to put its faith in market-based solutions—carbon taxes and pollution-trading schemes. If we could just get the incentives right, it believes, the economy will properly value everything that matters and nudge our self-interest down the proper channels. The best we can hope for is a greener version of the old invisible hand. Visible hands it has no use for.

But while some such grand scheme may well be necessary, it's doubtful that it   13
will be sufficient or that it will be politically sustainable before we've demonstrated
to ourselves that change is possible. Merely to give, to spend, even to vote, is not to
do, and there is so much that needs to be done—without further delay. In the judgment of James Hansen, the NASA climate scientist who began sounding the alarm
on global warming 20 years ago, we have only 10 years left to start cutting—not just
slowing—the amount of carbon we're emitting or face a "different planet." Hansen
said this more than two years ago, however; two years have gone by, and nothing
of consequence has been done. So: eight years left to go and a great deal left to do.

Which brings us back to the "why bother" question and how we might better   14
answer it. The reasons not to bother are many and compelling, at least to the cheap-
energy mind. But let me offer a few admittedly tentative reasons that we might put on
the other side of the scale:

If you do bother, you will set an example for other people. If enough other   15
people bother, each one influencing yet another in a chain reaction of behavioral
change, markets for all manner of green products and alternative technologies will
prosper and expand. (Just look at the market for hybrid cars.) Consciousness
will be raised, perhaps even changed: new moral imperatives and new taboos
might take root in the culture. Driving an SUV or eating a 24-ounce steak or
illuminating your McMansion like an airport runway at night might come to be
regarded as outrages to human conscience. Not having things might become cooler
than having them. And those who did change the way they live would acquire the
moral standing to demand changes in behavior from others—from other people,
other corporations, even other countries.

All of this could, theoretically, happen. What I'm describing (imagining would   16
probably be more accurate) is a process of viral social change, and change of this
kind, which is nonlinear, is never something anyone can plan or predict or count
on. Who knows, maybe the virus will reach all the way to Chongqing and infect my
Chinese evil twin. Or not. Maybe going green will prove a passing fad and will lose
steam after a few years, just as it did in the 1980s, when Ronald Reagan took down
Jimmy Carter's solar panels from the roof of the White House.

Going personally green is a bet, nothing more or less, though it's one we proba-   17
bly all should make, even if the odds of it paying off aren't great. Sometimes you have
to act as if acting will make a difference, even when you can't prove that it will. That,
after all, was precisely what happened in Communist Czechoslovakia and Poland,
when a handful of individuals like Vaclav Havel and Adam Michnik resolved that they
would simply conduct their lives "as if" they lived in a free society. That improbable
bet created a tiny space of liberty that, in time, expanded to take in, and then help
take down, the whole of the Eastern bloc.

So what would be a comparable bet that the individual might make in the   18
case of the environmental crisis? Havel himself has suggested that people begin to
(continued)

(continued)

"conduct themselves as if they were to live on this earth forever and be answerable for its condition one day." Fair enough, but let me propose a slightly less abstract and daunting wager. The idea is to find one thing to do in your life that doesn't involve spending or voting, that may or may not virally rock the world but is real and particular (as well as symbolic) and that, come what may, will offer its own rewards. Maybe you decide to give up meat, an act that would reduce your carbon footprint by as much as a quarter. Or you could try this: determine to observe the Sabbath. For one day a week, abstain completely from economic activity: no shopping, no driving, no electronics.

19   But the act I want to talk about is growing some—even just a little—of your own food. Rip out your lawn, if you have one, and if you don't—if you live in a high-rise, or have a yard shrouded in shade—look into getting a plot in a community garden. Measured against the Problem We Face, planting a garden sounds pretty benign, I know, but in fact it's one of the most powerful things an individual can do—to reduce your carbon footprint, sure, but more important, to reduce your sense of dependence and dividedness: to change the cheap-energy mind.

20   A great many things happen when you plant a vegetable garden, some of them directly related to climate change, others indirect but related nevertheless. Growing food, we forget, comprises the original solar technology: calories produced by means of photosynthesis. Years ago the cheap-energy mind discovered that more food could be produced with less effort by replacing sunlight with fossil-fuel fertilizers and pesticides, with a result that the typical calorie of food energy in your diet now requires about 10 calories of fossil-fuel energy to produce. It's estimated that the way we feed ourselves (or rather, allow ourselves to be fed) accounts for about a fifth of the greenhouse gas for which each of us is responsible.

21   Yet the sun still shines down on your yard, and photosynthesis still works so abundantly that in a thoughtfully organized vegetable garden (one planted from seed, nourished by compost from the kitchen and involving not too many drives to the garden center), you can grow the proverbial free lunch—CO_2-free and dollar-free. This is the most-local food you can possibly eat (not to mention the freshest, tastiest and most nutritious), with a carbon footprint so faint that even the New Zealand lamb council dares not challenge it. And while we're counting carbon, consider too your compost pile, which shrinks the heap of garbage your household needs trucked away even as it feeds your vegetables and sequesters carbon in your soil. What else? Well, you will probably notice that you're getting a pretty good workout there in your garden, burning calories without having to get into the car to drive to the gym. (It is one of the absurdities of the modern division of labor that, having replaced physical labor with fossil fuel, we now have to burn even more fossil fuel to keep our unemployed bodies in shape.) Also, by engaging both body and mind, time spent in the garden is time (and energy) subtracted from electronic forms of entertainment.

You begin to see that growing even a little of your own food is, as Wendell Berry   22
pointed out 30 years ago, one of those solutions that, instead of begetting a new set of
problems—the way "solutions" like ethanol or nuclear power inevitably do—actually
beget other solutions, and not only of the kind that save carbon. Still more valuable are
the habits of mind that growing a little of your own food can yield. You quickly learn
that you need not be dependent on specialists to provide for yourself—that your body
is still good for something and may actually be enlisted in its own support. If the experts
are right, if both oil and time are running out, these are skills and habits of mind we're
all very soon going to need. We may also need the food. Could gardens provide it? Well,
during World War II, victory gardens supplied as much as 40 percent of the produce
Americans ate.

But there are sweeter reasons to plant that garden, to bother. At least in this one   23
corner of your yard and life, you will have begun to heal the split between what you
think and what you do, to commingle your identities as consumer and producer and
citizen. Chances are, your garden will re-engage you with your neighbors, for you will
have produce to give away and the need to borrow their tools. You will have reduced
the power of the cheap-energy mind by personally overcoming its most debilitating
weakness: its helplessness and the fact that it can't do much of anything that doesn't
involve division or subtraction. The garden's season-long transit from seed to ripe
fruit—*will you get a load of that zucchini?!*—suggests that the operations of addition and multiplication still obtain, that the abundance of nature is not exhausted. The
single greatest lesson the garden teaches is that our relationship to the planet need
not be zero-sum, and that as long as the sun still shines and people still can plan and
plant, think and do, we can, if we bother to try, find ways to provide for ourselves
without diminishing the world.

Inquiring into the Essay

1. **Explore.** Pollan's essay is as much about the problem of problem solving
   as it is a proposal for planting gardens. What do we do with the feeling that
   as individuals there is little we can do to influence really big issues such as
   homelessness, hunger, war, or climate change? Who wants to be just a drop
   in the bucket? Explore this dilemma by having a conversation in writing
   with an imaginary companion on a big issue you care about. First, explain
   in writing what problem you think needs to be solved and why. And then
   respond to your companion's first question: *You don't think you could ever
   really do anything about it, do you?* Carry on the conversation with your
   skeptical companion as long as you can.

2. **Explain.** Test your understanding of Pollan's argument. After reading "Why
   Bother?" compose a fast paragraph that summarizes how Pollan answers his
   own question: Why bother?

3. **Evaluate.** Use both the "believing game" and the "doubting game" (see Chapter 2, "Inquiring into the Details: Reading Perspectives," on p. 48) to evaluate this claim from Wendell Berry and from Pollan: "the deep problem standing behind all the other problems of industrial civilization is 'specialization,'...the 'disease of the modern character' " (p. 208).

4. **Reflect.** Imagine "re-mixing" Pollan's article into other genres. For example, how might you use his essay as the basis for a YouTube video or radio documentary you might create on the importance of "doing" even when it feels like a drop in the bucket?

Seeing the Form

A Problem in Pictures

When members of the San Francisco Bicycle Coalition (SFBC) wanted to dramatize the problem of insufficient space for bikes on a city commuter train, they did it with pictures. It was a powerfully simple idea. They took shots of three morning trains, each overloaded with bicycles and nearly empty of passengers. The contrast is obvious. And so is the solution to the problem: Add more space for bicycles on trains. A few months later, transit authorities did just that.

No Space for Bikes:
A photo study of trains bumping cyclists out of SF.

1: Train 134: Sept 22 9:07 AM   2: Train 134: Sept 22 9:07 AM

Seeing the Form (*continued*)

3: Train 230: Sept 24 8:53 AM

4: Train 230: Sept 24 8:53 AM

5: Train 332: Sept 30 8:56 AM

6: Train 332: Sept 30 8:56 AM

Submitted to JBP Oct 2
by Benjamin Damm

6.3
Argue effectively for both the seriousness of the problem and the proposed solutions, using strong evidence.

THE WRITING PROCESS

Inquiry Project **Writing a Proposal**

Inquiry questions: What is the problem? What should be done?

Write a proposal to help resolve a problem that you care about. Make sure your proposal does the following (see also pp. 198–199 for typical features of proposals):

- Addresses a problem that is of consequence and of a manageable scale, including the problem's causes and effects.
- Provides evidence for the seriousness of the problem and for ways to solve it, justifying these solutions over alternatives. You can draw on your experience but should also use outside sources.
- Is appropriate in both form and content to your purpose and audience.
- Includes graphics if relevant.

Prose+

Design a web page for your proposal that has the following features:

- Links to relevant sites that provide additional evidence or information on the problem and/or solution.
- At least one image or graphic.
- A boxed feature with additional information, suggestions, helpful summaries, key ideas, etc.

(For more information on how to mock up a web page, see "Inquiring into the Details: Design Tips for Basic Web Pages" on p. 224.)

Turn your proposal into a radio documentary. Rewrite the proposal around interview clips with people who are affected by the problem or who are trying to solve it. Tell a story. (For more information on working with digital audio, see "Inquiring into the Details: Using Audacity to Record and Edit Audio" on p. 143.)

Using "Green Dining" (p. 203) as inspiration, develop a PowerPoint presentation on your proposal, combining images and text. It's also easy to embed video and audio files in a PowerPoint if relevant.

Alternatively, use the San Francisco Bicycle Coalition's visual proposal (p. 212) as inspiration and present your "problem in pictures."

What Are You Going to Write About?

Perhaps you already have a topic in mind for your proposal. But if you don't, or you want to explore some other possibilities, begin by generating a list of problems you'd like to solve. Don't worry too much about whether they're problems of consequence or about whether you have solutions to the problems. Try some of the generating exercises that follow.

The explosion of "how-to" and "self-help" books and articles is evidence of the popularity of writing that attempts to solve problems.

Opening Up

Play with some ideas about subjects for the proposal assignment. Remember not to judge the material at this stage.

Listing Prompts. Lists can be rich sources of triggering topics. Let them grow freely, and when you're ready, use an item as the focus of another list or an episode of fastwriting. The following prompts should get you started.

6.4

Use appropriate invention strategies to discover and develop a proposal topic.

1. Title a list "Things That Bug Me" and brainstorm as many things as you can think of for two minutes. Let the ideas come in waves.

2. Spend three minutes brainstorming a list of problems *on your campus, at your workplace*, or *in the local community* that affect you in some way or that you feel something about. Don't worry about repeating items from the list you made in Listing Prompt 1.

3. Explore some possible causes of a problem you listed, by finishing the following sentence as many times as you can: *One of the things causing this problem is* _____.

One Student's Response

Caesar's Journal

LISTING PROMPTS

Problems in my life

Procrastination
Can't stick to a budget
Credit card debt
Hate the winter
Failing calculus
Girlfriend prefers Hector
Balancing studying and social life
Can't afford to travel
Work too much

Problems on campus

No sense of community
Drying up of work-study funds
Not enough diversity
Lines at the registrar
Recent tuition hike
Legislature underfunds higher
   education
Lousy food at the SUB

One Student's Response (*continued*)

Textbooks are too expensive

Waiting list for child-care center

Problems in community

Overdevelopment of foothills

Litter and degradation of Boise River

Too few child-care options

Hate crimes

Concert venues inadequate

Traffic

Air pollution in Valley

Smell from sugar beet factory

Range fires

Fastwriting Prompts. In the early stages of generating possible topics for an essay, fastwriting can be invaluable, *if* you allow yourself to write badly. Initially, don't worry about staying focused; sometimes you find the best triggering topics by ranging freely. Once you've tentatively settled on something, use a more focused fastwrite to try to generate information and ideas within the loose boundaries of your chosen topic.

1. Pick any of the items from the preceding lists as a launching place for a five-minute fastwrite. Explore some of the following questions:

   - When did I first notice this was a problem?
   - What's the worst part about it?
   - What might be some of its causes?
   - What moment, situation, or scene is most typical of this problem? Describe it as if you're experiencing it by writing in the present tense.
   - How does this problem make me feel?
   - What people do I associate with it?

2. Depending on how familiar you are with a problem that interests you, do a five-minute focused fastwrite that explores solutions, beginning with the sentence I think one of the ways to deal with _____ is _____. Follow that sentence as long as you can. When the writing stalls, use the following prompt: Another possible solution to the problem of _____ might be _____.

Visual Prompts. Only a few problems have a single root cause. Use the following template to begin thinking about some of the possible causes of a problem. Describe the problem in the middle circle and then build arrows to as many explanations of possible causes as come to mind.

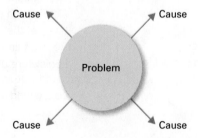

Research Prompts. Reading, observing, and talking to people can be great ways to discover a proposal topic. The following research prompts can help you along.

1. Interview your classmates about what they think are the biggest problems facing them as students. Interview student or faculty leaders or administrators about what they think are the biggest problems facing the university community. Do the same with community leaders.

2. Design an informal survey targeted to a particular group that you're interested in—students, student-athletes, local businesspeople, sports fans, migrant workers, and so on. This group may or may not be one to which you belong. Discover what they believe are the most serious problems they face.

3. Become a student of a local newspaper. In particular, pay attention to the letters to the editor and the local community pages. What seems to be a recurrent problem that gets people's attention? Clip articles, letters, or editorials that address the problem.

4. Google the following phrase: "solution to the problem of." Scan the results for topic ideas.

Narrowing Down

Feeling a little overwhelmed? See problems everywhere? It can be wearing to focus on what's wrong with your life, your university, and your community. But remember that your ultimate goal is to write a proposal that suggests ways these problems might be resolved. You may have already explored some of these solutions, but if you haven't, don't worry—you'll get the chance later. Begin by scrutinizing the material you generated for possible topics.

What's Promising Material and What Isn't? We've talked about some initial judgments you can make. Now look at the material you generated in the fastwrites, lists, research, or clusters, and ask yourself which of the problems listed *do you care about the most*, or which *are you most interested in*? Once you've selected some tentative topics for your proposal, narrow them down using the following questions:

- *Does someone aside from you have a stake in finding a solution? Is there an identifiable audience for proposals about solutions?*
- *Is the problem a manageable one?*
- *Have other people said something about the problem and possible solutions?*
- *Which subject offers you the most opportunity for learning?*

Questions About Audience and Purpose. This assignment asks you to craft a proposal appropriate to your audience and purpose. When you have identified

Awareness of the problem	If low, increase emphasis on dramatizing the problem.	If high, emphasize proposed solutions.
Initial disposition toward proposed solution	If favorably disposed, emphasize action that needs to be taken to implement solution. Emphasize pathos over logos.	If unfavorably disposed, offer balanced treatment of possible solutions before stating yours. Emphasize logos over pathos.
Attitude toward speaker	If positive, emphasize stronger action to solve the problem.	If negative, emphasize the views or experience speaker *does* share with audience.

Figure 6.2   Audience analysis chart. As with other forms of argument, the persuasiveness of a proposal depends on a rhetorical understanding of your audience. This is discussed in more detail in Chapter 7, where I introduce the rhetorical triangle, as well as *ethos, pathos*, and *logos* (see p. 241 for a discussion of those terms). See if you can do a rhetorical analysis on your proposal, and use what you discover to revise your essay.

an audience for your proposal, consider what exactly might be your purpose with respect to that audience. Do you want to:

- *Inform* them about the problem and explore possible solutions?
- *Advocate* certain solutions as the best ways to solve the problem?
- *Inform and advocate,* dramatizing the problem because your audience may not fully appreciate and understand it, and then persuading them to support the solutions you favor?

These purposes will shape your approach. And which you choose will depend partly on how your audience might already think and feel about the problem you're tackling and the solutions you offer. Use the chart in Figure 6.2.

Although it might be premature to decide the *form* your proposal will take, sometimes an awareness of purpose and audience will suggest an approach. Ask yourself this question: Given the problem I'm writing about, which audiences are (1) most affected by it and (2) most likely to contribute to the solution? Next, think about how to best reach one or both of those audiences. For example, suppose that Cheryl's purpose is to advocate for a new nontraditional student center on campus and her audience is school administrators. Her best approach for getting her message across might be to write her proposal in the form of a letter to the university's president.

Trying Out

Got a topic you want to try? Good. Let's do some focused work on that topic to generate some more material on it. Unless you've got a lot of personal experience with the problem you're thinking about writing about (and probably even if you do), you need to develop a working knowledge of the topic through some quick research.

Researching to Answer the *So What?* Question. To start with, you need to be able to establish that the problem you're interested in is significant. To do that, you'll need to answer a skeptic's question: *Okay, so what's the big deal about this?* That will be the focus of your initial research.

Using Google, Google Scholar, or library databases, find at least three sources online that show the significance of the problem you're interested in writing about. These sources may

a. Provide statistics or facts that suggest the seriousness of the problem.

b. Tell a story, case study, or anecdote about people who are affected by it.

c. Visually illustrate the effects of the problem.

d. Offer assertions by experts who are concerned with the problem.

Giving Your Answer on a PowerPoint. Using what you've learned, prepare a single PowerPoint slide that you would use to answer the question "So what's the big deal about this?" Here's a slide that one of my students, Andrea, developed to dramatize the problem of disappearing honeybees. While it isn't a very effective PowerPoint slide—there's too much text, for one thing—it's a really useful summary of the problem.

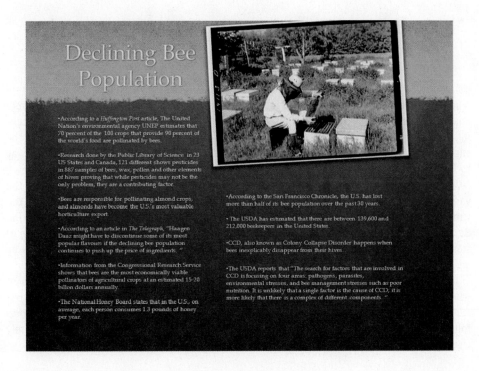

Use the material you generate from this exercise to help establish the significance of the problem in your sketch.

Writing the Sketch

Try out a tentative proposal topic by writing a sketch, a relatively brief early draft written with an audience in mind. Your sketch should:

- Have a tentative title.
- Use appropriate evidence (personal experience, facts, statistics, etc.) to dramatize the problem.
- Identify one or more causes of the problem and offer some tentative solutions for addressing those causes.
- Be written with an appropriate audience and purpose in mind.

You might also develop this sketch in a form that you think might be particularly effective given your purpose and audience. Your sketch might be an essay or a letter, a PowerPoint, a podcast, a web page, or the text of a brochure or ad.

▶ Student Sketch

Loving and Hating Reality TV
Jenna Appleman

1   When I moved into my own apartment without TV or cable, I assumed I'd be watching much less television. My TV consumption had never been a problem—I'd watch *Law & Order* and HBO when I was home, but didn't follow very much else. I prided myself on watching intelligent television, avoiding the low-culture reality series with a sneer. But in the silence of a studio apartment in the busiest semester of my college career, I needed a way to fill the space and blow off some steam. That's when I started watching reality TV.

2   There are TV channels dedicated exclusively to reality programming. Bravo houses the various *Real Housewives* series (my gateway), as well as their many spinoffs, E! plays the various Kardashian series, and reality competition shows like *The Biggest Loser* and *The Bachelor* rake in thousands of viewers on primetime. Certainly such success is indicative of something, and there are those who would disagree with my assumptions, but I stand by my initial negative cast on the cultural saturation of reality TV.

3   Reality television is (theoretically) unscripted and unacted, removing thousands of paying jobs for writers and actors from the market. I also sense that such excessive exposure can be exploitative. One show I have guiltily watched on Lifetime called *Dance Moms* follows a team of very young competitive dancers, between the ages of 7 and 14. Surely

having their emotional breakdowns and embarrassing parents on camera at that young age isn't helping their development.

And yet, I watch it. Frequently. But in public, I pretend I don't know the names of the Kardashians and roll my eyes wildly at front page news about the Housewives. For better or worse, I have grown accustomed to the comfort of curling up in bed with my cat and watching a marathon of *Millionaire Matchmaker* after an exhausting day. I watched an episode of *The Bachelor* while I was drafting this proposal, just to have some noise in the background to help me think. I want to hate it, but there's a lot about it I love.   4

I don't propose that we change the burgeoning culture of reality television entirely. That's far from realistic, and I have a feeling eventually this too will cycle out of popularity. But I do feel that I need to find a way to reconcile how I feel about reality TV with my penchant for it. The first step, I recognize, is admitting that I have a problem.   5

I don't propose that I stop watching reality television. But I do think it's important to clarify *why* I do—if it's to help me focus on schoolwork, that's a benefit. If I find it calming after a long day, that's okay too. But if I start watching because I simply *must* find out what's happening in these people's lives, if I begin to really stake weight in it, that's when I need a reality check. If I can accept the reasons why, then I can start feeling less guilty about it. I also think I should make a point to also watch other television; the normal kind that employs actors and writers. It would also be good to try to utilize my gym membership and watch these "guilty pleasures" on the cardio machines' TVs while I'm actually doing something physical. I should also recognize the shows that I find particularly exploitative, and avoid them, or at least view them with an intelligent, critical eye in order to form an opinion.   6

Moving from Sketch to Draft

Return to the inquiry questions behind a proposal: *What is the problem? What should be done?* How well does your sketch answer those questions? Is the problem clear, and would a skeptical reader be convinced that it is serious enough to address? Based on what you know now, do the solutions make sense? Explore these considerations in the next section.

Evaluating Your Own Sketch. Proposal sketches, no matter what the form, usually need work in the following areas:

- **Refining the problem.** It's too big and needs to be more focused.
- **Insufficient evidence.** More research is required to establish the seriousness of the problem, identify key causes, and/or support proposed solutions.

For example, Jason's sketch argued that people watch too much TV. Okay, but might that assertion be easier to write about if it were less general? Which people, exactly, watch too much TV? What do they watch too much? Violent programs? Advertising? Reality TV? What is "too much"? And finally, what are the consequences of watching that much? All of these questions require research. Jason might discover that the effects of TV watching are especially problematic for a

certain age group, or that certain kinds of advertising—say, snack food commercials aimed at children—are particularly troubling. So Jason can refine his problem from "People watch too much TV" to something more focused like "Television commercials for high-calorie snack foods contribute to childhood obesity." Now that's much easier to work with! Jason's much clearer about the problem and its consequences, and can now focus his research.

See if you can refine the problem statement in your sketch in similar ways. "Wh" questions (who, which, what, where, when, why) can help you pare down a big problem to something more manageable. Use the example above as a guide, applying the "Wh" questions to the problem you discussed in your sketch. Then restate the problem as Jason did, so that it's more specific.

Reflecting on What You Learned. The thing I like about sketches is that they are very early drafts—attempts, really—at trying out a topic, without a huge investment of time. At least they're not supposed to be huge investments of time. But pretty often I have students who approach nearly every writing assignment as if it required "perfection" or who have such harsh internal critics that writing is always kind of painful and slow. For these students, sketches are no cure. What about you? Do a journal entry in which you fastwrite for a few minutes about your experience writing this sketch. In particular, was it hard for you to accept that your sketch didn't meet your usual standards for writing something to hand in? What are your "usual standards," and do they get in the way of drafting and revising?

Developing

If you refined the problem you're exploring, stating it more clearly and concretely, then you've made it much easier to develop your draft. Developing your draft is a process that will require research.

Research. But what kind will you need to do? What are you looking for? The table below shows some key elements of proposals, and questions to think about for each. Consider these questions as guides for your research.

Element	Questions for Research
Problem	What's the evidence that it's serious? Who does it affect and under what circumstances?
Effects and causes	What will happen if nothing is done? Why is it happening? Why does this matter?
Solutions	What should be done? How do these proposals address key causes and effects?

Where should you look for the evidence to answer these questions?

- *Exploit local publications.* If you've chosen a topic of local interest, then sources such as the local daily newspaper, government reports, and university policies may be important sources for your proposal. Some of these, such as local newspapers and government documents, may be available in online databases at your library.

- *Interview experts.* In Chapter 4, you practiced interview skills. Here's a chance to put them to use again. One of the most efficient ways to collect information for your revision is to talk to people who have knowledge about the problem. These may be experts who have researched the problem or people affected by it.

- *Search for experience with similar solutions elsewhere.* If your proposal calls for an education program on binge drinking, what other universities might have tried it? What was their experience? Search for information using keywords that describe the problem you're writing about ("binge drinking"), and try adding a phrase that describes the solution ("binge drinking education programs"). Also check library databases that might lead you to articles in newspapers, magazines, and journals on the problem and its solutions.

A word of advice about solutions: Researching and thinking about solutions can be a bit like following a horse race: You might favor one solution until another one suddenly races up from behind as you learn more. In an inquiry project, that's normal. Make sure that the solutions you end up with are consistent with your own experience and with your values about the best ways to solve problems.

Focusing on the Justifications. In my part of the country, everyone has an opinion about wolves. Many people hate them. Wolf packs were reestablished in the West under the Endangered Species Act, and in recent decades wolves have extended their range well beyond the national parks and into ranching and agricultural areas. The problem is that some wolves kill livestock. What does one do with a wolf pack that won't stop killing sheep? Some popular solutions include: (1) Nothing—they were here first; (2) Capture them and relocate them away from populated areas; (3) Kill them.

Each of these solutions has problems of its own—and advocates and critics who will energetically argue over them. If you're working on an essay that focuses on a problem that affects people (and isn't that the definition of a problem?), then you will discover controversies over what to do about it. One thing your draft should not do is pretend that these controversies don't exist. On the contrary, your draft should not only justify the solutions you prefer, but also identify the solutions you've rejected and show why your solutions are better.

You've done some research on the problem and solutions. Develop your draft by focusing on the justifications for your solutions:

- Why are they the best solutions?
- How do they effectively address the causes and effects of the problem?
- What is evidence that they will work?
- What might critics say? Why are they wrong?

These *justifications* for your solutions will be a key part of your draft.

Inquiring into the Details

Design Tips for Basic Web Pages

You don't have to be an expert to build a web page. In addition to free sites such as Wix, Weebly, and Webs, which provide design templates and even hosting options, you can use a word processing program such as Word to create basic web pages.

When building a web page, consider these design tips:

- Maximize contrast.
- For readability go with 40–80 characters per line (65 is optimal).
- Avoid going over 200–400 words per page.
- Don't be afraid of blank space. Blank space makes it easier for your audience to focus on the content.
- Use titles that make sense and are relevant to your content.
- To offset text, make use of images that are relevant and can give a good visual representation of what your essay is saying.
- Use menus for content that is longer than three pages.
- Avoid fonts other than the standards such as Verdana, Arial, Courier, or Times. Font size should run 12–15 points. Use sans-serif type for body text, and serif for titles.
- Decide on a color scheme and stick with it.

Drafting

As you think about how to organize your draft, consider some of the suggestions below.

Watch
the Animation on
Organizing Proposals
in your MyLab

Methods of Development. As mentioned earlier in the chapter, a proposal often moves from problem to solution, and some proposals, like the research proposal, need to follow a specific form. But if the form of your proposal has not been specified, you can organize it in a number of ways. One way to think about how to organize your draft is to imagine the questions a typical reader of a proposal, or a problem-solution paper, might ask and the order in which they might ask them:

- What's the big deal?
- Who says it's a big deal besides you?
- What's at stake?
- What causes the problem? What are its effects?
- What solutions have people proposed? Are they justified?
- Which do you prefer? How do you justify it?
- What are the potential problems with the solution you like?
- Why do you still like it?
- If we do this, is everything going to be okay? Is there anything you're asking me to do?

You might play with the order in which you deal with these questions in your draft, but you will likely have to address all of them somewhere.

Using Evidence. You will answer the preceding questions with evidence that you've gathered from research (reading, interview, observation) and experience. Like much else, the evidence you use depends on your intended audience. In other words, choosing the strongest evidence in a proposal is an exercise in audience analysis:

- How much does your audience know about the problem?
- Is your audience likely to favor your idea, oppose it, or have no opinion?
- What kind of evidence is most likely to convince your audience?

The *amount* of evidence you need to provide depends on whether your audience is likely to be predisposed to agree or disagree with the solutions you propose. Obviously, if readers need convincing, you need to offer more justification. The *types* of evidence you provide depend on your assessment of what your audience will be most likely to believe. The "Inquiring into the Details: Evidence—A Case Study" box gives you a chance to think about audience in choosing among types of evidence. As you compose your draft, consider who your readers will be and the kinds of evidence they will find most persuasive.

Watch the Animation on **Investigating Assumptions** in your MyLab

Inquiring into the Details

Evidence—A Case Study

Suppose a proposal argues that the university needs an alternative or independent film series. The proposal, in the form of a memo, is written to the Student Activities Board, a group of students who decide how to spend student fee money collected at registration. Which of the following types of evidence used to justify such a film series might be *most* persuasive to that audience?

1. The writer's personal enjoyment of foreign films.
2. A petition signed by 100 people that supports the idea.
3. A quotation from Woody Allen about the educational and cultural virtues of independent films.
4. Information about the success of the independent film theater in town.
5. A quote from an English professor supporting the idea.
6. An estimate that shows that the cost of renting five independent films is half the cost of renting the same number of Hollywood films.
7. A survey of 200 students that indicates that 60 percent support the idea.
8. Data on good attendance at a similar series at another, larger university.

Do a quick audience analysis for your proposal topic. Who has most at stake in solving the problem, and who can influence the solution? Then make a list of the types of evidence that would be most convincing to those audiences

Workshopping

If your draft is subject to peer review, see Chapter 14 for details on how to organize workshop groups and decide on how your group can help you. To help you decide, use the guidance, starting on p. 578, in Chapter 14. Each workshop type is described more fully in that chapter.

Because a proposal is a form of argument, your workshop is a chance to test its persuasiveness with readers. One key thing to consider before the session is how much your peers already know about the problem you're writing about. The less they know, the more work your draft needs to do in these areas:

1. Convince readers of the seriousness of the problem.
2. Provide a context for the problem: who's involved, who's affected, what's been tried, how long it's been going on, what will happen if nothing is done.

Questions for Peer Reviewers	
1. Purpose	After reading the draft, what do you think is at stake? If nothing is done to solve the problem, what might be the consequences?
2. Meaning	In your own words, how does the essay answer the inquiry question *What should be done?* Play the doubting game for a moment: What potential problems do you see with the solution I'm proposing?

3. Persuade peers that your proposal is fair and reasonable. That not only means providing convincing evidence to support your solution, but also means considering the arguments of critics of your approach.

In addition to these concerns, when you workshop the first draft of your proposal, you should focus on what peers make of the purpose and meaning of your essay, using their responses to guide your revision. The following grid can help you frame these questions for your workshop group.

Reflecting on the Draft. Following your workshop, make an entry in your journal that follows these prompts:

- If I were going to write this over again, the one thing I think I'd do would be . . .
- The most important thing I learned about writing a proposal so far is . . .
- The most difficult part of the process for me was . . .
- The biggest question I have about the draft is . . .

Revising

Revision is a continual process—not a last step. You've been revising—"reseeing" your subject—from the first messy fastwriting in your journal. But the things that get your attention vary depending on where you are in the writing process. With your draft in hand, revision becomes your focus through what I'll call "shaping and tightening your draft."

6.5

Apply revision strategies that are effective for a proposal.

Chapter 13 contains strategies that can help you revise any inquiry project, and the "Guide to Revision Strategies" on page 229 can help you locate these strategies. There are also certain things to think about that are especially useful for shaping a proposal.

Shaping. Shaping involves, among other things, arranging and rearranging information so that it is organized around the main idea.

Analyzing the Information. One way to think about the structure of your review is to see the information you've collected in categories. In a proposal, remember that these typically include the following:

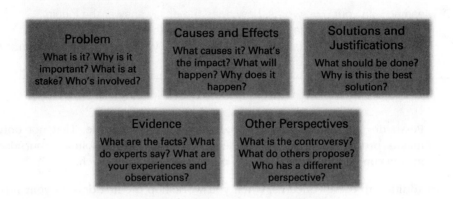

Problem
What is it? Why is it important? What is at stake? Who's involved?

Causes and Effects
What causes it? What's the impact? What will happen? Why does it happen?

Solutions and Justifications
What should be done? Why is this the best solution?

Evidence
What are the facts? What do experts say? What are your experiences and observations?

Other Perspectives
What is the controversy? What do others propose? Who has a different perspective?

This isn't a recipe for organizing your draft, but a way to look at whether you've included enough information in each category. One way to play around with the structure of your proposal is to use the "Frankenstein Draft" (Revision Strategy 13.18 in Chapter 13). Cut up your draft with scissors into pieces that fall into the categories mentioned here—problem, solution, evidence, and so on—and then play with the order. Worry about transitions later.

Other Questions for Revision. Proposals also have some fairly typical problems at this stage in the process, most of which can be addressed by repeating some of the steps in this chapter or selecting appropriate revision strategies in Chapter 13. Here are some questions to consider as you decide which of these strategies might be most helpful.

✓ Have you done enough to dramatize the problem if you're writing for an audience that may not be aware of it? Should you do more to establish how your readers have a stake in solving the problem?

✓ How well have you justified your solutions? Is there enough evidence? Is it appropriate evidence for your audience?

✓ Have you overemphasized one solution at the expense of others? Would your proposal be more balanced and persuasive if you considered alternatives, even if you ultimately reject them?

Polishing. Shaping focuses on things such as purpose, meaning, and design. No less important is looking more closely at paragraphs, sentences, and words. Are your paragraphs coherent? How do you manage transitions? Are your sentences fluent and concise? Are there any errors in spelling or syntax? The section of Chapter 13 called "Problems with Clarity and Style," on page 564, can help you focus on these issues.

Before you finish your draft, work through the following checklist:

✓ Every paragraph is about one thing.

✓ The transitions between paragraphs aren't abrupt.

✓ The length of sentences varies in each paragraph.

✓ Each sentence is concise. There are no unnecessary words or phrases.

✓ You've checked grammar, particularly verb agreement, run-on sentences, unclear pronouns, and misused words (*there/their, where/were*, and so on). (See the Handbook at the end of the book for help with these grammar issues.)

✓ You've run your spellchecker and proofed your paper for misspelled words.

Chapter 13 has strategies to help you solve all kinds of revision problems, large and small. Use the "Guide to Revision Strategies" below to know where to look in that chapter to both shape and tighten your draft.

Guide to Revision Strategies

Problems in the Draft (Chapter 13)	Page Number
Unclear purpose	538
■ Not sure what the essay is about? Fails to answer the *So what?* question?	
Unclear thesis, theme, or main idea	543
■ Not sure what you're trying to say? Proposal isn't clear?	
Lack of information or development	551
■ Needs more information to justify proposed solution?	
■ Evidence offered isn't persuasive enough?	
Disorganized	555
■ Doesn't move logically or smoothly from paragraph to paragraph?	
Unclear or awkward at the level of sentences and paragraphs	564
■ Seems choppy or hard to follow at the level of sentences or paragraphs?	

▶ Student Essay

Read
the
Interactive
Sales Proposal
in your MyLab

Jenna watches reality TV and feels guilty about it. But that's not the problem that interests her. She can see the appeal of programs such as *American Idol*, and she'd like to continue to watch them from time to time, but she would really like to watch reality shows that follow an ethical code of conduct. Jenna proposes that reality TV producers agree to a code that would minimize the emotional and physical injuries inflicted on participants, which she thinks is a problem on many of the shows.

Avoidable Accidents: How to Make Reality TV Safer

Jenna Appleman

1   When I moved into my own apartment without TV or cable, I assumed I'd be watching much less television. My TV consumption had never been a problem—I'd watch *Law & Order* and HBO when I was home, but didn't follow very much else. I prided myself on watching intelligent television, avoiding the low-culture reality series with a sneer. But in the silence of a studio apartment in the busiest semester of my college career, I needed a way to fill the space and blow off some steam. That's when I started watching reality TV.

2   There are TV channels dedicated exclusively to reality programming. Bravo houses the various *Real Housewives* series (my gateway), as well as their many spinoffs; E! plays the various Kardashian series; there are kid-centered shows like *Toddlers and Tiaras* on TLC and *Dance Moms* on Lifetime; and reality competition shows like *The Biggest Loser* and *The Bachelor* rake in thousands of viewers on prime time. Reality TV dominates American programming.

3   How dominant is it? According to the Nielson ratings for the week I'm writing this, seven of the top ten shows on cable were reality programs. *Jersey Shore* and *Pawn Stars* were one and two ("Top Tens"). On TV, *American Idol* is a perennial viewer favorite, often the most-watched program.

4   Yet my instinctive guilt about watching these shows is indicative of a pressing problem. "People are attracted to reality television because they know it has real consequences," said reality blurred editor Andy Dehnart. "You get the sense this is a real human being who could be hurt or injured" (Dehnart). And in August 2011, Russell Armstrong, the husband of Beverly Hills *Real Housewives'* Taylor Armstrong, committed suicide. While Amstrong's suicide is an extreme example, injuries on reality TV programs are rampant. A brawl on *Survivor* in 2010 resulted in a dislocated shoulder and broken toe. In 2011, an athlete on the reality show *Jump City* fell doing a stunt and shattered his wrist. Injuries on shows like *So You Think You Can Dance* are common.

5   Not only are contestants injured but viewers "inspired" by the programs are also at risk. Recently, for example, the American Medical Association warned that viewers of the

TV show *Extreme Makeover,* now off the air, might have had a distorted understanding of the risk of plastic surgery: "Heavily edited and selected scenes from reality TV have lulled the public into thinking there are no real risks or complications in these procedures. It's easy for viewers to forget that these are real people, who face the real risks—not just the benefits—of surgery" (216). All of this is a brash reminder that reality television is just that—*real.*

"These shows are Roman coliseums that we visit virtually," writes Matt Seitz of Salon.   6
"Participants in contact sports have corner men and doctors on hand to nurse their wounds, and determine if they are fit enough to step in the ring in the first place." So, too, then, should the participants of reality television shows.

To lower the risks to participants and viewers of watching reality TV, I propose the   7
following:

1. Possible candidates for a reality television show should be pre-screened, to ensure that they are fit emotionally and physically to withstand the rigors of a reality set.
2. Candidates with substance abuse, physical abuse, self-destructive behaviors, among others, would not be permitted to participate on the show *unless* they are provided with the following:
   a. Active counseling throughout the filming process
   b. Guaranteed after-care once filming ceases
   For example, *Hoarders* on A&E provides healthcare services during and after filming to the subjects it follows.
3. *All* participants should be provided with free after-care and counseling once filming wraps, for at least three months.
4. All participants should have immediate and total access to medical care, with the show absorbing all medical costs incurred during filming.
5. No footage of participants under the influence of alcohol should be used *if* the alcohol had been provided by producers.
6. Only non-incidental footage of minors should be used.
7. If a show focuses on minors (such as *Toddlers and Tiaras* and *Dance Moms*), counselors with training in adolescent and child psychology should be present during *all filming* and available to children before and after the conclusion of filming.
8. All participant contracts should be public.

An ethical code like this would admittedly be hard to implement and impossible to re-   8
quire. Further, as NPR's Linda Holmes writes, "there is . . . no solution for people who want to watch *The Real Housewives Of Beverly Hills* without guilt . . . you have to live with the fact that it exploits emotionally charged situations" (Holmes). Nonetheless, having an adopt-able ethical code for reality television producers, and public knowledge of which shows abide by the code, would at least put a modicum of power back in the hands of the viewer. We would be given the ability to make informed choices about which programs we choose

(continued)

(continued)

to watch—"to shop for ethical television the same way [we] might shop for ethically produced goods of any other kind, and to provide the financial incentives [for producers]," as Holmes says.

9   I will probably never stop feeling guilty for watching reality television, particularly the more exploitative shows. However, if I were given the option to watch reality programs that I could feel comfortable indulging in, knowing that there were an ethical code in place, I would like to think I'd choose those shows. Such a code wouldn't cure the problem, but at least it would empower viewers and encourage them to support less destructive programming.

Works Cited

D'Amico, Richard. "Plastic Surgery Is Real, Not Reality TV." *Virtual Mentor: American Medical Association Journal of Ethics* 9.3 (March 2007): 2150-218. Print.

Dehnart, Ann. "Real Housewives Cast Member Russell Killed Himself." *Realityblurred*. 16 Aug. 2011. Web. 20 Feb. 2012.

Holmes, Linda. "'Ethical Reality': A Proposed Code for Producers to Live By." *NPR*. 31 August 2011. Web. 11 Nov. 2011.

Seitz, Matt Zoller. "Reality TV: A Blood Sport That Must Change." *Salon*. 18 August 2011. Web. 20 Jan. 2012.

"Top Tens and Trends." *The Nielson Co.* 20 Feb. 2012. Web. 20 Feb. 2012.

Evaluating the Essay

1. A key part of a persuasive proposal is establishing the seriousness of the problem. Are you convinced that reality stars are at risk on these programs? If not, what would you suggest about strengthening that part of the essay?

2. Suppose Jenna were considering incorporating visuals—images, video, graphics, and tables—into the essay. What would you suggest?

3. What's your evaluation of the solution that she proposes? Is it convincing? Why or why not?

Using What You Have Learned

Let's revisit the list from the beginning of this chapter of things I hoped you'd learn about this form of writing.

1. **Describe a problem of consequence, framing it narrowly enough to explore convincing solutions.** It's hard to overstate the importance of this skill, not just for proposal writing, but also for most writing tasks. A fundamental problem with early drafts in any genre is that they're not focused enough; the writer takes a landscape shot when she needs to take a close-up. This is especially true with research-based writing such as proposals, when you're dealing with a lot of information. See if you can apply some of the things you learned here to, for example, a research essay.

2. **Identify the wide range of rhetorical situations that might call for a proposal argument.** There are all kinds of proposals—marketing proposals, business plans, grant proposals, policy proposals, and so on—but they are all in the service of the same question: What should be done? As you write for other college classes, you will probably have assignments that aren't called proposals but essentially ask you to answer this question.

3. **Argue effectively for both the seriousness of the problem and the proposed solutions, using strong evidence.** If you wrote a review for the previous chapter, then you already have some practice with making arguments, because evaluation is a form of argument. In this chapter, you built on those skills. Among other things, the proposal relies more heavily on research than does the review, and in subsequent assignments you'll be drawing on what you learned here, especially your understanding of what is appropriate evidence to support a claim.

4. **Use appropriate invention strategies to discover and develop a proposal topic.** The invention techniques themselves don't vary much from assignment to assignment. You've gotten considerable practice with fastwriting, clustering, listing, and so on. But with each assignment, you've cast a wider net for information. The proposal, for example, asked you to generate considerably more information from outside sources than, say, the profile or personal essay. Invention isn't just trying to get what's already in your head out on paper or screen. Invention is also techniques for *finding* information and thinking about what you make of it. This will become increasingly important with later assignments.

5. **Apply revision strategies that are effective for a proposal.** As we move towards more-argumentative forms of writing, revision is increasingly focused on considering how a skeptical audience might respond to what you say. In this chapter, you've spent time considering not only how to convince someone that a problem you care about is something he or she should care about, too, but also crafting proposals that are persuasive. Reviews, proposals, public arguments, and research essays are among the most reader-based forms, and it becomes even more important in revising these to imagine readers who may not think much like you.

Complete
Additional Exercises
and Practice on
Chapter 6
in your MyLab

Arguing is a civic duty. It is an essential activity in any democratic culture and a major element of academic discourse. Academic argument is one of the key means of making new knowledge.

Writing an Argument

Learning Objectives

In this chapter, you'll learn to

7.1 Identify the key elements of argument—reasons, claims, and evidence—and apply them in both reading and writing.

7.2 Understand how ethos, pathos, and logos combine in persuasion.

7.3 Use invention strategies appropriate to argument to discover and develop a topic.

7.4 Develop a question that is focused enough to lead to a strong claim and convincing evidence.

7.5 Use audience analysis and logical methods to help guide revision of an argument.

Writing to Persuade People

Where I live, public arguments about wolf reintroduction, saving salmon, property tax rates, and the need for a local community college are waged on the editorial pages of the local newspaper, *The Idaho Statesman*. The paper's editorials and op-ed articles (short persuasive essays that are literally on the opposite page from editorials) present usually well-reasoned arguments of 250 to 600 words, but the real slugfest takes place in the letters to the editor. Reading letters to the editor is a form of recreation here. One correspondent complained a few years ago that the song "Rain, Rain, Go Away" was objectionable because it made her children dislike precipitation. Another letter writer, an animal rights activist, is a regular who always generates heated rebuttals here in cattle country. Last week, she railed about the evils of "Rocky Mountain oysters" (fried cattle testicles), which were served up at the Eagle Fire Department fundraiser. I can't wait to see the responses to that one.

We resort to argument when we have strong feelings about something. We write a letter to the editor, or blog, or compose a paper in a college course, supporting our opinions with research. But in a way, all writing has elements of argument. As the writer Joan Didion once said, writing is, in a sense, a "hostile act." We want people to see the world the way we see it.

235

In arguments, however, this is more explicit, and sometimes the motive isn't just to convince an audience to see the world the way we see it, but also to convince them to actually *do something about it*. Support a certain candidate, join an organization, contact a legislator, give money.

We've already covered a couple of kinds of arguments, arising from different inquiry questions:

- **Review:** What is the value?
- **Proposal:** What should be done?

In this chapter, we'll work with another kind of argument essay, which answers this question: *What do I believe is true and why do I believe it?* An essay that addresses this inquiry question might be called a lot of things—a position paper, an opinion piece, or a claim–proof essay. Whatever it's called, an argument that states what a writer believes and why might be distinguished by its strong emphasis on factual *claims* and its attention to logic.

Here's the thing, though: While most of us think that argument involves starting with some strong opinion we have and then cherry-picking the evidence to build support for it, academic inquiry initially emphasizes exploration of the question *What is true?* Maybe you have strong feelings about privacy on the Internet. You think, for example, that while Google Street View is pretty cool, it violates privacy because someone might be accidentally photographed while walking down a street in their neighborhood. However, before you make that claim in an argument, it's important to spend considerable time listening in to the debate. What do experts say? What are counterclaims? Are there other, more troubling issues you hadn't considered?

Persuasive essays such as the op-ed are a great way to participate in public debates that affect your campus and community, and even your nation.

My point is this: *Inquiry always precedes argument.*

But what do we mean by argument?

What Is Argument?

Argument is not war.

When I was growing up, argument meant only one thing: indigestion. My father loved to argue at the dinner table, hotly pursuing any stray comment that would give him the chance to demonstrate his superior knowledge and logic. What I remember about these "arguments" was the hot-faced humiliation and anger I felt back then, and later, the feeling that I would prefer to avoid an argument at any cost. When I mention argumentative writing to my students, I think I recognize in the slumped shoulders and distant looks of some of them that they might have similar feelings.

Some of us think argument is impolite. It means uncomfortable conflict. It is the verbal equivalent of war.

And yet, we engage in argument every day, when we attempt to persuade an instructor to extend the deadline on a paper, try to convince our spouse to help more around the apartment, or seek a loan from a bank.

Arguments *can* involve conflict, but they are rarely combat—despite the war metaphors such as "finding ammunition" or "attacking a position." Far more often, the motives for arguing are more benign. We want others to consider seeing the world the way we see it. Or we want to encourage them to *do* something we believe is in their interests as well as ours. These motives were behind the attempts at persuasion in the review and proposal assignments you may have completed earlier in *The Curious Writer.*

In a sense, all writing is persuasive. *See the world my way*, we ask of readers, *at least for a moment.*

Two Sides to Every Argument?

TV talk shows stage "discussions" between proponents of diametrically opposed positions. Academic debating teams pit those for and those against. We are nurtured on language such as *win* or *lose, right* and *wrong*, and *either...or*. It's tempting to see the world this way, as neatly divided into truth and falsehood, light and dark. Reducing issues to two sides simplifies the choices. But one of the things that literature—and all art—teaches us is the delightful and nagging complexity of things. Huck Finn is a racist, and in *Huckleberry Finn* there's plenty of evidence in his treatment of Jim that confirms this. Yet there are moments in the novel when we see a transcendent humanity in Huck, and we can see that he may be a racist, *but...* It is this qualification—this modest word *but*—that trips us up in our apparent certainty. Rather than *either...or*, can it be *both...and*? Instead of two sides to every issue, might there be thirteen?

Here's an example:

One side: General education requirements are a waste of time because they are often irrelevant to the students' major goal in getting a college education—getting a good job.

The other side: General education requirements are invaluable because they prepare students to be enlightened citizens, more fully prepared to participate in democratic culture.

It's easy to imagine a debate between people who hold these positions, and it wouldn't be uninteresting. But it *would* be misleading to think that these are the only two possible positions on general education requirements in American universities.

One of the reasons why people are drawn to arguing is that it can be a method of discovery, and one of the most useful discoveries is some side to the story that doesn't fall neatly into the usual opposed positions. The route to these discoveries is twofold: *initially withholding judgment* and *asking questions.*

For instance,

What might be goals of a university education other than helping students get a good job and making them enlightened citizens?

Is it possible that a university can do both?

Are general education courses the only route to enlightenment?

Are there certain situations in which the vocational motives of students are inappropriate?

Are there certain contexts—say, certain students at particular schools at a particular point in their education—when general education requirements might be waived or modified?

As often happens with two-sided arguments, all of these questions, and others, tend to unravel the two sides of the argument and expose them for what they are: *starting points* for an inquiry, in this case, into the question *What good are general education requirements?*

The Machinery of Argument: Claims, Reasons, and Evidence

Claims: What You Want People to Believe

7.1

Identify the key elements of argument— reasons, claims, and evidence— and apply them in both reading and writing.

Watch the Animation on **Types of Claims** in your MyLab

"I have a headache" is simply a statement, and not a claim, because no one is likely to disagree with it. "Headaches can be caused by secondhand smoke" is a statement that is also a claim because reasonable people might agree or disagree with it.

Claims are at the heart of argument, and if you think about it, you already know this. Every time you make a judgment, interpretation, or evaluation, you make a claim. We do this daily: "Macs are better than PCs." "The food in this place sucks." "This town needs more buses." Because reviews and proposals, the forms in Chapters 5 and 6, are arguments, they involved claims. If you write a review, you make and support a *value claim*; if you write a proposal, you make and support a *policy claim*. In this chapter, we'll work with what's often called a *factual claim*.[1] Take this claim, for instance:

> *The rise of "Super PACs" in presidential politics is corrupting the electoral process.*

You probably can't definitively *prove* that claim is true, but you might find some good factual evidence to support it. Maybe you dig up some research on "attack ads" that are funded by these political action committees, demonstrating that they are often criticized for their inaccuracy. And perhaps you find some expert evidence that supports the claim: You interview a professor at your school, and she notes that most Super PACs are largely funded by huge contributions from a few wealthy individuals. Factual claims can be assertions about something in the present (e.g., "The electric car is unfairly subsidized," "Teaching to the test in high school English undermines the transition to college writing"). Supported by evidence, they can also make a prediction about what will happen; the Super PACs claim above, for example, concerns the future as well as the present. And finally, factual claims

---

[1]Philosophers distinguish between factual claims and conceptual claims. The former is something that can be proved with evidence; the latter a claim that is arrived at through careful reasoning but may never be proven.

can be about the past (e.g., "President Lincoln's abuse of the habeas corpus (laws protecting people from illegal imprisonment) was necessary to save the Union").

Watch
the Animation on
Appeals to Reason
in your MyLab

Reasons: The "Because..." Behind the Claim

I asked my first-year students what they thought of general education, or "core," classes at our university. It provoked a lively debate. Here's what one of them said:

> "I am all for the rant about higher education costing a fortune. The core classes are a joke, to be quite honest. Who hasn't had math, science, and history in high school?"

This student makes the claim that "core classes are a joke." She gives a reason: Students have already studied math, science, and history in high school. This is the "because" behind her claim. But notice that behind this reason there's an unstated assumption: Math, science, and history classes in high school are equivalent to university core classes in these subjects. Is this true? It may be. But it's certainly debatable, and because this assumption is never addressed, the claim that core classes are a joke is built on a pretty weak foundation.

Reasons—either stated or implied—hold up your claim. Your claim is what you believe is true, and your reasons are why you believe it is true. A claim and a reason can be linked with the word "because." So, stating its assumption explicitly as part of the reason, we could restate the claim and reason above as "Core classes are a joke *because* their content is similar to what most students learn in high school."

Evidence: Proof of the Point

When you're making a factual claim, you need evidence. The motive for making a claim is to persuade an audience to agree with it, and this depends on the quality of the evidence you offer. But what kind of evidence will be most persuasive?

Watch
the Animation on
Appeals to Authority
in your MyLab

The kind of evidence you need depends partly on the rhetorical situation, of course, but if you're making an argument to a general audience, then evidence for a factual claim might come from the following sources:

- Expert testimony (statements by authorities on the topic)
- Reliable data (facts from credible sources)
- Observation and personal experience (what you see and what has happened to you)
- Stories, case studies, anecdotes (the narratives of others that help you dramatize an issue or support a point)

Keep in mind that the kind of evidence that is persuasive will depend on the disposition of your audience—readers who are skeptical about your claim are harder to convince—and also on the discourse community you're writing in. Obviously, appropriate evidence for a biology article will be different from appropriate evidence for a philosophy article. For the purposes of this assignment, you're probably writing for peers (or a general audience) and, generally speaking, as you move from an expert audience to one that is less so, the rules of evidence get looser.

As important as using evidence persuasively is using it ethically. For example, you need to address—not omit—evidence that does not support your claim. Similarly, you need to avoid putting the evidence into a context that would distort its meaning (see the box "Seeing the Form: The 'Imagetext' as Argument"). Arguing ethically will contribute to your ethos, one of the elements of persuasion discussed next.

Read
the
Interactive Visual
Argument Sample
in your MyLab

Seeing the Form

The "Imagetext" as Argument

While model Kate Moss is likely disturbed by the appropriation of her image by advocates in the pro-anorexia ("pro-ana") movement, Moss's picture—along with those of other celebrities such as Calista Flockhart, Mary-Kate Olsen, and Keira Knightley—appear as "thinspiration" on websites that argue that eating disorders are a "lifestyle choice," not a disease. Some of these images (though not this one) are digitally altered to make the models seem even thinner than they really are. In an article on the "imagetexts" used by these controversial websites, Robin Jensen notes that in their new context, pictures like this one of Kate Moss are in effect given a "frame" quite different from the one originally intended. In this way, the meaning of the picture is manipulated to make an argument that serves the purpose of the pro-ana movement. In a sense, this is like quoting someone out of context, and raises a similar ethical question: Is it fair?

Kate Moss in ultra-thin pose.

Credibility, Emotion, and Logic

Persuasion, as Aristotle reminded us a few thousand years ago, depends not just on good reasoning (*logos*), but also on moving an audience (*pathos*) and making it believe the speaker is someone worth listening to on the subject (*ethos*). Figure 7.1 shows Aristotle's rhetorical triangle, a visual presentation of this idea. The triangle nicely illustrates that persuasion always incorporates all three appeals and that all three are always in relation to each other.

7.2

Understand how ethos, pathos, and logos combine in persuasion.

What may be a little misleading about the graphic is that it seems to suggest that the recipe for good argument is equal measures of ethos, pathos, and logos. Not at all. These are blended in varying amounts depending on the situation. One factor, for example, is the disposition of an audience toward your claim.

Watch
the Animation on
**Appeals to
Emotion**
in your MyLab

Figure 7.2 broadly indicates the balance between Aristotle's three categories of appeals in the three most common rhetorical situations: when an audience is resistant to what you're trying to say, neutral about it, or receptive. Consider each of these audiences:

- Direct-mail marketers trying to raise money for nonprofit groups and political causes cultivate lists of people who might be receptive to their messages. Direct-mail letters, therefore, are strong on emotional appeals (pathos): The humane society will include photographs of a sad-looking abandoned puppy, a conservative political action group will raise fears about threats to "family values," and so on. There's no need to spend a great deal reasoning (logos) with an audience that already agrees with your message. And because they agree with your message, they're already favorably disposed to the messenger (ethos). Move them with emotion!

- In contrast, resistant audiences will need to be convinced that you know what you're talking about (ethos), so your challenge here is to establish some common ground with the audience. But that's not enough. While a speaker or writer might earn a resistant audience's approval, gaining its assent to a claim depends on the quality of the reasoning (logos). Emotional appeals will be unlikely to move this audience, at least initially.

- Neutral audiences may be difficult to gauge. Sometimes an emotional appeal will spark its members' interest. Sometimes a well-reasoned argument will move them, and sometimes a neutral audience will be persuaded by the credibility of the speaker. Frequently, a careful combination of all three of Aristotle's appeals transforms a neutral audience into one that is receptive to what you have to say.

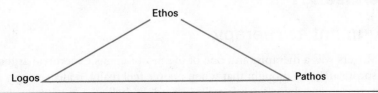

Figure 7.1   Aristotle's rhetorical triangle

Disposition of Audience	*Ethos*	*Pathos*	*Logos*
Resistant	Most important	Less important	Most important
Neutral	Important	Important	Important
Receptive	Less important	Most important	Less important

Figure 7.2   Audience and the balance of ethos, logos, and pathos

Analyzing Argument

How might you analyze this letter writer's argument?

Dear Editor,

As part of my required humanities class, I was forced to see the art exhibit "Home of the Brave" at the university gallery. As a combat veteran, what I saw there deeply offended me. I saw so-called "art" that showed great American military leaders such as General Petraeus with skulls superimposed on their faces, and a photo of a man with an American flag wrapped around his head and lashed with a plastic tie at his neck. It's popular to say these days that we should support the troops. Apparently, a group of artists who haven't defended our freedom feel free to use that freedom to be unpatriotic. I wonder if they would feel differently if they had to pay the real cost for freedom of speech.

Most arguments like this don't provoke an analytical response at first. We react emotionally: "This guy is so full of it!" or perhaps, "It's about time someone spoke up about the cost of freedom!" This letter, like many that raise controversial issues, triggers a whole set of deeply held beliefs about things such as patriotism, freedom of speech, and the purpose of art. These are things that *should* provoke discussion—and that inevitably trigger feelings. But without involving the head as well as the heart, it's impossible to have a civil discussion—one that will lead to new understanding. We need to understand not only what we ourselves believe, but also what the other guy believes. To see how this might work, try Exercise 7.1, based on some ideas about argument from American psychologist Carl Rogers.

Exercise 7.1

Argument as Therapy

Carl Rogers was a therapist and one of the most famous experts on argument theory. Not surprisingly, he thought that when people feel really, really strongly about something, reason just doesn't work well. Instead, he believed, a prerequisite to entering into an argument with someone else about a value-laden topic is to first listen and "say back" what you understand him or her to be saying. Let's do that here.

STEP ONE: Summarize what you understand to be the letter writer's basic argument. What claim is he making, and what seem to be the (implied) reasons behind it? You might use this as a template for your summary:

> *Because of _____ and _____, the letter writer argues that _____.*

STEP TWO: Now fastwrite for a few minutes in your notebook, exploring your own take on the validity of the claim and the reasons.

STEP THREE: Finally, write a brief analysis of the argument that includes the following:

1. Begin with your understanding of the letter writer's argument and something about the circumstances that might lead someone to make such claims.

2. Analyze the soundness of the reasons behind the argument. Do you agree or disagree with them? Is there a different way of thinking about them?

3. State your own position (e.g., What would you say about the relationship between art and politics?), including the reasons behind it.

One Student's Response

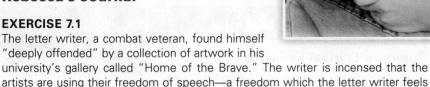

Rebecca's Journal

EXERCISE 7.1
The letter writer, a combat veteran, found himself "deeply offended" by a collection of artwork in his university's gallery called "Home of the Brave." The writer is incensed that the artists are using their freedom of speech—a freedom which the letter writer feels he has defended in war—to present "unpatriotic" images. Had these artists experienced combat firsthand, the writer claims, they might be less inclined to create these images.

In fact, it is partly the letter writer's experience of combat himself that has led to this intense reaction. The process of going to war is traumatic and singular—one a person can't understand unless they've experienced it first-hand. However, the artwork in the exhibition is not claiming to understand war from the perspective of a soldier, but rather to explore the issues from the artists' unique viewpoint in a creative way. The letter writer's argument that the artists might feel differently if they had been in combat is accurate—surely they would. However, such an argument doesn't invalidate the right of American citizens to express themselves and their diverse opinions through words and images.

I think this discussion is an important one, although I wish the letter writer had used it to spark debate. The vast disparity of experience in artist and audience is

> **One Student's Response (***continued***)**
>
> what makes art so valuable, encouraging reactions, discussions, and perhaps new understanding. I disagree with the letter writer that the artwork is unpatriotic—in fact, I think the artistic expression of a unique viewpoint is one of the greatest uses of freedom of speech. I also think that the artists could have something valuable to learn from the letter writer as a combat veteran, and I think such a meeting of opposing minds is one of the greatest reactions to art there is.

You can analyze an argument all kinds of ways, including by looking for logical fallacies (see "Inquiring into the Details: Common Logical Fallacies") or by using a method called Toulmin logic (see "Inquiring into the Details: Toulmin: A Method for Analyzing an Argument" on p. 276). But the Rogerian approach provides a wonderful introduction to argument analysis because it forces you to do something we don't typically do, particularly in the current climate of political division in the United States: *Understand and even empathize with the other guy.* That doesn't mean that you will agree. But it does make it more likely that you won't speak past each other. Later, you'll also see how essential it is to not only demonstrate understanding of others' arguments, but also to include some of them to make your own case more effectively.

Watch the Animation on **Logical Fallacies** in your MyLab

Inquiring into the Details

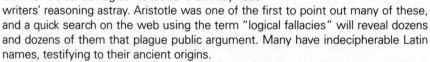

Common Logical Fallacies

An important way to evaluate the soundness of an argument is to examine its logic and, in particular, look for so-called logical fallacies that may lead writers' reasoning astray. Aristotle was one of the first to point out many of these, and a quick search on the web using the term "logical fallacies" will reveal dozens and dozens of them that plague public argument. Many have indecipherable Latin names, testifying to their ancient origins.

Here are ten of the most common logical fallacies. I think they cover about 90 percent of the ways in which writers stumble when making an argument.

1. ***Hasty generalization:*** We're naturally judgmental creatures. For example, we frequently make a judgment about someone after just meeting him or her. Or we conclude that a class is useless after attending a single session. These are generalizations based on insufficient evidence. Hasty generalizations *might* be true—the class might turn out to be useless—but you should always be wary of them.

Inquiring into the Details (*continued*)

2. **Ad hominem:** When arguments turn into shouting matches, they almost inevitably get personal. Shifting away from the substance of an argument to attack the person making it, either subtly or explicitly, is another common logical fallacy. It's also, at times, hard to resist.

3. **Appeal to authority:** We all know that finding support for a claim from an expert is a smart move in many arguments. But sometimes it's a faulty move because the authority we cite isn't really an expert on the subject. A more common fallacy, however, is when we cite an expert to support a claim without acknowledging that many experts disagree on the point.

4. **Straw man:** One of the sneakiest ways to sidetrack reason in an argument is to misrepresent or ignore the actual position of an opponent. Unfortunately, the "straw man" fallacy thrives in many political debates: "I can't support this proposal for universal health care," says politician A. "It's clear that politician A doesn't really take the problem of American health care seriously," says politician B. Huh?

5. **False analogy:** Analogies can be powerful comparisons in argument. But they can also lead us astray when the analogy simply doesn't hold. Are A and B *really* similar situations? For example, when a critic of higher education argues that a public university is like a business and should be run like one, are the two really analogous? Fundamentally, one is nonprofit and the other is designed to make money. Is this really a useful comparison?

6. **Post hoc or false cause:** Just because one thing follows another doesn't necessarily mean one *causes* the other. It might be coincidence, or the cause might be something else entirely. For example, if you're really keen on arguing that losing the football coach was the cause of the team's losing record, you might link the two. And it's possible that you're right, but it's also just as possible that the injury to the quarterback was one of the real reasons.

7. **Appeal to popularity:** In a country obsessed by polls and rankings, it's not hard to understand the appeal of reasoning that argues that because it's popular, it must be good or true. Advertisers are particularly fond of this fallacy, arguing that because their brand is most popular, it must be the best. In fact, this might not be the case at all. The majority can be wrong.

8. **Slippery slope:** I love the name of this one because it so aptly describes what can happen when reasoning loses its footing. You might start out reasonably enough, arguing, for example, that a gun control law restricts the rights of some citizens to have access to certain weapons, but pretty soon you start sliding toward conclusions that simply don't follow, such as that a gun control law is the beginning of the end of gun ownership in the country. Now you might really believe this, but logic isn't the route to get there.

9. **Either/or fallacy:** In a black-and-white world, something is right or wrong, true or false, good or bad. But ours is a colorful world with many shades. For instance, while it might be emotionally satisfying to say that opponents of the war in Afghanistan must not support the troops there, it is also possible that the

> **Inquiring into the Details** (*continued*)
>
> war's opponents are against the war *because* they're concerned about the lives of American service people. Rather than *either/or*, it might be *both/and*. We see this fallacy often in arguments that suggest that there are only two choices and each is opposite to the other.
>
> 10. ***Begging the question:*** This one is also called *circular reasoning*, because it assumes the truth of the arguer's conclusion without bothering to prove it. An obvious example of this would be to say that a law protecting people from Internet spam is good because it's a law, and laws should be obeyed. But why is it a good law?

Motives for Writing an Argument

Argument, obviously, is a part of everyday life. I'm constantly trying to persuade my wife, Karen, that it would be a good thing if I added another guitar to my acoustic collection. I was thinking a new Martin with mahogany back and sides and onboard Fishman electronics would be good.

"You've already got seven guitars," she says. "How many more do you need?"

We argue to get something we want—although these are often our less interesting arguments. More generally, developing arguments is the stuff of everyday life.

Classical rhetoricians such as Plato, Aristotle, and Cicero had a great deal to say about how to argue well. Their focus was largely on public speaking, although their ideas are foundational for a modern understanding of argument. For Aristotle, there were three arenas for persuasion—before the courts, before legislators and others who make public policy, and at social occasions.

Of course, there are plenty of other reasons to argue. As we have seen, common forms such as reviews and proposals are types of arguments. In academic and indeed much other writing, the writer sets out to assert and support a factual claim—whether about the past and what it tells us about the present, the current state of things, or what might happen.

Argument is also a civic duty, an essential activity in any democratic culture (for some examples of forums for argument today, see "Writing Beyond the Classroom: Public Argument in a Digital Age"). To participate fully in civic life, you need to know not only how to make a sound argument, but also how to analyze the arguments of others so you can decide what you believe. Classical rhetoric saw public engagement as a duty of people who speak well.

Finally, the most important motive behind writing and studying argument is that you care about something. Throughout this book, I've argued that the personal motive for writing is the most powerful one of all; in this case, you're passionate about a question or an issue, and building an argument channels that passion into prose that can make a difference.

Writing Beyond the Classroom

Public Argument in a Digital Age

An argument with Northwest Airlines over whether they owe you a lunch voucher after your flight was cancelled is typical of everyday uses of persuasion. But, more important, arguing well—and ethically— is a civic duty in a democratic society. A few thousand years ago, the Greeks and Romans created schools of rhetoric where people could learn the art of speaking persuasively in public settings.

These days, probably more than ever, argument is a vibrant part of civic life in the United States, particularly on the Internet. Here are a few of the many genres of public argument available to you for moving people to think or do something you consider important:

- **Op-ed essays:** These essays, ubiquitous in newspapers, remain among the most common brief argumentative essays for a general audience.

- **Letters to the editor:** Like op-ed essays, these appear in print or online publications; they're often a response to a previous contribution.

- **Blogs:** One of the newest forms of public argument is the blog. Hosted by such online sites as Google's "Blogger," the so-called blogosphere has grown so explosively that no one really knows how big it is anymore.

- **Photo essay:** Over one hundred years ago, Jacob Riis used photographs of immigrants' squalid conditions in New York City tenements to incite a public outcry—and policy change—on how we treat the poor.

- **YouTube:** It's not just a forum for published videos on weird cat tricks.

- **PowerPoint:** Former vice president Al Gore's slide presentation "An Inconvenient Truth" made the point that there really can be power in PowerPoint.

The Argument and Academic Writing

While proposals, reviews, and critical essays (discussed in the next chapter) are types of arguments you might write in college, you are most likely to write the type of argument we discuss here: arguments that address claims of fact. Whenever you're asked to write a position paper, an opinion piece, a cause-effect essay, and in some cases a reading response, you're asked to explore the topic, discover a claim that expresses what you think, and then assemble evidence that makes it convincing. In other words, you need to answer the question *What do you believe is true and why?*

> Argument is one of the key means of making new knowledge.

Academics value argument not because they're argumentative (though some are), but because it's the way that they "make knowledge," which is the central business of the university. Scholarly communities make discoveries through contesting what was once assumed to be true. Reasoned argument supported by research is the engine behind academic inquiry.

Fundamental to academic argument is an idea that isn't always obvious to newcomers at college: "Facts" can be contested. While it often seems that the facts we take for granted are immutable truths—as enduring as the granite peaks I can see through my office window—things often aren't that way at all. Our knowledge of things—how the planet was formed, the best ways to save endangered species, the meaning of a classic novel, how to avoid athletic injuries—is entirely made up of ideas that are *contested*. And the primary tool for shaping and even changing what we know is argument.

Features of the Form

Feature	Conventions of the Argument Essay
Inquiry question	What do I believe is true and why?
Motives	We hope to convince others to think as we do. Sometimes, however, we first need to convince ourselves, and argument is an invitation to *explore* as well as to persuade. A fundamental motive is discovery.
Subject matter	Any topic is fair game, but one thing is essential: Others must have a stake in the issue. An audience should be persuaded that whatever claim you're making might matter.
Structure	Like any form of writing, the design of arguments depends on the situation. However, outlines for arguments developed by rhetoricians share some of these features: • Background on the issue, especially what people seem to *agree* on. What's the controversy as most people understand it? • The inquiry question. • Claims and supporting reasons and evidence. • Acknowledgement of counterarguments and analysis of their significance. • Closing that refines the claim, summarizes it, or returns to the beginning to affirm how the argument addresses the issue.
Sources of information	Experts on your topic, sources of reliable data on your topic, your experiences and observations, and the stories of others can all potentially provide evidence for your argument.
Language	Who is the audience? Arguments for expert audiences are often formal. Arguments for the general public are much less formal, with relatively relaxed rules of evidence and casual language. The balance of appeals should be appropriate to the audience.

Prose+

Editorial cartoons such as this one are a popular form of argument, and one reason they're effective is a quality that comics share: By simplifying things, they amplify them. Cartoonist Scott McCloud notes that when we render something more abstractly—in this case, taking a coal mine and superimposing a graveyard and smoke—the details that were eliminated make the details that remain more obvious. Cartoons that make an argument, however, also have features typical of any argument: a claim (often implied) and reasons. The cartoon strip here, for example, combines drawings with very few words to make a pretty unambiguous claim: Wind power is preferable to nuclear, oil, and coal energy. The reason offered? The problems associated with wind power are relatively benign.

READINGS

▶ Argument 1

Bad?

> # Ways to Narrow the Question
>
> ❖ **Time**. Limit the time frame of your project. Instead of researching the entire Civil War, limit your search to the month or year when the most decisive battles occurred.
>
> ❖ **Place**. Anchor a larger subject to a particular location. Instead of exploring "senioritis" at American high schools, research the phenomenon at the local high school.
>
> ❖ **Person.** Use the particulars of a person to reveal generalities about the group. Instead of writing about the homeless problem, write about a homeless man.
>
> ❖ **Story.** Ground a larger story in the specifics of "smaller" one. Don't write about dream interpretation, write about a dream *you* had and use the theories to analyze it.
>
> ❖ **Relationship.** Find an interesting and relevant relationship between your topic and something else. Pose the question: **What is the relationship between ____ and ____?**

I've used PowerPoint for years. And I've misused it. I've loaded up PowerPoints with text and long lists of bullet points (see above). I've made presentations and read the text aloud directly from the slides. I've cluttered slides up with charts that are hard to read. Then I read a book called *Presentation Zen: Simple Ideas on Presentation Design and Delivery* and started to understand what I was doing wrong. What I needed, among other things, was handouts. Slides are not very good containers for information. I think my PowerPoint is better now, but you'd have to ask my students.

Edward Tufte, whose work in visual storytelling is legendary, hates PowerPoint, and the brief essay below elaborates on that sentiment. He argues that when meetings and classrooms turn to slideware to communicate information, bad things happen. You've undoubtedly used PowerPoint or other presentation software as a student, and you've certainly been an audience for plenty of slide presentations. What does your own experience tell you about the claims Tufte makes here?

PowerPoint Is Evil

Edward Tufte

1   Imagine a widely used and expensive prescription drug that promised to make us beautiful but didn't. Instead the drug had frequent, serious side effects: It induced stupidity, turned everyone into bores, wasted time, and degraded the quality and

credibility of communication. These side effects would rightly lead to a worldwide product recall.

Yet slideware—computer programs for presentations—is everywhere: in corporate America, in government bureaucracies, even in our schools. Several hundred million copies of Microsoft PowerPoint are churning out trillions of slides each year. Slideware may help speakers outline their talks, but convenience for the speaker can be punishing to both content and audience. The standard PowerPoint presentation elevates format over content, betraying an attitude of commercialism that turns everything into a sales pitch.

Of course, data-driven meetings are nothing new. Years before today's slideware, presentations at companies such as IBM and in the military used bullet lists shown by overhead projectors. But the format has become ubiquitous under PowerPoint, which was created in 1984 and later acquired by Microsoft. PowerPoint's pushy style seeks to set up a speaker's dominance over the audience. The speaker, after all, is making power points with bullets to followers. Could any metaphor be worse? Voicemail menu systems? Billboards? Television? Stalin?

Particularly disturbing is the adoption of the PowerPoint cognitive style in our schools. Rather than learning to write a report using sentences, children are being taught how to formulate client pitches and infomercials. Elementary school PowerPoint exercises (as seen in teacher guides and in student work posted on the Internet) typically consist of 10 to 20 words and a piece of clip art on each slide in a presentation of three to six slides—a total of perhaps 80 words (15 seconds of silent

(continued)

(continued)

Estimates of relative survival rates, by cancer site[19]

	% survival rates and their standard errors			
	5 year	10 year	15 year	20 year
Prostate	98.8 0.4	95.2 0.9	87.1 1.7	81.1 3.0
Thyroid	96.0 0.8	95.8 1.2	94.0 1.6	95.4 2.1
Testis	94.7 1.1	94.0 1.3	91.1 1.8	88.2 2.3
Melanomas	89.0 0.8	86.7 1.1	83.5 1.5	82.8 1.9
Breast	86.4 0.4	78.3 0.6	71.3 0.7	65.0 1.0
Hodgkin's disease	85.1 1.7	79.8 2.0	73.8 2.4	67.1 2.8
Corpus uteri, uterus	84.3 1.0	83.2 1.3	80.8 1.7	79.2 2.0
Urinary, bladder	82.1 1.0	76.2 1.4	70.3 1.9	67.9 2.4
Cervix, uteri	70.5 1.6	64.1 1.8	62.8 2.1	60.0 2.4
Larynx	68.8 2.1	56.7 2.5	45.8 2.8	37.8 3.1
Rectum	62.6 1.2	55.2 1.4	51.8 1.8	49.2 2.3
Kidney, renal pelvis	61.8 1.3	54.4 1.6	49.8 2.0	47.3 2.6
Colon	61.7 0.8	55.4 1.0	53.9 1.2	52.3 1.6
Non-Hodgkin's	57.8 1.0	46.3 1.2	38.3 1.4	34.3 1.7
Oral cavity, pharynx	56.7 1.3	44.2 1.4	37.5 1.6	33.0 1.8
Ovary	55.0 1.3	49.3 1.6	49.9 1.9	49.6 2.4
Leukemia	42.5 1.2	32.4 1.3	29.7 1.5	26.2 1.7
Brain, nervous system	32.0 1.4	29.2 1.5	27.6 1.6	26.1 1.9
Multiple myeloma	29.5 1.6	12.7 1.5	7.0 1.3	4.8 1.5
Stomach	23.8 1.3	19.4 1.4	19.0 1.7	14.9 1.9
Lung and bronchus	15.0 0.4	10.6 0.4	8.1 0.4	6.5 0.4
Esophagus	14.2 1.4	7.9 1.3	7.7 1.6	5.4 2.0
Liver, bile duct	7.5 1.1	5.8 1.2	6.3 1.5	7.6 2.0
Pancreas	4.0 0.5	3.0 1.5	2.7 0.6	2.7 0.8

A traditional table: rich, informative, clear

reading) for a week of work. Students would be better off if the schools simply closed down on those days and everyone went to the Exploratorium or wrote an illustrated essay explaining something.

5   In a business setting, a PowerPoint slide typically shows 40 words, which is about eight seconds' worth of silent reading material. With so little information per slide, many, many slides are needed. Audiences consequently endure a relentless sequentiality, one damn slide after another. When information is stacked in time, it is difficult to understand context and evaluate relationships. Visual reasoning usually works more effectively when relevant information is shown side by side. Often, the more

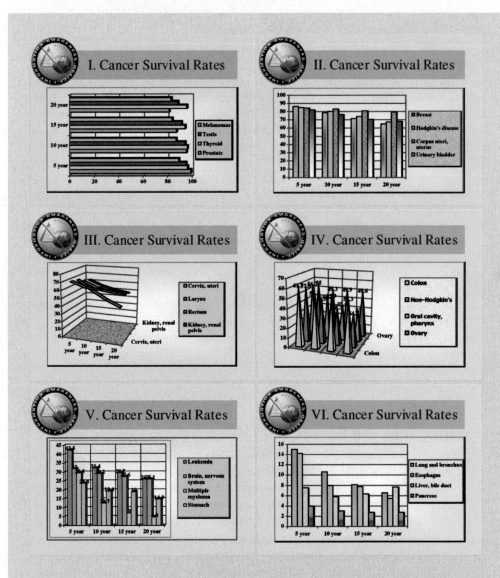

intense the detail, the greater the clarity and understanding. This is especially so for statistical data, where the fundamental analytical act is to make comparisons.

Consider an important and intriguing table of survival rates for those with cancer relative to those without cancer for the same time period. Some 196 numbers and 57 words describe survival rates and their standard errors for 24 cancers.   6

Applying the PowerPoint templates to this nice, straightforward table yields an analytical disaster. The data explodes into six separate chaotic slides, consuming   7

(continued)

(continued)

2.9 times the area of the table. Everything is wrong with these smarmy, incoherent graphs: the encoded legends, the meaningless color, the logo-type branding. They are uncomparative, indifferent to content and evidence, and so data-starved as to be almost pointless. Chartjunk is a clear sign of statistical stupidity. Poking a finger into the eye of thought, these data graphics would turn into a nasty travesty if used for a serious purpose, such as helping cancer patients assess their survival chances. To sell a product that messes up data with such systematic intensity, Microsoft abandons any pretense of statistical integrity and reasoning.

8   Presentations largely stand or fall on the quality, relevance, and integrity of the content. If your numbers are boring, then you've got the wrong numbers. If your words or images are not on point, making them dance in color won't make them relevant. Audience boredom is usually a content failure, not a decoration failure.

9   At a minimum, a presentation format should do no harm. Yet the PowerPoint style routinely disrupts, dominates, and trivializes content. Thus PowerPoint presentations too often resemble a school play—very loud, very slow, and very simple.

10   The practical conclusions are clear. PowerPoint is a competent slide manager and projector. But rather than supplementing a presentation, it has become a substitute for it. Such misuse ignores the most important rule of speaking: Respect your audience.

Inquiring into the Essay

1. **Explore.** Think back to the last time you created a slide presentation using PowerPoint or a similar software program. If it's still lurking there on your hard drive—take a look at it. Fastwrite for a few minutes about how you feel about the effectiveness of the presentation. Do you agree with Tufte that too often slide presentations "trivialize content"?

2. **Explain.** Identify some of the basic machinery of argument in "PowerPoint Is Evil." Identify what you think is Tufte's main claim, a reason supporting that claim, and several examples of evidence.

3. **Evaluate.** Look at "Inquiring into the Details: Common Logical Fallacies" on page 244, and use the list as a way of evaluating Tufte's argument. Do you think the argument commits any of these logical fallacies?

4. **Reflect.** It's fair to say that there is a fairly combative tone in "PowerPoint Is Evil," starting with the title. The speaker's tone is an element of ethos, of course; it influences how we *feel* about Tufte and, ultimately, how we feel about his argument. How did you feel about him? Are there any generalizations you might draw from your response to this essay about how speakers and writers might manage ethos?

▶ Argument 2

It's hard to imagine that one of the chief planners of the September 11, 2001, attacks on New York and Washington, DC, might invoke George Washington as his hero. In the excerpt that follows, Kahlid Sheikh Mohammed, a commander for al Qaeda who has been in custody since 2003, argues that Islamic extremists, like Washington, are just fighting for their independence. The language of war, says Mohammed, is universal, and that language is killing.

This partial transcript of Mohammed discussing his role in the 9/11 attacks, the murder of journalist Daniel Pearl, and the hotel bombings in Bali, was released by the U.S. Department of Defense and later appeared in *Harper's Magazine*.

The Language of War Is Killing
Khalid Sheikh Mohammed

I'm not making myself a hero when I said I was responsible for this or that. You know 1
very well there is a language for any war. If America wants to invade Iraq, they will not send Saddam roses or kisses. They send bombardment. I admit I'm America's enemy. For sure, I'm America's enemy. So when we make war against America, we are like jackals fighting in the night. We consider George Washington a hero. Muslims, many of them, believe Osama bin Laden is doing the same thing. He is just fighting. He needs his independence. Many Muslims think that, not only me. They have been oppressed by America. So when we say we are enemy combatants, that's right, we are. But I'm asking you to be fair with many detainees who are not enemy combatants. Because many of them have been unjustly arrested. You know very well, for any country waging war against their enemy, the language of the war is killing. If man and woman are together as a marriage, the others are kids, children. But if you and me, two nations, are together in war, the others are victims. This is the way of the language. You know forty million people were killed in World War I. Many people are oppressed. Because there is war, for sure, there will be victims. I'm not happy that three thousand have been killed in America. I feel sorry even. Islam never gives me the green light to kill people. Killing, in Christianity, Judaism, and Islam, is prohibited. But there are exceptions to the rule. When you are killing people in Iraq, you say, We have to do it. We don't like Saddam. But this is the way to deal with Saddam. Same language you use I use. When you are invading two thirds of Mexico, you call your war "manifest destiny." It's up to you to call it what you want. But the other side is calling you oppressors. If now we were living in the Revolutionary War, George Washington would be arrested by Britain. For sure, they would consider him an enemy combatant. But in America they consider him a hero. In any revolutionary war one side will be either George Washington or Britain. So we considered American Army bases in Saudi Arabia, Kuwait, Qatar, and Bahrain. This is a kind of invasion,

(continued)

(continued)

but I'm not here to convince you. I don't have to say that I'm not your enemy. This is why the language of any war in the world is killing. The language of war is victims. I don't like to kill people. I feel very sorry kids were killed in 9/11. What will I do? I want to make a great awakening in America to stop foreign policy in our land. I know Americans have been torturing us since the seventies. I know they are talking about human rights. And I know it is against the American Constitution, against American laws. But they said, Every law has exceptions. This is your bad luck—you've been part of the exception to our laws. So, for me, I have patience. The Americans have human rights, but enemy combatant is a flexible word. What is an enemy combatant in my language? The Ten Commandments are shared between all of us. We are all serving one God. But we also share the language of War. War started when Cain killed Abel. It's never gonna stop killing people. America starts the Revolutionary War, and then the Mexican, then the Spanish, then World War I, World War II. You read the history. This is life. You have to kill.

Inquiring into the Essay

1. **Explore.** Does Mohammed have a point when he compares Islamic extremists who fight for "freedom" to American revolutionaries such as George Washington who fought for independence? Fastwrite on this question in your journal for five minutes, exploring what you think. When you're done, skip a line and compose a one-sentence answer to this question: *What surprised you most about what you said in your fastwrite?*

2. **Explain.** Because of their very different topics and arguments, "The Language of War Is Killing" and "PowerPoint Is Evil," on page 250, use very different kinds of evidence. Compare the two essays. What kind of evidence does Mohammed use in his argument? How does it differ from the kind of evidence that Tufte uses? What conclusions do you draw about the relationship between claims and evidence in each of these two arguments?

3. **Evaluate.** One of the most influential methods of analyzing an argument is Stephen Toulmin's approach, which makes use of something called "warrants" (see "Inquiring into the Details: Toulmin: A Method for Analyzing an Argument"). Simply put, a warrant is an assumption that one needs to believe is true if a claim and the reason and evidence for it are to make sense. Example: Michelle must have a lot of money (claim) because she carries a lot of credit cards in her purse (reason and evidence). To buy this assertion, you would have to believe that there is a correlation between the numbers of credit cards one owns and wealth. That's a warrant. Discover the warrants in Mohammad's "The Language of War Is Killing." Start by stating what you think is one of his claims and pairing it with a reason behind it. The warrant is the assumption that you must believe to be true in order

to accept both the claim and the reason and evidence for it. What are some warrants here? Do you agree with them?

4. **Reflect.** The September 11 attacks have, understandably, made many Americans very emotional about terrorism and terrorists. What did you notice about your emotional reaction to Mohammed's argument in "The Language of War Is Killing"? Did you find it difficult to read the transcript analytically, as the previous questions asked you to do?

▶ Argument 3

Laredo businessman Loye Young agreed for the fall 2008 semester to teach a business management class at nearby Texas A&M International University (TAMIU). Like many instructors, he toiled over his syllabus, trying to make sure his course policies were clear, especially a section on the consequences of plagiarism in his class. Young warned that plagiarists would not only flunk the course but would also be reported to university officials. That's fairly standard punishment at most universities. What got critics' attention was Young's warning that he would publicly humiliate any student caught plagiarizing.

True to his word, when he caught six students plagiarizing a paper, Young published their names on his blog; and soon after, TAMIU officials fired him, arguing that he violated the Family Educational and Privacy Act, a policy designed to protect the confidentiality of certain student information. Young, a former attorney, strongly disagreed.

The firing ignited a national controversy and a wild debate in the blogosphere over whether Loye Young's decision to out students he suspected of academic dishonesty was effective, ethical, and fair. In response to one of his critics, Loye posted the following defense of his approach on his blog.

Is Humiliation an Ethically Appropriate Response to Plagiarism?

Loye Young

I'm a business owner in Laredo, Texas. I had never taught a college course before, and I never asked to teach. The department asked me to teach this course. I accepted because of my commitment to Laredo's future.

I worked hard on the syllabus, and everything in the syllabus was deliberate. Specifically, the language about dishonesty was based on moral and pedagogical

(continued)

(continued)

principles. The department chairman, Dr. Balaji Janamanchi, reviewed the syllabus with me line-by-line, and I made a few changes in response to his comments.

3   I was surprised by how common and blatant plagiarism turned out to be. Six students in one class is an extraordinarily high number. I thought and prayed about what to do for about a week before following through on my promise. I decided I had only one moral choice. I am certain it was right.

4   My decision was guided by two factors: What is good for the students themselves? and What is good for other students?

5   What is good for the students themselves?

6   I am cognizant of the extraordinary moral difficulty involved when deciding what is in another's best interests. Nonetheless, I am convinced that public disclosure, including the concomitant humiliation, is in the interests of the student because it is the best way to teach the student about the consequences of dishonesty and discourage the student from plagiarizing again. Humiliation is inextricably part of a well-formed conscience.

7   The Vice President-elect, Senator Joseph Biden, is perhaps the most well-known plagiarizer in recent history. Biden was caught plagiarizing while at Syracuse Law School. The school gave him an F, required him to retake the course, and subsequently treated the incident as confidential.

8   Unfortunately, Biden didn't learn his lesson at law school. He continued to plagiarize for another 20 years. During the 1988 presidential campaign, Senator Biden's career of plagiarizing came to light, and he was forced to end his presidential bid.

9   It is my belief that the Syracuse incident left a subtle and subliminal message in Biden's mind: plagiarism is not a deal breaker. Consequently, he continued to plagiarize. Unfortunately for the Senator, the facts came to public light at the worst possible time: when he was running for President.

10   I believe that had the Syracuse incident been available publicly, Mr. Biden would have actually learned his lesson and would not have plagiarized later. Twenty years later, if the incident had come up at all, the Senator would have plausibly and convincingly maintained that the incident was a youthful mistake.

11   There is yet another reason for publicity in such cases: unjustly accused students are protected, for two reasons. One, a professor will be more careful before blowing the whistle. I myself knew that posting the students' names would be appropriately subject to intense public scrutiny. Therefore, I construed every ambiguity in the students' favor. Two, public disclosure ensures that subsequent determinations by the university are founded on evidence and dispensed fairly.

12   What is good for other students?

13   On the second question, four reasons convince me: deterrents, fairness, predictability, and preparedness for life.

14   Deterrents—Only if everyone knows that violations of plagiarism will be exposed and punished will the penalties for plagiarism be an effective deterrent. (As a lawyer once told me after hearing of another lawyer's disbarment, "I'm damn sure not going to

do THAT again!") In fact, one of the six students had not plagiarized (to my knowledge) until the week before I announced my findings. Had I announced the plagiarism earlier, it is possible that student would not have plagiarized at all.

Fairness—Honest students should have, in fairness, the knowledge that their le-   15 gitimate work is valued more than a plagiarizer's illegitimate work. In my course, the students were required to post their essays on a public website for all to see. Thus, anyone in the world could have detected the plagiarism. Had another student noticed the plagiarism but saw no action, the honest student would reasonably believe that the process is unfair.

Predictability—By failing publicly to follow through on ubiquitous warnings   16 about plagiarism, universities have convinced students that the purported indigna- tion against deceit is itself deceitful and that the entire process is capricious. TAMIU's actions in this case have confirmed my suspicions that such a perception is entirely justified.

Preparedness for life—In the real world, deceitful actions have consequences,   17 and those consequences are often public. Borrowers lose credit ratings, employees get fired, spouses divorce, businesses fail, political careers end, and professionals go to jail. Acts of moral turpitude rightly carry public and humiliating consequences in real life, and students need to be prepared.

In closing, I submit that education died when educators came to believe that greater   18 self-esteem leads to greater learning. In fact, the causality is backwards: self-esteem is the result of learning, not the cause.

Inquiring into the Essay

1. **Explore.** If you accept that plagiarism is a problem, then what should an instructor do about it? What's a policy that you consider to be both ethical and potentially an effective deterrent? Fastwrite about this question in your journal for four minutes, exploring what you think.

2. **Explain.** Using the Rogerian approach discussed earlier (pp. 242–243), "say back" what you understand to be Young's argument. Can you imagine how his situation leads him to feel the way he does about punishing plagiarism?

3. **Evaluate.** Young writes, "Humiliation is inextricably part of a well-formed conscience." How would you evaluate that claim? Can you imagine the *reasons* why Young believes it's true? (Try filling in the blank in this sentence: *Because _____, humiliation is inextricably part of a well-formed conscience.*) Do you agree with those reasons?

4. **Reflect.** Young published this argument as a blog post. Reflect on the blog as a genre of argument. How would you distinguish it from, say, an op-ed essay or a letter to the editor?

Watch
the Animation on
**The Elements of
an Argument Essay**
in your MyLab

THE WRITING PROCESS

Inquiry Project **Writing an Argument**

Inquiry question: What do I believe is true and why?

Write an essay in which you make a factual claim about an issue or controversy that interests you. You are writing for an audience of nonexperts. Make sure your essay includes the following (see also p. 248 for typical features of arguments):

- Claims that are supported by clear reasons.
- Relevant evidence from your research, observations, and personal experience to support your claims and reasons.
- A strong sense of what is at stake for your readers. Why should they care as much as you do about the issue?
- At least some attention to counterarguments. What are other ways of looking at the issue, and why did you reject them?

Prose +

Make a visual argument. Consider the many ways you might do this:

- A photographic essay
- A PowerPoint
- An advertisement or poster
- A video
- A cartoon
- A t-shirt design

These will likely combine carefully crafted and purposefully selected text to go along with the images. There are *many* examples of visual arguments on the web.

If your argument topic affects people you can interview, develop a documentary podcast that uses interview clips as evidence. Record people who are affected by the issue and, if possible, experts who have interesting things to say about it. Documentary projects such as this one depend heavily on what people say, so consider collecting a lot of audio before you sketch out your argument. Then write your narration around the clips. Add music if you like. (See "Inquiring into the Details: Using Audacity to Record and Edit Audio" on page 143 for guidance on audio recording and editing).

What Are You Going to Write About?

Gun control, abortion rights, and other hot-button public controversies often make the list of banned topics for student essays. This is not because they aren't important public debates. Instead, the problem is much more that the writer has likely already made up his or her mind and sees the chance to ascend a soapbox.

Now, I have my own favorite soapboxes; people with strong convictions do. But as you think about subjects for your essay, consider that the soapbox may not be the best vantage point for practicing inquiry. If you've already made up your mind, will you be open to discovery? If you just want to line up ducks—assembling evidence to support an unwavering belief—will you be encouraged to think deeply or differently? Will you be inclined to filter the voices you hear rather than consider a range of points of view?

> The best argument essays make a clear claim, but they do it by bowing respectfully to the complexity of the subject, examining it from a variety of perspectives, not just two opposing poles.

The best persuasive essays often emerge from the kind of open-ended inquiry that you might have used writing the personal essay. What do you want to understand better? What issue or question makes you wonder? What controversies are you and your friends talking about? Be alert to possible subjects that you might write about *not* because you already know what you think, but because you want to find out. Or consider a subject that you might have feelings about but feel uninformed on, lacking the knowledge to know exactly what you think.

Opening Up

Play around with some ideas first by using some of the following triggers for thinking-through-writing in your journal. Suspend judgment. Don't reject anything. Explore.

7.3
Use invention strategies appropriate to argument to discover and develop a topic.

Listing Prompts. Lists can be rich sources of triggering topics. Let them grow freely, and when you're ready, use an item as the focus of another list or an episode of fastwriting. The following prompts should get you started.

1. In your journal, make a quick list of issues that have provoked disagreements between groups of people in your hometown or local community. What about on campus?

2. Think about these important areas of your life: school, family, work, hobbies, relationships. Title columns with each of these words in your journal or on your computer, and then make a fast list of whatever comes to mind when you think of *issues that threaten* each area.

3. Make a fast list of cultural trends. What's popular? What are the fads? What are people doing these days? Think about whether any of these trends raise interesting questions that might lead to an argument about their origins, meaning, or value.

One Student's Response

Rebecca's Journal

LISTS OF POSSIBLE ARGUMENT TOPICS

1. **Issues:** Gay marriage, rent control, cat calling on the street (or in restaurant jobs!), cleanliness, encouraging diversity vs. affirmative action, underage drinking, abortion rights
2. **School:** funding for the arts
3. **Family:** retirement/money issues, distance between family members, aging
4. **Work:** survival job vs. dream job, bad economy
5. **Hobbies:** too much work, NYC too expensive
6. **Relationships:** too much work, how to meet people?
7. **Cultural trends:** Twitter/Facebook/Tumblr/other social media, going to movies, drinking/clubbing, gossip

4. Jot down a list of the classes you're taking this semester. Then make a quick list of topics that prompt disagreements among people in the fields that you're studying. For example, in your political science class, did you learn that there are debates about the usefulness of the Electoral College? In your biology class, have you discussed global warming? In your women's studies class, did you read about Title IX and how it affects female athletes?

Fastwriting Prompts. Remember, fastwriting is a great way to stimulate creative thinking. Turn off your critical side and let yourself write "badly." Don't worry too much about what you're going to say before you say it. Write fast, letting language lead for a change.

1. Start with a fact that you find interesting, surprising, or disturbing. For example, here's some 2008 data on high school graduation rates in the United States from *Education Week*:

   > Nationally, about 71 percent of all students graduate from high school on time with a regular diploma, but barely half of African American and Hispanic students earn diplomas with their peers. In many states the difference between white and minority graduation rates is stunning; in several cases there is a gap of as many as 40 or 50 percentage points.

   Here are a few items from Harper's Index, a monthly feature in the magazine:

   > Percentage of all Americans who consider themselves part of the top 1 percent of U.S. earners: 13
   > Percentage of Hispanic Americans who do: 28

Percentage of 27- to 45-year-old women who have at least four sexual fantasies per week: 35
Percentage of 18- to 26-year-old women who do: 27

Fastwrite about one of these facts or one you chose, perhaps searching online. In your fastwrite, explore the following questions:

- Is this surprising?

- Does this fact seem true? If so, what would explain it? If not, what makes me skeptical?

- What is my personal experience with this? Does it remind me of any stories, people, situations?

- What can be done about it?

2. Use something from your lists in the preceding section for a focused fastwrite.

3. In a seven-minute fastwrite, explore the differences between your beliefs and the beliefs of your parents. Tell yourself the story of how your own beliefs about some question evolved, perhaps moving away from your parents' positions. Can you imagine the argument you might make to help them understand your point of view?

Visual Prompts. In your journal, cluster one or more of the following phrases:

"Things that seem unfair"

"Things that bug me the most"

"The worst thing about living here"

Let your cluster grow as many branches as possible; when one dies out, start another. Focus on ideas, people, places, facts, observations, questions, experiences, and details that pop into your mind when you focus on the words at the center of your cluster. Look for interesting argument topics when you're done. See Figure 7.3 for an example.

Research Prompts. By definition, argument essays deal with subjects in which people beyond the writer have a stake. And one of the best ways to collect ideas about such issues is to do a little quick and dirty research. Try some of the following research prompts:

1. Read the letters to the editor in your local paper a few days in a row. What issues have people riled up locally? Is there one that you find particularly interesting?

2. Do a Google search for terms or phrases on an issue that interests you, such as "global warming Greenland glaciers" or "pro-anorexia websites." Did you produce any results that make you curious or make you feel something about the issue, one way or another?

3. Your Facebook friends may list groups that support or oppose social causes. Browse some of them to see if one inspires an argument topic.

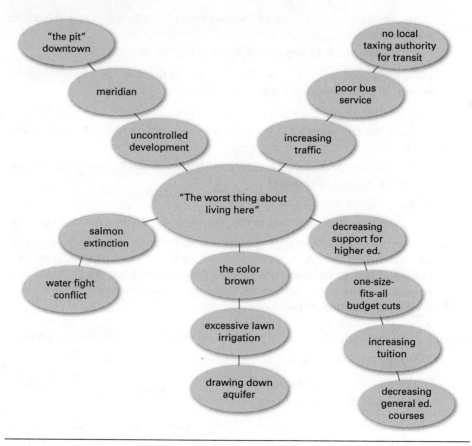

Figure 7.3 Sample cluster

Narrowing Down

Shift back to your more critical mind and sift through the material you generated. Did you discover a topic that might be interesting for your argument essay? Did you stumble over some interesting questions you'd like to explore further? Did anything you wrote or read make you *feel* something? Evaluate the raw material in your journal and keep the following things in mind as you zero in on a topic for your argument essay.

What's Promising Material and What Isn't? Let's take a critical look at the subjects you've generated so far. What promising topics might be lurking there for an argumentative essay? First, you simply must be interested in the topic, even if you know little about it. Also consider some of the following as you make your choice:

- *Evidence.* Do you think you'll be able to find facts, statistics, comments from experts, or stories about people affected by the issue?

■ *Disagreement.* A topic lends itself to argumentative writing if it leads to disagreement among reasonable people. *Is smoking bad for your health?* was once a question that was debatable, but now pretty much everyone concedes that this question has been answered. *Is your state's public anti-smoking initiative effective?*, however, is certainly a debatable question and therefore a potential topic.

■ *Inquiry.* Do you already have strong feelings about what you think about a topic? If so, consider another that provides more opportunities for learning and discovery.

Questions About Audience and Purpose. Persuasive writing is a very audience-oriented form. *To whom* you make your case in an argument matters a lot in *how* you make it, but audience also matters in *whether* one topic is a better choice for an essay than another topic. In choosing a subject, ask yourself:

■ *Do your readers have a stake in the question you're answering?* Readers may or may not realize that they have a *stake* in the question. Say you're writing for fellow students on your campus and your topic addresses whether a 12 percent hike in tuition is justified. In this case, your readers will know they have a stake in the question. Sometimes, however, you choose a topic because readers *need to know* that they have a stake in how a question is answered. For instance, the argument that new antiterrorist rules threaten online privacy may be something you believe your readers, most of whom surf the web, should consider.

■ *Can you identify what your readers might already believe?* One of the key strategies of persuasion is to find ways to link the values and attitudes of your audience with the position you're encouraging them to believe. Does your potential topic lend itself to this kind of analysis?

■ *Is your potential topic appropriate for encouraging readers to believe or do something?* As you know by now, one of the things that distinguishes argument essays such as the op-ed piece from other forms of writing is the writer's intention to change his or her audience.

Trying Out

Okay, you've got a tentative topic and inquiry question for your argument essay: *Do social media have an effect on society?* At this point, you're thinking that your claim might be that, yes, social media have an effect on society. This isn't a bad start. But your opening question is *huge*. Which social media? What kinds of effects? Which society? Like a lot of research-based projects, the argument essay should pose a question that will help you make the decision about what information to look for and what to ignore. It should be focused enough so that you can wade into a creek rather than a raging river of information. If you think your question might be too general, try the following activity to cut it down to size.

Kitchen Knives of Thought. Try the following steps in your journal:

STEP ONE: Write your tentative research question at the top of a page of your notebook, and circle or underline every general or vague term.

What is the (impact) of (social media) on (society?)

STEP TWO: "Wh" questions (who, what, which, when, where, why) are the kitchen knives of thought. They can help you cut abstractions and generalities down to size. For each circled word in your inquiry question, find an appropriate "Wh" question that might help you make your research question more specific. Then jot down a quick list of ideas to answer the question you pose. For example,

1. *What* **impacts** of social media exactly?
   - Friendship, relationships
   - "Arab spring"
   - Writing
2. *Which* **social media?**
   - Facebook
   - Twitter
   - Blogs
3. *What* **societies?**
   - High school kids
   - Middle East
   - Online dating

STEP THREE: Restate your inquiry question, making it more specific and focused.

How has Twitter proven a challenge to authoritarian regimes in the Middle East?

Research Considerations. While writing this argument essay does involve some research, it isn't exactly a research paper. A research paper is a much more extended treatment of a topic that relies on more-detailed and scholarly information than is usually needed for an argument essay. In addition to the research strategies in this section, in Chapter 11 you'll find more information that might be helpful, including on conducting effective Internet searches and evaluating the sources you find and on library resources.

To develop a working knowledge of the topic for your argument essay, focus your research on the following:

1. *The back story:* What is the history of the controversy? (When did it begin, who was involved, how was the issue addressed, and what were the problems?)
2. *Popular assumptions:* What do most people currently believe is true about the issue?

3. *The evidence:* Who has said what that seems to support your claim or provide backing for your assumptions?

4. *Opposing arguments:* Who offers a counterargument that you might need to consider?

Consider working through some of the following research strategies to find this information.

Researching on the Web

- Google (for relevant websites, online periodicals, and some newspapers)
- Google Scholar (if your topic is discussed by scholars)
- Google Blog Search (to get the gist of the public discussion of your topic)
- GPO Access (go to http://www.gpoaccess.gov/ to search for relevant federal documents)
- Online version of local newspaper (if your topic has a local angle)
- State and Local Government on the Net (go to http://www.statelocalgov .net/ if your topic is an issue of policy)

Researching in the Library

- General subject databases (these cover a wide range of subjects, and many include nonacademic publications as well)
- Newspaper databases (for example, National Newspaper Index or Newspaper Source)
- Newspapers on microfilm (your university library might archive copies of the local paper on microfilm, going back for many years)

Interviews. While both the web and the university library are great sources of information on your topic, often the best way to learn about it—and get some good quotes for your essay—is to find someone to talk to. Your reading will probably give you the best clues about who to contact. Who is often quoted in news stories? Who has been writing or blogging about the issue? You might also be able to find someone on your own campus. If you're writing, say, about measures that attempt to protect students from date rape on your campus, someone in the criminal justice department or in Student Affairs can tell you more about the issue in a few minutes than you might learn in a couple hours online.

Writing the Sketch

Now draft a sketch with the following elements:

- It has a tentative title.
- It makes at least one claim and offers several reasons that support the claim.
- It presents and analyzes at least one contrasting point of view.

■ It includes specific evidence to support (or possibly complicate) the reasons offered in support of the claim, including *at least* several of the following: an anecdote or story, a personal observation, data, an analogy, a case study, expert testimony, other relevant quotations from people involved, a precedent.

■ It includes a Work Cited or References page listing sources used.

▶ Student Sketch

Rebecca Thompson is a fan of social media, and in doing some quick research for the sketch that follows, she discovers that the Pope is too. At the same time, she concedes that there are many critics who believe that sites such as Facebook do harm by undermining our social relationships rather than enhancing them, as Rebecca starts to argue here. Her sketch is the seed of an argument: There's a claim, reasons that support it, evidence, and consideration of another point of view. We'll see how the argument develops from here later in the chapter.

Twitter a Profound Thought?

Rebecca Thompson

1   Facebook Chat. iPhone texting. Checking in on FourSquare. Twitter hashtags. Tumblr blogging. These days, there's no limit to the ways we can talk to each other. Suddenly, talking and listening is much more complicated. But is this a good thing?

2   I use social media regularly. I use my email, Facebook, Twitter, and iPhone in all areas of my life, from connecting with high school friends now scattered across the country, to networking and advertising projects I'm involved in, to keeping updated on news stories. When Hurricane Irene struck the East Coast, I was out of town. I kept tabs on my friends via Facebook, and followed the news stories by following the hashtag #HurricaneIrene on Twitter. It was a relief to be connected, even from far away. "At its core, it is about connections and community," said Mailet Lopez, the founder of the networking site I Had Cancer, to *Forbes* magazine. "Social networking provides an opportunity beyond physical support networks and online forums...because with a social network, people can connect based on whatever criteria they want, regardless of location."

3   Yet detractors argue that social media does the opposite of what Lopez claims—it encourages *disconnectivity*. By focusing more on the kind of communication based around gadgets and the internet, critics argue that social media deconstructs traditional methods of conversation and undermines interpersonal relationships. "Technology is threatening to dominate our lives and make us less human," writes Paul Harris, referencing Sherry Tunkle's book *Alone Together*. "Under the illusion of allowing us to communicate better, it is actually isolating us from real human interactions in a cyber-reality that is a poor imitation of the real world."

4   While there is certainly truth to this claim, I argue that social media sites have the potential, if used to their best advantage, to facilitate communication and networking.

Because I can respond to emails and texts on the go, I can plan ahead. I can keep in touch with my friends studying abroad when phones aren't an option. I get lost a *lot* less. Even the Pope has spoken of the benefits of the internet, social networking, and media. "Search engines and social networks have become the starting point of communication for many people who are seeking advice, ideas, information and answers," he said. "In our time, the internet is becoming ever more a forum for questions and answers...In concise phrases, often no longer than a verse from the Bible, profound thoughts can be communicated."

Works Cited

Harris, Paul. "Social networking under fresh attack as tide of cyber-skepticism sweeps US." *The Guardian.* 22 January 2011. Web. 10 February 2012.

John, Tracey. "New social network connects cancer survivors, patients, and supporters." *Forbes.* 25 August 2011. Web. 12 February 2012.

Shariatmadari, David. "Pope Benedict praises Twitter-like forms of communication." *The Guardian.* 24 January 2012. Web. 12 February 2012.

Moving from Sketch to Draft

A sketch is a useful starting point for an argument essay in any form because it helps you to focus your thinking on what you discovered. A successful sketch points the way to the next draft. But how can you get your sketch to point the way, particularly for an essay that makes an argument? One of the most useful things you can ask yourself about your sketch is this: *What is the balance between explaining what I think and presenting evidence to support it?* If your sketch is mostly what writing expert Ken Macrorie once called "explainery," then the most important thing you might do is refocus on research. Gather more information on your topic. Test your ideas against your current opinions.

Evaluating Your Own Sketch. There are some other, more specific ways of evaluating your sketch. For example, answering these questions should give you some guidance:

- **Is the question you started with narrow enough?** Does it use specific terms rather than general terms ("society," "people," etc.)? When you did some research, were you either overwhelmed with information or unsure of where to look? If you conclude that your question still isn't focused enough, try "Kitchen Knives of Thought," earlier in this chapter.

- **Does the sketch point to a S.O.F.T.?** What seems to be the main claim you're making based on the evidence you've gathered so far?

- **Is that claim linked to one or more reasons?** Remember that claims are built on reasons (e.g., Twitter played a key factor in the success of Egypt's "Arab spring" *because* the regime couldn't control it.).

Reflecting on What You've Learned. Based on your experience so far with developing an argument essay, make an entry in your journal that explores the following questions:

- What's the difference between a fact and an opinion? Between a claim and an opinion?

- Consider what you've always thought about making arguments. How has that changed since you started working on this project?

Developing

7.4
Develop a question that is focused enough to lead to a strong claim and convincing evidence.

Writing for Your Readers. You've read and written about an issue you care about. Now for the really hard part: getting out of your own head and into the heads of your potential readers, who may not care as much as you do. At least not yet. Successful persuasion fundamentally depends on giving an audience the right reasons to agree with you, and these are likely both logical and emotional, involving both logos and pathos, as you learned earlier in this chapter.

Another element of argument is the way the writer comes across to readers—his or her ethos. In the writing you've done so far on your topic, how do you think you might come off to an audience? Is your tone appealing, or might it be slightly off-putting? Do you successfully establish your authority to speak on this issue, or is the persona you project in the sketch somehow unconvincing, perhaps too emotional or not fair enough?

As we develop convictions about an issue, one of the hardest things to manage in early argument drafts is creating a persuasive persona (ethos). Another is finding ways to establish connections with our audience; this does not merely involve connecting writer and readers, but also includes creating some common ground between readers and *the topic*. There are many ways to do this, including the following:

1. Connecting your readers' prior beliefs or values with your position on the topic.

2. Establishing that readers have a *stake*, perhaps even a personal one, in how the question you've raised is answered; this may be self-interest, but it may also be emotional (remember the advertiser's strategy).

3. Highlighting the common experiences readers may have had with the topic and offering your claim as a useful way of understanding that experience.

4. Being reasonable. Do you devote time to looking at other points of views that you may not share?

Researching the Argument. The key to developing your draft is research. Though you might be able to use some of the information you gathered for your sketch, chances are that your focus or claims are shifting as you learn more. That means going back to the research well. In particular, you need enough information on the following:

- Evidence that supports your claims. Not just anything will do. Which evidence is most *persuasive*? You may have to look hard for this.

- Counterarguments from sources that take a view different from yours.

- Background information that establishes the *context* of the issue you're writing about. What's the debate? Who's involved? How long has this been going on? Why does it matter?

More Looking in the Library. One of the most useful things you can do to prepare for the draft is to spend forty-five minutes at the campus library searching for new information on your topic. Consider expanding your search from current newspapers and periodicals to books or government publications (see Chapter 11 for more information about searching for all kinds of sources, including government documents). In addition, you can refer to online almanacs such as Infoplease and the CIA's online World Factbook (http://www.odci.gov/cia/publications/factbook/), as well as statistical information available from sources such as the U.S. Census Bureau's American Fact Finder (http://factfinder.census.gov/home/saff/main.html?_lang=en), which is a wonderful resource that draws on the Bureau's massive database of information on U.S. trends.

Face-to-Face Interviewing. Try some interviews if you haven't already. People who are somehow involved in your topic are among the best sources of new information and lively material. An interview can provide ideas about what else you should read or who else you might talk to, as well as the quotations, anecdotes, and case studies that can make the next draft of your argument essay much more interesting. After all, what makes an issue matter is how it affects people. Have you sufficiently dramatized those effects? For more information on face-to-face interviewing, see Chapter 4, "Writing a Profile," as well as Chapter 11, "Research Techniques."

Using the Web to Obtain Interviews and Quotes. The Internet can also be a source for interview material. Look for e-mail links to the authors of useful documents you find on the web and write to them with a few questions. Interest groups, newsgroups, or electronic mailing lists on the web can also provide the voices and perspectives of people with something to say on your topic. Remember to ask permission to quote them if you decide to use something of theirs in your draft. For leads on finding web discussion groups on your topic, visit the following sites:

- **Google Groups**, allows you to search for online discussion groups on virtually any topic.

- **Yahoo Groups** offers a similar service, allowing you to search for groups by keyword.

- **Catalist**, the official catalog of electronic mailing lists, has a database of about 15,000 discussion groups.

Finding Images. When appropriate, look for images to dramatize your claims or your evidence. Images are easy to find using search engines such as Google Image Search. But any images you use must be specifically relevant to your argument. If you do use online images in your essay make sure to give the source credit in the text and the bibliography.

Drafting

Designing Your Argument Rhetorically. The argument essay is one of those forms of writing that is plagued by organizing formulas. The claim must go in the first paragraph. The reasons behind the claims should be topic sentences, followed by evidence. The conclusion should restate the claim. Take a look at any published arguments and you'll see how far these formulas are from the way they're actually written. For example, take a look again at Edward Tufte's "PowerPoint Is Evil" on page 250. The claim happens to be in the first paragraph, but it's pretty indirect:

> *Imagine a widely used and expensive prescription drug that promised to make us beautiful but didn't. Instead the drug had frequent, serious side effects: It induced stupidity, turned everyone into bores, wasted time, and degraded the quality and credibility of communication. These side effects would rightly lead to a worldwide product recall.*

Tufte's lead paragraph doesn't say, "This essay will argue that PowerPoint is evil." It doesn't need to.

On the other hand, arguments do typically have the features that we've discussed: a question, a claim that addresses it, reasons, evidence, counterclaims. Just don't ever imagine that you march through these things in some strict order. You need to decide the design of your argument. And what will help you most in doing this is thinking about audience, especially:

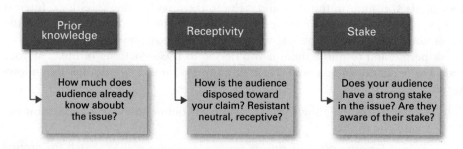

This rhetorical awareness of your audience has implications for what information you include—and especially what you emphasize—in your draft:

- **Prior knowledge.** If your audience knows little about your topic, then you'll spend more time with background and context than you might if they largely understand the issue.

- **Receptivity.** Audiences that are already inclined to strongly agree are less critical. They probably need less evidence to be convinced of your position than neutral readers do. A resistant audience is the toughest sell: Strong evidence, and lots of it, is key.

- **Stake.** Neutral audiences—the kind you're most likely to encounter—have little awareness that your topic matters to them. You have to make it matter, and make it matter quickly.

Methods of Development. While there is no formula for organizing an argument, there are some ways of developing parts—and sometimes all—of your essay.

Narrative. Telling a story is an underrated way of developing an argument. Can you imagine a way to present your topic in an extended story, perhaps by focusing on the experience of a particular person or group of people, in a particular place, at a particular time? Obviously, the story must somehow be logically linked to your claim.

There are other ways to use narrative, too. Anecdotes, or brief stories that illustrate an idea or a problem, are frequently used in argument essays. One effective way to begin your essay might be to tell a story that highlights the problem you're writing about or the question you're posing.

Question to Answer. Almost all writing is an attempt to answer a question. In the personal essay and other open forms of inquiry, the writer may never arrive at a definite answer, but an argument essay usually offers an answer. An obvious method of development, therefore, is to begin your essay by raising the question and end it by offering your answer.

Are there several key questions around which you might organize your draft, leading to your central claim at the end?

Problem to Solution. This variation on the question-to-answer structure can be particularly useful if you're writing on a topic readers may know very little about. In such cases, you might need to spend as much time establishing what exactly the problem is—explaining what makes it a problem and why the reader should care about it—as you do offering your particular solution.

Effect to Cause or Cause to Effect. At the heart of some arguments is the *relationship* between causes and effects; often what is at issue is pinpointing such a relationship. Once a relationship is pinpointed, solutions can be offered. Sadly, we know the effects of terrorism, but what are its causes? If you were to argue, as some do, that Islamic radicalism arose in response to U.S. policies in the Middle East, including its policies toward Israel and the Palestinians, then you would be arguing from effect to cause. As the solution, you might go on to propose a shift in foreign policy. Some arguments can be organized simply around an examination of causes and effects.

Combining Approaches. As you think about how you might organize your first draft, you don't necessarily have to choose between these various methods of development. In fact, most often they work well together.

Inquiring into the Details

What Evidence Can Do

Usually we think of using evidence only to support an idea or claim we're making. But evidence can be used in other ways, too. For example, it can do the following:

- *support* an idea, observation, or assertion
- *refute* or challenge a claim with which you disagree
- *show* that a seemingly simple assertion, problem, or idea is really more complex
- *complicate* or even contradict an earlier point you've made
- *contrast* two or more ways of seeing the same thing
- *test* an idea, hypothesis, or theory

Using Evidence. All writing relies on evidence—that is, on specific information that has some relationship to general ideas expressed. For some of these relationships, see "Inquiring into the Details: What Evidence Can Do." Although all these relationships are possible in an argumentative essay, especially common is the use of evidence to support ideas the writer wants the reader to believe. What *kind* of evidence to include is a rhetorical issue. To whom are you writing, and what kind of evidence will they be more likely to believe?

Generally speaking, the narrower and more specialized the audience, the more particular they will be about the types of evidence they'll find convincing. As you continue on in your chosen major, you'll find that the types of evidence that help you make a persuasive argument will be more and more prescribed by the field. In the natural sciences, the results of quantitative studies count more than case studies; in the humanities, primary texts count more than secondary ones.

The important thing for this argument essay, which you're writing for a more general audience, is that you attempt to *vary* your evidence. For example, rather than relying exclusively on anecdotes, include some quotes from an expert as well.

Workshopping

If your draft is subject to peer review, see Chapter 14 for details on how to organize workshop groups and decide on how your group can help you. To help you decide, use the guidance, starting on p. 578, in Chapter 14. Each workshop type is described more fully in that chapter.

Workshops on argument drafts can be lively affairs. People have opinions, and other people may disagree with them. Facts can be contested with counterfacts. As you prepare to share your draft, I'd encourage you to ask peers to speak to two separate issues:

1. Do you agree with my argument? What are your feelings about it?
2. No matter what your disposition is toward the argument in my draft, can you help me make it better?

Both discussions are important. But it may be hard to get to the second discussion if your workshop group is consumed by a debate over the issue itself.

As always, focus your peer review on the central concerns of a first draft: purpose and meaning. You can use the following grid.

Questions for Peer Reviewers	
Purpose	What is the question driving my argument? At what point in the draft do you first understand the question? Is that early enough?
Meaning	Do you understand the claim I'm making? Are the reasons I'm taking this position clear? Which do you find most convincing? Least convincing?

Reflecting on the Draft. After having spent time choosing an argument topic and developing and drafting your argument, what do you now understand about making effective arguments that you didn't when you started? If you were to make a single PowerPoint slide explaining that, what would it say?

Revising

Revision is a continual process—not a last step. You've been revising—"reseeing" your subject—from the first messy fastwriting in your journal. But the things that get your attention vary depending on where you are in the writing process. With your draft in hand, revision becomes your focus through what I'll call "shaping and tightening your draft."

7.5
Use audience analysis and logical methods to help guide revision of an argument.

Chapter 13 contains strategies that can help you revise any inquiry project, and the "Guide to Revision Strategies" on page 278 can help you locate these strategies. There are also certain things to think about that are especially useful for shaping an argument.

Shaping. In your draft, you made a tentative commitment to your topic, hoping that you could shape it into something that might have meaning for someone other than you. Fundamentally, you've been trying to figure out *what you're trying to say* and then rebuild your essay so that this is both clear and convincing. In an argument essay, you also want it to be convincing.

Shaping focuses first on the largest concerns of purpose and meaning—which you've already looked at if you workshopped your draft—and on the next-to-largest concerns of information and organization. It starts with knowing what your essay is about—your inquiry question and maybe your claim—and then revising to make every element of the draft focused on that question or assertion.

This chapter includes some useful tools that should help you shape the next draft, and in particular examine your reasoning strategies.

1. **Toulmin.** A helpful technique for revising the first draft of your argument essay is to use a method of analyzing argumentative reasoning, such as Toulminian or Rogerian logic. In an earlier exercise in this chapter, you may have experimented with a small element of Rogers' approach. Toulmin might be especially helpful for analyzing your draft. See "Inquiring into the Details: Toulmin: A Method for Analyzing an Argument," to see how you might apply his method.

2. **Logical fallacies.** Did you get yourself on any slippery slopes or beg a question? Find out by looking at the list in "Inquiring into the Details: Common Logical Fallacies," page 244.

3. **Rhetorical triangle.** We've talked about Aristotle's elements of persuasion: ethos, pathos, and logos (see Figure 7.1 and Figure 7.2). Is there an effective emphasis on each of these in your draft, and have you used them in proportions appropriate to your topic and audience?

Inquiring into the Details

Toulmin: A Method for Analyzing an Argument

Stephen Toulmin, an English philosopher, argued that arguments about any subject have features that include:

- claims
- evidence
- warrants
- backing

In an argument, the *claims* are supported by *evidence* (examples, observations, statistics, etc.). The most penetrating aspect of Toulmin's approach is the idea that claims and evidence are linked together by *warrants*—or assumptions about the way things are. In the example I gave on page 256, if the claim *Michelle must have a lot of money* is based on the evidence of the half-dozen credit cards in her purse, the person making the claim assumes there's a correlation between the number of credit cards one has and wealth. That's a warrant. To believe the claim based on this evidence, you would have to also believe the assumption. Essentially, then, a warrant is the answer to the question *What do you need to believe is true in order to accept the validity of a claim based on evidence?*

Inquiring into the Details (*continued*)

To see how this might work, consider how it applies to the letter to the editor on page 242. Let's find the implicit claim, the evidence, and then the warrants linking the two.

Claim: In times of war, artists, especially those who have never served, should not create art that is unpatriotic.

Evidence: Art pieces at an exhibition that showed General Petraeus with a skull superimposed on his face, a photograph of a man with a noose made from an American flag. These images, made by artists who had never been to war, were exhibited when servicepeople were deployed in battle overseas. The writer of the letter, a veteran, was deeply offended.

Warrant 1: During wartime, Americans should temper their criticism of the military.

Warrant 2: Those who haven't seen military service don't fully appreciate the costs associated with protecting freedom.

Warrant 3: Art can have the quality of being unpatriotic.

The strongest arguments provide "backing"—or factual support for some or all of the warrants in an argument. The first challenge, of course, is identifying the warrants in an argument. Then you can look for evidence to substantiate them if you believe they make sense.

Toulmin's approach might be visualized this way:

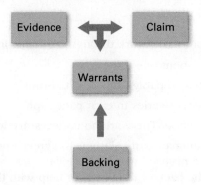

To analyze an argument using Toulmin's method, search for the often implied warrants in the text, beginning with this question: *What are the assumptions about what is true that I must agree with to buy the argument?*

Polishing. When you are satisfied with the shape of your draft, focus on paragraphs, sentences, and words. Are your paragraphs coherent? How do you manage transitions? Are your sentences fluent and concise? Are there any errors in spelling or syntax? The section of Chapter 13 called "Problems with Clarity and Style" can help you focus on these issues.

Guide to Revision Strategies

Problems in the Draft (Chapter 13)	Page Number
Unclear purpose	538
■ Not sure what the paper is about?	
Unclear thesis, theme, or main idea	543
■ Not sure what you're trying to say?	
Lack of information or development	551
■ Need more convincing evidence? Need to check for logical fallacies?	
Disorganized	555
■ Doesn't move logically or smoothly from paragraph to paragraph?	
Unclear or awkward at the level of sentences and paragraphs	564
■ Seems choppy or hard to follow at the level of sentences or paragraphs?	

Before you finish your draft, work through the following checklist:

✓ Every paragraph is about one thing.

✓ The transitions between paragraphs aren't abrupt.

✓ The length of sentences varies in each paragraph.

✓ Each sentence is concise. There are no unnecessary words or phrases.

✓ You've checked grammar, particularly verb agreement, run-on sentences, unclear pronouns, and misused words (*there/their, where/were*, and so on). (See the Handbook at the back of the book for help with these grammar issues.)

✓ You've run your spellchecker and proofed your paper for misspelled words.

▶ Student Essay

One of the things I really like about Rebecca Thompson's essay, "SocialNetworking SocialGood?" is that she readily concedes that there are downsides to social networking even though she's a fan of it. Rebecca could have quickly nodded to critics of her position in a sentence or two. But instead she explores the case against social media in some detail, quoting extensively from people who worry that they undermine conversations and personal relationships. Rebecca agrees with some of this. But she argues that, overall, media such as Facebook and Twitter have made her life better. Acknowledging opposing viewpoints is an important move in argumentative essay. But taking them seriously is rare. Because Rebecca recognizes the complexity of her topic, and tries to deal with it in her essay, the claim she does make seems more persuasive.

Social Networking Social Good?

Rebecca Thompson

Facebook Chat. iPhone texting. Checking in on FourSquare. Twitter hashtags. Tumblr blogging. OkCupid matchmaking. These days, there's no limit to the ways we can talk to each other. Suddenly, the basic human foundation of communication—talking and listening—has become much more complicated. It's incontrovertible that our society has changed in response to technological and media advancements. The day-to-day functions of our lives are different than they were even five years ago. We read differently (on Kindle or Nook), we watch differently (on Netflix, Hulu, or OnDemand), we hear differently (earbuds and surround sound), we even learn differently (smart boards, smart phones, Google). Despite the major advancements in rapid response, worldwide networking, as well as major shifts in the arts and sciences, many are concerned that there are major downfalls to the way that we, as a society, have begun to use social networking and media devices. Yet overall the explosion of social networking has provided unforeseen benefits, too. We can now find comfort in the company of strangers, erase the distance between far-flung friends, and most important, participate in conversations that spread new knowledge.

I use social media, like e-mail, Facebook, Twitter, and Wordpress, in all areas of my life, from connecting with high school friends now scattered across the country, to networking and advertising projects I'm involved in, to keeping updated on news stories. When Hurricane Irene struck the East Coast, I was out of town. I kept tabs on my friends via Facebook, and followed the news stories by following the hashtag #HurricaneIrene on Twitter. It was a relief to be connected, even from far away. Similarly, following the devastating tornado in Missouri in May 2011, so-called "small-media efforts" (such as Facebook, local radio, and Twitter) were the ones that led most mainstream media to the scene. Facebook groups formed instantaneously and expanded exponentially, featuring posts from families searching for survivors as well as complete strangers offering prayers and support. As one poster wrote, "On one hand, my heart is just aching for your loss and devastation...[O]n the other hand, seeing everyone pulling together reminds me how resilient the human spirit is." (Mustich)

In instances of catastrophe like Hurricane Irene and the tornados in the Midwest, social networking is put to effective use in networking relief efforts, gathering and spreading crucial information, and sharing messages of support. Few would argue the positive effects of these technological advances. However, social media also functions on a more personal level, connecting people on a one-on-one basis, often inviting them into the most clandestine parts of their lives. "At its core, it is about connections and community," said Mailet Lopez, the founder of the networking site I Had Cancer, to *Forbes* magazine. "Social networking provides an

(continued)

(continued)

opportunity beyond physical support networks and online forums...because with a social network, people can connect based on whatever criteria they want, regardless of location" (Tracey).

4   Thousands of anonymous viewers can read about the inner workings of thousands of other social media users, following their Twitter, subscribing to their blogs, mapping their location on FourSquare. This is a new phenomenon, thanks to the rapid developments in speed and accessibility in the technology, and is often cited as a cause of heightened disconnectivity and impersonality in human relationships. For some, though, social networking's seemingly impersonal associations actually provide great personal comfort. During the time her husband suffered from debilitating cancer and treatment, writer Lee Ann Cox chronicled her struggles on Twitter, her own "defiant cry to be seen, to testify, bearing witness to suffering in 140 characters or less." Cox tweeted about the mundane, the terror, and the absurdities of handling her husband's condition, and though she had followers, the simple act of tweeting in and of itself was her therapy. "Maybe I did get something I needed from Twitter," she writes. "With no one's permission, I gave myself a voice...I needed to say these things and imagine some heart in the Twittersphere absorbing my crazed reality" (Cox).

5   Social media critics see the downside of Cox's experience, arguing that rather than encouraging communication and interpersonal relationships, it diminishes them. These critics worry that social media deconstructs traditional methods of conversation and undermines interpersonal relationships. I have certainly sat in a room with four of my friends, all of us checking our iPhones and laptops, barely speaking. I've had more communication with some people on Facebook than I have with them in real life. I'm sure that the authors of certain blogs I follow have more "blog friends" than real friends. Certainly, this kind of distance makes communication easier. If there's an awkward pause in a conversation, pull out your phone. If you're too shy to actually talk to a boy you're interested in, poke him on Facebook. The risk that online conversations might impoverish actual conversations is real. However, as Susan Greenfield, director of the Royal Institution of Great Britain, put it

> Real conversation in real time may eventually give way to these sanitized and easier screen dialogues, in much the same way as killing, skinning and butchering an animal to eat has been replaced by the convenience of packages of meat on the supermarket shelf. Perhaps future generations will recoil with similar horror at the messiness, unpredictability and immediate personal involvement of a three-dimensional, real-time interaction. (qtd. in Mackey)

6   Greenfield's gruesome image exemplifies the lowered stakes of communication, and therefore, repercussions, online. In 2011, the *Oxford English Dictionary* put the term "cyberbullying" into its lexicons. With increasing anonymity, access to personal information, and expanded public forums, social media has opened the door to new forms of cruelty—and not just for kids. Take the Dharun Ravi case. He used his webcam to tape his college roommate Tyler Clementi in a homosexual encounter with another student, and then shared it online with his friends. Clementi subsequently committed suicide. The case is unusual because it was based primarily on records of online interaction. Both the prosecution and defense used mountains of electronic evidence, including numerous tweets

(some of which were tampered with), Facebook posts (including Clementi's final status update), text messages, screenshots, e-mails, and web chats. The sheer volume of evidence on social networking tools is beyond the scope of any other major bullying case in recent history. In many ways, this is a boon to the judicial process, as records of the students' online interactions are prime evidence for both the prosecution and defense. On the other hand, it is disturbing to note how the deteriorated relationship between these two boys "played out on social media with curiously few face-to-face exchanges" (Clayton).

Ravi's ability to quickly disperse the contraband video highlights is another inherent problem in social media. In mere seconds, an online post can be captured, saved, reposted, and shared. While a great boon for marketing and the quick dissemination of crucial information (such as in the case of a major natural disaster or a political event), there exists no system to judge the veracity and reliability of viral posts. The most viral video of all time is a 30-minute documentary made by the organization Invisible Children about Ugandan leader Joseph Kony, which received over 100 million hits in under a week when it was first posted in March 2012. However, after that first week had passed and certain critics began to look deeper, deep flaws in the message of the video emerged. "To call [Kony2012's] campaign a misrepresentation is an understatement," writes Angelo Izama, quoted in Time's "Global Spin" blog (Ishaan). The organization itself, Invisible Children, is under fire for its practices as an NGO. Most concerning to critics, though, is the extreme simplification and digestibility of the message itself. In this telling, to simply "know" about Kony...would be enough to bring him down," writes Ishaan Tharoor in "Global Spin." "That quest takes place in a world of moral simplicity, of good and evil, of innocence and horror...justice is about much more than manhunts and viral video crusades" (Ishaan).

I recall seeing the Kony post on Facebook, and watched a few minutes before closing it down. I almost reposted, but then figured I should perhaps watch the whole 30 minutes before showing my support to my friends and followers. Upon reading the criticism of the documentary, now nearly as viral as the video itself, it seems to me that knowledge has been disseminated, albeit in a non-traditional way. Social networking allows for great diversity of opinion, and also opens the door to conversation. "Knowledge consists of a network of people and ideas that are not totally in sync, that are diverse, that disagree," states David Weinberger in an interview with Salon's Thomas Rogers. "Books generally have value because they encapsulate some topic and provide you with everything you know, because when you're reading it you cannot easily leap out of the book to get to the next book. The Web only has value because it contains difference" (Rogers).

Weinberger elucidates precisely the problems with, and the importance of, social media and the way knowledge is shared. It has inherently changed our tools of communication and of functioning in modern society—we can't go back now. "Ask anybody who is in any of the traditional knowledge fields," states Weinberger.

> She or he will very likely tell you that the Internet has made them smarter. They couldn't do their work without it; they're doing it better than ever before, they know more; they can find more; they can run down dead ends faster than ever before...Now we have a medium that is as broad as our curiosity. (qtd. in Rogers)

(continued)

(continued)

10   I agree that social networking tools have the potential, if used to their best advantage, to facilitate communication, networking, and the spread of knowledge. It's made
functioning on a day-to-day basis much easier. Because I can respond to emails and texts
on the go, I can plan ahead. I can keep in touch with my friends studying abroad when
phones aren't an option. I get lost a lot less. Even the Pope has spoken of the benefits of
the Internet, social networking, and media. "Search engines and social networks have become the starting point of communication for many people who are seeking advice, ideas,
information and answers," he said. "In our time, the Internet is becoming ever more a
forum for questions and answers...In concise phrases, often no longer than a verse from
the Bible, profound thoughts can be communicated" (Shariatmadari).

Works Cited

Clayton, Mark. "Rutgers Spycam Case: Why It's Not Open and Shut." *Christian Science
    Monitor.* 22 February 2012. Web. 15 March 2012.

Cox, Lee Ann. "Losing My Husband, 140 Characters at a Time." *Salon.* 24 January 2012.
    Web. 12 March 2012.

Harris, Paul. "Social Networking Under Fresh Attack as Tide of Cyber-skepticism Sweeps
    US." *The Guardian.* 22 January 2011. Web. 12 March 2012.

John, Tracey. "New Social Network Connects Cancer Survivors, Patients, and Supporters."
    Forbes. 25 August 2011. Web. 15 March 2012.

Mackey, Robert. "Is Social Networking Killing You?" The Lede Blog: *New York Times.*
    24 February 2009. Web. 12 March 2012.

Mustich, Emma. "Joplin rescue efforts HQ: Facebook." *Salon.* 23 May 2011. Web.
    18 March 2012.

Rogers, Thomas. "Are We on Information Overload?" *Salon.* 1 January 2012. Web.
    14 March 2012.

Shariatmadari, David. "Pope Benedict Praises Twitter-like Forms of Communication."
    The Guardian. 24 January 2012. Web. 14 March 2012.

Tharoor, Ishaan. "Why You Should Feel Awkward About the 'Kony2012' Video." *Time.*
    8 March 2012. Web. 14 March 2012.

Evaluating the Essay

1. Rebecca claims that, overall, social media offers "comfort," eliminates "the
    distance between far-flung friends," and contributes to the creation of "new
    knowledge." Do you agree?

2. Use the rhetorical concepts of ethos, pathos, and logos to analyze the ef-
    fectiveness of the essay. If the claim is that social networking, despite its
    potential shortcomings, is beneficial, then what are the reasons Rebecca
    uses to support the claim? Which do you find most convincing? Least
    convincing?

Using What You Have Learned

Let's return to the learning objectives I outlined in the beginning of the chapter.

1. **Identify the key elements of argument—reasons, claims, and evidence— and apply them in both reading and writing.** The next time you listen to a friend argue that Boise State's football team isn't a BCS-worthy team, or that general education classes are a waste of time, or that the foreign aid budget is bankrupting the country, you'll have some tools with which to respond. Making and recognizing a claim in an argument isn't hard. But most of us aren't so good at crafting reasons for what we believe and using evidence to make them persuasive. You will find this understanding powerful, not just in school where you make arguments all the time, but in life, too, where we also make arguments all the time.

2. **Understand how ethos, pathos, and logos combine in persuasion.** These three concepts, borrowed from Aristotle, are fundamental to rhetorical analysis and can help you to not only evaluate your own arguments, but also analyze the arguments of others in all kinds of situations. Whenever you're assigned an argument in a college class, or express your opinion in a blog or other public form of argument, always ask yourself: How do I make myself credible to speak on this topic (ethos), do I use emotional appeals effectively (pathos), and is my reasoning sound (logos)? Remember that the answer to each of these questions depends on the situation and especially your audience.

3. **Use invention strategies appropriate to argument to discover and develop a topic.** As the writing assignments have moved from forms such as the personal essay that rely heavily on memory, experience, and observation to forms such as argument that rely especially on research, I hope that you see how invention strategies such as fastwriting can help you explore topics outside yourself. In this chapter, for example, you generated ideas from some random facts. These were starting points for generating ideas, not simply fodder for supporting an opinion. Approached openly, information is a source of discovery.

4. **Develop a question that is focused enough to lead to a strong claim and convincing evidence.** This is a consistent theme in *The Curious Writer.* Inquiry begins with questions. But not just any questions. You've learned that different kinds of questions spark different kinds of arguments. For instance, *What should be done?* might lead to a proposal. In this chapter, you've worked to narrow a question that would lead to claims of fact. The skills that you developed here of narrowing that question are essential in any research-based project, as you'll see if you tackle the ethnography and research essay later in the book.

5. **Use audience analysis and logical methods to help guide revision of an argument.** Argument is among the most audience-focused forms, and the kind of rhetorical analysis you did here as you revised your draft should prove invaluable whenever persuasion is a motive. If you found Toulmin's methods of analyzing your argument helpful, then you should look more closely at the abundant examples of applying Toulmin scattered across the web, because my treatment of his approach here was necessarily limited.

Complete
Additional Exercises
and Practice on
Chapter 7
in your MyLab

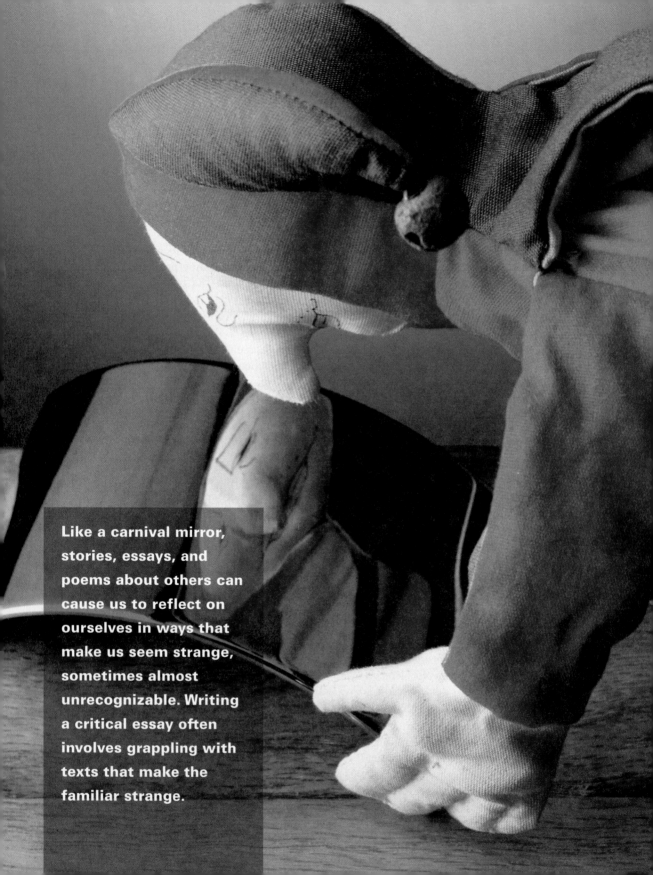

Like a carnival mirror, stories, essays, and poems about others can cause us to reflect on ourselves in ways that make us seem strange, sometimes almost unrecognizable. Writing a critical essay often involves grappling with texts that make the familiar strange.

Writing a Critical Essay

Learning Objectives

In this chapter, you'll learn to

8.1 Apply the methods of critical analysis not only to literature but anything whose meanings aren't apparent.

8.2 Use evidence from primary sources to argue effectively for a convincing interpretation.

8.3 Use appropriate invention strategies to discover a topic for a critical essay.

8.4 Apply revision strategies that are effective for the critical essay.

Writing About Literature

One of the world's shortest short stories was reputedly written by Ernest Hemingway in a wager: "For Sale: Baby Shoes. Never worn." While the origin of this six-word short story is disputed, it does point to a quality that much literature shares: It says more than it says. Taken literally, this is simply a classified ad for some never-used baby shoes. Yet it implies so much more. Beneath the fairly mundane facts is the echo of sudden loss. A baby has died before he or she had the chance to wear new shoes, and the parents, somewhat curiously, choose to sell them for what will likely be a pittance. Why would they do that? Who is this baby? Who are these parents? What happened?

Six words trigger a cascade of questions about what might be *inferred* from the literal facts, all seeding the larger inquiry question that is behind any act of interpretation: *What might it mean?*

What might it mean? is the kind of question we ask about things with ambiguous meanings—a painting, a film, a short story, a sculpture—but we might also ask it about a social interaction ("Why did he make that face when I said that?") or a cultural ritual. When we attempt to interpret something, we sense that there is more going on than meets the eye. An explanation of the literal facts—there are never-used baby shoes for sale— doesn't do justice to the thing we're looking at. What else is going on here? What is being implied, intentionally or unintentionally?

Here's something I hear nearly every semester: "Why do we have to analyze literature to death? Isn't it enough that it's just a good story?" I actually sympathize with this frustration. It *is* enough sometimes to simply indulge in the pleasure of a well-told story or a beautifully written essay. But reading a good story or essay and refusing the invitation to look underneath is like someone fond of fast cars failing to pop the hood. You can admire the beauty of a Porsche or Alpha from afar, but to really appreciate it fully you should look at what powers the thing.

We interpret literature, film, or art not because we're supposed to, but because it makes our encounter with those things richer and more pleasurable. Yet even if you never take another English course or read a short story, it's impossible to live life without asking, "What might it mean?" We interpret things all the time, and in this chapter, you'll learn some methods for doing it.

Motives for Writing a Critical Essay

8.1

Apply the methods of critical analysis not only to literature but anything whose meanings aren't apparent.

A critical essay makes an argument for a certain interpretation of something. Typically, we think of critical essays as a genre of the literature class, but it just as easily could be used in any writing situation that asks you to look closely at something—a photograph, a political strategy, or even animal behavior—and draw some conclusions about what it means. As I mentioned before, we do this informally all the time. A few days ago, my dog Ada, who is laying under my desk as I write this, suddenly refused to come back in the dog door. Going out was no problem. I watched her wrestle with the door, tentatively approaching and poking the plastic curtain, backing off and then trying again. It made no sense. What does this mean? She's suddenly neurotic? Something scared her? I can't ask the dog, so I may never know the real answer. But the situation called for interpretation: observing her behavior and speculating on its meaning. This is what humans do as we try to make sense of the things around us. The critical essay is a form for reporting such speculations.

The process of critical analysis looks something like Figure 8.1. We direct our gaze to a subject—say, a short story or film—and pay close attention to the particulars as we wonder *What might it mean?* Then, drawing on the evidence, we speculate, working towards an argument that our interpretation is a convincing one. This process, at least initially, is largely *inductive*. We work from the specifics to the general. In writing about literature, this means that we first look very closely at specifics in the work: certain words, lines, passages, scenes, characters, conflicts, and so on. Then we do what we always do in inquiry-based investigations: look for patterns.

To fully appreciate what authors are saying or what effects they're trying to create in an essay, poem, or story, you often need to look closely, and in doing so, you see beyond the obvious.

Recognizing patterns in literary texts (or anything we're not familiar with) is hard. But one of the things that helps enormously are theories about what to look for. Some of these that you're probably most familiar with from English classes suggest categories of things you might analyze: characters, theme, motifs, conflict, structure, language, etc. (See "Inquiring into the Details: Common Literary Devices" on p. 320). Other theories work from

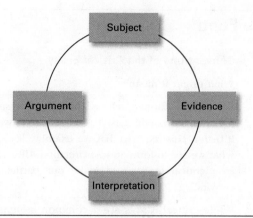

Figure 8.1 Critical analysis involves making inferences about the significance of something by examining it closely—a text, a painting, experimental data—and then enlisting the evidence to argue for a particular interpretation.

premises that might change your gaze altogether. For example, so-called feminist criticism encourages readers to see how gender operates in a story. What are the relations between men and women? How does each exercise authority? Later in this chapter, we'll look at a few of these (see "Inquiring into the Details: Why Literary Theory Is Not a Sleep Aid" on p. 309).

The Critical Essay and Academic Writing

Virtually all academic work—and much of daily life, for that matter—involves looking for patterns in an effort to make sense of things. One way to look for some of these patterns is to ask the interpretation question behind the critical essay: *What might it mean?* In virtually every class you take in college, interpreting from data is central. What differs from course to course is the source of this data. In English, for example, you'll often be drawing evidence from texts. In anthropology, you might observe social behavior and rituals in the field. In physics, you analyze experimental data.

> Critical essays are built around a main idea, claim, or interpretation you are making about a text.

While the term "critical essay" is most often used in literary studies, whenever you're asked to interpret or speculate from evidence, you are doing critical analysis. For example, if you write about an experiment you've conducted in biology, a section called "Discussion of Results" is critical analysis. What differs between the disciplines, obviously, are the theories that help you do this interpreting. A scientist might use statistical theories to interpret data. An anthropologist might use theories related to cultural ecology. For many of these disciplines, no matter what the theories that inform it, critical analysis is in the service of an argument that answers the question *What does this mean?*

8.2
Use evidence from primary sources to argue effectively for a convincing interpretation.

Features of the Form

Feature	Conventions of the Critical Essay
Inquiry question	What might it mean?
Motives	We turn to forms such as the critical essay whenever the meaning of something isn't obvious and we want to understand it better. This requires that we examine it more closely, using what we see to form an interpretation. Ultimately, the purpose in a critical essay is to make our particular interpretation convincing.
Subject matter	While critical essays are a common assignment in English, focusing on literary texts, they also might explore film, art, popular culture, or any subject matter whose meanings are uncertain.
Structure	There are three elements in most critical essays: 1. Review of what others have said about the thing being analyzed. What is the current conversation about it among other critics? 2. References to *specific* features of the object being analyzed (e.g. passages, language, images, etc.) that informed the interpretation. 3. Background summary for an audience not familiar with the story, poem, painting, etc., that is being analyzed.
Sources of information	This depends on what's being analyzed. An interpretation of a story, for example, would draw evidence from the story itself: lines, passages, scenes, characters. Critical essays, at least initially, are written *inductively*, through close analysis and observation of the object of study. This yields specific information that influences any interpretation. In addition, critical essays might include information from other critics or analysts who have contributed to the conversation about possible interpretations.
Language	The tone of a critical essay, as for most forms, depends on the audience. Formal essays, the kind assigned in literature classes, rarely use the first person, focusing readers' attention on the argument, not the writer. Less-formal response essays might use much more casual language.

Prose+

Charles Bukowski's touching poem "The Bluebird"—a meditation on how terrifying it can be to drop our masks and expose the face sweating beneath it—inspired a visual interpretation by the artist Monika Umba. This is one of four images that she created in response to the poem.

there's a bluebird in my heart that
wants to get out
but I'm too tough for him,
I say, stay in there, I'm not going
to let anybody see
you.
there's a bluebird in my heart that
wants to get out
but I pour whiskey on him and inhale
cigarette smoke
and the whores and the bartenders
and the grocery clerks
never know that
he's
in there.

there's a bluebird in my heart that
wants to get out
but I'm too tough for him,
I say,
stay down, do you want to mess
me up?
you want to screw up the
works?
you want to blow my book sales in
Europe?
there's a bluebird in my heart that
wants to get out
but I'm too clever, I only let him out
at night sometimes
when everybody's asleep.
I say, I know that you're there,
so don't be
sad.

then I put him back,
but he's singing a little
in there, I haven't quite let him
die
and we sleep together like
that
with our
secret pact
and it's nice enough to
make a man
weep, but I don't
weep, do
you?

Writing Beyond the Classroom

Book Groups

Here's an obscure writer's dream: She wrote a novel; let's call it *The Snowstorm in August*, which is published by an equally obscure publisher. Sales of the book are miniscule. But in this dream, Oprah appears, looking saintly, striding through a small bookstore, where she sees *The Snowstorm in August* on a remainder table. Oprah picks it up. She buys it. She makes it a selection for Oprah's Book Club. Our obscure writer is obscure no more.

While Oprah's Book Club is the largest and most influential of its kind, lovers of literature have plenty of other options for sharing their passion. Online book clubs are all over the Internet. Some focus on particular genres such as science fiction or biography, while others have more-general interests. Members not only get ideas for good reads, but also share their reviews and analyses of favorite books. Alternatively, there are book clubs meeting face-to-face in homes across America, including mine. Advice about how to organize these abound (just google "book clubs"). Major publishers also provide discussion guides for popular books in their lists, designed for these gatherings of friends.

Another variation of the book club is community-wide "read one book" programs, often sponsored by local libraries, which get everyone in town reading the same thing and gathering to discuss it. The Library of Congress's Center for the Book (http://www .loc.gov/loc/cfbook) has a state-by-state search engine for these programs.

READINGS

▶ Short Story 1

Watch
the Video on
**Reading a
Short Story**
in your MyLab

People love stories, and I think they always will. The oral tradition—someone tells a story to one or more listeners—was once a fundamental way to transfer knowledge about the world and how it worked. Then came writing. Now we compose stories in written prose, fixed on paper or a computer screen. There is no visible speaker, or particular occasion for the telling, and the story is static. It never changes. For Native American writers, such as Leslie Silko, who grew up in tribal communities where stories are still told orally, the two narrative traditions might seem to conflict. Instead, much contemporary Native American literature, while written, still preserves qualities and motives of speech.

Silko is widely recognized as one of the finest living Native American writers, and her novel *Ceremony*, published in 1977, received critical acclaim. She's also a talented poet and essayist. Above all, Leslie Marmon Silko is a storyteller in the Laguna tradition, using a kind of narrative that in many ways will be familiar to nonnative readers. There are characters and scenes and a significant event, but also notice how landscape figures into the telling of this story, and in particular what the narrator's relationship is with the natural world. One of the motives for telling a story like this is to deal with loss by seeking recovery through balance or harmony.

Lullaby
Leslie Marmon Silko

1   The sun had gone down but the snow in the wind gave off its own light. It came in thick tufts like new wool—washed before the weaver spins it. Ayah reached out for it like her own babies had, and she smiled when she remembered how she had laughed at them. She was an old woman now, and her life had become memories. She sat down with her back against the wide cottonwood tree, feeling the rough bark on her back bones; she faced east and listened to the wind and snow sing a high-pitched Yeibechei song. Out of the wind she felt warmer, and she could watch the wide fluffy snow fill in her tracks, steadily, until the direction she had come from was gone. By the light of the snow she could see the dark outline of the big arroyo a few feet away. She was sitting on the edge of Cebolleta Creek, where in the springtime the thin cows would graze on a grass already chewed flat to the ground. In the wide deep creek bed where only a trickle of water flowed in the summer, the skinny cows would wander, looking for new grass along winding paths splashed with manure.

2   Ayah pulled the old Army blanket over her head like a shawl. Jimmie's blanket—the one he had sent to her. That was a long time ago and the green wool was faded,

and it was unraveling on the edges. She did not want to think about Jimmie. So she thought about the weaving and the way her mother had done it. On the tall wooden loom set into the sand under a tamarack tree for shade. She could see it clearly. She had been only a little girl when her grandma gave her the wooden combs to pull the twigs and burrs from the raw, freshly washed wool. And while she combed the wool, her grandma sat beside her, spinning a silvery strand of yarn around the smooth cedar spindle. Her mother worked at the loom with yarns dyed bright yellow and red and gold. She watched them dye the yarn in boiling black pots full of beeweed petals, juniper berries, and sage. The blankets her mother made were soft and woven so tight that rain rolled off them like birds' feathers. Ayah remembered sleeping warm on cold windy nights, wrapped in her mother's blankets on the hogan's sandy floor.

The snow drifted now, with the northwest wind hurling it in gusts. It drifted up   3
around her black overshoes—old ones with little metal buckles. She smiled at the snow which was trying to cover her little by little. She could remember when they had no black rubber overshoes; only the high buckskin leggings that they wrapped over their elkhide moccasins. If the snow was dry or frozen, a person could walk all day and not get wet; and in the evenings the beams of the ceiling would hang with lengths of pale buckskin leggings, drying out slowly.

She felt peaceful remembering. She didn't feel cold any more. Jimmie's blanket   4
seemed warmer than it had ever been. And she could remember the morning he was born. She could remember whispering to her mother, who was sleeping on the other side of the hogan, to tell her it was time now. She did not want to wake the others. The second time she called to her, her mother stood up and pulled on her shoes; she knew. They walked to the old stone hogan together, Ayah walking a step behind her mother. She waited alone, learning the rhythms of the pains while her mother went to call the old woman to help them. The morning was already warm even before dawn and Ayah smelled the bee flowers blooming and the young willow growing at the springs. She could remember that so clearly, but his birth merged into the births of the other children and to her it became all the same birth. They named him for the summer morning and in English they called him Jimmie.

It wasn't like Jimmie died. He just never came back, and one day a dark blue se-   5
dan with white writing on its doors pulled up in front of the boxcar shack where the rancher let the Indians live. A man in a khaki uniform trimmed in gold gave them a yellow piece of paper and told them that Jimmie was dead. He said the Army would try to get the body back and then it would be shipped to them; but it wasn't likely because the helicopter had burned after it crashed. All of this was told to Chato because he could understand English. She stood inside the doorway holding the baby while Chato listened. Chato spoke English like a white man and he spoke Spanish too. He was taller than the white man and he stood straighter too. Chato didn't explain why; he just told the military man they could keep the body if they found it. The white man looked bewildered; he nodded his head and he left. Then Chato looked at her and shook his head, and then he told her, "Jimmie isn't coming home anymore," and

(continued)

(continued)

when he spoke, he used the words to speak of the dead. She didn't cry then, but she hurt inside with anger. And she mourned him as the years passed, when a horse fell with Chato and broke his leg, and the white rancher told them he wouldn't pay Chato until he could work again. She mourned Jimmie because he would have worked for his father then; he would have saddled the big bay horse and ridden the fence lines each day, with wire cutters and heavy gloves, fixing the breaks in the barbed wire and putting the stray cattle back inside again.

6   She mourned him after the white doctors came to take Danny and Ella away. She was at the shack alone that day they came. It was back in the days before they hired Navajo women to go with them as interpreters. She recognized one of the doctors. She had seen him at the children's clinic at Cañoncito about a month ago. They were wearing khaki uniforms and they waved papers at her and a black ball-point pen, trying to make her understand their English words. She was frightened by the way they looked at the children, like the lizard watches the fly. Danny was swinging on the tire swing on the elm tree behind the rancher's house, and Ella was toddling around the front door, dragging the broomstick horse Chato made for her. Ayah could see they wanted her to sign the papers, and Chato had taught her to sign her name. It was something she was proud of. She only wanted them to go, and to take their eyes away from her children.

7   She took the pen from the man without looking at his face and she signed the papers in three different places he pointed to. She stared at the ground by their feet and waited for them to leave. But they stood there and began to point and gesture at the children. Danny stopped swinging. Ayah could see his fear. She moved suddenly and grabbed Ella into her arms; the child squirmed, trying to get back to her toys. Ayah ran with the baby toward Danny; she screamed for him to run and then she grabbed him around his chest and carried him too. She ran south into the foothills of juniper trees and black lava rock. Behind her she heard the doctors running, but they had been taken by surprise, and as the hills became steeper and the cholla cactus were thicker, they stopped. When she reached the top of the hill, she stopped to listen in case they were circling around her. But in a few minutes she heard a car engine start and they drove away. The children had been too surprised to cry while she ran with them. Danny was shaking and Ella's little fingers were gripping Ayah's blouse.

8   She stayed up in the hills for the rest of the day, sitting on a black lava boulder in the sunshine where she could see for miles all around her. The sky was light blue and cloudless, and it was warm for late April. The sun warmth relaxed her and took the fear and anger away. She lay back on the rock and watched the sky. It seemed to her that she could walk into the sky, stepping through clouds endlessly. Danny played with little pebbles and stones, pretending they were birds eggs and then little rabbits. Ella sat at her feet and dropped fistfuls of dirt into the breeze, watching the dust and particles of sand intently. Ayah watched a hawk soar high above them, dark wings gliding; hunting or only watching, she did not know. The hawk was patient and he circled all afternoon before he disappeared around the high volcanic peak the Mexicans called Guadalupe.

Late in the afternoon, Ayah looked down at the gray boxcar shack with the paint all peeled from the wood; the stove pipe on the roof was rusted and crooked. The fire she had built that morning in the oil drum stove had burned out. Ella was asleep in her lap now and Danny sat close to her, complaining that he was hungry; he asked when they would go to the house. "We will stay up here until your father comes," she told him, "because those white men were chasing us." The boy remembered then and he nodded at her silently.

If Jimmie had been there he could have read those papers and explained to her what they said. Ayah would have known then, never to sign them. The doctors came back the next day and they brought a BIA policeman with them. They told Chato they had her signature and that was all they needed. Except for the kids. She listened to Chato sullenly; she hated him when he told her it was the old woman who died in the winter, spitting blood; it was her old grandma who had given the children this disease. "They don't spit blood," she said coldly. "The whites lie." She held Ella and Danny close to her, ready to run to the hills again. "I want a medicine man first," she said to Chato, not looking at him. He shook his head. "It's too late now. The policeman is with them. You signed the paper." His voice was gentle.

It was worse than if they had died: to lose the children and to know that somewhere, in a place called Colorado, in a place full of sick and dying strangers, her children were without her. There had been babies that died soon after they were born, and one that died before he could walk. She had carried them herself, up to the boulders and great pieces of the cliff that long ago crashed down from Long Mesa; she laid them in the crevices of sandstone and buried them in fine brown sand with round quartz pebbles that washed down the hills in the rain. She had endured it because they had been with her. But she could not bear this pain. She did not sleep for a long time after they took her children. She stayed on the hill where they had fled the first time, and she slept rolled up in the blanket Jimmie had sent her. She carried the pain in her belly and it was fed by everything she saw: the blue sky of their last day together and the dust and pebbles they played with; the swing in the elm tree and broom stick horse choked life from her. The pain filled her stomach and there was no room for food or for her lungs to fill with air. The air and the food would have been theirs.

She hated Chato, not because he let the policeman and doctors put the screaming children in the government car, but because he had taught her to sign her name. Because it was like the old ones always told her about learning their language or any of their ways: it endangered you. She slept alone on the hill until the middle of November when the first snows came. Then she made a bed for herself where the children had slept. She did not lie down beside Chato again until many years later, when he was sick and shivering and only her body could keep him warm. The illness came after the white rancher told Chato he was too old to work for him anymore, and Chato and his old woman should be out of the shack by the next afternoon because the rancher had hired new people to work there. That had satisfied her. To see how

(continued)

(continued)

the white man repaid Chato's years of loyalty and work. All of Chato's fine-sounding English talk didn't change things.

13   It snowed steadily and the luminous light from the snow gradually diminished into the darkness. Somewhere in Cebolleta a dog barked and other village dogs joined with it. Ayah looked in the direction she had come, from the bar where Chato was buying the wine. Sometimes he told her to go on ahead and wait; and then he never came. And when she finally went back looking for him, she would find him passed out at the bottom of the wooden steps at Azzie's Bar. All the wine would be gone and most of the money too, from the pale blue check that came to them once a month in a government envelope. It was then that she would look at his face and his hands, scarred by ropes and the barbed wire of all those years, and she would think, this man is a stranger; for forty years she had smiled at him and cooked his food, but he remained a stranger. She stood up again, with the snow almost to her knees, and she walked back to find Chato.

14   It was hard to walk in the deep snow and she felt the air burn in her lungs. She stopped a short distance from the bar to rest and readjust the blanket. But this time he wasn't waiting for her on the bottom step with his old Stetson hat pulled down and his shoulders hunched up in his long wool overcoat.

15   She was careful not to slip on the wooden steps. When she pushed the door open, warm air and cigarette smoke hit her face. She looked around slowly and deliberately, in every corner, in every dark place that the old man might find to sleep. The bar owner didn't like Indians in there, especially Navajos, but he let Chato come in because he could talk Spanish like he was one of them. The men at the bar stared at her, and the bartender saw that she left the door open wide. Snowflakes were flying inside like moths and melting into a puddle on the oiled wood floor. He motioned to her to close the door, but she did not see him. She held herself straight and walked across the room slowly, searching the room with every step. The snow in her hair melted and she could feel it on her forehead. At the far corner of the room, she saw red flames at the mica window of the old stove door; she looked behind the stove just to make sure. The bar got quiet except for the Spanish polka music playing on the jukebox. She stood by the stove and shook the snow from her blanket and held it near the stove to dry. The wet wool smell reminded her of new-born goats in early March, brought inside to warm near the fire. She felt calm.

16   In past years they would have told her to get out. But her hair was white now and her face was wrinkled. They looked at her like she was a spider crawling slowly across the room. They were afraid; she could feel the fear. She looked at their faces steadily. They reminded her of the first time the white people brought her children back to her that winter. Danny had been shy and hid behind the thin white woman who brought them. And the baby had not known her until Ayah took her into her arms, and then Ella had nuzzled close to her as she had when she was nursing. The blonde woman was nervous and kept looking at a dainty gold watch on her wrist. She sat on the bench near the small window and watched the dark snow clouds gather

around the mountains; she was worrying about the unpaved road. She was frightened by what she saw inside too: the strips of venison drying on a rope across the ceiling and the children jabbering excitedly in a language she did not know. So they stayed for only a few hours. Ayah watched the government car disappear down the road and she knew they were already being weaned from these lava hills and from this sky. The last time they came was in early June, and Ella stared at her the way the men in the bar were now staring. Ayah did not try to pick her up; she smiled at her instead and spoke cheerfully to Danny. When he tried to answer her, he could not seem to remember and he spoke English words with the Navajo. But he gave her a scrap of paper that he had found somewhere and carried in his pocket; it was folded in half, and he shyly looked up at her and said it was a bird. She asked Chato if they were home for good this time. He spoke to the white woman and she shook her head. "How much longer?" he asked, and she said she didn't know; but Chato saw how she stared at the boxcar shack. Ayah turned away then. She did not say good-bye.

She felt satisfied that the men in the bar feared her. Maybe it was her face and the way she held her mouth with teeth clenched tight, like there was nothing anyone could do to her now. She walked north down the road, searching for the old man. She did this because she had the blanket, and there would be no place for him except with her and the blanket in the old abode barn near the arroyo. They always slept there when they came to Cebolleta. If the money and the wine were gone, she would be relieved because then they could go home again; back to the old hogan with a dirt roof and rock walls where she herself had been born. And the next day the old man could go back to the few sheep they still had, to follow along behind them, guiding them, into dry sandy arroyos where sparse grass grew. She knew he did not like walking behind old ewes when for so many years he rode big quarter horses and worked with cattle. But she wasn't sorry for him; he should have known all along what would happen.   17

There had not been enough rain for their garden in five years; and that was when Chato finally hitched a ride into the town and brought back brown boxes of rice and sugar and big tin cans of welfare peaches. After that, at the first of the month they went to Cebolleta to ask the postmaster for the check; and then Chato would go to the bar and cash it. They did this as they planted the garden every May, not because anything would survive the summer dust, but because it was time to do this. The journey passed the days that smelled silent and dry like the caves above the canyon with yellow painted buffaloes on their walls.   18

He was walking along the pavement when she found him. He did not stop or turn around when he heard her behind him. She walked beside him and she noticed how slowly he moved now. He smelled strong of woodsmoke and urine. Lately he had been forgetting. Sometimes he called her by his sister's name and she had been gone for a long time. Once she had found him wandering on the road to the white man's ranch, and she asked him why he was going that way; he laughed at her and said, "You know they can't run that ranch without me," and he walked on determined,   19

(continued)

(continued)

limping on the leg that had been crushed many years before. Now he looked at her curiously, as if for the first time, but he kept shuffling along, moving slowly along the side of the highway. His gray hair had grown long and spread out on the shoulders of the long overcoat. He wore the old felt hat pulled down over his ears. His boots were worn out at the toes and he had stuffed pieces of an old red shirt in the holes. The rags made his feet look like little animals up to their ears in snow. She laughed at his feet; the snow muffled the sound of her laugh. He stopped and looked at her again. The wind had quit blowing and the snow was falling straight down; the southeast sky was beginning to clear and Ayah could see a star.

20   "Let's rest awhile," she said to him. They walked away from the road and up the slope to the giant boulders that had tumbled down from the red sand-rock mesa throughout the centuries of rainstorms and earth tremors. In a place where the boulders shut out the wind, they sat down with their backs against the rock. She offered half of the blanket to him and they sat wrapped together.

21   The storm passed swiftly. The clouds moved east. They were massive and full, crowding together across the sky. She watched them with the feeling of horses—steely blue-gray horses startled across the sky. The powerful haunches pushed into the distances and the tail hairs streamed white mist behind them. The sky cleared. Ayah saw that there was nothing between her and the stars. The light was crystalline. There was no shimmer, no distortion through earth haze. She breathed the clarity of the night sky; she smelled the purity of the half moon and the stars. He was lying on his side with his knees pulled up near his belly for warmth. His eyes were closed now, and in the light from the stars and the moon, he looked young again.

22   She could see it descend out of the night sky: an icy stillness from the edge of the thin moon. She recognized the freezing. It came gradually, sinking snowflake by snowflake until the crust was heavy and deep. It had the strength of the stars in Orion, and its journey was endless. Ayah knew that with the wine he would sleep. He would not feel it. She tucked the blanket around him, remembering how it was when Ella had been with her; and she felt the rush so big inside her heart for the babies. And she sang the only song she knew to sing for babies. She could not remember if she had ever sung it to her children, but she knew that her grandmother had sung it and her mother had sung it:

> The earth is your mother,
> she holds you.
> The sky is your father,
> he protects you.
> Sleep,
> sleep.
> Rainbow is your sister,
> she loves you.
> The winds are your brothers,

they sing to you.
Sleep,
sleep.
We are together always
We are together always
There never was a time
when this
was not so.

Inquiring into the Story

1. **Explore.** On the left page of your notebook, jot down at least five lines or passages that you believe were key to your understanding of the story. These may include details that seem important, moments that signify turning points, or feelings or ideas suggested by the narrator or another character. On the right page, openly fastwrite about the passages you collected. What do they seem to suggest about possible themes for the story? What do you notice about Ayah, the main character and narrator? What do you consider the significant events that affect all the characters and how do these events change the characters?

2. **Explain.** A recurring detail in the story is the blanket that Ayah received from her son, Jimmie. Trace every mention of the blanket in the story. What accumulated meaning does this detail acquire in the story?

3. **Evaluate.** Some critics have argued that "Lullaby" is a story of healing and recovery. Do you agree or disagree? What evidence in the story would you point to that either supports or contradicts that contention?

4. **Reflect.** When you studied literature in high school, you developed certain routines for writing analytical papers. What were they? Was your experience analyzing Silko's story different from what you're used to when you're asked to interpret literature?

One Student's Response

Noel's Journal

**DOUBLE-ENTRY JOURNAL
RESPONSE TO "LULLABY"**

"It was worse than if they had died: to lose the children and to know that somewhere, in a place called Colorado, in a place full of sick and dying strangers, her children were without her."

One Student's Response (*continued*)

"She stayed on the hill where they had fled the first time, and she slept rolled up in the blanket Jimmie had sent her."

I think this sets the tone of the whole story. She loses one son to the war and the other two were taken from her. Knowing that one son had died and wouldn't ever come home again. The other two were alive and well but they would not grow up with their mother and were kept from their own culture by the government.

After she lost all her children she finds comfort in the blanket her older son had sent her. She sleeps in the place where she spent the last moments with her other two children.

She carries the blanket with her wherever she goes. This is how she spent her time mourning her loss and memories.

▶ Short Story 2

Watch the Video on **Conflict in Literature** in your MyLab

A story is a good story if we can "relate to it." At least that's what I often hear, and there is, of course, some truth to this; we are drawn to what we know. However, when we encounter someone like the narrator of Gish Gen's story, "Who's Irish?," it's hard to see how this applies. The narrator is a Chinese immigrant who made a good life in America but never lost her cultural ties to China. Her daughter, now a successful banker, marries a man of Irish descent. Out of this ethnic stew arises questions of identity, such as What does it mean to be an Other in America? What is so compelling in this story is that we see these questions through the narrator's eyes, someone for whom Western ways still seem odd. In "Who's Irish?" the conflict over cultural identity ignites when the narrator is asked to care for her granddaughter, a child who is Chinese and not Chinese, Irish and not Irish, or simply American. Which is it? Those of us whose immigrant ancestors factor little into who we are today wouldn't seem to "relate to" such a dilemma. And yet, the narrator's point of view challenges us to see ourselves as others might. In this way, the story makes the familiar strange.

Who's Irish?

Gish Gen

1   In China, people say mixed children are supposed to be smart, and definitely my granddaughter Sophie is smart. But Sophie is wild, Sophie is not like my daughter Natalie, or like me. I am work hard my whole life, and fierce besides. My husband always used to say he is afraid of me, and in our restaurant, busboys and cooks all afraid of me too. Even the gang members come for protection money, they try to talk to my husband. When I am there, they stay away. If they come by mistake, they pretend they

are come to eat. They hide behind the menu, they order a lot of food. They talk about their mothers. Oh, my mother have some arthritis, need to take herbal medicine, they say. Oh, my mother getting old, her hair all white now.

I say, Your mother's hair used to be white, but since she dye it, it become black again. Why don't you go home once in a while and take a look? I tell them, Confucius say a filial son knows what color his mother's hair is.   2

My daughter is fierce too, she is vice president in the bank now. Her new house is big enough for everybody to have their own room, including me. But Sophie take after Natalie's husband's family, their name is Shea. Irish. I always thought Irish people are like Chinese people, work so hard on the railroad, but now I know why the Chinese beat the Irish. Of course, not all Irish are like the Shea family, of course not. My daughter tell me I should not say Irish this, Irish that.   3

How do you like it when people say the Chinese this, the Chinese that? she say.   4

You know, the British call the Irish heathen, just like they call the Chinese, she say.   5

You think the Opium War was bad, how would you like to live right next door to the British? she say.   6

And that is that. My daughter have a funny habit when she win an argument, she take a sip of something and look away, so the other person is not embarrassed. So I am not embarrassed. I do not call anybody anything either. I just happen to mention about the Shea family, an interesting fact: four brothers in the family, and not one of them work. The mother, Bess, have a job before she got sick, she was executive secretary in a big company. She is handle everything for a big shot, you would be surprised how complicated her job is, not just type this, type that. Now she is a nice woman with a clean house. But her boys, every one of them is on welfare, or so-called severance pay, or so-called disability pay. Something. They say they cannot find work, this is not the economy of the fifties, but I say, even the black people doing better these days, some of them live so fancy, you'd be surprised. Why the Shea family have so much trouble? They are white people, they speak English. When I come to this country, I have no money and do not speak English. But my husband and I own our restaurant before he die. Free and clear, no mortgage. Of course, I understand I am just lucky, come from a country where the food is popular all over the world. I understand it is not the Shea family's fault they come from a country where everything is boiled. Still, I say.   7

She's right, we should broaden our horizons, say one brother, Jim, at Thanksgiving. Forget about the car business. Think about egg rolls.   8

Pad thai, say another brother, Mike. I'm going to make my fortune in pad thai. It's going to be the new pizza.   9

I say, You people too picky about what you sell. Selling egg rolls not good enough for you, but at least my husband and I can say, We made it. What can you say? Tell me. What can you say?   10

Everybody chew their tough turkey.   11

I especially cannot understand my daughter's husband John, who has no job but cannot take care of Sophie either. Because he is a man, he say, and that's the end of the sentence.   *(continued)*   12

(continued)

13   Plain boiled food, plain boiled thinking. Even his name is plain boiled: John. Maybe because I grew up with black bean sauce and hoisin sauce and garlic sauce, I always feel something is missing when my son-in-law talk.

14   But, okay: so my son-in-law can be man, I am baby-sitter. Six hours a day, same as the old sitter, crazy Amy, who quit. This is not so easy, now that I am sixty-eight, Chinese age almost seventy. Still, I try. In China, daughter take care of mother. Here it is the other way around. Mother help daughter, mother ask, Anything else I can do? Otherwise daughter complain mother is not supportive. I tell daughter, We do not have this word in Chinese, supportive. But my daughter too busy to listen, she has to go to meeting, she has to write memo while her husband go to the gym to be a man. My daughter say otherwise he will be depressed. Seems like all his life he has this trouble, depression.

15   No one wants to hire someone who is depressed, she say. It is important for him to keep his spirits up.

16   Beautiful wife, beautiful daughter, beautiful house, oven can clean itself automatically. No money left over, because only one income, but lucky enough, got the baby-sitter for free. If John lived in China, he would be very happy. But he is not happy. Even at the gym things go wrong. One day, he pull a muscle. Another day, weight room too crowded. Always something.

17   Until finally, hooray, he has a job. Then he feel pressure.

18   I need to concentrate, he say. I need to focus.

19   He is going to work for insurance company. Salesman job. A paycheck, he say, and at least he will wear clothes instead of gym shorts. My daughter buy him some special candy bars from the health-food store. They say THINK! on them, and are supposed to help John think.

20   John is a good-looking boy, you have to say that, especially now that he shave so you can see his face.

21   I am an old man in a young man's game, say John.

22   I will need a new suit, say John.

23   This time I am not going to shoot myself in the foot, say John.

24   Good, I say.

25   She means to be supportive, my daughter say. Don't start the send her back to China thing, because we can't.

26   Sophie is three years old American age, but already I see her nice Chinese side swallowed up by her wild Shea side. She looks like mostly Chinese. Beautiful black hair, beautiful black eyes. Nose perfect size, not so flat looks like something fell down, not so large looks like some big deal got stuck in wrong face. Everything just right, only her skin is a brown surprise to John's family. So brown, they say. Even John say it. She never goes in the sun, still she is that color, he say. Brown. They say, Nothing the matter with brown. They are just surprised. So brown. Nattie is not that brown, they say. They say, It seems like Sophie should be a color in between Nattie and John. Seems funny, a girl named Sophie Shea be brown. But she is brown, maybe her name should

be Sophie Brown. She never go in the sun, still she is that color, they say. Nothing the matter with brown. They are just surprised.

The Shea family talk is like this sometimes, going around and around like a Christmas-tree train.   27

Maybe John is not her father, I say one day, to stop the train. And sure enough, train wreck. None of the brothers ever say the word brown to me again.   28

Instead, John's mother, Bess, say, I hope you are not offended.   29

She say, I did my best on those boys. But raising four boys with no father is no picnic.   30

You have a beautiful family, I say.   31

I'm getting old, she say.   32

You deserve a rest, I say. Too many boys make you old.   33

I never had a daughter, she say. You have a daughter.   34

I have a daughter, I say. Chinese people don't think a daughter is so great, but you're right. I have a daughter.   35

I was never against the marriage, you know, she say. I never thought John was marrying down. I always thought Nattie was just as good as white.   36

I was never against the marriage either, I say. I just wonder if they look at the whole problem.   37

Of course you pointed out the problem, you are a mother, she say. And now we both have a granddaughter. A little brown granddaughter, she is so precious to me.   38

I laugh. A little brown granddaughter, I say. To tell you the truth, I don't know how she came out so brown.   39

We laugh some more. These days Bess need a walker to walk. She take so many pills, she need two glasses of water to get them all down. Her favorite TV show is about bloopers, and she love her bird feeder. All day long, she can watch that bird feeder, like a cat.   40

I can't wait for her to grow up, Bess say. I could use some female company.   41

Too many boys, I say.   42

Boys are fine, she say. But they do surround you after a while.   43

You should take a break, come live with us, I say. Lots of girls at our house.   44

Be careful what you offer, say Bess with a wink. Where I come from, people mean for you to move in when they say a thing like that.   45

Nothing the matter with Sophie's outside, that's the truth. It is inside that she is like not any Chinese girl I ever see. We go to the park, and this is what she does. She stand up in the stroller. She take off all her clothes and throw them in the fountain.   46

Sophie! I say. Stop!   47

But she just laugh like a crazy person. Before I take over as baby-sitter, Sophie has that crazy-person sitter, Amy the guitar player. My daughter thought this Amy very creative—another word we do not talk about in China. In China, we talk about whether we have difficulty or no difficulty. We talk about whether life is bitter or not bitter. In America, all day long, people talk about creative. Never mind that I cannot even look at this Amy,   48

(continued)

(continued)

with her shirt so short that her belly button showing. This Amy think Sophie should love her body. So when Sophie take off her diaper, Amy laugh. When Sophie run around na-ked, Amy say she wouldn't want to wear a diaper either. When Sophie go shu-shu in her lap, Amy laugh and say there are no germs in pee. When Sophie take off her shoes, Amy say bare feet is best, even the pediatrician say so. That is why Sophie now walk around with no shoes like a beggar child. Also why Sophie love to take off her clothes.

49   Turn around! say the boys in the park. Let's see that ass!

50   Of course, Sophie does not understand. Sophie clap her hands, I am the only one to say, No! This is not a game.

51   It has nothing to do with John's family, my daughter say. Amy was too permis-sive, that's all.

52   But I think if Sophie was not wild inside, she would not take off her shoes and clothes to begin with.

53   You never take off your clothes when you were little, I say. All my Chinese friends had babies, I never saw one of them act wild like that.

54   Look, my daughter say. I have a big presentation tomorrow.

55   John and my daughter agree Sophie is a problem, but they don't know what to do.

56   You spank her, she'll stop, I say another day.

57   But they say, Oh no.

58   In America, parents not supposed to spank the child.

59   It gives them low self-esteem, my daughter say. And that leads to problems later, as I happen to know.

60   My daughter never have big presentation the next day when the subject of spanking come up.

61   I don't want you to touch Sophie, she say. No spanking, period.

62   Don't tell me what to do, I say.

63   I'm not telling you what to do, say my daughter. I'm telling you how I feel.

64   I am not your servant, I say. Don't you dare talk to me like that.

65   My daughter have another funny habit when she lose an argument. She spread out all her fingers and look at them, as if she like to make sure they are still there.

66   My daughter is fierce like me, but she and John think it is better to explain to Sophie that clothes are a good idea. This is not so hard in the cold weather. In the warm weather, it is very hard.

67   Use your words, my daughter say. That's what we tell Sophie. How about if you set a good example?

68   As if good example mean anything to Sophie. I am so fierce, the gang members who used to come to the restaurant all afraid of me, but Sophie is not afraid.

69   I say, Sophie, if you take off your clothes, no snack.

70   I say, Sophie, if you take off your clothes, no lunch.

71   I say, Sophie, if you take off your clothes, no park.

72   Pretty soon we are stay home all day, and by the end of six hours she still did not have one thing to eat. You never saw a child stubborn like that.

73   I'm hungry! she cry when my daughter come home.

What's the matter, doesn't your grandmother feed you? My daughter laugh.   74

No! Sophie say. She doesn't feed me anything!   75

My daughter laugh again. Here you go, she say.   76

She say to John, Sophie must be growing.   77

Growing like a weed, I say.   78

Still Sophie take off her clothes, until one day I spank her. Not too hard, but she cry   79
and cry, and when I tell her if she doesn't put her clothes back on I'll spank her again, she
put her clothes back on. Then I tell her she is good girl, and give her some food to eat. The
next day we go to the park and, like a nice Chinese girl, she does not take off her clothes.

She stop taking off her clothes, I report. Finally!   80

How did you do it? my daughter ask.   81

After twenty-eight years experience with you, I guess I learn something, I say.   82

It must have been a phase, John say, and his voice is suddenly like an expert.   83

His voice is like an expert about everything these days, now that he carry a leather   84
briefcase, and wear shiny shoes, and can go shopping for a new car. On the company,
he say. The company will pay for it, but he will be able to drive it whenever he want.

A free car, he say. How do you like that?   85

It's good to see you in the saddle again, my daughter say. Some of your family   86
patterns are scary.

At least I don't drink, he say. He say, And I'm not the only one with scary family   87
patterns.

That's for sure, say my daughter.   88

Everyone is happy. Even I am happy, because there is more trouble with Sophie, but   89
now I think I can help her Chinese side fight against her wild side. I teach her to eat
food with fork or spoon or chopsticks, she cannot just grab into the middle of a bowl
of noodles. I teach her not to play with garbage cans. Sometimes I spank her, but not
too often, and not too hard.

Still, there are problems. Sophie like to climb everything. If there is a railing, she   90
is never next to it. Always she is on top of it. Also, Sophie like to hit the mommies
of her friends. She learn this from her playground best friend, Sinbad, who is four.
Sinbad wear army clothes every day and like to ambush his mommy. He is the one
who dug a big hole under the play structure, a foxhole he call it, all by himself. Very
hardworking. Now he wait in the foxhole with a shovel full of wet sand. When his
mommy come, he throw it right at her.

Oh, it's all right, his mommy say. You can't get rid of war games, it's part of their   91
imaginative play. All the boys go through it.

Also, he like to kick his mommy, and one day he tell Sophie to kick his mommy too.   92

I wish this story is not true.   93

Kick her, kick her! Sinbad say.   94

Sophie kick her. A little kick, as if she just so happened was swinging her little   95
leg and didn't realize that big mommy leg was in the way. Still I spank Sophie and
make Sophie say sorry, and what does the mommy say?

(continued)

(continued)

96   Really, it's all right, she say. It didn't hurt.

97   After that, Sophie learn she can attack mommies in the playground, and some will say, Stop, but others will say, Oh, she didn't mean it, especially if they realize Sophie will be punished.

98   This is how, one day, bigger trouble come. The bigger trouble start when Sophie hide in the foxhole with that shovel full of sand. She wait, and when I come look for her, she throw it at me. All over my nice clean clothes.

99   Did you ever see a Chinese girl act this way?

100   Sophie! I say. Come out of there, say you're sorry.

101   But she does not come out. Instead, she laugh. Naaah, naah-na, naaa-naaa, she say.

102   I am not exaggerate: millions of children in China, not one act like this.

103   Sophie! I say. Now! Come out now!

104   But she know she is in big trouble. She know if she come out, what will happen next. So she does not come out. I am sixty-eight, Chinese age almost seventy, how can I crawl under there to catch her? Impossible. So I yell, yell, yell, and what happen? Nothing. A Chinese mother would help, but American mothers, they look at you, they shake their head, they go home. And, of course, a Chinese child would give up, but not Sophie.

105   I hate you! she yell. I hate you, Meanie!

106   Meanie is my new name these days.

107   Long time this goes on, long long time. The foxhole is deep, you cannot see too much, you don't know where is the bottom. You cannot hear too much either. If she does not yell, you cannot even know she is still there or not. After a while, getting cold out, getting dark out. No one left in the playground, only us.

108   Sophie, I say. How did you become stubborn like this? I am go home without you now.

109   I try to use a stick, chase her out of there, and once or twice I hit her, but still she does not come out. So finally I leave. I go outside the gate.

110   Bye-bye! I say. I'm go home now.

111   But still she does not come out and does not come out. Now it is dinnertime, the sky is black. I think I should maybe go get help, but how can I leave a little girl by herself in the playground? A bad man could come. A rat could come. I go back in to see what is happen to Sophie. What if she have a shovel and is making a tunnel to escape?

112   Sophie! I say.

113   No answer.

114   Sophie!

115   I don't know if she is alive. I don't know if she is fall asleep down there. If she is crying, I cannot hear her.

116   So I take the stick and poke.

117   Sophie! I say. I promise I no hit you. If you come out, I give you a lollipop.

118   No answer. By now I worried. What to do, what to do, what to do? I poke some more, even harder, so that I am poking and poking when my daughter and John suddenly appear.

119   What are you doing? What is going on? say my daughter.

Put down that stick! say my daughter.   120

You are crazy! say my daughter.   121

John wiggle under the structure, into the foxhole, to rescue Sophie.   122

She fell asleep, say John the expert. She's okay. That is one big hole.   123

Now Sophie is crying and crying.   124

Sophie, my daughter say, hugging her. Are you okay, peanut? Are you okay?   125

She's just scared, say John.   126

Are you okay? I say too. I don't know what happen, I say.   127

She's okay, say John. He is not like my daughter, full of questions. He is full of an-   128
swers until we get home and can see by the lamplight.

Will you look at her? he yell then. What the hell happened?   129

Bruises all over her brown skin, and a swollen-up eye.   130

You are crazy! say my daughter. Look at what you did! You are crazy!   131

I try very hard, I say.   132

How could you use a stick? I told you to use your words!   133

She is hard to handle, I say.   134

She's three years old! You cannot use a stick! say my daughter.   135

She is not like any Chinese girl I ever saw, I say.   136

I brush some sand off my clothes. Sophie's clothes are dirty too, but at least she   137
has her clothes on.

Has she done this before? ask my daughter. Has she hit you before?   138

She hits me all the time, Sophie say, eating ice cream.   139

Your family, say John.   140

Believe me, say my daughter.   141

A daughter I have, a beautiful daughter. I took care of her when she could not hold   142
her head up. I took care of her before she could argue with me, when she was a little
girl with two pigtails, one of them always crooked. I took care of her when we have
to escape from China, I took care of her when suddenly we live in a country with
cars everywhere, if you are not careful your little girl get run over. When my husband
die, I promise him I will keep the family together, even though it was just two of us,
hardly a family at all.

But now my daughter take me around to look at apartments. After all, I can cook,   143
I can clean, there's no reason I cannot live by myself, all I need is a telephone. Of
course, she is sorry. Sometimes she cry, I am the one to say everything will be okay.
She say she have no choice, she doesn't want to end up divorced. I say divorce is terrible, I don't know who invented this terrible idea. Instead of live with a telephone,
though, surprise, I come to live with Bess. Imagine that. Bess make an offer and, sure
enough, where she come from, people mean for you to move in when they say things
like that. A crazy idea, go to live with someone else's family, but she like to have some
female company, not like my daughter, who does not believe in company. These days
when my daughter visit, she does not bring Sophie. Bess say we should give Nattie
time, we will see Sophie again soon. But seems like my daughter have more presentation than ever before, every time she come she have to leave.

(continued)

(continued)

144   I have a family to support, she say, and her voice is heavy, as if soaking wet. I have a young daughter and a depressed husband and no one to turn to.

145   When she say no one to turn to, she mean me.

146   These days my beautiful daughter is so tired she can just sit there in a chair and fall asleep. John lost his job again, already, but still they rather hire a baby-sitter than ask me to help, even they can't afford it. Of course, the new baby-sitter is much younger, can run around. I don't know if Sophie these days is wild or not wild. She call me Meanie, but she like to kiss me too, sometimes. I remember that every time I see a child on TV. Sophie like to grab my hair, a fistful in each hand, and then kiss me smack on the nose. I never see any other child kiss that way.

147   The satellite TV has so many channels, more channels than I can count, including a Chinese channel from the mainland and a Chinese channel from Taiwan, but most of the time I watch bloopers with Bess. Also, I watch the bird feeder—so many, many kinds of birds come. The Shea sons hang around all the time, asking when will I go home, but Bess tell them, Get lost.

148   She's a permanent resident, say Bess. She isn't going anywhere.

149   Then she wink at me, and switch the channel with the remote control.

150   Of course, I shouldn't say Irish this, Irish that, especially now I am become honorary Irish myself, according to Bess. Me! Who's Irish? I say, and she laugh. All the same, if I could mention one thing about some of the Irish, not all of them of course, I like to mention this: Their talk just stick. I don't know how Bess Shea learn to use her words, but sometimes I hear what she say a long time later. Permanent resident. Not going anywhere. Over and over I hear it, the voice of Bess.

Inquiring into the Story

1. **Explore.** We all have "identities assigned" to us "by society," Gish Jen said in an interview, and sometimes these can be "very irritating." As the child of immigrant parents, Jen was acutely aware of these "assigned" identities, but we all have them. Whether our identity is football player, theater major, southerner with an accent, or pretty woman, it's hard to escape the identities imposed on us. But which of these is irritating? Explore that in your journal. How does this writing help you to see Jen's story differently?.

2. **Explain.** Talking about her upbringing as a child of Chinese immigrants to the U.S., Jen said that she "came from a world where—in every sentence—in everything they did there was this idea that there were obstacles everywhere that one could not simply go out and do what one wanted. That one had to be canny and one had to be smart because the world opposed you. And then I would go out into the mainstream world where it was assumed that you got what you wanted. Wasn't that what the world was for? To provide for us?" Explain some of the ways these ideas are implied in "Who's Irish?" Point to particular passages.

3. **Evaluate.** America is a "melting pot," a place where people can eventually abandon ethnic and culture differences and merge into a "harmonious whole." No, others argue, one of the great virtues of America is its diversity. Differences should be celebrated, not erased. Use "Who's Irish?" to make an argument that addresses these assertions.

4. **Reflect.** One of the most common criterion for registering our like or dislike for something we read is that we can—or can't—"relate to it." What does this mean? And how does that idea apply to Gish Jen's story? Can we also find stories compelling that we can't "relate to?"

Inquiring into the Details

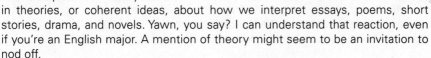

Why Literary Theory Is Not a Sleep Aid

The discipline of literary studies is interested in theories, or coherent ideas, about how we interpret essays, poems, short stories, drama, and novels. Yawn, you say? I can understand that reaction, even if you're an English major. A mention of theory might seem to be an invitation to nod off.

But here's a way to understand the relevance of theory in any discipline, including literary studies. Good theories help you understand and explain what you see. Here's an example of what I mean. A group of scholars has always been interested in how we tell stories, and one of these scholars, Joseph Campbell, was a mythologist who developed ideas about how most of the stories we tell are variations on the same story that has been told forever: the hero's journey. This journey has identifiable stages, Campbell argued, including this progression: (1) First we see the hero in his or her ordinary world, then (2) the hero is presented with a challenge, (3) he or she resists the challenge, (4) the hero gets encouraged by a wise mentor, (5) and the hero embarks, encountering the first test, and so on until the journey is completed and the hero returns to the ordinary world again, but transformed and possessing something that makes that world better. Think *Star Wars*.

Campbell's theory that stories conform to the outlines of this basic journey can be used to analyze a novel, film, short story, or even personal essay. His ideas provide a framework—better yet, an optic instrument such as a microscope that helps to reveal in a text what you wouldn't ordinarily see.

There are many literary theories that you can turn to when you want to direct your gaze in a certain way at a particular work.

■ *New criticism:* It isn't really new anymore, but still influential. These theories encourage readers to look at a poem or story as an object that can be analyzed independently from the author's intentions or historical contexts.

■ *Reader-response criticism:* You can't understand a work independently of a reader's response to it, say reader response theorists. Whatever meaning exists

> ### Inquiring into the Details (*continued*)
>
> is necessarily a transaction between, say, the short story and the reader's experience of the short story, an experience informed by the reader's personal history and other texts he or she has read.
>
> ■ ***Feminist criticism:*** This diverse body of theory argues, among other things, that gender figures prominently in writing and reading literature. A critic might notice, for example, how male authors have historically depicted female characters in their work, or find in often-neglected women writers an alternative view of female characters and even methods of storytelling.
>
> ■ ***New historicism:*** We're used to interpreting a poem or story by seeing it in historical context. If you want to understand *Huck Finn*, for instance, consider the history of racial conflict in the American South. New historicism proposes that this way of using history to interpret literature is way too simplistic. New historicists believe that, while history is a useful way to interpret literature, it's only one of many interrelated "discourses" a critic should consider.
>
> If you want to apply a literary theory to your analysis of a work, you don't have to read a score of books about it. You can find excellent summaries of each theory's methods online, including some examples of how to apply them.

▶ Film Criticism

A confession: I'm obsessed with the app "Call of Duty: Nazi Zombies." Or at least I was for about a year. And that's why the James Parker essay "Our Zombies, Ourselves" was so interesting to me. Why are zombies lurching through our minds these days, grasping and groping their way into our cultural imagination? Zombies are featured in video games, films, and popular television shows. What's up with that? The simplistic answer is that zombies are easy to hate and fun to kill. They are no longer human, after all, so it's nearly impossible to step out of bounds morally. Slaughter them with abandon.

Parker suggests our cultural obsession with zombies is more complex than that. They first plodded into a 1968 film, *Night of the Living Dead*, and what surprises Parker is that they took so long to arrive. We *need* zombies, he argues, projecting all of our own anxieties on a creature that is blank enough to provide plenty of room for whatever fears we want to inscribe.

"Our Zombies, Ourselves" analyzes a number of films, especially the *Night of the Living Dead*. Parker is interested in the zombie phenomenon, not only as it is reflected in film, but in other forms as well—books, TV, video games. He asks the inquiry question behind most critical essays: *What does this mean?* In this case, he wonders (as I do) why, now more than never, zombies have captured our imaginations.

A few of the Nazi zombies who lurch through the computer game "Call of Duty: Black Ops."

Our Zombies, Ourselves

James Parker

The most surprising thing about the modern zombie—indeed, the only surprising thing about the modern zombie—is that he took so long to arrive. His slowness is a proverb, of course: his museumgoer's shuffle, his hospital plod. Plus he's a wobbler: the shortest path between two points is seldom the one he takes. Nonetheless, given all that had been going on, we might reasonably have expected the first modern zombies to start showing up around 1919. Twentieth-century man was already moaning and scratching his head; shambling along with bits falling off him; desensitized, industrialized, hollowed out, metaphysically evacuated....And yet not until 1968, at the dawning of the Age of Aquarius, did the zombie as we know him really make the scene.

Look: there he is, out of focus and deep in the shot, in the fifth minute of George A. Romero's *Night of the Living Dead*. He's wandering through a cemetery, wearing a shabby blazer, with the air of a distracted groundskeeper. In the foreground are two soberly dressed young people, Barbara and Johnny. They are visiting their father's

(continued)

(continued)

grave. Barbara kneels and bows her head, but Johnny's a scoffer. "Hey, c'mon, Barb—church was this morning, huh? Hey, I mean praying's for church, huh?" Sniffs Barbara: "I haven't seen you in church lately." A breeze rises. Dark, frondy tree limbs wave above them like seaweed in the black-and-white afternoon, and the zombie draws near. He has begun to reel and lurch. He grabs Barbara. There's death in his skin tone, but his face is alive with a kind of stricken fixity. He bashes Johnny against a tombstone. Barbara flees in a car, but wrecks it. And now we really see him, framed disastrously in the skewed rear windshield, advancing toward us at an off-kilter zombie trot. No mistaking the message: the world is out of whack, the car is off the road, here comes the zombie.

3   And he's never stopped coming. After fertile decades bumbling in the gore/horror subbasement, he veered toward the mainstream in the early 2000s and currently enjoys a cultural profile unmatched even by his fancy-pants cousin, the vampire. Sure, we've all enjoyed *Twilight, True Blood,* vampire love, the pallor and the pangs, etc.—but it's the zombie, Old Reliable, who's really bringing home the bacon. He's the one who rides the best-seller lists and consumes the pop unconscious, whose titles spatter the humor section of your local bookstore: *Zombie Haiku, The Zen of Zombie, It's Beginning to Look a Lot Like Zombies: A Book of Zombie Christmas Carols.* People, sometimes hundreds of people, go on processional "zombie walks." Video gamers are mowing down fresh multitudes of zombies with a fervor undimmed by habit: And AMC's zombie series, *The Walking Dead*—the DVD of which is released this month—was the surprise cable smash of last year. Are we approaching, have we already reached, a zombie saturation point, or "burnout," as Max Brooks, author of the (very good) 2006 zombie novel *World War Z,* has put it? I say no. The zombie keeps on: it's what he does.

4   His origins, we learn—we who dabble in the recklessly expanding field of zombie studies—are in Caribbean folk nightmare. For the people of Haiti, the *zombi* was one who had died and been buried, only to be malignantly revived and enslaved by a sorcerer, or *bokor.* Look: there's the zombie in 1929, the year William Seabrook published his sensational account of Haitian voodoo lore, *The Magic Island.* He's working in the cane fields, his eyes like "the eyes of a dead man" but his hands "callused, solid, human." And there he is in 1932, in the Halperin Brothers' *White Zombie*—his cinematic debut—trudging with alienated obedience behind his dark master (played by Béla Lugosi). At night he works with other zombies in the sugar mill. The blades of the great thresher groan magnificently, zombifically, as they turn. A zombie falls in. Oh well.

5   So Romero did not invent the zombie. But he cut him loose: the graveyard zombie in *Night of the Living Dead* may be punishing Johnny, in the finest horror-flick tradition, for being cheeky on hallowed ground, but he himself is no longer a supernatural figure. No demon or magus possesses him, no enchantment holds him. The zombifier seems to be technology: radioactive contamination from an exploded space probe. Zombiedom runs amok, moving virally through the population. The zombie wants live human flesh, and those still in possession of it are advised, via TV and radio, to barricade themselves indoors. Romero was laying down the new canons

of zombiehood: the wobbliness of the zombie, the terrible mobility of the virus, the pockets of survival, the squall of information as the grid collapses.

Severed thus from his heritage, sent freewheeling into postmodernity with nothing to say on his own behalf (because he can't talk, because he's a *zombie*), our hero would seem to be in a position of great semiotic vulnerability. And so it has proved: all manner of meanings have been and continue to be plastered onto the zombie. Much can be made of him, because he makes so little of himself. He is the consumer, the mob, the Other, the proletariat, the weight of life, the dead soul. He is too many e-mails in your inbox, a kind of cosmic spam. He is everything rejected and inexpugnable. He comes back, he comes back, feebly but unstoppably, and as he drags you down, a fatal lethargy overtakes you.

None of this is to ignore the plentiful variations that have been worked upon Romero's zombie theme since 1968. Recent years, for example, have given us both the Sprinting or Galloping Zombie of Danny Boyle's *28 Days Later* and Zack Snyder's *Dawn of the Dead* remake, and the Comic-Existential Zombie of Edgar Wright's *Shaun of the Dead*. In the Boyle/Snyder model, the zombie is wild-eyed and very fast. The virus, too, has been ferally accelerated: now, scant seconds after having your throat ripped out, you stand up snarling and race off in search of prey. *Shaun of the Dead* is gentler and more profound: here zombiedom seems to germinate through a fog of hangovers, Monday mornings, lapses in conversation. Shaun refuses to *become*; his job (selling televisions) demeans him; his nice girlfriend wants him to give up smoking and stop spending so much time down the pub. He will not, he cannot, and the dead throng the streets. As the future peters out, the present blooms with zombies.

But sometimes a zombie is just a zombie. Strike that: a zombie is always just a zombie. The blow-'em-all-away success of *The Walking Dead* is no mystery: the show, and the comic-book series by Robert Kirkman on which it's based, mark a triumphant return to zombie orthodoxy, to the non-galloping zombie and his icons. Once again, and with great gladness, we see shotguns, frantically tuned radios, smoke pillars of apocalypse on the horizon—the full zombie opera. The zombie himself has never looked better, dripping with wounds, full of conviction. With his dangling stethoscope, or his policeman's uniform, or his skateboard, he exhibits the pathos of his ex-personhood. He flaps and sighs. He crookedly advances. He's taking his time. But he'll get there.

Inquiring into the Essay

1. **Explore.** You really can't avoid zombies (or vampires, for that matter). They're everywhere we look these days. The question is this: Why? In this essay, James Parker writes that "much can be made of [the zombie] because he makes so little of himself." In your journal, spend some time exploring your thinking about this. Parker has given you some of his ideas. What do you make of them? What is he missing? How would you explain the cultural fascination with these hobbling, slack-jawed, flesh-eating creatures of the night?

2. **Explain.** Try to "say back" what you take to be Parker's thesis in his essay. First, identify the passage in "Our Zombies, Ourselves" that is key to your understanding of the main thing the essay is trying to say. Then use this and any other relevant passages to summarize the key ideas in the essay.

3. **Evaluate.** Is this essay persuasive? Based on your own experiences and observations, along with the exploratory writing you did in response to the first question, what do you find most and least convincing about Parker's argument?

4. **Reflect.** We typically think of the critical essay—if we think about it at all—as a creature of the English class, a form of writing about literature. It is that, to be sure, but as this essay demonstrated, critical analysis can also analyze cultural trends, and pose the same question we ask about literature: What might it mean? Social undercurrents, like zombie love, are always changing. Literature, on the other hand, seems static; after all, Hemingway isn't coming out with another version of *Old Man and the Sea*. Is it true that a published short story or essay has relatively fixed meanings?

Seeing the Form

Young Ladies on the Banks of the Seine by Gustave Courbet

If a photograph can be thought of as a form of nonfiction, then a painting compares well with fiction or poetry. The painting certainly has a strong relationship to the real; after all, the painter sees the world we all live in and expresses that vision in the work. That expression may be realistic, impressionistic, or abstract, but it is firmly rooted in things that can be seen, smelled, heard, and touched. Yet unlike photographers who work with the visual materials presented to them through the viewfinder, the painter can transform these materials through invention. If it works better that the woman's dress is pink rather than blue, then pink it shall be. Similarly, fiction writers' primary obligation is to the story, not reality, and they invent characters and make them do things that contribute tension and meaning to the narrative.

Interpreting a painting, then, such as Gustave Coubet's painting, *Young Ladies on the Banks of the Seine*, is much like interpreting fiction. The painting acts as a text that, like a short story, is a complete invention and whose meaning is implicit rather than explicit. Therefore "reading" Coubet's painting should involve the kind of interpretive moves you might employ in reading any literature.

In analyzing *Young Ladies on the Banks of the Seine* and other paintings, it can be helpful to consider the following basic terms and concepts:

- **Line:** In artistic composition, the line is the direction the viewer's gaze travels when looking at the painting, something that is managed by the placement of forms and their relative size. In a good painting, the viewer's eye is directed to the main focal point of the picture, and away from unimportant elements. Some questions to ask about line include whether the painting succeeds in encouraging your gaze to move smoothly to the main objects of interest,

Other Ways of Seeing (*continued*)

Young Ladies on the Banks of the Seine River (1856), Gustave Courbet. Oil on canvas. Petit Palais, Musée Des Beaux-Arts De La Ville De Paris. The Bridgeman Art Library/Getty Images.

or whether the line is confusing, making you feel as if you're not quite sure where to look. Do things flow visually?

- ■ *Hierarchy:* Do you sense that some visual elements are more important than others? In a well-composed painting, you should. Artists can manage this in a number of ways, including with the size and location of various objects in the painting, and in doing so they are communicating something important about the overall theme of the work. What, for example, might the emphasis on certain objects in the painting imply about its meaning? What is the relationship among these things, and what does that imply?

- ■ *Color:* The arrangement of color in a painting influences its mood. Certain colors are cool—blues, greens, purples, and their many combinations—and these tend to recede in a painting. Other colors—yellows, oranges, and reds—are warm and can be perceived as coming forward. Color is obviously enormously expressive when handled well. How do the colors the artist chose affect the mood of the work? How might that mood contribute to its overall theme or idea?

Other Ways of Seeing (*continued*)

- ▪ ***Value:*** To create the sense of dimension, artists use light and dark tones. In a black-and-white drawing, these tones are white to black and all the shades of gray in between. In a color painting, value is often managed by using various shades of a color. Without value, a painting looks flat, one-dimensional. With it, the subjects look more realistic. How much emphasis is there on value in the painting? How realistic is the image?

- ▪ ***Composition:*** All of these qualities—line, color, value, hierarchy—and more contribute to a painting's composition. One of the key qualities of composition is balance, and this can be achieved in a number of ways, including arranging visual elements symmetrically or asymmetrically. Or this can be done using something called the "golden mean," an ancient mathematical concept that has historically influenced art and architecture and which represents proportions often seen in nature, including the spiral of a sea shell and the proportions of the human body. What do you notice about the composition of the painting? How is it arranged to influence your feelings, and how does it seem to contribute to the overall theme or idea?

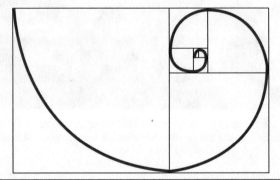

Figure 8.2   The golden mean is a mathematical formula that when applied to a rectangle creates spatial relationships that are particularly pleasing to the eye. This is the so-called golden rectangle. For centuries, artists have exploited this principle, creating proportions in paintings and buildings based on these calculations. Can you see how Coubet's painting is visually organized to adhere to the golden rectangle?

THE WRITING PROCESS

Inquiry Project **Writing a Critical Essay**

Inquiry Question: What might it mean?

Write an essay about a poem, short story, or essay—maybe one of the works in this chapter or something your instructor recommends. Alternatively, do a critical analysis of a visual work of art—a painting, photograph, or film. Whatever the subject, make sure your essay does the following:

■ Focuses on an *aspect* of the subject. While you begin with the inquiry question *What does it mean?* your paper should be focused on exploring that, by looking closely at a few things in the work.

■ Argues for a particular interpretation of the work, using specifics from it to support your assertion.

■ If possible, uses the work of other critics, when relevant, to develop your argument.

▸ Watch
the Animation on
**Writing a
Rhetorical Analysis**
in your MyLab

Prose+

■ Build a web page around your critical essay, embedding video or audio of interviews with the author of the work and links to the work of other critics who comment on it. You might also add images, including those that you think echo the interpretation you're arguing for. Other features might include a bibliography with links to the sources you used, a list of other featured works by the author or artist, a sidebar that highlights an important passage, etc.

■ Develop a PowerPoint or Pages presentation for your critical essay, or as a supplement to it. This would be especially effective if you're analyzing a visual work, because you can include close-ups of significant features that are key to your interpretation. But a slide presentation can be effective for conventional literary analysis, too. Consider developing slides that provide background on the work, a statement of your thesis, and then slides of key passages or quotes from criticism that you're using as evidence.

■ Using a program such as Microsoft's Photo Story 3 or iMovie, develop a photographic interpretation of a piece of music that you like. Importing the soundtrack and drawing on your own digital photographs or those you find online, create a visual story that reflects your particular interpretation of the music. Add text to some of the images, if relevant.

What Are You Going to Write About?

In the conversation between what a text says and what it might be saying, you discover fresh understandings of what you read.

It's likely that your instructor will ask you to write a critical essay on one or more of the readings in this chapter, or perhaps an assigned reading from another book. But if your assignment is more open-ended, possible subjects are everywhere. Anything that is confusing or ambiguous invites interpretation: a photograph, sculpture, film, cultural trend such as the popularity of reality TV or zombies, etc. The following prompts should help you explore some of these possibilities and consider ways of analyzing an assigned text.

Opening Up

8.3

Use appropriate invention strategies to discover a topic for a critical essay.

Listing Prompts. First, spend some time playing with ideas, without censoring yourself. Lists can be rich sources for triggering topics. Let them grow freely, and when you're ready, use an item as the focus of another list or an episode of fastwriting. Divide your notebook into columns with the following headings

Cultural trends	Great songs	Favorite movies	Favorite books, stories, essays	Memorable pictures, paintings, images

In each column, generate a fast list of things that come to mind. What cultural trends do you find hard to explain, what songs do you find strangely moving, what films or TV shows capture your interest? Are there books you love, paintings or photographs you remember?

If you're writing about a work of literature, try making the following list:

1. Brainstorm a list of questions about the work that you find puzzling.

2. List the names of every important character or person in the story or essay. Choose one or two that seem most important. Under each name, make two new headings: Dreams and Problems. Under Dreams, list the things that character seems to desire most, even if he or she isn't fully aware of it. Under Problems, list everything that seems to be an obstacle to that character's achieving those desires.

3. List details or particulars from the story that seem to say more than they say. In other words, do any details recur? Do any objects have particular significance to one or more characters? Do any descriptions suggest the feelings, dispositions, or values of a particular character?

Fastwriting Prompts. Remember, fastwriting is a great way to stimulate creative thinking. Turn off your critical side and let yourself write "badly."

1. Choose one of the items in a column from your listing prompts to write about. Fastwrite about your experience with that thing. What do you remember? What do you notice? Do you feel something about this? Why?

If you're writing about a work of literature, try these prompts:

2. Write a narrative of thought. Begin with *When I first read this story or essay, I thought…And then I thought…And then…And then…*

3. Choose three lines or passages that are key to your current understanding of the themes or ideas behind the story or essay. Write these down on the left page of your notebook. On the opposing right page, fastwrite about each, beginning with *The first thing I notice about this passage is…And then…And then…And then…* When the writing stalls, write about the next line or passage until you've written about all three.

4. Use one of the following "seed sentences" as a prompt for fastwriting:

   - What is the relationship between _____ and _____?
   - The most important scene in the story is _____ because _____.
   - The title of the work might be significant because _____.
   - If I was going to divide the poem, story, or essay into parts, the first part would be _____.
   - The narrator in the work seems to want _____.

Visual Prompts. Visual thinking might help you play with ideas about how to analyze the work you're studying. Try these prompts to explore your response to a literary work:

1. Create a cluster using the name of the main character as the core word. Reread the story and then build as many associations as you can from that character. Think about feelings and ideas you associate with that person as well as any particulars you remember from the story.

2. Make a visual map of the story. Begin by placing a brief description of what you believe is the most significant moment in the story at the center of a blank page. This might be a turning point, or the point of highest tension, or perhaps the moment when the main character achieves his or her desires and dreams. Consider that moment the destination of the story. Now map out events or details in the narrative that threaten to lead the protagonist away from that destination, and those that appear to lead the protagonist toward it.

Research Prompts. Critical analysis usually involves working with primary sources: the poem, novel, essay, photograph, or painting. Sometimes, especially if the work isn't a text, you have to observe the object, performance, or behavior. If you're looking for a subject like these for your critical essay, then you need to go out and look. This field work might include

1. Attending a performance (e.g., watching the modern dance, going to see the drama, etc.)

2. Observing a behavior (e.g., observing how people behave in a certain social situation)

3. Going to the museum (e.g., browsing paintings)

4. Seeing the films or shows (e.g., an evening watching zombie films)

On the other hand, if you're looking for a literary text to analyze, you can research your favorite authors' work online, but you can also research top-ten lists of short stories, poems, and essays. There are annual "Best of" collections published every year in your university library.

Inquiring into the Details

Common Literary Devices

Many key concepts provide useful frameworks for analyzing literature. The key is to see the following ideas as an angle for viewing an essay, story, or poem much as you might move around a subject with a camera. Each provides a different way of seeing the same thing. In addition, each becomes a platform from which to pose a question about a text.

■ *Plot and significant event:* This is what happens in a story that moves it forward. One way of thinking about plot is to consider this: What are the key moments that propel the story forward? Why do you consider them key? How do they add tension to the story? In an essay, these moments often give rise to the question the writer is exploring. In short stories, there is often a significant event that may happen in or outside of the story, but the entire narrative and its characters act or think in response to that event.

■ *Characters:* Imagine a still pond upon which small paper boats float. Someone throws a rock in the pond—big or small—and the ripples extend outward, moving the boats this way and that. Depending on the size of the ripples, some of the boats may list or capsize, sinking slowly. Characters in a short story are like those boats, responding in some way to something that happened, some significant event that is revealed or implied. They move almost imperceptibly, or quite noticeably, or even violently. Is there logic to their response? How exactly are they changed? How do they relate to each other?

■ *Setting:* Where a story takes place can matter a lot or a little, but it always matters. Why? Because where a story takes place signals things about characters and who they are. A story set in rural Wyoming suggests a certain austere, ranching culture in which the characters operate. Even if they're not ranchers, they must somehow deal with that culture. Similarly, a story set in Chicago's predominantly black South Side introduces another set of constraints within which characters must operate. In some cases, setting might even become a kind of character.

■ *Point of view:* In nonfiction essays, point of view is usually straightforward—we assume the narrator is the author. But in fiction, it's much more complicated; in fact, *how* a story is told—from what perspective—is a crucial aesthetic decision. Stories told from the first-person point of view in the present tense

Inquiring into the Details (*continued*)

give the story a sense of immediacy—this feels like it's happening *now*—but at the same time limit our understanding of other characters, because we can't get into their heads. So-called omniscient narrators can introduce a feeling of distance from the action, but they are also gratifyingly godlike because they can see everything, hovering above all the action and even entering characters' minds at will. Why might an author have chosen a particular point of view? Is the narrator trustworthy? What might be his or her biases, and how might they affect the telling?

■ ***Theme:*** One way to understand a story or essay is to consider that everything—character, point of view, and setting—all contribute to a central meaning. In a good story, everything is there for a purpose—to say something to the reader about what it means to be human. In essays, this theme may be explicit, because essays both show *and* tell. Short stories, and especially poems, are often short on explanation of theme, operating with more ambiguity. The writer hopes the reader can *infer* certain ideas or feelings by paying close attention to what he or she *shows* the reader. To get at the theme, begin with the simple question *So what?* Why is the author telling this story or sharing this experience? What significance are we supposed to attach to it?

■ ***Image:*** Stories and poems ask us to see. When I read them, I imagine that writers take my face in their hands and gently—or sometimes brutally—direct my gaze. What are they insisting that I look at, and how do they want me to see it? Images that recur may also be significant.

Narrowing Down

Now that you've opened up possibilities for review topics, there are choices to make. Which do you want to write about?

What's Promising Material and What Isn't? Try out a possible topic for your critical essay by doing some more-focused writing and by thinking about it.

First, generate some thinking-through-writing.

■ **First thoughts?** Interpretation is inspired by this question: *What might it mean?* And that's not a bad question to start with. Spend some time rereading, observing, or studying the work you've tentatively chosen, and if you're using a double-entry journal, collect notes (e.g., key passages, lists of observations, descriptions, etc.) on the left-facing page of your journal. Then, on the right, fastwrite for as long as you can, exploring and speculating about possible interpretations. When the writing stalls, pick up on something in your notes on the left page. This writing should be very open-ended; you don't need to come to conclusions yet.

Now judge what you've generated:

- Can you refine your question? Reread your fastwrite. Do you see hints that you might explore about a relationship between two things? For example, what's the relationship between the author's description of the setting in the story and the idea you think is at its heart? Craft a relationship question from your fastwrite, using a template like this:

  What's the relationship between _____ and _____?

- Drawing on your thinking so far, can you turn the interpretation question (What does it mean?) into an assertion? For example, in the poem "The Bluebird" by Charles Bukowski, the narrator's "secret pact" with the "little" bird represents the bargain that many men in this culture make with themselves to conceal feelings using "toughness."

Considering doing some research to generate ideas on your tentative topic. In addition to searching for relevant material on Google and Google Scholar, search the databases at the university library for published articles or books on the author of your work and criticism of the particular piece you're analyzing. For this research, use specialized databases in the appropriate fields. For example,

- **Literary works.** Search the *MLA International Bibliography.*
- **Art.** Check databases such as ARTstor and ARTbibliographies Modern for criticism of contemporary work, or Art and Architecture Complete.
- **Film.** The AFI Catalog is a definitive database on American films. Many arts and humanities indexes also cover film studies.

Questions About Audience and Purpose. One basic rhetorical question is this: Is your audience familiar with the work you're interpreting? If not, should you provide background so that they share enough knowledge of it to appreciate your analysis? This might include things like

- **Background on the work.** When was it published or created? How was it received? What was it compared to?
- **Summary or description.** What is the basic plot? What happens? What does it say? What does it look like?
- **Background on the author.** Significance in literary or artistic circles? How the thing being analyzed fits into the body of work?

Another key rhetorical consideration is finding ways to interest readers in the work you're analyzing, especially if they're unfamiliar with it. Why should they care about your analysis of Charles Bukowski's poem or your interpretation of the relationship between personality and how people hold a beer? Think about ways in which the thing you're studying is relevant to understanding everyday experience. That's not so hard with your interpretations of barroom behavior. But a poem? Make it interesting. Why is this poem important? How does it speak to how we might live and feel? How does it speak to you?

Inquiring into the Details

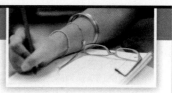

What Is a "Strong Reading"?

A big difference between literary texts and other kinds of texts is that when we read literature, we expect ambiguity. When I was reading the instructions for how to set the alarm on my daughter's iPod clock radio the other day, I would not have tolerated ambiguity. I'm interested in only one meaning for the word *plug*. But if I were reading the same word in a poem, I might imagine something other than the thing with two flat metal prongs that fit into a wall socket.

If a literary work can have multiple meanings, isn't the author's intended meaning the "right" way to interpret it? While discerning the author's intention, particularly in nonfiction, is a factor in interpreting a work's meaning, it is hardly the only one. What the reader *brings* to the text—his or her experiences, cultural biases, reading habits, and so on—is probably even more important.

That must mean that *any* interpretation of a literary text is fair game, right? Of course not. It has to be a *plausible* interpretation, one that the reader can explain convincingly using evidence from the text, the work of other critics, historical context, or the author's body of work. Readers must make arguments for their interpretations of literature, and the best arguments not only use strong evidence, but also account for as much of the work as possible.

A "strong reading" of a literary work should be your goal.[*] This is a reading that goes "against the grain." A story, poem, or essay may seem to beg to be read and interpreted a particular way. If you want to know which way that is, simply take a quick look at the literary essays for sale on the Internet on any popular work. These kinds of readings—which are usually the most obvious interpretations—are often reflections of stories about ourselves that we like to believe or that feel familiar. They might be what we often call "universal themes." A strong reading is one that recognizes this reflex and offers alternative, often less obvious interpretations. A strong reading is one that begins to notice the ways a work *breaks* with our usual understandings of things: "At first, this story seemed to reflect what I felt about growing up, but in these ways it helped me to understand that differently."

---

[*]Flower, Linda, Kathleen McCormick, and Gary Waller. *Reading Texts: Reading, Responding, Writing.* Lexington, MA: Heath, 1987. Print.

Writing the Sketch

We'll begin again with an early draft, a sketch that represents an initial attempt to discover what you want to focus on and what you might have to say about the work (or works) you've chosen.

Watch
the Animation on
Analyzing Texts
in your MyLab

Develop your sketch with the following things in mind:

- It should have a tentative title.
- It should be at least 500 to 600 words.

- Write it with the appropriate audience in mind. Are you writing for readers who are familiar with the text?

- Consider writing your sketch as a narrative of thought that tells the story of how you arrived at your current interpretation of the work you're studying. *When I began analyzing _____, I thought _____. And then . . . And then . . . And now . . .*

▶ Student Sketch

When Julie Bird read Leslie Marmon Silko's short story "Lullaby" for the first time, she said "It almost made me cry." In class, we talked a little about some of the traditions in Native American literature, and you can see in her sketch how she tries out several of the ideas we talked about: the importance of the storytelling tradition, the ways in which identity is tied to going home, and the healing power of the natural world. There are all kinds of literary traditions that are lenses through which you can read a story.

But the most important thing is to pay close attention to the text itself. What *exactly* does the story say, and what might it mean? Julie doesn't incorporate many passages from "Lullaby" in her sketch; she's thinking through some ideas about key themes in the story. She underlines several ideas that emerged in this first look. Now she has to return to the story and test the ideas against what the text actually says.

What Is the Role of Nature in "Lullaby"?

Julie Bird

1   "Lullaby," written by Leslie Marmon Silko, is an intriguing story about the life of a Navajo woman by the name of Ayah and her life. Ayah bared her soul to tell this story, an act of special meaning in a culture that passes on history by oral means. The Navajos often connect their identity to family, home, and nature. When the white man came to take away her children, Ayah, not fully understanding why, grabbed them and ran up the long slope of the mesa, to wait for her husband to come home. While she was waiting, she allowed the sun to relax her and felt as if "she could walk into the sky, stepping through clouds endlessly." The connection of peace to the natural world is key to the essay's theme.

2   Ayah, using the wool blanket as an instrument, created strong parallels between her mother (the past) and her son Jimmie (her present). This generational timeline establishes her identity by correlating the comfort of the past with the warmth of the present. The wool blanket is the object of that unbroken line. At the end of the story, Ayah is searching for her husband and she is thinking, "She did this because she had the blanket, and there

would be no place for him except with her and the blanket in the old abode barn near the arroyo." The blanket is significant to the characters in revealing the importance of family ties to the Navajos.

The overall theme of the essay relates to the sorrow and loss Ayah feels at the hands of the white man, and her inability to do anything about it. First, a government man comes to tell her that her son Jimmie was killed at war. Next, more government officials dupe her into signing her name in order to take away her children. To this she states, "Because it was like the old ones always told her about learning their language or any of their ways: it endangered you." When Chato was too old to work, the rancher made them move out of their home, and they had to go to the barn.   3

Through all of the sorrow put upon her, Ayah was able to turn to her identity and connection with her heritage, nature, and roots to find peace and strength to continue on.   4

Moving from Sketch to Draft

How well does your sketch lead you to an assertion about the meaning of the work or situation you're analyzing? Do you have a clear focus?

Evaluating Your Own Sketch. Among the key concerns in evaluating this early draft of your critical essay is whether you've discovered a workable focus and whether you're beginning to get some clear idea of what you're trying to say. One of the best things you can do at this point is to use your sketch to craft a tentative thesis *or* the question that will be the focus of the next draft.

- **Thesis.** On the back of your sketch, in a sentence or two (but no more), state the main thing you're trying to communicate in answer to the question *What does it mean?*

- **Inquiry question.** Compose a question that reflects what you want to focus on in your interpretation. A relationship? The significance of certain recurring elements? An analysis based on a certain context—when the work was written or a tradition or theory?

Reflecting on What You've Learned. At the beginning of this chapter, I talked about some of the basic elements of critical analysis (see p. 288) and said that a close examination of *evidence* leads to inferences about what the evidence might mean. This leads to an *interpretation* that you think makes sense, and, drawing on the evidence, an *argument* that convinces someone else of the soundness of your interpretation. How well did you incorporate those three elements into your sketch? What needs more development in the next draft? What does this tell you about the act of interpretation? Does the critical essay encourage a kind of thinking that can be distinguished from the thinking encouraged by other forms of writing?

Developing

To develop your sketch into a draft, work on two fronts:

1. Closer analysis of the primary work or phenomenon
2. Research in secondary sources on the context of the thing you're writing about: what other critics say, theories that guide the analysis, relevant background on the work or situation

Analysis. Interpretation is an inductive process. By looking closely at the specifics, you develop ideas about patterns in the work that might be significant. If you're studying a text, for example, then your analysis must be grounded in what exactly you see in the poem, story, or essay. In literary analysis, for example, you might focus on common devices such as setting and characters (see "Inquiring into the Details: Common Literary Devices" on p. 320). What *exactly* is the setting? What do the characters say *exactly* and when? What you look at will depend, of course, on your thesis or inquiry question. This evidence is the foundation of any critical essay, because it helps writers discover the *reasons* that support a particular interpretation.

Research. Any significant work of art—a painting or novel or a cultural artifact such as reality TV or Facebook profile pictures—exists in context. These contexts include:

- **Historical.** When was it created? Is it part of a tradition? In what ways does the work or performance reflect the politics and culture of its time?
- **Theoretical.** What are some critical methods for analyzing the thing (for literary works, for example, see "Inquiring into the Details: Why Literary Theory Is Not a Sleep Aid" on p. 309).
- **Biographical.** Who created the work? What does the author say about it or about his or her aesthetic intentions?
- **Critical.** What do other critics who have studied the work or phenomenon say about it?

To do this research on the context of the thing you're analyzing, you'll rely most heavily on scholarly sources in your university library. For example, here are some academic sources typically used in analyzing a literary work. Search as well for books on your author, work, or topic.

Historical	*Oxford Encyclopedia of American Literature, Cambridge History of English and American Literature, The Literary Encyclopedia*
Theoretical	*MLA International Bibliography, Magill's History of Literary Criticism*
Biographical	*Dictionary of Literary Biography, Biography Index Past and Present, Contemporary Authors*
Critical	*MLA International Bibliography, Book Review Index, Essay & General Literature Index, Magill's Bibliography of Contemporary Literary Criticism*

Drafting

Because a critical essay is an argument, your draft needs to make one. If you're writing a formal critical paper, then your thesis—the interpretation that is at the heart of your argument—should be stated explicitly pretty early in your paper. In a less formal critical essay (see "Our Zombies, Ourselves" earlier in the chapter), the thesis isn't necessarily a fixture of the introduction. You might work your way to it, like the unraveling of a ball of string. The question that is driving your essay, however, should be clear in the beginning (e.g., What does the popularity of zombies in American film say about us?)

Methods of Development. Like most writing, there is no formula for structuring your critical essay, but if you're writing for an audience that is relatively unfamiliar with your subject, you might imagine that your draft needs to answer a series of questions in roughly the following order:

- What do you find particularly interesting in the work or phenomena that inspired your analysis? (Show something specific.)
- What's the question that interests you? (Your thesis that answers that question?)
- Can you summarize or describe what you're analyzing?
- What have other critics or experts said about it? (Maybe some alternative interpretations, different from yours?)
- What's a reason behind your interpretation? What's the evidence that led you to see it?
- What's another reason? And the evidence?
- Can you tell me again what your close analysis or observation helped you to see about the meaning of the work or phenomenon?

   What are some of the other ways you might organize your critical essay?

Narrative. An entirely different approach is to use your question as the starting point for a story you tell about how you arrived at an answer. This approach is more essayistic in the sense that it provides the story of *how* you came to know rather than reporting *what* you think. A narrative essay might also involve relevant autobiographical details that influenced your analysis. For example, what feelings or experiences do you *bring* to the reading of a text?

Question to Answer. Because the assignment is designed around a question you're trying to answer about the topic, the question-to-answer design is an obvious choice. Consider spending the first part of your essay highlighting the question you're interested in. The key is to convince readers that yours is a question worth asking, and that the answer might be interesting to discover.

Compare and Contrast. Critical essays often benefit from this method of development. The approach might be to compare and contrast certain elements within the work. In a story there might be several characters, symbols or metaphors, plot developments, and so on—or you might compare the work to others by the same or even different authors. These comparisons have to be relevant to the question you're asking.

Combining Approaches. Frequently, a critical essay uses several or even all of the methods of development mentioned here: question to answer, comparison and contrast, and narrative. Consider how you might put them all to work, especially in certain sections of your draft.

Using Evidence. You need to consider two main kinds of evidence in a critical essay: evidence that comes from so-called *primary* sources—especially the work itself, but also letters or memoirs by the author; and evidence that comes from *secondary* sources, or books, articles, and essays by critics who are also writing about the work or author. Primary sources are generally most important. In more-personal literary responses, however, your personal associations, anecdotes, stories, or feelings may be used as evidence, if they're relevant to the question you're posing.

Workshopping

If your draft is subject to peer review, see Chapter 14 for details on how to organize workshop groups and decide on how your group can help you. To help you decide, use the guidance, starting on page 578, in Chapter 14. Each workshop type is described more fully in that chapter.

As you know, a critical essay argues for a particular interpretation of a text or phenomenon. As you prepare to share your draft, you want to look for some of these weak links in your argument; consider asking peer reviewers whether you've addressed them:

- **Insufficient evidence.** Remember that this is a form of writing that works mostly with *primary sources*—the short story, the film(s), the firsthand observations, etc. Most of the information in your essay should be your close examination of the primary sources you're focusing on.

- **Broad focus.** Even lengthy critical essays look only at *certain aspects* of the primary source that most contributed to the writer's interpretation.

- **General interpretation.** After all your analysis, you're not going to write something like "zombies are everywhere in film and are an interesting cultural phenomenon" as your thesis. That might be a setup for your thesis, which must be an interpretation with a much sharper edge: *The rise of the zombie in American film is testimony to the growing cultural nightmare that there are no safe places anymore, especially with the spread of nuclear weapons.*

In addition to these concerns, when you workshop the first draft of your critical essay, you should focus first on what peers make of the purpose and meaning of your essay, both of which guide your revision. The following grid can help you frame these questions for your workshop group.

Questions for Peer Reviewers	
1. Purpose	After reading the draft, can you explain back to me why I think the topic I chose to analyze is significant? Do I convince you that it might be significant to you, too?
2. Meaning	In your own words, how does the essay answer the inquiry question *What does it mean?* What evidence did you find most convincing in support of this interpretation? Least convincing?

Reflecting on the Draft. Take a look at the draft before you and circle the passage you think is the best in the essay so far. Now circle the passage that you think is weakest.

In your notebook, fastwrite for five minutes about both passages. What seems to be working in the better passage? What problems do you notice about the weaker one? Does either one address the question you're writing about? If so, how? If not, how might it? When you compare the two passages, what do you notice about the differences? How might you make the weaker passage more like the stronger one? How might you make the rest of the essay stronger?

Revising

Revision is a continual process—not a last step. You've been revising—"reseeing" your subject—from the first messy fastwriting in your journal. But the things that get your attention vary depending on where you are in the writing process. With your draft in hand, revision becomes your focus through what I'll call "shaping and tightening your draft."

8.4
Apply revision strategies that are effective for the critical essay.

Chapter 13 contains strategies that can help you revise any inquiry project, and the "Guide to Revision Strategies" on page 331 can help you locate these strategies. There are also certain things to think about that are especially useful for shaping a critical essay.

Shaping. When we shape a draft, the focus is on design—the order of information, the chain of reasoning, the coherence of paragraphs and their contribution to the whole composition. In a critical essay, one of the basic units of reasoning is the moments of analysis in your essay, or those places where you actually work with a primary source to tease out its implications.

Here's an example from a critical essay I once wrote on how American Indian writers seem to use memory in their fiction, poetry, and nonfiction. My focus here was on Sherman Alexie's work, and his character Thomas-Builds-the-Fire, who appears in several of the writer's stories.

Interpretation

Evidence

> I think that the implications of this—that tribal memory and personal memory merge—are profound. Perhaps that's why nobody wants to listen to the stories of Thomas Builds-the-Fire in Spokane/Coeur d'Alène writer Sherman Alexie's recent works, *Reservation Blues* and *Tonto and the Lone Ranger Fistfight in Heaven*. Thomas, whose stories came to him before he "had the words to speak" (*Reservation* 73), tells stories that many of the Indians on the Spokane reservation refuse to hear, "stealth stories" that work their way into dreams and into "clothes like sand, [that] gave you itches that could not be scratched" (15). I wonder if the antipathy to Thomas's stories is really resistance to the hegemonic power of someone else's story to structure and contain individual experience and memory. Is that why Victor and Junior, two Spokanes who are adrift, unable to find the symmetry between personal past, history, and legend that Momaday discovers in *Rainy Mountain*, "tried to beat those stories out of Thomas, tied him down and taped his mouth shut" (*Reservation* 15).

Notice how the analysis here is *layered*. An interpretation is introduced and then explicated with evidence, which then leads to an elaboration of the initial interpretation and ends with some supporting evidence.

Examine your own paragraphs in a similar way. Take a highlighter and use two different colors, one for interpretation (assertion) and the other for evidence. Look to see if your analysis is layered—working back and forth from your ideas about a work or phenomenon and the evidence from the text or your observations—and if not, revise to encourage that quality in paragraphs or passages of your draft.

Polishing

Shaping focuses on things such as purpose, meaning, and design. No less important is looking more closely at paragraphs, sentences, and words. Are your paragraphs coherent? How do you manage transitions? Are your sentences fluent and concise? Are there any errors in spelling or syntax? Chapter 13 can help you focus on these issues.

Before you finish your draft, work through the following checklist:

✓ Every paragraph is about one thing.

✓ The transitions between paragraphs aren't abrupt.

✓ The length of sentences varies in each paragraph.

✓ Each sentence is concise. There are no unnecessary words or phrases.

✓ You've checked grammar, particularly verb agreement, run-on sentences, unclear pronouns, and misused words (*there/their, where/were*, and so on). (See the Handbook at the back of this book for help with these grammar issues.)

✓ You've run your spellchecker and proofed your paper for misspelled words.

Chapter 13 is a buffet of revision strategies that will help you solve all kinds of revision problems, large and small. Use the "Guide to Revision Strategies" below to know where to look in that chapter to both shape and tighten your draft.

Guide to Revision Strategies

Problems in the Draft (Chapter 13)	Page Number
Unclear purpose	538
■ Not sure what the paper is about?	
■ Not focused enough?	
Unclear thesis, theme, or main idea	543
■ Not sure what you're trying to say?	
Lack of information or development	551
■ Need more convincing evidence?	
Disorganized	555
■ Doesn't move logically or smoothly from paragraph to paragraph?	
Unclear or awkward at the level of sentences and paragraphs	564
■ Seems choppy or hard to follow at the level of sentences or paragraphs?	

▶ Student Essay

Julie Bird's sketch earlier in this chapter about Leslie Marmon Silko's short story "Lullaby" showed traces of the ideas behind this draft. Julie touches on the question behind her inquiry into the story—how does the character Ayah recover from her many losses?—and finds a tentative answer: Ayah finds peace in nature. Sketches are just that—roughly drawn glimpses into our own thinking about something. When they're most helpful, this "bad" writing can help us discover what we want to say, as it did here for Julie.

But notice how Julie takes the idea that nature is a powerful force in the story and extends and deepens it in the draft. The result is that her thesis is richer and more interesting. How did she do this? By returning to the dialectical process—that motion between creative thinking and critical thinking—and immersing herself in the story itself. Julie also did some research on Silko and Native American literature, testing her assertions. She found not only evidence to support them, but new ways of thinking about what she wants to say.

Nature as Being: Landscape in Silko's "Lullaby"

Julie Bird

1   Leslie Marmon Silko, the author of "Lullaby," is a Native American writer from the Laguna Pueblo culture in New Mexico. Silko's story is about a Navajo woman, Ayah, and how she copes with the loss of her children—one dies in war, several others die in infancy, and two more are taken by the "white doctors" who suspect the children may have been exposed to tuberculosis. How is Ayah, condemned to poverty and surrounded by white indifference or hatred, able to recover from these losses?

2   Reflecting the "interrelatedness of man and nature that permeates Native American literature" (Schweninger 49), it is in the landscape that Ayah finds peace in old age. Arizona's natural environment, such as snow and the slope of the mesa, is an integral character in "Lullaby" that shows the intricate relationship between humans and the natural world.

3   Even the structure of the story echoes these themes. Silko writes her story from the end, to the beginning, to the end in the same cyclical fashion as life in the natural world and on the reservation. The writer portrays this cyclical structure of storytelling beautifully when describing Ayah as an old woman, as she reflects on the birth of her children through to the death of her husband.

4   Trying to find peace in the harmony of the natural world, Ayah turned herself to the memories of a happier past, and the rituals and rhythms of the earth's cycle. When saddened by thoughts of her dead son Jimmie, lost in some faraway war, Ayah wraps herself in a wool blanket that he had sent to her. This unconscious gesture invariably brings the memory of sitting with her grandma and mother and combing twigs from the freshly washed wool while they weaved it into blankets. Ayah fondly remembers that "the blankets...were soft and woven so tight that rain rolled off them like birds' feathers" (Silko 44). Through Ayah's reference to the feathers, Silko is making the connection to her own beliefs in the natural world. In a sense, Ayah becomes a bird.

5   When Ayah runs into the foothills of the "juniper trees and black lava" (45) in order to get her children away from the white doctors, she is seeking the place of refuge that is a constant source of comfort. It is her ritual to return to this spot. Ayah comes to the mesa when her son Jimmie dies, when she buries her children who died too soon, when the doctors take her children; in other words, when she is looking for balance. To Ayah, "the sun's warmth relaxed her and took the fear and anger away....It seemed to her that she could walk into the sky, stepping through clouds endlessly" (46).

6   This harmony that Ayah shares with the natural world is what makes her who she is; it is her identity as a Navajo woman. This is especially obvious at the end of the story when she is sitting with her dying husband, a man crushed by hopelessness and alcoholism. Silko writes that "The light was crystalline....She breathed the clarity of the night sky; she smelled the purity of the half moon and the stars" (51). Silko makes a point

that upon the death of her husband, Ayah at last felt a clear ("crystalline") understanding. With the passing of the storm, "steely blue-gray horses startled across the sky" (51), and with the passing away of the last of her family, Ayah was finally free to find her own peace. In old age, Ayah finally achieved her balance with the harmony of nature and was ready for it.

Just hearing the word "snow" evokes images of "freezing" and "icy," but Silko uses snow to project Ayah's feelings of warmth and comfort. Music, like nature, is a very integral part of some Native American cultures, and Silko expresses the correlation between music and the natural world throughout the story. For example, when Ayah is waiting for her husband to return home from a bar, she "sat down with her back against the wide cottonwood tree...and listened to the wind and snow sing a highpitched Yeibechei song" (43).   7

We learn from Silko that the Yeibechei song is the Navajo Night Chant and is a ceremony of healing. The fact that the snow sings such a song further reinforces the idea that nature is a healing force in the story. When Ayah is watching as the "snow drifted...with the northwest wind hurling it in gusts," and "she smiled at the snow which was trying to cover her little by little" (44), Silko suggests that the snow, like the blanket, is a source of comfort to Ayah. And when Ayah is sitting next to her dying husband, the snow storm clears up and the night is still and clear. This is significant in that it parallels the clearing of Ayah's troubles, the passing of the figurative storm within herself.   8

At the end, Ayah sings her lullaby: "The earth is your mother,...the sky is your father,...rainbow is your sister,...the winds are your brothers" (51). It is hard to miss the balance of nature with humanity that is a part of the Navajo heritage. But Ayah's lullaby also points to Silko's particular vision of the role of nature. Landscapes aren't something to be looked at as separate from people. As the critic Karen E. Waldron notes, "Silko's poems, essays, and novels manifest the relationship between the human being and his or her surroundings as one of *being* rather than viewing" (179) [emphasis added].   9

The most interesting but subtle way in which the story is written deals with Silko's use of color, scent, and smell to make the story come alive and to further reinforce the images of nature as a benign and loving force. When describing the birth of one of Ayah's children, Silko writes, "The morning was already warm ever before dawn and Ayah smelled the bee flowers blooming and the young willow growing at the springs" (44). This passage correlates birth with the smell of spring flowers, very much in the tradition of human harmony with the natural world.   10

Silko, in trying to show Ayah's relationship to the natural world, uses every sense at her disposal to paint a vivid picture to the reader. When reading "Lullaby" you can feel the snow landing gently about you, hear the screech of the hawk as it patiently circles above, and smell the pungent odor of the juniper trees. Silko is also able to make the reader feel the intense pain of loneliness associated with the loss of Ayah's family and culture at the hands of the white man. In the story, Silko weaves the natural world into every nook and cranny of the narrative so the reader is unaware of its existence but can feel its essence   11

(continued)

(continued)

as its own entity; in this case it's an entity that is not separate from Ayah but merges with her. Both are "beings"; both share consciousness. And in the end, she finds comfort in that.

Works Cited

Schweninger, Lee. "Writing Nature: Silko and Native Americans as Nature Writers." *Mellis* 18 (1993): 47–60. Print.

Silko, Leslie Marmon. "Lullaby." *Storyteller*. New York: Arcade, 1981. 43-51. Print.

Waldron, Karen E. "The Land as Consciousness." *Such News of the Land: U.S. Women Nature Writers*. Ed. Thomas S. Edwards and Elizabeth A. De Wolfe. Hanover, NH: UP of New England, 2001. 179–190. Print.

Evaluating the Essay

1. Compare Bird's earlier sketch and her draft. What do you notice about her revisions? In particular, do you think the draft is more insightful than the sketch? Why?

2. One of the temptations in writing about Native American literature (or any literature by someone from another or unfamiliar culture) is to make assumptions about what "they" believe or how "they" think. Many of these are based on certain cultural commonplaces that we pick up without thinking much about them. One of these is that Indians have strong ties to nature. Does Bird find support for her assumptions about that? How do you avoid simply accepting such assumptions?

3. When you write about literature, the most important source of information is the text you're writing about—the story, poem, essay, or novel. How well does Bird use evidence from "Lullaby" to convince you that what she says about the story is a reasonable interpretation?

Using What You Have Learned

1. **Apply the methods of critical analysis not only to literature but anything whose meanings aren't apparent.** If you're not an English major, why should you learn to write a critical essay? I hope the answer is obvious by now. The act of interpretation is a fundamental part of making sense of the world; it's also an essential academic skill. In the future, you'll be asked to interpret data, field observations, historical narratives, case studies, and

many other primary sources. Interpretation is a method of thought you can't practice enough.

2. **Use evidence from primary sources to argue effectively for a convincing interpretation.** The last three chapters—the proposal, the argument, and now the critical essay—are all persuasive forms of writing. In some ways, you build arguments in all three forms in very similar ways. But with a critical essay, you've composed an argument that works with a particular kind of evidence: primary sources. This is a more scholarly approach to argument that builds on the foundations of persuasive writing you've developed in previous chapters.

3. **Use appropriate invention strategies to discover a topic for a critical essay.** Though research has been part of the invention toolbox since the first assignment chapter on the personal essay, it has become increasingly important as we move towards writing on subjects outside our experience and knowledge. Because it relies on close reading and observation, the critical essay is mostly research. By now it should be apparent that research (reading, interview, observation) *is* an invention strategy—a source of discovery—not just a move to build support for what you already know. This becomes even more obvious if you write a research paper or ethnography in later chapters.

4. **Apply revision strategies that are effective for the critical essay.** Research is, of course, not only an invention strategy but a revision strategy, especially with a form such as the critical essay. When we "do research," particularly on the web, it often seems haphazard—looking here and there unsystematically, hoping to stumble into something usable. In the final two chapters, I hope you see that revising with research is, well, strategic. There are certain *categories* of information that you should look for. For example, in this chapter we talked about this in terms of context: historical, theoretical, biographical, and critical. Various forms of writing—and types of inquiry questions—give you guidance about types of information to research as you draft and revise. Look at your future research-based assignments rhetorically: What are the features of this kind of writing, and are there recognizable categories of information that are typically present?

Complete
Additional Exercises
and Practice on
Chapter 8
in your MyLab

Writing an ethnographic essay will test your research skills by bringing them out of the library and into the field. That might be to the park where skateboarders gather, a hall where World War II veterans meet, a mall where fifteen-year-olds congregate, or the fields where migrant workers toil.

Writing an Ethnographic Essay

9

Learning Objectives

In this chapter, you'll learn to

9.1 Understand the idea of culture as a "web," and apply techniques of field research to describe it.

9.2 Use appropriate features of an ethnographic essay in a project that interprets how a social group sees itself and its world.

9.3 Use relevant methods of invention to identify a local culture to study.

9.4 Analyze and interpret qualitative information.

9.5 Apply revision strategies that are effective for an ethnographic essay.

Writing About Culture

My daughter used to hate spiders. In fact, she was so repulsed by spiders she refused to utter the word, calling them "s-words" whenever she spotted one of the bugs. In sadistic moments, I wanted to explain to her that there are invisible webs everywhere and that we walk into them all the time. In fact, we may spin a few threads ourselves occasionally. Like the spiders in our basement, subcultures abound right under our very noses. We just have to learn to see the webs they weave.

The "web of culture" is a good metaphor because, like spider webs, the many cultures and subcultures we encounter in our everyday lives are often difficult to detect. These webs are also something in which we are all enmeshed, whether we know it or not. To some extent they limit our movements, shape our beliefs, and determine our traditions.

Ethnography is a method of inquiry into culture that exposes cultural webs much the way the morning dew exposes the intricacies of a spider web in your backyard. In this chapter, you'll practice this approach to research and learn some ways that you can apply ethnographic techniques to all kinds of research projects. The real value of trying ethnography isn't that you'll be writing lots of ethnographies in other classes. Instead, writing an ethnographic essay will expand your research skills by bringing them out of the library and into the field. That might be to the park where skateboard-ers gather, a hall where World War II veterans meet, a mall where fifteen-year-olds congregate, or the fields where migrant workers toil. You might even wander online, where electronic subcultures abound. You'll learn to be a more careful observer. And ethnography will also raise interesting questions about whether all research can be objective.

Motives for Writing Ethnography

Ethnography may be new to you, but you've almost certainly enjoyed its nonaca-demic versions. Magazine articles on other cultures in *National Geographic* and *Discover* have some elements of ethnography, and arguably so do some of the reality TV shows. In a way, *Jersey Shore* has elements of ethnography in its im-plicit insistence that "Guidos" and "Guidettes" represent a certain type of Italian American youth culture that really exists. Programs such as *Jersey Shore* or *Orange County Housewives* invite us into cultural worlds that we may not know or rec-ognize. I think that's one reason they're popular. Reality TV may be staged, over-dramatized, and sometimes jaw-droppingly stupid, but in their own ways these programs do some of the things that ethnography does: show us types of people in the social setting they live in, doing what they do to find meaning in their lives. There are also traces of ethnographic methods in some photographic essays, mov-ies, podcasts, and documentaries; whenever someone goes into the field with a camera, microphone, or pen to document a culture—including those in their own communities—they're doing ethnographic work.

Of course, the world is not a laboratory. You can't control the many variables that influence what people say and what they do. But that's the point. From the outset, ethnography concedes that social communities are complicated. Fieldwork will never be able to completely untangle them. But it can unknot a few strands. Ethnographers try to do this while acknowledging their own bias. Like much "qualitative" research, ethnography is subjective, but in many ways this adds to the richness of the results. We get a truer look at the chemistry between the observer and the observed, something that is always present in research with human sub-jects but frequently hidden behind the veil of "objectivity."

Ethnography and Academic Writing

9.1

Understand the idea of culture as a "web," and apply techniques of field research to describe it.

Interest in academic ethnography has boomed in recent years, something you'll prob-ably discover if you take an anthropology course. But you may also encounter ethno-graphic ways of seeing—or interest in the ways social groups behave and believe—in sociology, English, and even the visual arts, where something called "visual ethnogra-phy" might be practiced in formal or informal ways. Some researchers are using both film and still photography to capture a subculture in action, something you might consider as you work on your own ethnographic project.

ethnographic: use film & photography to capture subculture in action.

Increasingly, ethnography is going online to study online cultures such as YouTube or using the web to report findings in multimedia formats. Studying social communities on the web is a relatively new form of ethnography, and it often has very practical implications. For example, marketing specialists who study how consumers behave when shopping for a product online can harvest invaluable data that help them sell things. Usability experts want to know how people interact with a website, to refine its features. Sociologists might use online ethnography to study gay culture and other groups that in certain countries may be hard to reach otherwise.

More than in other forms of inquiry, ethnographers must spend time in the field simply watching and taking notes

As I mentioned earlier, ethnography is what scholars call *qualitative* research. Instead of experimental data, ethnographers analyze case studies, artifacts (things that are meaningful to a particular group), and especially the first-hand observations they've collected in field notes. Quantitative research often isn't the best way to study people, because variables are hard to control and we're really complicated subjects to study. Qualitative research such as ethnography is better suited to providing a picture of social communities; it may lack the authority of quantitative methods, but it provides a much richer picture.

[handwritten: Use, case studies artifacts, things that have meaning to group and 1st hand observation]

In this chapter, you won't be tackling a formal ethnographic project. Save that for your anthropology class. Instead, you'll attempt to create an ethnographic *essay* or project that uses some of the basic methods of that kind of research, including:

- Field (or online) observations
- Interviews
- Photographs, video, audio recordings
- Collection and study of artifacts
- Background research on the culture you're studying

*[handwritten: *for an ethnographic project!]*

Features of the Form

9.2
Use appropriate features of an ethnographic essay in a project that interprets how a social group sees itself and its world.

Feature	Conventions of the Ethnographic Essay
Inquiry question →	How do the people in a social group or culture see themselves and their world?
Motives →	We put people in categories all the time: This person is a "geek," or that person is a "skater." But is there actually evidence that justifies a social category, a culture with which certain people identify? The only way to find out is to observe, interview, and describe members of these groups. What do they say and do? What things do they value?

(continued)

[handwritten: — important —]

(continued)

Motives:

	How do they see each other? The motives for doing this might include practical purposes: • Discovering the best ways to understand and communicate with a particular audience. • Proposing policies that incorporate how affected people see the problems. • Improving products and services targeted to certain groups. Or more academic purposes: • Developing an informed understanding of cultural groups and theories that explain their beliefs and behaviors.
Subject matter	We all belong to subcultures that we don't recognize we belong to—or perhaps refuse to acknowledge. But ethnography tends to focus on people who, at least when pressed, freely identify with a specific group. Cultures for study can be as remote as a Pacific island or as close as the researcher's neighborhood. Student projects have described skateboarders, international students, quilters, truck drivers, thirteen-year-old cheerleaders, football fans, and birdwatchers. Whatever the cultural group you choose, what's key is that you *study it in its local setting*.

Structure	Projects that use ethnographic methods often tell a story. For this project, consider using one or more of the following structures:
	
	    • A typical day: What does it look like for group members?
	    • Collage: a series of richly described scenes
	    • Narrative: the story of your understanding of the culture from your research

Sources of information	Above all, evidence is gleaned from field research. Sources of information include: • Field observations • Interviews • Artifacts • Images, recordings, video • Research, including statistics and background information on the group

use these

very important to ethnographic's

Language	Because the researcher is inevitably a part of the research, ethnography is often openly subjective. Researchers may use the first person and, in their role as narrators of their findings, write up their work in something like a literary style—scenes, descriptions, dialogue, and so on. Imagine for this project that your audience is nonexpert; they're not anthropologists or authorities on the culture you're studying. The language you use may be informal, speculative, and personal.

Prose+

While visual ethnography as an academic field is relatively new, filmmakers and photographers have long been interested in documenting cultures. Films such as *Nanook of the North* (1922), an early documentary about the Inuit people in the Arctic, is one famous example. Today, visual methods—especially photographs—are often a part of more conventional studies, but the wide availability of digital video, audio, and images have made visual ethnography an important subdiscipline. To explore some of the possibilities, browse the many video ethnographies on YouTube—many of them produced by students. For example, here's a screen shot from a video ethonography of jugglers.

READINGS

▶ Ethnographic Essay 1

Identity, as any fifteen-year-old knows, is a transaction. You give a little and you get a little from the social groups you like, and you don't do business with those you don't, except maybe to make sure you don't look or act like "one of them." This is not, however, free enterprise. Certain identities carry more social power. In my high school, those were not just the varsity football and basketball players, but also the well-to-do kids whose homes had huge "rec rooms" in the basement, where they held parties for a select few.

You don't have a choice, however, about belonging to some groups. For example, you may be African American, Latina, or Native American. Perhaps you are disabled. While there's more tolerance of difference these days, Judith Ortiz Cofer observes in "The Myth of the Latin Woman," it is nearly impossible, as someone who is different, to escape the assumptions others have about who you are. Sometimes these perceptions have serious consequences: You aren't hired or you can't rent the house. What can you do about this? Understandably, you might get angry. In her essay, Cofer suggests another response: Sometimes it is "custom,…not chromosomes," that helps explain difference. Cofer's essay, like the others in this chapter, is not a formal ethnography, but it is a great introduction to ethnography as a form of inquiry. "The

Myth of the Latin Woman" helps us to see how the people we observe look back at us. Because we are visitors in their world, doing ethnography means working hard to understand that world in *their* terms, not ours.

The Myth of the Latin Woman: I Just Met a Girl Named Maria

Judith Ortiz Cofer

2

On a bus trip to London from Oxford University where I was earning some graduate credits one summer, a young man, obviously fresh from a pub, spotted me and as if struck by inspiration went down on his knees in the aisle. With both hands over his heart he broke into an Irish tenor's rendition of "Maria" from *West Side Story*. My politely amused fellow passengers gave his lovely voice the round of gentle applause it deserved. Though I was not quite as amused, I managed my version of an English smile: no show of teeth, no extreme contortions of the facial muscles—I was at this time of my life practicing reserve and cool. Oh, that British control, how I coveted it. But Maria had followed me to London, reminding me of a prime fact of my life: you can leave the Island, master the English language, and travel as far as you can, but if you are a Latina, especially one like me who so obviously belongs to Rita Moreno's gene pool, the Island travels with you.

1

This is sometimes a very good thing—it may win you that extra minute of someone's attention. But with some people, the same things can make *you* an island—not so much a tropical paradise as an Alcatraz, a place nobody wants to visit. As a Puerto Rican girl growing up in the United States and wanting like most children to "belong," I resented the stereotype that my Hispanic appearance called forth from many people I met.

2

Our family lived in a large urban center in New Jersey during the sixties, where life was designed as a microcosm of my parents' casas on the island. We spoke in Spanish, we ate Puerto Rican food bought at the bodega, and we practiced strict Catholicism complete with Saturday confession and Sunday mass at a church where our parents were accommodated into a one-hour Spanish mass slot, performed by a Chinese priest trained as a missionary for Latin America.

3

As a girl I was kept under strict surveillance, since virtue and modesty were, by cultural equation, the same as family honor. As a teenager I was instructed on how to behave as a proper señorita. But it was a conflicting message girls got, since the Puerto Rican mothers also encouraged their daughters to look and act like women and to dress in clothes our Anglo friends and their mothers found too "mature" for our age. It was, and is, cultural, yet I often felt humiliated when I appeared at an American friend's party wearing a dress more suitable to a semiformal than to a playroom birthday celebration.

4

(continued)

(continued)

At Puerto Rican festivities, neither the music nor the colors we wore could be too loud. I still experience a vague sense of letdown when I'm invited to a "party" and it turns out to be a marathon conversation in hushed tones rather than a fiesta with salsa, laughter, and dancing—the kind of celebration I remember from my childhood.

5   I remember Career Day in our high school, when teachers told us to come dressed as if for a job interview. It quickly became obvious that to the barrio girls, "dressing up" sometimes meant wearing ornate jewelry and clothing that would be more appropriate (by mainstream standards) for the company Christmas party than as daily office attire. That morning I had agonized in front of my closet, trying to figure out what a "career girl" would wear because, essentially, except for Marlo Thomas on TV, I had no models on which to base my decision. I knew how to dress for school: at the Catholic school I attended we all wore uniforms; I knew how to dress for Sunday mass, and I knew what dresses to wear for parties at my relatives' homes. Though I do not recall the precise details of my Career Day outfit, it must have been a composite of the above choices. But I remember a comment my friend (an Italian-American) made in later years that coalesced my impressions of that day. She said that at the business school she was attending the Puerto Rican girls always stood out for wearing "everything at once." She meant, of course, too much jewelry, too many accessories. On that day at school, we were simply made the negative models by the nuns who were themselves not credible fashion experts to any of us. But it was painfully obvious to me that to the others, in their tailored skirts and silk blouses, we must have seemed "hopeless" and "vulgar." Though I now know that most adolescents feel out of step much of the time, I also know that for the Puerto Rican girls of my generation that sense was intensified. The way our teachers and classmates looked at us that day in school was just a taste of the culture clash that awaited us in the real world, where prospective employers and men on the street would often misinterpret our tight skirts and jingling bracelets as a come-on.

6   Mixed cultural signals have perpetuated certain stereotypes—for example, that of the Hispanic woman as the "Hot Tamale" or sexual firebrand. It is a one-dimensional view that the media have found easy to promote. In their special vocabulary, advertisers have designated "sizzling" and "smoldering" as the adjectives of choice for describing not only the foods but also the women of Latin America. From conversations in my house I recall hearing about the harassment that Puerto Rican women endured in factories where the "boss men" talked to them as if sexual innuendo was all they understood and, worse, often gave them the choice of submitting to advances or being fired.

7   It is custom, however, not chromosomes, that leads us to choose scarlet over pale pink. As young girls, we were influenced in our decisions about clothes and colors by the women—older sisters and mothers who had grown up on a tropical island where the natural environment was a riot of primary colors, where showing your skin was one way to keep cool as well as to look sexy. Most important of all, on the island, women perhaps felt freer to dress and move more provocatively, since, in most cases, they were protected by the traditions, mores, and laws of a Spanish/Catholic system of morality and machismo whose main rule was: *You may look at my sister, but if*

you touch her I will kill you. The extended family and church structure could provide a young woman with a circle of safety in her small pueblo on the island; if a man "wronged" a girl, everyone would close in to save her family honor.

This is what I have gleaned from my discussions as an adult with older Puerto Rican women. They have told me about dressing in their best party clothes on Saturday nights and going to the town's plaza to promenade with their girlfriends in front of the boys they liked. The males were thus given an opportunity to admire the women and to express their admiration in the form of *piropos*: erotically charged street poems they composed on the spot. I have been subjected to a few piropos while visiting the Island, and they can be outrageous, although custom dictates that they must never cross into obscenity. This ritual, as I understand it, also entails a show of studied indifference on the woman's part; if she is "decent," she must not acknowledge the man's impassioned words. So I do understand how things can be lost in translation. When a Puerto Rican girl dressed in her idea of what is attractive meets a man from the mainstream culture who has been trained to react to certain types of clothing as a sexual signal, a clash is likely to take place. The line I first heard based on this aspect of the myth happened when the boy who took me to my first formal dance leaned over to plant a sloppy over-eager kiss painfully on my mouth, and when I didn't respond with sufficient passion said in a resentful tone: "I thought you Latin girls were supposed to mature early"—my first instance of being thought of as a fruit or vegetable—I was supposed to *ripen*, not just grow into womanhood like other girls.

It is surprising to some of my professional friends that some people, including those who should know better, still put others "in their place." Though rarer, these incidents are still commonplace in my life. It happened to me most recently during a stay at a very classy metropolitan hotel favored by young professional couples for their weddings. Late one evening after the theater, as I walked toward my room with my new colleague (a woman with whom I was coordinating an arts program), a middle-aged man in a tuxedo, a young girl in satin and lace on his arm, stepped directly into our path. With his champagne glass extended toward me, he exclaimed, "Evita!"

Our way blocked, my companion and I listened as the man half-recited, half-bellowed "Don't Cry for Me, Argentina." When he finished, the young girl said: "How about a round of applause for my daddy?" We complied, hoping this would bring the silly spectacle to a close. I was becoming aware that our little group was attracting the attention of the other guests. "Daddy" must have perceived this too, and he once more barred the way as we tried to walk past him. He began to shout-sing a ditty to the tune of "La Bamba"—except the lyrics were about a girl named María whose exploits all rhymed with her name and gonorrhea. The girl kept saying "Oh, Daddy" and looking at me with pleading eyes. She wanted me to laugh along with the others. My companion and I stood silently waiting for the man to end his offensive song. When he finished, I looked not at him but at his daughter. I advised her calmly never to ask her father what he had done in the army. Then I walked between them and to my room. My friend complimented me on my cool handling of the situation. I confessed to her that I really

(continued)

8

9

10

(continued)

had wanted to push the jerk into the swimming pool. I knew that this same man—probably a corporate executive, well educated, even worldly by most standards—would not have been likely to regale a white woman with a dirty song in public. He would perhaps have checked his impulse by assuming that she could be somebody's wife or mother, or at least *somebody* who might take offense. But to him, I was just an Evita or a María: merely a character in his cartoon-populated universe.

11   Because of my education and my proficiency with the English language, I have acquired many mechanisms for dealing with the anger I experience. This was not true for my parents, nor is it true for the many Latin women working at menial jobs who must put up with stereotypes about our ethnic group such as: "They make good domestics." This is another facet of the myth of the Latin woman in the United States. Its origin is simple to deduce. Work as domestics, waitressing, and factory jobs are all that's available to women with little English and few skills. The myth of the Hispanic menial has been sustained by the same media phenomenon that made "Mammy" from *Gone with the Wind* America's idea of the black woman for generations; María, the housemaid or counter girl, is now indelibly etched into the national psyche. The big and the little screens have presented us with the picture of the funny Hispanic maid, mispronouncing words and cooking up a spicy storm in a shiny California kitchen.

12   This media-engendered image of the Latina in the United States has been documented by feminist Hispanic scholars, who claim that such portrayals are partially responsible for the denial of opportunities for upward mobility among Latinas in the professions. I have a Chicana friend working on a Ph.D. in philosophy at a major university. She says her doctor still shakes his head in puzzled amazement at all the "big words" she uses. Since I do not wear my diplomas around my neck for all to see, I too have on occasion been sent to that "kitchen," where some think I obviously belong.

13   One such incident that has stayed with me, though I recognize it as a minor offense, happened on the day of my first public poetry reading. It took place in Miami in a boat-restaurant where we were having lunch before the event. I was nervous and excited as I walked in with my notebook in my hand. An older woman motioned me to her table. Thinking (foolish me) that she wanted me to autograph a copy of my brand new slender volume of verse, I went over. She ordered a cup of coffee from me, assuming that I was the waitress. Easy enough to mistake my poems for menus, I suppose. I know that it wasn't an intentional act of cruelty, yet of all the good things that happened that day, I remember that scene most clearly, because it reminded me of what I had to overcome before anyone would take me seriously. In retrospect I understand that my anger gave my reading fire, that I have almost always taken doubts in my abilities as a challenge—and that the result is, most times, a feeling of satisfaction at having won a convert when I see the cold, appraising eyes warm to my words, the body language change, the smile that indicates that I have opened some avenue for communication. That day I read to that woman and her lowered eyes told me that she was embarrassed at her little faux pas, and when I willed her to look up at me, it was my victory, and she graciously allowed me to punish her with my full attention.

We shook hands at the end of the reading, and I never saw her again. She has probably forgotten the whole thing but maybe not.

Yet I am one of the lucky ones. My parents made it possible for me to acquire a   14
stronger footing in the mainstream culture by giving me the chance at an education.
And books and art have saved me from the harsher forms of ethnic and racial prejudice
that many of my Hispanic *compañeras* have had to endure. I travel a lot around the
United States, reading from my books of poetry and my novel, and the reception I most
often receive is one of positive interest by people who want to know more about my
culture. There are, however, thousands of Latinas without the privilege of an education
or the entrée into society that I have. For them life is a struggle against the misconceptions perpetuated by the myth of the Latina as whore, domestic or criminal. We cannot
change this by legislating the way people look at us. The transformation, as I see it, has
to occur at a much more individual level. My personal goal in my public life is to try to
replace the old pervasive stereotypes and myths about Latinas with a much more interesting set of realities. Every time I give a reading, I hope the stories I tell, the dreams
and fears I examine in my work, can achieve some universal truth which will get my
audience past the particulars of my skin color, my accent, or my clothes.

I once wrote a poem in which I called us Latinas "God's brown daughters." This   15
poem is really a prayer of sorts, offered upward, but also, through the human-to-human channel of art, outward. It is a prayer for communication, and for respect. In
it, Latin women pray "in Spanish to an Anglo God / with a Jewish heritage," and they
are "fervently hoping / that if not omnipotent, / at least He be bilingual."

Inquiring into the Essay

1. **Explore.** Being different and being born different are two quite different
   things. But different from what? Who gets to decide what is "normal" or
   "conventional"? And is there anything we can do about it? Fastwrite about
   these questions for four minutes without stopping.

2. **Explain.** Imagine that Cofer's essay is "data" for an ethnographic project on
   Latina culture, specifically first-generation Puerto Rican girls who attend an
   urban high school. In your own words, summarize what this "subject" (Cofer)
   contributes to your effort to understand those girls' world.

3. **Evaluate.** One thing that makes this essay interesting to read is Cofer's reliance on anecdote, and especially scenes, as a way of making her argument.
   This essay both shows and tells. Choose one of these moments (e.g., the
   London bus trip, high school Career Day, the hotel encounter, the poetry
   reading) and explain why you found it particularly persuasive.

4. **Reflect.** Reflect on this problem: Ethnography doesn't pretend to be "objective." The writer/observer is intimately involved in collecting and interpreting
   the data. And yet, like all "qualitative" research, ethnographers hope to produce accurate insights. How can the ethnographer attempt to minimize bias?

▶ **Ethnographic Essay 2**

A few years ago, an anthropology professor in her fifties decided to move into the freshman dorm at her university. She registered as a freshman with an undeclared major and spent an academic year doing exactly what other freshmen did: attending parties, going to classes, making new friends. But she was also quietly collecting data on her experience for an ethnography about student life that was then published as a book, *My Freshman Year.*

The professor, Cathy Small, assumed a pseudonym for her project, Rebekah Nathan, and managed to conduct her research without arousing the suspicion of fellow freshmen at the school, Northern Arizona University. Her research was based not only on extensive observations, but also on a number of interviews with fellow students, including international students who attended the school. In the excerpt that follows, Small reports on how students from England, Germany, Japan, Mexico, India, China, and the United Arab Emirates (UAE) viewed an American college and its students. It isn't often that we can see ourselves as these students see us, and the portrait is revealing.

 # 3.

My Freshman Year:
Worldliness and Worldview
Rebekah Nathan

1   The single biggest complaint international students lodged about U.S. students was, to put it bluntly, our ignorance. As informants described it, by "ignorance" they meant the misinformation and lack of information that Americans have both about other countries and about themselves. Although most international students noted how little other students asked them about their countries, almost all students had received questions that they found startling: "Is Japan in China?" "Do you have a hole for a bathroom?" "Is it North Korea or South Korea that has a dictator?" "Where exactly is India?" "Do you still ride elephants?" "Do they dub American TV programs into British?"

2   These are just a few of the questions American students actually asked of international students. While they no doubt came from the less sophisticated among their classmates, it was clear that international students across the board felt that most Americans—even their own friends—are woefully ignorant of the world scene. It is instructive to hear how students from diverse countries discuss their perceptions of American students' views of themselves and the world.

JAPAN: Really, they don't know very much about other countries, but maybe it's just because a country like Japan is so far away. Japanese probably don't know about the Middle East. Sometimes, students keep asking about ninjas.

UAE: American students are nice, but they need to stop being so ignorant about other countries and other cultures. Americans need to look at the world around them, and even the cultures around them in their own country.

MEXICO: The U.S. is not the center of the world. [Americans] don't know anything about other countries. Many of them don't have an interest in learning about other cultures. The only things students ever ask me about in my culture is food.

CHINA: Americans know very little about China or its culture. Most people think China is still very poor and very communist-controlled, with no freedom. There is a very anticommunist feeling, and people know little about today's China, which is quite changing and different. New Zealanders know much more about China—perhaps it's their proximity. I think that older people here have more of a sense of history, and that history, about the wars, about the cold war, makes them understand more about the world. Younger people seem to have no sense of history.

ENGLAND: People here know surprisingly little about England, and they assume a lot of things, some true, some not. People's impressions of me when I say I'm from England is that I might drink tea off a silver tray, and maybe live in a castle, and use a red telephone box. That's the honest truth. The questions that I've been asked are unbelievable.

MALAYSIA: I tell people that I am Muslim, and they take for granted that I'm an Arab. How can they not realize that not all Muslims are Arabs when they have many Muslims here who are American?

GERMANY: American students are much more ignorant of other countries and cultures. I suppose it's because it's so big, and knowing about California for you is like us knowing about France. It's a neighbor. The U.S. is less dependent on other cultures, and maybe that's why they need to know less. Still, Americans come across as not interested in other cultures, like they don't really care about other countries. So they think things like Swedish people are only blonds.

INDIA: Somebody asked me if we still ride on elephants. That really bothered me. If I say I'm Indian, they ask which reservation? I say I'm from Bombay. "Where is Bombay?" Some people don't even know where India is. A friend of mine and I tried to make these Americans see what it was like and we asked them where they're from. They said California. And we said, Where was that?

FRANCE: People here don't know where anything is. For World War II, the teacher had to bring in a map to show where Germany and England are—it was incredible! I read somewhere a little research that said only 15 to 20 percent of Americans between the ages eighteen to twenty-five could point out Iraq on a map. The country will go to war, but it doesn't know where the country is!

Despite the critical consensus in these comments, it would be unfair of me to represent international student perspectives as roundly negative. In general, students from outside the United States warmly appreciated the American educational system as well as the spirit of the American college student. The criticisms that they did have, though, were pointed and focused. Taken together, they amounted to nothing less than a theory of the relationship among ignorance, intolerance, and ethnocentrism in this

(continued)

[handwritten margin note: Americans form culture judgements]

[handwritten margin note: 3]

(continued)

country, one that international eyes saw bordering on profound self-delusion. When I asked the linked questions, "What would you want American students to see about themselves?" and "What advice would you give them?" one German student stated succinctly what many students communicated to me at greater length: "Americans seem to think they have the perfect place to live, the best country, the best city. I hear that all the time. I used to think you just got that from politicians, but now I see it's from regular people too. The patriotism thing here really bothers me."

4   It is sobering to hear these words from a German student, whose country's historical experience in the 1930s and 1940s taught him the dangers of hypernationalism. To his fellow U.S. students he offered this recommendation: "I'd give them advice to live elsewhere. They should recognize that the way of living in the U.S. is fine, but it isn't necessarily the best way for everyone. I don't like to evaluate, and I'd like that applied to me. Be more informed. Information leads to tolerance."

5   It bothered a Chinese student who read in an article that American students don't want to study a foreign language because they believe that the world language will be English. "I think they need to learn about the world, to learn a foreign language," he urged. It bothered a British student, who lamented how much of world music American students seem to miss. "Everything here [on his corridor] is either black gangster rap or punk rock, and that's basically it. They don't want to hear other music—contemporary music from around the world."

6   The connection between lack of information and intolerance translated occasionally into personal stories of frustration, hitting home in the lives of some students. "I wish they [his hall mates] were accepting of more different music," said an Indian student. "I play my own music. I play it loud just like they do—Arabic and Punjabi and other stuff—and they complain to the RAs. But it's my right to play that too. Why don't they understand that?"

7   "They don't accept other cultures," speculated one Japanese student.

> Once I was eating the food I had made—Japanese noodles—and we Japanese eat noodles with a noise. Somebody else in the kitchen area looked at me funny. She asked, "Why are you making so much noise?" I told her that's the way Japanese eat their noodles, and I can see by her face that she is disapproving. It hurt me to see that. Some Americans don't care about other worlds.

8   One key toward creating a more positive cycle of information, self-awareness, and tolerance was for many the university and university education itself. Learn a foreign language and study overseas, many recommended for individual students. Use your education to expand your purview beyond your own country. For the university, other students recommended a greater emphasis on self-awareness, including a more critical eye directed to our own institutions and history.

9   For one Chinese student, the need to be more reflective about the media representation of news and issues was critical: "Media coverage has a very great influence here. In China, it has less influence because everyone knows it's propaganda. Here it is not seen

that way because there is a free press. But it's curious." In American newspaper articles and TV news, "the individual facts are true often, but the whole is not sometimes. I can see how Americans need to question the way stories are being represented to them."

A French student beseeched us to examine our own educational system: 10

> Americans teach like the only important thing is America. There is no required history course in college. The history course I took on Western civ. at AnyU was middle-school level, and it was very biased. I mean they taught how, in World War II, America saved France and saved the world, how they were so great. The courses don't consider what Americans have done wrong. All the current events here is news about America and what America is doing. If it's about another country, it's about what America is doing there. There's nothing about other countries and their histories and problems. [In France] we had lots of history and geography courses, starting very young. I learned about France, but then we had to take a course in U.S. industrialization, in China, Russia, Japan, too. We got the history and geography of the world, so we could see how France now fits into the bigger picture.

For the international students I interviewed, American college culture is a world   11
of engagement, choice, individualism, and independence, but it is also one of cross-cultural ignorance and self-delusion that cries out for remediation. It was a Somali student who summed up all of their hopes for "America": "You have so much here, and so many opportunities. I wish America would ask more what this country can do to make the world a better place."

Inquiring into the Essay

1. **Explore.** International students, according to Nathan's research, feel that many American college students are "ignorant" about the world, even ethnocentric, often feeling as if the United States is the only place worth living in. This sometimes translates into a kind of supernationalism or patriotism that further feeds Americans' isolation from other cultures. This is a strong assertion. Fastwrite for seven minutes about whether you believe this is true, turning your writing whenever you can to your own personal experiences with other cultures on and off campus.

2. **Explain.** Would-be members of a culture learn what it is they need to do to join and, later, how they should behave to maintain their status. These international students are obviously confused about what it takes to belong to American student culture. Explain how they've got it wrong, and how they've got it right.

3. **Evaluate.** Ethnography and most other qualitative research attempts to infer from the few what might be true of the many. Evaluate the generalizability of the data reported here about international students and how they view us. Do you find Nathan's findings plausible? Why or why not?

4. **Reflect.** Reflect on the methodology of this ethnography. Imagine, for example, that you were one of the students who lived on the same dorm floor as Rebekah Nathan. How would you have responded to her presence? How reliable do you think were the data she collected?

Seeing the Form

German Cowboys

Photographer Eric O'Connell has been visually documenting the dress and lifestyles of a group of former East Germans, where some residents have embraced the American cowboy. O'Connell notes that "emerging from Communist rule, their self-determination found new identity with the spirit of the Wild West." This picture is one of a series O'Connell shot of these Germans, who live near the Czech border. O'Connell is a professional photographer enrolled in the University of Southern California's graduate program in visual anthropology. Read ethnographically, images such as this one are rich sources of "data."

THE WRITING PROCESS

Inquiry Project **Writing the Ethnographic Essay**

Inquiry Question: How do the people in a culture see themselves and their world?

Watch the Animation on **Writing Observations** in your MyLab

Write an essay that uses field research and reading as the basis for an interpretation of how a subculture sees itself and others. This necessarily will be a limited picture, so it should focus on some aspect of the culture that emerges from your observations.

The essay should also have the following qualities:

- Have a limited focus.
- Be organized around some thesis or interpretation of how this culture sees things. For example, how does the culture view authority figures, or what constitutes a leader in the group? (See the "Inquiring into the Details: Questions Ethnographers Ask" box, page 359.)
- Offer a rationale for why this group constitutes a distinct culture.
- Provide enough evidence from your field observations to make your interpretations and commentary convincing.

Prose+

- The digital camera is a great tool for ethnography. Focus your fieldwork on collecting as many images as you can of your study subjects doing things that are meaningful for that group (e.g., athletes putting on gear to play, quilters at work on a coverlet, etc.). Incorporate these into your essay or make them the centerpiece of your analysis of the culture. Describe in detail what you see in the images and how they're relevant to your inquiry question.
- One approach to ethnography is to present a "day in the life" of a subject, trying to capture some of the ordinary rituals, habits, customs, conversations, and activities of someone who might be representative of the larger social group. This one-day snapshot can certainly be done in words alone, but it also lends itself to multimedia approaches—particularly audio and video. Imagine, for example, following your subject around one day with a digital recorder, collecting conversations and sounds that you later edit into an audio documentary. Audio clips would be surrounded by your narration, explaining the significance of what listeners hear.
- Another exciting development in the last decade is "hypermedia ethnography," or projects that combine images, videos, audio, and graphics in web pages rich with hyperlinks between the materials. Can you imagine creating a web page for your project that both helps you think about the connections between your findings and helps viewers to see those connections?

What Are You Going to Write About?

9.3

Use relevant methods of invention to identify a local culture to study.

Possible subjects for your ethnography are all around you. We are all enmeshed—or wish to be—within intricate webs of cultures. Might your professional interests be relevant to this project? Say you want to be a police officer; might it be enlightening to hang out with a few officers to find out what the life is like? If you're a student at an urban campus, then the possibilities are nearly limitless, but even if you attend a rural university, you can still find a culture to study on your own campus. However, there are two conditions that you should keep in mind when deciding on a group to study:

1. Do members of the group identify with it? Is it a social group with some cohesion?

2. Is it accessible? Will you be able to talk to and describe group members in the field in the coming few weeks?

Opening Up

Begin exploring possible subjects for a review by generating material in your notebook. This should be an open-ended process, a chance to use your creative side without worrying too much about making sense or trying to prejudge the value of the writing or the subjects you generate. In a sense, this is an invitation to play around.

Listing Prompts. Lists can be rich sources of triggering topics. Let them grow freely, and when you're ready, use an item as the focus of another list or an episode of fastwriting. The following prompts should get you started.

Writing Beyond the Classroom

Commercial Ethnography

Ethnography isn't just for academics. Increasingly, businesses are using the method to analyze consumer behavior, and they are finding that ethnography is often better than the usual surveys, questionnaires, and focus groups. Why? Because the information researchers get from observing people where they work and live is a more accurate measure of what they think. Even more important, because ethnographers are interested in watching how people behave, not just in surveying their attitudes, they get a much more realistic picture than other researchers about what people are willing to actually *do*. Using video, photographs, audio, interviews, and observation, commercial application of ethnography gives designers and marketers a glimpse into cultural norms or can reveal some of the ways a product may—or may not—fit into our ordinary lives.

1. In class or in your journal, create a four-column table, labeling the first column Trends, the second Hobbies, the third Community Groups, and the fourth Campus Groups (see the following example). Brainstorm a list of *cultural trends* that are a visible part of American culture in the new millennium. Write the name of each trend under the first column in the table. Create a similar list for popular hobbies (it's okay to repeat items in different columns), and write the name of each hobby in the second column. Finally, brainstorm a list of identifiable social groups in the community and on campus—fraternities, truck drivers, goths, and so on. Write these, respectively, in the third and fourth columns of your table.

Trends	Hobbies	Community Groups	Campus Groups
Snowboarding	Fly fishing	Kiwanis	Fraternities
Blogging (participating in web logs)	Ballroom dancing	Pentecostal church	Black student alliance
	Computer games	Gospel singers	
Atkins/South Beach/low-carb diet craze	Autograph collecting	Truck drivers	Graduate students
Reality TV programming			

2. Create a new three-column table, labeling the first column Artifacts, the second Language, and the third Rituals. Now choose one of the trends, hobbies, community groups, or campus groups from your first table, and under the first column of the new table list all of the artifacts—tools, equipment, devices, clothing—that you can think of that people typically use when they participate in the activity/group you have selected. In the second column, list the language—special terms, jargon, and other words or phrases—that group members regularly use. In the third column, list the rituals—habits, patterns of behavior, or traditions—that are typical of the activity/group. Creating the new table will help you expose some of the threads of a particular activity's or group's culture. Objects that group members typically use, their ways of speaking, and the traditions and rituals that govern their behavior are three key elements you need to consider when writing an ethnographic essay. The accompanying table identifies some of the artifacts, language, and rituals of fly fishing.

Fly Fishing

Artifacts	Language	Rituals
Fly rod (not "pole")	"Working water"	Keeping physical distance from other fly fishers
Artificial fly	"Skunked"	Catch and release of fish
Vest	"Meat fisherman"	Winter fly tying

Fastwriting Prompts. Choose an item from one of your lists as a fastwrite prompt. Write quickly, exploring each of the following questions:

1. What are your own experiences and observations with this trend, hobby, or group?

2. What are your presuppositions, biases, or assumptions about this trend, hobby, or group? What do you assume about the kind of people who participate in it, for example, and what might their motives be for belonging?

3. Based on what you know now, what things—or artifacts—seem particularly important to participants?

4. What questions do you have about why this trend exists, or why people participate in the group or hobby?

Visual Prompts. Sometimes the best way to generate material is to see what we think represented in something other than sentences.

1. If you like to take photographs, go through your collection looking for suggestive pictures you've captured of subcultures. Perhaps you took pictures of an on-campus or community event, or you have some shots of people back home that represent certain social groups.

2. Take a word or phrase from the table you created from the first question in the "Listing Prompts" section and use it as a nucleus word for a cluster on a blank page of your journal. When you cluster a hobby, cultural trend, or community or campus group, build associations using the five *W*'s: *What, When, Where, Who,* and *Why. Where* do participants of this hobby, group, or trend gather, and *when*? *Who* are the kind of people who belong? *What* are their activities and rituals? *Why* do people belong?

Research Prompts. Research can be helpful even this early in the process. New or more-detailed information might trigger ideas about possible topics for your paper that you otherwise would never have considered. At this stage, your research will be open-ended and not particularly methodical. Just enjoy poking around.

1. In the United States, there's a magazine for nearly every subculture. Go online and survey the hobby and special-interest magazines. The web also has

useful sites with links to resources on American subcultures or information on cultural trends (see "Inquiring into the Details: Researching Trends and Subcultures on the Web"). Do any of these interest you?

2. There are a number of historical archives online that provide primary materials such as interview transcripts, letters and photographs, video interviews, and sound files of people who belong to identifiable groups: former slaves, 9/11 survivors, World War II veterans, Depression-era farmers, etc. Start with the digital collections at the Library of Congress. Is there enough data there for an essay?

3. One quick way to gain entry to a culture you don't belong to is to find someone in your class who is a member. Stay alert to what others in the class say about their own identification with certain social groups, and interview any who belong to a culture that interests you.

Narrowing Down

The generating process may produce the messy, incoherent writing that would earn you bad grades in most classes. Its virtue, however, should be obvious by now:

Inquiring into the Details

Researching Trends and Subcultures on the Web

If you're browsing for ideas about a topic, or researching the cultural group you've chosen to investigate, a number of sites on the Internet can help.

- **The Pew Internet and American Life Project** features up-to-date information on trends in Internet use. http://www.pewinternet.org

- **The Statistical Abstract of the United States** is an annual Census Bureau publication that is a gold mine of data on all kinds of trends. http://www.census.gov/compendia/statab

- **The Gallup Poll** website features recent survey results on social trends.

- **The Open Directory Project**, a subject catalog of web information, includes a useful directory on subcultures as varied as geeks and polygamists. http://dmoz.org/Society/Subcultures/

- **The Google Directory** also lists subcultures, with links to resources on the web.

- **Wikipedia**, the "free encyclopedia," isn't necessarily a good source for academic writing, but it is the "largest reference site on the Web." The list of subcultures is impressive. http://en.wikipedia.org/wiki/Category:Subcultures

"Bad" writing gives a writer material to work with. And while it's always better to work from abundance rather than scarcity, this material still must be judged, shaped, and evaluated.

What's Promising Material and What Isn't? Earlier, I mentioned two conditions that are key: Your study subject is a cohesive cultural group and one that is accessible to you in the next few weeks for field observations. There's another key issue to consider now, too: Should this be a group to which you belong? Ethnographic methods ask that writers be *participant-observers.* As the term implies, you're not just watching, but also involved in some way in the activities of the group you're studying (with their permission). Participation is easy if you're an insider, and you're likely to get considerable access, which is no small thing as you'll be doing this project relatively quickly. On the other hand, being an outsider makes you a better observer. Because of your unfamiliarity with your study subjects, you're likely to notice things an insider would miss, and you'll also be freer from bias. Weigh the advantages and disadvantages before you decide.

Finally, consider how much data you'll be able to gather.

- Does the cultural group you want to study meet regularly?

- Is there any background research on the group in the library or online that might provide additional information?

- Will there be any privacy issues? For example, do members of the group engage in activities (legal or otherwise) that would make them reluctant to talk to you?

9.4

Analyze and interpret qualitative information.

Questions About Audience and Purpose. No matter how fascinated you are by the people who do medieval battle reenactments at the park, you still have to have something *to say* about the subculture to readers who may not share your fascination. Most academic ethnographies are written to fellow experts. Researchers, to some extent, assume prior knowledge and interest in their subjects. However, you're writing an ethnographic *essay*—a much shorter, less extensively researched, and more reader-friendly work. Imagine an audience that may know something about your subject (after all, most of us are aware of many social groups), but your essay should help readers to see what perhaps they've seen before in a way they haven't seen it. Good essays make the familiar strange. And good ethnographies don't simply describe—they *analyze*.

How do you do this?

1. *Look hard and look closely.* If you're going to see anything new, you have to have as much data as you can. That means doing as much fieldwork as you can.

2. *Focus on what is less obvious.* If you're going to surprise your audience, you need to surprise yourself. What are you noticing about those battle reenactors that you never noticed before?

3. *Find the question.* What aspect of your culture are you most interested in exploring?

4. *Discover one main thing you're trying to say.* You can't know what this is until you've done a lot of fieldwork and some reading. But in the final draft, the main idea you're trying to get across about the group you observed should be clear.

5. *Tell stories, provide profiles, use dialogue, incorporate heavy description.* To bring the culture you studied to life for readers, try to employ some of the literary techniques you know from good storytelling.

Trying Out

Prepare to do fieldwork by confirming the best places to conduct observations of the culture in which you're interested. Sometimes that's easy to figure out: Snowboarders hang out at the lodge, surfers at the beach, fraternity brothers at the fraternity house, homeless men at the shelter. But there will also be less-obvious gathering places, locations you may only learn of through interviews with group members. Are there other locations where group members gather to socialize, plan activities, celebrate successes, or learn from each other?

Writing ethnographically requires that you expand your repertoire of research to include interviews and fieldwork.

Inquiring into the Details

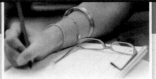

Questions Ethnographers Ask

When you study a social group, whether it's skateboarders or opera singers, there are certain basic things you want to find out about how that group operates. For example,

- How do group members view outsiders?
- What motivates members to belong?
- What artifacts are present, how are they typically used, and what significance is attached to them?
- What is the nature of gender relations in the group?
- Where does the group gather and why?
- What is the group's social hierarchy, and how is it organized and maintained?
- What's the relationship between this local culture and the larger culture with which it identifies?
- Does this group seem to define itself *in opposition to* other groups, and if so, why?
- What are the culture's most symbolic or significant rituals? Why is meaning assigned to them?
- Is there an initiation of some kind?

If the sites you want to visit aren't public, you may need permission to conduct your observation. In addition, make sure you plan for your own safety. While it's unlikely that you'll study a city gang or a gun-toting right-wing militia or some similar group that can be dangerous to outsiders, make sure that you will be safe wherever you go. Bring a friend with you; tell others where you'll be and for how long.

Taking Notes. The most important source of information for your essay will be the observation notes you take in the field. You've practiced note taking during the profile assignment, but the notes for the ethnography project will involve more observation. In the initial stages, focus on your first impressions of the group you're studying. Jot down everything, including:

- Conversations, both formal and informal. What do people say, where, and who does the talking?

- Topics or issues that arise that might merit follow-up interviews.

- Things that members of the group often talk about, or things that they say that surprise you.

- Detailed descriptions of activities, especially those that happen regularly or that have particular significance for the group you're studying.

Inquiring into the Details

Ethnography and Ethics

Unlike most other undergraduate research projects, an ethnography involves work with human subjects. As you might imagine, this raises some ethical issues. How open should you be with your research subjects about your project? Do you need their permission? What responsibility do you have to protect your subjects' identities?

For faculty who do research with people, a university review board charged with protecting human subjects must approve the project. That probably won't be necessary for your ethnographic essay, but there are still ethical guidelines you should follow:

1. Let your research subjects know what you're doing and why you're doing it.

2. Obtain their permission to be included in your research. While a written "informed consent" may not be necessary, there should at least be a clear verbal understanding between you and the people you're studying.

3. Protect their anonymity. You have an obligation to make certain that your subjects' identities are protected. It's often a wise practice to use pseudonyms in your research.

For the American Anthropological Association's ethical guidelines, visit http://www.aaanet.org/committees/ethics/ethcode.htm.

▶ Field Notes

Rita Guerra hasn't bowled often in the past twenty years, but she has fond memories of holding birthday parties at the local bowling alley when she was a girl, and now her own children clamor from time to time to do some ten-pin bowling. Guerra remembers her hometown bowling alley as a social and cultural center for her small town. Wouldn't such a place be a great site to do some fieldwork for her ethnographic essay?

What follows are Guerra's field notes following her first visit to Emerald Lanes—"The Best Alley in the Valley." At this stage, she is focused on collecting data—transcribing conversations she hears, carefully describing what she sees, jotting down text from signs and notices, mapping the space, and simply watching to see what happens when. She uses double-entry field notes. On the left are her observations, and on the right are her impressions or ideas about what she sees, hears, smells, or feels. Notice that she gets a dialogue going between the two columns—speculating, interpreting, and raising questions on the right in response to specific information she collected on the left.

The success of your ethnographic essay depends on the success of your field notes. Always collect more information than you can use—which probably means multiple visits to your field sites—and push yourself to reflect on what you've found as you collect the information. Rita Guerra's field notes are a good model.

Field Notes on Friday Afternoon at Emerald Lanes
Rita Guerra

OBSERVATIONS OF
4/9/04
4:32 Sounds of balls hitting maple lanes, thundering toward pins. There is a constant hum of noise—rolling balls, lane chatter, country music, clanking of pins. Smells like cigarettes and beer. Smoking is allowed throughout the alley.

IDEAS ABOUT

A Friday afternoon at Emerald Lanes appears to be more family oriented, no league play. But I was impressed by how many strong bowlers, mostly young couples played. Emerald Lanes seems a family-friendly place though I was surprised that the entire place allowed smoking. This might be indicative of the bowling culture—smoking is still okay.

(continued)

(continued)

"That will be a triple," says a woman in shorts and green tank top. She is bowling with two other young couples and they all bowl well, alternating between strikes and spares. Successful frame usually produces a kind of dance, clenched fists, "yessss!" Poor frame—silence, stone faced.

Scores are tallied electronically on monitors above each lane. Large number of families on Friday afternoon, including birthday party in far lanes.

"Got it right where I wanted to," says young player with girlfriend. He cups the ball underneath before his swing and when releasing it gives it a spin. Ball breaks from left to right. Wears own bowling shoes, no rentals, and black wrist band. Spends very little time preparing but picks up his ball, sights the pins, and goes into motion within 15 seconds.

"The Best Alley in the Valley"
"The Bowling Guy's Pro Shop" Ball polisher
Tropical theme—three plastic palm trees between lanes.
Budweiser sign: Welcome to Emerald Lanes. Good Family Fun?
Movement

Need to check for "bowling lingo" on the Internet. What is a "triple"? Three strikes in a row? I was really interested in watching the preparation and releases of bowlers. Seems like you could tell the experienced bowlers from inexperienced ones by the smoothness of their release and especially the velocity of the ball. But maybe more than anything, I began to interpret their reactions to a good frame and bad frame. Strike produces a "yesss!" and clenched fist but not extended celebration. Bad frame a stony face. No anger, no laughter. Seemed to be no difference in this between men and women. Less experienced bowlers would react with more exaggeration.

I need to learn more about the theories behind introducing spin in releasing the ball. The ability to do this seems to distinguish the more skilled from the less skilled bowlers. This player consistently produced a left-to-right break by cupping the ball and obviously spinning it right before he releases it.

Might be interesting to actually time how long it takes for bowlers to prepare to bowl when it is their turn. My impression is that more experienced bowlers waste very little time; novices diddle and dawdle.

Like a lot of bowling alleys I've seen this one seems a bit tacky from the outside, and inside seems friendly but with an atmosphere of Budweiser beer and smoke. On a Friday afternoon, though, it seemed family friendly. Need to plan next visit for a Saturday night during league play. I have a sense that it's an entirely different culture.

Writing the Sketch

Write a sketch that provides a verbal snapshot of the culture you're studying. Using the ethnographer's questions (posed earlier) as guides for your field observation, go to a place where you can observe your culture in action. Collect observations and interviews that will allow you to create a snapshot of your group in action. For example, if you're interested in gender relations among young skateboarders, go to the skateboard park and carefully observe how the boys and girls interact. If possible, talk to some of them. Take lots of notes, and consider taking photographs as visual records, too.

Try working through the following three steps in your journal in preparation for drafting your sketch.

1. **Narrative of thought.** In your notebook, tell the story of how your thinking has evolved. When you first chose your subject, what did you think about that culture? What assumptions did you make, and what did you expect to find? And then? And then? And then? And how about now?

2. **Look at strands in the web.** Which of the following features of a culture apply to the one you're studying?

   - *Shared language* (for instance, are there insider phrases and words that have significance to group members?)

   - *Shared artifacts* (for instance, are there objects that have particular significance to group members?)

   - *Common rituals and traditions* (for instance, are there patterns of behavior that surround certain activities, or are there historical understandings of how something must be done?)

   - *Shared beliefs and attitudes* (for instance, are there common attitudes toward other insiders, toward outsiders, toward new initiates; do group members share beliefs in the significance of the group and its activities?)

   - *Common motivations* (for instance, do members participate for some of the same reasons?)

3. **Examine one strand.** Choose *one* of the preceding features. In your notebook/journal, generate specific evidence from your research or fieldwork that supports your finding.

After you complete the above steps, write a sketch that describes what you saw and heard during one or more of your field experiences. The key is not to simply *explain* what you noticed, but to *show* it, too. In addition:

- Choose a title for your sketch.
- Whenever possible, *show* what you observed or heard using description, scene, dialogue, and similar literary devices.
- Offer a tentative theory about a belief or attitude that group members seem to share, based on your initial field observations and interviews.

Moving from Sketch to Draft

If it was successful, your sketch provided an initial snapshot of the group you're studying. The draft, of course, will provide a fuller picture. But what should that picture focus on? What kind of information should you try to gather now? Your sketch can provide some useful clues.

Evaluating Your Own Sketch. To read your sketch for these clues, focus on your strongest impressions, working through the following questions in your journal:

1. *What is my strongest impression of the group so far? What kinds of things did I see, hear, or read that gave me that impression?*
2. *What is another impression I have?*
3. *Which one of these two impressions might be a focus for the next draft?*
4. *What do I most want to know now about the culture I'm observing? What questions do I have?*

Reflecting on What You've Learned. Make a schedule that describes your plan for additional research and field observations over the next few weeks. For example:

Sunday	Monday	Tuesday	Wednesday	Thursday	Friday	Saturday
2–4 Field observa-tions at the park		3 PM Pick up photos		7 PM Library research		10–12 Field observations, Interview w/ Karen

Developing

The most important thing you can do to improve the next draft of your ethnography is return to the field for more observations and interviews. This project doesn't permit the kind of immersion in a culture that most ethnographic researchers enjoy, so it's essential that you focus on gathering as much data as you can in the time you have. This will take careful planning and scheduling, and your schedule will help. (In fact, your instructor may ask you to hand in your schedule.)

Sources of Data. Your field notes will be the richest source of information for your project. *You should plan to make repeated visits to places members of your group frequent.* It's hard to overstate the importance of your first-hand observations. But there are other sources of information you might consider as well.

Photographs. Visual ethnography uses photographs, film, or video to document local culture. These can be enormously rich records, because pictures extend our perception and preserve information for later study and analysis. In addition, sharing the photographs we take with our study subjects can yield valuable insight about the significance of the images. A twelve-year-old skateboarder, for example, might look at the picture of someone attempting a trick and offer a commentary about the rider's motives and techniques, and the meanings of his moves. Digital photography has made it possible to instantaneously share this material.

Bring your camera along on your site visits and record what you see. When you print the pictures, attempt to place them in a meaningful order. Try to establish relationships among the pictures. Do they fall into certain categories of activity or significance? In addition, study the photographs for information that you might have missed in your field notes. What do you notice about artifacts, clothing, or the context in which the action is taking place?

Interviews. There is only so much we can see. Simply observing people won't tell us what they think or feel; we have to ask. Your earlier practice with interviews will have prepared you for this method of collecting information; see Chapter 4 and Chapter 11 for more information on interview methods and techniques.

Artifacts. If you can, collect or describe things from the site or things that people in this culture routinely make, talk about, or use. For example, if you're studying a truck stop, collect menus, placemats, and so on. If you're studying people in a bowling league, describe the differences among bowling balls or collect score sheets. Photographs can also be helpful in identifying artifacts that you can't haul away. Collecting such things can help you to determine what meaning, if any, is assigned to them by group members. For example, do members of a male bowling league see the weight of a bowling ball as a measure of not only a bowler's strength but also his manhood?

Maps. One way to analyze a group's social relationships and the context in which activities take place is to observe where and how members occupy space. Imagine, for example, your own family dinner table as you were growing up. Did everyone sit in the same chair every night? Was there any logic to that arrangement? Does it say anything about the social role of each family member? If you were to draw a map of your family's seating arrangement, and then add arrows that follow the movement of each member of your family during a typical meal, what would that suggest about social roles and relationships? In my family, my mother's chair was always nearest the kitchen, and she moved far more than the rest of us, mostly back and forth, to and from the oven, table, and sink. Consider making similar maps of your study site, noting the arrangement of things and people, as well as their movements.

Reading Research. Because you have weeks rather than months to write your ethnographic essay, you will probably need to rely somewhat on the work of others who have formally or informally studied the culture in which you're interested. This may include reading the hobby or specialty magazines that group members read; visiting websites, newsgroups, chat rooms, and electronic mailing lists that group members frequent online; and searching the library databases for any academic research that scholars may have published on the culture you're

Inquiring into the Details

Useful Library Databases for Ethnography

Don't forget to research existing ethnographies that may be published about the culture you're studying. If your library has them, the following specialized databases are worth checking:

- Anthropological Index Online
- EHRAF Collection of Ethnography
- Sociological Abstracts
- Ethnographic Bibliography of North America
- Abstracts in Anthropology
- Abstracts of Folklore Studies
- International Bibliography of the Social Sciences

studying (see the box "Inquiring into the Details: Useful Library Databases for Ethnography," above). You'll be surprised at how much work has been done on local culture in the United States.

Analyzing the Data. Analyze the data that you're gathering as you collect it. In particular, look at two kinds of patterns: recurrences and categories. As you look at your data, what things seem to recur? Do your subjects keep telling you the same stories? Are there certain ways that they describe or say something that you often hear? What themes keep coming up?

Categories will help you to organize your data. In the table below, I suggest some categories that *may* apply to your project. Come up with your own, too.

Type of analysis	What to look for
Recurrences	What ideas, themes, stories, phrases, behaviors keep coming up in your field notes and interviews?
Categories	• Social relationships • Interactions • Use of space • Rules of behavior • Authority and power • Beliefs • Rituals and customs • Language and expressions • History

Finally, don't forget to continue library and Internet research. Consult specialized indexes and databases you might have skipped earlier (see "Inquiring into the Details: Useful Library Databases for Ethnography"). What can you learn from what others have observed and said about the culture you're studying?

Drafting

Academic ethnographies often take months or even years to complete. Field notes, video, photographs, and artifacts might fill a stack of storage boxes and gigabytes of space on a researcher's hard drive. This project, obviously, is much more modest. But if you're going to write a strong essay that uses ethnographic methods, the one thing you can't have is too much information. Collect, describe, observe, record, read, photograph, and listen as much as you can in the timeframe you have for the assignment. If you have enough information, and you've analyzed it (see the previous section), your draft must *interpret* what you've found. What does it mean? In particular, you're trying to answer this inquiry question:

> *What do I understand about how the people in this culture see things?*

Like much research, ethnography is *inductive*. You make inferences from the data. What did people say, do, or use, and what does this say about how that culture seems to see things? You might start to answer this question by focusing on one of the categories you used to analyze your data. For example, what patterns did you see in social relationships within the culture you observed? Can you offer a theory about what they might mean?

The practical problem is this: You're not writing a book. You can't give a very thorough picture of the group you studied; it will be necessarily limited. So how might you organize your draft with this in mind?

Methods of Development. As an extended form of inquiry, the ethnographic essay will probably combine some of the methods of development described here.

Narrative Structures. Because ethnography often involves scene or setting, character, dialogue, and action, it's a form that naturally accommodates storytelling. Try one or more of these narrative techniques.

1. *A typical day.* One way to capture your culture is to describe, in some detail, what happened on a single day that seems representative. This focus on a particular time, place, and people gives your ethnographic essay a dramatic and limited focus.

2. *Collage.* Sometimes it's effective to generate a series of significant snapshots of your subjects in their natural setting. For example, an ethnography of eighth-grade cheerleaders might feature a collage of scenes with titles like "Making the Team" or "The Squad's Social Hierarchy."

3. *Narrative of thought.* Tell the story of your initial presumptions about the culture and how your observations and research influenced those. Or state an initial theory and then tell the story of whether the evidence supported it.

Question to Answer. The inquiry question driving your project—*How do members of the group you studied see themselves and their world?*—will need to be more focused in your essay or project. You'll look at *some aspect* of how they see things.

Begin by establishing your focusing question (e.g., "What is the social hierarchy of dog handlers, and how is it maintained?"). Then consider including some or all of the following:

- Provide some background from research about other studies (if any) that have directly or indirectly addressed the question.

- Explain the writer's interest in the question. What observations, interviews, or readings suggest that the social hierarchy of dog handlers might be interesting or significant to look at?

- Explain the methods the writer used to focus on the question.

- Offer a theory, a possible answer to the question. For example: *Based on my initial impressions, handlers and trainers who have established reputations as successful breeders tend to get the most respect.*

Compare and Contrast. When I teach graduate workshops in creative nonfiction, I often wonder how gender shapes my students' responses to each other and the work being discussed. If I conducted a study that focused on such a question, I probably would find a range of ways in which men and women interact with each other. One useful way of exploring these would be to look for similarities and differences, to compare and contrast. In fact, it's hard to imagine any ethnography not exploiting this method of development in at least a small way, and it's easy to imagine that comparisons might form the backbone of some essays.

Using Evidence. We've already talked a lot about the kind of evidence an ethnographic essay draws on. This is largely *primary* research. It will draw heavily on your field notes, photographs, videos, maps, and artifacts. But don't forget to search for *secondary* sources as well. What has been published in journals, in magazines, and online about the culture you're studying?

Workshopping

If your draft is subject to peer review, see "Models for Writing Workshops" (p. 578) in Chapter 14 for details on how to organize workshop groups and consult "Methods of Responding" (p. 584) to help you decide on how your group can help you.

Peer review of ethnography projects is almost always fun. The diversity of the topics, the interesting findings from fieldwork, and the interest we all have in the lives of others makes this workshop pretty fascinating for everyone. But there are often problems in these first drafts, and the most common one is that there simply isn't enough information to draw enough interesting inferences. Focus the workshop, as always, on whether the purpose and meaning of your project is clear. The grid below might help.

Questions for Peer Reviewers	
1. Purpose	If my topic (e.g., women volleyball players) is the landscape, is it clear what *part* of that landscape I'm focused on?
2. Meaning	If you had assumptions about the culture I'm studying before you read my essay, how did reading it change those assumptions? In your own words, how would you summarize my answer to the inquiry question: *How do members of this group see themselves and their world?*

Reflecting on the Draft. Go back to the categories listed in the "Analyzing the Data" section on page 366. Reflect on which of these categories seem central to your project, and for those that are, think about which need to be the focus of the next draft. Write in your journal about what you plan to do to generate more data in the key categories.

Revising

Revision is a continual process—not a last step. You've been revising—"reseeing" your subject—from the first messy fastwriting in your journal. But the things that get your attention vary depending on where you are in the writing process. With your draft in hand, revision becomes your focus through what I'll call shaping and tightening your draft.

9.5

Apply revision strategies that are effective for an ethnographic essay.

Chapter 13 contains strategies that can help you revise any inquiry project, and the "Guide to Revision Strategies" on page 371 can help you locate these strategies. There are also certain things to think about that are especially useful for shaping an argument.

Shaping. In your draft, you made a tentative commitment to your topic, hoping that you could shape it into something that might have meaning for someone other than you. Fundamentally, you've been trying to figure out *what you're trying to say* and then rebuild your essay so that this is both clear and convincing. Shaping focuses first on the largest concerns of purpose and meaning—which you've already looked at if you workshopped your draft—and on the next-to-largest concerns of information and organization. It starts with knowing what your essay is about—your inquiry question and maybe your claim—and then revising to make every element of the draft focused on that question or assertion.

As you know, the inquiry question that drives ethnography is how members of a culture see themselves and their world. But your essay should have a more specific focusing question, and this will be the key to shaping your essay. For example, in Kersti Harter's ethnographic essay at the end of this chapter, she asks *Is it true that homosexual men have more finely tuned "gaydar," or the ability to recognize other gay men based on location, behavior, clothing and taste?"* This question is sufficiently focused to provide Kersti with great guidance as she shapes her essay. It tells her,

1. **Who exactly are the subjects of her study:** gay men (not all gay or transgender people)

2. **The types of information she will include (and, of course, what to exclude):** data about locations, behavior, clothing, and taste

3. **A key term and concept that needs defining:** "gaydar"

4. **The theory she hopes to test:** that gay men are particularly good at recognizing other gay men whose sexual preference is unknown based on limited knowledge

If you haven't done so already, explicitly identify the question that you're focusing on in your study. Then use it to limit your essay's subject and to decide what to put in and what to take out, what terms and concepts need explaining, and what theory or idea you are exploring.

- Does the draft try to say things about the group rather than focus on a single main thesis, interpretation, or question?

- If your time for fieldwork was limited, did you make up for it by finding some useful research about the culture you studied in the library or on the web?

Polishing. When you are satisfied with the shape of your draft, focus on paragraphs, sentences, and words. Are your paragraphs coherent? How do you manage transitions? Are your sentences fluent and concise? Are there any errors in spelling or syntax? The section of Chapter 13 called "Problems with Clarity and Style," p. 564, can help you focus on these issues.

Before you finish your draft, work through the following checklist:

✓ Every paragraph is about one thing.

✓ The transitions between paragraphs aren't abrupt.

✓ The length of sentences varies in each paragraph.

✓ Each sentence is concise. There are no unnecessary words or phrases.

✓ You've checked grammar, particularly verb agreement, run-on sentences, unclear pronouns, and misused words (*there/their, where/were*, and so on). (See the Handbook at the end of the book for help with these grammar issues.)

✓ You've run your spellchecker and proofed your paper for misspelled words.

Guide to Revision Strategies

Problems in the Draft (Chapter 13)	Page Number
Unclear purpose	538
▪ Not sure what the paper is about?	
Unclear thesis, theme, or main idea	543
▪ Not sure what you're trying to say?	
Lack of information or development	551
▪ Need more-convincing evidence?	
Disorganized	555
▪ Doesn't move logically or smoothly from paragraph to paragraph?	
Unclear or awkward at the level of sentences and paragraphs	564
▪ Seems choppy or hard to follow at the level of sentences or paragraphs?	

▶ Student Essay

The term *gaydar* entered the American lexicon in the past decade or two, though few thought the idea that gay men and women can intuitively distinguish gay from straight was much more than urban legend. Recent research, however, seems to confirm that there just might be something to it. The ethnographic essay that follows asks whether gay men use means other than intuition to make judgments about the sexual orientation of strangers.

This study of four Boise gays is a fascinating look at gay culture. But it's a limited one, too. Like all qualitative research, "Beyond Gaydar" hopes to find useful insight into the many by looking at the few. This project, like most ethnographies conducted in a composition class, is based on only several weeks of fieldwork, rather than the years that most ethnographies require. Still, the essay offers a useful glimpse at the world of young gay men, and it seems to amplify some of the published research. Kersti Harter's essay is cited using APA guidelines.

Kersti Harter

Beyond "Gaydar": How Gay Males Identify Other Gay Males

A Study with Four Boise, Idaho, Men

Introduction

1   While people who do not fit into the codified norms of behavior in contemporary urban life are often marginalized by the mainstream, this very fact often serves to empower and reinforce the behavior of its members in marginalized groups. This is the case within gay male culture in United States urban society. Because gay males remain heavily stigmatized, they have formed a large "outside" group with subtle yet unmistakably designated patterns and categories of behavior, action, clothing, and taste. These patterns and behaviors may not be identifiable to the larger society, but they are well-known among gay men. One of these social rituals is the patterns through which gay men attempt to identify other gay males. I had very little prior knowledge that this pattern existed, but through interviews and observations of several gay men in Boise, Idaho, aged 18–25, I discovered how some gay males identify others who are gay.

I was able to model this pattern and the categories of behavior that exist within it.

Background

2   Several studies suggest that so-called "gaydar," the use of intuition to determine the sexual orientation of someone without asking the person outright whether he or she is gay, might have a basis in fact. A recent study (Lawson, 2005) demonstrated that when provided with "neck-up" photographs of strangers who weren't wearing jewelry or makeup, homosexuals were better than heterosexuals in making the correct identification of the stranger's sexual orientation, making

BEYOND GAYDAR   2

this judgment in 2 seconds or less (p. 30). Martins et al. (2005) also reported that "gay men were found to be particularly good at detecting the scent of other gay men" (p. 694). In addition, another study argued that "eye gaze," with distinct variations, is "crucial to forces that either trigger or reinforce one gay's perception of another gay's identity during social encounters" (Nicholas, 2004).

Identifying Other Gay Males: Place

There are, however, other methods of gay identification used by male homosexuals that don't rely on "gaydar" or intuition. One such method, depicted in Figure 1, relies on contextual cues or markers. The number one identifier among the four contextual cues is place: if he's in the gay bar, he's likely gay. But

3

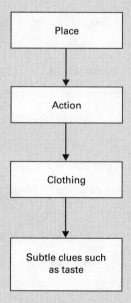

Figure 1. The sequence of judgments used by gay men to identify other gay men

BEYOND GAYDAR   3

this does not mean for sure that any man in a gay club is gay. Julian recounted a

story in which he accidentally "hit on" a straight male who was in a gay club:

> It was at a gay club, so I'm not entirely at fault. This guy was just sitting
> there, kind of like, I don't know, just sitting there at the bar, looking kind
> of, well, sitting there sulking I guess. And I thought he was pretty good
> looking, so I thought I'd go talk to him, I wasn't going to pick him up or
> anything. And so I went up and was talking to him, and he would answer
> me in one-syllable replies. And I just walked off and I found out that he
> was actually the bouncer that worked there and he had the night off.

4   Julian's story suggests that "gaydar" isn't always reliable. Sexual orienta-

tion signaling is based on more than intuition. It also means that place is not

the only identifier of gay males, although it is often accurate. So what happens

when the identifier of place fails to confirm sexual orientation?

Action

5   Then we must move onto appearance. I use "appearance" here because

my participants claimed that movement as well as personal style played into

identifying whether a man is gay. I have subdivided appearance into action, or

movements and other behaviors, and clothing, which I discuss below. During

my group interview, both Aaron and Steven claimed that movement is the more

important part of appearance in determining a man's orientation:

> Me: Does clothing or movement clue you in more to whether or not a person
> is gay? Aaron: Movement... You can tell by the way a person gesticulates,
> by how they walk. I can tell how I walk... I'm like God, everyone knows
> I'm a homo [laughs]! Like I like it, but yeah, it's definitely how they move.

6   It seems that certain movements are ingrained qualities that help gay

males identify other gay males. So, in Figure 1, I've identified the next step

BEYOND GAYDAR   4

my subjects might use to identify another gay male as "Action." Some of these
movements are evident even to straight observers, and occasionally the actions
have to do with associations with other gay men. For example, another participant, Jeff, pointed out, "Well, if they are with a guy, then yeah, they're gay."

If action is not enough to identify the man's orientation, an observer   7
might move on to more subtle parts of clothing style or even personal tastes.
But this would probably not happen in such a situation, and actions are likely
telling enough.

Clothing and Personal Style

There are times, however, when gay men are in places less exclusively   8
gay, or in places not defined as gay at all. Then one must skip to the latter steps,
identifying the less obvious markers of sexual orientation such as personal style.

When I began my research, I sat with my friend Steven in a popular   9
downtown Boise coffee shop, The Flying M. While being widely known as
the "gay" coffee shop, it is not exclusively so. Wednesday, according to
Steven, has become known to some in the gay community as "Gay Night."
This Wednesday was the first time that I met his friend Aaron, who later
helped me in the group interview. I would ask Steven, "Is that guy over there
gay?" and so on, and he would answer yes, because the man was simply at
this coffee shop on Gay Night, or because he acted a certain way, or dressed
a certain way.

When he would identify them as gay because of the way they looked, David   10
would often cite things like button-down Abercrombie and Fitch shirts or spiky
hair. There was a definite gay look that he was able to identify. Steven was able
to identify gay males, even though we were in a setting that was not necessarily exclusively gay. Clothing, though it is used less than place and action, still

BEYOND GAYDAR   5

can provide clues about sexual orientation. There are also categories of gay male dress style that the men that I interviewed identified.

Stylistic Stereotypes Among Gay Males

11   To outsiders, clothing and personal style would be one of the easiest identifiers of gay males. But it is actually, according to my subjects, a less obvious marker than place or action. Personal style also comes in many shapes and forms in the gay community. It's as if there is a set of emic values (distinctions that members of a group recognize that may not be apparent to outsiders) that are stereotypical of the gay male. This is an instance where the pattern of behavior in the group is broken down into diverse categories.

12   For example, Green and Ashmore, in "Taking and Developing Pictures in the Head: Assessing the Physical Stereotypes of Eight Gender Types" (1998), asked college students to picture various stereotypes in their heads and describe what they saw. They asked them to picture both "nerd" and "homosexual," and they found that:

> Perceivers have similar pictures of the homosexual and the nerd in their
> heads. Both were frequently described as being slender and of average height,
> wearing glasses, and wearing the "uniform" of the male college student
> (e.g., button-down shirt, pants or jeans, sneakers or casual shoes). (p. 1627)

13   Though these college students pictured "the nerd" and "the homosexual" together, the men I talked with identified a picture of the homosexual that was quite different from the one these college students identified. The men also emphasized that there were many different types of gay male style, not just one. They all identified several emic stereotypes, and disagreed with the "nerd" and "homosexual" being lumped together in similar stylistic categories.

BEYOND GAYDAR　　　　　　　　　　　　　　　　　　　　　　6

14
When I mentioned this article to Julian, he explained to me why people might lump the "nerd" with the "homosexual":

> In Europe they used to associate Jews and homosexuals, they were kind of lumped together. And so maybe whoever's on the outside is kind of labeled together...I don't think that's a look that gay guys go for as far as trying to look like that...there's sort of that geek chic that a lot of people do, pretty much if you see that you know they're straight.

15
According to Julian, though the outside sees homosexuals and nerds having similar styles because of their roles as the "outsiders," homosexuals have a different view of their styles, one that is much more rich and varied.

16
In the essay "Gay Masculinity in the Gay Disco," Cheseboro and Klenk (1981) identify several categories of symbol-using in the gay disco. Though written more than twenty-five years ago, it gives insight into some incipient analyses of stylistic categories that gay men employ. Cheseboro and Klenk describe "The Virility Component":

> One concept asserted in the gay disco is an exaggerated, if not flagrant, form of masculinity in appearance...an extreme case of this composite image includes an explicitly displayed, muscularly developed body, a flannel shirt, a leather vest, denim or leather pants, construction or cowboy boots. (p. 95)

17
Though perhaps less in vogue now, the hyper-masculine male look is still a symbolic type that some gay males employ. At first, I described these men as "bears," a more masculine type of gay male, but Julian corrected me and said that perhaps I was referring to something more like a butch. Julian thought that perhaps butch gay males care about their appearance and attempt to look masculine while bears don't really care about their appearance at all, and are more like the general straight male.

BEYOND GAYDAR   7

18   Julian's uncertainty about what exactly the hyper-masculine gay man would be called perhaps reflects current fashion. With the rise of more males in high fashion, the advent of television programs such as *Queer Eye for the Straight Guy*, and the heterosexual adaptation of the homosexual stereotype, or the "metrosexual," it seems that the bear style has fallen out of favor. It seems that now, instead of taking its fashion cues from the heterosexual world, homosexuals are creating styles that are being used by the world of high fashion and by straight people, who dress more in the mainstream. Julian expressed this concern:

> Me and some of my friends were talking and we were mad because we feel that straight people are stealing our stuff, like have you noticed the guys wearing pink shirts? Yeah, I just don't think they have a right to do that. Like my friends and I were joking that we might go up to one of these guys and be like, "You better have put that in the laundry with something red," you know like it was white before.

19   There is a feeling of resentment within the gay community that symbols are being appropriated by the larger population. In *Gays, Lesbians, and Consumer Behavior* (1996), Wardlow explains the cause of this resentment:

> When the symbolism of the community becomes framed as the basis for a target market from an "outside" perspective, the styles become divorced of the meanings they once held...and the style takes on new or more vague meanings. Based on the perspectives expressed in our interviews, the issue is not so much that meaning has become diluted or that a symbol has been stolen, as it is that manufacturers are selling the product as "cool" or "hip" without reference to its meaning. (pp. 99–100)

BEYOND GAYDAR   8

The manufacturing world is taking symbols highly popularized in the gay com-   20
munity and making them available for the mainstream, for example, the pink shirts
that Julian cited which are becoming increasingly popular with heterosexual males.

Appealing to both a homosexual and a heterosexual (or perhaps metrosex-   21
ual) audience is a good strategy for a clothing manufacturer; it can target two
highly valuable markets at once. Based on my research, it's obvious that no other
company does this better than Abercrombie and Fitch, as every interviewee cited
the popular clothing company and its ubiquity among gay males. This leads me
to the associated stereotypes of "flamer" and "Abercrombie bitch." Both of these
types would wear Abercrombie and Fitch clothing, but the flamer would not wear
it exclusively. These two types would perhaps, if we could put all the different
gay styles on a spectrum, fall closer to femininity than butch or bear would.

What happens when place, action, and personal style all fail to disclose a   22
man's sexual orientation, or when one of these categories is missing or fragmen-
tary? Then clues can be found in personal taste, or habitus.

Subtle Clues in Personal Taste

Among the gay men I interviewed, I found that there is a distinct musi-   23
cal taste that gay males recognize is characteristically gay. I focused on musical taste because my interviewees discussed it the most when I brought up gay
preferences in things other than clothing. During the group interview, I asked
them to comment on gay musical taste. Jeff mentioned that "they all listened to
techno" and expressed his exasperation over it. They cited Barbara Streisand as
gay music. Steven stressed that, "You can't be gay and not have Cher."

So how could musical taste signal sexual orientation? It's difficult to imag-   24
ine such a situation when place, action, and personal style would fail to show

BEYOND GAYDAR   9

sexual orientation. Personal taste might be a more cultivated part of the gay habitus, one which would be formed later after the other qualifications were met, and therefore would not be present without the other gay qualities. In other words, musical taste cannot be seen as only a signal to other gay men of a man's orientation. For example, a man who contradicted the other gay qualities regarding place, action, and personal style would probably not be viewed by the others as gay, if he simply expressed an affection for alternative music.

Conclusions

25   In interviewing four gay males in Boise, Idaho, over a period of a month, I saw some general patterns emerge. I discovered that the most importance in discovering sexual orientation was placed on the actual location where a man was seen. Behaviors and movements were also highly important, though being in a gay location might outweigh any straight symbolism that a certain man would possess, e.g., Julian's experience of assuming a man in a gay bar was gay, when in reality he was straight. Clothing can also be a signal to other males of sexual orientation, but it is not as telling as place and action. Personal tastes in things like music are less of a signal of sexual orientation and more of a cultivated gay taste.

26   In concluding my research, I also should point out that these things I have observed have merely scratched the surface of gay male identification. I do not even attempt to explain verbal behavior and its relation to nonverbal clues. I did not consider hearsay among the gay community or when gay males have simply identified themselves verbally. I do not assume that these are the only ways that gay males identify each other or that they are the most commonly used. I also do not want to trivialize intuition or conclude that there is absolutely nothing to "gaydar."

BEYOND GAYDAR   10

References

Cheseboro, J. W., and Klenk, K. L. (1981). Gay masculinity and the gay disco. In J. W. Cheseboro (Ed.), *Gayspeak: Gay male and lesbian communication* (pp. 87–103). New York: Pilgrim Press.

Green, R. J., and Ashmore, R. D. (1998). Taking and developing pictures in the head: Assessing the physical stereotypes of eight gender types. *Journal of Applied Social Psychology, 28*(17), 1609–1636.

Lawson, W. (November–December 2005). Gay men really do find it easier to spot other gays. *Psychology Today,* 30.

Martins, Y., Crabtree, C. R., Runyan, Vainius, A. A., and Wysocki, C. J. (2005). Preference for human body odors is influenced by gender and sexual orientation. *Psychological Science, 16,* 694–701.

Nicholas, C. L. (2004). Gaydar: Eye-gaze as identity recognition among gay men and lesbians. *Sexuality and Culture, 8* (Winter), 60–86.

Wardlow, D. L. (1996). *Gays, lesbians, and consumer behavior: Theory, practice, and research issues in marketing.* New York: Harrington Park Press.

(All references to "Julian," Steven, Jeff, or Aaron come from either participant observation or interviews collected between November 3, 2004, and November 29, 2004.)

Evaluating the Essay

1. As its author admits, "Beyond Gaydar" is based on a month of interviews and observations and therefore "only scratches the surface" of how gay men identify other gay men. If you were going to redesign the study in ways to make its findings more authoritative, what would you suggest?

2. Your own feelings about homosexuality may have strongly affected your reading of this research. Part of becoming a sophisticated reader is developing an awareness of how your own biases and predispositions influence your understandings of and reactions to what you read. Reflect on this. Can you identify particular ideas in the essay that you resisted or didn't evaluate critically because of how you felt?

3. What are the ethical issues the student author of this essay needed to address?

Using What You Have Learned

Let's return to the learning objectives I outlined in the beginning of the chapter.

1. **Understand the idea of culture as a "web," and apply techniques of field research to describe it.** What was once relatively invisible in your everyday life—the often fine threads of culture in which we are all caught—is now something you see everywhere. But what do you do with this knowledge? For one thing, it gives you a powerful rhetorical tool for analyzing your audience. When we begin to see the affiliations people feel with each other, we know what matters to them, what they value, and how they might be persuaded.

2. **Use appropriate features of an ethnographic essay in a project that interprets how a social group sees themselves and their world.** In this chapter, you've not only used some of the techniques used to generate qualitative research, but you've also *applied* what you found, working inductively to draw some conclusions from the data. These are techniques that will significantly expand your skills as an academic researcher. They should also prove useful whenever you're asked to present findings to any audience.

3. **Use relevant methods of invention to identify a local culture to study.** When you started *The Curious Writer*, you generated topics mostly from memory (personal essay); then you used interviews (profile), observation (review), and reading (proposal, argument, critical essay). Now in a single essay you've generated material from all sources of information. To write with all four sources of information—memory, interview, observation, and reading—is now something you might do with any essay, no matter what the genre. How far you cast your net for information depends, as you know now, on what question you are asking, not the type of writing you're doing.

4. **Analyze and interpret qualitative information.** In a small but significant way, you've done what all academic researchers do: generate data, identify patterns in it, and try to draw some inferences about what they mean. This is an inductive process, and it is the basic work of all science.

5. **Apply revision strategies that are effective for an ethnographic essay.** When you have a lot of information to work with, problems with organization are often the hardest to solve. In this chapter, you learned some approaches to this that you can apply in other research projects as well: limiting your focus by refining your question, and exploiting the promise of *narrative* structures. We don't often use "narrative" and "research" in the same breath. But telling a story—either about the subjects of your research and/or your own discoveries along the way—can be a powerful way to organize many research-based projects.

Complete
Additional Exercises
and Practice on
Chapter 9
in your MyLab

3

INQUIRING DEEPER

What is the relationship between jazz and African music? How is jazz related to hymns and spirituals? Is there a connection between jazz and the history of slavery? Questions like these motivate effective research projects. The best reason to investigate something is because you genuinely wonder about it.

Writing a Research Essay

10

Learning Objectives

In this chapter, you'll learn to

10.1 Apply what you've learned about writing shorter inquiry-based papers to an extended research project.

10.2 Identify different forms of researched writing and the purposes behind them.

10.3 Practice reading, analyzing, and writing with a limited number of sources on a single topic.

10.4 Use invention techniques for discovering a researchable question.

10.5 Refine a research question to narrow the topic focus and lead to a judgment.

10.6 Use audience and purpose to make decisions about the structure of the work and the types of information to use in it.

Writing with Research

In a way, there's no such thing as a research paper. Research is a source of information, not a form of writing, and it's a source you've been using all along in the inquiry projects here. And yet, instructors assign "research papers" all the time. So what are they talking about? Usually, a research paper is a thesis-driven, documented essay that draws on multiple sources of information relevant to the topic. It is modeled in some ways after the scholarly articles that your professors write.

What isn't apparent is that much scholarship reports on the *products* of the inquiry process—what the researcher concluded from exploring a topic—and so it's easy to assume that writing a research paper means abandoning the goal of most academic inquiry: discovery. Yet that is the goal of scholarship—and it's the goal of the research paper, too—so in an effort to lift the curtain on the process of inquiry, I'll introduce you in this chapter to a variation of researched writing: the research *essay*. As you'll see, the research essay begins with the motive that

> Research is something writers naturally do whenever they have questions they can't answer on their own.

385

drives any essay—the desire to find out something about a topic. Later, this may lead to argument—the intention to prove something—but essaying begins with exploration, the beating heart of inquiry.

Research Essays, Research Papers, and Research Reports

10.1

Apply what you've learned about writing shorter inquiry-based papers to an extended research project.

While any piece of writing can be researched—including things such as short stories, blogs, and personal essays—academic research assignments typically fall into one of three categories (see Figure 10.1):

[handwritten: 3 categories for academic research]

- ▪ Research reports
- ▪ Research (or term) papers
- ▪ Research essays

The less common of these in college is the research report. This is the familiar paper many of us wrote in high school that simply explains—Wikipedia-like—what is known about some topic. The writer of a research report isn't trying to *use* the information to make a point or investigate a question. There is, however, a version of the research report, called the *literature review*, that is sometimes a first step in the research process. A literature review summarizes how others have addressed the question you're exploring.

[handwritten: Outside sources —] A far more common college writing assignment is the research paper, a term that is loosely used to describe an essay that is an extended argument on some topic. It's like the essay you might have tackled in Chapter 8—the argument—except that the research paper leans much more heavily on outside sources and is intended for a more academic audience. Its goal is to prove a thesis using the evidence the writer gathers.

The research essay is the most obviously inquiry-based of the three genres. While the research paper certainly can involve an open-ended investigation, the paper itself usually reports conclusions rather than the questions that gave rise to

10.2

Identify different forms of researched writing and the purposes behind them.

	Research Report	**Research Paper**	**Research Essay**
Purpose	To explain	To prove	To discover
Thesis	None	Up front	Delayed
Documentation	Yes	Yes	Usually
Organization	Summary-explanation	Thesis-support	Question-answer
Use of "I"	No	Sometimes	Usually
Inquiry	Low	High	Highest

Figure 10.1 Three genres of academic research

them. Both the research paper and research essay have a thesis, but in the essay it might appear late in the work, as the writer works through questions and evidence to arrive at an understanding of the topic. While it may be a less common assignment than the argumentative research paper, the research essay is much more likely to encourage the habits of mind that encourage genuine inquiry. It invites writers to begin with questions rather than answers, to suspend judgment, and to accept that ambiguity—even confusion—is a natural part of the research process.

> The research essay is likely to encourage the habits of mind that encourage genuine inquiry and accepting ambiguity as a natural part of the process.

Start w/ questions, not always w/ aunsers.

Motives for Writing a Research Essay

I was in the market for a new guitar, and for several weeks I'd been studying back issues of an acoustic guitar magazine, searching the web for guitar makers, and talking to people who play. My process was driven by particular questions I had: *What are the best tone woods for a classical guitar? What are the various models and how much do they cost? What are the sound qualities to consider when selecting an instrument?* Questions like these—factual or informational questions—are often where we naturally begin when we begin research. Everyday research, things like shopping for a guitar or investigating the museums in a new city before vacationing there, may never go beyond basic information seeking: What is already known? While inquiry-based investigations often begin with factual questions, they rarely stop there. The motive behind writing a research essay—or term paper, for that matter—is to *do* something with the information you find. It's to make an argument, explore a hunch, or answer a more specific question. The research is always in the service of what a writer might be trying to *say* about a topic.

The Research Essay and Academic Writing

The research paper is a fixture in high school courses, usually lodged in the junior or senior English class and advertised as preparation for The College Research Paper. (Even my nine-year-old daughter wrote research papers.) Research-based writing assignments are probably among the most common in college, across the curriculum. In fact, at my own university, almost three-quarters of the faculty surveyed said they assign an "academic paper that requires research." That's one reason you're writing a research essay in your composition class—to help prepare you to write papers in other courses.

   You've already had some practice with some of the genres of researched writing that you might encounter in college: proposals, reviews, critical essays, and argumentative essays. But the researched academic paper is usually longer, with more sources, and it features some scholarly conventions such as citation of sources and, in some cases, a formal organization. You might imagine the conventional college research paper as organized in three acts:

- **Act I:** Establish the significance of the research question, review what has already been said by others about it, and introduce the thesis proposed to answer the research question.

- **Act II:** "Prove" the thesis by bringing the evidence on stage. Actors might include expert testimony from those who support your main idea, experiences and comments from those affected by the issue you're investigating, and especially your own analysis about how this information supports your thesis. All of this is set against the backdrop of relevant data, statistics, and factual findings.

- **Act III:** The last act unfolds as an inevitable conclusion. There's a summary of key findings, while the original thesis is revisited. Unanswered questions might make a brief appearance, along with thoughts about other directions for the research.

The research *essay* might roughly follow these three acts as well, but it may focus on the drama of discovering the answer to your research question. What is your motive for exploring the question? What's the story of the research, and why did your discoveries lead to your conclusions? This is the process of inquiry that is typically invisible when we read conventional scholarship, which often argues from conclusions stated early on.

The research essay is common in nonacademic writing, and particularly in creative nonfiction—the kinds of essays and articles you might read in a magazine. But even if documented research essays aren't usually assigned in college classes, I think they're a powerful *introduction* to academic inquiry, because they place emphasis on the process of coming to know. How did your thinking lead to the research question that drove your investigation into the topic? And how did your thinking evolve as you began to consider the evidence? Though the initial motive behind a research essay is *to find out*, it may end with an attempt *to prove*—the purpose behind most conventional research papers. Inquiry precedes argument, and it is the best way to discover a thesis that grows from evidence rather than thin air.

Features of the Form

Feature	Conventions of the Research Essay
Inquiry questions	What does the evidence suggest is true? What is the relationship?
Motives	Academic inquiry always begins with the desire to find out something. Sometimes the researcher has a theory about what might be true—a hypothesis—a hunch that arises

[handwritten margin note: these will help while writing paper!]

from an initial investigation. Sometimes the researcher merely begins with a question: What could be the cause of this? What is this like or unlike? What might explain it? While the initial motive is to *find out*, a subsequent motive may be *to prove*. In academic writing, this is usually the argument a researcher makes to convince others that an explanation, claim, or theory is true.

Subject matter	While academic fields often fence off certain territories of knowledge that they are particularly interested in, any topic is researchable if the researcher has a good question.
Structure	Research begins with questions, not answers. Later in this chapter, we'll explore what makes a good question, something that may be the most important thing you can learn about writing with research. Research papers and research essays (see Figure 10.1) have some different features (e.g., the thesis is delayed in a research essay), but they also have similar features, including: • A review of what has already been said by others about the research question. • A proposed answer to the question based on appropriate evidence. • Citations that signal which ideas and information belong to the writer and which belong to sources. • Information from multiple sources, analyzed by the writer for its relevance to the research question and/or thesis.
Sources of information	Informal research essays—those intended for an audience of nonexperts—may rely on all four sources of information: personal experience, observation, interview, and reading. In more-formal forms, the writer's personal experiences may not be used at all. What's key is to understand what is meant by "appropriate" evidence. This is the information that is most likely to be viewed by a particular audience as most reliable, relevant, and convincing. The more knowledgeable your audience is about your topic, the more restrictive the rules of evidence.
Language	We often assume that all researched writing should sound "objective." It should scrupulously avoid the first person, use formal diction, and employ the passive voice. As you'll see in the next section, however, the language of researched writing, like any other kind, is determined by the answer to a rhetorical question: For whom am I writing and why?

Prose+

Research is gray: blocks of text with tables of data and long lists of sources. At least that's the way we usually see it. But digital media now allow us to take even the most somber data—say, statistics on bumblebee flight patterns—and make them come to life. *National Geographic Magazine*, from which "Bumblebee Math" was taken, is a leader in turning research into visually appealing and understandable infographics. And it's not just the power of images and colorful graphics that make this presentation on the flight of the bumblebee so appealing. It's also the text, which is written so we not only "get it," but think the research is pretty cool, too.

Now

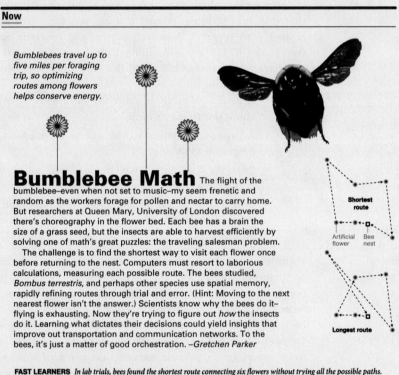

Bumblebees travel up to five miles per foraging trip, so optimizing routes among flowers helps conserve energy.

Bumblebee Math
The flight of the bumblebee–even when not set to music–my seem frenetic and random as the workers forage for pollen and nectar to carry home. But researchers at Queen Mary, University of London discovered there's choreography in the flower bed. Each bee has a brain the size of a grass seed, but the insects are able to harvest efficiently by solving one of math's great puzzles: the traveling salesman problem.

The challenge is to find the shortest way to visit each flower once before returning to the nest. Computers must resort to laborious calculations, measuring each possible route. The bees studied, *Bombus terrestris*, and perhaps other species use spatial memory, rapidly refining routes through trial and error. (Hint: Moving to the next nearest flower isn't the answer.) Scientists know why the bees do it– flying is exhausting. Now they're trying to figure out *how* the insects do it. Learning what dictates their decisions could yield insights that improve out transportation and communication networks. To the bees, it's just a matter of good orchestration. –*Gretchen Parker*

Shortest route

Artificial flower   Bee nest

Longest route

FAST LEARNERS *In lab trials, bees found the shortest route connecting six flowers without trying all the possible paths. Each bee was tested 80 times and used the shortest route more frequently over time.*

● Attempt ● Shortest route taken

Bee 1
2
3
4
5
6
7
8

First ten attempts
Average distance traveled 215 ft

Final ten attempts
126 ft

GRAPHICS: LAWSON PARKER, NGM STAFF. SOURCE: NIGEL RAINE, ROYAL HOLLOWAY, UNIVERSITY OF LONDON

READINGS: FACEBOOK AND DEPRESSION

A lot of things have changed since I wrote my first research papers as an undergraduate. But one thing hasn't and never will: You still have to *do* something with the information you collect. You have to select what's relevant, understand what you've read, and use it in your writing. Experts who study student writing recently reported that when they analyzed research papers from composition classes, they found that the students seemed to struggle a lot with integrating sources. For one thing, students rarely—if ever—summarized a source. They paraphrased, copied, or "patchwrote," mixing in their own words with the words of a source in a way that sometimes crossed the line into plagiarism, usually unintentionally.

10.3

Practice reading, analyzing, and writing with a limited number of sources on a single topic.

The real problem, the experts argued, is that students have too little practice analyzing, interpreting, and evaluating the information they find. This is the essential intellectual work of researched writing. Years ago, the "controlled research paper" was all the rage. Students didn't do their own research on a topic; they were given the research on a single topic—usually collected in a book—and then asked to write a paper on it. We'll try that in a much more limited way, as an exercise (a much better approach, I think) to get a conversation going about how to use sources in your writing. So in a break with past chapters, the readings in Chapter 10 will all be focused on one inquiry question that will involve analyzing, interpreting, and evaluation. In Exercise 10.1, I'll encourage you, as always, to write about what you read but also to *combine* the readings into a flash (or very short) research essay.

Exercise 10.1

Flash Research on Facebook and Depression

Most of us have Facebook accounts, and if we don't, it's usually because we have strong feelings about *why* we don't. Here's an inquiry question that might interest users and nonusers alike:

> *Is there a relationship between Facebook use and depression?*

You'll be reading and writing about this question, working towards some idea of your own about it that uses the sources here.

STEP ONE: First Thoughts

To start with, what are your first thoughts about the inquiry question? Based on your own personal experiences and observations, do you think there's a connection between Facebook use and depression, and if so, what might it be? Fastwrite in your journal about this for at least four minutes.

After you're done, read all four of the selections that follow, using your journal to respond to the questions that follow each reading.

[handwritten annotation: Use primary sources, so you know material is Real.]

▶ Reading 1: Web Page

Like a lot of websites that would turn up if you googled "Facebook and depression," the article that follows from LiveScience summarizes recent findings on the topic. This is a secondary source, one step removed from the original research it discusses. That means you have to trust someone else's analysis of the original work. It's a little like the game "telephone," where someone whispers something into someone else's ear and the message gets passed along to others the same way. At the end of the line, of course, the original message is laughably contorted. That's why academic research-ers want to avoid the whispering and go to the *primary source*—the study itself.

However, some whisperers are better than others, and Stephanie Pappas isn't too bad. She writes for the website LiveScience, which supplies scientific news to major news outlets, and while she's not an expert on Facebook or psychology, she does have relevant degrees and a background in science writing. In "Facebook with Care," Pappas summarizes the findings of three studies that investigate the relationship between Facebook and users' feelings about themselves.

Facebook with Care: Social Networking Site Can Hurt Self-Esteem

Stephanie Pappas

1   Facebook's initial public offering of stock is likely to make a lot of developers and designers of the site very wealthy. But for many users, frequent Facebooking may not be so beneficial.

2   According to three new studies, Facebook can be tough on mental health, offering an all-too-alluring medium for social comparison and ill-advised status updates. And while adding a friend on the social networking site can make people feel cheery and connected, having a lot of friends is associated with feeling worse about one's own life.

3   The thread running through these findings is not that Facebook itself is harmful, but that it provides a place for people to indulge in self-destructive behavior, such as trumpeting their own weaknesses or comparing their achievements with those of others.

The status (update) trap

4   Take status updates. Most people know that their Facebook friends tend to craft these online-wall memos on what they're up to in a way that puts their lives in the best light, said Mudra Mukesh, a doctoral candidate in marketing at the Instituto de Empresa in Madrid. But when it comes down to actually using the site, reading other people's status updates still makes Facebookers feel worse. [Facebook's Global Reach (Infographic)]

In research presented earlier this month at the annual meeting of the Society for Personality and Social Psychologists (SPSP) in San Diego, Mukesh and her co-author Dilney Goncalves found that when people think about the last time someone asked to friend them on Facebook, they get a boost in feelings of belonging and social connectedness—the kind of feeling that makes people "sing 'Kumbaya,'" Mukesh told LiveScience.

5

But once you've collected all those friends, viewing their status updates is a downer, Mukesh said. When asked how they felt about their place in life and their achievements, people with lots of Facebook friends gave themselves lower marks if they'd just viewed their friends' status updates, compared with people who hadn't recently surfed the site.

6

For people with just a few friends, viewing status updates wasn't a problem.

7

"A small number of friends means a low probability of viewing others showing off," Mukesh said. For people with lots of friends, though, the Facebook Newsfeed turns into a parade of good news about other people's live: promotions, engagements, weddings and new babies. Even if someone knows intellectually that people use Facebook to show off, Mukesh said, all of this information can make them feel worse about their own achievements or lack thereof.

8

(In Mukesh's study, 354 friends was the cut-off point for when participants started to feel bad about viewing status updates. But that's not a universal number, she cautioned, just the number that applied given the statistics of her sample.)

9

Comparisons and competitions

In another study presented at the SPSP conference, researchers at the University of Houston surveyed college students and found that time spent on Facebook is linked to depressive symptoms. That doesn't mean Facebook causes depression, but that depressed feelings and lots of Facebooking tend to go hand in hand, for whatever reason. For young men, the study found, the link seemed to be a tendency to compare oneself with others.

10

"It appears as if males, when they socially compare themselves on Facebook, they tend to experience depressive symptoms," study researcher and University of Houston doctoral student Mai-Ly Nguyen told LiveScience.

11

In this case, Facebook seems to be a new medium for men to compete with one another, Nguyen said. Outside the digital realm, men often compare themselves with one another, she said. It may be that women more often use the site to connect with one another and men to compete with one another.

12

Woe is me

Some people, however, don't use their Facebook status updates to pump themselves up. Instead, they complain.

13

People with low self-esteem view Facebook as a safer place to express themselves than in face-to-face interactions, according to new research published in the March

14

(continued)

(continued)

issue of the Journal of Psychological Science. All this venting may actually alienate friends.

15   Researchers led by Amanda Forest of the University of Waterloo in Ontario collected recent status updates from 117 participants who also reported their average time spent on Facebook and answered questions to reveal their self-esteem levels. Some statuses were chipper, such as "[Poster] is lucky to have such terrific friends and is looking forward to a great day tomorrow!" Others wallowed in bad news: "[Poster] is upset b/c her phone got stolen :@."

16   Next, the researchers had another group of participants read the status updates and rate how much they liked the person who wrote each. Unsurprisingly, people responded more positively to posters whose updates were positive.

17   Of course, you'd expect friends to be a little more caring than strangers. So the researchers set up another experiment in which they collected recent status updates from 98 undergraduates and also asked the students to submit the number of likes and number of comments on each.

18   It turned out that for users with high self-esteem, a negative post garnered more responses than a positive one, presumably because those people's friends were concerned about the out-of-character update. For users with low self-esteem, though, negative posts seemed to exhaust friends: They got few responses.

19   "Indeed, [low-self-esteem users'] friends rewarded their posts with more validation and attention the more *positive* they were, perhaps trying to encourage this atypical behavior," Forest and her colleagues wrote.

Forgoing Facebook?

20   The takeaway of all this work is not to dump your Facebook account—the site has its benefits, some psychological. But researchers suggest being mindful about your online social life, just as most people are about friends in the real world.

21   "You have to be careful," said University of Houston psychologist Linda Acitelli, who advised Nguyen on the social comparison study. "I think parents, especially if they have teenage kids, need to be monitoring how much time they spend on Facebook."

22   Because Facebook provides more opportunities to peer into others' lives, it helps to keep Facebook pitfalls in mind, according to the Instituto de Empresa's Mukesh. She found that reminding people in the moment of what they already know—that people brag on Facebook—can ease the self-recriminations that come with hearing about friends' accomplishments.

23   "At the end of the day, have more friends, there's no problem with that. Just be sure to remember that when you start feeling crappy about your life, think about the fact that you have a large number of friends and that increases your probability of viewing more ostentatious information," Mukesh said. "So, it's not you, it's them."

Inquiring into the Essay

1. **Explore.** Among other things, the studies Pappas cites suggest that people with a lot of Facebook friends are more likely to be depressed by others' status updates than those with fewer friends. She also speculates that some men use Facebook to "compete with one another" rather than connect, as women do, and that these men are more likely to feel down on themselves. What's your own take on this? Try both the believing game and the doubting game. In what ways might these things be true? In what ways do you think they aren't true? Fastwrite for at least five minutes in your journal, exploring your thinking about this.

2. **Explain.** The "takeaway" from this recent research, Pappas writes, "is not to dump your Facebook account," but to be careful how you use it. This seems a sensible, if uninteresting, conclusion. Explain your takeaway from the article. What did you find most interesting and relevant to the research question we're addressing?

3. **Evaluate.** Return to the initial assumptions or first thoughts you had about the research question: *Is there a relationship between Facebook and depression?* Using ideas, information, and, if helpful, quotes from the article, write a fat paragraph about how the article influenced your thinking.

   - Did it confirm or contradict your initial theories about the connection between Facebook and depression. If so, how?

   - Did it revise your thinking? What in the article seemed particularly influential?

   - Did it give you a new idea about what you think about the connection? Did another, more specific inquiry question arise that interests you?

4. **Reflect.** As I mentioned earlier, you'll harvest a lot of web pages like "Facebook with Care" while doing online research; these secondary sources can be useful *if* you can trust the source to report on and interpret others' findings accurately. The question is, though, what exactly makes a secondary source trustworthy? How would you evaluate that?

▶ Reading 2: Journal Article

In 2011, *Pediatrics*, the journal of the American Academy of Pediatrics (AAP), published a "clinical report" on "The Impact of Social Media on Children, Adolescents, and Families." AAP, concerned with suspected links between the use of social networks and depression, among other things, wanted to give pediatricians some guidance about how to help families deal with the problem. This isn't exactly a study; it's a scholarly review of the findings of others who have looked at how children and adolescents inhabit "the digital world." The list of references at the end of the article is where you'll find the research the authors reviewed. (In any academic article, the bibliography is often a buffet of potentially useful sources already laid out for you to pick through.) As you'll see, "The Impact of Social Media" is pretty balanced, acknowledging both benefits and drawbacks to using social networks. But it also coins the controversial term "Facebook depression," an idea that's certainly relevant to your inquiry question.

The Impact of Social Media on Children, Adolescents, and Families

Gwenn Schurgin O'Keeffe, Kathleen Clarke-Pearson, and Council on Communications and Media

Abstract

1   Using social media Web sites is among the most common activity of today's children and adolescents. Any Web site that allows social interaction is considered a social media site, including social networking sites such as Facebook, MySpace, and Twitter; gaming sites and virtual worlds such as Club Penguin, Second Life, and the Sims; video sites such as YouTube; and blogs. Such sites offer today's youth a portal for entertainment and communication and have grown exponentially in recent years. For this reason, it is important that parents become aware of the nature of social media sites, given that not all of them are healthy environments for children and adolescents. Pediatricians are in a unique position to help families understand these sites and to encourage healthy use and urge parents to monitor for potential problems with cyberbullying, "Facebook depression," sexting, and exposure to inappropriate content. *Pediatrics* 2011; 127:800–804

Social Media Use by Tweens and Teens

2   Engaging in various forms of social media is a routine activity that research has shown to benefit children and adolescents by enhancing communication, social connection, and even technical skills.[1] Social media sites such as Facebook and MySpace offer multiple daily opportunities for connecting with friends, classmates, and people with shared interests. During the last 5 years, the number of preadolescents and adolescents using such sites has increased dramatically. According to a recent poll, 22% of teenagers log on to their favorite social media site more than 10 times a day, and more than half of adolescents log on to a social media site more than once a day.[2] Seventy-five percent of teenagers now own cell phones, and 25% use them for social media, 54% use them for texting, and 24% use them for instant messaging.[3] Thus, a large part of this generation's social and emotional development is occurring while on the Internet and on cell phones.

3   Because of their limited capacity for self-regulation and susceptibility to peer pressure, children and adolescents are at some risk as they navigate and experiment with social media. Recent research indicates that there are frequent online expressions

of offline behaviors, such as bullying, clique-forming, and sexual experimentation,[4] that have introduced problems such as cyberbullying,[5] privacy issues, and "sexting."[6] Other problems that merit awareness include Internet addiction and concurrent sleep deprivation.[7]

Many parents today use technology incredibly well and feel comfortable and capable with the programs and online venues that their children and adolescents are using. Nevertheless, some parents may find it difficult to relate to their digitally savvy youngsters online for several reasons. Such parents may lack a basic understanding of these new forms of socialization, which are integral to their children's lives.[8] They frequently do not have the technical abilities or time needed to keep pace with their children in the ever-changing Internet landscape.[8] In addition, these parents often lack a basic understanding that kids' online lives are an extension of their offline lives. The end result is often a knowledge and technical skill gap between parents and youth, which creates a disconnect in how these parents and youth participate in the online world together.[9]

Benefits of Children and Adolescents Using Social Media

Socialization and Communication

Social media sites allow teens to accomplish online many of the tasks that are important to them offline: staying connected with friends and family, making new friends, sharing pictures, and exchanging ideas. Social media participation also can offer adolescents deeper benefits that extend into their view of self, community, and the world, including[1,10]:

1. opportunities for community engagement through raising money for charity and volunteering for local events, including political and philanthropic events;
2. enhancement of individual and collective creativity through development and sharing of artistic and musical endeavors;
3. growth of ideas from the creation of blogs, podcasts, videos, and gaming sites;
4. expansion of one's online connections through shared interests to include others from more diverse backgrounds (such communication is an important step for all adolescents and affords the opportunity for respect, tolerance, and increased discourse about personal and global issues); and
5. fostering of one's individual identity and unique social skills.[11]

Enhanced Learning Opportunities

Middle and high school students are using social media to connect with one another on homework and group projects.[11] For example, Facebook and similar social media programs allow students to gather outside of class to collaborate and exchange ideas about assignments. Some schools successfully use blogs as teaching tools,[12] which has the benefit of reinforcing skills in English, written expression, and creativity.

(continued)

4

5

6

(continued)

Accessing Health Information

7   Adolescents are finding that they can access online information about their health concerns easily and anonymously. Excellent health resources are increasingly available to youth on a variety of topics of interest to this population, such as sexually transmitted infections, stress reduction, and signs of depression. Adolescents with chronic illnesses can access Web sites through which they can develop supportive networks of people with similar conditions.[13] The mobile technologies that teens use daily, namely cell phones, instant messaging, and text messaging, have already produced multiple improvements in their health care, such as increased medication adherence, better disease understanding, and fewer missed appointments.[14] Given that the new social media venues all have mobile applications, teenagers will have enhanced opportunities to learn about their health issues and communicate with their doctors. However, because of their young age, adolescents can encounter inaccuracies during these searches and require parental involvement to be sure they are using reliable online resources, interpreting the information correctly, and not becoming overwhelmed by the information they are reading. Encouraging parents to ask about their children's and adolescents' online searches can help facilitate not only discovery of this information but discussion on these topics.

Risks of Youth Using Social Media

8   Using social media becomes a risk to adolescents more often than most adults realize. Most risks fall into the following categories: peer-to-peer; inappropriate content; lack of understanding of online privacy issues; and outside influences of third-party advertising groups.

Cyberbullying and Online Harassment

9   Cyberbullying is deliberately using digital media to communicate false, embarrassing, or hostile information about another person. It is the most common online risk for all teens and is a peer-to-peer risk.

10   Although "online harassment" is often used interchangeably with the term "cyberbullying," it is actually a different entity. Current data suggest that online harassment is not as common as offline harassment,[15] and participation in social networking sites does not put most children at risk of online harassment.[16] On the other hand, cyberbullying is quite common, can occur to any young person online, and can cause profound psychosocial outcomes including depression, anxiety, severe isolation, and, tragically, suicide.[17]

Sexting

11   Sexting can be defined as "sending, receiving, or forwarding sexually explicit messages, photographs, or images via cell phone, computer, or other digital devices."[18] Many of these images become distributed rapidly via cell phones or the Internet. This phenomenon does occur among the teen population; a recent survey revealed that

20% of teens have sent or posted nude or seminude photographs or videos of themselves.[19] Some teens who have engaged in sexting have been threatened or charged with felony child pornography charges, although some states have started characterizing such behaviors as juvenile-law misdemeanors.[20,21] Additional consequences include school suspension for perpetrators and emotional distress with accompanying mental health conditions for victims. In many circumstances, however, the sexting incident is not shared beyond a small peer group or a couple and is not found to be distressing at all.[4]

Facebook Depression

Researchers have proposed a new phenomenon called "Facebook depression," defined as depression that develops when preteens and teens spend a great deal of time on social media sites, such as Facebook, and then begin to exhibit classic symptoms of depression.[22–27] Acceptance by and contact with peers is an important element of adolescent life. The intensity of the online world is thought to be a factor that may trigger depression in some adolescents. As with offline depression, preadolescents and adolescents who suffer from Facebook depression are at risk for social isolation and sometimes turn to risky Internet sites and blogs for "help" that may promote substance abuse, unsafe sexual practices, or aggressive or self-destructive behaviors.

12

Privacy Concerns and the Digital Footprint

The main risk to preadolescents and adolescents online today are risks from each other, risks of improper use of technology, lack of privacy, sharing too much information, or posting false information about themselves or others.[28] These types of behavior put their privacy at risk.

13

When Internet users visit various Web sites, they can leave behind evidence of which sites they have visited. This collective, ongoing record of one's Web activity is called the "digital footprint." One of the biggest threats to young people on social media sites is to their digital footprint and future reputations. Preadolescents and adolescents who lack an awareness of privacy issues often post inappropriate messages, pictures, and videos without understanding that "what goes online stays online."[8] As a result, future jobs and college acceptance may be put into jeopardy by inexperienced and rash clicks of the mouse. Indiscriminate Internet activity also can make children and teenagers easier for marketers and fraudsters to target.

14

Influence of Advertisements on Buying

Many social media sites display multiple advertisements such as banner ads, behavior ads (ads that target people on the basis of their Web-browsing behavior), and demographic-based ads (ads that target people on the basis of a specific factor such as age, gender, education, marital status, etc.) that influence not only the

15

(continued)

(continued)

buying tendencies of preadolescents and adolescents but also their views of what is normal. It is particularly important for parents to be aware of the behavioral ads, because they are common on social media sites and operate by gathering information on the person using a site and then targeting that person's profile to influence purchasing decisions. Such powerful influences start as soon as children begin to go online and post.[29] Many online venues are now prohibiting ads on sites where children and adolescents are participating. It is important to educate parents, children, and adolescents about this practice so that children can develop into media-literate consumers and understand how advertisements can easily manipulate them.

On Too Young: Mixed Messages from Parents and the Law

16   Many parents are aware that 13 years is the minimum age for most social media sites but do not understand why. There are 2 major reasons. First, 13 years is the age set by Congress in the Children's Online Privacy Protection Act (COPPA), which prohibits Web sites from collecting information on children younger than 13 years without parental permission. Second, the official terms of service for many popular sites now mirror the COPPA regulations and state that 13 years is the minimum age to sign up and have a profile. This is the minimum age to sign on to sites such as Facebook and MySpace. There are many sites for preadolescents and younger children that do not have such an age restriction, such as Disney sites, Club Penguin, and others.

17   It is important that parents evaluate the sites on which their child wishes to participate to be sure that the site is appropriate for that child's age. For sites without age stipulations, however, there is room for negotiation, and parents should evaluate the situation via active conversation with their preadolescents and adolescents.

18   In general, if a Web site specifies a minimum age for use in its terms of service, the American Academy of Pediatrics (AAP) encourages that age to be respected. Falsifying age has become common practice by some preadolescents and some parents. Parents must be thoughtful about this practice to be sure that they are not sending mixed messages about lying and that online safety is always the main message being emphasized.

References

1.   Ito M, Horst H, Bittani M *Living and Learning With New Media: Summary of Findings From the Digital Youth Project.* Chicago, IL: John D. and Catherine T. MacArthur Foundation Reports on Digital Media and Learning; 2008. Available at: http://digitalyouth.ischool.berkeley.edu/files/report/digitalyouth-TwoPageSummary .pdf. Accessed July 16, 2010

2. Common Sense Media. *Is Technology Networking Changing Childhood? A National Poll*. San Francisco, CA: Common Sense Media; 2009. Available at: www .commonsensemedia.org/sites/default/files/CSM_teen_social_media_080609_ FINAL.pdf. Accessed July 16, 2010

3. Hinduja S, Patchin J. Offline consequences of online victimization: school violence and delinquency. *J Sch Violence*. 2007;6(3):89–112

4. Lenhart A. *Teens and Sexting*. Washington, DC: Pew Research Center; 2009. Available at: http://pewinternet.org/Reports/2009/Teens-and-Sexting.aspx. Accessed August 4, 2010

5. Patchin JW, Hinduja S. Bullies move beyond the schoolyard: a preliminary look at cyberbullying. *Youth Violence Juv Justice*. 2006;4(2):148–169

6. A thin line: 2009 AP-TVT digital abuse study. Available at: www.athinline.org /MTV-AP_Digital_Abuse_Study_Executive_Summary.pdf. Accessed July 16, 2010

7. Christakis DA, Moreno MA. Trapped in the net: will internet addiction become a 21st century epidemic? *Arch Pediatr Adolesc Med*. 2009;163(10):959–960

8. Palfrey J, Gasser U, Boyd D. *Response to FCC Notice of Inquiry 09*–94: "Empowering Parents and Protecting Children in an Evolving Media Landscape." Cambridge, MA: Berkman Center for Internet and Society at Harvard University; 2010. Available at: http://cyber.law.harvard.edu/sites/cyber.law.harvard.edu/files/Palfrey_Gasser_ boyd_response_to_FCC_NOI_09-94_Feb2010.pdf. Accessed July 16, 2010

9. Jenkins H, Clinton K, Purushotma R, Robinson AJ, Weigel M. *Confronting the Challenges of Participatory Culture: Media Education for the 21st Century*. Chicago, IL: John D. and Catherine T. MacArthur Foundation Reports on Digital Media and Learning; 2006. Available at: http://digitallearning.macfound.org/ atf/cf/{7E45C7E0-A3E0-4B89-AC9C-E807E1B0AE4E}/JENKINS_WHITE_PAPER.PDF. Accessed July 16, 2010

10. Boyd D. Why youth (heart) social network sites: the role of networked publics in teenage social life. In: Buckingham D, ed. *MacArthur Foundation Series on Digital Learning: Youth, Identity, and Digital Media Volume*. Cambridge, MA: MIT Press; 2007. Available at: www.danah.org/papers/WhyYouthHeart.pdf. Accessed July 16, 2010

11. Boyd D. *Taken Out of Context: American Teen Sociality in Networked Publics* Berkeley, CA: University of California; 2008. Available at: www.danah.org/papers /TakenOutOfContext.pdf. Accessed July 16, 2010

12. Borja RR. "Blogs" catching on as tool for instruction: teachers use interactive Web pages to hone writing skills. *Educ Week*. December 14, 2005. Available at: www.iapsych.com/edblogs.pdf. Accessed July 16, 2010

13. Lenhart A, Purcell K, Smith A, Zickur K. *Social Media and Young Adults*. Washington, DC: Pew Research Center; 2010.Available at: http://pewinternet .org/Reports/2010/Social-Media-and-Young-Adults.aspx. Accessed July 16, 2010

14. Krishna S, Boren SA, Balas EA. Healthcare via cell phones: a systematic review. *Telemed E Health*. 2009;15(3):231–240

(continued)

(continued)

15. Lenhart A. *Cyberbullying*. Washington, DC: Pew Research Center; 2007. Available at: www.pewinternet.org/Reports/2007/Cyberbullying.aspx. Accessed July 16, 2010

16. Ybarra ML, Mitchell KJ. How risky are social networking sites? A comparison of places online where youth sexual solicitation and harassment occurs. *Pediatrics*. 2008;121(2). Available at: www.pediatrics.org/cgi/content/full/121/2/e350

17. Hinduja S, Patchin JW. Bullying, cyberbullying, and suicide. *Arch Suicide Res*. 2010;14(3):206–221

18. Berkshire District Attorney. *Sexting*. Pittsfield, MA: Commonwealth of Massachusetts; 2010. Available at: www.mass.gov/?pageID=berterminal&L=3&L0=Home&L1=Crime+Awareness+%26+Prevention&L2=Parents+%26+Youth&sid=Dber&b=terminalcontent&f=parents_youth_sexting&csid=Dber. Accessed September 7, 2010

19. National Campaign to Prevent Teen and Unplanned Pregnancy. *Sex and Tech: Results of a Survey of Teens and Young Adults*. Washington, DC: National Campaign to Prevent Teen and Unplanned Pregnancy; 2008. Available at: www.thenationalcampaign.org/SEXTECH/PDF/SexTech_Summary.pdf. Accessed July 16, 2010

20. Gifford NV. *Sexting in the USA*. Washington, DC: Family Online Safety Institute Report; 2009. Available at: www.fosi.org/cms/downloads/resources/Sexting.pdf. Accessed July 16, 2010

21. Walker J. Child's play or child pornography: the need for better laws regarding sexting. *ACJS Today*. 2010;XXXV(1):, 3–9. Available at: www.acjs.org/pubs/uploads/ACJSToday_February_2010.pdf. Accessed July 16, 2010

22. Davila J, Stroud CB, Starr LR, et al. Romantic and sexual activities, parent-adolescent stress, and depressive symptoms among early adolescent girls. *J Adolesc*. 2009;32(4):909–924

23. Selfhout MHW, Branje SJT, Delsing M, ter Bogt TFM, Meeu WHJ. Different types of Internet use, depression, and social anxiety: the role of perceived friendship quality. *J Adolesc*. 2009;32(4):819–833

24. Melville K. Facebook use associated with depression. *Science A Go Go*. February 3, 2010. Available at: www.scienceagogo.com/news/20100102231001data_trunc_sys.shtml. Accessed September 7, 2010

25. Irvine C. Excessive chatting on Facebook can lead to depression in teenage girls. *Daily Telegraph*. January 31, 2010. Available at: www.telegraph.co.uk/technology/facebook/4405741/Excessive-chatting-on-Facebook-can-lead-to-depression-inteenage-girls.html. Accessed September 7, 2010

26. Herr J. Internet entangles college students in a web of loneliness and depression. *Truman State University Index*. February 27, 2007. Available at: www.trumanindex.com/2.10111/internet-entangles-collegestudents-in-a-web-of-loneliness-anddepression-1.1462681. Accessed September 7, 2010

27. Sturm S. Social networking psych studies: research shows teen Facebook users prone to depression. *TrendHunter*. Available at: www.trendhunter.com/trends /depressionfrom-facebook. Accessed September 7, 2010

28. Barnes S. A privacy paradox: social networking in the United States. *First Monday*. 2006;11(9). Available at: http://firstmonday.org/htbin/cgiwrap/bin/ojs/index.php /fm/article/view/1394/1312. Accessed July 16, 2010

29. Kunkel D, Wilcox BL, Cantor J, Palmer E, Linn S, Dowrick P. Report of the APA Task Force on Advertising and Children. Section: psychological aspects of commercial- ization of childhood. February 2004. Available at: www.chawisconsin.org/Obesity /O2ChildAds.pdf. Accessed July 16, 2010

30. American Academy of Pediatrics. Talking to kids and teens about social media and sexting. Available at: www.aap.org/advocacy/releases/june09socialmedia .htm. Accessed September 7, 2010

31. American Academy of Pediatrics. Safety net. Available at: http://safetynet.aap.org. Accessed September 7, 2010

32. American Academy of Pediatrics. Internet safety. Available at: www.healthychildren .org/english/search/pages/results.aspx?Type=Keyword&Keyword=internet+safety. Accessed September 7, 2010

Inquiring into the Essay

1. **Explore.** Immediately after reading the article, open your journal and quickly tell the story of your thinking about the research question. This will be especially helpful if you read the first reading as well. Start your fastwrite with: *When I first started thinking about the connections between Facebook and depression, I thought...And then I thought...And then...And now I'm thinking...*

2. **Explain.** Summarize, in your own words, what you take away from this article that's relevant to our research question.

3. **Evaluate.** The reliability of this "clinical report," like a lot of reviews of exist- ing scholarship, depends on which articles the authors chose upon which they based their conclusions. Evaluate the references the authors use in their discussion of "Facebook depression." (If you can, find them on the web using the URLs provided.) What's your judgment about their quality?

4. **Reflect.** As most academic writing goes, this isn't particularly dense and difficult to read. But it does have some typical features of "academic dis- course" that aren't features of the other readings here. Which of these do you notice?

▶ **Reading 3: Reference**

Definition of a "Major Depressive Episode"

The *Diagnostic and Statistical Manual for Mental Disorders** (*DSM*), the key reference for professionals in the psychiatric field, defines a "major depressive episode" in the following ways. Someone presents at least five symptoms that persist for at least fourteen days, and must include at least one of the following two symptoms: a "depressed mood or loss of interest or pleasure." The *DSM* notes that these should also "represent a change from previous functioning." A "depressed mood" is something we may all feel from time to time but the *DSM* notes that in a "major depressive episode" the symptom is persistent over time "most of the day, nearly every day," and in children might present as irritability. The other key factor, the feeling that nearly every activity is joyless, persists in much the same way as depression. The *DSM* lists an additional seven symptoms in people with severe depression, and these include the following:

- Sleeplessness or sleeping excessively
- Changes in body weight (e.g., unintended weight loss or gain and shifts in appetite)
- Frequent thoughts about death or dying
- Fatigue
- Restlessness, or its opposite, "slowing down"
- Daily feelings of "worthlessness or inappropriate guilt"
- Inability to focus or "indecisiveness"

Finally, the *DSM* qualifies the diagnosis by adding that these symptoms shouldn't be caused by medical condition, drugs, or grief from "the loss of a loved one."

---

*"Criteria for Major Depressive Episode." *Diagnostic and Statistical Manual of Mental Disorders*. 4th ed. Washington: American Psychological Association, 1994. 327. Print.

▶ **Reading 4: Blog**

Anyone can write a blog. So it certainly can be an unreliable source for academic writing. But like anything else online, the quality of blogs can vary widely. Take the one that follows: "Pediatrics Gets It Wrong About 'Facebook Depression.'" The author, John Grohol, who writes for the online site PyschCentral, has excellent credentials and, in a move you don't see often with blogs, he includes a bibliography. But what's especially interesting for us is that the article takes exception—pretty strong exception—to an article we read earlier that appeared in the journal *Pediatrics*. Grohol calls it "shoddy research."

No matter what topic you research, you'll find situations like this, where reputable scholars and researchers disagree (though rarely this strongly), contesting findings that to the rest of us seem to be presented pretty convincingly. This is how knowledge is advanced, of course—an ongoing conversation between people who have a stake in trying to establish the truth about a topic. Most often, the "truth" is temporary. In Grohol's blog, he assails the implication that there *is* something called "Facebook depression" and that it is causal. In other words, is it true that Facebook *causes* users to be depressed? Grohol doesn't think so. See what you think.

Pediatrics Gets It Wrong About "Facebook Depression"

John Grohol

You know it's not good when one of the most prestigious pediatric journals, *Pediatrics,* can't differentiate between correlation and causation. 1

And yet this is exactly what the authors of a "clinical report" did in reporting on the impact of social media on children and teens. Especially in their discussion of "Facebook depression," a term that the authors simply *made up* to describe the phenomenon observed when depressed people use social media. 2

Shoddy research? You bet. That's why *Pediatrics* calls it a "clinical report"—because it's at the level of a bad blog post written by people with a clear agenda. In this case, the report was written by Gwenn Schurgin O'Keeffe, Kathleen Clarke-Pearson and the American Academy of Pediatrics Council on Communications and Media (2011). 3

What makes this bad a report? Let's just look at the issue of "Facebook depression," their made-up term for a phenomenon that doesn't exist. 4

The authors of the *Pediatrics* report use six citations to support their claim that social media sites like Facebook actually *cause* depression in children and teens. Four of the six citations are thirdparty news reports on research in this area. In other words, *the authors couldn't even bother with reading the actual research to see if the research actually said what the news outlet reported it said.* 5

I expect to see this sort of lack of quality and laziness on blogs. Hey, a lot of time we're busy and we just want to make a point—that I can understand. 6

When you go to the trouble not only of writing a report but also publishing it in a peer-reviewed journal, you'd think you'd go to the trouble of reading the research—not other people's reporting on research. 7

(continued)

(continued)

8   Here's what the researchers in *Pediatrics* had to say about "Facebook depression:"

Researchers have proposed a new phenomenon called "Facebook depression," defined as depression that develops when preteens and teens spend a great deal of time on social media sites, such as Facebook, and then begin to exhibit classic symptoms of depression.

Acceptance by and contact with peers is an important element of adolescent life. The intensity of the online world is thought to be a factor that may trigger depression in some adolescents. As with offline depression, preadolescents and adolescents who suffer from Facebook depression are at risk for social isolation and sometimes turn to risky Internet sites and blogs for "help" that may promote substance abuse, unsafe sexual practices, or aggressive or self-destructive behaviors.

9   Time and time again researchers are finding much more nuanced relationships between social networking sites and depression. In the Selfhout et al. (2009) study they cite, for instance, the researchers only found the correlation between the two factors in people with *low quality* friendships. Teens with what the researchers characterized as high quality friendships showed no increase in depression with increased social networking time.

10   The *Pediatrics* authors also do what a lot of researchers do when promoting a specific bias or point of view—they simply ignore research that disagrees with their bias. Worse, they cite the supposed depression-social networking link as though it were a forgone conclusion—that researchers are all in agreement that this actually exists, and exists in a causative manner.

11   There are a multitude of studies that disagree with their point of view, however. One longitudinal study (Kraut et al., 1998) found that, over a period of 8–12 months, both loneliness and depression increased with time spent online among adolescent and adult first-time Internet users. In a one-year follow-up study (Kraut et al., 2002), however, the observed negative effects of Internet use had disappeared. In other words, this may not be a robust relationship (if it even exists) and may simply be something related to greater familiarity with the Internet.

12   Other research has shown that college students'—who are often older teens—Internet use was directly and indirectly related to **less depression** (Morgan & Cotten, 2003; LaRose, Eastin, & Gregg, 2001).

13   Furthermore, studies have revealed that Internet use can lead to online relationship formation, and thereby to more social support ([Nie and Erbring, 2000], [Wellman et al., 2001] and [Wolak et al., 2003])—which may subsequently lead to less internalizing problems.

14   In another study cited by the *Pediatrics* authors, simply reading the news report should've raised a red flag for them. Because the news report on the study quoted the study's author who specifically noted her study could not determine causation:

According to Morrison, pornography, online gaming and social networking site users had a higher incidence of moderate to severe depression than other users. "Our research indicates that excessive Internet use is associated with depression, but what we don't know is which comes first–are depressed people drawn to the Internet or does the Internet cause depression? What is clear is that for a small subset of people, excessive use of the Internet could be a warning signal for depressive tendencies," she added.

The other citations in the *Pediatrics* report are equally problematic (and one citation has nothing to do with social networking and depression [Davila, 2009]). None mention the phrase "Facebook depression" (as far as I could determine), and none could demonstrate a **causative relationship between use of Facebook making a teenager or child feel more depressed.** Zero.   15

I'm certain depressed people use Facebook, Twitter and other social networking websites. I'm certain people who are already feeling down or depressed might go online to talk to their friends, and try and be cheered up. This in no way suggests that by using more and more of Facebook, a person is going to get more depressed. That's just a silly conclusion to draw from the data to date, and we've previously discussed how use of the Internet has not been shown to *cause* depression, only that there's an association between the two.   16

If this is the level of "research" done to come to these conclusions about "Facebook depression," the entire report is suspect and should be questioned. This is not an objective clinical report; this is a piece of propaganda spouting a particular agenda and bias.   17

The problem now is that news outlets everywhere are picking up on "Facebook depression" and suggesting not only that it exists, but that researchers have found the online world somehow "triggers" depression in teens. *Pediatrics* and the American Academy of Pediatrics should be ashamed of this shoddy clinical report, and retract the entire section about "Facebook depression."   18

References

Davila, Joanne; Stroud, Catherine B.; Starr, Lisa R.; Miller, Melissa Ramsay; Yoneda, Athena; Hershenberg, Rachel. (2009). Romantic and sexual activities, parent–adolescent stress, and depressive symptoms among early adolescent girls. *Journal of Adolescence, 32(4), 909-924.*

Kraut, R., S. Kiesler, B. Boneva, J. N. Cummings, V. Helgeson and A. M. Crawford. (2002). Internet paradox revisited. *Journal of Social Issues, 58, 49–74.*

Kraut, R., M. Patterson, V. Lundmark, S. Kiesler, T. Mukophadhyay and W. Scherlis. (1998). Internet paradox: a social technology that reduces social involvement and psychological well-being? *American Psychologist, 53, 1017–1031.*

LaRose, R., Eastin, M. S. and Gregg, J. (2001). Reformulating the Internet paradox: social cognitive explanations of Internet use and depression. *Journal of Online Behavior, 1, 1–19.*

Maarten H. W. Selfhout Susan J. T. Branje1, M. Delsing Tom F. M. ter Bogt and Wim H. J. Meeus. (2009). Different types of Internet use, depression, and social anxiety: The role of perceived friendship quality. *Journal of Adolescence, 32(4), 819-833.*

(continued)

(continued)

Morgan, C. & Cotten, S. R. (2003). The relationship between Internet activities and depressive symptoms in a sample of college freshmen. *CyberPsychology and Behavior, 6, 133–142.*

Nie, NH and Erbring, L. (2000). Internet and society: A preliminary report, Stanford Inst. of Quant. Study Soc., Stanford, CA.

O'Keeffe et al. (2011). Clinical Report: The Impact of Social Media on Children, Adolescents, and Families (PDF). *Pediatrics. DOI: 10.1542/peds.2011-0054*

Wellman, B., A. Quan-Haase, J. Witte and K. Hampton. (2001). Does the Internet increase, decrease, or supplement social capital? Social networks, participation, and community commitment. *American Behavioral Scientist, 45, 436–455.*

Wolak, J., K. J. Mitchell and D. Finkelhor. (2003). Escaping or connecting? Characteristics of youth who form close online relationships. *Journal of Adolescence, 26, 105–119.*

Inquiring into the Essay

1. **Explore.** If you've read all four of the readings on our research question, you have a better understanding of what the connections might be between Facebook use and depression. Now would be a great time to return to where you started: the journal entry with your "first thoughts" on the question. Read over what you wrote, and finish the following sentence:

   When I first thought about the relationship between Facebook use and depression, I thought _____. But now I think _____.

   Repeat this sentence, using different ideas in the blanks each time. Try to do this at least three times.

2. **Explain.** Summarize the argument that Grohol makes in his blog about the relationship between Facebook use and depression.

3. **Evaluate.** Drawing on your understanding of all four readings and your own analysis of the findings and claims in each, draft a thesis that addresses the original inquiry question:

   Is there a relationship between Facebook use and depression?

4. **Reflect.** When you encounter articles from experts that seem to disagree as strongly as the two articles here—the one in *Pediatrics* and this blog—how you do you determine which to believe?

Exercise 10.1 (Continued from p. 391)

STEP TWO: **Flash Research**

Now *do* something with all that journal writing that you generated in response to the readings in this section. Write a 250-word argument that addresses the inquiry question *Is there a relationship between Facebook use and depression?* This flash research essay should:

- Make a claim (have a thesis)
- Incorporate *at least* two of the readings through summary, paraphrase, and/or quotation (see Chapter 12 for more on how to approach each)
- For now, use a simplified citation. For example, put a parenthetical citation after borrowed material with the last name(s) of the article's author(s) and the paragraph number of the relevant passage. For example, (Grohol para. 5).

STEP THREE: **Talking About It**

Share the drafts of your flash research essays in class or online. Discuss the following:

- How did you decide when to quote and when to paraphrase or summarize?
- Do you notice any significant differences in how people interpreted the readings?
- Who in class had the most interesting thesis? What seem to be the qualities of a strong thesis?
- What did you notice about how people used sources *differently*? In particular, did anyone use one of the readings as something other than support for a point they were trying to make?
- What questions arose about what should be cited and how?

THE WRITING PROCESS

Inquiry Project **Writing a Research Essay**

⊙
⌐ **Watch** ⌐
the Animation on
Planning Research
in your MyLab

Inquiry questions: What does the evidence suggest is true? What is the relationship?

Write a research essay on a topic of your choice. Choose a subject because you want to find out something about it; avoid things you *already* have a strong opinion about. This essay should

- Be based on a "researchable" inquiry question.

- Have a S.O.F.T., or a central thesis that represents your best answer to your research question. This thesis may be delayed rather than parked in the introduction.

- Use appropriate and relevant sources based on your own experiences, observations, interviews, and reading, or all four sources of information.

- Be cited using the conventions recommended by your instructor.

- Be written for an audience of peers rather than experts on the topic.

Prose+

- Make data beautiful by creating an infographic like "Bumblebee Math" on page 390. Identify some key statistics on your topic that you'd like to visually summarize. In addition to text, include things such as graphs, timelines, flowcharts, diagrams, size comparisons, and images. This will be a pretty basic infographic, as most of us have little experience with design, but even with a program such as Word and Excel it's possible to tell a visual story. For those who want to experiment with free graphics software that will help with design, download Inkscape (inkscape.org).

- If your research topic has a local angle—it affects people in your community or there are local experts—then consider creating a radio documentary styled after those on NPR's *This American Life*. You'll need a microphone (laptop, smartphone, or digital recorder) and editing software. Audacity (audacity.sourceforge.net) is free and relatively easy to use (See "Inquiring into the Details: Using Audacity to Record and Edit Audio" on page 143). Interview a person (or people) affected by your topic and write the narration, incorporating the best interview clips. You might even add a music track.

- Slide software such as PowerPoint and Keynote can supplement your research essay by reimagining your findings for a public presentation. Avoid bland bullet-point-riddled slides by creating a handout to go along with your presentation. Instead, use the slides to incorporate text, images, and even sound to emphasize key points that you'll make orally or, better yet, to help you tell a story about your topic. The key questions to address for the audience of your presentation is this: *Why should I care about this topic? What stake do I have in the question you're exploring? In other words:* So what?

What Are You Going to Write About?

This choice may be wide open, or your instructor might ask you to focus on a broad theme, perhaps one on which your class is focused. Either way, the same principle applies:

10.4
Use invention techniques for discovering a researchable question.

There are no boring topics, only poor questions.

There is no topic—dust mites, fruit cake, Elvis, nuclear fusion, or basketballs—that won't yield to the right question. (We'll take up the characteristics of a good question later.) But there's another condition upon which the success of your research project depends: your curiosity. Whatever the question that eventually becomes a focus for inquiry, it must be one that you find interesting. Typically, this means that you choose a topic because it holds the promise of discovery.

Ask yourself this: *What have I seen, read, experienced, or heard about that raises interesting questions that research might help answer?*

Approaching your research project this way is exactly the impulse that might have motivated you to write a personal essay on growing up with an autistic sibling or a persuasive essay on the downside of recruiting NCAA athletes at your school. It's the same motive that inspires all genuine inquiry: *How do I feel about this? What do I think about this? What do I want to know?*

While inquiry-based investigations often begin with factual questions, they rarely stop there.

Opening Up

Use your notebook to generate some material. As in previous inquiry projects, at this stage don't prejudge anything you come up with. Let yourself play around with possibilities.

Listing Prompts. Lists can be rich sources of triggering topics. Let them grow freely, and when you're ready, use an item as the focus of another list or an episode of fastwriting. The following prompts should get you started.

1. Inventory your interests by creating five separate lists on a page of your notebook. Choose among the following words as a general category for each of the five lists you will create: Places, Trends, Things, Technologies, People, Controversies, History, Jobs, Habits, Hobbies. In each of the five categories you choose, brainstorm a list of words or phrases that come to mind when you think about *what you know and what you might want to know.* For example, under Places, I would put "pigeons in Florence," because I want to know more about their impact on Renaissance buildings. Under Hobbies, I would put "fly fishing," because that's something I know about. Spend about fifteen minutes building these lists.

2. Look over your lists and ask yourself, *Are there research topics implied by a few of the items on these lists?* In other words, what here raises questions that more research might answer? What is it about this item that I wonder about?

3. Finally, choose a promising item from one of the lists and generate questions about it that you'd love to have answered. Perhaps you already know something about the topic but would like to learn more. Don't worry yet about whether all the questions are great.

Listen
to the Audio on
**Finding a
Research Topic**
in your MyLab

Fastwriting Prompts. Remember, fastwriting is a great way to stimulate creative thinking. Turn off your critical side and let yourself write "badly."

1. Choose an item from your lists and use it as a prompt for a seven-minute fastwrite. Begin by telling yourself the story of when, where, and why you first got interested in the subject. When the writing stalls, write the following phrase, and follow it for as long as you can: *Among the things I most want to learn about this are . . .*

2. Interesting research questions can emerge from the most ordinary experiences. Take eating, for instance, or friendship, running, dreaming, depression, texting, infatuation, insomnia, listening to music, body language, butterflies, intelligence, addiction, etc. The key is to figure out what you might want to know about ordinary experiences that research might help answer. Take one of the subjects above—or another that you think of—and begin a fastwrite with this phrase: *The thing that I've always found interesting about* _____ *is* _____. *For example,* _____ . . . Follow this writing until it stalls, and then pick another ordinary experience and do it again.

Visual Prompts. Sometimes the best way to generate material is to see what we think represented in something other than sentences. Boxes, lines, webs, clusters, arrows, charts, and even sketches can help us to see more of the landscape

One Student's Response

Julian's Journal

TOPIC: JAZZ

My dad was into jazz. Would listen to it all night long after working all day long. He listened to all kinds of jazz—Bird, Miles Davis, Billy Holiday, Monk. It took me years to really appreciate the music but now it's my favorite kind. **Among the things I most want to learn about** jazz is its connection to African music and slave songs. It makes me wonder whether the uniqueness of jazz, its spontaneity especially, has something to do with the hymns and spirituals of the slaves. **Among the other things I want to learn** is whether jazz was accepted in the early days. I seem to remember my dad saying that the . . .

of a subject, especially connections among fragments of information that aren't as obvious in prose.

> Do an image search using Google on some person, place, thing, or event that interests you. Might one of the pictures you find be the focus of an investigation? Who was that guy? What was going on when this happened? Why did it happen?

Research Prompts. Should you do some research before you begin your research? Absolutely. By exploring what others have said or done or wondered about, you might discover an interest in something you wouldn't have otherwise considered.

1. Surf the Net, perhaps beginning with a subject directory such as the Internet Public Library (http://ipl.org). Start by clicking on a subject area that interests you. Keep following the links as you branch more deeply into the subcategories and subdisciplines of that area of knowledge. Look for specific subject areas that intrigue you. For example, you might have begun in the broad subject of history, clicked the link for medieval history (maybe you've always wondered what was dark about the Dark Ages), and ended up reading some fascinating articles on the home life of medieval women. Does this raise some questions you'd like to explore?

2. Study the local newspaper, which may be available online. Devote some time to reading the paper to discover a local controversy that intrigues you. Say there was an article on the impact of Title IX on the university's athletic department, and you wonder, *Is the elimination of the men's wrestling team really the result of shifts in funding to women's sports?* Or perhaps there's a letter to the editor about the condition of housing for migrant workers in the valley. *Are things really that bad?*

3. Use Google Scholar. Type in a topic or a phrase that reflects an interest of yours. For example, I've been interested in peoples' beliefs in alien abduction. What might explain their persistence? Google Scholar will often surprise you, serving up results on even less-academic-seeming topics. There's some fascinating stuff on alien abduction, as you'll see on the following page.

Narrowing Down

The great thing about simply generating material is that you can turn off your critical mind and simply muck about all sorts of possible topics for your essay. But, as always, the process depends on taking a more analytical look at whether you've discovered anything genuinely useful. Remember your goal at this stage: You want to identify a possible topic—and maybe, if you're lucky, a research question—that will move your investigation forward in the next few days. All writing projects need to be focused, and this is especially important with any project such as the research essay, in which you're dealing with a lot of information. Focusing your project on an initial question that is narrow enough has enormous practical value.

10.5

Refine a research question to narrow the topic focus and lead to a judgment.

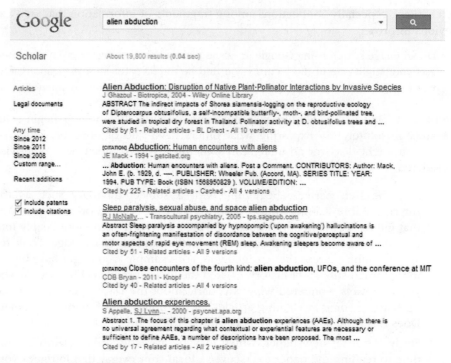

In case you doubted that there are scholarly articles on nearly any subject, you can see here that Google Scholar generated nearly 20,000 results from the keyword search "alien abduction."

It helps you control the floodgates. The more specific your question, the easier it is to manage the information and to decide what information you can ignore. This is a huge advantage when you're dealing with a flood of information. For example, using the topic I mentioned earlier—belief in alien abduction—there's a big difference between this question

Why do people believe in alien abduction?

and this question

What's the relationship between belief in alien abduction and the creation of "false memories"?

On the other hand, if you're exploring a topic about which you know little, it will be hard to come up with a focused research question until you learn more. (I got my question about the relationship between belief in alien abduction and false memory from a quick Google Scholar search). Start by developing a "working knowledge" of your tentative topic, exploring questions of fact and definition first: *What is known about this? What is it?* When you know something about you're topic, it's infinitely easier to find a focus.

What's Promising Material and What Isn't? The most promising subject is one you're curious about. But that's not enough. Consider the following:

- *Has something already been said about it?* Is there information on your topic and is it accessible?
- *Does it raise more questions?* It shouldn't have a simple answer.
- *Does it matter to someone other than you?* Other people should have a stake in the question you're exploring.
- *Do you already know what you think?* Why inquire into a topic you've already got figured out?
- *Is it appropriate for the assignment?* Will you be able to find images for an infographic, scholarly sources for an academic paper, or people to interview for an audio documentary?

Questions About Audience and Purpose. When you imagine an audience for your research project, ask yourself this:

> *Am I writing up? Am I writing down? Am I writing across?*

When you "write up," you're assuming readers who are experts on your topic, people who already know *more* than you do. When you "write down," you're imagining an audience that knows *less* than you, at least after you've done some research. Scholarly research, the kind you find in academic journals and books, is written "across," to fellow experts. Unless you're an expert writing to others with considerable knowledge about your topic, then the scholarly article isn't a model you should try to emulate in your research essay. On the other hand, there might be situations in which you're writing up for a professor, presenting research in his or her field, perhaps in a class on the subject. But for this assignment, you're likely writing down—to peers—trying to make your discoveries relevant and interesting to nonexperts.

    Which audience it is makes a huge difference (as always) in how you write your essay, including:

1. The tone and formality of the language.
2. How much background on the topic you need to provide.
3. What kinds of evidence you can use.
4. The need to present an "original" finding.
5. The methods you use to come up with a finding.

A research essay is written "down" for an audience of nonexperts. A conventional research paper may be written "up" or "across." Some of the implications of this are summarized here:

10.6
Use audience and purpose to make decisions about the structure of the work and the types of information to use in it.

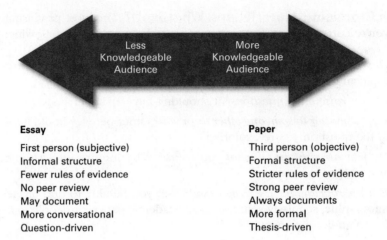

Essay

First person (subjective)
Informal structure
Fewer rules of evidence
No peer review
May document
More conversational
Question-driven

Paper

Third person (objective)
Formal structure
Stricter rules of evidence
Strong peer review
Always documents
More formal
Thesis-driven

Trying Out

You've got a tentative topic. The next step is to develop a "working knowledge" of the topic so you can come up a with a focused research question. What's a working knowledge? It's a basic factual understanding: What is known about _____? OR How is _____ defined? This understanding is hardly comprehensive, but it's enough to be able to tell someone about your topic for five minutes without stopping. Steps for developing working knowledge—and later, focused knowledge—are covered on pages 448 through 455 in Chapter 11.

Refining the Question. Once you've got at least a working knowledge of your topic, try developing a more focused research question. You might try fitting your topic into one of the two inquiry questions that are often explored in research essays:

1. What does the evidence suggest that might explain _____?
2. What might be the relationship between _____ and _____? Does _____ cause _____? Is _____ similar (or dissimilar) to _____?

Focus Like a Journalist. Another way to find a narrower focus for your project is to try anchoring your subject to a particular story, person, place, event, or time period (see graphic below). This is something journalists do all the time. Sometimes they combine particular stories, in particular places, with particular people, at particular times, to focus on a large, complex problem. For example, if journalists want to cover the issue of climate change, they might tell the story of what's happening on one small island in the Pacific. If they want to explore a problem such as the costs of college tuition, they tell the story of a single student at Lane Community College in Oregon. If they want to show the dangers of coal mining, they write about a day in a Kentucky mine. Think about which of these—a story, a person, a place, or a time period—might focus your larger topic.

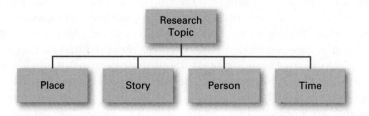

Writing a Proposal. Rather than writing a sketch, draft a proposal on your research topic, with the following elements:

1. **What's known?** What controversies, questions, or schools of thought are there on your topic? Who is involved, and what do they say? What do you find most interesting and significant?

2. **What's at stake?** Provide some background on why your research question is relevant to people. You may be curious about the topic, but why should the rest of us care? How does it affect us? What might we learn that we will find useful or interesting?

3. **What's the question, and what's your hunch?** What's your opening question for the inquiry project? What do you want to know? Based on what you know now, what are your assumptions about answers to the question you pose? What do you think you'll find and why?

4. **Bibliography.** Provide a list of references you've consulted so far. You can find information about how to format these citations in Chapter 11. Your instructor may ask you to annotate this bibliography as well, providing short summaries of what each source says that's relevant to your question.

▶ Sample Research Proposal

Research Essay Proposal: What is the relationship between Facebook use and depression?

1. What's known?

Most observers believe that the number of users of Facebook is now well over 100 million worldwide, with particularly heavy use by people who are between the ages of 18 and 25. Coincidentally, the National Institute of Mental Health notes that this is also the age group that is particularly vulnerable to depression ("major depressive disorder"). Depression rates among college students, a group who are heavy Facebook users, has also increased significantly in the past six years (Moreno et. al 447). Though there is some dispute about the term "Facebook depression," a recent "clinical report" claims that teenagers who turn to social networks to overcome feelings of social isolation may find "triggers" for their depression online (O'Keefe, Clarke-Pearson 802). I know from my own experience, for example, that people compare themselves to others on Facebook, often feeling badly about themselves when friends post announcements about achievements (Pappas). I've also observed that certain people are more likely to share Facebook posts about their personal struggles, and there is some research that suggests that people see social networks as offering "a sense of security and belonging which allow users to disclose thoughts and feelings that are normally hidden" (Hollaran 11). Depending on the responses that depressed posters get from others, they may find comfort or more distress. A number of researchers are also looking at whether Facebook can be used to predict clinical depression. One study said that about 27% of the Facebook users profiled showed symptoms of depression (Moreno 447).

2. What's at stake?

I think this is an issue that obviously affects a lot of people, particularly people from teen to college age. If the research I've read so far is right, then the number of depressed college-age students is increasing, and most of these have a presence on Facebook. Does social networking help or hurt? Facebook can be a way to detect symptoms, a way to make them worse, or a way to destigmatize the problem. But which is it? The answer could make a significant difference in whether Facebook use should be encouraged for people with symptoms of depression.

3. What's the question? What's my hunch?

In general, I'm interested in the relationship between depression and Facebook use. More specifically, I'm wondering whether users who are already depressed might be particularly vulnerable. Will Facebook make their depression worse? My hunch is that it depends. I suspect I'll find that Facebook helps some depressed users and hurts others. What might be interesting is to look at the online conditions that *do* make people more depressed.

4. Working Bibliography

Baker, Levi R. and Debra L. Oswald. "Shyness and Online Networking Services." *Journal of Social and Personal Relationships* 27.7 (2010): 873–889. Print.

Grohol, John. "Pediatrics Gets It Wrong About 'Facebook Depression.'" Pyschcentral .com. No date. Web. 20 April 2012.

"Major Depressive Disorder Among Adults." National Institute of Mental Health. No date. Web. 4 April 2012.

Moreno, Megan A., Lauren Jelenchick, Katie Egan, Elizabeth Cox, Henry Young, Kerry Gannon, and Tara Becker. "Feeling Bad on Facebook: Depression Disclosures by College Students on Social Networking Site." *Depression and Anxiety* 28 (2011): 447–455. Print.

O'Keefe, Gwen Schurgin, Kathleen Clarke-Pearson. "The Impact of Social Media on Children, Adolescents, and Families." *Pediatrics* (2011): 800–804. 28 March 2011. Web. 4 April 2012.

Pappas, Stephanie. "Facebook with Care: Social Networking Site Can Hurt Self-Esteem." LiveScience. 6 February 2012. Web. 15 April 2012.

Moving from Proposal to Draft

If you developed a proposal, then you've got a tentative destination for your research essay; you know what it is you might want to know about your topic. Obviously, the next step is to continue your research, developing what I call "focused knowledge" on your topic. Take a look at the strategies for developing focused knowledge in Chapter 11, on pages 451 through 455.

Remember that the proposal is just your first stab at pinning down your project. As you learn more about the topic, your research question will evolve, and how successful you are at revising the question is the one thing that will most determine the success of your project. Remember that your initial questions are often questions of fact (What is known about _____?) or definition (What *is* _____?). These are necessary for developing a working knowledge. But they don't produce essays. They produce reports. In your proposal, you've posed a question that will hopefully guide you to some kind of judgment about your topic. Does it?

Evaluating Your Proposal. Let's look at the inquiry question in the sample research proposal, on pages 417–418.

What is the relationship between Facebook use and depression?

This is a pretty good question, and here are a few reasons:

✓ It isn't a question of fact or definition.

✓ It is likely to lead to some kind of judgment (e.g., Does Facebook use *cause* users to get depressed?)

✓ The question narrows the writer's sights, at least some (e.g., it isn't asking about *all* social networks, but Facebook; it isn't speculating about *all* emotional responses, but depression).

Now examine your own research question. Does it do similar things for you?

Reflecting on What You've Learned. Though you haven't been working on your project for long, you've been at it long enough to start to tell yourself the story of how your thinking about the topic has evolved. In your journal, spend a few minutes telling yourself this story: *When I first chose this topic, I thought...And then I thought...And then...And now I'm thinking...* Do this "narrative of thought" on your topic periodically, because it will help you to figure out what you think and, ultimately, what you might be trying to say in your draft.

Developing

Discovery is what drives inquiry-based research. This is why having a good question matters so much, and finding a good question for your project depends on knowing something about your topic. "Working knowledge" seeds this effort. A working knowledge will give you an encyclopedia-like view of your topic—what is the terrain, what are the controversies or the questions, who is influential—and from this you can frame a question that interests you.

But this is just the beginning. As you explore your research question in the coming weeks, you'll go beyond working knowledge to "focused knowledge," finding information that drills down more deeply into your topic's terrain. Good questions are sharper drills. However, this is an open-ended process, and your goal at this stage is to use what you discover to continually shape what you want to see. As you become more informed, you'll revise your approach, refining your question, developing ideas about what you think, and always searching for the answers to this simple question: *So what?*

Writing *while you research* will help you figure this all out and even help you get a start on drafting your essay. I'm not talking about simply taking notes on the information that you find in the coming weeks. Writing about what you *think* about what you're reading or hearing is the best incubator of insight. The double-entry journal, which was introduced to you earlier in *The Curious Writer*, is one method that encourages this kind of writing.

Tools for Developing the Research Essay Draft. Chapter 11 is full of tools for developing your research draft. Here's a summary of some of those helpful topics.

Quick Guide to Research Techniques

Topic	Purpose	Pages
Search terms	How to focus and improve the quality of search results	442–447
Working knowledge	Strategies for collecting information on questions of fact and definition	448–450
Developing "focused knowledge"	Strategies for searching more narrowly and deeply into a limited topic	451–455
Evaluating sources	Methods for determining the reliability and authority of sources	455–460
Interviews and surveys	How to gather information from people	460–468

| Note taking | Using double-entry journals, research logs, and other techniques for "writing in the middle" | 470–473 |
| Citing sources | How to know when to cite a source and how | MLA, 486–512
APA, 512–529 |

Drafting

Sara was a compulsive collector of information. She researched and researched, collecting more books and articles and web sources until the desk in her apartment looked like a miniature version of downtown Chicago—towering piles of paper and books everywhere. She never felt as if she knew enough to begin writing her essay, and would only begin drafting when forced to—when the paper was due tomorrow. Neal figured he could find most of what he needed pretty quickly on the Internet. He printed out a few articles and web pages and felt confident he could write his paper using those. He didn't feel pressured to begin writing until the due date loomed. When Neal started writing and realized that he probably wouldn't be able to get the required page length, he widened the margins.

Sara and Neal obviously use different strategies for getting to the draft. Sara relies on accumulating great quantities of information, trusting that aggressively collecting sources will make the writing easier—the main source of anxiety for her—although she probably doesn't really believe that. On the other hand, Neal suffers from overconfidence. He figures he can make do with a few sources and doesn't look around much. Both Neal and Sara do what research paper writers have done forever: wait until the last minute. Neither of these writers will be happy with the result.

It's easy to avoid this situation if you begin the draft after you've accomplished the following:

- *You've done some writing before you start writing.* In other words, have you exploited the double-entry journal or an alternative note taking method to both collect useful information and to explore your reaction to what it says?

- *You are working from abundance (but not overabundance).* Neal is much more typical than Sara. He is trying to compose his draft by drawing from a nearly empty well. Almost any writing—and particularly research writing—depends on working from abundance. You need to collect more information than you can use. But not too much. Don't let endless collecting become an avoidance tactic.

- *Your research question has helped you exclude information.* A good question is a guide. It will help you see the relevance of certain portions of the sources you've collected and give you reason to ignore the rest. If you sense that this is happening consistently as you review your sources, you're probably ready to write.

■   *You have a tentative idea about what you think.* By now, you know enough about your topic to have some feelings or ideas about a possible answer to the question behind your investigation. Remember that the draft may make you change your mind—that's fine—but begin composing with at least a tentative point of view.

Methods of Development. How you decide to organize your draft begins with the question of motive. Is your purpose to *find out* or *to prove,* to explore or to argue? The first motive is often the purpose of a research essay, the latter the motive when we write a conventional research paper. Though both forms share a considerable number of qualities, the structure of each may differ. For example, an essay frequently has a delayed thesis, appearing somewhere towards the end of the piece as the writer reports what he or she has discovered. The research paper typically has a thesis that is stated somewhere in the beginning, as a claim or assertion that the paper will prove. You might imagine it this way:

The Development of an Exploratory Research Essay

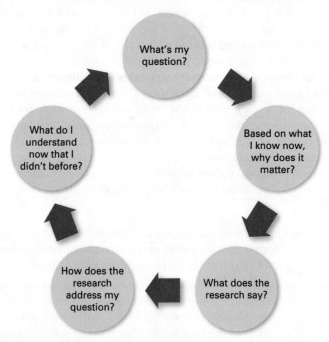

The Development of an Argumentative Research Paper

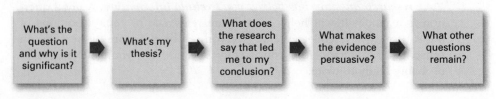

As you can see, a research essay might have the qualities of a narrative: What did I want to know initially, what's the story of what I found out, and what do I understand now? The argumentative paper is a bit more linear, working from claim to proof. Let's look a little more closely at microstructures that could be present in either form.

Narrative. We don't usually associate narrative structure with research papers, but research-based writing tells stories all the time. Perhaps one of the most common techniques is the use of the case study, which can be an excellent way to begin your paper. Case studies or anecdotes about people involved or affected by a topic often bring that topic to life by moving it closer to the everyday *lives* of people. But as I already mentioned, narrative might also be used as the backbone of a research essay. Sometimes an essay tells the story of what the writer wanted to know and what she found out—a kind of narrative of thought.

Question to Answer. Because much of the research process is devoted to developing a good question to drive the inquiry, it makes sense to consider organizing your essay around what that question is, where it came from, and what has already been said about it, and then reporting what you've discovered about possible answers to the question that triggered the investigation. A lot of formal academic research is organized this way, although there might be an added section about the methods the investigator chose to try to seek the answers.

Known to Unknown. This is a variation on the question-to-answer structure that might be particularly useful if you're writing about a complex topic about which much remains unknown. Your research might have led to the discovery that the question you're interested in is one that has very speculative or limited answers. For example, Andy was writing about the use of psychiatric medicine such as antidepressants and antipsychotics on children, because his family physician had recommended them for one of his own kids. Andy quickly discovered that this was a relatively new use for such drugs and that much mystery surrounded both the diagnosis and the treatment of children with emotional problems. It became clear that the purpose of his essay was not to offer a definitive answer to his question, but to suggest areas that still needed further study.

Using Evidence. What kind of information should you use in your research project? That depends in part on how you answered the audience question I posed earlier. Are you writing "down" to people who know less than you do? Or are you writing "up" or "across" to experts? The more knowledgeable your audience, the stricter the rules of evidence. However, if you're writing your paper for peers ("down"), the types of evidence you could use are looser. For example, you might use relevant personal experiences or observations, the kind of thing that might not be strong evidence in a more academic paper. The key is this: *Vary your sources.* The weakest research essays draw heavily from one well—maybe using a single source over and over again, or a single *type* of source: e.g., popular web pages or online articles with no authors.

The table below gives you an idea about the *range* of sources you might draw on in a research project. Some, such as experimental data, are evidence that you won't use here, as you aren't doing a study. But as you begin developing your essay, consider incorporating several of the different types of evidence you see here.

Type of Evidence	Source	Description	Examples
Anecdotal	From personal experience, story someone told you or reported from published source.	Examples drawn from limited number of sources, usually involving stories.	Case studies, personal experiences and observations, profiles, interviews with people affected.
Statistical	From expert or research institution directly, or reported in secondary source.	Relevant facts and findings, often quantitative.	Tables, statistics in government reports, size comparisons, growth data, numbers affected, etc.
Expert testimony	From transcript, scholarly article or book, personal interview, or secondary source.	Quotes, claims, and ideas from individuals or institutions with expertise in the topic.	An argument by an influential scholar, a quote from a personal interview, a quoted passage from a book, etc.
Experimental	Data generated by the researcher to test a hypothesis.	Studies conducted with an approved methodology that often produces quantitative results.	A lab experiment, survey, transcript analysis, etc.
Textual	Interpretation and analysis of writing, images, and other kinds of texts.	Close "reading" of a text to interpret its meaning, test a theory, analyze it's structure, or evaluate its effectiveness.	Interpretation of a poem or short story, analysis of an advertisement or photograph, rhetorical analysis of a speech.
Observation	Close observation in a controlled setting or in the field.	Methodological descriptions of what subjects do in response to a task, problem, question, or event. Or "deep descriptions" of people in natural settings, to interpret behaviors, status, social roles, etc.	Analyzing video to determine usability of software, field observations of bowling-league members or an Alcoholics Anonymous meeting. Detailed description of study site, or description of the scene of a significant event.

Workshopping

If your draft is subject to peer review, see Chapter 14 for details on how to organize workshop groups and decide on how your group can help you. See "Models for Writing Workshops" (p. 578) for details on how to organize workshop groups. Each workshop type is described more fully in that section.

There are a couple of key things to consider as you prepare for this workshop.

- **Is it boring?** There's no reason to write an extended essay, such as the one for this project, that bores everybody to death. Why would you want to do that? You might identify passages or pages in the draft that you think seem to drag and see if your group agrees and can suggest what you might do about it.

- **Is the question clear?** The organizing force of the research essay is the writer's research question: What is it she wants to know? This must be obvious at the beginning of the essay, or in a page or two readers *will* get bored because they don't know where it's headed.

- **Does it suggest an answer?** If you're going to ask readers to peddle your bike for more than a few pages, then they not only need to know in what direction you're steering, but also that you'll have something to say when you get there. We often call this the thesis. Whatever you call it, your draft must ultimately make a judgment, and make it clearly.

Questions for Peer Reviewers	
1. Purpose	What is the research question that is driving this project? Is it clear? Is it interesting? Is there another question that might be better?
2. Meaning	In your own words, what do you think I'm trying to say? Did the draft hint at another idea that I might develop in the next draft?

Reflecting on the Draft. A draft is a thing the wind blows through. That might be especially true of the full first draft of your research essay. After all, this project involves juggling a lot more than most other inquiry projects: controlling information and the ideas from a wide variety of sources, the challenge of trying to surround that outside material with your own ideas, worries about following citation conventions, and the struggle not to let the whole project get away from your own purposes and questions. Spend a little time reflecting on how all this went.

In your notebook or on a separate piece of paper you'll attach to the draft when you hand it in, answer the following questions:

- What's the most important thing you learned about your topic after the research and writing you've just completed? Is this important understanding obvious in the draft?

■ Choose two paragraphs that incorporate outside sources—one that you think is written pretty well, and another written less well. What differences do you notice between the two? Can you identify at least one problem you need to work on in the next draft that will help you improve the way you integrate sources?

Revising

Revision is a continual process—not a last step. You've been revising—"reseeing" your subject—from the first messy fastwriting in your journal. But the things that get your attention vary depending on where you are in the writing process. With your draft in hand, revision becomes your focus through what I'll call shaping and tightening your draft.

Chapter 13 contains strategies that can help you revise any inquiry project, and the "Guide to Revision Strategies" on page 427 can help you locate these strategies. There are also certain things to think about that are especially useful for shaping a research essay.

Shaping. When we shape a draft, the focus is on design—the order of information, the chain of reasoning, the coherence of paragraphs, and their contribution to the whole composition. The architecture of a research essay is particularly important, because it's longer and carries a heavy load of information. Earlier in the chapter, we discussed in general terms the different ways an exploratory research essay and an argumentative research paper might be organized. Now you've got some material to work with, and one of the best ways to consider ways to shape the material is through literally cutting it apart.

One of the most effective revision exercises for a research essay is what I call the "Frankenstein Draft." This is modeled after a cut-and-paste revision exercise by writing theorist Peter Elbow. Cut up your draft with scissors, dividing it into the different elements (description, judgments, criteria, evidence), and then play with the order. What seems to be most effective? Worry about transitions later. You'll find instructions for this revision activity in Chapter 13, on page 562. Try it and play with the design of your essay.

Polishing. Shaping focuses on things such as purpose, meaning, and design. No less important is looking more closely at paragraphs, sentences, and words. But for this project, in particular, you also need to make sure that you cited sources correctly. You'll get plenty of help with that in Chapter 12, "Using and Citing Sources." Refer to it for help with how to properly quote, paraphrase, summarize, and control information. You will also find guidelines for citation using MLA and APA styles.

Before you finish your draft, work through the following checklist:

✓ Every paragraph is about one thing.

✓ The transitions between paragraphs aren't abrupt.

✓ The length of sentences varies in each paragraph.

✓ Each sentence is concise. There are no unnecessary words or phrases.

✓ You've checked grammar, particularly verb agreement, run-on sentences, unclear pronouns, and misused words (*there/their, where/were,* and so on).

✓ You've run your spellchecker and proofed your paper for misspelled words.

✓ You've double-checked your citations and Works Cited or References page to ensure that the formatting is correct.

Guide to Revision Strategies

Problems in the Draft (Chapter 13)	Page Number
Unclear purpose	538
■ Not sure what the paper is about?	
Unclear thesis, theme, or main idea	543
■ Not sure what you're trying to say?	
Lack of information or development	551
■ Need more-convincing evidence? Need to check for logical fallacies?	
Disorganized	555
■ Doesn't move logically or smoothly from paragraph to paragraph?	
Unclear or awkward at the level of sentences and paragraphs	564
■ Seems choppy or hard to follow at the level of sentences or paragraphs?	

▶ Student Essay

Like some of the best research, Gordon Seirup's essay "College Dating" grows from his own experience with his topic—as a student at a large western university. Building on his own observations, interviews with peers, and reading, Seirup goes on to describe five distinct patterns in college dating. One of the basics of any research project is to do exactly that: *Look for patterns in the data and attempt to describe them.* Seirup's writing here is accessible, interesting, and informative—not the usual qualities we expect in a conventional research paper. He also does a great job varying his sources: drawing from web pages, interviews, and academic articles. Goron Seirup's essay is cited using MLA guidelines.

Seirup 1

Gordon E. Seirup

Professor Ballenger

English 101

6 October 2006

College Dating

1   First there was the passing notes, hand holding, and name-calling of middle school. Then you survived your first heartbreak when your high school sweetheart decided it would be best to "just be friends." Now swept away in college life you hardly take the time to step back and ask yourself, "What am I doing here? Whose bed did I just wake up in, and how the hell did I get here?!" If you have not yet taken the time to ponder what it is you plan to do with the so-called best four years of your life, besides studying and eating dorm food, perhaps it is about time you did. What do you want to be accomplishing in these prime dating years? More importantly, is that what you are accomplishing? In short, my purpose is to discuss the question: "What role should dating play in college students' lives?"

2   If you assume that most college students have thought how their dating decisions today might affect them tomorrow, think again. The students I spoke with informally here on the Colorado State University campus all hesitated when asked to simply "define dating." Once done struggling through that answer, they were asked, "What is the purpose of dating in college?" These students' answers ranged from "getting laid!" to "discover more about yourself through others" to "find the person you want to marry" to "I have no clue." Are the college masses blissfully unaware of exactly what it is they are doing when they pursue relationships?

3   First, what is dating? For my purposes, dating is defined as seeing someone socially in a one-on-one setting. Other terms used within the following pages are

Seirup 2

"hooking up" and "courtship," defined as noncommittal sexual acts and nonserial exclusive dating with the intention of marriage, respectively. What I mean
by "nonserial" dating is that when you choose to date someone, you intend to
marry that person. While this may not work out, and might lead you to enter this
process again, you sincerely choose each person you date as a potential spouse.
While you may court more than one person, it isn't your intention to do so.

I have defined five major approaches to college dating based on their common
purpose, values, and motivations, in addition to their general line of reasoning:
Casual Dating, Exclusive Dating, Courting, Cannot Date, and Hooking Up.

Casual dating was popular during the American 1950s, although Beth Bailey
notes that "between 1890 and 1925, dating—in practice and in name—had
gradually, almost imperceptibly, become a universal custom in America" (19).
The emergence of public dating rituals coincided with the emergence of mass
media, especially TV and magazines that made dating a feature of the typical
American romance (Bailey 9). Casual dating was modeled on popular TV shows,
and analyzed in mostly women's magazines—where to go, how much to spend,
when to allow a first kiss. A major motive for dating was, according to Bailey,
public competition to spend the most, choose the best partner, and so on.

However, dating these days is much less ritualized. Rather than focusing on
public display, these days casual daters value meeting new people, discovering and/
or reinventing who you are as a person, and enjoying yourself. The original scenario
for casual dating typically went something like this: Guy meets Girl, decides he would
like to see her socially, and asks her to join him at the diner for hamburgers and a
shared milkshake. If this date goes well, they may see each other again. After about
three dates there is a good chance Guy would be graced with a goodnight kiss.

4

5

6

Seirup 3

7   These dates did not imply exclusivity or any concrete commitment at all. While social enjoyment is the driving force behind the Casual Dating approach, there are two other important aspects: meeting new people and discovering yourself. By the simple act of participating in these dates, each party naturally learns more about himself and herself through their interaction. "Dating one-on-one gives you a chance to become comfortable with new people," says Julie Baugher, Georgetown University's premier relationship columnist (Baugher, "'Rules'").

8   The key to developing sufficient attachment for a couple to want to date multiple times is that elusive quality called "chemistry." One study that attempted to pin down exactly what college students mean by chemistry suggested that it involves similarity of interests and backgrounds, as well as "reciprocity," or the feeling that both partners are giving something to each other (Peretti and Abplanalp 5).

9   But chemistry isn't necessarily a scarce phenomenon, and it's possible to find it with more than one person. According to Lee Ann Hamilton, a health educator at the University of Arizona, "College is the time to re-invent yourself and try new things; many people don't want to be tied down" (qtd. in Hill). It is very important to keep in mind that not being "tied down," as Ms. Hamilton put it, is a fundamental aspect of the Casual Dating approach.

10   Columnist Julie Baugher has laid out some guidelines helpful to circumventing our typical defensive maneuvers when it comes to dating. (It may be useful to remember these next time you are asked out for a date.) "Don't think about whether you want to Date him with an uppercase 'D' (meaning exclusive dating). Don't conclude that he isn't 'Your type.' Don't assume this is the beginning of a long-term relationship that you're not ready for" (Baugher, "Dating"). Approaching it casually, couples may date as many people as there are nights available in the week, so long as all parties involved know the arrangement.

Seirup 4

Similar to the Casual Dating approach is the Exclusive Dating approach.   11
Both parties value dating as an activity for social enjoyment, as well as self-
education. Exclusive dating may be thought of as the "next step" from casual
dating, and indeed commonly tends to grow out of casual dating. When exclusively dating, you are not only learning more about yourself, but also consciously
aware of what you are learning about your partner. Which characteristics can you
see yourself living with for the rest of your life? Which make you want to run
away and never date again? "Through several short-term relationships, students
can find personalities with which they are most compatible," claims Matt West,
a writer at the University of Virginia. "Relationships at this age allow you to explore what you like and don't like in a partner," agrees Mary Anne Knapp, a clinical social worker. Through a series of exclusive relationships, one forms a model
of the ideal spouse (qtd. in Pleiss).

However, here is the crucial detail for this approach: This flirtation with   12
long-term commitment is solely a mental exercise. Marriage is not a goal of the
exclusive dating approach. Exclusively dating college students are aware of their
proximity to marriage; however, they are not going to let that detail dominate
their lives. The goal is gaining knowledge. This distinction is memorably worded
by Jennifer Graham, a senior staff writer at Stanford University: "I think I'm
going to put marriage on the backburner and, at least for the time being, refrain
from appraising my peers' credentials for parenthood. There's no need to sap
all the joy from life." Don't misinterpret Graham as saying she wishes to ignore
completely her peers' credentials for parenthood; rather the issue is at which
stage in the dating process qualifications for marriage become important. When
making the choice of whether or not to date someone, these marriage-related
thoughts are minimally important. However, while in a relationship, it would

be wise to consider these credentials to learn what you are looking for when you are shopping for a spouse.

13   Expert testimony supports the Exclusive Dating approach. Clinical social worker Mary Anne Knapp says these exclusive relationships are healthy and "serve more of a purpose than just having a permanent date every Friday night," since "having a supportive partner, someone who knows you and is on your side, is good for a positive outlook on life" (qtd. in Pleiss 1).

14   The premise of the Courting approach is that dating should play no role in the lives of college students. Believers in courtship argue for a return to the practice of courtship rather than dating, and hold marriage absolutely paramount. Furthermore, proponents argue that this courtship should take place after college. In general, students who advocate the Courting approach share strong religious backgrounds, and actively use their faith to both justify their opinion and denounce others'. In fact, the approach is as much their adamant opposition to dating as it is their support of courtship, saying casual dating is "a bankrupt convention...a training ground for divorce [and]...a cheap imitation of the love and intimacy of a real marriage" (Jensen). Furthermore, they believe that the practice of casual dating is futile: "If the couple never intends to get married in the first place, then breaking up is a foregone conclusion, and their relationship is doomed" (Jensen).

15   Advocates of this approach value the unique bonds that are formed between husband and wife as well as purity upon entering marriage. Courtship "is the only way to date with true love, respect and honesty because it is rooted in a desire to take the relationship to its complete and glorious fulfillment" (Jensen). Those seeking courtship seek others who seek the same; assuming that if you have kept pure in pursuit of marriage, you should expect the same of your

spouse to-be—though today the selection of potential partners may be slim. "It's hard enough to meet somebody who doesn't have a past relationship that is like a skeleton in her closet," says Matt Sweet, finance major at the University of Virginia (qtd. in Jensen). According to those who take the Courting approach, if more college students adopted their strategy, this wouldn't be a problem.

Believers in courtship share both a wholehearted commitment to a relationship that will lead to marriage and the best possible education while in college. Value is placed on the concept of college students being just that—students. During college they have neither the time nor energy to responsibly court a spouse. Therefore, it is best for people to engage in courtship only after graduation and they are settled into their careers.   16

Proponents of the Cannot Date approach also believe that dating should play no role in the lives of college students. They don't oppose dating, but these students have tried to date, or at least wanted to, but deemed it to be impossible. Like the Courting approach, these students value their standing as students and hold education as a very high priority. This approach is aptly described by a student at the University of Arizona: "While pursuing a double major, interning, working, maintaining a social life and attending school full time," Danielle Demizjian, a business economics and finance senior, finds "exclusive dating too much of a commitment" (qtd. in Hill). This is a common complaint among college students. Despite their desire to date, exclusively or casually, there just does not seem to be the time, though time alone is not the only issue. For those students advanced in their time management skills, the emotional burden may be too great. Jaime Dutton, a sophomore at Johns Hopkins University, says, "It's hard enough to have fun here with all the work you have to do, [and] there's no reason   17

Seirup 7

to have the extra drama in your life" (qtd. in Saxe). Nicole Kucewitz, a writer for the *Rocky Mountain Collegian*, agrees: "Relationships take time and patience, and in college, both of these can be very limited."

18   Finally, there is the Hooking Up approach. This last group has an alternate social structure to replace traditional dating. Their philosophy is this: At the college level, formal dating is unnecessary. For social activities, in contrast with the one-on-one date, groups are ideal. As for sexual needs, noncommittal hooking up is not only acceptable, it's preferred. Common values amongst this group include enjoying yourself socially with friends, casually fulfilling sexual needs, and avoiding commitment. This "new age" form of dating is the solution that has flourished as a result of the gripes of the Cannot Date approach.

19   Many of the students who Hook Up see the dating arena as split into two distinct groups: "People are either single or practically married" (Burney). Hooking Up is the solution for those people who wish to largely retain their single status while still satisfying their social and sexual needs, and avoiding the "marriage-type" exclusive relationship. Dan, a student at Duke University, puts it this way: "In the real world, there is an expectation that after the third date, you might get a hookup. At Duke, there is the expectation that after the third hookup, you might get a date" (qtd. in Beckett). So perhaps once college students reach the "real world" this approach will fade away, but it remains wildly popular on campus.

20   One reason for its popularity is that Hooking Up avoids potential complications of exclusive dating or even casual dating. With this approach, future hookup partners spend time in groups and get to know each other in a friendlier context first, avoiding the awkward chesslike strategies common to the predate period. Or even simpler, the story goes like this: "Now all a guy in a decent

fraternity has to do to hookup on a Saturday night is to sit on the couch long enough at a party. It's slow at first, but eventually a girl will plop herself down beside him, they'll sit there drinking, he'll make a joke, she'll laugh, their eyes will meet, sparks will fly, and the mission is accomplished. And you want me to tell this guy to call a girl, spend $100 on dinner and hope for a goodnight kiss" (qtd. in Beckett)? This trend is perpetuated by "the beds [being] short walks from the parties. This increases the likelihood of the drunken hookup, while simultaneously decreasing the frequency of actual dates," according to Tom Burney, a columnist and student at Duke University (qtd. in Beckett).

With this tendency to go from partying to hooking up, a critic may be quick   21
to draw the conclusion that sex is the driving force behind this approach. On the contrary, students' motives are often to get to know potential partners as friends (at least superficially) first. David Brunkow, computer science major at Colorado State University, attests to this: "Most of the people I've been with were already my friends...It's so much easier that way. You already know they're a good person and that they're not going to screw you over. Also, if things don't work out, you don't lose your friend" (qtd. in Borra).

Research seems to confirm Brunkow's contention. According to Paul and   22
Hayes, the best hookups were more likely to be prefaced by hanging out, flirting, mutual attraction, and talking. The worst hookups often resulted from a friend's instigation (Paul and Hayes 648).

Of the five categories I've offered to describe college dating, Hooking Up   23
is both the most common and the most controversial. In a recent study, three quarters of students interviewed reported that they had hooked up at least once and at least a third said this involved sex with a stranger or a new acquaintance

Seirup 9

(Paul, McManus, and Hayes 84). Students who choose Hooking Up may not believe that there are other, socially sanctioned choices, as this paper suggests. Do participants think Hooking Up is a good thing? One would assume so since it's so popular these days. But there is some evidence that the practice is driven by "pluralistic ignorance" or the mistaken assumption that their discomfort with the behavior is unique. This is particularly true of women (Lambert, Kahn, and Apple 132), a situation which could lead to abuses.

24

While no one approach is clearly ideal for all students, there seems to be one to suit everyone, despite a wide range of personal beliefs. Casual Dating, Exclusive Dating, Courting, Cannot Date, and Hooking Up represent distinct alternatives to college students, difficult choices that add to the complexities—both academic and non-academic—that college students find themselves caught up in every day. But it's crucial that students at least be aware that there are choices to make.

Works Cited

Bailey, Beth. "The Worth of a Date." *From Front Porch to Back Seat: Courtship in Twentieth-Century America*. 1998. Baltimore: Johns Hopkins University Press. Print.

Baugher, Julia. "Dating with a Lower Case 'd.'" *Hoya* 4 Oct. 2002. Web. 8 Oct. 2003.

Baugher, Julia. "'Rules' Teach Ladies Tricks to Winning Love." *Hoya* 15 Nov. 2002. Web. 7 Oct. 2003.

Beckett, Whitney. "What Lies Between the Hookup and Marriage?" *Chronicle* 5 Sept. 2003. Web. 13 Oct. 2003.

Borra, Jessup. "The 'He-Said-She-Said' on Dating." *Rocky Mountain Collegian* 17 Oct. 2002. Web. 19 Oct. 2003.

Burney, T. "Dating Sea Nuggets." *Chronicle* 26 Mar. 2003. Web. 13 Oct. 2003.

Seirup 10

Graham, Jennifer. "Graduation Time: Cap and Gown or Wedding Gown?" *Stanford Daily* 17 July 2003. Web. 13 Oct. 2003.

Hill, Tessa. "UA students Have Lost That Lovin' Feeling." *Arizona Daily Wildcat* 30 Jan. 2003. Web. 8 Oct. 2003.

Jensen, Mark. "A Return to Courtship." *Cavalier Daily* 26 Apr. 2002. Web. 19 Oct. 2003.

Kucewicz, Nicole. "Ins and Outs of the College Dating Game: Fun or Forever?" *Rocky Mountain Collegian* 15 Aug. 2001. Web. 19 Oct. 2003.

Lambert, Tracy, Arnold Kahn, and Kevin Apple. "Pluralistic Ignorance and Hooking Up." *Journal of Sex Research* 40.2 (2003): 129–33. Print.

Paul, Elizabeth, Brian McManus, and Allison Hayes. "Hookups: Characteristics and Correlates of College Students' Spontaneous and Anonymous Sexual Experiences." *Journal of Sex Research* 37.1 (2000): 76–88. Print.

Paul, Elizabeth, and Kristen Hayes. "The Casualties of Casual Sex: A Qualitative Exploration of the Phenomenology of College Student Hookups." *Journal of Social and Personal Relationships* 19 (2002): 639–61. Print.

Peretti, Peter, and Richard Abplanalp, Jr. "Chemistry in the College Dating Process: Structure and Function." *Social Behavior and Personality* 32.2 (2004): 147–54. Print.

Pleiss, Carissa. "Couples Can Offer Support, Comfort." *Collegian* 11 Feb. 2003. Web. 17 Oct. 2003.

Saxe, Lindsay. "Books before Relationships?" *Johns Hopkins News–Letter* 28 Mar. 2003. Web. 8 Oct. 2003.

West, Matt. "Steering clear of marriage until after college." *Cavalier Daily* 26 Apr. 2001. Web. 19 Oct. 2005.

Evaluating the Essay

1. I've been saying all along that in a research essay you try to *do* something with the information you've collected that leads, ultimately, to some kind of judgment: What's true? What's important? What's the relationship? We usually look for a thesis as an explicit statement of that judgment. One of the interesting things about "College Dating," though, is that the thesis isn't that obvious. Is this a problem? Does the essay make judgments in other ways?

2. Seirup presents "five major approaches" to college dating. Do these make sense to you? Is there another category he's missing?

3. Was this an interesting piece of writing? Why or why not?

Using What You Have Learned

Let's return to the learning goals I identified in the beginning of the chapter.

1. **Apply what you've learned about writing shorter inquiry-based papers to an extended research project.** In some ways, the research essay is the culmination of a long journey from kinds of writing that used fewer sources of information to one that uses multiple sources. Researched writing is also most likely to use conventions of academic scholarship such as citation. But in some ways, writing a research paper is simply a longer version of something you've been doing all along: identifying a question that interests you and then exploring possible answers. Discovery is the "heart of the enterprise." I hope you take that fundamental concept into nearly any writing assignment you get in the future, no matter how formal.

2. **Identify different forms of researched writing and the purposes behind them.** You might have begun this project assuming that *all* research papers have certain qualities in common: They are formally structured, you should know your thesis before you begin, never use "I," etc. By now, you should know that the rhetorical considerations—especially purpose and audience—provide the best guidance for your approach in any writing situation, including The College Research Paper.

3. **Practice reading, analyzing, and writing with a limited number of sources on a single topic.** I've become convinced that practice working with a limited number of sources in collaboration with others can be a useful way to learn some strategies for working with sources. Was that true?

4. **Use invention techniques for discovering a researchable question.** By now, you know the drill. Before you make a judgment about what to write about, open up the possibilities. This may be especially important with researched essays, because it's essential that you are *curious* about the topic

you're exploring. Whenever you receive a research assignment in another class, take time to use some of these invention strategies. It may have more to do with the success of your project than anything else you can do.

5. **Refine a research question to narrow the topic focus and lead to a judgment.** There's some scholarly evidence that the thing that students struggle most with in an inquiry-based investigation is coming up with a good question. Whenever you're working with a lot of information—as you often are in a research project—the quality of the question has huge practical implications. Will it help you decide what to ignore?

6. **Use audience and purpose to make decisions about the structure of the work and the types of information to use in it.** In this final assignment chapter, you've gone from seeing that all writing uses information to recognizing that in academic writing we evaluate this information as evidence. The quality of evidence differs. And those differences matter more when you're writing for an audience that knows something about your topic. When you get writing assignments in other classes, make sure you know what kinds of evidence you should use in your papers by clarifying to whom you are writing.

Complete
Additional Exercises
and Practice on
Chapter 10
in your MyLab

To be conscious of your process is to get control over it, and to see the *choices* you might make in particular writing or reading situations. Research is a process, too. And you'll find that many of the routines you brought with you to college may not serve you well.

Research Techniques

11

Learning Objectives

In this chapter, you'll learn to

11.1 Identify the "research routines" you've typically used, and practice new ones appropriate to college-level research.

11.2 Refine and improve the effectiveness of search terms.

11.3 Apply research strategies for developing "working knowledge" and "focused knowledge" on your topic.

11.4 Use a method to analyze and evaluate research sources.

11.5 Understand and apply new note-taking strategies that will help you analyze sources *while* you're researching.

Methods of Collecting

This chapter should tell you everything you need to know about finding what you need in the university library and on the web. It is particularly useful for collecting information for research essays, but research is a source of information that can make *any* essay stronger. Every assignment in *The Curious Writer*, therefore, includes suggestions for research as you're searching for a topic and writing your draft. Research also can be an especially useful revision strategy for any essay.

Use this chapter much as you would a toolbox—a handy collection of tips and research tools that you can use for all assignments. Refer to it whenever you discover a topic that raises questions that research can help answer, or whenever it would be helpful to hear what other people say about the things you're thinking about. Below is a quick reference guide for finding information in this chapter on key topics.

Topic	Pages
Crafting effective search terms	442–447
Developing "working knowledge" of a topic	448–450
Developing "focused knowledge" of a topic	451–455
Evaluating sources	455–460

Research in the Electronic Age

The digital revolution has profoundly changed the way we do research, and it's mostly a wonderful thing. It's extraordinary, for example, how much information I can access on any topic from right here at my desk. But research in the electronic age has also created some new challenges. For example,

There's strong evidence that college undergraduates use some pretty standard "research routines" when given a paper assignment, no matter what the assignment says.

- An extraordinary amount of information, while more accessible than ever, is really, really bad, at least for academic research.

- The information that is accessible online is as disorganized as a hoarder's closet.

What this means is (1) that you need to spend more time critically evaluating what you find when searching online, (2) that the quality of the search terms you use will make a big difference in how easy it is to find reliable and relevant information, (3) that the library, which exists in part to *organize* information so it's easier to find, is more important than ever. In this chapter, I'll cover each of these and offer some advice about how to develop your skills.

Research Routines

11.1

Identify the "research routines" you've typically used, and practice new ones appropriate to college-level research.

But first, consider "research style," or ways you typically approach writing a research paper, some of which you might have imported from high school. In your journal or on an online discussion board, answer the following questions about your typical habits when asked to write a research paper.

1. In the past, when you got a research assignment, what's the first thing you did to get started?

2. At what point did you come up with a thesis? How did you decide what your thesis was?

3. What sources did you typically use in your research papers? What were some of the ways that you evaluated sources to help you decide whether to use them in your paper?

4. Did you use the library? How?

There's strong evidence that college undergraduates use some pretty standard "research routines" when given a paper assignment, no matter what the assignment says. One of these, according to a study group, Project Information Literacy, is writing a thesis and making an outline early on in the process. In some cases, this isn't a bad approach. But if your goal is discovery—and that, after all, is the motive behind academic inquiry—then dreaming up a thesis before you've done much research defeats the purpose of doing research in the first place. You might have other routines as well, such as consulting Wikipedia first, waiting until the night before the paper is due before doing any writing, relying exclusively on Google and skimming only the first few sources that appear.

I'm a lousy dancer. I pretty much do the same moves over and over again and try not be self-conscious. Similarly, writers who keep using the same routines never discover new moves that will help them adapt to new demands. In Chapter 1 and Chapter 2, you thought about your writing and reading habits, some of which you may have developed in high school, or simply by accident. To be conscious of your process is to get control over it and seeing the *choices* you might make in particular writing or reading situations. Research is a process, too. And you'll find that many of the routines you brought with you to college may not serve you well. But how could you know what you need to *unlearn* if you don't think about your process? Reflect often on what you're noticing about ways of doing research. You'll then learn more dance moves, whatever the music.

Power Searching Using Google

Say I'm researching why people believe in alien abduction. For better or worse, most of us start with Google. So I type the following in the search window:

11.2

Refine and improve the effectiveness of search terms.

I get 5.87 million hits. Okay, that's a lot of stuff to scroll through. If you're like most people, you'll just harvest the first few relevant results on the opening page or two. But that would squander the power of the search engine, ignoring lots of even better potential sources. But how do you find them?

Add a word or two:

That's a little better. Now I've got less than a million results. I might refine the search further by adding some words and putting a few terms in quotation marks. The quotes tell Google that I want documents with that exact phrase. Still, I'd like fewer and better results, from sources I am likely to trust. Here's where some of the more advanced commands can help. Suppose I want to get information from a particular site—say, NASA. What does the federal government's space agency have to say about belief in alien abduction? To do this, I'd begin with the operator *site: (website)*.

Ninety-seven hits! This more focused search also produced some more reliable sources.

Say I stumbled on a really great article on belief in alien abduction from the website *Psychology Today* and I'd like to see if its website has any related articles on the topic. Or perhaps I'm interested in sources that cite the original article. The operator *related: (URL of site and search terms)* will help you do this:

Watch
the Animation on
**Conducting
Online Keyword
Searches**
in your MyLab

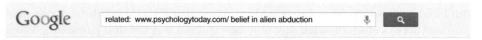

You can also search for particular kinds of documents such as the formats pdf, jpg, doc, etc., by beginning your query with *filetype: (jpg, doc, pdf, etc., and search terms)*. To summarize, then, here are some Google search tools you should use:

1. Play with terms, including, perhaps, searching for an exact phrase using quotation marks.
2. Focus your search using some of the following operators:
   a. site:
   b. filetype:
   c. related:

Google Scholar. But perhaps the most useful thing you can do is to try Google Scholar to see if there is any scholarly work published on your topic. You will be amazed at the things that academics research, including belief in alien abduction, and the results you get will produce sources with the highest quality for an academic essay. *To use Google Scholar, the first thing you should do is link with your university library using a setting in Preferences.* Once you do this, the results will allow you to retrieve documents from your campus library without paying for them. To do this, open Google Scholar, open "scholar preferences," and scroll down to "library links." Enter the name of your university or college. Click on your school, and then you may have to enter your login credentials. Now you will see links to your own library on your results pages when a document is available (see screenshot on facing page).

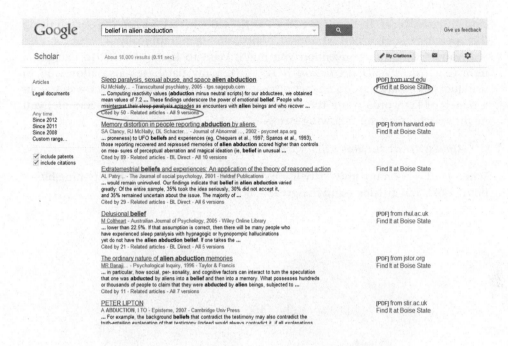

Notice, too, that if you do find a relevant article, you can quickly discover who has cited it (leading you to other potentially useful sources) and "related" work. It's hard to overstate how useful this is for college research.

Power Searching in the Library

Many of us just search electronic card catalogs and library databases using our web-searching routines. And to some extent that will work. But you're going to search far more efficiently if you understand something called "controlled language searches" and "Boolean operators." Library databases often use both, so they're good to know, and they are less complicated than they sound.

Combing Terms Using Boolean Searching. George Boole, an eighteenth-century mathematician, came up with a system for using words like AND, OR, and NOT to help researchers craft logical search queries. Searches still use these words, though it isn't always obvious. Remember that I did a keyword search on *alien abduction* using Google in the previous section? What wasn't obvious is that Google assumes there is an AND between the two terms even if I don't write it; in other words, Google searches for online documents that contain *all* terms whenever I just type a bunch of keywords in the search window. On the other hand, if I had typed *alien OR abduction*, I would be telling Google to find materials that contain *either* term. In that case, I had to *tell* Google to broaden the search using the operator *OR*. Figures 11.1 and 11.2 show the idea graphically:

Another Boolean convention you might want to know is *NOT*, to exclude a term (e.g., *alien* AND *abduction* NOT *ufos*). Many databases also allow you to use quotation marks around exact phrases. What you end up with is a way to join a bunch of keywords using the operators to get better results. For example, you might search using the following string:

Alien AND *abduction* AND *stories* NOT *ufos*

When I did that on my university library's websites, I came up with fifty-nine hits—both books and articles—and the great majority were relevant.

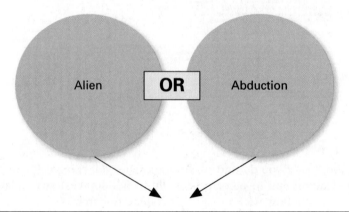

Figure 11.1 Using the *OR* operator in a keyword search yields results that contain one keyword or the other.

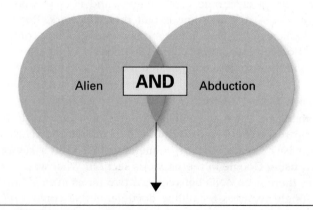

Figure 11.2 Using the *AND* operator (which is often implied) yields results that include all the keywords.

Using Controlled Language Searches. Mostly, we search using keywords—terms that we come up with, usually through trial and error, that seem to give us the best results. But in libraries there's another option: controlled language searches (see Figure 11.3). These are the preferred words that librarians use to organize and find information. But how would you know what those authorized terms are? There are two ways to find out:

1. *Library of Congress Subject Headings.* This is the standard that reference librarians use to identify which terms to use to yield the best results on any topic. You can search the *LCSH* online (authorities.loc.gov). Enter in your keywords, and voilà, there's a list of preferred headings you might use to search library databases. I found out that *alien abduction* was the favored search term, but I also discovered a list of twenty variations, some of which I hadn't thought to use in a database search. For example,

   ▪ Alien abduction in literature

   ▪ Alien abduction-prevention-case studies

   ▪ Alien abduction-psychological aspects

2. *Do a keyword search.* Sometimes you can also find the authorized terms by doing a keyword search on your library database and looking in the results to see if the *LCSH* or other preferred vocabulary is listed in one of the relevant results.

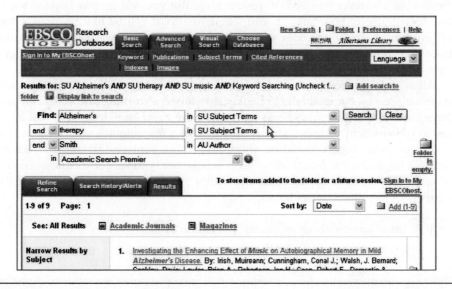

Figure 11.3 Advanced search pages such as EBSCOhost database allow you to exploit Boolean terms using drop-down menus. Further refinements allow the researcher to link terms to different kinds of searches or sources.

Developing Working Knowledge

11.3

Apply research strategies for developing "working knowledge" and "focused knowledge" on your topic.

Every day we make decisions about how much we need to know about something. Twenty-five years ago, I decided to know enough to tune up my own car, which I did badly. Later, I decided I wasn't interested in keeping up with the changes in electronic ignitions and fuel injection, so now I leave car repair to Davey at State Street Auto. A scholar is someone who, like Davey, has committed his or her professional life to keeping up with the knowledge in his or her field. College professors possess *expert knowledge* of their discipline. In a way, we are all experts on at least one thing: ourselves. Five hundred years ago, the French philosopher Michel de Montaigne argued that it is most important to be a "scholar of the self." Having this expertise can help us in writing insightful personal essays. But if our research projects lead us into unfamiliar territory—and inquiry projects almost always do—then we need to know something about our subjects. But how much?

How much we need to know about a subject is, in part, a personal choice, but a college education does at least two things: It challenges you to develop new knowledge about things that will make you a better citizen and a more productive professional, and it teaches you *how* to better acquire the new knowledge that you might seek by choice. A research project such as the one in this chapter is driven by both goals—you'll be challenged to go beyond superficial knowledge about a meaningful topic, and you'll learn some of the methods for doing that.

You will not end up a scholar on anorexia, college dating, the medical effects of music, or whatever topic you're researching. But you will go way beyond superficial knowledge of your subject; and when you do, it will be like opening a door and entering a crowded room of intelligent strangers, all deep in conversation about your topic. At first you simply listen in before you speak, and that process begins with a *working knowledge*.

All of us know how to develop a working knowledge of something, especially when we need to. For example, I recently developed a working knowledge of podcasting software for a course I was teaching. Now I can knowledgeably talk about how to use Audacity to edit digital recordings for a few minutes without repeating myself. An audio expert would be unimpressed, but someone unfamiliar with the software might find it informative. As a researcher, you've got to know enough about your topic in order to come up with a strong research question, and this begins with two simple questions:

1. What is known about my topic? (Question of fact)
2. What *is* it? (Question of definition)

Exploring the answer to these questions will give you some essential background on your topic (see Figure 11.4), and this will help you develop a more focused and interesting research question.

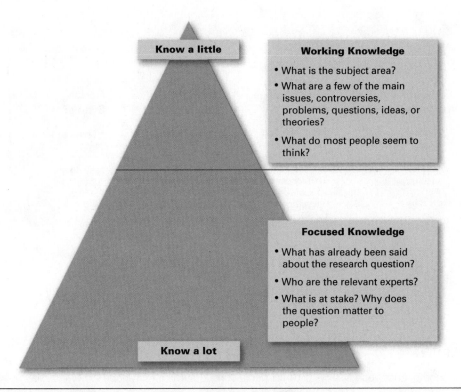

Know a little

Working Knowledge

• What is the subject area?

• What are a few of the main issues, controversies, problems, questions, ideas, or theories?

• What do most people seem to think?

Focused Knowledge

• What has already been said about the research question?

• Who are the relevant experts?

• What is at stake? Why does the question matter to people?

Know a lot

Figure 11.4   Working and focused knowledge. Inquiry projects often encourage you to choose a research topic you don't know much about. But you must quickly develop at least a *working knowledge* in order to come up with a good question. Guided by that question, you'll later develop a more *focused knowledge* of your topic and then discover what you have to say about it.

A Strategy for Developing Working Knowledge

It's hard to beat the Internet as a quick-and-dirty way to develop working knowledge about nearly any topic. But the library can play an important role, too. Combine the two to develop a good working knowledge of your topic, efficiently. There are many ways to do this, but here's a sequence of research steps I recommend (see examples of specific sources in Figure 11.5).

Refine the Research Question. With a working knowledge of your topic, you're now ready to craft a stronger research question that will guide your investigation over time *and* lead to some kind of judgment. It's hard to overstate how important this step is; a good question is the difference between a successful research project and one that flounders. (See pages 416–417 in Chapter 10 for advice on how to use your working knowledge to refine your research question).

Watch
the Animation on
Finding Sources
in your MyLab

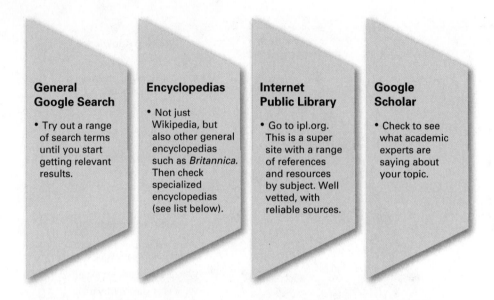

General Google Search

• Try out a range of search terms until you start getting relevant results.

Encyclopedias

• Not just Wikipedia, but also other general encyclopedias such as *Britannica*. Then check specialized encyclopedias (see list below).

Internet Public Library

• Go to ipl.org. This is a super site with a range of references and resources by subject. Well vetted, with reliable sources.

Google Scholar

• Check to see what academic experts are saying about your topic.

Source	Examples
General Encyclopedias	Encyclopedia.com, Columbia Encyclopedia, Wikipedia, Oxford Reference, Encyclopedia Britannica
Specialized Encyclopedias	Encyclopedia of Psychology, Encyclopedia of World Art, Encyclopedia of Sociology, Encyclopedia of the Environment, Encyclopedia of Women and Sports, Encyclopedia of African American Culture and History, Encyclopedia of Democracy, Encyclopedia of Science and Technology, Encyclopedia of Children, Adolescents, and the Media
Google (or other search engines)	Google, Mamma, Dogpile
Internet Public Library	ipl.org
Google Scholar	Google Scholar

Figure 11.5 Examples of sources that will help you develop a working knowledge of your topic

Now is also a good time to begin building a "working bibliography." (See the "Inquiring into the Details: The Working Bibliography" feature on page 456 for tips on how to do that.)

Developing Focused Knowledge

If working knowledge equips you to sustain a one-minute monologue on your topic, then focused knowledge is enough for you to make a fifteen-minute presentation to your class and to answer most of their questions. Knowing this much doesn't make you an expert, but it does make you far more informed than most people on your topic. Focused knowledge grows from a well-crafted research question, one that isn't too general and allows you to *ignore* information that isn't relevant. With focused knowledge, you should be able to answer some of the following questions about your topic.

- Who are key people who have influenced the published conversation on your topic? (Example: *Among the key advocates for a playoff system in college football was long-time Penn State coach Joe Paterno and even President Barack Obama.*)

- What has already been said about the topic? Up until now, what are the major themes of the conversation? (Example: *Among the arguments against a playoff system is that student athletes will miss too much class. Others add that such a system will lead to the "NFL-ization" of college football, extending the season and compounding the academic problems of student athletes, who already spend as many as forty hours a week on football.*)

- What is at stake for people? Why is the research question significant? (Example: *Thousands of student athletes in the United States are wedged between two conflicting goals for college football: the public hunger for big-time entertainment and the athletes' desire to complete a degree.*)

A Strategy for Developing Focused Knowledge

To move to this next level of knowing about your topic, launch your research on three fronts:

Library Research. While the web is an intoxicating source of information, academic research still fundamentally depends on library work. Much of this work you can do online. Libraries offer database indexes to magazines, journals, and books that are accessible from your computer at home or at school, and in some cases you can retrieve and print out full-text articles.

But there are still reasons to walk into the university library. Here are six:

1. That's where the books are.
2. Some of the best articles on your topic aren't available as full-text PDFs.
3. Browsing the stacks in your topic's subject area will produce books you won't find any other way.
4. You can read current periodicals not yet online.
5. The reference room has books and other resources that aren't available anywhere else.
6. Reference librarians are irreplaceable.

So you'll want to go to the library—online and on foot—but you won't want to waste your time. The two best ways to avoid this are to have a good research question, one that will allow you to focus your efforts, and to have a handful of good search terms to try. Don't forget to use "controlled language searches," or searches that use the terms librarians have chosen to organize access to materials on every subject (see pp. 445–447). As you recall, you discover these terms in the Library of Congress Subject Headings. Find this online (search for "Library of Congress Authorities") or look for bound copies in the library, which are often called the "big red books" by librarians.

Where should you begin? When you developed working knowledge, you started with more-general sources such as encyclopedias and then shifted to more-specialized sources such as Google Scholar, trying to drill down a little ways into your subject. Now it's time to drill more deeply. For focused knowledge, you can start anywhere—really—especially because you've already got some background knowledge on your research question. The key is to cover a lot of ground.

Searching for Books. Every library has an online index for books (also available at computers in the library, naturally), and using the right search terms, you'll get an instantaneous list of relevant books on your topic and "call numbers" that will help you find them in the stacks. Your results will also tell you if the book is checked out, missing, or unavailable in your college library. If any of these apply to a book you're really hankering for, don't despair. You've got several options:

- *Recall.* Make an online request that the book be returned (usually in a few weeks) by the person who has checked it out.

- *Interlibrary loan.* This is a wonderful, underutilized service, often provided by campus libraries at no charge to students. You can request, usually online, a call-out to a large network of university libraries for the book (or article) you need. It is delivered to you, sometimes within days.

- *Check another library.* If the campus library doesn't have it, check the community library's index online.

The book search form on your university's website, like most search portals, has simple and advanced options. The advanced page is pretty cool because it makes it easy to do a Boolean search on your topic. You can also put "limiters" on the terms, allowing you to control the results for things such as author, title, date, and so on. Learning to use the Advanced Search will really pay off after enduring the initial brief learning curve.

Searching for Periodicals and Newspapers. It's hard to imagine a research question or topic that isn't covered by periodicals. You'll want to check those databases, too. These are organized into four broad categories:

1. General subject databases, or indexes to periodicals across disciplines.

2. Specialized databases, or indexes that are discipline-specific.

3. Genre-specific databases such as Newspaper Source.

4. Government document databases.

Quite often, general subject databases include periodicals that may not be considered scholarly, including magazines such as *Discover, Newsweek,* and *Psychology Today.* These databases are a good place to start. To drill down further, use specialized databases, which are much more likely to produce the most interesting results on your research question because they are written by specialists in the fields of interest. They will also produce articles that can be a chore to understand if you don't know the jargon. That's when your working knowledge on your topic will really pay off. Also consider databases that warehouse certain types of content—plays, government documents, dissertations, and so on. You can see examples of all of these databases in the table starting below.

Web Research. Web research for inquiry projects should be motivated by the following principles:

1. Maximize coverage.

2. Maximize relevant results.

3. Find stable sources.

4. Find quality sources.

Later in this chapter, I'll elaborate on what I mean by stable, quality sources, but examples would include: web pages and documents with .edu, .gov, or .org domains; those that are routinely updated; and those that might include a bibliography of references that document claims.

On the other hand, depending on your topic, you might seek a range of types of sources. For instance, suppose you're writing about green design and a blog from an architect in Texas has an interesting proposal for using turbines on a highway in Austin, powered by passing cars. The proposal is interesting, and other sites refer to the blogger's idea. While this isn't a conventional academic source, the architect's blog is certainly a relevant and useful one for your essay.

Consider other types of online content as well: images, video, podcasts, discussion boards, and so on. For example, iTunes includes iTunesU, a remarkable collection of lectures, interviews, and video clips on a range of subjects, uploaded from universities around the United States.

The challenge is to find this stuff. Though Google is the dominant player in everyday research, good academic researchers shouldn't limit themselves to a single search service. Google is just the beginning. Try some of the alternative search portals or directories listed here.

Database Type	Examples
Interdisciplinary/general subject databases	Academic Search Premier, Academic One File, JSTOR, ArticleFirst, Project Muse, MasterFILE Premier, WorldCat, Web of Science, ProQuest Central

Discipline-specific databases	ABI/INFORM (business), AnthroSource, America: History and Life, ArtSTOR, Applied Science and Technology, Biography Index, BioOne, Communication and Mass Media, ERIC (education), Health Reference Center, MLA Bibliography (languages and literature), Philosopher's Index, PsycINFO, Sociological Abstracts, Worldwide Political Science Abstracts
Genre-specific databases	National Newspaper Index, Newspaper Source, New York Times Index, Dissertation Abstracts International, Book Review Digest, Literature Criticism Online, Play Index
Government documents	Fed in Print, GPO Monthly Catalog, LexisNexis Government Periodicals Index

Search Type	Examples
General search engines	Google, Ask, Yahoo!, Bing
Metasearch engines	Dogpile, Clusty, SurfWax, Mamma
Subject directories	Yahoo!, About.com, Google, botw.org
Academic search engines or directories	Google Scholar, infomine.ucr.edu, www.academicinfo.net, www.academicindex.net
Search engines for particular content	VideoSurf, Google Books, Google Blogs, Google Images, www.newslink.org, www.internetarchive.org (audio, video, education, etc.), www.usa.org (federal government)

Inquiring into the Details

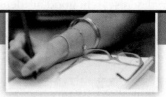

Full-Text Articles and the Convenience Trap

We're spoiled by full-text articles that are served up by some databases. Not only do you get a citation, but also there is the huge bonus of actually looking at the article and printing it out. More and more indexes provide this service, and every database will allow you to filter your search so that you only get full-text results. This is all good except for one

> **Inquiring into the Details** (*continued*)
>
> thing: Many articles still aren't available as instantly downloadable PDF or web files. It's pretty common, in fact, to discover that the article you really need—the one that seems right on topic—isn't available online. That often means that student researchers ignore the really good article and just go for the one that's instantly available, even if it isn't quite right. Convenience isn't the highest value in academic research.
>
> The commercial owners of periodical databases do not convert citations to include full-text articles on the basis of their significance to the subject. It's much more random than that. So you can't be sure, if you rely only on full-text versions, that you're getting the best information.
>
> Finding those articles that aren't immediately available online requires a trip to the library, where, armed with the citation information, you can find the piece in bound volumes of the journal or on microfilm. It might seem a bit old-fashioned, but that's the best way to get good information that isn't available digitally. Alternatively, you can order the article through the library's interlibrary loan service.

Evaluating Library Sources

One of the huge advantages of finding what you need at the campus library is that nearly everything there was chosen by librarians whose job it is to make good information available to academic researchers. Now that many of the university library's databases are available online, including full-text articles, there really is no excuse for deciding to exclusively use web pages you downloaded from the Internet for your essays.

11.4
Use a method to analyze and evaluate research sources.

In general, the more specialized the audience for a publication, the more authoritatively scholars view the publication's content. Academic journals are at the bottom of this inverted pyramid because they represent the latest thinking and knowledge in a discipline, and most of the articles are reviewed by specialists in the field before they are published. At the top of the inverted pyramid are general encyclopedias and general-interest magazines such as *Newsweek* and *Time*. These have broader audiences and feature articles that are written by nonspecialists. They are rarely peer-reviewed. As a rule, then, the lower you draw from the inverted pyramid mentioned above, the more authoritative the sources are from an academic point of view. Here are some other guidelines to consider:

- *Choose more-recent sources over older ones.* This is particularly good advice, obviously, if your subject is topical; the social and natural sciences also put much more emphasis on the currency of sources than do humanities disciplines.

Watch
the Animation on
Evaluating Sources
in your MyLab

- *Look for often-cited authors.* Once you've developed a working knowledge of your topic, you'll start noticing that certain authors seem to be mentioned

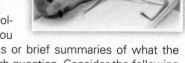

Inquiring into the Details

The Working Bibliography

A working bibliography lists sources you've collected that you think will be helpful when you
draft your essay. These may include annotations or brief summaries of what the
source says that you find relevant to your research question. Consider the following
examples:

TOPIC: RELATIONAL AGGRESSION

PRINT SOURCES

Simmons, Rachel. *Odd Girl Out: The Hidden Culture of Aggression in Girls*. New York:
Harcourt, 2002.

   Simmons argues that the "secret world of girls' aggression"—the backstab-
bing, the silent treatment, the bartering of friendship for compliance to a group's
"rules"—can be just as bad as the less subtle aggression of boys. Her basic
thesis is that girls in American culture are supposed to be "nice" and therefore
have no outlet for their anger except for exploiting the one thing they do covet:
relationships. Because my essay focuses on the popularity phenomenon in high
school—How does it affect girls when they become adults?—Simmons's chapter
on parents of these girls seems particularly useful because it shows how the
parents' responses are often shaped by their own experiences in school.

WEB SOURCES

"What Is Relational Aggression?" *The Ophelia Project*. 22 Sept. 2003 http://www
.opheliaproject.org/issues/issuesRA.shtml.

   The page defines relational aggression by contrasting it with physical aggression. It argues that most research, naturally, has focused on the latter because of need to limit physical injury between children. But girls tend to avoid
physical aggression and instead indulge in actions that harm others by disrupting
their social relationships, like giving someone the silent treatment. The Ophelia
Project is a nonprofit group created in 1997 by parents who wanted to address
the problem.

or cited fairly frequently. These are likely to be the most listened-to authors,
and may also be considered the most authoritative on your topic.

■ *If possible, use primary sources over secondary sources.* In literary research,
primary sources are the original words of writers—their speeches, stories, novels, poems, memoirs, letters, interviews, and eyewitness accounts. Secondary
sources would be articles that discuss those works. Primary sources in other
fields might be original studies or experiments, firsthand newspaper accounts,
marketing information, and so on.

Advanced Internet Research Techniques

In a previous section, you saw how to use some advanced search techniques on Google. Don't forget to use this as you probe more deeply for sources on your research question. There are also a few other things you should try, and one of the most productive might be to use multiple search tools.

Go Beyond Google

There are lots of other search portals, and there's evidence that varying your search engines *will* produce unique results. It's worth your time to try them. Here are a few suggestions:

- AltaVista
- Ask
- Bing
- Hotbot
- Lycos
- Yahoo! Search

In addition, there are so-called "metasearch" tools that can search multiple services at one time. Try a few of these:

- Dogpile
- Mamma
- Search.com
- SurfWax
- Yippy

Finally, you might also try out some specialized search tools (sometimes called "vertical" search engines) that focus on particular topics and kinds of content. Google Scholar is one of these. To find more, visit Noodletools and click on "Choose the Best Search."

Evaluating Web Sources

One of the more amusing sites on the web is titled "Feline Reactions to Bearded Men." At first glance, the site appears to be a serious academic study of the physiological responses of cats—heartbeat, respiration, and pupil dilation—to a series of photographs of men with beards. The researchers are listed with their affiliations to respected universities. The article includes an abstract, a methodology, and a results section, as well as a lengthy list of works cited.

Watch
the Animation on
**Evaluating
Online Sources**
in your MyLab

A cat reacts to a picture of a bearded man from the study "Feline Reactions to Bearded Men."

The conclusions seem genuine and include the following:

1. Cats do not like men with long beards, especially long dark beards.

2. Cats are indifferent to men with shorter beards.

3. Cats are confused and/or disturbed by men with beards that are incomplete and, to a lesser degree, by men whose beards have missing parts.

The study is a hoax, a fact that is pretty obvious to anyone who critically examines it. For one thing, it was "published" in the *Annals of Improbable Research*, but I can usually fool about a third of my class with the site for five to ten minutes as I discuss the conventions of academic research, some of which are accurately reproduced in the "study."

Everyone knows to be skeptical of what's on the web. But this is even more crucial when using web sources for college writing. Because it's dominated by commercial sites, much of the World Wide Web has limited usefulness to the academic researcher; and although very few online authors are out to fool researchers with fake scholarship, many have a persuasive purpose. Despite its "educational" mission, for example, the purpose of the Consumer Freedom website is to promote industry views on laws relating to food and beverages. That doesn't make the information it offers useless, but a careful researcher would be wary of the site's claims and critical of its studies. At the very least, the information provided by Consumer Freedom should be attributed as a proindustry view.

Imagine, as you're researching on the web, that you've been dropped off at night in an unfamiliar neighborhood. You're alert. You're vigilant. And you're careful about whom you ask for directions. You can also be systematic about how you approach evaluating online sources. In general, follow these principles:

- *Favor governmental and educational sources over commercial ones.* These sites are more likely to have unbiased information. How can you tell which are institutional sites when it's not obvious? Sometimes the domain name—the abbreviation *.edu*, *.org*, or *.gov* at the end of an Internet address—provides a strong clue, as does the absence of ads on the site.

- *Favor authored documents over those without authors.* There's a simple reason for this: You can check the credentials of authors if you know who they are. Sometimes sites provide e-mail links so you can write to authors, or you can do a search on the Internet or in the library for other materials they've published.

- *Favor documents that are also available in print over those available only online.* Material that is published in both forms generally undergoes more scrutiny. An obvious example would be newspaper articles, but also some articles from journals and magazines are available electronically and in print.

- *Favor web sources that document their claims over those that don't.* This familiar academic convention is strong evidence that the claims an online author is making are supported and verifiable.

- *Favor web pages that have been recently updated over those that haven't changed in a year or more.* Frequently at the bottom of a web page there is a line indicating when the information was posted to the Internet and/or when it was last updated. Look for it.

An Evaluation Process for Web Sources

1. **Relevance.** Is this web source relevant to my research question?
2. **Authors.** Are there any? If so, can I trust them? Are they recognized experts on the subject? Do they have a bias? Do they say sensible things? If there aren't authors, are there other things about the source that make it credible?
3. **Source.** What's the domain: .edu, .gov, .org.? If it's a commercial site, is the content still useful because of its author, content, or relevance?
4. **Verifiability.** Can you contact the authors? Is there a bibliography of references? Do other credible sites refer to this one?
5. **Stability.** How long has the website been around, and how often is it updated?

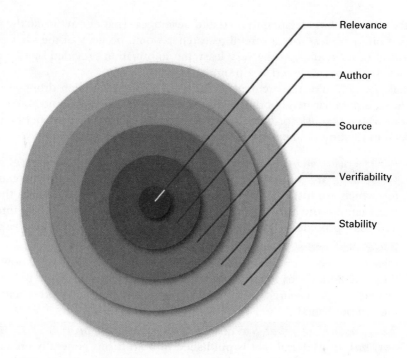

Relevance

Author

Source

Verifiability

Stability

Another way to think about evaluating web sources is to imagine a series of questions you ask yourself, beginning with the relevance of a site or document to your project and then working outward to some judgments about the author, the source, the verifiability of the information, and its stability.

Research with Living Sources: Interviews, Surveys, and Fieldwork

Sometimes the best way to get information about something is to ask someone. Sometimes the best way to see what happens is to go out and look. And sometimes the best way to find out what people think or believe is to invite them to tell you. While we often assume that research means reading, much research also involves interviews, observations, and surveys. Consider whether your research project can benefit from collecting information from these sources.

> Tethered as we are these days to the electronic world of the web and the increasingly digital university library, it's easy to forget an old-fashioned source for research: a living, breathing human being.

Interviews

Tethered as we are these days to the electronic world of the web and the increasingly digital university library, it's easy to forget an old-fashioned source for research: a living, breathing human being. People are often the best sources of information because you can have a real conversation rather than the imagined one simulated by the double-entry notebook. Some kinds

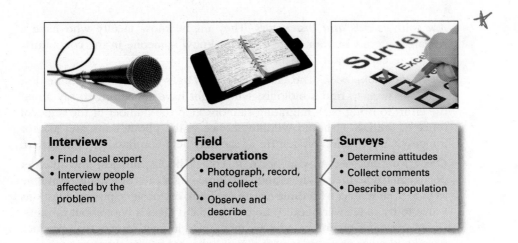

Interviews
- Find a local expert
- Interview people affected by the problem

Field observations
- Photograph, record, and collect
- Observe and describe

Surveys
- Determine attitudes
- Collect comments
- Describe a population

of writing, such as the profile, fundamentally depend on interviews; with other genres, such as the personal essay or the research paper, interviews are one of several sources of information. But they can be central to bringing writing to life, because when we put people on the page, abstract ideas or arguments suddenly have a face and a voice. People on the page make ideas matter.

Arranging Interviews. Whom do you interview? Basically, there are two kinds of interviews: (1) the interviewee is the main subject of your piece, as in a profile; (2) the interviewee is a source of information about another subject.

The interviewee as a source of information is the far more common type of interview, and it usually involves finding people who either are experts on the topic you're writing about or have been touched or influenced in some way by it. For example, Tina was writing a research essay on the day-care crisis in her community. Among those affected by this issue were the parents of small children, their day-care teachers, and even the kids themselves; all were good candidates for interviews about the problem. Experts were a little more difficult to think of immediately. The day-care teachers might qualify—after all, they're professionals in the area—but Tina also discovered a faculty member in the College of Health and Social Sciences who specialized in policies related to child care. Interviewing both types of people—experts and those influenced by the issue—gave Tina a much richer perspective on the problem.

How do you find experts in your topic? Here are a few strategies for locating potential interviewees:

- *Check the faculty directory on your campus.* Many universities publish an annual directory of faculty and their research interests, which may be online. In addition, your university's public information office might have a similar list of faculty and areas of expertise.

- *Cull a name from an online discussion group.* Use a specialized search engine such as Google Group's search to search by topic and find someone interesting who might be willing to do an e-mail interview.

- *Ask your friends and instructors.* They might know faculty who have a research interest in your topic or might know someone in the community who is an expert on it.

- *Check the phone book.* The familiar *Yellow Pages* can be a gold mine. For example, want to find a biologist who might have something to say about the effort to bring back migrating salmon? Find the number of the regional office of the U.S. Fish and Wildlife Service in the phone book and ask for the public information officer. He or she may help you find the right expert.

- *Check your sources.* As you begin to collect books, articles, and Internet documents, note their authors and affiliations. I get calls or e-mails from time to time from writers who came across my book on lobsters, posing questions I love to try to answer because no one in Idaho gives a hoot about lobsters. Google searches of authors who are mentioned in your sources may produce e-mail addresses or websites with e-mail links that you might query.

- *Check the* Encyclopedia of Associations. This is another underused book and database in your university's reference room that lists organizations in the United States with interests as varied as promoting tofu and saving salmon.

Conducting the Interview. The kinds of questions you ask fundamentally depend on what type of interview you're conducting. In a profile, your questions will focus on the interview subject (see Chapter 4). To some extent, this is also true when you interview nonexperts who are *affected* by the topic you're writing about. For example, Tina is certainly interested in what the parents of preschoolers *know* about the day-care crisis in her town, but she's also interested in the feelings and *experiences* of these people. Gathering this kind of information leads to some of the questions you may have used in a profile, but with more focus on the subject's experience with your topic:

- What was your first experience with _____? What has most surprised you about it?

- How does _____ make you feel?

- Tell me about a moment that you consider most typical of your experience with _____.

More often, however, your motive in an interview will be to gather information. Obviously, this will prompt you to ask specific questions about your topic as you try to fill in gaps in your knowledge. But some more general, open-ended questions may also be useful to ask. For example:

- What is the most difficult aspect of your work?

- What do you think is the most significant popular misconception about _____?

- What are the significant current trends in _____?

- If you had to summarize the most important thing you've learned about _____, what would that be?

- What is the most important thing other people should know or understand?
- What do you consider the biggest problem?
- Who has the power to do something about it?
- What is your prediction about the future? Ten years from now, what will this problem look like?

Once you have a list of questions in mind, be prepared to ignore them. Good interviews often take turns that you can't predict, and these journeys may lead you to information and understandings you didn't expect. After all, a good interview is like a good conversation; it may meander, speed up or slow down, and reveal things about your topic and your interview subject that you don't expect. But good interviewers also attempt to control an interview when the turns it's taking aren't useful. You do this through questions, of course, but also with more-subtle tactics. For example, if you stop taking notes, most interview subjects notice, and the astute ones quickly understand that what they're saying has less interest to you. A quick glance at your watch can have the same effect.

E-mail interviews produce a ready-made text with both your questions and the subject's answers. This is pretty wonderful. Live interviews, on the other hand, require more skill. It's usually a good idea to use a tape recorder (with your subject's permission), but never rely exclusively on it, especially as machines can fail and batteries can expire unexpectedly. *Always take notes.* Your notes, if nothing else, will help you know where on the tape you should concentrate later, transcribing direct quotations or gathering information. Note taking during interviews is an acquired skill; the more you do it, the better you get, inventing all sorts of shorthand for commonly occurring words. Practice taking notes while watching the evening news.

Most of all, try to enjoy your interview. After all, you and your interview subject have something important in common—you have an interest in your topic—and this usually produces an immediate bond that transforms an interview into an enjoyable conversation.

Using the Interview in Your Writing. Putting people on the page is one of the best ways to bring writing to life. This is exactly what information from interviews can do—give otherwise abstract questions or problems a voice and a face. One of the most common ways to use interview material is to integrate it into the lead or first paragraph of your essay. By focusing on someone involved in the research question or problem you're exploring, you immediately capture reader interest. For example, here's the beginning of a *Chronicle of Higher Education* essay, "What Makes Teachers Great?"* Quite naturally, the writer chose to begin by profiling someone who happened to be a great teacher, using evidence from the interviews he conducted.

> When Ralph Lynn retired as a professor of history at Baylor University in 1974, dozens of his former students paid him tribute. One student, Ann Richards, who became the governor of Texas in 1991, wrote that Lynn's classes were like "magical

---

*Ken Bain, "What Makes Teachers Great?" *Chronicle of Higher Education* (April 9, 2004): B7-B9.

tours into the great minds and movements of history." Another student, Hal Wingo, the editor of *People* magazine, concluded that Lynn offered the best argument he knew for human cloning. "Nothing would give me more hope for the future," the editor explained, "than to think that Ralph Lynn, in all his wisdom and wit, will be around educating new generations from here to eternity."

This is a strong way to begin an essay, because the larger idea—the qualities that make a great teacher—is then grounded in a name and a face. But information from interviews can be used anywhere in an essay—not just at the beginning—to make an idea come to life.

Information from interviews can also provide strong evidence for a point you're trying to make, especially if your interview subject has expertise on the topic. But interviews can also be a *source* of ideas about what you might want to say in an essay. The essay on great teaching, for instance, offers seven qualities that great teachers embrace in their classrooms—things such as "create a natural critical learning environment" and "help students learn outside of class." All of these claims grew from interviews with sixty professors in a range of disciplines.

The principal advantage of doing interviews is that *you* ask the questions that you're most interested in learning the answers to. Rather than sifting through other sources that may address your research questions briefly or indirectly, interviews generate information that is often relevant to and focused on the information needs of your essay. In other words, interviews are a source of data that can also be a *source* of theories or ideas on your topic. And this is often the best way to use interview material in your essay.

Surveys

Watch
the Animation on
Writing Surveys
in your MyLab

The survey is a fixture in American life. We love surveys. What's the best economical laptop? Should the president be reelected? Who is the sexiest man alive? What movie should win Best Picture? Some of these are scientific surveys with carefully crafted questions, statistically significant sample sizes, and carefully chosen target audiences. In your writing class, you likely won't be conducting such formal research. More likely it will be like Mike's—fairly simple, and although not necessarily statistically reliable, your informal survey will likely be more convincing than anecdotal evidence or your personal observation, particularly if it's thoughtfully developed.

Defining a Survey's Goals and Audience. A survey is a useful source of information when you're making some kind of claim regarding "what people think" about something. Mike observed that his friends all seem to hate pennies, and he wanted to generalize from this anecdotal evidence to suggest that most people probably share that view. But do they? And which people are we really talking about? As we discussed this in his writing group, Mike pointed out that his grandfather grew up during the Great Depression and that he has a very different perspective on money than Mike does. "So your grandfather would probably pick up a penny in the parking lot, right?" I asked. "Probably," Mike said.

Quickly, Mike not only had a survey question but began to think about qualifying his claim. Maybe younger adults—Mike's generation—in particular share this attitude about the lowly penny. To confirm this, Mike's survey had both a purpose (to collect information about how people view pennies) and an audience (students on his campus). If he had the time or inclination, Mike could conduct a broader survey of older Americans, but for his purposes the quad survey would be enough.

Types of Survey Questions

1. *Open-ended questions*. Open-ended questions often produce unexpected information, while direct questions are easier to analyze. Open-ended questions are like those on the narrative evaluations students might fill out at the end of the semester, such as "What did you learn in this course?" and "What were the instructor's strengths and weaknesses?"

2. *Direct questions*. Direct questions are the kind used on quizzes and tests, the kind that have a limited number of answers. The simplest, of course, would be a question or statement that people might agree or disagree with: Would you pick up a penny if you saw it lying on the street? Yes? No? You don't know?

How do you decide which types of questions to ask? Here are some things to consider:

- *How much time do you have to analyze the results?* Open-ended questions obviously take more time, while direct questions often involve mere tabulation of responses. The size of your sample is a big factor in this.

- *How good are you at crafting questions?* Direct questions need to be more carefully crafted than open-ended ones because you're offering limited responses. Are the responses appropriate to the question? Have you considered all the alternative ways of responding?

- *Do you want statistical or qualitative information?* Qualitative information—anecdotes, stories, opinions, case studies, observations, individual perspectives—are the stuff of open-ended questions. This can be wonderful information, because it is often surprising and it offers an individual's voice rather than the voiceless results of statistical data. On the other hand, statistical information—percentages, averages, and the like—is easily understood and can be dramatic.

Crafting Survey Questions. To begin, you want to ask questions that your target audience can answer. Don't ask a question about a campus alcohol policy that most students in your survey have never heard of. Second, keep the questions simple and easy to understand. This is crucial because most respondents resist overly long survey questions and won't answer confusing ones. Third, make sure the questions will produce the information you want. This is a particular hazard of open-ended questions. For example, a broad, open-ended question such as "What do you think of the use of animals in the testing of cosmetics?" will probably produce a verbal shrug or an answer of "I don't know." A better question is

Inquiring into the Details

Types of Survey Questions

These are a few of your options when deciding what type of questions to ask in a survey.

1. **Limited choice**

   Do you believe student fees should be used to support campus religious organizations?

   _____ Yes

   _____ No

   _____ I'm not sure

   At what point in the writing process do you usually get stuck?

   _____ Getting started

   _____ In the middle

   _____ Finishing

   _____ I never get stuck

   _____ Other: _____

2. **Scaled response**

   The Student Film Board should show more foreign films.

   _____ Strongly agree

   _____ Agree

   _____ Neither agree nor disagree

   _____ Disagree

   _____ Strongly disagree

3. **Ranking**

   Which of the following do you consider important in designing a classroom to be conducive to learning? Rank them from 1 to 5, with the most important a 1 and the least important a 5.

Comfortable seating	
Natural light from windows	
Carpeting	
Effective soundproofing	
Dimmable lighting	

4. **Open-ended**

   Describe three things you learned in this course.

   What steps do you think the university should take to increase attendance at women's soccer games?

more focused: "What do you think about the U.S. Food and Drug Administration's claim that animal testing by cosmetic companies is 'often necessary to provide product safety'?"

Such a question could be an open-ended or direct question, depending on the kind of responses you're seeking. Focusing the question also makes it more likely to generate information that will help you compose your essay on the adequacy of current regulations governing animal testing. Also note that the question doesn't necessarily betray the writer's position on the issue, which is essential—a good survey question isn't biased or "loaded." Imagine how a less neutral question might skew the results: "What do you think of the federal bureaucrats' position that animal testing for cosmetics is 'often necessary to provide product safety'?" An even more subtle bias might be introduced by inserting the term *federal government* rather than *Food and Drug Administration* in the original question. In my part of the world, the Rocky Mountain West, the federal government is generally not viewed favorably, no matter what the issue.

Keep your survey questions to a minimum. It shouldn't take long—no more than a few minutes at most—to complete your survey, unless you're lucky enough to have a captive audience such as a class.

Finally, consider beginning your survey with background questions that establish the identity of each respondent. Typical information you might collect includes the gender and age or, with student-oriented surveys, the class ranking of the respondent. Depending on your topic, you might be interested in particular demographic facts, such as whether someone has children or comes from a particular part of the state. All of these questions can help you sort and analyze your results.

Conducting a Survey

1. **If you can, test it first.** People who design surveys for a living always test them first. Invariably this turns up problems: A survey is too long, a question is poorly worded, the response rate to a particular question is low, and so on. You won't be able to test your draft survey nearly as thoroughly as the experts do, but before you put your faith in an untested survey, ask as many people as you can to try it out and describe their experience answering your questions. Was there any confusion? How long did it take? Is the survey generating relevant information?

2. **Find a way to reach your audience.** Once you're confident in the design of your survey, plan how you'll distribute it. There are several options:

   a. *Distribute in a likely location.* Begin by asking yourself whether your target audience tends to conveniently gather in a particular location. For example, if you're surveying sports fans, then surveying people by the main gate at the football stadium on Saturday might work. If your target audience is first-year college students and your university requires freshman English composition, then surveying one or more of those classes would be a convenient way to reach them. In some situations, you can leave your survey forms in a location that might produce responses from your target audience. For example, a student at my university wanted to survey people about which foothill's hiking trails they liked best, and she left an envelope with the forms and a pencil at several trailheads.

b. *Distribute it online.* Software for designing online surveys is available now, but unless the survey is linked to a website that is visited by the target audience whose opinions you seek, the response rates will most likely be low. Still, it might be possible for you to direct traffic to your online survey by posting a notice on social networks such as Facebook or online discussion groups relevant to the topic. There is free software available on the web to do limited online surveys. The best known is probably Survey Monkey.

Using Survey Results in Your Writing. The best thing about conducting an informal survey is that you're producing original and interesting information about your topic's local relevance. This can be an impressive element of your essay and will certainly make it more interesting.

Because analysis of open-ended questions can be time consuming and complicated, consider the simplest approach: As you go through the surveys, note which responses are worth quoting in your essay because they seem representative. Perhaps the responses are among the most commonly voiced in the entire sample, or they are expressed in significant numbers by a particular group of respondents.

In a more detailed analysis, you might try to nail down more specifically the *patterns* of responses. For example, perhaps you initially can divide the survey results into two categories: people who disagree with the university's general-education requirements and those who agree with it, Group 1 and Group 2. The next step might be to further analyze each of these groups, looking for particular patterns. In particular, pay attention to responses you didn't expect, responses that might enlarge your perspective about what people think about your topic.

Your analysis of the responses to direct questions will usually be pretty simple—probably a breakdown of percentages. In a more sophisticated analysis, you might try to break the sample down, if it's large enough, to certain categories of respondents—men and women, class ranking, respondents with high or low test scores, and so on—and then see if any response patterns correlate to these categories. For example, perhaps a much higher percentage of freshmen than seniors sampled agreed that a good job was the most important reason to go to college.

What might this difference mean? Is it important? How does it influence your thinking about your topic, or how does it affect your argument? Each of these questions involves interpretation of the results, and sample size is the factor that most influences the credibility of this kind of evidence.

Fieldwork: Research on What You See and Hear

In many disciplines, field observations are at the heart of research. You might remember, for example, that the ethnographic essay in Chapter 9 is focused on describing how human cultures operate in natural settings. Field research is essential. There are a lot of inquiry projects that might benefit from direct observation and description, especially if you're researching something that has a local angle and there might be something relevant to see. Would your essay on farmer's markets, for instance, benefit from listening to and observing people at the Saturday market downtown?

There are two kinds of fieldwork:

1. **Participant observation.** You are involved in the thing you are describing as an active participant.

2. **Direct observation.** You unobtrusively observe the settings or phenomena.

Because you're not doing formal scholarship for this project, whichever method you use as your approach will probably be casual rather than carefully planned and methodologically strict. What you *are* trying to do that is common to all fieldwork is look for patterns in what you see. In particular, you might want to describe what is either *typical* (e.g., a common behavior, complaint, attitude, problem, etc.) or *exceptional* (e.g., significant differences, nonconformance, unusual circumstances, etc.). Remember, too, that you're not limited to making these observations with a notebook and pen alone. You might also digitally record, video, and photograph the things you see for analysis later.

The Ethics of Fieldwork. Because fieldwork often involves research on people, you should always be careful to protect the privacy and wishes of your subjects. For a relatively informal project such as this one—something that isn't likely to be published—there are fewer ethical concerns, but there are some principles that should guide you. The least complicated ethical situation is direct observation in a public setting. In this case, you don't need an invitation from anyone to observe unless you directly approach the people you're observing. Sometimes, though, especially when you're a participant-observer, you'll be actively seeking permission to come watch, record, and interview. How should you handle those situations?

- Make your study subjects aware of the purpose of your project.

- Preserve the anonymity of the people you observe unless they give you permission to use their names.

Note-Taking Strategies. Write down and document in detail what you see and hear. This includes behaviors, descriptions of activities and settings, conversations, maps of movements, etc. This is the raw data you'll analyze for patterns. In addition to looking for things that seem "typical" and "exceptional," consider the following frames for analysis:

- Evidence that confirms, contradicts, or qualifies the theories and claims you've read about in your research.

- What do people do or say during moments of particular significance?

- What "artifacts" seem important? What things do people use?

- *How* do the people you observe talk about themselves or the activity they are participating in?

Using Field Research in Your Writing. The observations and descriptions you gather from the field can be powerful additions to your research project. For example,

- **Give your topic a face.** Use a description of an individual who is affected by the problem you're writing about, as a way to dramatize its impact.
- **Make a scene.** Help your readers *see* what you're writing about.
- **Incorporate images.** Even a written research essay can benefit by pictures, which can be dropped into the text and analyzed.
- **Develop a multimodal essay.** Might your research project be transformed into an audio documentary, or a video podcast? Could you create an online slide show?

Writing in the Middle: Note-Taking Techniques

11.5
Understand and apply new note-taking strategies that will help you analyze sources while you're researching.

Like most students, when I wrote undergraduate research papers I never did any writing until the end—usually late at night with all of my sources fanned out across my desk like cards at a blackjack table. I'm going to propose an alternative that will work much better, and it looks something like this: It's not the night before, but *weeks* before the paper is due, and I'm writing like mad in my notebook *as* I'm reading an article. I'm not exactly writing my paper—I'm using writing to think about what I'm reading, to understand the source, and to *converse* with it.

Throughout *The Curious Writer*, I've promoted what's termed "dialectical thinking"—moving back and forth between suspending judgments and making judgments—and this method is particularly useful when writing about what you read. One way to do this as you research is to use something called the "double-entry journal."

Whatever method you use for "writing in the middle," these things are key:

Watch
the Animation on
**Effective Note
Taking**
in your MyLab

1. You write as—or immediately after—you read something that's relevant to your project.

2. You use the writing to talk to yourself and *to the source* about what you understand it to be saying, what you find particularly interesting, how you might agree or disagree, what questions the source raises.

3. You carefully jot down bibliographic information so you build your list of references as you research.

I think the double-entry journal makes a great research notebook. You collect passages, ideas, statistics, summaries, and so on from the source on the left facing page, and explore what you make of what you've collected on the right facing page. You can do this in a paper notebook or in a Word document using columns. In the double-entry journal that follows, you can see how this might work.

Double-Entry Journal

In the sample double-entry journal below, notice how the writer collects material in the left column, and then explores in the right, looking left whenever the writing stalls to find traction on something else from the source.

Page	Source Notes	First Thoughts
140	"Carl Sagan suggested that the 'pay dirt' of space alien abduction accounts is not in what they might tell us about alien visitation but in what they might tell us about ourselves."	Really interesting article that summarizes the research, as of 1996, on alien abduction memories. Point seems to be the ways in which these don't necessarily tell us anything about aliens but a lot about ourselves. But what? I think the evidence here suggests that it isn't necessarily some kind of psychiatric problem, but how vulnerable we are to suggestion. The stop sign case, for example. Even when the visual clearly has a yield not a stop sign, the mere suggestion it's a stop sign made people confidently believe it. But maybe the most interesting thing here to me is the dynamic of having a memory of something that is challenged, which is a kind of threat, and as a result we believe even a false memory more strongly. We believe what we want to believe and then actively seek out information that reinforces it, particularly in the face of challenge.
141	"the misinformation effect" Describes "classic experiment" to demonstrate this: a pedestrian accident in which slide shows yield sign but respondents "subtly" told was stop sign. Majority claimed stop sign was there with "high degree of confidence."	
142	"… humans can cook up false memories …" But why aliens? ✓ variety of sources in popular culture of "true" abduction stories ✓ most reported under hypnosis, and this makes it seem more "real" to the abductee because it evokes "strong visual imagery" ✓ when belief is challenged, holder of belief clings to it more strongly ✓ reinforced by other "support groups" of believers	The thing about hypnosis being the source of most abduction reports, and how this might deepen an abductee's belief in it, is also something I need to look into more.
	Clark, Steven E. and Elizabeth F. Loftus. "The Construction of Alien Abduction Memories." *Psychological Inquiry* 7.2 (1996): 140–143. Print.	

Research Log

Another method of note taking that also exploits dialectical thinking is the research log. Rather than using opposing pages, you'll layer your notes and responses, one after another. This is a particularly useful method for those who would prefer to work with a keyboard rather than a pencil. Here's how it works:

1. Begin by taking down the full bibliographic information on the source, something you may already have in your working bibliography.

2. Read the article, book chapter, or web page, marking up your personal copy as you typically do, perhaps underlining key facts or ideas or information relevant to your research question.

3. Your first entry in your notebook or on the computer will be a fastwrite, an open-ended response to the reading under the heading What Strikes Me Most. As the title implies, you're dealing with first thoughts here.

4. Next, take notes on the source, jotting down summaries, paraphrases, quotations, and key facts you glean from it. Title this section Source Notes.

5. Finally, follow up with another episode of fastwriting. Title this The Source Reconsidered. This is a *more focused* look at the source; fastwrite about what stands out in the notes you took. Which facts, findings, claims, or arguments shape your thinking now?

One Student's Response

Claude's Research Log

SOURCE

Letawsky, Nicole R., et al. "Factors Influencing the College Selection Process of Student Athletes." *College Student Journal* 37.4 (2003): 604–11. *Academic Search Premier.* EBSCOhost Databases. Albertson's Lib. 5 Apr. 2004.

WHAT STRIKES ME MOST

Really interesting article that studied about 130 student athletes at a large 1-A university. Noted that there have been a lot of research studies on why students choose a particular school but not so much on why student-athletes choose a school. Everyone assumes, of course, that student-athletes go somewhere because they're wined and dined and promised national TV exposure. In other words, it all has to do with the glamour of playing 1-A, particularly the so-called revenue sports like basketball and football. But this study had some surprising findings. They found that the number one reason that student-athletes chose a school was the degree options

One Student's Response (*continued*)

it offers. In other words, the reasons student-athletes choose a school aren't that much different than the reason regular students choose one. The study also found that the glamour stuff—getting awards, getting on TV, and future professional possibilities—mattered the least to the student-athletes. This study challenges some of the myths about student recruiting, and should be read by recruiters especially. If you want to get a blue-ribbon player at your school, tell him or her about the academic opportunities there.

SOURCE NOTES (CUT AND PASTED FROM ELECTRONIC VERSION)

"This study found that the most important factor for student-athletes was the degree program options offered by the University. Other important factors were the head coach, academic support services, type of community in which the campus is located, and the school's sports traditions. Two of the top three factors were specifically related to the academic rather than athletic environment. This is a key finding and should be understood as recruiting efforts should be broad based, balancing academics and athletics if they are to be effective."

"A somewhat surprising result of the study concerned relatively low ratings associated with factors considered essential to 'Big-Time College Sports.' Television exposure, perceived opportunity to play immediately, and perceived future professional sporting opportunities were among the lowest-ranked factors. Furthermore, the participants rated athletic rewards (a 5-item survey scale containing these and other reward items) consistently lower than both the campus and athletic environment. These results may be due to the fact that respondents were from each of the sports offered by the University. Many of the sports (e.g., swimming, track), although funded and supported similar to the other sports, do not receive the national attention, large crowds, and television exposure."

THE SOURCE RECONSIDERED

This article did more than anything I've read so far to make me question my thesis that big-time college sports recruiting is way out of control. It's pretty convincing on the point that athletes care about the academic programs when they're choosing a school. But then the second quotation has an interesting part that I just noticed. This study surveyed athletes in all sports, not just the big-time sports like football and basketball at the university where the study was conducted. It seems to me that that would really skew the findings because someone participating in a sport like tennis that doesn't get a lot of attention and doesn't necessarily lead to professional opportunities after school *would* be more interested in academics. They're not dreaming of making a name for themselves, but getting a scholarship to pay for school. Seems like a better study would focus on the big-time sports...

Using What You Have Learned

Let's return briefly to the learning outcomes listed at the beginning of the chapter.

1. **Identify the "research routines" you've typically used, and practice new ones appropriate to college-level research.** Since the beginning of *The Curious Writer*, I've encouraged you to look at the habits you use, often without thinking, to read and write. You have "research routines," too, often learned in high school; while some of these might still serve you well, many may not, particularly in college. This "unlearning" is an essential part of developing your abilities, not just in academic tasks, but also with anything you want to do that is guided by habits you rarely examine.

2. **Refine and improve the effectiveness of search terms.** This is a skill that will not only help make your academic research more efficient, but will aid you with everyday research as well. And the ability to refine search languages will become even more important as information continues to expand on the web and in library databases.

3. **Apply research strategies for developing "working knowledge" and "focused knowledge."** I've tried to encourage you to look at any research project as a developmental process, one in which how much knowledge

you have about a topic will determine how effectively you can write about it. If you don't know much, which is often the case in an inquiry-based class, then you need to quickly learn enough to come up with a strong research question. From there, you can mine more deeply into your topic, developing "focused" knowledge with more-advanced research strategies. This a process you can use in nearly any research project.

4. **Use a method to analyze and evaluate research sources**. There are a lot of methods for doing this, and in this chapter you learned just one. But the key is that you actually *use* a method, one that will consistently help you to find credible sources. As we do more and more research online, it's hard to overstate what an essential skill this is.

5. **Understand and apply new note-taking strategies that will help you analyze sources *while* you're researching.** The double-entry journal and research log are two systems for note-taking that I recommend here, but the important thing is that you do some writing *as* you do your research. This is likely a major break with your research routine, but it will make a huge difference in helping you to think about what you're reading and in beginning to build your essay. This is yet another application of the "bad" writing—exploratory, open-ended fastwriting—that you've learned to use in previous assignments.

Complete
Additional Exercises
and Practice on
Chapter 11
in your MyLab

Will you control the outside sources in your research essay, or will they control you? The appropriate use of sources is really a matter of control. Writers who put research information to work for them see outside sources as serving a clear purpose.

Using and Citing Sources 12

Learning Objectives

In this chapter, you'll learn to

12.1 Use sources effectively and control sources so they don't control you.

12.2 Practice summarizing, paraphrasing, and quoting and apply these to your own work.

12.3 Understand and identify plagiarism to avoid it in your own work.

12.4 Cite sources using MLA and APA documentation styles.

Controlling Information

The first college paper that really meant something to me was an essay on whaling industry practices and their impacts on populations of humpback and sperm whales. Writing from the place of itchy curiosity and strong feelings is a wonderful thing. It will motivate you to read and learn about your topic, and when it comes to writing the draft, you might find that you have little trouble enlisting the voices of your sources to make your point. More often, however, you've chosen a topic because you don't know what you think or feel about it—the inquiry-based approach—or you've been assigned a general topic that reflects the content of a course you're taking. In these cases, writing with sources is like crashing a party of strangers that has been going on for a long time. You shyly listen in, trying to figure out what everyone is talking about, and look for an opening to enter the conversation. Mostly you just feel intimidated, so you hang back feeling foolish.

This kind of writing situation is really a matter of control. Will you control the outside sources in your research essay, or will they control you? Will you enter the conversation and make a contribution to it, or will you let others do all the talking? The easiest way to lose control is simply to turn long stretches of your paper over to a source, usually one with long quotations. I've seen a quotation from a single source run more than a full page in some drafts. Another way to lose control is to do what one of my colleagues calls a "data dump." Fill the truck with a heavy load of information, back it up to the paper, and dump in as much as you can, without analysis, without carefully selecting what is relevant and what isn't, without much thought at all. The writer in this situation sees his or her essay as a hole that must be filled with information.

When you introduce a voice other than your own, make it clear what this new voice adds to the conversation you have going about your topic.

Using Sources

The appropriate use of sources is also a matter of control. Writers who put research information to work for them see outside sources as serving a clear purpose. There are at least five of these purposes:

12.1

Use sources effectively and control sources so they don't control you.

Purpose	Description
Support a claim or idea	The motive we usually imagine for using information in academic writing.
Provide background	What does your audience need to know about your topic to understand why your inquiry question is significant?
Answer a question	Periodically asking relevant questions—and answering them with information from research—creates a structure built on reasoning.
Complicate things	This is the most counterintuitive use of information. Why would you use information that might *not* support your thesis? Because things are *always* complicated, and that's what makes them interesting.

Let's see how this works in an actual passage. In an essay that asks, "Why Did God Make Flies?" writer Richard Conniff argues that the answer might be as a punishment for human arrogance. In the middle of the essay, he draws on research to provide some background for this claim by establishing the long and sometimes unhappy relationship between the housefly and human beings.

The true housefly, *Musca domestica*, does not bite. (You may think this is something to like about it, until you find out what it does instead.) *M. domestica*, a drab fellow of salt-and-pepper complexion, is the world's most widely distributed insect species and probably the most familiar, a status achieved through its pronounced fondness for breeding in pig, horse, and human excrement. In choosing at some point in the immemorial past to concentrate on the wastes around human habitations, *M. domestica* made a major career move. Bernard Greenberg of the

University of Illinois at Chicago has traced human representations of the housefly back to a Mesopotamian cylinder seal from 3000 B.C. But houseflies were probably with us even before we had houses, and they spread with human culture.

Here Conniff demonstrates exquisite control over outside sources, marshalling them in the service of his larger point. But he does this by not simply quoting extensively or going on and on explaining the relevant information, but also by *finding his own way of saying things*. For example, rather than writing that the housefly's fondness for associating with people had significant ecological implications for the insect, Conniff writes that it was "a major career move."

Summarizing

A summary is usually much shorter than the original. For example, consider the following summary of the earlier extract paragraph about the relationship between houseflies and human beings:

> The common housefly is among the "most familiar" insects because it found its long partnership with human beings, one that goes back thousands of years, extremely beneficial.

Can you see how the summary captures the main idea of the longer paragraph? Also note that when the summary refers to identical language in the original—the phrase "most familiar"—the writer is careful to use quotation marks. Finally, the summary uses original language that breaks with the source, describing the relationship between people and flies as a "long partnership."

12.2
Practice summarizing, paraphrasing, and quoting and apply these to your own work.

Tips for Crafting a Summary

1. Academic articles in the social sciences often include abstracts, or ready-made summaries of a study. Books frequently explain their purpose in a preface or introduction. Start there. Then check the concluding chapter.

2. If your aim is to summarize a passage of a longer work, remember to look for the author's most important ideas where he or she is most likely to put them: the first and last sentences of paragraphs or a concluding paragraph.

3. Summary has little to do with your opinion. Try, as best you can, to capture your understanding of the *source's* meaning or argument.

4. Typically, a summary includes the name(s) of the author(s) or the title of the work, usually attached to a verb that characterizes its nature: so-and-so *argues, finds, explains, speculates, questions*, and so on.

Paraphrasing

Of the three forms of note taking, paraphrasing requires the most attention and the greatest care. Your goal is to craft a restatement, in your own words, of what an original source is saying, in roughly the same length as the original.

Here's a paraphrase of the earlier extract paragraph on houseflies.

Houseflies, according to Richard Conniff, have had a long partnership with human beings. They are also among "the world's most widely distributed insect species," two factors that explain our familiarity with *Musca domestica*, the housefly's Latin name. This partnership may have been cultivated for thousands of years, or certainly as long as humans—and their animal companions—produced sufficient excrement in which the flies could breed. Ironically, these pests have benefited enormously from their "fondness" for human and animal wastes, and unwittingly we have contributed to their success at our own expense.

Tips for Crafting a Paraphrase

1. Make sure to find your own way of saying things, quoting phrases that you borrow from the source.

2. Try the "look away" strategy. Carefully read the passage several times, then set it aside. Compose your paraphrase without looking at the source, trusting that you'll remember what's important. Then check the result against the passage, changing or quoting any borrowed language and refining your prose.

3. Like summary, introduce paraphrased material in your essay by attributing the author or the work.

Quoting

When should you turn to quotation in your essay? There are two main situations:

1. When the source says something in a distinctive way that would be lost by putting it in your own words.

2. When you want to analyze or emphasize a particular passage in the source, and the exact words of the author matter.

For instance, the excerpt from "Why Did God Make Flies?" is eminently quotable because Richard Conniff, its author, writes with such a lively voice. Consider his sentence:

The true housefly is the world's most widely distributed insect species and probably the most familiar, a status achieved through its pronounced fondness for breeding in pig, horse, and human excrement.

What is it about this that seems quotable? Maybe the way it goes along with fairly straightforward exposition until the second half of the sentence, when suddenly the fly seeks status and feels fondness for you know what.

When you bring someone else's voice into your own writing, it's usually a good idea to introduce the source and provide some justification for making such a move. For instance, you might introduce the preceding quote by saying something like this:

Richard Conniff, whose popular studies of invertebrate animals have made even leeches lovable, observes that the familiarity of the housefly is no accident. He writes...

It's even more important in academic writing to follow up quoted text with your own commentary. What would you like the reader to notice about what the quotation says? What seems most relevant to your own research question or point? How does the quotation extend an important idea you've been discussing or raise an important question? What does it imply? What do you agree with? What do you disagree with? In other words, when you introduce a voice other than your own, make it clear what this new voice adds to the conversation you have going about your topic.

Tips for Handling Quotations

Integrate quoted material in your essay in the following ways:

1. **Separate it.** There are two ways to do this. Provide an introductory tag that ends in a comma or a colon. *According to Carl Elliott (82), the new drug pushers "are officially known as 'pharmaceutical sales representatives' but everyone calls them 'sales reps.' " Or, Carl Elliott (82) observes that drug salespeople are easy to spot: "Drug reps today are often young, well groomed, and strikingly good looking. Many are women..."*

2. **Embed it.** Integrate quoted material in your own sentence something like this:

   Carl Elliott calls drug reps "the best dressed people in the hospital."

3. **Block it.** Extended quotations (more than 40 words in APA style and more than four lines in MLA) should be indented five spaces in APA style and ten spaces in MLA style in a block. Quotation marks, except those used in the source, are omitted. For instance:

   Carl Elliott, in "The Drug Pushers," highlights the perks doctors have historically received:

   > *Gifts from the drug industry are nothing new, of course. William Helfand, who worked in marketing for Merck for thirty-three years, told me that company representatives were giving doctors books and pamphlets as early as the late nineteenth century. "There is nothing new under the sun," Helfand says, "There is just more of it." The question is: Why is there so much more of it just now? And what changes occurred during the past decade to bring about such a dramatic increase in reps bearing gifts? (86)*

Watch
the Video on
Citing Sources
in your MyLab

Citing Sources

Of all the rules some of my students believe were invented to torture composition students, requirements that they carefully cite their sources in research papers may cause the most anguish. They rarely question these requirements; they seem like divine and universal law. In fact, these aren't rules but conventions, hardly as old as the Greeks, and historically quite new. For many centuries, writers freely borrowed from others, often without attribution, and the appropriation of some-one else's words and ideas was considered quite normal. This is still the view in some non-Western cultures; some students, for example, are quite puzzled in their English as a Second Language classes when they have to cite a source in their re-search essays.

This convention of explicitly acknowledging the source of an idea, quota-tion, piece of data, or information with a footnote or parenthetical citation and bibliography arose in the past 150 years. It began when mostly German univer-sities began promoting the idea that the purpose of research was not simply to demonstrate an understanding of what already was known, but to *make a contri-bution of new knowledge*. Researchers were to look for gaps in existing scholar-ship—questions that hadn't yet been asked—or to offer extensions of what had already been posed by someone else. Knowledge making became the business of the research writer, and, like gardeners, scholars saw themselves as tending a living thing, a kind of tree that grew larger as new branches were grafted onto existing limbs.

Just as a child clambering up a tree in the park is grateful for the sturdy limbs under his or her feet, research writers acknowledge the limbs they are standing on that have helped them to see a little more of their subjects. That's why they cite their sources. This is an act of gratitude, of course, but it also signals to readers on whose authority the writer's claims, conclusions, or ideas are based. Citation helps readers locate the writer's work on a specific part of the tree of knowledge in a discipline; it gives a useful context of *what has already been said* about a question or a topic.

Student writers cite for exactly the same reasons: not because it's required in most college research writing, but because it makes their research writing more relevant and more convincing to the people who read it.

> Citation helps readers locate the writer's work on a specific part of the tree of knowledge in a discipline; it gives a useful context of *what has already been said* about a question or a topic.

There are quite a few conventions for citing, and these con-ventions often vary by discipline. Humanities disciplines such as English often use the Modern Language Association (MLA) conventions, while the social sciences use the American Psychological Association (APA) methods. Both of these docu-mentation styles are detailed later in this chapter. Although there are differences between the two styles, the purpose of each is the same: to acknowledge those from whom you have borrowed ideas and information.

Avoiding Plagiarism

Watch
the Animation on
Avoiding Plagiarism
in your MyLab

Modern authors get testy when someone uses their work without giving them credit. This is where the concept of intellectual property comes from, an idea that emerged with the invention of the printing press and the distribution of multiple copies of an author's work. In its most basic form, plagiarism is stealing someone else's words, ideas, or information. Academic plagiarism, the kind that gets a lot of ink these days, especially with the rise of the Internet, usually refers to more-specific misdeeds. Your university probably has an academic honesty or plagiarism policy posted on the web or in a student handbook. You need to look at it. But it probably includes most or all of the following forms of plagiarism:

> Intentional plagiarism stems from an intellectual laziness and dishonesty that sooner or later are bound to catch up with the person doing it.

1. Handing in someone else's work—a downloaded paper from the Internet or borrowed from a friend—and claiming that it's your own.
2. Using information or ideas that are not common knowledge from any source and failing to acknowledge the source.
3. Handing in the same paper for two different classes.
4. Using the exact language or expressions of a source and not indicating through quotation marks and citation that the language is borrowed.
5. Rewriting a passage from a source using minor substitutions of different words but retaining the same syntax and structure of the original.

Most plagiarism is unintentional. The writer simply didn't know or pay attention to course or university plagiarism policies. Equally common is simple carelessness. How can you avoid this trap? Check out the "Tips for Avoiding Plagiarism" box.

Intentional plagiarism, of course, is a different matter. Many websites offer papers on thousands of topics to anyone willing to pay for them. College instructors, however, have tools for identifying these downloaded papers. The consequences of buying and handing in online papers are often severe, including flunking the course and even expulsion—an academic Hades of sorts. Moreover, even if a person is not caught committing this academic crime, intentional plagiarism stems from an intellectual laziness and dishonesty that sooner or later are bound to catch up with the person doing it. Just don't go there.

12.3
Understand
and identify
plagiarism to
avoid it in your
own work.

Tips for Avoiding Plagiarism

- **Don't procrastinate.** Many careless mistakes in citation or proper handling of source material occur in the rush to finish the draft in the wee hours of the morning.

- **Be an active note taker.** Work in the middle of the process to take possession of the material you read, especially exploring your responses to sources *in your own words* and *for your own purposes*.

- **Collect bibliographic information first.** Before you do anything else, take down complete publication information for each source, including the page numbers from which you borrowed material.

- **Mark quoted material clearly.** Whenever you quote a source directly, make sure that it's obvious in your notes.

- **Be vigilant whenever you cut and paste.** The great usefulness of cutting and pasting passages in electronic documents is also the downfall of many research writers. Is the copied material directly borrowed, and if so, is it properly cited?

Exercise 12.1

Watch
the Animation on
**Avoiding Plagiarism
While Using
Quotations**
in your MyLab

The Accidental Plagiarist

Most plagiarism problems are accidental. The writer simply isn't aware that he or she has stumbled into the problem. Here's a low-stakes exercise that can test your understanding of how to avoid the simplest—and most common—types of accidental plagiarism. Get this wrong and the grammar police won't accost you in the middle of the night, throw you against the wall, and make you spell difficult words. You'll just learn something.

Using the words and ideas of others in your own writing is essential in most research essays and papers. Doing this without plagiarizing isn't exactly like walking through a minefield, but you do have to step carefully. For example, Beth is exploring the question "What might explain the high rate of divorce in the early years of marriage?" She's interested in divorce because she just went through one. In her research, Beth encounters Diane Ackerman's book, *The Natural History of Love*, and finds the following paragraph:

"Philandering," we call it, "fooling around," "hanky-panky," "skirt chasing," "man chasing," or something equally picturesque. Monogamy and adultery are both hallmarks of being human. Anthropologist Helen Fisher proposes a chemical basis for adultery, what she calls "The Four-Year Itch." Studying the United Nations survey of marriage and divorce around the world, she noticed that divorce usually occurs early in marriage, during the couple's first reproductive and parenting years. Also, that this peak time for divorce coincides with the period in which infatuation normally ends, and a couple has to decide if they're going to call it quits or stay together as companions. Some couples do stay together and have other children, but even more don't. "The human animal," she concludes, "seems built to court, to fall in love, and to marry one person at a time; then, at the height of our reproductive years, often with a single child, we divorce them; then, a few years after, we remarry once again."

Beth thought this was pretty interesting stuff, and in her draft she summarized the paragraph in the following way:

> According to Diane Ackerman, a hallmark of being human is "monogamy and adultery," and she cites the period right after infatuation subsides—about four years for most couples—as the time when they call it quits.

STEP ONE: In small groups, analyze Beth's summary. Does Beth plagiarize the original passage, and if so, do you have ideas about how she could fix it? Revise the summary on a piece of newsprint and post it on the wall.

STEP TWO: Discuss the proposed revisions. How well do they address any plagiarism problems you see in Beth's summary?

STEP THREE: Now compare the following paraphrases of the same Ackerman passage. Which has plagiarism problems and which seems okay?

PARAPHRASE 1

Divorce may have a "chemical basis," something that may kick in after four years of marriage and ironically when partners are reaching their highest potential for having children. Researcher Helen Fisher calls it "The Four-Year Itch," the time that often signals a shift from infatuation into a more sober assessment of the relationship's future: Are they going to stay together or "call it quits"? Most end up deciding to end the relationship.

PARAPHRASE 2

When infatuation fades and couples are faced with the future of their relationship, bio-chemistry may help them decide. According to researcher Helen Fisher, "divorce usually occurs early in marriage, during the couple's first reproductive and parenting years" (Ackerman 165). She suggests that this is often about four years into the relationship, and argues that humans may be designed to behave this way because the pattern seems so entrenched (Ackerman 166).

STEP FOUR: In class, discuss which paraphrase seems acceptable and which does not. Note that the problems are pretty subtle.

STEP FIVE: Now practice your own *summary* of the following passage, applying what you've learned so far in the exercise about ways to avoid plagiarism when using the words and ideas of other people. This passage in Ackerman's book follows the passage you worked with earlier.

> Our chemistry makes it easy to follow that plan, and painful to avoid it. After the seductive fireworks of first attraction, which may last a few weeks or a few years, the body gets bored with easy ecstasy. The nerves no longer quiver with excitement. Nothing new has been happening for ages, why bother to rouse oneself? Love is exhausting. Then the attachment chemicals roll in their thick cozy carpets of marital serenity. Might as well relax and enjoy the calm and security some feel. Separated even for a short while, the partners crave the cradle of the other's embrace. Is it a chemical craving? Possibly so, a hunger for the soothing endorphins that flow when they're together. It is a deep, sweet river, just right for dangling one's feet in while the world waits.

MLA Documentation Guidelines

12.4
Cite sources
using MLA
and APA
documentation
styles.

Watch
the Animation on
**Citing Sources Using
MLA Guidelines**
in your MyLab

The professional organization in charge of academic writing in literature and languages, the Modern Language Association (MLA), uses one of two methods of citing sources that you should be familiar with. The second, the American Psychological Association (APA) system, is described in the next section. Your English class will most likely use the MLA system.

The guidelines presented in this section are based on the seventh edition of the *MLA Handbook for Writers of Research Papers* (2009).

You must cite a source in your paper in the following situations:

1. Whenever you quote from an original source.

2. Whenever you borrow ideas from an original source, even when you express them in your own words by paraphrasing or summarizing.

3. Whenever you borrow factual information from a source that is not common knowledge (see the "Inquiring into the Details: The Common Knowledge Exception" box below).

Inquiring into the Details

The Common Knowledge Exception

The business about common knowledge causes much confusion. Just what does this term mean? Basically, *common knowledge* means facts that are widely known and about which there is no controversy.

Sometimes, it's really obvious whether something is common knowledge. The fact that the Super Bowl occurs in late January and pits the winning teams from the American and National Football Conferences against each other is common knowledge. The fact that former president Ronald Reagan was once an actor and starred in a movie with a chimpanzee is common knowledge, too. And the fact that most Americans get most of their news from television is also common knowledge, although this information is getting close to leaving the domain of common knowledge.

But what about a writer's assertion that most dreaming occurs during rapid eye movement (REM) sleep? This is an idea about which all sources seem to agree. Does that make it common knowledge?

It's useful to ask next, *How common to whom? Experts in the topic at hand or the rest of us?* As a rule, consider the knowledge of your readers. What information will not be familiar to most of your readers or may even surprise them? Which ideas might even raise skepticism? In this case, the fact about REM sleep and dreaming goes slightly beyond the knowledge of most readers, so to be safe, it should be cited. Use common sense, but when in doubt, cite.

Citing Sources

The foundation of the MLA method of citing sources *in your paper* is putting the last name of the author and the page number of the source in parentheses as closely as possible to the borrowed material. For example,

> Researchers believe that there is an "infatuation chemical" that may account for that almost desperate attraction we feel when we're near someone special (Ackerman 164).

The parenthetical citation tells a reader two things: the source of the information (for example, the author's name) and where in the work to find the borrowed idea or material. A really interested reader—perhaps an infatuated one—who wanted to follow up on this would then refer to the Works Cited at the back of the paper. This would list the work by the author's last name and all the pertinent information about the source:

> Ackerman, Diane. *A Natural History of Love*. New York: Vintage, 1994. Print.

Here's another example of parenthetical author/page citation from another research paper. Note the differences from the previous example:

> "One thing is clear," writes Thomas Mallon, "plagiarism didn't become a truly sore point with writers until they thought of writing as their trade....Suddenly his capital and identity were at stake" (3–4).

The first thing you may have noticed is that the author's last name—Mallon—was omitted from the parenthetical citation. It didn't need to be included, because it had already been mentioned in the text. *If you mention the author's name in the text of your paper, then you only need to parenthetically cite the relevant page number(s).* This citation also tells us that the quoted passage comes from two pages rather than one.

Where to Put Citations. Place the citation as close as you can to the borrowed material, trying to avoid breaking the flow of the sentences, if possible. To avoid confusion about what's borrowed and what's not—particularly in passages longer than a sentence—mention the name of the original author *in your paper*. Note that in the next example the writer simply cites the source at the end of the paragraph, not naming the source in the text. Doing so makes it hard for the reader to figure out whether Blager is the source of the information in the entire paragraph or just part of it:

> Though children who have been sexually abused seem to be disadvantaged in many areas, including the inability to forge lasting relationships, low self-esteem, and crippling shame, they seem advantaged in other areas. Sexually abused children seem to be more socially mature than other children of their same age group. It's a distinctly mixed blessing (Blager 994).

In the following example, notice how the ambiguity about what's borrowed and what's not is resolved by careful placement of the author's name and parenthetical citation in the text:

> Though children who have been sexually abused seem to be disadvantaged in many areas, including the inability to forge lasting relationships, low self-esteem, and crippling shame, they seem advantaged in other areas. According to Blager, sexually abused children seem to be more socially mature than other children of their same age group (994). It's a distinctly mixed blessing.

In this latter version, it's clear that Blager is the source for one sentence in the paragraph, and the writer is responsible for the rest. Generally, use an authority's last name, rather than a formal title or first name, when mentioning him or her in your text. Also note that the citation is placed *inside* the period of the sentence (or last sentence) that it documents. That's almost always the case, except at the end of a blocked quotation, where the parenthetical reference is placed after the period of the last sentence.

Inquiring into the Details

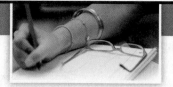

Citations That Go with the Flow

There's no getting around it—parenthetical citations can be like stones on the sidewalk. Readers stride through a sentence in your essay and then have to step around the citation at the end before they resume their walk. Yet citations are important in academic writing because they help readers know whom you read or heard that shaped your thinking.

Inquiring into the Details (*continued*)

However, you can minimize citations that trip up readers and make your essay more readable by doing the following:

- Avoid lengthy parenthetical citations by mentioning the name of the author in your essay. That way, you usually have to include only a page number in the citation.

- Try to place citations where readers are likely to pause anyway—for example, the end of the sentence or right before a comma.

- Remember that you *don't* need a citation when you're citing common knowledge or referring to an entire work by an author.

- If you're borrowing from only one source in a paragraph of your essay and all of the borrowed material comes from a single page of that source, don't bother repeating the citation over and over again with each new bit of information. Just put the citation at the end of the paragraph.

The citation can also be placed near the author's name, rather than at the end of the sentence, if it doesn't unnecessarily break the flow of the sentence. For example:

Blager (994) observes that sexually abused children tend to be more socially

mature than other children of their same age group.

When You Mention the Author's Name. It's generally good practice in research writing to identify who said what. The familiar convention of using attribution tags such as "According to Fletcher,..." or "Fletcher argues that..." and so on helps readers attach a name to a voice, or an individual to certain claims or findings. When you mention the author of a source, you can drop his or her name from the parenthetical citation and just list the page number. For example,

Robert Harris believes that there is "widespread uncertainty" among students

about what constitutes plagiarism (2).

You may also list the page number directly after the author's name.

Robert Harris (2) believes that there is "widespread uncertainty" among students

about what constitutes plagiarism.

When There Is No Author. Occasionally, you may encounter a source in which the author is anonymous—where the article doesn't have a byline or for some reason the author hasn't been identified. This isn't unusual with pamphlets, editorials, government documents, some newspaper articles, online sources, and short filler articles in magazines. If you can't parenthetically name the author, what do you cite?

Most often, cite the title (or an abbreviated version, if the title is long) and the page number. If you choose to abbreviate the title, begin with the word under which it is alphabetized in the Works Cited. For example:

According to the Undergraduate Catalog, "the athletic program is an integral

part of the university and its total educational purpose" (7).

Here is how this publication would be listed at the back of the paper:

Works Cited

Undergraduate Catalog, Boise State University 2012–2013.

Boise, ID: BSU, 2012. Print.

For clarity, it's helpful to mention the original source of the borrowed material in the text of your paper. When there is no author's name, refer to the publication (or institution) you're citing or make a more general reference to the source. For example:

An article in *Cuisine* magazine argues that the best way to kill a lobster is to

plunge a knife between its eyes ("How to Kill" 56).

or

According to one government report, with the current minimum size limit, most

lobsters end up on dinner plates before they've had a chance to reproduce ("Size

at Sexual Maturity" 3–4).

Works by the Same Author. Suppose you end up using several books or articles by the same author. Obviously, a parenthetical citation that merely lists the author's name and page number won't do, because it won't be clear *which* of several works the citation refers to. In this case, include the author's name, an abbreviated title (if the original is too long), and the page number. For example:

One essayist who suffers from multiple sclerosis writes that "there is a subtle

taxonomy of crippleness" (Mairs, *Carnal Acts* 69).

The Works Cited list would show multiple works by one author as follows:

Works Cited

Mairs, Nancy. *Carnal Acts*. Boston: Beacon, 1996. Print.

- - -. *Voice Lessons*. Boston: Beacon, 1994. Print.

It's obvious from the parenthetical citation which of the two Mairs books is the source of the information. Note that in the parenthetical reference, no punctuation separates the title and the page number, but a comma follows the author's name. If Mairs had been mentioned in the text of the paper, her name could have been dropped from the citation.

Also notice that the three hyphens used in the second bibliographic entry are meant to signal that the author's name in this source is the same as in the preceding entry.

When One Source Quotes Another. Whenever you can, cite the original source for material you use. For example, if an article on television violence quotes the author of a book and you want to use the quote, try to hunt down the book. That way, you'll be certain of the accuracy of the quote and you may find some more usable information.

Sometimes, however, finding the original source is not possible. In those cases, use the term *qtd. in* to signal that you've quoted or paraphrased a quotation from a book or article that you found elsewhere. In the following example, the citation signals that Bacon's quote was culled from an article by Guibroy, not Bacon's original work:

Francis Bacon also weighed in on the dangers of imitation, observing that "it

is hardly possible at once to admire an author and to go beyond him" (qtd. in

Guibroy 113).

Personal Interviews. If you mention the name of your interview subject in your text, no parenthetical citation is necessary. On the other hand, if you don't mention the subject's name, cite it in parentheses after the quote:

Instead, the recognizable environment gave something to kids they could

relate to. "And it had a lot more real quality to it than, say, *Mister Rogers*...,"

says one educator. "Kids say the reason they don't like *Mister Rogers* is that it's

unbelievable" (Diamonti).

Regardless of whether you mention your subject's name, you should include a reference to the interview in the Works Cited. In this case, the reference would look like this:

Works Cited

Diamonti, Nancy. Personal interview. 5 Nov. 1999.

Several Sources in a Single Citation. Suppose two sources both contributed the same information in a paragraph of your essay. Or perhaps even more common is when you're summarizing the findings of several authors on a certain topic—a fairly common move when you're trying to establish a context for your own research question. You cite multiple authors in a single citation in the usual fashion, using author name and page number, but separating each with a semicolon. For example,

> A whole range of studies have looked closely at the intellectual development of
>
> college students, finding that they generally assume "stages" or "perspectives"
>
> that differ from subject to subject (Perry 122; Belenky et al. 12).

If you can, however, avoid long citations, because they can be cumbersome for readers.

Sample Parenthetical References for Other Sources. MLA format is pretty simple, and we've already covered some of the basic variations. You should also know five additional variations, as follow:

AN ENTIRE WORK

If you mention the author's name in the text, no citation is necessary. The work should, however, be listed in the Works Cited.

> Leon Edel's *Henry James* is considered by many to be a model biography.

A VOLUME OF A MULTIVOLUME WORK

If you're working with one volume of a multivolume work, it's a good idea to mention which volume in the parenthetical reference. The following citation attributes the passage to volume 2, page 3, of a work by Baym and three or more other authors. The volume number always precedes the colon, which is followed by the page number:

> By the turn of the century, three authors dominated American literature: Mark
>
> Twain, Henry James, and William Dean Howells (Baym et al. 2: 3).

SEVERAL SOURCES FOR A SINGLE PASSAGE

Occasionally, a number of sources may contribute to a single passage. List them all in one parenthetical reference, separated by semicolons:

> American soccer may never achieve the popularity it enjoys in the rest of the
>
> world, an unfortunate fact that is integrally related to the nature of the game
>
> itself (Gardner 12; "Selling Soccer" 30).[1]

---

[1] Jason Pulsifer, University of New Hampshire, 1991. Used with permission

A LITERARY WORK

Because so many literary works, particularly classics, have been reprinted in so many editions, it's useful to give readers more information about where a passage can be found in one of these editions. List the page number and then the chapter number (and any other relevant information, such as the section or volume), separated by a semicolon. Use arabic rather than roman numerals, unless your teacher instructs you otherwise:

> Izaak Walton warns that "no direction can be given to make a man of a dull
>
> capacity able to make a Flie well" (130; ch. 5).

When citing classic poems or plays, instead of page numbers, cite line numbers and other appropriate divisions (book, section, act, scene, part, etc.). Separate the information with periods. For example, (*Othello* 2.3.286) indicates act 2, scene 3, line 286 of Shakespeare's work.

AN ONLINE SOURCE

Online sources frequently don't have page numbers. So how can you cite them parenthetically in your essay? Most of the time, you won't include page numbers, particularly when you're citing web pages.

Rarely, digital documents include paragraph numbers. If so, use the abbreviation *par.* or *pars.*, followed by the paragraph number or numbers you're borrowing material from. For example:

> In most psychotherapeutic approaches, the personality of the therapist can have
>
> a big impact on the outcome of the therapy ("Psychotherapy," par. 1).

Sometimes the material has an internal structure, such as sections, parts, chapters, or volumes. If so, use the abbreviation *sec., pt., ch.,* or *vol.* (respectively), followed by the appropriate number.

In many cases, a parenthetical citation can be avoided entirely by simply naming the source in the text of your essay. A curious reader will then find the full citation to the article on the Works Cited page at the back of your paper. For example:

> According to Charles Petit, the worldwide effort to determine whether frogs are
>
> disappearing will take somewhere between three and five years.

Finally, if you don't want to mention the source in text, parenthetically cite the author's last name (if any) or article title:

> The worldwide effort to determine whether frogs are disappearing will take
>
> somewhere between three and five years (Petit).

Format

Watch
the Animation on
**Formatting Papers
in MLA Style**
in your MyLab

The Layout. A certain fussiness is associated with the look of academic papers. The reason for it is quite simple—academic disciplines generally aim for consistency in format so that readers of scholarship know exactly where to look to find what they want to know. It's a matter of efficiency. How closely you must follow the MLA's requirements for the layout of your essay is up to your instructor, but it's really not that complicated. A lot of what you need to know is featured in Figure 12.1.

Printing. Compose your paper on white, $8^1/_2$" × 11" printer paper. Make sure the printer has sufficient ink or toner.

Margins and Spacing. The old high school trick is to use big margins. That way, you can meet your page length requirements with less material. Don't try that trick with this paper. Leave half-inch margins at the top and one-inch margins at the bottom and sides of your pages. Indent the first line of each paragraph five spaces, and blocked quotes ten spaces. Double-space all of the text, including blocked quotes and Works Cited.

Title Page. Your paper doesn't need a separate title page. Begin with the first page of text. One inch below the top of the page, type your name, your instructor's name, the course number, and the date (see the following). Below that, type the title, centered on the page. Begin the text of the paper below the title.

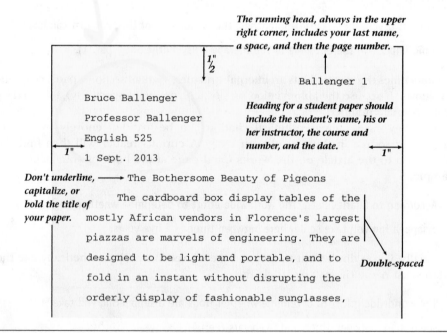

Figure 12.1 The basic look of an MLA-style paper

Julie Bird

Professor Ballenger

English 102

1 June 2013

Nature as Being: Landscape in Silko's "Lullaby"

Leslie Marmon Silko, the author of "Lullaby," is a Native American writer from

the Laguna Pueblo culture...

Note that every line is double-spaced. The title is not underlined (unless it includes the name of a book or some other work that should be underlined) or boldfaced.

Pagination. Make sure that every page, including the first one, is numbered. That's especially important with long papers. Type your last name and the page number in the upper right corner, flush with the right margin: Ballenger 3. Don't use the abbreviation *p.* or a hyphen between your name and the number.

Placement of Tables, Charts, and Illustrations. With MLA format, papers do not have appendixes. Tables, charts, and illustrations are placed in the body of the paper, close to the text that refers to them. Number illustrations consecutively (Table 1 or Figure 3), and indicate sources below them (see Figure 12.2). If you use a chart or illustration from another text, give the full citation. Place any table caption above the table, flush left. Captions for illustrations or diagrams are usually placed below them.

Handling Titles. The MLA guidelines about the style of titles are, as the most recent *Handbook* observes, "strict." The general rule is that the writer should capitalize the first letters of all principal words in a title, including any that follow dashes. The exceptions are articles (*a, an*, and *the*), prepositions (*for, of, in, to*), and coordinating

Table 1   Percentage of Students Who Self-Report Acts of Plagiarism

Acts of Plagiarism	Never/Rarely	Sometimes	Often/Very Freq.
Copy text without citation	71	19	10
Copy paper without citation	91	5	3
Request paper to hand in	90	5	2
Purchase paper to hand in	91	6	3

Source: Scanlon, Patrick M., and David R. Neumann. "Internet Plagiarism Among College Students." *Journal of College Student Development* 43.3 (2002): 379.

Figure 12.2   Example of format for a table

conjunctions (*and, or, but, for*). These exceptions apply *only if the words appear in the middle of a title*; capitalize them if they appear at the beginning or end.

The rules for underlining a title or putting it in quotation marks are as follows:

1. *Italicize the Title* if it is a book, play, pamphlet, film, magazine, TV program, CD, audiocassette, newspaper, or work of art.

2. "Put the Title in Quotes" if it is an article in a newspaper, magazine, or encyclopedia; a short story; a poem; an episode of a TV program; a song; a lecture; or a chapter or essay in a book.

Here are some examples:

The Curious Researcher (Book)

English Online: The Student's Guide to the Internet (CD-ROM)

"Once More to the Lake" (Essay)

Historic Boise: An Introduction into the Architecture of Boise, Idaho (Book)

"Psychotherapy" (Encyclopedia article)

Idaho Statesman (Newspaper)

"One Percent Initiative Panned" (Newspaper article)

Under the most recent guidelines (the *MLA Handbook, Seventh Edition)*, the underlining of titles is out and the use of italics is in. Now, for instance, your Works Cited page would list the book title <u>Bombproof Your Horse</u> as *Bombproof Your Horse*. (And yes, that's horse not house.)

Language and Style

Names. Though it may seem as if you're on familiar terms with some of the authors you cite by the end of your research project, it's not a good idea to call them by their first names. Typically, initially give the full names of people you cite, and then only their last names if you mention them again in your essay.

Ellipsis Dots. Those are the three (always three unless you're omitting material that comes at the end of a sentence, where they join a period) dots that indicate you've left out a word, phrase, or even whole section of a quoted passage. It's often wise to do this because you want to emphasize only certain parts of a quotation rather than burden your reader with unnecessary information, but be careful to preserve the basic intention and idea of the author's original statement. The ellipsis dots can come at the beginning of a quotation, in the middle, or at the end, depending where it is you've omitted material. For example,

"After the publication of a controversial picture that shows, for example, either

dead or grieving victims..., readers, in telephone calls and in letters to the

editor, often attack the photographer for being tasteless...."

Quotations. Quotations that run more than four lines long should be blocked, or indented ten spaces from the left margin. The quotation should be double-spaced and quotation marks should be omitted. In an exception from the usual convention, the parenthetical citation is placed *outside* the period at the end of the quotation. A colon is a customary way to introduce a blocked quotation. For example,

> Chris Sherman and Gary Price, in *The Invisible Web*, contend that much of the
>
> Internet, possibly most, is beyond the reach of researchers who use conventional
>
> search engines:
>
> > The problem is that vast expanses of the Web are completely invisible to
> >
> > general-purpose search engines like AltaVista, HotBot, and Google. Even
> >
> > worse, this "Invisible Web" is in all likelihood growing significantly faster
> >
> > than the visible Web that you're familiar with. It's not that search engines
> >
> > and Web directories are "stupid" or even badly engineered. Rather, they
> >
> > simply can't "see" millions of high quality resources that are available
> >
> > exclusively on the Invisible Web. So what is this Invisible Web and why
> >
> > aren't search engines doing anything about it to make it visible? (xxi)

Preparing the Works Cited Page

The Works Cited page ends the paper. Several other lists of sources may also appear at the end of a research paper, though these are much less common in college research essays. An Annotated List of Works Cited not only lists the sources used in the paper, but also includes a brief description of each. A Works Consulted list includes sources that may or may not have been cited in the paper but shaped your thinking. A Content Notes page, keyed to superscript numbers in the text of the paper, lists short commentaries or asides that are significant but not central enough to the discussion to be included in the text of the paper.

The Works Cited page is the workhorse of most college papers. The other source lists are used less often. Works Cited is essentially an alphabetical listing of all the sources you quoted, paraphrased, or summarized in your paper. If you have used MLA format for citing sources, your paper has numerous parenthetical references to authors and page numbers. The Works Cited page provides complete information on each source cited in the text for the reader who wants to know. (In APA format, this page is called References and is only slightly different in how items are listed.)

If you've been careful about collecting complete bibliographic information—author, title, editor, edition, volume, place, publisher, date, page numbers—then preparing your Works Cited page will be easy. If you've recorded that information on notecards, all you have to do is put them in alphabetical order and then transcribe them into your paper. If you've been careless about collecting that information, you may need to take a hike back to the library.

Format

Alphabetizing the List. Works Cited follows the text of your paper on a separate page. After you've assembled complete information about each source you've cited, put the sources in alphabetical order by the last name of the author. If the work has multiple authors, use the last name of the first listed. If the source has no author, then alphabetize it by the first key word of the title. If you're citing more than one source by a single author, you don't need to repeat the name for each source; simply place three hyphens followed by a period (- - -.) for the author's name in subsequent listings.

Indenting and Spacing. Type the first line of each entry flush left, and indent subsequent lines of that entry (if any) five spaces. Double-space between each line and each entry. For example:

Works Cited

Bianchi, William. "Education by Radio: America's Schools of the Air." *TechTrends: Linking Research & Practice to Improve Learning* 52.2 (2008): 36–44. Print.

Campbell, Gardener. "There's Something in the Air: Podcasting and Education." *EDUCAUSE Review,* 40.6 (November/December 2005): 32–47. Print.

Checho, Colleen. "The Effects of Podcasting on Learning and Motivation: A Mixed Method Study of At-Risk High School Students." Diss. University of Nevada, Reno. Ann Arbor, UMI, 2007. Print.

Davis, Anne, and Ewa McGrail. "'Proof-Revising' With Podcasting: Keeping Readers in Mind as Students Listen to and Rethink Their Writing." *The Reading Teacher* 62.6 (2009): 522–29. Print.

Grisham, Dana L., and Thomas Devere Wolsey. "Writing Instruction for Teacher Candidates: Strengthening a Weak Curricular Area." *Literacy Research and Instruction* 50.4 (2011): 348–64. Print.

Klaus, Carl H. *The Made-Up Self: Impersonation in the Personal Essay.* Iowa City: University of Iowa Press, 2010. Print.

"What Is Educational Podcasting?" *Educate.* Russell Educational Consultancy and Productions. No date. Web. 7 July 2012.

Citing Books. You usually need three pieces of information to cite a book: the name of the author or authors, the title, and the publication information. If you're citing an e-book, however, some additional information may be required. See below.

CITING A BOOK IN PRINT	CITING AN E-BOOK
1. Author(s)	1. Author(s)
2. *Title*	2. *Title*
3. Edition and/or volume (if relevant)	3. Edition and/or volume (if relevant)
4. Where published, by whom, and date	4. If also in print, where published, by whom, and date; in any case, sponsoring organization, date of electronic publication
5. Medium: Print	5. Medium: Web
	6. Date of access
SAMPLE CITATION: BOOK IN PRINT	**SAMPLE CITATION: E-BOOK (WEB ONLY)**
Donald, David H. *Lincoln.* New York: Simon, 1995. Print.	Lincoln, Abraham. *The Writings of Abraham Lincoln.* B & R Samisdat Express. 2009. Web. 28 Jan. 2011.

Title. Titles of books are italicized, with the first letters of all principal words capitalized, including those in any subtitles. Titles that are not italicized are usually those of pieces found within larger works, such as poems and short stories in anthologies. These titles are set off by quotation marks. Titles of religious works (the Bible, the Qur'an, etc.) are neither underlined nor enclosed within quotation marks. (See the guidelines in the earlier "Handling Titles" section.)

Edition. If a book doesn't indicate an edition number, then it's probably a first edition, a fact you don't need to cite. Look on the title page. Signal an edition like this: *2nd ed., 3rd ed.*, and so on.

Publication Place, Publisher, and Date. Look on the title page to find out who published the book. Publishers' names are usually shortened in the Works Cited list: for example, *St. Martin's Press Inc.* is shortened to *St. Martin's*.

It's sometimes confusing to know what to cite about the publication place, because several cities are often listed on the title page. Cite the first.

The date a book is published is usually indicated on the copyright page. If several dates or several printings by the same publisher are listed, cite the original publication date. However, if the book is a revised edition, give the date of that edition. One final variation: If you're citing a book that's a reprint of an original edition, give both dates. For example:

Stegner, Wallace. *Recapitulation*. 1979. Lincoln: U of Nebraska P, 1986. Print.

This book was first published in 1979 and then republished in 1986 by the University of Nebraska Press.

Page Numbers. You don't usually list page numbers of a book. The parenthetical reference in your paper specifies that. But if you use only part of a book—an introduction or an essay—list the appropriate page numbers following the publication date. Use periods to set off the page numbers. If the author or editor of the entire work is also the author of the introduction or essay you're citing, list her by last name only the second time you cite her. For example:

Lee, L. L., and Merrill Lewis. Preface. *Women, Women Writers, and the West*. Ed.

Lee and Lewis. Troy, MI: Whitston, 1980. v–ix. Print.

Publication Medium. A recent update to the MLA's guidelines now requires that you include the type of source. In most cases, a book citation will end with the word "Print." An online book would end with "Web."

Sample Book Citations
A BOOK BY ONE AUTHOR

Keen, Sam. *Fire in the Belly*. New York: Bantam, 1991. Print.

In-Text Citation: (Keen 101)

A BOOK BY TWO AUTHORS

Ballenger, Bruce, and Barry Lane. *Discovering the Writer Within*. Cincinnati:

Writer's Digest, 1996. Print.

In-Text Citation: (Ballenger and Lane 14)

A BOOK WITH MORE THAN THREE AUTHORS
If a book has more than three authors, list the first and substitute the term *et al.* for the others.

Belenky, Mary Field, et al. *Women's Ways of Knowing*. New York: Basic Books,

1973. Print.

In-Text Citation: (Belenky et al. 21–30)

SEVERAL BOOKS BY THE SAME AUTHOR

Baldwin, James. *Going to Meet the Man*. New York: Dell-Doubleday, 1948. Print.

- - -. *Tell Me How Long the Train's Been Gone*. New York: Dell-Doubleday, 1968.

Print.

In-Text Citation: (Baldwin, *Going* 34)

A COLLECTION OR ANTHOLOGY

Crane, R. S., ed. *Critics and Criticism: Ancient and Modern*. Chicago: U of Chicago

P, 1952. Print.

In-Text Citation: (Crane xx)

A WORK IN A COLLECTION OR ANTHOLOGY

The title of a work that is part of a collection but was originally published as a book should be italicized. Otherwise, the title of a work in a collection should be enclosed in quotation marks.

Bahktin, Mikhail. *Marxism and the Philosophy of Language. The Rhetorical*

Tradition. Ed. Patricia Bizzell and Bruce Herzberg. New York: St. Martin's,

1990. 928–44. Print.

In-Text Citation: (Bahktin 929–31)

Jones, Robert F. "Welcome to Muskie Country." *The Ultimate Fishing Book*. Ed. Lee

Eisenberg and DeCourcy Taylor. Boston: Houghton, 1981. 122–34. Print.

In-Text Citation: (Jones 131)

AN INTRODUCTION, PREFACE, FOREWORD, OR PROLOGUE

Scott, Jerie Cobb. Foreword. *Writing Groups: History, Theory, and Implications*. By

Ann Ruggles Gere. Carbondale: Southern Illinois UP, 1987. ix–xi. Print.

In-Text Citation : (Scott ix–xi)

Rich, Adrienne. Introduction. *On Lies, Secrets, and Silence*. By Rich. New York:

Norton, 1979. 9–18. Print.

In-Text Citation: (Rich 12)

A BOOK WITH NO AUTHOR

American Heritage Dictionary. 3rd ed. Boston: Houghton, 1994. Print.

In-Text Citation: (*American Heritage Dictionary* 444)

AN ENCYCLOPEDIA

"Passenger Pigeon." *Encyclopedia Britannica Online.* Encyclopedia Britannica,

Inc., 2012. Web. 26 June 2012.

In-Text Citation: ("Passenger Pigeon")

"City of Chicago." *Encyclopaedia Britannica.* 1999 ed. Print.

In-Text Citation: ("City of Chicago" 397)

A BOOK WITH AN INSTITUTIONAL AUTHOR

Hospital Corporation of America. *Employee Benefits Handbook.* Nashville: HCA,

1990. Print.

In-Text Citation: (Hospital Corporation of America 5–7)

A BOOK WITH MULTIPLE VOLUMES
Include the number of volumes in the work between the title and publication information.

Baym, Nina, et al., eds. *The Norton Anthology of American Literature.* 5th ed. 2

vols. New York: Norton, 1998. Print.

In-Text Citation: (Baym et al. 2: 3)

If you use one volume of a multivolume work, indicate which one, along with the page numbers, followed by the total number of volumes in the work.

Anderson, Sherwood. "Mother." *The Norton Anthology of American Literature.* Ed. Nina

Baym et al. 5th ed. Vol. 2. New York: Norton, 1998. 1115–31. 2 vols. Print.

In-Text Citation: (Anderson 1115)

A BOOK THAT IS NOT A FIRST EDITION
Check the title page to determine whether the book is *not* a first edition (2nd, 3rd, 4th, etc.); if no edition number is mentioned, assume it's the first. Put the edition number right after the title.

Ballenger, Bruce. *The Curious Researcher.* 7th ed. Boston: Longman, 2011. Print.

In-Text Citation: (Ballenger 194)

Citing the edition is necessary only for books that are *not* first editions. This includes revised editions (*Rev. ed.*) and abridged editions (*Abr. ed.*).

A BOOK PUBLISHED BEFORE 1900

For a book this old, it's usually unnecessary to list the publisher.

Hitchcock, Edward. *Religion of Geology*. Glasgow, 1851. Print.

In-Text Citation: (Hitchcock 48)

A TRANSLATION

Montaigne, Michel de. *Essays*. Trans. J. M. Cohen. Middlesex, England: Penguin,

1958. Print.

In-Text Citation: (Montaigne 638)

GOVERNMENT DOCUMENTS

Because of the enormous variety of government documents, citing them properly can be a challenge. Because most government documents do not name authors, begin an entry for such a source with the level of government (U.S. Government, State of Illinois, etc.)—unless it is obvious from the title—followed by the sponsoring agency, the title of the work, and the publication information. Look on the title page to determine the publisher. If it's a federal document, then the *Government Printing Office* (abbreviated *GPO*) is usually the publisher.

United States. Bureau of the Census. *Statistical Abstract of the United States*.

Washington: GPO, 2005. Print.

In-Text Citation: (United States, Bureau of the Census 79–83)

A BOOK THAT WAS REPUBLISHED

A fairly common occurrence, particularly in literary study, is to find a book that was republished, sometimes many years after the original publication date. In addition, some books first appear in hardcover, and then are republished in paperback. To cite, put the original date of publication immediately after the book's title, and then include the more current publication date, as usual, at the end of the citation. Do it like so:

Didion, Joan. *Slouching Towards Bethlehem*. 1968. New York: Farrar, 1992. Print.

In-Text Citation: (Didion 31)

Badke, William. *Research Strategies: Finding Your Way through the Information*

Fog. Lincoln, NE: Writers Club P, 2000. Web. 12 July 2009.

In-Text Citation: (Badke)

Citing Periodicals. These days, you're more likely to find an article through a library database or on the web than in a print journal or magazine. Citation of each type of source is quite similar, with the differences listed in the table below.

PRINT ARTICLE	ARTICLE FROM A DATABASE OF THE WEB
1. Author(s)	1. Author(s)
2. "Article Title"	2. "Article Title"
3. *Periodical Title*	3. *Periodical Title*
4. Volume and issue	4. Volume and issue
5. Date published	5. Date published
6. Page numbers	6. Page numbers, if any (usually present in versions also in print)
7. Medium: Print	7. *Website, Database* or Sponsor
	8. Medium: Web
	9. Date of access
SAMPLE CITATION: PRINT ARTICLE	**SAMPLE CITATION: DATABASE ARTICLE**
Newcomb, Matthew. "Sustainability as a Design Principle for Composition." *College Composition and Communication* 63.4 (2012): 593–614. Print.	Pereira, Tony. "The Transition to a Sustainable Society: A New Social Contract." *Environment, Development and Sustainability* 14.2 (2012): 273–281. *Crossref.* Web. 26 June 2012.

Format. Citations for magazines, journals, newspapers, and the like aren't much different from citing books. MLA's 2009 update, however, introduced some significant changes in how you handle online periodicals (see the table).

Author's Name. List the author(s) as you would for a book citation.

Article Title. Unlike book titles, article titles are usually enclosed in quotation marks.

Periodical Title. Italicize periodical titles, dropping introductory articles (*Aegis*, not *The Aegis*). If you're citing a newspaper your readers may not be familiar with, include in the title—enclosed in brackets but not italicized—the city in which it was published. For example:

Barber, Rocky. "DEQ Responds to Concerns About Weiser Feedlot." *Idaho Statesman* [Boise] 23 Apr. 2004: B1. Print.

Volume and Issue Numbers. Most scholarly journals have both. The latest MLA guidelines require that you include both in your citation. These will appear as weird decimals after the journal title. For example, the sixth volume and third issue of the journal *Diseases of the Dairy Cow* would be 6.3. Popular periodicals frequently don't have issue numbers, and you're not required to use them.

Name of Website, Database, or Sponsor. If the name of the site is different from the title of the piece you're citing, include that name in italics. In addition, if the the website's name is different from the organization that hosts it include the sponsor's name as well. The name of the site's sponsor isn't always obvious. Try looking at the bottom of the page or click on the "About Us" link if there is one. If the publisher is unclear include *n.p.* (for "no publisher") in your citation. If you do include a publisher's name, don't italicize it. Finally, if your source is from a library database, identify it (e.g. *ProQuest, JSTOR, Google Scholar,* etc.).

Date. When citing popular periodicals, include the day, month, and year of the issue you're citing—in that order—following the periodical name. Academic journals are a little different. Because the volume number indicates when the journal was published within a given year, just indicate that year. Put it in parentheses following the volume number and before the page numbers (see examples in "A Journal Article" section on following page).

Page Numbers. Include the page numbers of the article at the end of the citation, followed by a period. Just list the pages of the entire article, omitting abbreviations such as *p.* or *pp*. It's common for articles in newspapers and popular magazines *not* to run on consecutive pages. In that case, indicate the page on which the article begins, followed by a "+" (*12+*).

Newspaper pagination can be peculiar. Some papers wed the section (usually a letter) with the page number (*A4*); other papers simply begin numbering anew in each section. Most, however, paginate continuously. See the sample citations for newspapers that follow, for how to deal with these peculiarities.

Online sources, which often have no pagination at all, present special problems. For guidance on how to handle them, see the "Citing Online and Other Sources" section.

Publication Medium. Indicate the form in which you found the periodical, usually either "Print" or "Web."

Date of Access. If you did find the journal or magazine online, end your citation with the date you first accessed it.

Sample Periodical Citations
A MAGAZINE ARTICLE

Elliot, Carl. "The New Drug Pushers." *Atlantic Monthly* Apr. 2006: 82–93. Print.

In-Text Citation: (Elliot 92)

Williams, Patricia J. "Unimagined Communities." *Nation* 3 May 2004: 14. Print.

In-Text Citation: (Williams 14)

Citations for magazines that you find online should also include the publication medium ("Web") and the date you accessed the material. For example,

Kaufman, Ken. "Stopover Country." *Audubon Magazine* May–June 2009. Web. 1

July 2009.

In-Text Citation: (Kaufman)

Notice that both the website's name and its publisher are included in the on-line article below.

Schoen, John W. "Jobless Consumers Will Hold Up Recovery." *Msnbc.com.*

Microsoft, 2 July 2009. Web. 3 July 2009.

In-Text Citation: (Schoen)

A JOURNAL ARTICLE

There's a good chance that you found a journal article using your library's online database. If so, include the database name, italicized, in your citation. Remember to also include the volume and issue number whenever you cite any journal.

Here's an article from a library database.

Niservich, P. M. "Training Tips for Vegetarian Athletes." *IDEA Fitness Journal* 6.4

(2009). *Physical Education Index.* Web. 2 July 2009.

In-Text Citation: (Niservich)

Here is sample citation for an article in print:

Allen, Rebecca E., and J. M. Oliver. "The Effects of Child Maltreatment on

Language Development." *Child Abuse and Neglect* 6.1 (1982): 299–305. Print.

In-Text Citation: (Allen and Oliver 299–300)

A NEWSPAPER ARTICLE

Some newspapers have several editions (morning edition, late edition, national edition), and each may feature different articles. If an edition is listed on the mast-head, include it in the citation.

Mendels, Pamela. "Internet Access Spreads to More Classrooms." *New York Times*

1 Dec. 1999, morning ed.: C1+. Print.

In-Text Citation: (Mendels C1)

Some papers begin numbering pages anew in each section. In that case, include the section number if it's not part of pagination.

Brooks, James. "Lobsters on the Brink." *Portland Press* 29 Nov. 2005, sec. 2: 4.

Print.

In-Text Citation: (Brooks 4)

The decline of print newspapers means you are more likely to find an article online. Because these often lack page numbers, you can omit them; but don't forget to include the website's name, publisher (if different), and the date you accessed the article.

Wald, Matthew. "Court Backs EPA on Emissions Rulings." *New York Times*. New

York Times, 26 June 2012. Web. 26 July 2012.

In-Text Citation: (Wald)

AN ARTICLE WITH NO AUTHOR

"The Understanding." *New Yorker* 2 Dec. 1991: 34–35. Print.

In-Text Citation: ("Understanding" 35)

AN EDITORIAL

"Downward Mobility." Editorial. *New York Times* 27 Aug. 2006: 31. Print.

In-Text Citation: ("Downward" 31)

AN OPINION PIECE

Vanden Heuvel, Katrina. "Women Who Don't Have Anything Close to 'It All.'"

Washingtonpost.com. The Washington Post, 26 June 2012. Web. 4 July

2012.

In-Text Citation: (Vanden Heuvel)

A LETTER TO THE EDITOR

Boulay, Harvey. Letter. *Boston Globe* 30 Aug. 2006: 14. Print.

In-Text Citation: (Boulay 14)

A letter to the editor you find online would be cited like this:

Willett, Catherine. "Go Ahead and Test but Spare the Animals." *NYTimes.com*.

New York Times, 2 July 2009. Web. 2 July 2009.

In-Text Citation: (Willett)

A REVIEW

Page, Barbara. Rev. of *Allegories of Cinema: American Film in the Sixties*, by David

E. James. *College English* 54 (1992): 945–54. Print.

In-Text Citation: (Page 945–46)

AN ABSTRACT

> Edwards, Rob. "Air-Raid Warning." *New Scientist* 14 Aug. 1999: 48–49. Abstract.
>
> *MasterFILE Premier*. Web. 1 May 2002.

In-Text Citation: (Edwards)

The following citation is from another useful source of abstracts, the *Dissertation Abstracts International*. In this case, the citation is from the print version of the index.

> McDonald, James C. "Imitation of Models in the History of Rhetoric: Classical,
>
> Belletristic, and Current-Traditional." U of Texas, Austin. *DAI* 48 (1988):
>
> 2613A. Print.

In-Text Citation: (McDonald 2613A)

Citing Online and Other Sources
AN INTERVIEW

If you conducted the interview yourself, list your subject's name first, indicate what kind of interview it was (telephone, e-mail, or personal interview), and provide the date.

> Kelley, Karen. Personal interview. 1 Sept. 2012.

In-Text Citation: (Kelley)

Or avoid parenthetical reference altogether by mentioning the subject's name in the text: According to Lonny Hall, ...

If you're citing an interview done by someone else (perhaps from a book or article) and the title does not indicate that it was an interview, you should, after the subject's name, include *Interview*. Always begin the citation with the subject's name.

> Stegner, Wallace. Interview. *Conversations with Wallace Stegner*. By Richard
>
> Eutlain and Wallace Stegner. Salt Lake: U of Utah P, 1990. Print.

In-Text Citation: (Stegner 22)

If there are other works by Stegner on the Works Cited page:

(Stegner, *Conversations* 22)

As radio and TV interview programs are increasingly archived on the web, these can be a great source of material for a research essay. In the following example, the interview was on a transcript I ordered from the Fresh Air website. Note that the national network, National Public Radio, *and* the local affiliate that produced the program, WHYY, are included in the citation along with the airdate.

> Mairs, Nancy. Interview by Terry Gross. *Fresh Air*. Radio. NPR. WHYY,
>
> Philadelphia. 7 June 1993.

In-Text Citation: (Mairs)

The following citation is for an interview published on the web. The second date listed is the date of access.

Messner, Tammy Faye Bakker. Interview. *The Well Rounded Interview.* Well

Rounded Entertainment. Aug. 2000. 14 July 2002. Web.

In-Text Citation: (Messner)

SURVEYS, QUESTIONNAIRES, AND CASE STUDIES
If you conducted the survey or case study, list it under your name and give it an appropriate title.

Ball, Helen. "Internet Survey." Boise State U, 2012.

In-Text Citation: (Ball)

RECORDINGS
Generally, list a recording by the name of the performer and italicize the title. Also include the recording company, catalog number, and year. (If you don't know the year, use the abbreviation *n.d.*)

Orff, Carl. *Carmina Burana.* Cond. Seiji Ozawa. Boston Symphony. RCA, 6533–2-RG,

n.d. CD.

In-Text Citation: (Orff)

TELEVISION AND RADIO PROGRAMS
List the title of the program (italicized), the station, and the broadcast date. If the episode has a title, list that first in quotation marks. You may also want to include the name of the narrator or producer after the title.

"Congress Takes Student Loans, Highway Bill to the Wire." *All Things Considered.*

Natl. Public Radio, Washington, DC, 26 June 2012. Radio.

In-Text Citation: ("Congress Takes Student Loans")

ONLINE AUDIO OR VIDEO

Sarah Palin 20/20 Interview with Charlie Gibson, Part 2/4. YouTube. YouTube,

12 Sept. 2008. Web. 3 July 2009.

In-Text Citation: (*Sarah Palin 20/20 Interview*)

"Bad Bank." *This American Life.* Prod. Ira Glass. *NPR.* Chicago Public Radio,

27 Feb. 2009. Web. 3 July 2009.

In-Text Citation: ("Bad Bank")

ONLINE IMAGES

"Passenger Pigeon." Online image. 26 June 2012. *Sarroffillustration.com*.

2 July 2012.

In-Text Citation: ("Passenger Pigeon")

BLOG

O'Brien, Terence. "EPA May Have Suppressed Global Warming Study." *Switched*.

AOL News, 2 July 2009. Web. 3 July 2009.

In-Text Citation: (O'Brien)

PODCAST

Kermode, Mark. "Drag Me to Hell." *5 Live*. BBC Radio, 12 May 2009. Web.

3 July 2009.

In-Text Citation: (Kermode)

WIKI

"Emily Dickinson." *Wikipedia*. Wikipedia Foundation, 2009. Web. 3 July 2009.

In-Text Citation: ("Emily Dickinson")

FILMS, VIDEOTAPES, AND DVD

Begin with the title (italicized), followed by the director, the distributor, and
the year. You may also include names of writers, performers, or producers. End
with the date and any other specifics about the characteristics of the film or video-
tape that may be relevant (length and size).

Saving Private Ryan. Dir. Steven Spielberg. Perf. Tom Hanks, Tom Sizemore, and

Matt Damon. Paramount, 1998. DVD.

In-Text Citation: (*Saving*)

You can also list a video or film by the name of a contributor you'd like to
emphasize.

Capra, Frank, dir. *It's a Wonderful Life*. Perf. Jimmy Stewart and Donna Reed. RKO

Pictures, 1946. Film.

In-Text Citation: (Capra)

ARTWORK

List each work by artist. Then cite the title of the work (italicized) and where
it's located (institution and city). If you've reproduced the work from a published
source, include that information as well.

Homer, Winslow. *Casting for a Rise*. Hirschl and Adler Galleries, New York. *Ultimate*

Fishing Book. Ed. Lee Eisenberg and DeCourcy Taylor. Boston: Houghton,

1981. Print.

In-Text Citation: (Homer 113)

LECTURES AND SPEECHES

List each by the name of the speaker, followed by the title of the address (if any) in quotation marks, the name of the sponsoring organization, the location, and the date. Only indicate what kind of address it was (Lecture, Speech, etc.) when no title is given.

Naynaha, Siskanna. "Emily Dickinson's Last Poems." Sigma Tau Delta, Boise, ID.

15 Nov. 1999. Lecture.

Avoid the need for parenthetical citation by mentioning the speaker's name in your text.

PAMPHLETS

Cite a pamphlet as you would a book.

New Challenges for Wilderness Conservationists. Washington, DC: Wilderness

Society, 2006. Print.

In-Text Citation: (New Challenges)

A Sample Paper in MLA Style. Most of the student essays in *The Curious Writer* use MLA style. For a fully documented research paper, see Gordon Seirup's essay, "College Dating," in Chapter 10.

MLA VERSUS APA: SOME BASIC DIFFERENCES

MLA Approach	APA Approach
(Author page #)—Example:	**(Author, year)—Example:**
According to Ackerman, there is an infatuation chemical (164).	According to Ackerman (1994), there is an infatuation chemical.
Usually no title page.	Usually title page and abstract. An abstract is a short summary of the paper's content, always less than 120 words in APA style.
	(continued)

MLA Approach	APA Approach
Pagination uses writer's last name and page number. For example:	Pagination uses running head and page number. A "running head" is the paper's abbreviated title. For example:
Smith 5	EXPORTING JOBS 5
Figures and tables included within the paper.	Figures and tables included in section at the end of the paper.
Bibliography called Works Cited page.	Bibliography called References page.

APA Documentation Guidelines

The American Psychological Association's (APA) citation conventions are the other dominant approach to acknowledging sources. If you're headed for courses in the social sciences, then this is the system you'll use. It's no harder than the MLA; in fact, the two systems are quite similar. Both use parenthetical citations. Both organize the bibliography (or References page) in very similar ways. But there are a few significant differences, some of which are summarized in the accompanying table. Detailed descriptions of the APA system then follow.

Watch
the Animation on
Formatting
Papers in APA Style
in your MyLab

How the Essay Should Look

Page Format. Papers should be double-spaced, with at least one-inch margins on all sides. Number all pages consecutively, beginning with the title page; put the page number in the upper right corner. Above or five spaces to the left of the page number, place an abbreviated title of the paper on every page, in case pages get separated. As a rule, the first line of all paragraphs of text should be indented five to seven spaces.

Title Page. Unlike a paper in MLA style, an APA-style paper has a separate title page, containing the following information: the title of the paper, the author, and the author's affiliation (e.g., what university she is from). Each line of information should be centered and double-spaced. (See Figure 12.3.) At the top of the title page, flush left and in uppercase letters, you may also include a *running head*, or an abbreviation of the title (fifty characters or less, including spaces). A page header, which uses the first two or three words of the title followed by the page number, begins on the second page. This is different from the running head, which tends to be longer and appears only on the title page.

Abstract. Although it's not always required, many APA-style papers include a short abstract (no longer than 120 words) following the title page. (See Figure 12.4.) An abstract is essentially a short summary of the paper's contents.

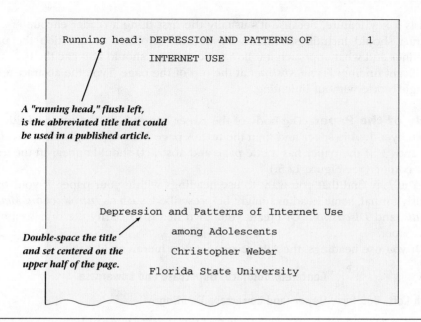

Figure 12.3 Title page in APA style

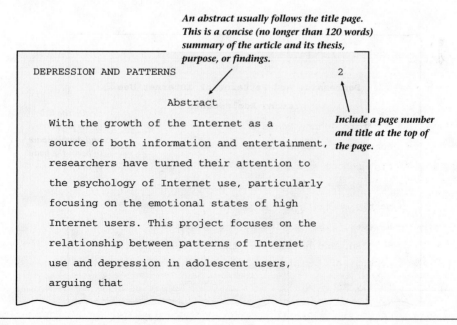

Figure 12.4 The abstract page

This is a key feature, because it's usually the first thing a reader encounters. The abstract should include statements about what problem or question the paper examines and what approach it follows; the abstract should also cite the thesis and significant findings. Type *Abstract* at the top of the page. Type the abstract text in a single block, without indenting.

Body of the Paper. The body of the paper begins with the centered title, followed by a double space and then the text. A page header (usually an abbreviated title and "3" if the paper has a title page and abstract) should appear in the upper right corner. (See Figure 12.5.)

You may find that you want to use headings within your paper. If your paper is fairly formal, some headings might be prescribed, such as *Introduction, Method, Results,* and *Discussion.* Or create your own heads to clarify the organization of your paper.

If you use headings, the APA recommends a hierarchy like this:

Centered, Boldface, Uppercase and Lowercase

Flush Left, Boldface, Upper- and Lowercase Heading

   Indented, boldface, lowercase except first letter of first word

   Indented, boldface, italicized, lowercase except first letter of first word

   Indented, italicized, lowercase except first letter of first word

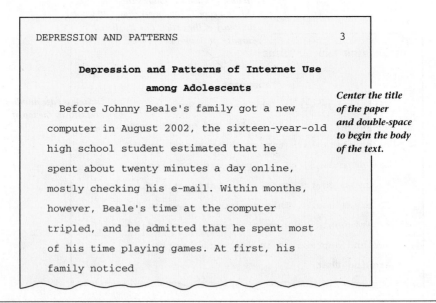

Figure 12.5   The body of the paper in APA style

Papers rarely use all five levels of headings; two or three is probably most common, particularly in student papers. When you use multiple levels, always use them consecutively. In other words, a level 1 heading would always be followed by a level 2 heading (if there is one).

For example,

The Intelligence of Crows

Current Understandings of Crow Intelligence

References Page. All sources cited in the body of the paper are listed alphabetically by author (or title, if anonymous) on the page titled *References*. See Figure 12.6. This list should begin a new page. Each entry is double-spaced; begin each entry flush left, and indent subsequent lines five to seven spaces. Explanation of how to cite various sources in the references follows in the "Preparing the References List" section.

Appendix. This is a seldom-used feature of an APA-style paper, although you might find it helpful for presenting specific or tangential material that isn't central to the discussion in the body of your paper: a detailed description of a device described in the paper, a copy of a blank survey, or the like. Each item should begin on a separate page and be labeled *Appendix*, followed by *A, B*, and so on, consecutively, if there is more than one item.

Notes. Several kinds of notes might be included in a paper. The most common is *content notes*, or brief commentaries by the writer keyed to superscript numbers in the body of the text. These notes are useful for discussion of key points that

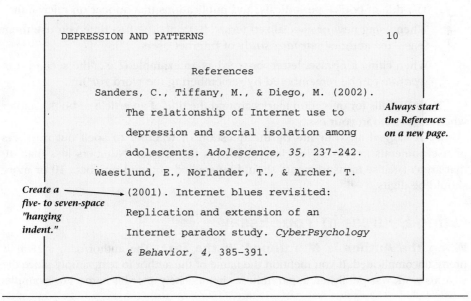

Figure 12.6 The References page

are relevant but might be distracting if explored in the text of your paper. Present all notes, numbered consecutively, on a page titled *Endnotes*. Each note should be double-spaced. Begin each note with the appropriate superscript number, keyed to the text. Indent each first line five to seven spaces; consecutive lines run the full page measure.

Tables and Figures. The final section of an APA-style paper features tables and figures mentioned in the text. Tables should all be double-spaced. Type a table number at the top of the page, flush left. Number tables Table 1, Table 2, and so on, corresponding to the order in which they are mentioned in the text. A table may also include a title. Each table should begin on a separate page.

Figures (illustrations, graphs, charts, photographs, drawings) are handled similarly to tables. Each should be titled *Figure* and numbered consecutively. Captions may be included, but all should be typed on a separate page, clearly labeled *Figure Captions*, and listed in order. For example:

Figure Captions

Figure 1. A photograph taken in the 1930s by Dorothea Lange.

Figure 2. Edward Weston took a series of green pepper photographs like this one. This is titled "No. 35."

Language and Style. The APA is comfortable with the italics and bold functions of modern word processors, and underlining is a thing of the past. The guidelines for *italicizing* call for its use when writing the following:

- The title of books, periodicals, and publications that appear on microfilm.
- When using new or specialized terms, but only the first time you use them (e.g., "the authors' *paradox study* of Internet users...").
- When citing a phrase, letter, or word as an example (e.g., "the second *a* in *separate* can be remembered by remembering the word *rat*").

The APA calls for quotation marks around the title of an article or book chapter when mentioned in your essay.

Been nagged all your life by the question of whether to spell out numbers or use numerals in APA style? Here, finally, is the answer: Numbers less than 10 that aren't precise measurements should be spelled out, and numbers 10 or more should be digits.

Citing Sources in Your Essay

Watch
the Animation on
Citing Sources
in APA Style
in your MyLab

When the Author Is Mentioned in the Text. The author/date system is pretty uncomplicated. If you mention the name of the author in text, simply place the year his work was published in parentheses immediately after his name. For example:

Herrick (1999) argued that college testing was biased against minorities.

When the Author Isn't Mentioned in the Text. If you don't mention the author's name in the text, then include that information parenthetically. For example:

A New Hampshire political scientist (Sundberg, 2012) recently studied the state's

presidential primary.

Note that the author's name and the year of her work are separated by a comma.

When to Cite Page Numbers. If the information you're citing came from specific pages, chapters, or sections of a source, that information may also be included in the parenthetical citation. Including page numbers is essential when quoting a source. For example:

The first stage of language acquisition is called "caretaker speech" (Moskowitz,

1985, pp. 50–51), in which children model their parents' language.

The same passage might also be cited this way if the author's name is mentioned in the text:

Moskowitz (1985) observed that the first stage of language acquisition is called

"caretaker speech" (pp. 50–51), in which children model their parents' language.

A Single Work by Two or More Authors. When a work has two authors, always mention them both whenever you cite their work in your paper. For example:

Allen and Oliver (1998) observed many cases of child abuse and concluded that

maltreatment inhibited language development.

If a source has more than two authors but fewer than six, mention them all the first time you refer to their work. However, any subsequent references can include the surname of the first author followed by the abbreviation *et al.* When citing works with six or more authors, *always* use the first author's surname and *et al.*

A Work with No Author. When a work has no author, cite an abbreviated title and the year. Place article or chapter titles in quotation marks, and *italicize* book titles. For example:

The editorial ("Sinking," 2012) concluded that the EPA was mired in bureaucratic

muck.

Two or More Works by the Same Author. Works by the same author are usually distinguished by the date; works are rarely published the same year. But if they are, distinguish among works by adding an *a* or *b* immediately following the year in the parenthetical citation. The reference list will also have these suffixes. For example:

> Douglas's studies (1986a) on the mating habits of lobsters revealed that the
>
> females are dominant. He also found that the female lobsters have the uncanny
>
> ability to smell a loser (1986b).

This citation alerts readers that the information came from two studies by Douglas, both published in 1986.

An Institutional Author. When citing a corporation or agency as a source, simply list the year of the study in parentheses if you mention the institution in the text:

> The Environmental Protection Agency (2012) issued an alarming report on ozone
>
> pollution.

If you don't mention the institutional source in the text, spell it out in its entirety, along with the year. In subsequent parenthetical citations, you can abbreviate the name as long as the abbreviation will be understandable. For example:

> A study (Environmental Protection Agency [EPA], 2012) predicted dire conse-
>
> quences from continued ozone depletion.

And later:

> Continued ozone depletion may result in widespread skin cancers (EPA, 2012).

Multiple Works in the Same Parentheses. Occasionally, you'll want to cite several works at once that speak to a topic you're writing about in your essay. Probably the most common instance is when you refer to the findings of several relevant studies, something that is a good idea as you try to establish a context for what has already been said about your research topic. For example,

> A number of researchers have explored the connection between Internet use and
>
> depression (Sanders, Field, & Diego, 2000; Waestlund, Norlander, & Archer, 2001).

When listing multiple authors within the same parentheses, order them as they appear in the references. Semicolons separate each entry.

Interviews, E-Mail, and Letters. Interviews and other personal communications are not listed in the references at the back of the paper, because they are not *recoverable data*, but they are parenthetically cited in the text. Provide the initials and surname of the subject (if not mentioned in the text), the nature of the communication, and the complete date, if possible.

Nancy Diamonti (personal communication, November 12, 2012) disagrees with

the critics of *Sesame Street*.

In a recent e-mail, Michelle Payne (personal communication, January 4, 2012)

complained that...

New Editions of Old Works. For reprints of older works, include both the year of the original publication and that of the reprint edition (or the translation).

Pragmatism as a philosophy sought connection between scientific study and real

people's lives (James, 1906/1978).

A Website. When referring to an *entire* website (see the following example), cite the address parenthetically in your essay. As for e-mail, it isn't necessary to include a citation for an entire website in your references list. However, you will cite online documents that contribute information to your paper (see the "Citing Online and Other Sources" section).

One of the best sites for searching the so-called Invisible Web is the Librarians

Index to the Internet (http://www.lii.org).

Preparing the References List

All parenthetical citations in the body of the paper correspond to a complete listing of sources on the References page. The format for this section was described earlier (see the "References Page" section).

Order of Sources. List the references alphabetically by author or by the first key word of the title if there is no author. The only complication may be if you have several articles or books by the same author. If the sources weren't published in the same year, list them in chronological order, the earliest first. If the sources were published in the *same* year, include a lowercase letter to distinguish them. For example:

Lane, B. (1991a). Verbal medicine...

Lane, B. (1991b). Writing...

While the alphabetical principle—listing authors according to the alphabetical placement of their last names—works in most cases, there are a few variations you should be aware of.

- If you have several entries by the same author, list them by year of publication, beginning with the earliest.

■ Because scholars and writers often collaborate, you may have several references in which an author is listed with several *different* collaborators. List these alphabetically using the second author's last name. For example,

Brown, M., & Nelson, A. (2002)

Brown, M., & Payne, M. (1999)

Order of Information. A reference to a periodical or book in APA style includes this information, in order: author, date of publication, article title, periodical title, and publication information.

Electronic sources include some additional information. If you're harvesting your books and articles online or from a library database, you need to cite in a way that makes it clear how readers can find the book or document. That seems simple, right? It isn't always. Typically, you include the URL for an online document in your citation, even if it's long and ugly. But URLs can change, and they are vulnerable to transcription mistakes. To solve this problem, the APA created something called the Digital Object Identifier (see description on facing page). This is a number that is a permanent link to the document. But not all documents have them, and if not, use their URLs.

One other bit of information you usually include in a citation for an electronic document is the retrieval date, or exactly when you accessed the work online. This can be omitted, however, when the document you're citing is "archival." An archival copy is a final version, and it's usually the version that appeared in print.

Author. List up to eight authors using last name, comma, and then initials. Invert all authors' names. Use commas to separate authors' names and add an ampersand (&) before the last author's name. When citing more than eight authors, list the first six, then add ellipses ("…") and add the last name. When citing an edited book, list the editor(s) in place of the author(s), and add the abbreviation Ed. or Eds. in parentheses following the initials. End the list of names with a period.

Date. List the year the work was published, along with the date if it's a magazine or newspaper (see the following "Sample References" section), in parentheses, immediately after the last author's name. Add a period after the closing parenthesis.

Article or Book Title. APA style departs from MLA here, at least with respect to periodicals. In APA style, only the first word of the article title is capitalized and appears without italics or quotation marks. Book titles are italicized; capitalize only the first word of the title and any subtitle. End all titles with periods.

Periodical Title and Publication Information. Italicize the complete periodical title; type it using both uppercase and lowercase letters. Add the volume number (if any), also italicized. Separate the title and volume number with a comma (e.g., *Journal of Mass Communication, 10,* 138–150). If each issue of the periodical starts with page 1, then also include the issue number in parentheses immediately after the volume number (see examples following). End the entry with the page numbers of the article. Use the abbreviation *p.* or *pp.* if you are citing a newspaper. Other APA-style abbreviations include the following:

chap.	p. (pp.)
Ed./Eds. (Editor/Editors), ed. (edition)	Vol.
Rev. ed.	No.
2nd ed.	Pt.
Trans.	Suppl.

For books, list the city and state or country of publication (use postal abbreviations) and the name of the publisher; separate the city and publisher with a colon. End the citation with a period. The following cities do not require state or country abbreviations:

Baltimore	Amsterdam
Boston	Jerusalem
Chicago	London
Los Angeles	Milan
New York	Moscow
Philadelphia	Paris
San Francisco	Rome
	Stockholm
	Tokyo
	Vienna

Remember that the first line of each citation should begin flush left, and all subsequent lines should be indented five to seven spaces. Double-space all entries.

Retrieval Date. If you're citing an electronic document, you often indicate when you accessed the book or article. This is important because online documents can change, and the retrieval date gives readers a "snapshot" of what version you were looking at when you did your research. Retrieval dates can be omitted when you're citing a permanent or "archival" version of the work.

DOI or URL. These are more ingredients for your alphabet soup. So readers can locate the electronic documents you're citing, you need to tell them where you found them. You frequently do this by including the URL. But more and more documents in the social sciences include something called the Digital Object Identifier (DOI), a permanent link to the work. The DOI is often listed on the article's first page. It may also be hidden under the "Article" button that appears with the work on certain library databases.

Here's a summary of the similarities and differences in APA style when citing print and electronic journals and magazines:

Print Periodical	Electronic Periodical
• Author(s) • (Date) • Article title • Periodical title • Issue and volume number • Page numbers	• Author(s) • (Date) • Article title • Periodical title • Issue and volume number • Page numbers • Retrieval date (unless archival) • DOI (if available) or URL (if DOI unavailable)

Sample References: Articles
A JOURNAL ARTICLE

When citing an online article, include information about how readers can find it. Use the DOI, if available. For example,

Mori, K., Ujiie, T., Smith, A., & Howlin P. (2009). Parental stress associated with

caring for children with Asperger's syndrome. *Pediatrics International, 51*(3),

364–370. doi:10.1111/j.1442-200X-2008.0278.x

In-Text Citation: (Mori, Smith, & Howlin, 2009); (Mori et al., 2009) in subsequent citations. If authors are quoted, include page numbers.

If there is no DOI, include the document's URL.

Wing, L. (1981). Asperger's syndrome: A clinical account. *Psychological Medicine,*

11(1), 115–129. Retrieved from http://search.ebscohost.com/login

.aspx?direct=true&db=psyh&AN=1981-30537-001&site=ehost-live

In-Text Citation: (Wing, 1981)

Cite a print journal article like this:

Blager, F. B. (1979). The effect of intervention on the speech and language of

children. *Child Abuse and Neglect, 5,* 91–96.

In-Text Citation: (Blager, 1979)

If the author is mentioned in the text, just parenthetically cite the year:

Blager (1979) stated that...

If the author is quoted, include the page number(s):

(Blager, 1979, p. 92)

A MAGAZINE ARTICLE

Maya, P. (1981, December). The civilizing of Genie. *Psychology Today*, 28–34.

In-Text Citation: (Maya, 1981)

Maya (1981) observed that...

When citing a magazine article from a database, include the URL. Many databases include a "permanent link" to the article on the citation page. Use that if available. Notice also that the database name is no longer included.

Horowitz, A. (July, 2008). My dog is smarter than your dog. *Discover Magazine*

219(9), 71. Retrieved from http://search.ebscohost.com.libproxy.boisestate

.edu/login.aspx?direct=true&db=aph&AN=32580478&site=ehost-live

In-Text Citation: (Horowitz, 2008). If quoting, include page numbers: (Horowitz, 2008, p. 71)

AN ARTICLE ON A WEBSITE

This article has no author, so the citation begins with the title.

Enhancing male body image. (2006). *Nationaleatingdisorders.org.* Retrieved

July 9, 2009, from http://www.nationaleatingdisorders.org/

In-Text Citation: ("Enhancing," 2006)

If quoting, include the page number(s): (Maya, 1981, p. 28)

A NEWSPAPER ARTICLE

Honan, W. (2004, January 24). The war affects Broadway. *New York Times*, pp. C15–16.

In-Text Citation: (Honan, 2004)

Honan (2004) argued that...

Honan (2004) said that "Broadway is a battleground" (p. C15).

If there is no author, a common situation with newspaper articles, alphabetize using the first "significant word" in the article title. The parenthetical citation would use an abbreviation of the title in quotation marks, then the year.

There's a good chance that you'll find newspaper articles online. Here's how you cite them:

Jennings, D. (2009, July 7). With cancer, you can't hurry recovery. *The New York*

Times. Retrieved from http://www.nytimes.com

In-Text Citation: (Jennings, 2009)

Sample References: Books
A BOOK

> Lukas, A. J. (1986). *Common ground: A turbulent decade in the lives of three*
>
> *American families.* New York: Random House.

In-Text Citation: (Lukas, 1986)

According to Lukas (1986), . . .

If quoting, include the page number(s).

AN ONLINE BOOK

If you're citing an entire book you found online, include the URL. Sometimes, however, the Internet address may not lead to the work itself, but rather information on how to find it. In that case, use the phrase "Available from" rather than "Retrieved from." For example,

> Suzuki, D. T. (1914). *A brief history of early Chinese philosophy.* Available from
>
> http://www.archive.org/details/briefhistoryofea00suzuuoft

In-Text Citation: (Suzuki, 1914)

When citing a chapter from an online book, include a bit more information, including the name of the database (if any) from which you retrieved it.

> Hollin, C. R. (2002). Criminal psychology. In Hollin, C. R., *Oxford handbook of crim-*
>
> *inology* (pp. 144–174). Retrieved from Academic Research Premier database.

In-Text Citation: (Hollin, 2002)

A SOURCE MENTIONED BY ANOTHER SOURCE

Frequently you'll read an article that mentions another article you haven't read. Whenever possible, track down that original article and read it in its entirety. But when that's not possible, you need to make it clear that you know of the article and its findings or arguments indirectly. The APA convention for this is to use the expression *as cited in* parenthetically, followed by the author and date of the indirect source. For example, suppose you want to use some information from Eric Weiser's piece that you read about in Charlotte Jones's book. In your essay, you would write something like:

> Weiser argues (as cited in Jones, 2002) that . . .

A BOOK OR ARTICLE WITH MORE THAN ONE AUTHOR

> Rosenbaum, A., & O'Leary, D. (1978). Children: The unintended victims of marital
>
> violence. *American Journal of Orthopsychiatry, 4,* 692–699.

In-Text Citation: (Rosenbaum & O'Leary, 1978)

Rosenbaum and O'Leary (1978) believed that...

If quoting, include the page number(s).

A BOOK OR ARTICLE WITH AN UNKNOWN AUTHOR

The politics of war. (2004, June 1). *New York Times*, p. 36.

In-Text Citation: ("Politics," 2004)

Or mention the source in the text:

In "The Politics of War" (2004), an editorialist compared Iraq to...

If quoting, provide page number(s) as well.

The Chicago manual of style (14th ed.). (1993). Chicago: University of Chicago

Press.

In-Text Citation: (*Chicago Manual of Style*, 1993)

According to the *Chicago Manual of Style* (1993),...

If quoting, include the page number(s).

A BOOK WITH AN INSTITUTIONAL AUTHOR

American Red Cross. (1999). *Advanced first aid and emergency care*. New York:

Doubleday.

In-Text Citation: (American Red Cross, 1999)

The book *Advanced First Aid and Emergency Care* (American Red Cross, 1999)

stated that...

If quoting, include the page number(s).

A BOOK WITH AN EDITOR

Crane, R. S. (Ed.). (1952). *Critics and criticism*. Chicago: University of Chicago Press.

In-Text Citation: (Crane, 1952)

In his preface, Crane (1952) observed that...

If quoting, include the page number(s).

A SELECTION IN A BOOK WITH AN EDITOR

McKeon, R. (1952). Rhetoric in the Middle Ages. In R. S. Crane (Ed.), *Critics and*

criticism (pp. 260–289). Chicago: University of Chicago Press.

In-Text Citation: (McKeon, 1952)

McKeon (1952) argued that...

If quoting, include the page number(s).

A REPUBLISHED WORK

James, W. (1978). *Pragmatism*. Cambridge, MA: Harvard University Press.

(Original work published 1907).

In-Text Citation: (James, 1907/1978)

According to William James (1907/1978),...

If quoting, include the page number(s).

AN ABSTRACT

The growth of online databases for articles has increased the availability of full-text versions and abstracts of articles. Although the full article is almost always best, sometimes an abstract alone contains some useful information. If the abstract was retrieved from a database or some other secondary source, include information about it. Aside from the name of the source, this information might involve the date, if different from the year of publication of the original article, an abstract number, or a page number. In the following example, the abstract was retrieved from an online database, Biological Abstracts.

Garcia, R. G. (2002). Evolutionary speed of species invasions. *Evolution, 56,*

661–668. Abstract retrieved from Biological Abstracts.

In-Text Citation: (Garcia, 2002), or Garcia (2002) argues that...

A BOOK REVIEW

Dentan, R. K. (1989). A new look at the brain [Review of the book *The dreaming*

brain]. *Psychiatric Journal, 13,* 51.

In-Text Citation: (Dentan, 1989)

Dentan (1989) argued that...

If quoting, include the page number(s).

An online book review would include the same information below, but with the review's URL and the phrase ("Retrieved from...").

ONLINE ENCYCLOPEDIA

Turner, B. S. (2007). Body and society. In G. Ritzer (Ed.), *Blackwell encyclopedia*

of sociology. Retrieved July 7, 2009, from http://blackwellreference.com

In-Text Citation: (Turner, 2007)

Because they are collaboratively written, Wikipedia articles have no single author. Usually, therefore, the citation will begin with the article title. For example,

Ticks (n.d.). Retrieved July 9, 2009 from Wikipedia: http://en.wikipedia.org

/wiki/Ticks

In-Text Citation: ("Ticks," n.d.)

Sample References: Other

A GOVERNMENT DOCUMENT

U.S. Bureau of the Census. (2004). *Statistical abstract of the United States* (126th

ed.). Washington, DC: U.S. Government Printing Office.

In-Text Citation: (U.S. Bureau of the Census, 2004)

According to the U.S. Census Bureau (2004),...

If quoting, include the page number(s).

A LETTER TO THE EDITOR

Hill, A. C. (2006, February 19). A flawed history of blacks in Boston [Letter to

the editor]. *The Boston Globe*, p. 22.

In-Text Citation: (Hill, 2006)

Hill (2006) complained that...

If quoting, include page number(s).

A PUBLISHED INTERVIEW

Personal interviews are not cited in the References section of an APA-style paper, unlike published interviews. Here is a citation for a published interview:

Cotton, P. (2004, April). [Interview with Jake Tule, psychic]. *Chronicles*

Magazine, 24–28.

In-Text Citation: (Cotton, 2004)

Cotton (2004) noted that...

If quoting, include the page number(s).

A FILM OR VIDEOTAPE

Hitchcock, A. (Producer & Director). (1954). *Rear window* [Motion Picture].

Los Angeles: MGM.

In-Text Citation: (Hitchcock, 1954)

In *Rear Window*, Hitchcock (1954)...

PODCAST, VIDEO, AND AUDIO

> Shier, J. (Producer and Director). (2005). Saving the grizzly: One hair at a
>   time. *Terra: The nature of our world*. Podcast retrieved from http://www
>   .lifeonterra.com/episode.php?id=1

In-Text Citation: (Shier, 2005)

> Uhry, A. (2009, July 6). Private education in America. *The Economist*. Podcast
>   retrieved from http://podcast.com/episode/40782102/5356/

In-Text Citation: (Uhry, 2009)

A TELEVISION PROGRAM

> Burns, K. (Executive Producer). (1996). *The west* [Television broadcast]. New
>   York and Washington, DC: Public Broadcasting Service.

In-Text Citation: (Burns, 1996)

In Ken Burns's (1996) film,...

For an episode of a television series, use the scriptwriter as the author, and provide the director's name after the scriptwriter. List the producer's name after the episode.

> Hopley, J. (Writer/Director), & Shannon, J. (Writer/Director). (2006). Buffalo
>   burrito/Parkerina [Television series episode]. In J. Lenz (Producer),
>   *Mr. Meaty*. New York: Nickelodeon.

In-Text Citation: (Hopley & Shannon, 2006)

Fans were appalled by the second episode, when Hopley and Shannon (2006)...

A MUSICAL RECORDING

> Wolf, K. (1986). Muddy roads [Recorded by E. Clapton]. *On gold in California*
>   [CD]. Santa Monica, CA: Rhino Records. (1990).

In-Text Citation: (Wolf, 1986, track 5)

In Wolf's (1986) song,...

A COMPUTER PROGRAM

> OmniPage Pro 14 (Version 14) [Computer software]. (2003). Peabody, MA: Scansoft.

In-Text Citation: (OmniPage Pro, Version 14, 2003)

Scansoft's new software, OmniPage Pro, (2003) is reputed...

DISCUSSION LISTS

Discussion lists abound on the Internet. They range from groups of flirtatious teenagers to those with a serious academic purpose. Although virtually all of these discussion lists are based on e-mail, they do vary a bit. The most useful lists for academic research tend to be e-mail discussion lists. Newsgroups, or Usenet groups, are extremely popular among more-general Internet users. Various search engines can help you find these discussion groups on your topic. You can join or monitor the current discussion or, in some cases, search the archives for contributions that interest you. Google is a great search tool for newsgroups and includes an archive for many of them. *If there are no archives, don't include the citation in your references, because the information isn't recoverable.* However, you may still cite these in your essay as personal communications.

The method of citation varies slightly if it's a newsgroup, an online forum, or an electronic mailing list. For example, a newsgroup posting would be cited like this:

Hord, J. (2002, July 11). Why do pigeons lift one wing up in the air? [Msg 5].

Message archived at rec.pets.birds.pigeons

In-Text Citation: (Hord, 2002), or Hord asks (2002) . . .

Note that the citation includes the subject line of the message as the title and the message number of the "thread" (the particular discussion topic). The prefix for this newsgroup is *rec*, which indicates the list is hobby oriented.

Electronic mailing lists would be cited this way:

Cook, D. (2002, July 19). Grammar and the teaching of writing. Message posted

to the CompTalk electronic mailing list, archived at http://listserv.comptalk

.boisestate.edu

In-Text Citation: (Cook, 2002), or According to Cook (2002) . . .

E-MAIL

E-mail is not cited in the list of references. But you should cite e-mail in the text of your essay. It should look like this:

In-Text Citation: Michelle Payne (personal communication, January 4, 2012) argued that responding to personal writing . . .

BLOG

Notice in the example that the blogger uses a screen name.

Rizaro. (7 July, 2009). Anxiety and suicide. Message posted to *HelptoHealth.co.cc*

A Sample Paper in APA Style. To see a documented student research paper in APA style, go to Kersti Harter's ethnographic essay "Beyond 'Gaydar'" on pages 372–381 in Chapter 9. Professional essays formatted using APA style include "Why Bother?" by Michael Pollan in Chapter 6.

Using What You Have Learned

1. **Use sources effectively and control sources so they don't control you.** In college you'll be writing about subjects you know little about. As a novice researcher in these domains, this is a juggling act. You need to understand what you read, evaluate its relevance, assess its credibility, and then deploy it in your own work. That's a lot. This is one reason why it's so tempting to throw up your hands and simply "dump" information into your writing without thinking much about it. Now you have some tools to avoid this, and one of the most important is writing *while* you collect and read information. Assert control over information before you start a draft and you'll find the draft much easier to write.

2. **Practice summary, paraphrase, and quotation and apply these to your own work.** The Citation Project published a study recently that reviewed the research routines of college students writing research papers. One of their findings was that students almost never summarize their sources. What they do is something called "patchwriting," in which students essentially reproduce what they read, changing some words and maybe some grammatical structures. Patchwriting may not be plagiarism, but it doesn't involve much critical understanding of the source. Of the three—summary, paraphrasing, and quotation—summary may be the most academically useful because it requires a reader to understand and think about a source. When you can, always use summary as you're reading—and after you've read—something you want to use in your writing.

3. **Understand and identify plagiarism to avoid it in your own work.** It's no secret that plagiarism is a huge problem on college campuses. What is less well-known is that the vast majority of it is *unintentional*. If you ever have any questions about what constitutes plagiarism, return to this chapter and reread the definition on page 483. And if you ever have questions, don't hesitate to ask your instructor.

4. **Cite sources using MLA and APA documentation styles.** Citation can be mind-numbing. I find it so. But remember that it's not just about following rules but telling a story. When you cite an author, you are signaling where the ideas came from that changed the way you think. When you get these authors in conversation with each other, you are creating a scene that's probably never been staged before between these particular authors. And the best part? It's *your* story.

Complete
Additional Exercises
and Practice on
Chapter 12
in your MyLab

4

RE-INQUIRING

Revision is work. But it's also an opportunity for surprise. The trick is to see what you have written in ways you haven't seen it before.

Revision Strategies 13

Learning Objectives

In this chapter, you'll learn to

13.1 Understand the meaning—and value—of revision and apply it to your own work when appropriate.

13.2 Recognize five types of revision and apply most relevant strategies to a particular draft.

Why Revise?

One draft and done. That was Shauna's motto about revision, and when she said it nearly everyone in the class nodded. "I know I should revise but usually I write papers at the last minute so I don't really have the time," she added.

Surprisingly, one of the least discussed topics in writing classes is *time*. Perhaps no other factor influences a writer's success than having the time to do the work, and the academic culture doesn't provide a lot of time to write. You may have multiple writing assignments at the same time in different classes with deadlines that may land on the same day. Getting a single draft done on the due date seems like a major accomplishment, much less a revision. And in some classes (though not this one), it isn't even clear that instructors expect students to revise their work before they hand it in. Why do it?

The motive for revision is like a photographer's inclination to take more than one shot—both writer and photographer know not to trust their first look at something.

Before I make a pitch for revision, let's be clear on a few things. Revision isn't a virtue, nor is it always a necessary step in the writing process, and it also doesn't always occur at the end of the process. Revision is also more than "fixing" things. In Figure 13.1, you can see that "proofreading" and "editing," while very important parts of rewriting, may not involve revision. They are things that help burnish the surface of prose and make it easier to see the subject underneath it.

Revision involves "re-seeing." You started with a certain idea about what you were writing about and you realize, no, that's not it at all. Or perhaps when you began writing you had one inquiry question, but the draft tells you there's another, better question lurking there. "Deep revision" might lead you to start all over, or shift subjects entirely, or even switch

533

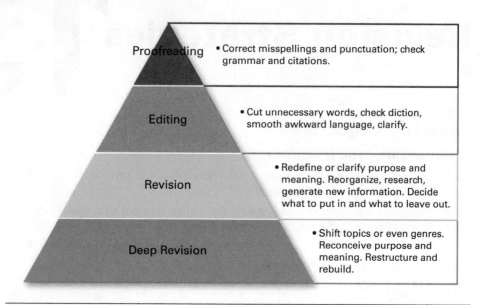

Figure 13.1 Four levels of rewriting

genres. Sometimes revision helps you to re-see not just the subject but the draft itself: It's apparent that the beginning is all wrong, or that there is essential information missing, or that the strongest part of the paper is something you can build on in the next draft.

One of the most powerful analogies for revision comes from photography, a word from Greek that means "light writing." Typically, most of us take only one picture of a subject, even in the digital age when it's cheap and easy to shoot multiple images. In other words: one draft and done. But what would happen if you took ten pictures of the same subject—say, an old wagon in a field—varying angle, distance, and time of day? Your first shot would likely be the most obvious image, the one everyone takes of the wagon. But by the fourth or fifth image, you're have to strain a bit to get the shot. Maybe you lie on the ground and shoot upwards, or you try a close-up of the wooden wheel in the evening when the light is thick. The more shots you take, the more likely it is that you will start seeing your subject in a way that you hadn't initially seen it. The wagon becomes infinitely more interesting. That's the payoff for re-seeing, for what we call *revision* when we talk about writing. The motive for revision is like a photographer's inclination to take more than one shot—both writer and photographer know not to trust their first look at something. They also know that the longer they look, the more likely it is that they will see something interesting.

Why revise? Not because it's necessary, or it's good for you, or someone expects you to. Revise because there's more to learn and think about. Revise because you really care about what you're saying and you want to say it well. Revise because it yields the unexpected—new insights, new perspectives, new ways of seeing.

Divorcing the Draft

Sometimes I ask my students to generalize about how they approach the writing process for most papers by asking them to divide a continuum into three parts corresponding to how much time, roughly, they devote to prewriting, drafting, and rewriting. Then I play "writing doctor" and diagnose their problems, particularly resistance to revision. Figure 13.2 depicts a typical example for most of my first-year writing students.

> Revision, as the name implies, is a *re-seeing* of the paper's topic and the writer's initial approach to it in the draft.

The writing process shown in Figure 13.2 obviously invests lots of time in the drafting stage and very little time in prewriting or rewriting. For most of my students, this means toiling over the first draft, starting and then starting over, carefully hammering every word into place. For students who use this process, strong resistance to revision is a typical symptom. It's easy to imagine why. If you invest all that time in the first draft, trying to make it as good as you can, you'll be either too exhausted to consider a revision, delusional about the paper's quality, or, most likely, so invested in the draft's approach to the topic that revision seems impossible or a waste of time.

There also is another pattern among resistant revisers. Students who tend to spend a relatively long time on the prewriting stage also struggle with revision. My theory is that some of these writers resist revision as a final stage in the process because *they have already practiced some revision at the beginning of the process.* We often talk about revision as occurring only after you've written a draft, which of course is a quite sensible idea. But the process of revision is an effort to *re-see* a subject, to circle it with questions, to view it from fresh angles; and many of the open-ended writing methods we've discussed in *The Curious Writer* certainly involve revision. Fastwriting, clustering, listing, and similar invention techniques all invite the writer to re-see. Armed with these discoveries, some writers may be able to write fairly strong first drafts.

What is essential, however, whether you revise at the beginning of the writing process or, as most writers do, after you craft the draft, is achieving some separation from what you initially thought, what you initially said, and how you said it. To revise well, writers must divorce the draft.

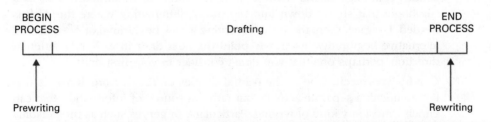

Figure 13.2 How some writers who resist revision typically divide their time among the three elements of the writing process: prewriting, drafting, and rewriting. The most time is devoted to writing the first draft, but not much time is given to prewriting and rewriting.

Strategies for Divorcing the Draft

You can do some things to make separation from your work easier, and spending less time on the first draft and more time on the revision process is one of them. But aside from writing fast drafts, what are other strategies for re-seeing a draft that already has a hold on you?

1. **Take some time.** Absolutely the best remedy for revision resistance is setting the draft aside for a week or more. Professional writers, in fact, may set a piece aside for several years and then return to it with a fresh, more critical perspective. Students simply don't have that luxury. But if you can take a week or a month—or even a day—the wait is almost always worth it.

2. **Attack the draft physically.** A cut-and-paste revision that reduces a draft to pieces is often enormously helpful, because you're no longer confronted with the familiar full draft, a version that may have cast a spell on you. By dismembering the draft, you can examine the smaller fragments more critically. How does each piece relate to the whole? Might there be alternative structures? What about gaps in information? (See Revision Strategy 13.18 later in this chapter for a useful cut-and-paste exercise.)

3. **Put it away.** Years ago I wrote a magazine article about alcoholism. It was about twenty-five pages long and it wasn't very good. I read and reread that draft, completely puzzled about how to rewrite it. One morning, I woke up and vowed I would read the draft just once more, then put it away in a drawer and start all over again, trusting that I would remember what was important. The result was much shorter and much better. In fact, I think it's the best essay I've ever written. Getting a troublesome draft out of sight—literally—may be the best way to find new ways to see it.

Watch
the Video on
**Revising After
Peer Review**
in your MyLab

4. **Ask readers to respond.** Bringing other people's eyes and minds to your work allows you to see your drafts through perspectives other than your own. Other people have a completely different relationship with your writing than you do. They will see what you don't. They easily achieve the critical distance that you are trying to cultivate when you revise.

5. **Write different leads.** The nonfiction writer John McPhee once talked about beginnings as the hardest thing to write. He described a lead as a "flashlight that shines down into the story," illuminating where the draft is headed. Imagine, then, the value of writing a new beginning, or even several alternative beginnings; each may point the next draft in a slightly different direction, perhaps one that you didn't consider in your first draft.

6. **Conduct research.** One of the central themes of *The Curious Writer* is that research isn't a separate activity, but rather a source of information that can enrich almost any kind of writing. Particularly in genres such as the personal essay, in which the writer's voice, perspective, and experience dominate the draft, listening to the voices and knowledge of others about a topic can deepen and shift the writer's thinking and perspectives.

7. **Read aloud.** I always ask students in workshop groups to read their drafts aloud to each other. I do this for several reasons, but the most important is the effect that *hearing* a draft has on a writer's relationship to it. In a sense, we often hear a draft in our heads as we compose it or reread it, but when we read the words aloud, the draft comes alive as something separate from the writer. As the writer listens to herself—or listens to someone else read her prose—she may cringe at an awkward sentence, suddenly notice a leap in logic, or recognize the need for an example. Try reading the work aloud to yourself, and the same thing may happen.

8. **Write in your journal.** One of the strategies you can use to divorce the draft is to return to your notebook and fastwrite to yourself about what you might do to improve the piece. You can do this by asking yourself questions about the draft and then—through writing—attempting to answer them. The method can help you see a new idea that may become key to the structure of your next draft. Too often we see the journal exclusively as a prewriting tool, but it can be useful throughout the writing process, particularly when you need to think to yourself about ways to solve a problem in revision.

Later in this chapter, we'll build on some of these basic strategies, with specific revision methods that may work with particular kinds of writing and with drafts that have particular problems. All of these methods encourage a separation between the writer and his or her draft, or rely on that critical distance to be effective.

Five Categories of Revision

The following kinds of writers are typically ones who most need to revise:

1. Writers of fast drafts
2. Writers who compose short drafts
3. Writers who indulge in creative, but not critical, thinking
4. Writers who rarely go past their initial way of seeing things
5. Writers who have a hard time imagining a reader other than themselves
6. Writers who rely on limited sources of information
7. Writers who still aren't sure what they're trying to say
8. Writers who haven't found their own way of saying what they want to say
9. Writers who haven't delivered on their promises
10. Writers who think their draft is "perfect"

13.2
Recognize five types of revision and apply most relevant strategies to a particular draft.

These are the usual suspects for revision, but there are many more. In general, if you think there's more to think about, more to learn, more to say, and better ways to say it, then revision is the route to surprise and discovery. Most writers agree that rewriting is a good idea, but where should they start?

Problems in drafts vary enormously. But the diagnosis tends to involve concerns in five general areas: purpose, meaning, information, structure, and clarity and style. Here are some typical reader responses to drafts with each kind of problem:

1. **Problems with Purpose**
   - "I don't know why the writer is writing this paper."
   - "The beginning of the essay seems to be about one thing, and the rest of it is about several others."
   - "I think there are about three different topics in the draft. Which one do you want to write about?"
   - "So what?"

2. **Problems with Meaning**
   - "I can't tell what the writer is trying to say in the draft."
   - "There doesn't seem to be a point behind all of this."
   - "I think there's a main idea, but there isn't much information on it."
   - "I thought the thesis was saying something pretty obvious."

3. **Problems with Information**
   - "Parts of the draft seemed really pretty vague or general."
   - "I couldn't really *see* what you were talking about."
   - "It seemed like you needed some more facts to back up your point."
   - "It needs more detail."

4. **Problems with Structure**
   - "I couldn't quite follow your thinking in the last few pages."
   - "I was confused about when this happened."
   - "I understood your point, but I couldn't figure out what this part had to do with it."
   - "The draft doesn't really flow very well."

5. **Problems with Clarity and Style**
   - "This seems a little choppy."
   - "You need to explain this better. I couldn't quite follow what you were saying in this paragraph."
   - "This sentence seems really awkward to me."
   - "This doesn't have a strong voice."

Problems with Purpose

A draft that answers the *So what?* question is a draft with a purpose. Often enough, however, writers' intentions aren't all that clear to readers, so they don't have a strong reason to keep reading.

It's a little like riding a tandem bike. The writer sits up front and steers while the reader occupies the seat behind, obligated to pedal but with no control over where the bike goes. As soon as the reader senses that the writer isn't steering anywhere in particular, then the reader will get off the bike. Why do all that pedaling if the bike seems to be going nowhere?

Frequently, when you begin writing about something, you don't have any idea where you're headed; that's exactly *why* you're writing about the subject in the first place. When we write such discovery drafts, revision often begins by looking for clues about your purpose. What you learn then becomes a key organizing principle for the next draft, for trying to clarify this purpose for your readers. The first question, therefore, is one writers must answer for themselves: "Why am I writing this?" Of course, if it's an assignment, it may be hard to get past the easy answer—"Because I have to"—but if the work is going to be any good, there must be a better answer than that. Whether your topic is open or assigned, you have to find your own reason to write about it, and what you discover becomes an answer to your bike partner's nagging question, yelled into the wind from the seat behind you: "If I'm going to pedal this hard, you better let me know where we're going."

In general, writers' motives behind writing often involve more than one of these following four purposes.

1. **To explore.** One way to handle complicated questions is to approach the answers in an open-ended way; the writer writes to discover what he thinks or how he feels and then reports to the reader on these discoveries.

2. **To explain.** Much of the writing we encounter in daily life is meant simply to provide us with information: This is how the coffeemaker works, or this is the best way to prepare for a trip to New Zealand. Expository writing frequently explains and describes.

3. **To evaluate.** In a sense, all writing is evaluative, because it involves making judgments. For instance, when you explain how to plan a New Zealand vacation, you're making judgments about where to go. But when the explicit purpose is to present a judgment about something, the writer encourages readers to see the world the way the writer does. He or she may want the reader to think or behave a certain way: It makes sense to abolish pennies because they're more trouble than they're worth, or you should vote for the bond issue because it's the best way to save the foothills.

4. **To reflect.** Less frequently, we write to stand back from what we're writing about and consider *how* we're thinking about the subject, the methods we're using to write about it, and what we might learn from this writing situation that might apply to others.

Revision Strategy 13.1: The Motive Statement

It may help to begin a revision by attempting to determine your *primary motive* for the next draft. Do you want to explore your topic, explain something to your readers, offer a persuasive judgment, or step back and reflect on what you're saying or how you're saying it? The genre of writing has a great deal to do with this (see the following table). If you're writing a personal essay, your purpose is likely to be exploratory. If you're writing a review, a proposal, a critical essay, or an argument essay, it's likely that your primary motive is to evaluate. One way, then, to get some basic guidance for the next draft is to carefully craft the second half of the following sentence: *My primary motive in writing this paper is to explore/ evaluate/explain/reflect about* _____

GENRE	PRIMARY MOTIVE
Personal essay	Explore
Profile	Explore or explain
Review	Evaluate
Proposal	Evaluate
Argument	Evaluate
Critical essay	Evaluate
Ethnographic essay	Explore or evaluate
Research essay	Explore or evaluate
Reflective essay	Reflect

Of course, any one essay may involve all four motives, but for the purpose of this exercise, choose your *main* purpose in writing the essay. Composing the second half of the sentence above may not be so easy, because it challenges you to limit your subject. For instance, the following is far too ambitious for, say, a five-page essay: *My main motive in writing this paper is to evaluate the steps taken to deal with terrorism and judge whether they're adequate.* That's simply too big a subject for a brief persuasive paper. This is more reasonable: *My main motive in writing this paper is to evaluate passenger screening procedures in Europe and decide whether they're better than those in the United States.*

Because largely exploratory pieces often are motivated by questions, a writer of a personal essay might compose the following sentence: *My main motive in writing this essay is to explore why I felt relieved when my father died.*

After you craft your motive sentence, put it on a piece of paper or an index card and post it where you can see it as you revise the draft. Periodically ask yourself, *What does this paragraph or this section of the draft have to do with my main motive?* The answer will help you decide what to cut and what needs more development in the next draft. Remember, the essay should be organized around this motive from beginning to end.

Revision Strategy 13.2: What Do You Want to Know About What You Learned?

Because inquiry-based writing is usually driven by questions rather than answers, one way to discover your purpose in a sketch or draft is to generate a list of questions it raises for you. Of course, you hope that one of them might be behind your

One Student's Response

Julia's Draft

What do I understand about this topic now that I didn't understand before I started writing about it?

    After writing this essay, I understand more clearly that there's a relationship between a girl's eating disorders and how her father treats her as a child.

LIST OF QUESTIONS

- Why the father and not the mother?
- What is it about father/daughter relationships that make them so vulnerable to feminine body images?
- Is the father's influence on a girl's body image greater at certain ages or stages in her life?
- How can a father be more informed about his impact on a daughter's body image?

purpose in the next draft. Try the following steps with a draft that needs a stronger sense of purpose.

1. Choose a draft or sketch you'd like to revise, and reread it.

2. On the back of the manuscript, craft an answer to the following question: *What do I understand about this topic now that I didn't understand before I started writing about it?*

3. Next, if you can, build a list of questions—perhaps new ones—that this topic still raises for you. Make this list as long as you can, and don't censor yourself (see "One Student's Response" above).

4. Choose one or more of the questions as a prompt for a fastwrite. Follow your writing to see where it leads and what it might suggest about new directions for the revision.

5. If you can't think of any questions, or find you didn't learn much from writing about the topic (step 2), you may have several options. One is to abandon the draft altogether. Is it possible that this topic simply doesn't interest you anymore? If abandoning the draft isn't possible, then you need to find a new angle. Try Revision Strategy 13.3.

Revision Strategy 13.3: Finding the Focusing Question

The best topics, and the most difficult to write about, are those that raise questions for you. In a sketch or first draft, you may not know what these questions are. But if your subsequent drafts are going to be purposeful and focused, then discovering the main question behind your essay is essential. This is particularly important in essays that are research based, because the drafts are longer and you're often trying to manage a lot of information. This revision strategy works best when it's a class activity.

1. Begin by simply putting your essay topic on the top of a large piece of paper such as newsprint or butcher paper. If yours is a research topic—say, Alzheimer's disease—jot that down. Post your paper on the classroom wall.

2. Spend a few minutes writing a few sentences explaining why you chose to write about this topic in the first place.

3. Make a quick list of everything you *already know* (if anything) about your topic—for instance, surprising facts or statistics, the extent of the problem, important people or institutions involved, key schools of thought, common misconceptions, familiar clichés that apply to the topic, observations you've made, important trends, and typical perspectives. Spend about five minutes on this.

4. Now spend fifteen or twenty minutes brainstorming a list of questions about your topic that you'd love to learn the answers to. Make this list as long as possible.

5. As you look around the room, you'll see a gallery of topics and questions on the walls. You can help each other. Circulate around the room and do two things: Add a question that you're interested in about a particular topic, and check the question (yours or someone else's) that seems most interesting.

When you return to your own newsprint or butcher paper, it should be covered with questions. How will you decide which of them might provide the best focus for the next draft? What you're going to see are mostly factual questions. Generally, there are two kinds of questions: factual questions and questions that attempt to *do* something with information. When we know little about a topic, it's natural to begin with fact or definition questions: What is known about this? What *is* it? Look at your list and identify which factual questions you might want to pursue. Ultimately, though, for a research essay you'll need to use what you're learning about your topic and frame a *doing* question, a question that will purposefully *use* the information you've gathered. These include the following:

- What should be done about this? (policy question)
- What is the value of this? (value question)
- What might this mean? (interpretation question)
- What is the relationship? (relationship question)
- Might this be true? (hypothesis question)

If you can, try to draft a question about your topic that might fit into one of these doing question categories. Because relationship questions are particularly powerful guides to research, the next exercise looks more closely at how your topic might use cause-effect or comparison-contrast to analyze your topic.

Revision Strategy 13.4: What's the Relationship?

One of the more common purposes for all kinds of essays is to explore a relationship between two or more things. We see this in research all the time. What's the relationship between AIDS and IV drug use in China? What's the relationship between gender and styles of collaboration in the workplace? What's the social class relationship between Huck and Tom in *The Adventures of Huckleberry Finn*?

One way, then, to clarify your purpose in revision is to try to identify the relationship that may be at the heart of your inquiry. Relationships between things can be described in a couple different ways.

- *Cause and effect*. What is the relationship between my father's comments about my looks and my eating disorder when I was a teenager? What is the relationship between the second Iraqi war and destabilization in Saudi Arabia? What is the relationship between the decline of the Brazilian rain forest and the extinction of the native eagles? What is the relationship between my moving to Idaho and the failure of my relationship with Kevin?

- *Compare and contrast*. How is jealousy distinguished from envy? How might writing instruction in high school be distinguished from writing instruction in college? What are the differences and similarities between my experiences at the Rolling Stones concert last month and my experiences at the Stones concert fifteen years ago?

Review your sketch or draft to determine whether what you're really trying to write about is the relationship between two (or more) things. In your journal, try to state this relationship in sentences similar to those listed here. With this knowledge, return to the draft and revise from beginning to end with this purpose in mind. What do you need to add to the next draft to both clarify and develop the relationship you're focusing on? What should you cut that is irrelevant to that focus?

Problems with Meaning

Fundamentally, most of us write something in an attempt to say something to someone else. The note my wife, Karen, left for me yesterday said it in a sentence: "Bruce—could you pick up some virgin olive oil and a loaf of bread?" I had no trouble deciphering the meaning of this note. But it isn't always that easy. Certain poems, for example, may be incredibly ambiguous texts, and readers may puzzle over them for hours, coming up with a range of plausible interpretations of meaning. (See Figure 13.3.)

Where Does Meaning Come From?

Depending on the writing situation, you may know what you want to say from the start or you may *discover* what you think as you write and research. Inquiry-based projects usually emphasize discovery, while more-conventional argument

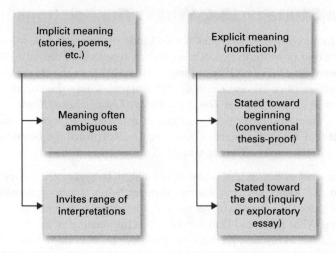

Figure 13.3 Depending on the genre, writers say it straight or tell it slant. In short stories, for example, the writers' ideas may be ambiguous, inviting interpretation. Nonfiction genres—the kind you will most often write in college and beyond—usually avoid ambiguity. Writers say what they mean as clearly and as persuasively as they can.

papers may rely on arriving at a thesis earlier in the process. It's something like the difference between sledding with a saucer or a flexible flyer. The saucer is likely to veer off course, and you might find yourself somewhere unexpected, yet interesting.

Terms to Describe Dominant Meaning

- Thesis
- Main point
- Theme
- Controlling idea
- Central claim or assertion

No matter what you think about a topic when you start writing—even when you begin with a thesis to which you're committed—you can still change your mind. You *should* change your mind if the evidence you've gathered leads you away from your original idea. Unfortunately, writers of thesis-driven papers and other deductive forms are far more resistant to any change in their thinking. In some writing situations—say, essay exams—this isn't a problem. But it's often important in academic writing, including arguments, to always be open to new insight.

Ideas about what we want to say on a writing topic grow from the following:

1. **Thesis.** This is a term most of us know from school writing, and it's most often associated with types of writing that work deductively from a main idea. Here's a sample thesis:

   The U.S. Securities and Exchange Commission is incapable of regulating an increasingly complex banking system.

2. **Theory.** We have strong hunches about how things work all the time, but we're not certain we're right. We test our theories and report on the accuracy of our hunches. Here's an example of a theory:

   Certain people just "don't have a head" for math.

3. **Question.** In a question-driven process, the emphasis is on discovery, and you might work more inductively. You see or experience something that makes you wonder. Here's a question that led a writer to ideas about girls, advertising, and sexuality.

   Why does my ten-year-old want to dress like a hooker?

The revision strategies that follow assume either that you've got a tentative thesis and want to refine it or that you're still working on discovering what you want to say.

Methods for Discovering Your Thesis

Use the following strategies if you're not quite sure whether you know what you're trying to say in a sketch or draft. How can you discover clues about your main point or meaning in what you've already written?

Revision Strategy 13.5: Find the "Instructive Line"

It may seem odd to think of reading your own drafts for clues about what you mean. After all, your writing is a product of your own mind. But often a draft can reveal to us what we didn't know we knew—an idea that surfaces unexpectedly, a question that we keep asking, or a moment in a narrative that seems surprisingly significant. Part of the challenge is to recognize these clues to your own meanings and understand what they suggest about the revision.

This isn't always easy, which is one reason it's often so helpful to share your writing with other readers; they may see the clues that we miss. However, this revision strategy depends on reading your own drafts more systematically for clues about what your point might be. What do you say in this draft that might suggest what you really want to say in the next one?

1. **Find the "instructive line."** Every draft is made up of many sentences. But which of these is *the most important sentence or passage*? What do I mean by *important*? Which line or passage points to a larger idea, theme, or feeling that seems to rise above much of the draft and illuminates the

significance or relevance of many other lines and passages? The writer Donald Murray calls this the "instructive line," the sentence that seems to point upward toward the meaning of what you've set down. Underline the instructive line or passage in your draft. It may be subtle, only hinting at larger ideas or feelings, or quite explicitly stated. In a narrative essay, the instructive line might be a moment of stepping back to reflect: "As I look back on this now, I understand that..." In a review or persuasive essay, it might be an assertion of some kind: "American moviegoers are seduced by the 'twist' at the end of a film, and learn to expect it."

2. **Follow the thread of meaning.** If the instructive line is a ball of string, tightly packed with coils of meaning that aren't readily apparent, then to get any guidance for revision you need to try to unravel it. At the top of a journal page, write the line or passage you selected in your draft as most important. Use it as a prompt for five minutes of exploratory writing, perhaps beginning with the following seed sentence: I think/feel this is true because... and also because... and also... and also...

3. **Compose a thesis.** Reread your fastwriting in the preceding step and, keeping your original passage in mind, craft a single sentence that best captures the most important idea or feeling you'd like to bring into the next draft. For example, *Because of the expectation, encouraged by Hollywood, that every good movie has a surprise ending, American moviegoers often find even superior foreign films a disappointment.*

4. **Post it.** Put this thesis on the wall above your computer, or use a Post-it note and place the thesis on your computer screen. Revise with the thesis in mind, from beginning to end. Add information that will *illustrate, extend, exemplify, complicate, clarify, support, show, provide background*, or *prove* the thesis. Cut information from the draft that does none of these things.

Revision Strategy 13.6: Looping Toward a Thesis

I've argued throughout *The Curious Writer* for a dialectical approach to writing: moving back and forth between creative and critical modes of thinking, from your observations of and your ideas about, from generating and judging, from specifics and generalities. This is how writers can make meaning. The approach can also be used as a revision strategy, this time in a technique called *loop writing*. When you loop write, you move back and forth dialectically between both modes of thought—opening things up and then trying to pin them down. I imagine that this looks like an hourglass. (See Revision Strategy 13.7 for a variation on loop writing.)

1. Reread the draft quickly, and then turn it upside down on your desk. You won't look at it again but will trust that you'll remember what's important.

2. **Narrative of thought.** Begin a three-minute fastwrite on the draft, in which you tell yourself the story of your thinking about the essay. When you first

started writing it, what did you think you were writing about, and then what, and then...? Try to focus on your ideas about what you were trying to say and how it evolved.

3. **Summary.** Sum up what you said in your fastwrite by answering the following question in a sentence: *What seems to be the most important thing I've finally come to understand about my topic?*

4. **Examples.** Begin another three-minute fastwrite. Focus on scenes, situations, case studies, moments, people, conversations, observations, and so on that stand out for you as you think about the draft. Think especially of specifics that come to mind that led to the understanding of your topic that you stated in the preceding step. Some of this information may be in the draft, but some may *not* yet be in the draft.

5. **Summary.** Finish by restating the main point you want to make in the next draft. Begin the revision by thinking about a lead or introduction that dramatizes this point. Consider a suggestive scene, case study, finding, profile, description, comparison, anecdote, conversation, situation, or observation that points the essay toward your main idea (see the "Inquiring into the Details: Types of Leads" box on page 561). For example, if your point is that your university's program to help second-language learners is inadequate, you could begin the next draft by telling the story of Maria, an immigrant from Guatemala who was a victim of poor placement in a composition course that she was virtually guaranteed to fail. Follow this lead into the draft, always keeping your main point or thesis in mind.

Revision Strategy 13.7: Reclaiming Your Topic

When you do a lot of research on your topic, you may reach a point when you feel awash in information. It's easy at such moments to feel as if you're losing control of your topic—besieged by the voices of experts, a torrent of statistics and facts, and competing perspectives. Your success in writing the paper depends on making it your own again, gaining control over the information for your own purposes, in the service of your own questions or arguments. This revision strategy, a variation of Revision Strategy 13.6, should help you gain control of the material you collected for a research-based inquiry project.

1. Spend ten or fifteen minutes reviewing all of the notes you've taken and skimming key articles or passages from books. Glance at your most important sources. If you have a rough draft, reread it. Let your head swim with information.

2. Now clear your desk of everything but your journal. Remove all your notes and materials. If you have a rough draft, put it in the drawer.

3. Now fastwrite about your topic for seven full minutes. Tell the story of how your thinking about the topic has evolved. When you began, what did you

think? What were your initial assumptions or preconceptions? Then what happened, and what happened after that? Keep your pen moving.

4. Skip a few lines in your notebook, and write *Moments, Stories, People, and Scenes*. Now fastwrite for another seven minutes, this time focusing more on specific case studies, situations, people, experiences, observations, facts, and so on that stand out in your mind from the research you've done so far, or perhaps from your own experience with the topic.

5. Skip a few more lines. For another seven minutes, write a dialogue between you and someone else about your topic. Choose someone who you think is typical of the audience you're writing for. If it helps, think of someone specific—an instructor, a fellow student, a friend. Don't plan the dialogue. Just begin with the question most commonly asked about your topic, and take the conversation from there, writing both parts of the dialogue.

6. Finally, skip a few more lines and write this two-word question in your notebook: *So what?* Now spend a few minutes trying to summarize the most important thing you think your readers should understand about your topic, based on what you've learned so far. Distill this into a sentence or two.

As you work your way to the last step, you're reviewing what you've learned about your topic without being tyrannized by the many voices, perspectives, and facts in the research you've collected. The final step, step 6, leads you toward a thesis statement. In the revision, keep this in mind as you reopen your notes, reread your sources, and check on facts. Remember in the rewrite to put all of this information in the service of this main idea—as examples or illustrations, necessary background, evidence or support, counterexamples, and ways of qualifying or extending your main point.

Revision Strategy 13.8: Believing and Doubting

In persuasive writing such as the argument, review, proposal, or research paper, we often feel that a thesis involves picking sides—"the play was good" or "the play was bad," "the novel was boring" or "the novel was fun to read." Instead of *either/or*, consider *both/and*. This might bring you to a more truthful, more sophisticated understanding of your subject, which rarely is either all bad or all good. One way to do this is to play Peter Elbow's doubting game and believing game.

1. Set aside ten to twelve minutes for two episodes of fastwriting in your journal or on the computer. First, spend a full five minutes playing the "believing game" (see the following prompts), exploring the merits of your subject even if (and especially if) you don't think it has any. Then switch to the "doubting game." Write fast for another five minutes using a skeptical mind.

THE BELIEVING GAME	THE DOUBTING GAME
Give the author, performer, text, or performance the benefit of the doubt. Suspend criticism.	Adopt a critical stance. Look for holes, weaknesses, omissions, problems.
1. What seems true or truthful about what is said, shown, or argued?	1. What seems unbelievable or untrue?
2. How does it confirm your own experiences or observations of the same things?	2. What does it fail to consider or consider inadequately?
3. What did you like or agree with?	3. Where is the evidence missing or in-sufficient, or where do the elements not work together effectively?
4. Where is it strongest, most compel-ling, most persuasive?	4. How does it fail to meet your criteria for good in this category of thing?
5. How does it satisfy your criteria for being good, useful, convincing, or moving?	5. Where is it the least compelling or persuasive? Why?

2. From this work in your notebook, try to construct a sentence—a thesis—that is more than a simple statement of the worth or worthlessness of the thing you're evaluating, but an expression of *both* its strengths and weaknesses: *Although _____ succeeds (or fails) in _____, it mostly _____.* For example: *Although reality television presents viewers with an often interesting glimpse into how ordinary people handle their fifteen minutes of celebrity, it mostly exaggerates life by creating drama where there often is none.*

Methods for Refining Your Thesis

You may emerge from writing a draft with a pretty clear sense of what you want to say in the next one. But does this idea seem a little obvious or perhaps too general? Does it fail to adequately express what you really feel and think? Use one or more of the following revision strategies to refine a thesis, theme, or controlling idea.

Revision Strategy 13.9: Questions as Knives

Imagine that your initial feeling, thesis, or main point is like an onion (see Figure 13.4). Ideas, like onions, have layers, and to get closer to their hearts you need to cut through the most obvious outer layers to reveal what is less obvious, probably more specific, and almost certainly more interesting. Questions are to ideas as knives are to onions: They help you slice past your initial impressions. The most important question—the sharpest knife in the drawer—is simply *Why? Why* was the Orwell es-say interesting? *Why* do you hate foreign films? *Why* should the university do more for second-language speakers? *Why* did you feel a sense of loss when the old corn-field was paved over for the mall?

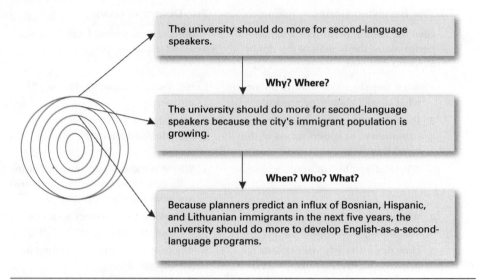

The university should do more for second-language speakers.

Why? Where?

The university should do more for second-language speakers because the city's immigrant population is growing.

When? Who? What?

Because planners predict an influx of Bosnian, Hispanic, and Lithuanian immigrants in the next five years, the university should do more to develop English-as-a-second-language programs.

Figure 13.4   Why? Where? When? Who? and What? Using questions to narrow the focus of a thesis is like using a knife to cut into the heart of an onion.

Why may be the sharpest knife in the drawer, but there are other *W* questions with keen blades, too, including *What?, Where?, When?,* and *Who?* In Figure 13.4 you can see how these questions can cut a broad thesis down to size. The result is a much more specific, more interesting controlling idea for the next draft.

1. Subject your tentative thesis to the same kind of narrowing. Write your theme, thesis, or main point as a single sentence in your notebook.
2. Slice it with questions and restate it each time.
3. Continue this until your point is appropriately sliced; that is, when you feel that you've gone beyond the obvious and stated what you think or feel in a more specific and interesting way.

As before, rewrite the next draft with this new thesis in mind, reorganizing the essay around it from beginning to end. Add new information that supports the idea, provides the necessary background, offers opposing views, or extends it. Cut information that no longer seems relevant to the thesis.

Revision Strategy 13.10: Qualifying Your Claim

In your research you discovered that, while 90 percent of Americans think that their fellow citizens are too "fat," only 39 percent would describe themselves that way. This evidence leads you to make the following claim: *Although Americans agree that obesity is a national problem, their response is typical: It's somebody else's problem—an attitude that will cripple efforts to promote healthier lifestyles.* This seems like a logical assertion if the evidence is reliable. But if you're going to try to build an argument around it, a claim should be rigorously examined. Toulmin's approach to analyzing arguments provides a method for doing this.

1. Toulmin observes that sometimes a claim should be *qualified* to be more accurate and persuasive. The initial question is simple: *Is what you're asserting always or universally true?* Essentially, you're being challenged to examine your certainty about what you're saying. This might lead you to add words or phrases to it that acknowledge your sense of certainty: *sometimes, always, mostly, in this case, based on available evidence*, and so on. In this case, the claim is already qualified by specifying that it is limited to Americans, but it is also based on evidence from a single source. The claim, therefore, might be qualified to say this: *Although one survey suggests that Americans agree that obesity is a national problem, their response is typical: It's somebody else's problem—an attitude that will cripple efforts to promote healthier lifestyles.*

2. Imagining how your claim might be rebutted is another way to strengthen it. How might someone take issue with your thesis? What might be the exceptions to what you're saying is true? For example, might someone object to the assertion that Americans "typically" respond by putting their heads in the sand when personally confronted with problems? You must decide, then, whether this clever aside in your claim is something you're prepared to support. If not, cut it.

Problems with Information

Writers who've spent enough time generating or collecting information about their topics can work from abundance rather than scarcity. This is an enormous advantage, because the ability to throw stuff away means you can be selective about what you use, and the result is a more focused draft. But as we revise, our purpose and point might shift, and we may find ourselves in the unhappy position of working from scarcity again. Most of our research, observation, or fastwriting was relevant to the triggering subject in the initial sketch or draft, not to the generated subject we decide is the better direction for the next draft. In some cases, this might require that you research the new topic or return to the generating activities of listing, fastwriting, clustering, and so on that will help provide information for the next draft.

More often, however, writers don't have to begin from scratch in revision. Frequently, a shift in the focus or refining a thesis in a first draft just means emphasizing different information or perhaps filling in gaps in later drafts. The strategies that follow will help you solve this problem.

Revision Strategy 13.11: Explode a Moment

The success of personal essays that rely on narratives frequently depends on how well the writer renders an important scene, situation, moment, or description. When you're telling a story from experience, not all parts of the story are equally important. As always, emphasis in a narrative depends on the writer's purpose in the essay. For example, Matt's essay on the irony of the slow poisoning of Butte, Montana, his hometown, by a copper mine that once gave the city life would emphasize those parts of the story that best highlight that irony. Or a description of the agonizing death of the snow geese that unwittingly landed on the acid pond—their white beauty set against the deadly dark water—might be an important scene in Matt's next draft; it nicely portrays life and death, beauty and ugliness in much the same way the town and the mine might be contrasted. Matt should "explode that moment" because it's an important part of the story he's trying to tell about his Montana hometown.

If you're trying to revise a draft that relies on narratives, this revision strategy will help you first identify moments, scenes, or descriptions that might be important in the next draft, and then develop these as more-important parts of your story.

1. Choose a draft that involves a story or stories.

2. Make a list in your journal of the moments (for example, scenes, situations, and turning points) that stand out in the narrative.

3. Circle one that you think is most important to your purpose in the essay. It could be the situation that is most telling, a dramatic turning point, the moment of a key discovery that is central to what you're trying to say, or a scene that illustrates the dilemma or raises the question you're exploring in the draft.

4. Name that moment at the top of a blank journal page (for example, *the snow geese on the acid pond*).

5. Now put yourself back into that moment and fastwrite about it for seven full minutes. Make sure that you write with as much detail as possible, *drawing on all your senses*. Write in the present tense if it helps.

6. Use this same method with other moments in the narrative that might deserve more emphasis in the next draft. Remember that real time means little in writing. An experience that took seven seconds can easily take up three pages of writing if it's detailed enough. Rewrite and incorporate the best of the new information in the next draft.

Revision Strategy 13.12: Beyond Examples

When we add information to a draft, we normally think of adding examples. If you're writing a research essay on living with a sibling who suffers from Down syndrome, you might mention that your brother typically tries to avoid certain cognitive challenges. Members of your workshop group wonder, "Well, what kind of challenges?" In revision, you add an example or two from your own experience, to clarify what you mean. This is, of course, a helpful strategy; examples of what you mean by an assertion are a kind of evidence that helps readers more fully understand your work. But also consider other types of information it might be helpful to add to the next draft. Use the following list to review your draft for additions you might not have thought of for revision.

- **Presenting counterarguments.** Typically, persuasive essays include information that represents an opposing view. Say you're arguing that beyond "avoidance" behaviors, there really aren't personality traits that can be attributed to most people with Down syndrome. You include a summary of a study that says otherwise. Why? Because it provides readers with a better understanding of the debate, and enhances the writer's ethos because you appear fair.

- **Providing background.** When you drop in on a conversation between two friends, you initially may be clueless about the subject. Naturally, you ask questions: "Who are you guys talking about? When did this happen? What did she say?" Answers to these questions provide a context that allows you to understand what is being said and to participate in the conversation. Such background information is often essential in written communication, too. In a personal essay, readers may want to know when and where the event occurred or the relationship between the narrator and a character. In a critical essay, it might be necessary to provide background on the short story because readers may not have read it. In a research essay, it's often useful to provide background information about what has already been said on the topic and the research question.

- **Establishing significance.** Let's say you're writing about the problem of obesity in America, something that most of us are generally aware of these days. But the significance of the problem really strikes home when you add information from research suggesting that 30 percent of American adults are overweight, up from 23 percent just six years ago. It is even more important to establish the significance of a problem about which there is little awareness or consensus. For example, most people don't know that America's national park system is crumbling and in disrepair. Your essay on the problem needs to provide readers with information that establishes the significance of the problem. In a profile, readers need to have a reason to be interested in someone—perhaps your profile subject represents a particular group of people of interest or concern.

- **Giving it a face.** One of the best ways to make an otherwise abstract issue or problem come to life is to show what it means to an individual person. We can't fully appreciate the social impact of deforestation in Brazil without being introduced to someone such as Chico Mendes, a forest defender who was murdered for his activism. Obesity might be an abstract problem until we meet Carl, a 500-pound 22-year-old who is "suffocating in his own fat." Add case studies, anecdotes, profiles, and descriptions that put people on the page, to make your essay more interesting and persuasive.

- **Defining it.** If you're writing about a subject your readers know little about, you'll likely use concepts or terms that readers will want you to define.

What exactly do you mean, for example, when you say that the Internet is vulnerable to cyberterror? What exactly is cyberterror anyway? In your personal essay on your troubled relationship with your mother, what do you mean when you call her a narcissist? Frequently, your workshop group will alert you to things in the draft that need defining, but also go through your own draft and ask yourself, *Will my readers know what I mean?*

Revision Strategy 13.13: Research

Too often, research is ignored as a revision strategy. We may do research for the first draft of a paper or essay but never return to the library or search the web to fill in gaps, answer new questions, or refine the focus of a rewrite. That's crazy, particularly because well-researched information can strengthen a draft of any kind. That has been one of the themes of *The Curious Writer* since the beginning of the book: Research is not a separate activity reserved only for the research paper, but a rich source of information for any type of writing. Try some of these strategies:

1. For quick facts, visit refdesk.com. This enormously useful website is the fastest way to find out the exact height of the Great Wall of China or the number of young women suffering from eating disorders in America today.

2. Return to the *Library of Congress Subject Headings*, the reference mentioned in Chapter 11 that will help you pinpoint the language you should use to search library databases on your topic. Particularly if the focus of your next draft is shifting, you'll need some fresh information to fill in the gaps. The *LCSH* will help you find more of it, more quickly.

3. To maximize web coverage, launch a search on at least three different search engines (for example, Google, Bing, and Yahoo!), but this time search using terms or phrases from your draft that will lead you to more-specific information that will fill gaps in the draft.

4. Interview someone relevant to your topic. (See Chapter 11.)

5. To ferret out some new sources on your topic, search library databases under author rather than keyword. Focus on authors that you know have something to say on your topic.

6. Return to any of the steps in Chapter 11 that involve developing deeper knowledge about your topic.

Revision Strategy 13.14: Backing Up Your Assumptions

Targeted research is particularly important when you're making an argument. In addition to providing evidence that is relevant to your thesis, frequently an argument rests on the assumptions behind that assertion. Stephen Toulmin calls these assumptions *warrants*. A warrant bridges the evidence with a related claim by revealing the assumptions on which it rests. A warrant essentially answers this question: What do you have to believe is true to believe a claim? For example, suppose your claim is the following: *Reading a lot makes people better writers.* And here's the evidence supporting the claim: *English majors read a lot and they are also strong writers.* What do you need to assume is true to believe this assertion? Lots. One particularly key warrant is that what's true of English majors is true of all "people." Warrants are often implicit, so it can be really helpful to tease them out into the open and see if they're sound.

1. Write your claim on the top of a journal page, and then list the assumptions or warrants on which it seems to rest. For example, the claim about obesity includes an assumption that most Americans equate the words *obesity* and *fat*. Also, there's an assumption that public attitudes—particularly the view that there is a problem but it isn't my problem—hinder progress on public policy.

2. Which of the warrants behind your claim would be stronger if there were "backing" or evidence to support them? This will give you new direction for research. It might strengthen the argument on the obesity problem, for example, to draw on evidence from the civil rights struggle. Is there any evidence that attitudes toward personal responsibility for racism lagged behind acknowledgment of racial inequality as a national problem? Was progress finally made when this gap narrowed?

Problems with Structure

When it's working, the structure of a piece of writing is nearly invisible. Readers don't notice how the writer is guiding them from one piece of information to the next. When structure is a problem, the writer asks readers to walk out on a shaky bridge and trust that it will help them get to the other side, but the walkers can think of little else but the shakiness of the bridge. Some professional writers, such as John McPhee, obsess about structure, and for good reason; when you're working with a tremendous amount of information, as McPhee often does in his research-based essays, it helps to have a clear idea about how you'll use it.

It's helpful to distinguish two basic structures for writing. One typically organizes the information of experience, and one organizes our thinking so that it's clear and convincing. Typically, we use narrative, and especially chronology, to organize our experiences, though how we handle time can vary considerably. Writing that presents information based on the writer's reasoning—perhaps making an argument or reporting on an experiment—is logically structured. The most common example is the thesis-example, or thesis-proof, paper. Much formal academic writing relies on logical structures that use deduction or induction.

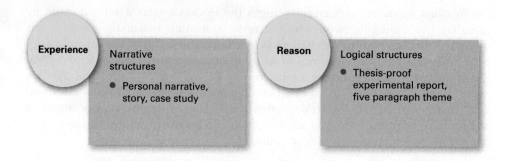

And yet some kinds of writing, such as the researched essay or ethnography, may *combine* both patterns, showing how the writer reasoned through to the meaning of an experience, observation, reading, and so on. These essays tell a "narrative of thought."

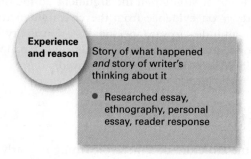

Formal Academic Structures

In some academic writing, the structure is prescribed. Scientific papers often have sections—Introduction, Methodology, Results, Discussion—but within those sections writers must organize their material. Certain writing assignments may also require you to organize your information in a certain way. The most common of these is the thesis/support structure. In such essays, you typically establish your thesis in the first paragraph, spend the body of the paper assembling evidence that supports the thesis, and conclude the essay with a summary that restates the thesis in light of what's been said.

Thesis/support is a persuasive form, so it lends itself to arguments, critical essays, reviews, proposals, and similar pieces. In fact, you may have already structured your draft using this approach. If so, the following revision strategy may help you tighten and clarify the draft.

Beginning

- Establishes purpose (answers So what? question)
- Introduces question, dilemma, problem, theory, thesis, claim (sometimes dramatically)
- Helps readers understand—and feel—what's at stake for them

Middle

- Tests theory, claim, thesis against the evidence
- Develops reasons, with evidence, for writer's thesis or claim
- Tells story of writer's inquiry into question, problem, or dilemma

End

- Proposes answer, even if tentative, for writer's key question
- Revisits thesis or claim, extending, qualifying, contradicting, or reconfirming initial idea
- Raises new questions, poses new problems, or offers new understanding of what is at stake for readers

Revision Strategy 13.15: Beginnings, Middles, Ends, and the Work They Do

Stories, we are often told, always have a beginning, middle, and end. This may be the most fundamental structure of all, and it doesn't just apply to narratives. The illustration above explains what a beginning, middle, and end might contribute to making nearly any piece of writing coherent and convincing. Apply some of these ideas to your draft.

1. Divide into three parts a draft you'd like to revise—beginning, middle, and end—by drawing lines on the paper to distinguish each section. Where you decide to divide the draft is entirely up to you; there's no formula to this. But you may change your mind as you go along.

2. Now use the illustration above to analyze your beginning, middle, and end. Does each section do at least *one* of the listed tasks? If not, revise that section so that it does. This may involve adding a sentence or two—or possibly a couple of paragraphs—of new information, perhaps moving some from elsewhere in the draft.

3. Generally speaking, the middle of an essay does the most work, and so proportionally it should have the most information. For example, many essays look like this:

If you find, for example, that your beginning takes three pages of a five-page essay, then you might want to cut away at the first few pages and concentrate on developing the body of your essay.

Revision Strategy 13.16: Reorganizing Around Thesis and Support

Because the thesis/support structure is fairly common, it's useful to master. Most drafts, even if they weren't initially organized in that form, can be revised into a thesis/support essay (personal essays would be an exception). The order of information in such an essay generally follows this design:

- **Lead paragraph:** This paragraph introduces the topic and explicitly states the thesis, usually as the last sentence in the paragraph. For example, a thesis/support paper on the deterioration of America's national parks system might begin this way:

> Yellowstone National Park, which shares territory with Idaho, Montana, and Wyoming, is the nation's oldest park and, to some, its most revered. Established on March 1, 1872, the park features the Old Faithful geyser, which spouts reliably every 76 minutes on average. What isn't nearly as reliable these days is whether school groups will get to see it. Last year 60% of them were turned away because the park simply didn't have the staff. <u>This essay</u>

will argue that poor funding of our national parks system is a disgrace that
threatens to undermine the Park Service's mission to preserve the areas "as
cumulative expressions of a single national heritage" ("Famous Quotes").

The thesis (underlined) is the final sentence in the paragraph, for emphasis.

■ **Body:** Each succeeding paragraph until the final one attempts to prove or
develop the thesis. Often, each paragraph is devoted to a single *reason*
why the thesis is true, frequently stated as the topic sentence of the paragraph. Specific information then explains, clarifies, and supports the reason. For example, here's a typical paragraph from the body of the national
parks essay:

One aspect of the important national heritage at risk because of poor
funding for national parks is the pride many Americans feel about these
national treasures. *Newsweek* writer Arthur Frommer says the national park
system is among the "crowning glories of our democracy." He adds, "Not
to have seen them is to have missed something unique and precious in
American life" (12). To see the crumbling roads in Glacier National Park, or
the incursion of development in Great Smoky Mountains National Park, or
the slow strangulation of the Everglades is not just an ecological issue; it's
a sorry statement about a democratic nation's commitment to some of the
places that define its identity.

The underlined sentence is the topic sentence of the paragraph and is an
assertion that supports and develops the thesis in the lead of the essay.
The rest of the paragraph offers supporting evidence of the assertion, in
this case a quotation from a *Newsweek* writer who recently visited several
parks.

■ **Concluding paragraph:** This paragraph reminds the reader of the central argument, not simply by restating the original thesis from the first
paragraph, but also by reemphasizing some of the most important points.
This may lead to an elaboration or restatement of the thesis. One common
technique is to find a way at the end of the essay to return to the beginning. Here's the concluding paragraph from the essay on national park
funding:

We would never risk our national heritage by allowing the White House
to deteriorate or the Liberty Bell to rust away. As the National Park Service's
own mission states, the parks are also "expressions" of our "single national

heritage," one this paper contends is about preserving not only trees, animals, and habitats, but also our national identity. The Old Faithful geyser reminds Americans of their constancy and their enduring spirit. What will it say about us if vandals finally end the regular eruptions of the geyser because Americans didn't support a park ranger to guard it? What will we call Old Faithful then? Old Faithless?

Note that the underlined sentence returns to the original thesis but doesn't simply repeat it word for word. Instead, it amplifies the original thesis, adding a definition of "national heritage" to include national identity. It returns to the opening paragraph by finding a new way to discuss Old Faithful. Revise your draft to conform to this structure, beginning with a strong opening paragraph that explicitly states your thesis and concluding with an ending that somehow returns to the beginning without simply repeating what you've already said.

Revision Strategy 13.17: Multiple Leads

A single element that may affect a draft more than any other is the beginning. There are many ways into the material, and of course you want to choose a beginning or lead that a reader might find interesting. You also want to choose a beginning that makes some kind of promise, providing readers with a sense of where you intend to take them. But a lead also has less-obvious effects on both readers and writers. How you begin often establishes the voice of the essay; signals the writer's emotional relationship to the material, the writer's ethos; and might suggest the form the essay will take.

This is, of course, why beginnings are so hard to write. But the critical importance of where and how we begin also suggests that examining alternative leads can give writers more choices and more control over their essays. To borrow John McPhee's metaphor, if a lead is a "flashlight that shines down into the story," then pointing that flashlight in four different directions might reveal four different ways of following the same subject. This can be a powerful revision strategy.

1. Choose a draft that has a weak opening, doesn't have a strong sense of purpose, or needs to be reorganized.

2. Compose four *different* openings to the *same* draft. One way to generate ideas for this is to cluster your topic and write leads from four different branches. Also consider varying the type of lead you write (see the "Inquiring into the Details: Types of Leads" on facing page).

3. Bring a typed copy of these four leads (or five if you want to include the original lead from the first draft) to class and share them with a small

group. First, simply ask your classmates to choose the beginning they like best.

4. Choose the lead *you* prefer. It may or may not be the one your classmates chose. Find a partner who was not in your small group and ask him or her the following questions after sharing the lead you chose:

   ▪ Based on this lead, what do you predict that this paper is about?

   ▪ Can you guess the question, problem, or idea I'm writing about in the rest of the essay?

   ▪ Do you have a sense of what my thesis might be?

   ▪ What is the ethos of this beginning? In other words, how do I come across to you as a narrator or author of the essay?

If the predictions were fairly accurate using the lead you preferred, this might be a good alternative opening to the next draft. Follow it in a fastwrite in your

Inquiring into the Details

Types of Leads

Writer John McPhee says beginnings—or leads— are "like flashlights that shine down into the story." If you imagine that information about your topic is collected in a darkened room, then where and how you choose to begin an essay will, like a flashlight, illuminate some aspect of that room. Different beginnings point the flashlight in different directions and imply the different directions the essay might develop. Consider a few types of leads:

1. *Announcement.* Typical of a thesis/support essay, among others. Explicitly states the purpose and thesis of the essay.

2. *Anecdote.* A brief story that nicely frames the question, dilemma, problem, or idea behind the essay.

3. *Scene.* Describe a situation, place, or image that highlights the question, problem, or idea behind the essay.

4. *Profile.* Begin with a case study or description of a person who is involved in the question, problem, or idea.

5. *Background.* Provide a context through information that establishes the significance of the question, problem, or idea.

6. *Quotation or Dialogue.* Begin with a voice of someone (or several people) involved or whose words are relevant.

7. *Comparison.* Are there two or more things that, when compared or contrasted, point to the question, problem, or idea?

8. *Question.* Frame the question the essay addresses.

notebook to see where it leads you. Go ahead and use the other leads elsewhere in the revision, if you like.

If your reader's predictions were off, the lead may not be the best choice for the revision. However, should you consider this new direction an appealing alternative for the next draft? Or should you choose another lead that better reflects your current intentions rather than strike off in new directions? Either way, follow a new lead to see where it goes.

Revision Strategy 13.18: The Frankenstein Draft

One way to divorce a draft that has you in its clutches is to dismember it; that is, cut it into pieces and play with the parts, looking for new arrangements of information or new gaps to fill. Writing teacher Peter Elbow's cut-and-paste revision can be a useful method, particularly for drafts that don't rely on narrative structures (although sometimes playing with alternatives, particularly if the draft is strictly chronological, can be helpful). Research essays and other pieces that attempt to corral lots of information seem to benefit the most from this strategy.

1. Choose a draft that needs help with organization. Make a one-sided copy.

2. Cut apart the copy, paragraph by paragraph. (You may cut it into smaller pieces later.) Once you have completely disassembled the draft, shuffle the paragraphs to get them wildly out of order so the original draft is just a memory.

3. Now go through the shuffled stack and find the *core paragraph*. This is the paragraph the essay really couldn't do without because it helps answer the *So what?* question. It might be the paragraph that contains your thesis or establishes your focusing question. It should be the paragraph that explains, implicitly or explicitly, what you're trying to say in the draft. Set this aside.

4. With the core paragraph directly in front of you, work your way through the remaining stack of paragraphs and make two new stacks: one of paragraphs that don't seem relevant to your core (such as unnecessary digressions or information) and those that do (they support the main idea, explain or define a key concept, illustrate or exemplify something important, or provide necessary background).

5. Put your reject pile aside for the moment. You may decide to salvage some of those paragraphs later. But for now focus on your relevant pile, including the core paragraph. Now play with order. Try new leads, ends, and middles. Consider trying some new methods of development as a way to organize your next draft (see the "Methods of Development" box). As you spread the paragraphs out before you and consider new arrangements, don't worry about the lack of transitions; you can add those later. Also look for gaps, places where more information might be needed. Consider some of the information in the reject pile as well. Should you splice in *parts* of paragraphs that you initially discarded?

6. As a structure begins to emerge, begin taping together the fragments of paper. Also splice in scraps in appropriate places and note what you might add in the next draft that is currently missing.

Methods of Development

- Narrative
- Problem to solution
- Cause to effect, or effect to cause
- Question to answer
- Known to unknown, or unknown to known
- Simple to complex
- General to specific, or specific to general
- Comparison and contrast
- Combinations of any of these

Now you've created a Frankenstein draft. But hopefully this ugly mess of paper and tape and scribbled notes holds much more promise than the monster did. On the other hand, if you end up with pretty much the original organization, perhaps your first approach wasn't so bad after all. You may at least find places where more information is needed.

Revision Strategy 13.19: Make a PowerPoint Outline

While outlines can be a useful tool for planning a formal essay, they can also help writers revise a draft. One of the best tools for doing this is a program such as PowerPoint that challenges you to develop brief slides in sequence. The ease of moving the slides around, the imperative to be brief and to the point, and the visual display of your logic all combine to make the program an ideal medium for playing with the order of information. This is often helpful even if you don't ever make a presentation.

Your goal in creating a PowerPoint outline isn't to transfer all your text to slides and then move it around, though you could do that if you thought it helpful. Your aim is to exploit the software to help you develop a logical outline. You have several options for doing this. One is to title separate slides using some of the conventional structures of academic essays, and then make bulleted lists of the information you might include in each (see the sample slide on the following page). For example, these could be slide titles:

- Abstract, Introduction, Literature Review, Thesis/Purpose, Methods, Results, Discussion, Conclusion
- The Problem/Question, Purpose of the Essay, Claim, Reasons and Evidence (separate slide for each reason), Conclusion

Sample PowerPoint slide outlining a plan for an essay.

- Introduction, Thesis, Example 1, Example 2, Example 3, etc., Conclusion
- Lead/Introduction, Background, Research Question, Significance of the Problem or Question, Other Voices on the Question, Thesis, Conclusion

Alternatively, you might use less-formal methods of parsing the information in the draft onto slides. For example, can you label categories of information? In a narrative essay, it might be a particular scene, description, or reflection. In an argument, it might be claims, warrants or assumptions, evidence, and counterarguments. A literary essay might be grouped on slides using key passages, the main idea, textual background, information on the author, and so on.

Whichever method you use, once you are able to disassemble your draft onto PowerPoint slides using some logic, don't just play with the order. Consider moving some of the information from slide to slide, too.

Problems with Clarity and Style

One thing should be made clear immediately: Problems of clarity and style need not have anything to do with grammatical correctness. You can have a sentence that follows all the rules and still lumbers, sputters, and dies like a

Volkswagen bug towing a heavy trailer up a steep hill. Take this sentence, for instance:

> Once upon a point in time, a small person named Little Red Riding Hood initiated plans for the preparation, delivery, and transportation of foodstuffs to her grandmother, a senior citizen residing at a place of residence in a wooded area of indeterminate dimension.

This beastly sentence opens Russell Baker's essay "Little Red Riding Hood Revisited," a satire about the gassiness of contemporary writing. It's grammatically correct, of course, but it's also pretentious, unnecessarily wordy, and would be annoying to read if it wasn't pretty amusing. This section of the chapter focuses on revision strategies that improve the clarity of your writing and will help you consider the effects you want to create through word choice and arrangement. Your questions about grammar and mechanics can be answered in the Handbook at the back of the book.

Strong writing at the sentence and paragraph levels always begins with clarity.

Maybe because we often think that work with paragraphs, sentences, and words always involves problems of correctness, it may be hard to believe at first that writers can actually manage readers' responses and feelings by using different words or rearranging the parts of a sentence or paragraph. Once you begin to play around with style, however, you will discover that it's much more than cosmetic. In fact, style in writing is a lot like music in movies. Chris Douridas, a Hollywood music supervisor who picked music for *Shrek* and *American Beauty*, said recently that he sees "music as an integral ingredient to the pie. I see it as helping to flavor the pie and not as whipped cream on top." Certainly people don't pick a movie for its music, but we know that the music is central to our experience of a film. Similarly, *how* you say things in a piece of writing powerfully shapes the reader's experience of *what* you say.

But style is a secondary concern. Strong writing at the sentence and paragraph levels always begins with clarity. Do you say what you mean as directly and economically as you can? This can be a real problem, particularly with academic writing, in which it's easy to get the impression that a longer word is always better than a shorter word and that the absence of anything interesting to say can be remedied by sounding smart. Nothing could be further from the truth.

Solving Problems of Clarity

Begin by revising your draft with one or more revision strategies that will make your writing more direct and clear.

Revision Strategy 13.20: The Three Most Important Sentences

Writers, like car dealers, organize their lots to take advantage of where customers are most likely to look and what they're most likely to remember. In many essays and papers, there are three places to park important information and to craft your very best sentences. These are,

- the very first sentence
- the last line of the first paragraph
- the very last line of the essay

The First Sentence. Obviously, there are many other important places in a piece of writing—and longer essays, especially, have more and different locations for your strongest sentences. But in an informal piece of modest length, the first sentence not only should engage the reader, it should, through strong language and voice, introduce the writer as well. For example, here's the first line of Richard Conniff's researched essay "Why Did God Make Flies?": "Though I've been killing them for years now, I have never tested the folklore that, with a little cream and sugar, flies taste very much like black raspberries." In more formal writing, the first line is much less about introducing a persona than introducing the subject. Here's the first line of an academic piece I'm reading at the moment: "Much of the international debate about the relationship between research and teaching is characterized by difference." This raises an obvious question—"What is this difference?"—and this is exactly what the author proposes to explore.

The Last Line of the First Paragraph. The so-called "lead" (or "lede" in journalism speak) of an essay or article does three things: It establishes the purpose of the work, raises interesting questions, and creates a register or tone. A lead paragraph in a shorter essay is just that—the first paragraph—while a lead in a longer work may run for paragraphs, even pages. Whatever the length, the last sentence of the lead launches the work and gets it going in a particular direction. In conventional thesis-proof essays, then, this might be the sentence where you state your main claim. In inquiry-based forms such as the essay, this might be where you post the key question you're exploring or illuminate the aspect of the problem you want to look at.

The Last Line of the Essay. If it's good, this is the sentence readers are most likely to remember.

Try this revision strategy:

1. Highlight or underline each of the three key sentences in your draft.
2. Ask yourself these questions about the first line and, depending on your answers, revise the sentence:
   - Is the language lively?
   - Does it immediately raise questions the reader might want to learn the answers to?
   - Will they want to read the second sentence, and why?

3. Analyze the last sentence of your "lead" paragraph for ideas about revision. Ask yourself this:

   ▪ Is the sentence well crafted?

   ▪ Does it hint at or explicitly state your motive for asking readers to follow along with you in the paragraphs and pages that follow?

4. Finally, scrutinize your last sentence:

   ▪ Is this one of the best-written sentences in the piece?

   ▪ Does it add something?

Revision Strategy 13.21: Untangling Paragraphs

One of the things I admire most in my friends David and Margaret is that they both have individual integrity—a deep understanding of who they are and who they want to be—and yet they remain just as profoundly connected to the people close to them. They manage to exude both individuality and connection. I hope my friends will forgive the comparison, but good paragraphs have the same qualities: Alone they have their own identities, yet they are also strongly hitched to the paragraphs that precede and that follow them. This connection happens quite naturally when you're telling a story, but in expository writing the relationship between paragraphs is more related to content than time.

The following passage is the first three paragraphs from Paul de Palma's essay on computers, with the clever title "http://www.when_is_enough_enough?.com." Notice the integrity of each paragraph—each is a kind of mini-essay—as well as the way each one is linked to the paragraph that precedes it.

In the misty past, before Bill Gates joined the company of the world's richest men, before the mass-marketed personal computer, before the metaphor of an information superhighway had been worn down to a cliché, I heard Roger Schank interviewed on National Public Radio. Then a computer science professor at Yale, Schank was already well known in artificial intelligence circles. Because those circles did not include me, a new programmer at Sperry Univac, I hadn't heard of him. Though I've forgotten details of the conversation, I have never forgotten Schank's insistence that most people do not need to own computers.

That view, of course, has not prevailed. Either we own a personal computer and fret about upgrades, or we are scheming to own one and fret about the technical marvel yet to come that will render our purchase obsolete. Well, there are worse ways to spend money, I suppose. For all I know, even Schank

(continued)

A paragraph should be unified, focusing on a single topic, idea, or thing. It's like a mini-essay in that sense.

Note how the first sentence in the new paragraph links with the last sentence in the preceding one.

As before, the first sentence links with the last sentence in the previous paragraph.

The final sentence is the most important one in a paragraph. Craft it carefully.

(continued)

owns a personal computer. They're fiendishly clever machines, after all, and they've helped keep the wolf from my door for a long time.

It is not the personal computer itself that I object to. What reasonable person would voluntarily go back to a typewriter? The mischief is not in the computer itself, but in the ideology that surrounds it. If we hope to employ computers for tasks more interesting than word processing, we must devote some attention to how they are actually being used, and beyond that, to the remarkable grip that the idol of computing continues to exert.

Well-crafted paragraphs such as these create a fluent progression, all linked together like train cars; they make readers feel confident that this train is going somewhere. This might be information that clarifies, extends, proves, explains, or even contradicts. Do the paragraphs in your draft work well on their own and together?

1. Check the length of every paragraph in your draft. Are any too long, going on and on for a full page or more? Can you create smaller paragraphs by breaking out separate ideas, topics, discussions, or claims?

2. Now examine each paragraph in your draft for integrity. Is it relatively focused and unified? Should it be broken down further into two or more paragraphs because it covers too much territory?

3. In Figure 13.5, note the order of the most important information in a typical paragraph. Is each of your paragraphs arranged with that order in mind? In particular, how strong is the final sentence in each paragraph? Does it prepare readers to move into the next paragraph? In general, each paragraph adds some kind of new information to the old information in the paragraphs preceding it. This new material may clarify, explain, prove, elaborate on, contrast, summarize, contradict, or alter time. Sometimes you should signal the nature of this addition using transition words and phrases (see the "Inquiring into the Details: Transition Flags" box). Are there any awkward transitions? Should you smooth them using transition flags?

Revision Strategy 13.22: Cutting Clutter

"Once upon a point in time—at coordinates as yet too sensitive to disclose—a small person named Little Red Riding Hood initiated an operation involving the preparation, transportation, and delivery of foodstuffs to her grandmother, a senior citizen residing in a forest of indeterminate dimension."

Russell Baker's overinflated version of "Little Red Riding Hood," excerpted above, suffered from what writer and professor William Zinsser called "clutter."

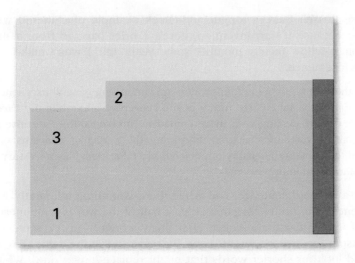

Figure 13.5   Order of important sentences in a paragraph. Often the first sentence is the second most important sentence in a paragraph. The third most important sentence follows immediately thereafter. The most important sentence usually comes at the end of the paragraph.

This disease afflicts much writing, particularly in academic settings. Clutter, simply put, is saying in three or four words what you might say in two, or choosing a longer word when a shorter one will do just as well. It grows from the assumption that simplicity means simplemindedness. This is misguided. Simplicity is a great virtue in writing. It's respectful of the readers, for one thing, who are mostly interested in understanding what you mean without unnecessary detours or obstacles.

Inquiring into the Details

Transition Flags

One way to connect paragraphs is to signal to a reader with words what the relationship is between them.

- **Clarifying:** *for example, furthermore, specifically, also, to illustrate, similarly*
- **Proving:** *in fact, for example, indeed*
- **Time:** *first...second...finally, subsequently, following, now, recently*
- **Cause or effect:** *therefore, consequently, so, accordingly*
- **Contrast or contradiction:** *on the other hand, in contrast, however, on the contrary, despite, in comparison*
- **Summarizing:** *finally, in the end, in conclusion, summing up, to conclude*

In case Russell Baker's tongue-and-cheek example of cluttered writing isn't convincing because it's an invention, here's a brief passage from a memo I received from a fellow faculty member some years ago. I won't make you endure more than a sentence.

> While those of us in the administration are supporting general excellence and consideration of the long-range future of the University, and while the Faculty Senate and Caucus are dealing with more immediate problems, the Executive Committee feels that an ongoing dialogue concerning the particular concerns of faculty is needed to maintain the quality of personal and educational life necessary for continued educational improvement.

That's a 63-word sentence, and while there is nothing inherently wrong with long sentences, I'm pretty sure that at least half of the words are unnecessary. For the fun of it, see if you can cut at least thirty words from the sentence without compromising the writer's intent. Look for ways to say the same things in fewer words, and look for shorter words that might replace longer ones. What kinds of choices did you make to improve the clarity of the sentence?

Now shift your attention to one of your own drafts and see if you can be as ruthless with your own clutter as you were with the memo writer's.

1. One of the most common kinds of clutter is stock phrases, things we mindlessly say because we've simply gotten in the habit of saying them.

STOCK PHRASE	SIMPLER VERSION
Due to the fact that...	Because
At the present time...	Now
Until such time as...	Until
I am of the opinion that...	I think
In the event of...	When
Referred to as...	Called
Totally lacked the ability to...	Couldn't
A number of...	Many
In the event of...	If
There is a need for...	Must

2. Another thing to consider is choosing a shorter, simpler word rather than a longer, more complicated word. For example, why not say *many* rather than *numerous*, or *ease* rather than *facilitate*, or *do* rather than *implement*, or *found* rather than *identified*? Go through your draft and look for opportunities such as these to use simpler, more direct words.

3. In his book *Style: Ten Lessons in Clarity and Grace*, Joseph Williams cleverly calls the habit of using meaningless words "verbal tics." My favorite verbal tic is the phrase *in fact*, which I park at the front of a sentence when I feel like I'm about to clarify something. Williams mentions a few common ones, including *kind of, actually, basically, generally, given, various*, and *certain*.

Go through your draft and search for words and phrases that you use out of habit, and cut them if they don't add meaning.

Revision Strategy 13.23: The Actor and the Action Next Door

I live in a relatively urban neighborhood, and so I can hear Kate play her music across the street and Gray powering up his chainsaw to cut wooden pallets next door. I have mixed feelings about this. Kate and I have different taste in music and Gray runs the saw at dusk. But I am never confused about who is doing what. That's less obvious in the following passage:

> A conflict that was greeted at first with much ambivalence by the American public, the war in Iraq, which caused a tentativeness that some experts call the "Vietnam syndrome," sparked protests among Vietnam veterans.

The subject, or actor, of the sentence (*the war in Iraq*) and the action (*sparked protests*) are separated by a few city blocks. In addition, the subject is buried behind a long introductory clause. As a result, it's a bit hard to remember who is doing what. Putting actor and action next door to each other makes the writing livelier, and bringing the subject up front helps clarify who is doing what.

> The war in Iraq sparked protests among Vietnam veterans even though the conflict was initially greeted with public ambivalence. Some experts call this tentativeness the "Vietnam syndrome."

Review your draft to determine whether the subjects in your sentences are buried or are in the same neighborhood as the verbs that modify them. If they're too far away, rewrite to bring the actors up front in your sentences and to close the distance between actors and actions.

Improving Style

These revision strategies will improve the style of your writing. Writers adopt a style because it serves a purpose, perhaps encouraging a certain feeling that makes a story more powerful, enhancing the writer's ethos to make an essay more convincing, or simply giving certain information particular emphasis. For example, here's the beginning of an article about Douglas Berry, a Marine drill sergeant.

> He is seething, he is rabid, he is wound up tight as a golf ball, with more adrenalin surging through his hypothalamus than a cornered slum rat, he is everything these Marine recruits with their heads shaved to dirty nubs have ever feared or ever hoped a drill sergeant might be.

The style of this opening is calculated to have an obvious effect—the reader is pelted with words, one after another, in a breathless sentence that almost simulates the experience of having Sgt. Douglas Berry in your face. There's no magic to this. It is all about using words that evoke action and feeling, usually verbs or words based on or derived from verbs.

Revision Strategy 13.24: Actors and Actions

Academic writing sometimes lacks strong verbs, relying instead on old, passive standbys such as *it was concluded by the study* or *it is believed*. Not only are the verbs weak, but the actors—the people or things engaged in the action—are often missing completely from the sentences. *Who* or *what* did the study? *Who* believes?

This is called *passive voice*, and while it's not grammatically incorrect, it can suck the air out of a room. One of the easiest ways to locate passive voice in your drafts is to conduct a *to be* search. Most forms of the verb *to be* usually signal passive voice.

1. Conduct a *to be* search of your own draft. Whenever you find passive construction, try to put the actor into the sentence.

2. Try to use lively verbs as well. Can you replace weak verbs with stronger ones? How about *discovered* instead of *found*, or *seized* instead of *took*, *shattered* instead of *broke*. Review every sentence in the draft and, when appropriate, revise with a stronger verb.

Revision Strategy 13.25: Smoothing the Choppiness

Consider the following sentences, each labeled with the number of syllables:

> When the sun finally rose the next day I felt young again.(15) It was a strange feeling because I wasn't young anymore.(15) I was fifty years old and felt like it.(10) It was the smell of the lake at dawn that thrust me back into adolescence.(19) I remembered the hiss of the waves.(9) They erased my footprints in the sand.(9)

The cause of the plodding rhythm is the unvarying length of the pauses. The last two sentences in the passage each have nine syllables, and the first two sentences are nearly identical in length as well (fifteen syllables each).

Now notice how this choppiness disappears by varying the lengths of the pauses through combining sentences, inserting other punctuation, and dropping a few unnecessary words.

> When the sun finally rose the next day I felt young again,(15) and it was a strange feeling because I wasn't young.(13) I was fifty years old.(6) It was the smell of the lake at dawn that thrust me back into adolescence and remembering the hiss of the waves as they erased my footprints in the sand.(39)

The revision is much more fluent, and the reason is simple: The writer varies the pauses and the number of syllables within each of them—15, 13, 6, 39.

1. Choose a draft of your own that doesn't seem to flow or seems choppy in places.

2. Mark the pauses in the problem areas. Put slash marks next to periods, commas, semicolons, dashes, and so on—any punctuation that prompts a reader to pause briefly.

3. If intervals between seem similar in length, revise to vary them, combining sentences, adding punctuation, dropping unnecessary words, or varying long and short words.

Revision Strategy 13.26: Fresh Ways to Say Things

It goes without saying that a tried-and-true method of getting to the heart of revision problems is to just do or die. Do you know what I mean? Of course you don't, because the opening sentence is laden with clichés and figures of speech that manage to obscure meaning.

Removing clichés and shopworn expressions from your writing will make it sound more as if you are writing from your own voice rather than someone else's.

1. Reread your draft and circle clichés and hand-me-down expressions. If you're not sure whether a phrase qualifies for either category, share your circled items with a partner and discuss them. Have you heard these things before?

2. Cut clichés and overused expressions and rewrite your sentences, finding your own way to say things. In your own words, what do you really mean by "do or die" or "striking while the iron is hot" or becoming a "true believer"?

Using What You Have Learned

Take a few moments to reflect on what you have learned in this chapter and how you can apply it.

1. **Understand the meaning—and value—of revision and apply it to your own work when appropriate.** Even if an instructor doesn't explicitly require a revision for a writing assignment, you now have experience with what a difference it can make in the quality of your work.

2. **Recognize five types of revision and apply most-relevant strategies to a particular draft.** As you continue to develop as a writer, you'll become a more critical reader of your own work, and this judgment gets easier. Learn to recognize your weaknesses—maybe you're not great at organizing drafts or you're wordy—and find strategies that help you address those problems.

Complete
Additional Exercises
and Practice on
Chapter 13
in your MyLab

Writers rarely experience the impact their writing has on readers. When they do experience this in a writing workshop, the idea of writing for an audience ceases to be an abstraction.

The Writer's Workshop

14

Learning Objectives

In this chapter, you'll learn to

14.1   Understand the purpose of peer review.

14.2   Select peer review strategies that are most likely to address problems in a draft.

14.3   Recognize typical problems with group work and solutions that will address them.

Making the Most of Peer Review

Sharing your writing with strangers can be among the most frightening and gratifying social experiences. It can be a key to the success of the next draft or a complete waste of time. One thing sharing your writing can't be, however, is avoided—at least in most composition courses, which these days frequently rely on small- and large-group workshops to help students revise. This is a good thing, I think, for three reasons:

1. It's useful to experience *being read* by others.
2. Workshops can be among the most effective ways for writers to divorce the draft.
3. The talk about writing in workshops can be enormously instructive.

Being Read

Being read is not the same thing as being read to. As we share our writing, sometimes reading our own work aloud to a group, we are sharing ourselves in a very real way. This is most evident with a personal essay, but virtually any piece of writing bears our authorship—our particular ways of seeing and saying things—and included in this are our feelings about ourselves as writers.

Last semester, Matthew told me that he felt he was the worst writer in the class, and that seemed obvious when I watched him share his writing in his workshop group. Matthew was quiet and compliant, readily accepting suggestions with little comment, and he seemed to rush the conversation about his draft as if to make the ordeal end sooner. When Matthew's drafts were discussed, his group always ended in record time, and yet he always claimed that they were "helpful."

Tracy always began presenting her drafts by announcing, "This really sucks. It's the worst thing I've ever written." Of course it wasn't. But this announcement seemed intended to lower the stakes for her, to take some of the pressure off of her performance in front of others, or, quite possibly, it was a hopeful invitation for Tracy's group members to say, "You're too hard on yourself. This is really good."

> In a workshop, you can actually hear the murmurs, the sighs, and the laughter of your readers as you read to them.

To be read in a workshop group can mean more than a critique of your ideas or sentences; for students like Matthew and Tracy, it is an evaluation of *themselves*, particularly their self-worth as writers. Of course, this isn't the purpose of peer review at all, but for those of us with sometimes nagging internal critics, it's pretty hard to avoid feeling that both your writing and your writing self are on trial. This is why it's so helpful to articulate these fears before being read. It's also helpful to imagine the many positive outcomes that might come from the experience of sharing your writing.

While taking workshop comments about your writing personally is always a risk, consider the really rare and unusual opportunity to *see* readers respond to your work. I often compare my published writing to dropping a very heavy stone down a deep well and waiting to hear the splash. And waiting. And waiting. But in a workshop, you can actually hear the murmurs, the sighs, and the laughter of your readers as you read to them; you can also see the smiles, puzzled expressions, nodding heads, and even tears. You can experience your readers' experiences of your writing in ways that most published authors never can.

What is so valuable about this, I think, is that audience is no longer an abstraction. After your first workshop, it's no stretch to imagine the transaction that most writing involves—a writer's words being received by a reader who thinks and feels something in response. And when you take this back to the many solitary hours of writing, you may feel you have company; that members of your workshop group are interested in what you have to say.

This is a powerful thing. In some ways, it's the most important thing about the workshop experience.

Divorcing the Draft

Our writing relationships include our emotional connection to drafts, and this often has to do with the time we spent writing them. In Chapter 13, I described the ways we can get entangled in first drafts that blind us to other ways of seeing a topic. Sometimes we need to divorce a draft, and the best remedy for this is time away from it. But students rarely have that luxury.

Workshops provide an alternative to time away from a draft and are effective for the same reason some people see therapists—group members offer an "outsider's" perspective on your work that may give it new meanings and raise new possibilities. If nothing else, readers offer a preview of whether your current meanings are clear and whether what you assume is apparent *is* apparent to someone other than yourself. It's rare when a workshop doesn't jerk writers away from at least a few of their assumptions about a draft, and the best of these experiences inspire writers to want to write again. This is the outcome we should always hope to attain.

14.1
Understand the purpose of peer review

Instructive Talk

Consider a few comments I overheard during workshops recently:

- "I don't think the focus is clear in this essay. In fact, I think there are at least two separate essays here, and it's the one on the futility of antiwar protests I'm most interested in."

- "Do you think that there's a better lead buried on the third page, in the paragraph about your sister's decision to go to the hospital? That was a powerful scene, and it seemed to be important to the overall theme."

- "I was wondering about something. What is it about the idea that we sometimes keep silent not only to protect other people but also to protect ourselves that surprised you? I mean, does knowing that change anything about how you feel about yourself as a parent?"

- "I loved this line. Simply loved it."

The talk in workshops is not always about writing. The "underlife" of the classroom often surfaces in workshops, a term one educator uses to describe the idle talk about the class itself. Most writing classes ask students to step out of their usual student roles. Rather than quietly listen to lectures or study a textbook, in a writing course you are asked to make your own meanings and find your own ways of making meaning. Whenever we are asked to assume new roles, some resistance can set in, and workshops can become an occasion for talk about the class, often out of earshot of the instructor. This talk isn't always complaining. Often, workshops are opportunities to share understandings or approaches to assignments, and especially experiences with them. They can also be a chance for students to try out new identities—"I really liked writing this. Maybe I'm an okay writer after all."

While this kind of talk may not be directly about a draft, it can help you negotiate the new roles you're being asked to assume in your writing class. This is part of becoming better writers who are confident that they can manage the writing process in all kinds of situations. However, the main purpose of workshop groups is to help students revise their drafts. But why seek advice from writers who are clearly less experienced than the instructor?

1. By talking with other students about writing, you get practice using the language you're learning in the writing classroom—language that helps you describe important features of your own work.

2. Because writing is about making choices among a range of solutions to problems in a draft, workshop groups are likely to surface possibilities that never occurred to you (and perhaps wouldn't occur to the instructor, either).

3. Your peers are also student writers, and because they come from similar circumstances—demands of other classes, part-time jobs, and perhaps minimal experience with college writing—they are in a position to offer practical and realistic revision suggestions.

4. Finally, in most writing courses, the students in the class are an important audience for your work. Getting firsthand responses makes the rhetorical situation real rather than imagined.

Will you get bad advice in a peer workshop? Of course. Your group members will vary in their experience and ability to read the problems and possibilities in a draft. But in the best writing workshops, you learn together, and as time goes by, the feedback gets better and better. Paradoxically, it pays off in your own writing to be generous in your responses to the work of others.

Models for Writing Workshops

14.2

Select peer review strategies that are most likely to address problems in a draft.

The whole idea of peer review workshops in writing classes has been around for years. Collaboration is hardly a novelty in the professional world, but small-group work in academia is a relatively recent alternative to lecture and other teaching methods in which the student listens to a professor, takes notes on what is said, and later takes a test of some kind. You won't learn to write well through lecture, although it may be a perfectly appropriate approach for some subjects. Because collaboration in the writing classroom fits in perfectly with the class's aim of generating knowledge about the many ways to solve writing problems, peer review of drafts in small groups is now fairly common. You'll find workshops in writing classes ranging from first-year composition to advanced fiction writing.

What will workshops be like in your course? Your instructor will answer that question, but the workshop groups will likely reflect one or more of the following models.

Full-Class Workshops

Sometimes you may not work in small groups at all. Depending on the size of your class and your instructor's particular purposes for using peer review, you may share your work with everyone in a full-class session. This approach is popular in creative writing classes, and it's typically used in composition classes to introduce students to the process of providing responses to other students' work. It also can work nicely in small classes with ten students or fewer.

In a full-class workshop, you'll choose a draft to share, and you (or your instructor) will provide copies for everyone either a few days before the workshop or at the beginning of the workshop session. On drafts you receive days ahead of the session, you're often expected to read them and bring written comments to class with you. If you receive the draft at the beginning of the workshop session, you might make notes while the draft's author reads the piece aloud, or take some time to write some comments either immediately after the draft is read or following the group discussion.

Reading your draft aloud to your workshop group is a common convention in all kinds of workshop groups, large or small. This might be something you resist at first. It will quickly become apparent, however, how useful it is to read your own work aloud. It's an entirely different reading, to literally give voice to your words. You'll stumble over passages in your draft that seemed fine when you read them silently, and you may notice gaps you glossed over. You'll hear what your writing voice sounds like in this particular essay, and whether it works for you and your readers.

Your instructor may lead the discussion in a full-class workshop, or she may sit back and wait while students share their responses. There may be guidelines and ground rules for responses as well (for some examples of these, see "The Reader's Responsibilities" section later in the chapter). If your draft is being discussed, your instructor may ask you to simply listen. Sometimes it's best to avoid defending certain choices you made in a draft and simply take in the range of responses you receive to what you have done. In other cases, you may be asked to present the large group with questions to consider. It certainly can be scary sharing your work with twenty or twenty-five people, but imagine the range of perspectives you'll get!

Small-Group Workshops

Far more typical is the workshop group of between three and seven members, either chosen randomly by your instructor or self-selected. These groups may stay together all semester or part of the semester, or you may find yourself working with fresh faces every workshop session. Each of these alternatives has advantages and disadvantages, all of which your instructor has considered in making a choice.

Ideally, your workshop group will meet in a circle, because when everyone, including the writer presenting a draft, is facing each other, you'll have more of a conversation and be able to engage each other directly (see Figure 14.1). Like so many writing group methods, this is a basic principle of teamwork borrowed from the business world.

Some of the methods of distributing drafts apply to the small group as well as to the full-class workshop discussed earlier: Writers will distribute copies of their drafts either a few days before their workshops or at the beginning of the sessions. You will provide written comments to each writer either before or after the workshop.

One-on-One Peer Review

Your instructor also may ask you to work with a partner, exchanging drafts and discussing them with each other. While you lose some of the range and quantity of

Watch
the Video on
Peer Review
in your MyLab

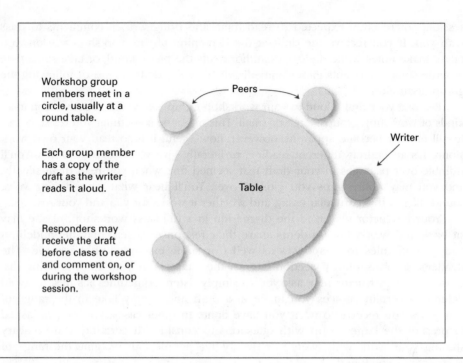

Workshop group members meet in a circle, usually at a round table.

Each group member has a copy of the draft as the writer reads it aloud.

Responders may receive the draft before class to read and comment on, or during the workshop session.

Peers

Writer

Table

Figure 14.1   The small-group workshop

feedback by working with a single reader, this conversation is often richer because each of you is reading the other's work with particular care and attention. You'll probably also have more time to talk, because you'll be discussing only two rather than four or five drafts.

One variation of this kind of one-on-one peer review is the draft exchange. Your instructor will ask you to make a pile of drafts at the front of the room and ask you to take a draft from the pile, comment on it, return it, and then take another. You may return multiple times to collect, comment on, and return a draft, and the result is that each draft may have three or four readers during the class session.

The Writer's Responsibilities

No matter what model your instructor chooses, the success of the workshop depends largely on the writers themselves. Sure, it can be harder to get what you need from some groups, but in the end, you can always get *some* help with a draft if you ask the right questions and seek certain kinds of responses.

How should you prepare for a workshop to make the most of it, and what are your responsibilities during the workshop? Here's a list you might find helpful:

■ Make sure everyone in the group gets a copy of the draft in a timely way.

■ Reread and reflect on the draft before the workshop session. What kinds of responses would be most helpful from your group? What questions do you have about the draft's possible problems?

■ Time the discussion so that your draft gets the allotted time and no more, particularly if there are other drafts to discuss.

■ Avoid getting defensive. Listen to comments on your work in an open-minded way. Your obligation is simply to listen, not to take all the advice you're offered.

■ Take notes. There are two reasons for this. First, it will help you remember other students' comments, and second, it will signal that you take those comments seriously. This increases everyone's engagement with your work.

The Reader's Responsibilities

▶ Watch
the Video on
Peer Review:
Global Responses
in your MyLab

Tina poured her heart and soul into her personal essay draft, and she was eager to get some response to it. When it was her turn to workshop the piece, however, one of the group's members was absent, and two others failed to write her the required response. "It was so lame," she told me. "It was as if no one cared about my essay. It sure makes me feel less inclined to read their stuff carefully." If this workshop group were at Hewlett-Packard or any of the thousands of businesses that encourage teamwork, the slackers would be in trouble. But teamwork in the writing class depends more on internal motivation—a sense of responsibility to others—than any external reward or punishment. There is some external motivation: It pays to be generous with your responses to others' work because you'll learn more about your own.

You can increase your own learning in a workshop and contribute to a writer's positive experience by taking the following responsibilities seriously:

■ Always read and respond to a writer's draft in a timely way. The writer may suggest the type of response that would be most helpful; if so, always keep that in mind.

■ Whenever possible, focus your responses on particular parts or passages of the draft, but, except in an editorial workshop, avoid a focus on grammar or mechanics.

■ Offer suggestions, not directives. The word *could* is usually better than *should*. Remember that the purpose of the workshop is to help identify the range of choices a writer might make to improve a draft. There is almost always more than one option.

■ Identify strengths in the draft. This is often a good place to begin because it sets writers at ease, but, more important, writers often build on strengths in revision.

■   Consider varying the roles you play in conversation with your group (see the "Inquiring into the Details: Finding a Role" box). It's easy to fall into a rut in group work, pretty much sticking to saying the same kinds of things or developing certain patterns of response. Stay vigilant about this, and try deliberately shifting the role you play in the workshop group.

What Can Go Wrong and What to Do About It

14.3
Recognize typical
problems with
group work and
solutions that will
address them.

Lana is not a fan of workshops. In an argument essay, she complained that they "lack quality feedback," and sometimes workshop groups encourage "fault finding" that can hurt the writer and the writing. Things can go wrong in workshops, of course,

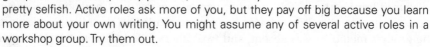

Inquiring into the Details

Finding a Role

"Slacker" is a role that's easy to slide into in small-group work. It's completely passive, and it's really pretty selfish. Active roles ask more of you, but they pay off big because you learn more about your own writing. You might assume any of several active roles in a workshop group. Try them out.

ROLES THAT HELP GROUPS GET THINGS DONE

Initiators: "Here's how we might proceed with this."

Information seekers: "What do we need to know to help the writer?"

Information givers: "This seems to be an important example."

Opinion seekers: "What do you think, Al?"

Opinion givers: "I think this works."

Clarifiers: "We all seem to be saying that the lead doesn't deliver, right?"

Elaborators: "I agree with Tom, and would add..."

Summarizers: "I think we've discussed the thesis problem enough. Should we move on to the evidence?"

ROLES THAT HELP MAINTAIN GROUP HARMONY

Encouragers: "I love that idea, Jen."

Expressivists: "My silence isn't because I'm not moved by the essay, but I'm still trying to figure out why. Is that why you're quiet, Leah?"

Harmonizers: "I think we disagree about this, but that's okay. Let's move on to discussing this next page."

Compromisers: "Maybe both Richard and Joseph are right, particularly if we look at it this way..."

Gatekeepers: "Jon, we haven't heard anything from you yet."

and when they do, students like Lana feel burned. Typically, unsuccessful workshop groups suffer from two major problems: lack of commitment by group members and lack of clarity about the process of giving feedback. It's like a cold and a runny nose—when a group is afflicted with one problem, it usually suffers from the other.

Lack of commitment is easy to see. The writer whose draft is to be discussed forgets to make copies for the rest of her group. Members who were supposed to provide written responses to a writer's draft before class hastily make notes on his manuscript as it's being discussed. The group is supposed to allot fifteen minutes to discuss each draft but finishes in five. Members are frequently absent and make no effort to provide responses to drafts they missed. Discussion is limited to general, not particularly thoughtful, compliments: "This is really good. I wouldn't change a thing," or "Just add a few details."

This lack of commitment is contagious and soon infects nearly every group meeting. Things rarely improve; they frequently get worse. Part of the problem may be that workshop participants are not clear on what is expected of them, a problem that should be minimized if you reviewed the checklists about the writer's and reader's responsibilities in workshop, discussed in the preceding sections. A solution that is beyond your control is that the instructor evaluates or even grades workshop participation, but a group can evaluate itself, too. Questions members should ask when evaluating their group can include: How effectively does your group work together? How would you evaluate the participation of group members? How do you feel about your own performance? How satisfied were you with the responses to your draft?

Groups that work together over a period of time should always monitor how things are going, and the group evaluations can be particularly helpful for this. If problems persist, the instructor may intervene or the group might consider an intervention of its own (consider Exercise 14.1 as one option). Remember, the best workshops have a simple but powerful effect on writers who share their work: *It makes them want to write again*.

Exercise 14.1

Group Problem Solving

If group evaluations reveal persistent problems, devote ten minutes to exploring possible solutions.

STEP ONE: Choose a facilitator and a recorder. The facilitator times each step, directs questions to each participant, and makes sure everyone participates. The recorder takes notes on newsprint.

1. Discuss the patterns of problems identified by group members. Do writers seem dissatisfied? Do readers feel like they're performing poorly?

2. What is behind these problems? Brainstorm a list.

3. What might be done to change the way the group operates? You must come up with *at least* one concrete idea that you agree to try.

One Student's Response

Amy's Perspective on Workshops

WHEN THINGS GO RIGHT
In both small and large workshops things are most
productive when the conversation delves deep into
a couple of issues instead of skimming the surface on a broad range of topics.
My best experiences have been in small workshops because the groups were willing
to get more deeply involved in a piece. It probably helps that there aren't too many
ideas in a small group and the ones that get thrown out for debate are well considered. I always appreciate it when the group writes notes on my paper for future reference and my absolute best workshops have been multiple sessions with the same
small group. Assessing each other's progress really helps in the revision stages.

WHEN THINGS GO WRONG
Especially in a small workshop people can take things too personally and ruin the
objective atmosphere, letting their own agenda take precedence over progression.
In one of the worst workshops I've been a part of, we were assessing an essay
by a writer who chose to write about her relationship with God. The essay had
many problems, she used very vague metaphorical language, and the attempted
symbolism didn't really work. It was a bit hard to read because of the overly senti-
mental tone of the piece. Instead of discussing these points, though, the workshop
turned into an argument about outside topics and became pretty vicious. The writer
was very open to most of the comments I made about some major changes that
needed to happen in the piece, but very defensive (understandably) to the personal
attacks. The communication simply broke down due to varying personal beliefs
when they could have been a strength of the group.

In a large group a fine balance must be achieved. It is important that the conversation runs deep, but also that it covers more than one topic. Because of the multitude
of opinions in a large group, the entire workshop can get stuck on one topic or section
of the piece. Not only is it unproductive when the debate gets stuck, but it's also really
hard to sit through.

STEP TWO: At the next workshop session, set aside five minutes at the end to discuss whether the change improved the group's performance. Is there something
else you should try?

Methods of Responding

One thing I don't need with an early draft is someone telling me that I misspelled the word *rhythm*. It is a word I'll never be able to spell, and that fact
makes me eternally grateful for spellcheckers. I do like to know whether an

early draft delivers on its implied promises to the reader, and especially whether there is another angle or another topic lurking there that I might not have noticed. But I don't want my wife, Karen, to read my stuff until I have a late draft to show her, because I sometimes find her comments on early drafts discouraging.

> The kinds of responses we seek to our writing in workshops depend on at least two things: where we are in the writing process and how we feel about the work in progress.

The *kinds* of responses we seek to our writing in workshops depend on at least two things: where we are in the writing process and how we feel about the work in progress. This is not particularly surprising. After all, certain kinds of problems arise during different stages of the writing process, and sometimes what we really need from readers of our work is more emotional than practical. We want to be motivated, encouraged, or validated, or feel any number of things that will help us work well.

Experiential and Directive Responses

It makes sense, then, to invite certain kinds of readings of your work that you'll find timely. In general, these responses range from experiential ("this is how I experienced your draft") to more directive ("this is what you could do to make it better"). Which of these two forms would make reader comments on your work most helpful? For example, depending on who you are and how you work, it may be most helpful to get less-directive responses to your work early on. Some people feel that very specific suggestions undermine their sense of ownership of rough drafts. They don't want to know what readers think they should do in the revision, but how readers experienced their draft. What parts were interesting? What parts were confusing? On the other hand, other writers feel particularly lost in the early stages of the writing process; they could use all the direction they can get. You decide (or your instructor will make suggestions), choosing from the following menu of workshop response methods. These range from the most experiential methods of response to those that invite your readers to offer quite specific suggestions about the revision (see Figure 14.2).

Response Formats

The following formats for responding to workshop drafts begin with the least directive, most experiential methods and move to the more directive approaches. While many of these formats feature some particular ways of responding to drafts, remember that the writer's and reader's responsibilities described earlier apply to all of them. Participate thoughtfully and ethically (see the box "The Ethics of Responding") and you'll be amazed at what you learn about your own writing from talking with other writers about theirs.

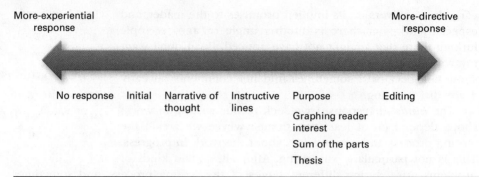

Figure 14.2   Range of Responses. Depending on your feelings about a draft and your stage in the process of writing it, you will need peer responses that range from simply reporting on the experience of reading it to offering directions about how the draft might be improved. The response formats described here fall somewhere on that continuum.

The Ethics of Responding

- Respect the writer.
- Everyone contributes.
- Say "could" rather than "should."
- Say "I" rather than "you," as in "I couldn't follow this" rather than "You weren't very clear."

The No-Response Workshop. Sometimes the most useful response to your work comes from simply reading it aloud to your group and asking them to just listen—nothing more. Why? You may not be ready for comments because the work is unformed and you're confident that'll you discover the direction you want to go in with the next draft. Comments may confuse or distract you. It's always helpful to read your work aloud to yourself, but it's also valuable to read to an audience even if you don't invite a response. You will read with more attention and awareness. Finally, you may simply feel unprepared for a response because your confidence is low.

The method couldn't be simpler. You read your draft with little or no introduction while your group quietly listens. They will not comment unless they want you to repeat something because it was inaudible. Remember to read slowly and clearly.

The Initial-Response Workshop. Robert Brooke, Ruth Mirtz, and Rick Evans[1] suggest a method that is useful for "maintaining your motivation to write while indirectly learning what to improve in your text." It might also be appropriate for an early draft.

---

[1] Robert Brooke, Ruth Mirtz, and Rick Evans, *Small Groups in Writing Workshops* (Urbana, IL: NCTE, 1994).

They suggest that you invite three kinds of responses to your work: a "relating" response, a "listening" response, and a "positive" response. These three types of response to a draft could be made in writing, in workshop discussion, or both.

- **Relating response.** As the name implies, group members share what personal associations the writer's topic inspires. Perhaps they've had a similar or a contradictory experience. Maybe they've read something or seen something that is relevant to what the writer is trying to do in the draft.

- **Listening response.** This is much like the "say back" method some therapists use with patients. Can you summarize what it is that you hear the writer saying in the draft? Is this something that is helpful to know?

- **Positive response.** What parts of the draft really work well and why? Might these be things the writer could build on in the next draft?

The Narrative-of-Thought Workshop. A writer who hears the story of readers' thinking *as they experienced the draft* can get great insight about how the piece shapes readers' expectations and how well it delivers on its promises. This method borrows a term from Peter Elbow—"movie of the mind"—to describe the creation of such a narrative response to a piece of writing.

The easiest way to create stories of your readers' experiences is to prepare your draft ahead of time to accommodate them. Before you make copies for your workshop group, create 2- to 3-inch white spaces in the manuscript immediately after the lead or beginning paragraph and then again in the middle of the essay. Also leave at least that much white space after the end of the piece.

You will read your draft episodically, beginning by just reading the lead or introductory paragraph, then allowing three or four minutes for your group's members to respond in writing in the space you provided for some of the following questions. The writer should time this and ask everyone to stop writing when it's time to read the next section of the draft. Repeat the process, stopping at the second patch of white space after you've read roughly half of the essay. Give your group the same amount of time to respond in writing, and then finish the essay to prompt the final episode of writing.

- **After hearing the lead:** What are your feelings about the topic or the writer so far? Can you predict what the essay might be about? What questions does the lead raise for you that you expect might be answered later? What has struck you?

- **After hearing half:** Tell the story of what you've been thinking or feeling about what you've heard so far. Has the draft fulfilled your expectations from the lead? What do you expect will happen next?

- **After hearing it all:** Summarize your understanding of what the draft is about, including what it *seems* to be saying (or not quite saying). How well did it deliver on its promises in the beginning? What part of your experience of the draft was most memorable? What part seemed least clear?

Discuss with your group each of the responses—after the lead, after the middle, and at the end of the draft. This conversation, and the written comments you receive when you collect their copies of your draft, should give you strong clues about how well you've established a clear purpose in your essay and sustained it from beginning to end. The responses also might give you ideas about directions in which to take the next draft that you hadn't considered.

The Instructive-Lines Workshop. Most essays balance on a thesis, theme, question, or idea. Like the point of a spinning top, these claims, ideas, or questions are the things around which everything else revolves. Essay drafts, however, may easily topple over because they lack such balance—there is no clear point, or there are too many points, or some of the information is irrelevant. In discovery drafts especially, a writer may be seeking the piece's center of gravity—or *centers* of gravity—and a useful response from a workshop group is to help the writer look for the clues about where that center might be.

This format for a workshop invites the members to try to identify the draft's *most important lines and passages,* by clearly marking them with underlining or highlighting. What makes a line or passage important? *These are places where writers explicitly or implicitly seem to suggest what they're trying to say in a draft,* and they may include the following:

- A line or passage where the writer seems to state his or her thesis.
- A part of a narrative essay when the writer adopts a critical stance and seems to be trying to pose a question or speculate about the meaning of an experience or some information.
- A part of the draft in which the writer seems to make an important claim.
- A scene or comparison or observation that hints at the question the writer is exploring (or could explore).
- A comment in a digression that the writer didn't seem to think was important, but you think might be.

These portions of the text become the subject of discussion in the workshop session. Questions to consider include the following: Why did this particular line seem important? What does it imply about what you think is the meaning of the essay? Do the different underlined passages speak to each other—can they be combined or revised into a controlling idea or question for the next draft—or do they imply separate essays or treatments. Could the writer underline something else? How might the different interpretations of the draft be reconciled?

The Purpose Workshop. Sometimes writers know their purpose in a draft: "I'm trying to argue that the Enron collapse represented the failure of current methods of compensating CEOs," or "I'm proposing that having vegetarian fast-food restaurants would reduce American obesity," or "This essay explores the question of why I was so relieved when my father died." What these writers may need most from their workshop groups is feedback on how well the draft accomplishes particular purposes.

Before the workshop session, the writer crafts a statement of purpose similar to those in the preceding paragraph—a sentence that clearly states what the writer is trying to do in the draft. This statement of purpose should include a verb that implies what action the writer is trying to take—for example, *explore, argue, persuade, propose, review, explain*, or *analyze*. As you probably guessed, these verbs are usually associated with a particular form of inquiry or genre.

The writer should include this sentence *at the end* of the draft. It's important that you make group members aware of your purpose only after they've read the entire piece and not before. Discussion and written responses should then focus on some of the following questions:

- Were you surprised by the stated purpose, or did the essay prepare you for it?
- If the stated purpose did surprise you, what did you think the writer was trying to do in the draft instead?
- Does the lead explicitly state or hint at the stated purpose?
- What parts or paragraphs of the draft seemed clearly relevant to the stated purpose, and which seemed to point in another direction?
- Did the draft seem to succeed in accomplishing the writer's purpose?

If more-directive responses would be helpful to you, consider also asking some questions such as whether there might not be a stronger beginning or lead buried elsewhere in the draft, or soliciting suggestions about which parts or paragraphs should be cut or what additional information might be needed. Which parts of the draft seemed to work best in the context of the writer's stated purpose, and which didn't work so well?

The Graphing-Reader-Interest Workshop. What commands readers' attention in a draft and what doesn't? This is useful to know, obviously, because our overall aim is to engage readers from beginning to end—which is difficult to do, particularly in longer drafts, and reader attention often varies from paragraph to paragraph in shorter drafts. But if three or four paragraphs or a couple of pages of your draft drone on, then the piece isn't working well and you need to do something about it in revision.

One way to know this is to ask your workshop group members to graph their response to your essay, paragraph by paragraph, and then discuss what is going on in those sections that drag.

For this workshop, consecutively number all the paragraphs in your draft. You or your instructor will provide each member of your group with a "reader-interest chart" (see Figure 14.3), on which the corresponding paragraph numbers are listed. On the vertical axis is a scale that represents reader interest, with 5 being high interest and 1 being low interest in that particular paragraph. As you slowly read your draft aloud to your group's members, they mark the graph after each paragraph, to roughly indicate their interest in what the paragraph says and how it says it.

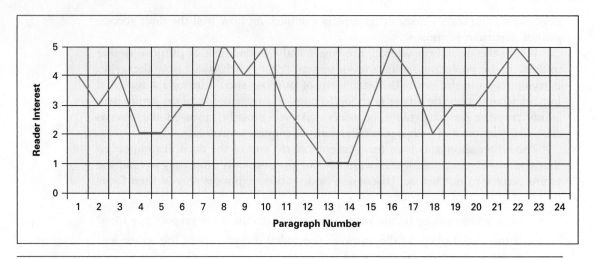

Figure 14.3   Reader-interest chart

When you're finished, you'll have a visual representation of how the essay worked, paragraph by paragraph, but the important work is ahead. Next, you need to discuss with your group *why* a paragraph or section of the draft failed to hold some readers' attention. What is going on in those parts of the draft?

- Are they confusing?
- Do they needlessly digress?
- Is the prose awkward?
- Is there too much or too little explanation?
- Are they too loaded with facts and not enough analysis?
- Does the writer seem to lose his voice?

One way to find out what's going on with the weaker parts of your essay is to look at the stronger ones. What do you notice about those paragraphs that were rated 4 or 5 by your group members? What are the particular strengths of these sections? Can you do more of that in other, less lively sections of the draft?

The Sum-of-the-Parts Workshop. Like a watch, a well-written essay moves fluently forward because all of its parts work together. In workshops, you can never talk about all those parts; there is too little time, and often it's hard to tease apart all the gears and the springs that make an essay go. But you can try to be as thorough as you can during a workshop, essentially running through a check-list of some of the most important elements, including purpose, theme, structure, information, and style. In this workshop, you attempt to cover as much territory as possible, so the responses you get will have breadth but not depth. You also invite some directive responses from your readers—suggestions for the revision, especially for specific areas of confusion—as well as their interpretation of your purpose and theme.

One of the best ways to solicit this information is to use a worksheet like the one that follows. Typically, this worksheet would be filled out by your group's members outside class and before you workshop the draft. It would then be attached to the copies of your draft and returned to you after the group discusses the work. If your peers respond thoughtfully to the worksheet, it can generate a wealth of information for you about your draft.

Workshop Worksheet

Purpose: In your own words, what is the writer's motive in the draft? Use one of the following verbs to describe this in a sentence: *explore, explain, argue, analyze, review, report, propose, persuade, reflect.*

Theme: State in your own words what you think the thesis, main point, or central question is in this draft. What question does this idea or question raise for you?

Information: Name at least two specific places in the draft where you wanted more information to fully appreciate what the writer was trying to say. What kind of information do you suggest (anecdote, story, fact, detail, background, example, interview, dialogue, opposing perspective, description, case study, etc.)?

Design: Identify *at least* one paragraph or passage that seemed out of place. Any suggestions about where it belongs?

Style: Place brackets [ ] around several sentences or passages in the draft that seemed awkward or confusing to read.

The Thesis Workshop. An alternative to the sum-of-all-parts format is to focus on a single element of the draft that you are particularly concerned about, and no part is more important than the thesis. An essay without an implicit theme or an explicit thesis is an essay without meaning. No one is particularly interested in reading a pointless story or research essay, nor are most readers interested in points that seem unrelated to the information in the draft or that are painfully obvious. For example, the idea that the death of your Aunt Trudy was sad for you is a much less compelling theme to build an essay around than the idea that her death—and the deaths of family members generally—upset the family system in ways that helped you to take on new roles, new identities.

A thesis workshop will help you make sure there is a controlling idea or question behind the draft, and help you think more deeply about what you're trying to say. Your workshop members can help with this because they bring a range of perspectives and experiences to a conversation about your theme that might make it richer and more informative for you.

In this workshop, group members receive the drafts ahead of time. Before the workshop session, they should underline the thesis, main idea, theme, or question that seems to be behind the draft. This will be the *main thing* the writer seems to be saying or exploring. This isn't particularly difficult in essays with explicit thesis statements, such as arguments or proposals, but in personal essays and other more literary pieces, the theme may not be so explicit. In that type of essay, they should underline the passage that seems central to the meaning of the essay. This may be a reflective passage or it might be a scene or moment.

Second, at the top of a piece of paper, they should write down in a sentence or two—at most—the thesis or theme as they understand it. This may involve simply copying it down from the draft. However, if the thesis or theme is not that clear or explicit, each reader should write it down in his or her own words, trying to capture the main point of the draft.

Then members should fastwrite for five minutes about their own thoughts and experiences about the writer's thesis or theme, constantly hunting for questions it raises for them. Say the draft's thesis is that the university athletic programs have become too powerful and have undermined the university's more important academic mission. In the fastwrite, explore what you've noticed about the football team's impact on the school. Where does the football program get funds? Does it compete with academic programs? Then fastwrite about what you've heard—for instance, that athletics have strong alumni support. Keep the fastwrite focused on the thesis; if it helps, stop and reread it for another prompt.

The workshop session that follows will be a conversation largely focused on what people thought was the point of the draft, and their own thoughts and feelings about it. The writer should facilitate the conversation without comment and make sure the following two things are discussed, in this order:

1. What seems to be the thesis, theme, or question behind the essay? Is it clear? Are there alternative ideas about what it might be?

2. What does each group member think or feel about what the writer seems to be saying? How do the reader's experiences and observations relate to the writer's main point or question? And especially, what questions should the writer consider in the next draft?

Although it may be hard to keep quiet if your draft is being discussed, the conversation will probably surprise you. You may discover that several of your group members either failed to understand what you were trying to say in the draft or give you a completely new idea about what you were up to. At its best, the thesis workshop inspires you to think more deeply about your theme or main idea as you consider the range of experiences and questions that other people have about it. Take lots of notes.

The Editing Workshop. In a late draft, the larger issues—for example, having a clear purpose, focus, and point, as well as appropriate information to support it—may be resolved to your satisfaction, or you may feel that you already have some pretty good ideas about how to deal with them. If so, what you may need most from your workshop group is editorial advice: responses to your work at the sentence and paragraph levels.

In the editing workshop, you invite your group members to focus on style and clarity (and perhaps grammar and mechanics). The questions that direct the reading of the draft might include some or all of the following:

- Did you stumble over any awkward passages that seemed to interrupt the fluency of the writing?
- Were there any sentences or passages that you had to read a few times to understand?
- Could any long paragraphs be broken down into smaller ones? Did any paragraphs seem to be about more than one thing?
- Are the first and last lines of the essay well crafted? Are the last lines of paragraphs strong enough?
- Were there any abrupt transitions between paragraphs?
- Was the voice or tone of the draft consistent?
- (Optional) Did you notice any patterns of grammatical problems, including run-on sentences, unclear pronoun references, or lack of subject–verb agreement?

Group members who see any of these problems should bracket [ ] the sentence or passage and refer to it when discussing the editorial issue with the group. The workshop discussion has the following ground rules:

- Be respectful of the writer's feelings. Some of us feel that style is a very personal issue and that grammar problems are related somehow to our self-worth.
- Don't have arguments about editorial judgments. Group members don't have to agree. In fact, you probably won't agree about a lot of things. Offer your comments on style as suggestions and then move on, although don't hesitate to offer a differing opinion.
- Make sure to identify places in the draft where the writing is working just fine. Editorial workshops need not focus exclusively on problems. Sentences, paragraphs, or passages that work well stylistically can often help the writer see how to revise the less effective parts.
- If readers have some comments about larger issues in the draft—things such as purpose or theme—ask the writer first if he or she welcomes that kind of feedback. Otherwise, keep the workshop focused on editorial matters.

An editing workshop may sound a little harrowing. It really isn't, particularly if the group knows the ground rules. My students often tell me that these conversations about style are some of the best workshops they have had. Everybody learns something—not just the writer—a principle that applies to many workshop formats and another reason why peer review is such a useful practice in the writing classroom.

Reflecting on the Workshop

The real work follows the workshop. Then you have the task of mulling over the things you've heard about your draft and deciding how you're going to rewrite it.

Watch
the Video on
**Revising After
Peer Review**
in your MyLab

This calls for a way of inquiring—reflection—that you've already practiced. As soon as possible after your workshop session, reread your notes and your readers' comments, then go to your journal and fastwrite for five minutes. Choose one of the following prompts to get—and keep—you going.

- What did I hear that seemed most useful? What did I hear that I'm not sure about?

- What responses to my draft do I remember most? Why?

- What did I think I needed to do to revise the draft before the workshop? Did my peer review experience change my mind? Did it reinforce my initial plans?

- What do I plan to do to revise this draft to make it stronger?

Using What You Have Learned

1. **Understand the purpose of peer review.** At first, it may have seemed crazy that it would be useful to have peers offer responses to your work rather than have the instructor "correct" it. Will this continue in other classes outside of English? Perhaps not. But you will always bring along with you the rhetorical knowledge you gained having peers read your work, including valuable experience witnessing how audiences respond to your writing. For example, how did changing the "lead" of an essay change your readers' understanding of your purpose? Based on your workshop experiences, what kinds of evidence works best in building an academic argument? You've written for teachers all of your school life. Now you know what it's like to write for other audiences. You'll reap the benefits of this for years to come.

2. **Select peer review strategies that are most likely to address problems in a draft.** You've learned about a range of responses you might invite to your writing, from open-ended responses to more directive ones. You've also got some practice deciding which will be most helpful to you, depending on how you're feeling about the work and the stage in the drafting process you're in. You've applied this knowledge in class workshops, but it will always be useful in the much more common informal situations when you invite someone—a roommate, friend, spouse, instructor—to read and respond to your work.

3. **Recognize typical problems with group work and solutions that will address them.** Collaboration in the workplace is the norm, not the exception. So what you've learned in this chapter about making writing workshop groups effective is knowledge you can use in any setting that involves teamwork. Perhaps the most important principle I emphasized here is the simplest: Unless you luck out with really effective collaborators, group work is rarely successful unless you take the time to *reflect* and *evaluate* how it's going. This chapter should give you some tools to do that in future classes and in the workplace.

Complete
Additional Exercises
and Practice on
Chapter 14
in your MyLab

Appendix A

THE WRITING PORTFOLIO

Michelle Payne, English Department Chair, Boise State University

What Is a Portfolio?

You've probably heard about stock portfolios and artist portfolios, but the term *writing portfolio* may be something new. *Portfolio* in these three examples means a collection of stocks, photographs or paintings, or writings that represent something about the compiler. For example, if you have a stock portfolio in which 75 percent of your money is invested in high-risk growth funds and the other 25 percent is in safe bond funds, then you might be showing that you're a risk taker. If you are an artist and you select a range of photographs taken over a long period of time, you might be showing how you've developed and changed as a photographer.

Writing portfolios can reflect similar things about their authors. As a collection of the work you've done for a writing class, a portfolio can demonstrate how you've developed as a writer, it can show specific writing principles you've learned, or it can illustrate the range of genres you have worked with (to name a few). Often it will be worth a large percentage of your course grade, so you will have revised the work several times. You might be asked to reflect on your assembled work, exploring what you want the portfolio to illustrate. In fact, the whole idea of using a portfolio to evaluate your work emphasizes the principles of inquiry and reflection at the heart of this book.

Instructors use portfolios in different ways: Some require certain essays and assignments to be included, some allow *you* to choose what to include, others ask that you choose according to particular guidelines (for example, pieces that demonstrate your ability to conduct research, to put a lesson plan together if it's a teaching portfolio, or to revise). It's important that you understand what kind of portfolio your instructor is requiring and why. We'll talk about why later. Let's look first at the different kinds of portfolios you might be asked to assemble.

Types of Portfolios

It's important here to distinguish between *unevaluated* and *evaluated* portfolios. An unevaluated portfolio would be one in which you are collecting all your work for the course, like a journal or working folder, but your instructor will not be evaluating the material. You keep class notes, doodles, drafts of essays, exercises, and anything else that relates to the course. From that folder, you then might be asked to *choose specific assignments*, continue working on them, and turn them in for your final portfolio. A final portfolio is one type of evaluated portfolio. Your instructor either gives you the evaluation criteria for it or helps the class develop those criteria with him or her. You turn in selected pieces from the course, either freely chosen by you or required by your instructor. The work is "final" in that you have stopped revising, done your best to make it as effective as possible, and are ready to have it graded. Unevaluated portfolios, then, are places in which you experiment with, collect, and play around with your ideas and your writing, not worrying about evaluation as much as you would when you assemble an evaluated portfolio. All the activities in this book, for example, would be part of a writing journal or working folder that your instructor might not evaluate. Then, as you develop essays from those exercises, you revise them into final products that your instructor can grade.

Unevaluated Portfolios

The unevaluated portfolios you are most likely to encounter in your college writing are the following:

- **A journal or working folder.** In this type of unevaluated portfolio, you keep all your work for your writing course—everything that you do in and out of class, all your assignments and drafts. It's a place where you can track your progress as a writer because you have everything there. Some instructors ask you to turn this type of portfolio in for a holistic grade (that is, the entire body of work is evaluated, not individual pieces), based on criteria that are different from the criteria used for evaluating a portfolio of final drafts (for example, in evaluating a writing journal, your instructor might consider whether you've completed all the assignments, taken risks in your writing, and experimented).

- **A learning portfolio.** For this type of unevaluated portfolio, you collect materials from your course and possibly other places that reflect something about your learning process. Let's say your writing instructor wants you to keep a record of your learning in another course, such as sociology. You might include class notes that changed the way you understood a concept, restaurant napkins scribbled with conversations you've overheard, a paper you've been assigned to write, and some reflections on how the theories you've been learning affect how you perceive your world. You can include both print and nonprint materials, such as photos or music.

Learning portfolios often allow for free choice, so you have to carefully select what you will include and why. This type of portfolio may be helpful as you apply the concepts you learn in this course—about inquiry, essay writing, and reflection—to another course.

Evaluated Portfolios

Evaluated portfolios include the following types:

- **A midterm portfolio.** As the name suggests, you assemble this portfolio at midterm. Your instructor might ask you to include particular assignments—such as your two best reading responses and a revised essay—and write a cover letter that explains, for example, what you've learned about writing that is reflected in these pieces. You might also be asked to evaluate the portfolio yourself and discuss your goals for the rest of the course. A midterm portfolio might be evaluated, but it might also be used as a practice run for the final portfolio at the end of the course and not be evaluated.

- **A final portfolio—limited choice.** Your instructor may require you to include specific assignments and essays in the portfolio you turn in at the end of the course. Let's say your university's writing program requires all students to write a research essay in their first-year writing course and to demonstrate that they can use documentation effectively, support their claims with evidence, and do more than simply string information together. Your instructor, then, would ask you to include one or more research essays in the final portfolio so he or she can assess whether you have learned what is required. That might be the only required essay and you would have some choice about what else to include. Or you might be required to include a profile, an argument, and an ethnographic essay, as well. In addition, instructors might ask you to include a reflective essay with your "open choice" final portfolio (explained in more detail next). In general, a final portfolio emphasizes the final products of the course, the revised and polished work that shows what you've learned for the entire term.

- **A final portfolio—open choice.** Although you will revise and polish all your work, your instructor may ask you to choose your best writing for the course and not require particular essays. She might ask that you choose only from the essays you've written or that you choose from the informal writing you've done, as well (such as the writing exercises in this book). She may require a certain number of pages (say, twenty to twenty-five pages) or a certain number of assignments (three out of the five essays required in the course) or leave the length and number of assignments open. Here are a couple of examples: If you feel your research essay is better than your ethnographic essay, then you might include it and not work any further on your ethnographic essay. You might also include your personal essay, an argument, and your response to particular writing exercises. You would include these pieces because you believe they are your best work, but be sure you can talk specifically about *why* they are the best and *what* they show your instructor about what you've learned. For instance, do you want to show your growth, your success in using writing as inquiry, or what you've learned about crafting paragraphs?

Why Require a Portfolio?

Before we talk more about how to choose the materials to include in your portfolio, we should talk about why you will be expected to assemble one. If you are keeping an unevaluated portfolio, your instructor wants to emphasize your learning process at least as much as your final product. We rarely take the time to reflect on how we learn, but doing so can help you learn better in your other courses. Are you a visual learner? Do you learn best when you have a relationship with your teacher or when the teacher is more removed? If you learn more outside school, why? Learning portfolios enable you to develop even better learning strategies and understand why you might struggle with certain learning situations. The same is true for a writing journal or working folder. As you collect everything you do in a writing course, you can pause periodically and reflect on which writing strategies seem to sabotage your efforts, which seem to work well, how you might work through writer's block, or what principles about writing you've been learning. Many of the exercises in this book prompt you to reflect on your writing process, your reading strategies, and your learning and thinking, so if you've been doing them, you have already seen the benefits of reflecting on your process.

In both kinds of unevaluated portfolios, the *process* of whatever you're doing is being emphasized and valued. You don't have to worry about writing beautifully styled sentences the first time around or having a complicated reading all figured out the first time through. An unevaluated portfolio allows for—in fact encourages—the messiness of writing and thinking instead of focusing only on polished work. These kinds of portfolios emphasize risk, experimentation, and reflection on the process of writing and learning, all of which are central to the ideas in this book. These types of portfolios, then, reflect and reinforce what you've been learning about writing so far.

Evaluated portfolios are important for very similar reasons. To get your drafts ready to be evaluated, you are encouraged all term to experiment, rewrite, and critique them. In fact, most of the term you are working in your writing journal, exploring ideas, commenting on peers' drafts in workshops, revising your own drafts, and taking them apart again, all in an effort to learn more about writing and make your essays more effective. Portfolios allow you to do all that over a long period and in a relatively "evaluation-free" zone, so you are graded based on your final product at the end—not in the middle—of the process.

Your final product, though, is the result and reflection of all that work you did throughout the semester. In addition, the reflection exercises in this book have had you thinking about your learning all term. You will be more conscious of the writing and reading strategies that work best for you, and so will be better prepared to write the reflective essay that your instructor may require in the portfolio.

Of course, the final product is what is evaluated in a final portfolio, so while this kind of portfolio reinforces the process of inquiry and reflection, it also emphasizes the way a writer crafts a sentence, organizes an essay, and explores an idea. A portfolio, then, allows an instructor to evaluate *both* the process of writing and the quality of the final product.

Organizing Portfolios

Because a writing portfolio emphasizes the *process* of writing and learning as much as the final product, you'll want to keep your course materials—that is, the materials that reflect your process—organized. Whether or not your instructor assigns a journal or working folder, it's a good idea to keep one yourself. You can do this on the computer or in a notebook. You can organize your writing journal or working folder in several ways, including these options:

1. **Organize by chronological order.** Keep everything that you do in the course in the order you complete it.

2. **Organize by assignments.** Within each category, include all the writing you've done (fastwriting, drafts, exercises), peer and teacher responses, notes, research materials, and so on. As an example, your portfolio might be broken out into the following categories:

   - Profile
   - Ethnographic essay
   - Review
   - Argument
   - Reflective exercises
   - Reading responses
   - Essay exam

3. **Organize by subjects.** Here you place your writing into categories defined by the subject or theme of the writing. For example:

   - Racism (profile, research essay)
   - Italy trip (personal essay, review, argument)

   With this approach, you have a better sense of how you've explored a topic through different genres, comparing what you've learned about the subject as well as about the form.

4. **Organize by stage of process.** Here you place your writing into categories based on what place in the writing process it falls, starting with your

fastwriting and journal writing and ending with your final drafts and reflective writing. For example:

- Fastwriting/journal writing
- Exercises
- Sketches
- Early drafts
- Peer responses
- Instructor responses
- Revisions
- Final drafts
- Reflective writing

You can also create your own categories to organize your class work. However you choose to organize your writing, be sure to keep everything you write for the course; don't throw anything away. If you are using a computer, *save all of your writing files and keep a separate backup copy.*

If you are expected to include a reflective letter or essay as a preface to your portfolio, it's a good idea to create a separate section in your journal or folder for all the reflective writing you've done in the class. You can do all the reflective exercises in that separate section, or you can include them for each separate assignment. However you do it, keeping your reflective writing in one place will make it easier to compose your reflective letter or essay.

Writing a Reflective Letter or Essay

You may have to preface your final portfolio with a letter or essay that introduces the pieces you've included and reflect on what you've learned about writing, reading, and inquiry. For some instructors, this letter or essay is crucial in evaluating

TYPICAL PROBLEMS IN REFLECTIVE ESSAYS/LETTERS

- Use of overly general and vague comments.
- Not enough specific details.
- Giving the teacher only what you think he or she wants, whether it's true or not.
- Critiquing the course (usually this is reserved for end-of-term evaluations that are confidential and anonymous); it's not wise to risk criticizing the person who is evaluating you.
- Comments that suggest you don't take the assignment seriously.

the whole portfolio because it gives coherence and purpose to the material and articulates what you've learned. In my own classes, the reflective essay can make the difference of half a letter grade in the overall evaluation of the portfolio. As always, clarify with your instructor what is expected in the reflective letter or essay and how it will be weighed in the portfolio grade. While some instructors require a five- to seven-page essay or letter that begins the portfolio, others may require a prefatory letter for *each piece* you include in the portfolio. Some want only a reflection on the writing process for each essay; others may want only a narrative of how your thinking changed about each subject you wrote about. Regardless, you'll want to spend some time going through your writing journal or folder and reflecting on what you notice. Here are some questions that might help:

- **Patterns.** As you flip through the pages of your writing journal or folder, what patterns do you notice? What seems to happen frequently or stand out to you? For example, you might notice that you always begin your essays the same way, or you ended up writing about the same subject the whole semester without realizing it, or you got better at organizing your essays and using significant detail.

- **Reflective writing.** As you look only at the reflective writing you've done throughout the course (and the reflective exercises in this book), what do you notice? What five things have you learned about writing, reading, and inquiry based on that early reflective writing?

- **Change over time.** How did you describe your writing process (and/or reading process) at the beginning of the course? How would you describe it now? If it has changed, why and how?

- **Writing principles.** List five to seven principles about writing that you have learned in this course—the five to seven most important things you've learned about writing, reading, and inquiry. Or, list five to seven strategies for writing and reading that you will take with you into other writing situations.

- **Revision.** For each of the essays you are including in your portfolio, what would you do differently if you had more time?

- **Writing processes.** For each of the essays in your portfolio, describe the writing and thinking process that led to the final product. Emphasize the most important changes you made and why you made them.

- **Most and least effective writing.** Which essay in the portfolio is your strongest? Your weakest? Why?

- **Effect of peer response.** How have your peers and other readers of your work affected the revisions you've made?

- **Showing what you've learned.** What does your portfolio demonstrate about you as a writer, a student, a reader, a researcher? How? Be as specific as possible.

- **What's missing.** What is *not* reflected in your portfolio that you believe is important for your instructor to know?

- **Expectations.** How does your portfolio meet the expectations for effective writing defined in your class?
- **Applying the textbook.** How have you applied the principles about each essay form that are outlined in this textbook?
- **Personal challenge.** In what ways did you challenge yourself in this course?

Your instructor might ask you to address only three or four of these questions in the letter or essay itself, but it's a good idea to do some fastwriting on all of them. Doing so will help your essay or letter be more specific, thoughtful, and persuasive.

As with any essay, you'll want to take this one through several revisions and get feedback from readers before you include it in the portfolio. Your instructor might even ask you to workshop a draft of this with your group. If you've done some fastwriting on the preceding questions, you are in good shape to compose a first draft of your reflective letter or essay. Keep in mind who your audience is—your teacher, teachers unknown to you, and/or your peers—and address what that audience expects. Be as specific as possible, citing examples from your work and drawing on the terms and principles you've discussed in class and read about in this book.

If you've been doing reflective writing all term, you will have plenty of material to draw from to make your reflective essay or letter concrete, substantive, and as honest as it can be (given the circumstances). You'll probably surprise yourself with all that you've learned.

Final Preparations

Before you turn your portfolio in, take time to proofread it carefully, possibly asking one of your peers for help. Check again to be sure you've met all the criteria for the portfolio, including what is required, assembling it appropriately, and formatting it as required. This is work that you are proud of, so the way you present it should reflect that pride. It should meet high standards for presentation and quality.

Appendix B

THE ANNOTATED BIBLIOGRAPHY

Michelle Payne, English Department Chair, Boise State University

What Is an Annotated Bibliography?

You've had experience putting together a Works Cited or References page for your research essays, but you may not have had experience writing an annotated bibliography, which includes descriptions and comments about each of your sources. It is a list in which each citation is followed by a short descriptive and sometimes evaluative paragraph or annotation. Many scholars use published annotated bibliographies during their research to help them narrow down the material that seems most relevant to their work, but you might be asked to write one as part of a larger project for a class, sometimes in preparation for a literature review or a research proposal. Annotated bibliographies, then, can serve a lot of different purposes, so if you are assigned one, be sure you understand your role as a researcher and writer.

We will examine four types of annotated bibliographies in this appendix.[1] Their purposes include indicating content and coverage, describing thesis and argument, evaluating the work, and a combination of these three. If you have looked at published annotated bibliographies, you have probably seen one of these types. When you are assigned to write an annotated bibliography, you'll need to decide which of the following four forms is the most appropriate, but you can also consider using these at various stages of your own research process.

Indicative Bibliography. Are you being asked *to indicate* what the source contains or simply to identify the topic of the source, but *not to evaluate or discuss the argument and evidence*? If so, explain what the source is about (e.g., "This article explores gender in Shakespeare's tragedies."). List the main ideas it discusses—this may include chapter titles, a list of authors included if the source is an anthology, or the main ideas included in the subsections if it's an article (e.g., "Topics covered include male homosocial desire, women as witches, and conceptions of romantic love."). Usually, in a descriptive annotation, you don't evaluate the source's argument or relevance, nor do you describe its overall thesis.

---

[1]The four forms discussed are found on the Writing Center website for the University of Wisconsin–Madison (http://www.wisc.edu/writing/Handbook/AnnBib_content.html).

WHY WRITE AN ANNOTATED BIBLIOGRAPHY?

- It can help you compile a list of sources on your subject that will need to be sorted through later. It can also help you decide if you want to return to a source later in your process.
- If you have been keeping a dialogue journal for your research project, you can refer to it in composing these annotations. This type of bibliography can help you further think through your own developing thesis or conclusions.
- This type of bibliography will help you develop your own thesis, and it will help you write a literature review, as well.

Informative Bibliography. Are you being asked *to summarize the argument* for each source? If so, briefly state each work's thesis, the primary assertions and evidence that support the main argument, and any conclusions the author makes. You are not evaluating the effectiveness of the argument, nor are you delineating the content of the source (as you would in an indicative form); instead, you are informing your audience about the works' arguments and conclusions.

Evaluative Bibliography. Are you being asked *to evaluate the sources* you find? If so, your annotations will include a brief summary of the arguments and conclusions and then move on to critically evaluate them: How useful is the source to your particular project? What are the limitations of the study or argument? What are the strengths? How reliable are the conclusions? How effective are the research methods? The criteria you use for evaluating each source depend on the purpose of the bibliography—whether you are compiling it to help focus your research project and sort out the most important articles or you are writing it to help others decide what is most relevant in the subject area. Be sure you are clear about the evaluation criteria.

Combination of Types. Are you being asked *to be both informative and evaluative*? Many annotated bibliographies have multiple purposes, so you will be combining the preceding forms. Because most annotations can be up to 150 words, you need to devote only a sentence or two for each purpose—in other words, a few lines to summarize and describe, a few to evaluate and comment. However, you may be told exactly what to include in the annotations and how many words or sentences to use. Your instructor might, for example, ask that you write one sentence summarizing each work's argument and then another sentence describing how the work relates to your own developing thesis.

How to Write an Annotated Bibliography

Before you can begin writing an annotated bibliography, you must choose a subject on which to focus. From there you will move to gathering materials, applying reading strategies, and finally writing the annotated bibliography.

Gathering Materials

See Chapter 11, "Research Techniques," to help you find material relevant to your subject. Are you supposed to find a wide range of materials, such as reviews, scholarly articles, and books? Are you to focus only on materials from the last five years? What are the parameters for your research? Be sure to clarify these issues with your instructor.

Reading Strategies

You'll again use the critical reading strategies you've learned as you read the sources you've decided to include in your bibliography. If the materials you've gathered will later become part of a research essay, then you will be taking notes and writing about them as discussed in Chapter 11. But to create your annotated bibliography, you'll have an additional purpose for reading your sources. If you simply need to describe the content of the sources (indicative form), you will do little critical evaluation; instead, you'll focus on explanation. Once you determine the focus for your annotations, use the following questions (which apply primarily to evaluative forms of annotation, but also can help with informative and indicative forms) to guide your reading.

- Who is the intended audience for this article, review, or book?
- What central research question or claim does the material address? Write it out in one or two sentences.
- What kind of evidence is used to support the conclusions, argument, and thesis? How valid is it, given what the intended audience values? For example, literary examples wouldn't be taken seriously as evidence in a biology paper, nor would anecdotal evidence about an experiment.
- How effectively has the author addressed the central question or claim?
- Sketch out the main argument in a brief outline. Note the main subjects covered, the authors listed (if it's a collection of articles), and the general organization of the work.
- What is known about the credibility of this author(s)? Have you seen her name appear in other works on this subject? Is she publishing in her area of expertise?
- Note the dates of publication, usually on the copyright page. Is the material current? Does it need to be? Is this a revised edition?
- Compare the source to others on the same subject. Are the ideas similar enough to suggest that this author is working with accepted knowledge?
- If they aren't, do you find them valid, significant, or well researched? Is one source on this subject better than another, and why or why not? Does the source build on the ideas of others, critique them, and add new knowledge?
- How effectively is the source written?

■ If you can, try to find reviews of the material or commentaries from other scholars in the area. This will give you a sense of how the work was received, what (if any) controversy it has generated, and what about it has been lauded and/or criticized.

Writing the Annotated Bibliography

Because annotations are so brief, it's tempting to think that they are easy to write. But, as in any writing project, you need to have a lot of material to draw from—in this case, substantive notes and reflective writing about each work. It is better to work from abundance than from scarcity—remember, you need material to work with if you are going to identify what's worth keeping and what should be dropped.

Length. Depending on the requirements for and purposes of the annotations, each entry could be one paragraph or only a few sentences, so choose your words carefully and use specific details judiciously. Clarify with your instructor the kind of writing style he expects; that is, does he want brief phrases, almost like a bulleted list of main points, or full sentences and paragraphs?

Content. Begin with the proper citation form for the source, following the guidelines for the specific documentation style your instructor requires (APA or MLA). Organize this list alphabetically. After each source, compose a paragraph or two that addresses your purpose for the bibliography. That purpose, again, will depend on the requirements your instructor has given you. If you are describing the content of the source, for example, begin with an overview of the work and its thesis; then select the specific points you want to highlight about it (such as chapter titles, subjects covered, authors included). If you are explaining the main argument of the work, begin with the central thesis and then include the main claims, evidence, research methods, and conclusions. Finally, if you are evaluating the source, add comments that summarize your critique.

Sample Student Annotated Bibliography

In the example that follows, Lauren Tussing wanted to apply what she's learned about feminist theory to the film *Lost in Translation*, and her annotated bibliography helped her focus her research question and decide which of the sources would be most useful in composing her essay. Notice that she has written an annotated bibliography that combines the informative and evaluative forms—she primarily summarizes the main argument of each source and then discusses its relevance to her research project.

Lauren Tussing

Instructor Michelle Payne

Engl 497

18 April 2004

Annotated Bibliography

Doane, Mary Ann. "Film and the Masquerade: Theorising the Female Spectator."

Feminism and Film. Ed. E. Ann Kaplan. Oxford: Oxford, 2000. 418–36. Print.

This is an article in a collection of articles on feminist film theory. In the essay, Doane works to create a theory for the female spectator, moving away from prior focus on the male spectator. Doane does, however, reintroduce the idea of Laura Mulvey's binary opposition of passive/female and active/male that she introduced in her essay "Visual Pleasure and Narrative Cinema." Doane applies the notion of distance to Mulvey's binary opposition.

This essay, written for an academic audience, is esoteric and sometimes difficult to understand, but it might be helpful for my paper if I decide to talk about the female spectator. Despite my difficulty with this essay, Doane did give me some ideas about how to think about *Lost in Translation*, the film that I discuss in my essay. A woman directs this film, so I wonder how her direction affects the gaze. Is there a uniquely female gaze for this film? Or does the film conform to the male gaze? How might viewers, both male and female, gaze upon this film?

Gaines, Jane. "White Privilege and Looking Relations: Race and Gender." *Feminism*

and Film. Ed. E. Ann Kaplan. Oxford: Oxford, 2000. 336–55. Print.

This essay, also included in the same collection as the above essay, argues that psychoanalysis isn't a good way to critique films, particularly because it overlooks racial and sexuality issues. Even when theorists use psychoanalysis to describe black family interaction, they impose "an erroneous universalisation and inadvertently reaffirm white middle-class norms" (337). When feminist theory uses gender first and foremost in discussing oppressions, it "helps to reinforce white middle-class values" (337). Also, Gaines argues, because feminist theory universalizes white middle-class values, it ideologically hides other forms of oppression from women.

This essay has given me new ideas about how to read *Lost in Translation*. Although I wasn't initially going to talk about issues of race, I might want to. Race actually plays a big role in the movie because it is about white people in an Asian country. Also, I think this essay is helpful in its critique of psychoanalysis. In my research of feminist film theory, I have found that you can't escape psychoanalysis. I don't particularly like psychoanalysis, but I realize that it is an important theory to understand. It is at the basis of many articles on feminist film theory. However, I don't think I will be discussing psychoanalysis in my essay.

Jayamanne, Laleen, ed. *Kiss Me Deadly: Feminism and Cinema for the Moment.*
　　Sydney: Power Institute of Fine Arts, 1995. Print.

　　This is a collection of articles about feminism and film. The articles in this book focus mostly on directors, such as Kathryn Bigelow, Rainer Werner Fassbinder, Alexander Kluge, and Nicolas Roeg. Before looking at this book, I had never heard of any of these directors. I didn't find this book particularly helpful, especially because, as Jayamanne notes in the introduction, some of the directors and films discussed are "foreign to the semi-official canons of feminist film theory" (14).

Johnston, Claire. "Dorothy Arzner: Critical Strategies." *Feminism and Film.*
　　Ed. E. Ann Kaplan. Oxford: Oxford, 2000. 139–50. Print.

　　In this essay, Johnston discusses Dorothy Arzner, a director from the 1920s to the 1940s who was nearly the only woman during her time to create a lucid bulk of work in Hollywood. Because not many studies have been written about Arzner—especially in male–dominated film studies—Johnston's purpose is to explore various approaches to Arzner's work and to discuss how her films are important for contemporary feminists.

This essay also gave me a new idea about how to look at the film I will be discussing in my paper. I'd like to discuss the director of *Lost in Translation*. Are her films, particularly *Lost in Translation*, important for contemporary feminists?

Kaplan, E. Ann, ed. *Women in Film Noir*. London: British Film Institute, 1978. Print.

This book is a collection of articles about film noir. Because the book is aimed at scholars who are educated in feminist film theory, it does not actually give a definition of film noir, and I didn't know what film noir was, so I looked it up in the Oxford English Dictionary. According to the Oxford English Dictionary, film noir is "a cinematographic film of a gloomy or fatalistic character." I don't think the film I will be discussing falls into this category, so I don't think I will be using this source for my essay.

———*Feminism and Film*. Oxford: Oxford University Press, 2000. Print.

This is a collection of articles on feminist film theory. Many of the essays in this book are esoteric and difficult to understand, but I think this is an invaluable resource to my research essay because of the range of essays it includes. The book is split into four phases: (1) Pioneers and Classics, (2) Critiques of Phase 1 Theories: New Methods, (3) Race, Sexuality, and Postmodernism in Feminist Film Theory, and (4) Spectatorship, Ethnicity, and Melodrama. By employing these different "phases" of feminist film theory, the book allows the reader to see the conversations within feminist film theory and its subsequent evolutions. I have summarized a few of the articles contained in this collection above.

Kuhn, Annette. *Women's Pictures: Feminism and Cinema.* London: Verso, 1994.
Print.

In this book, Kuhn argues that "feminism and film, taken together, could provide the basis for new forms of expression, providing the opportunity for a truly feminist alternative cinema in terms of film language, of reading that language and of representing the world." The book provides a systematic view of film. First, Kuhn discusses the dominant cinema. Then, she explores "rereading dominant cinema" from a feminist stance. Finally, she discusses "replacing dominant cinema" with feminist film.

I think this book will be helpful when I attempt to understand where *Lost in Translation* fits into film culture. Is the film part of dominant cinema? How can it be read from a feminist viewpoint? How is it a feminist film? How isn't it a feminist film?

Appendix C
THE ESSAY EXAM

Michelle Payne, English Department Chair, Boise State University

The following table explains the differences between essay exams and the essays you write for class assignments. From this we can figure out which writing and reading strategies will be most useful when you're sitting in a classroom with only fifty minutes to craft an argument on one of Shakespeare's plays or apply an economic theory to a specific scenario.

	Essay Exam	Essay for Class Assignment
Time	Usually limited to a class period (60–75 minutes), within which time you have to generate ideas, focus, plan, draft, and revise.	Usually several days to several weeks to generate ideas, explore and focus them, draft, workshop, and revise.
Purpose	To show your instructor how well you know class material and how well you can *analyze and apply it.*	Depending on the subject, genre, and focus of the class, this can vary from demonstrating competency at certain writing strategies to mastering a particular genre to making a persuasive argument.
Choice	While you may have a choice of which essay questions you'll respond to, often your choice of subject is limited by the question. Within the question you might have some choice of texts or materials to which you will refer.	Often students have a wider range of choices for subjects when writing for a class assignment.

(continued)

	Essay Exam	Essay for Class Assignment
(continued)		
Process	Your writing process is truncated into a shorter period, so you might go right to drafting an outline, drafting the response to the question, and then revising. You won't have time to experiment or explore ideas; your goals are to demonstrate your knowledge, not explore it.	More time to explore ideas, experiment, revise, and get feedback from other writers.
Methods of Inquiry	You will have little if any time for reflecting or even exploring ideas; instead, you will have to focus on explaining and evaluating, stating a claim, and providing explanation and evidence.	At various times you will use all the methods of inquiry: exploring, reflecting, explaining, and evaluating. The methods used in a particular paper depend on the assignment, the audience, the form, and the subject.
Form	Depending on the nature of the exam question, the form expected is something similar to a five-paragraph thesis essay: an introduction that states your thesis; supporting paragraphs that "prove" it using details from class materials; and a conclusion that wraps everything up (this is not true for short-answer essay questions). Essay exams are often expected to be close-ended forms.	The form depends on the subject and audience—from narrative to thesis-example structure, open-ended to closed-ended form. You have much more flexibility in choosing a form that fits the material than in an essay exam.
Thesis	Many instructors expect a thesis statement in the first paragraph.	Some instructors expect a thesis to be implied (as in the personal essay and the profile); others expect it to be explicit (as in the critical essay). How explicit it is depends on the genre, purpose, audience, and subject.

How to Write Essay Exams

Essay exams and the essays you write for class assignments call for different forms of writing; therefore, they call for specific strategies, including some of the following.

Gathering Materials

Because the purpose of an essay exam is different from that of a regular essay, the sources of information are going to be different. This may seem obvious, but it's crucial to understanding how to prepare for the exam. For a research essay, textbooks are rarely considered good reference sources, and while class lectures can be used in a course paper, they cannot form the basis of the paper. Yet these sources are often the sole basis for essay exams, and you usually can't have these sources open at your side as you write. So how do you figure out what is important to focus on in this rhetorical context?

Let's talk first about the purposes of essay exams. For many instructors, the essay exam offers a forum for students to demonstrate one or more of the following achievements:

- Students *understand* the main course concepts.
- Students can *apply* those concepts to other kinds of information, situations, or problems.
- Students can *evaluate and support* their evaluation with relevant evidence and criteria.
- Students can *analyze* a subject; this includes *synthesizing and summarizing* a range of information, as well as *making connections* among the pieces of information by considering cause/effect and using comparison and contrast.

Anticipating the Exam

If you've been paying attention to the main ideas of the course and the methods of inquiry your instructor seems to value, then you are in good shape to anticipate the questions that might be on the exam. One of the best ways to prepare for an exam is to play the role of your instructor. Consider the following questions:

- What does she want you to learn and why?
- What kinds of questions has she asked on previous exams?
- What kinds of questions would best show how you've met the course goals?

After you've thought about these questions, generate a list of possible exam questions and then answer them, either alone or in a small study group. You'll quickly discover what you need to go back and learn in more depth. You may just find some version of these questions on the exam.

Because your instructor is your only audience and will be forming the questions, you might ask him about the kinds of questions you can anticipate: How long will they be? What kinds of questions will there be? What criteria will he use for evaluating the answers? And, if they are available, look over previous exams from the same course and instructor.

If you've been engaging in inquiry throughout the course, then you will most likely have a good grasp of the main ideas in the course and your judgments about them. Inquiry can reduce the amount of time you spend memorizing the course material. You will have already been doing more than simply collecting facts and theories while your instructor lectures; you will have been posing questions, making connections, evaluating, and exploring, and then reflecting on what you know and what more you need to know. You will, in short, understand the material. By the time you sit down to commit some key concepts and details to memory, you'll remember them better because you understand their purpose and relationship to each other.

Analyzing Essay Questions

When you get the exam, read through all of it before you do anything else, and consider the following factors before you start writing your answers:

Time. Make some choices about how much time you will spend on each question based on:

- **Point value.** How many points is each question assigned? Prioritize them based on how much they are worth so you spend more time on the questions that are worth more. If you run out of time, then the questions you haven't responded to won't hurt you quite as much.

- **Priority.** Based on your priorities, divide the time up for each question. Spend more time on questions worth more points. Try to stick to the time limits you've given yourself.

- **Ability to answer the question.** If you have a choice of questions, consider carefully which one you will answer. To decide, quickly brainstorm in the margins your ideas for each question. That will tell you how much you know about each and whether you can do what the question asks. For example, you might be able to explain a concept but not compare it to something else, which is what the exam question actually demands that you do.

Key Phrases/Verbs. Once you've tentatively decided which questions you'll answer and how much time you'll devote to each, analyze the questions as quickly as you can. Your first step is to figure out what a question is asking you to *do*. Circle the key verbs that indicate your purpose when writing your answer. One way to understand what an essay question is asking you to do is to think of it in terms you already know: the ways of inquiring. In general, essay exams ask you to evaluate or explain. The accompanying table lists some of the verbs that imply one or the other way of inquiring.

Verbs of Evaluation	Required Action
Prove/justify/support	Offer reasons and evidence in support of a position.
Argue	Like *prove* and *justify*, this verb demands that you present an argument with reasons and evidence, but often the essay question gives you a position to take or asks you to choose a particular position.
Evaluate/assess	Make a judgment about the value or importance of a particular idea or subject, being clear about the criteria you're using for evaluation and supporting your claim with reasons and evidence.
Analyze	Usually this means you examine the parts of something—such as an argument—breaking it into sections and discussing the relationships among them; sometimes it may mean assessing those parts, or explaining your response. The rest of the question should indicate how much you should describe the parts and how much you should judge them.
Critique	To analyze and evaluate the subject in the essay question (an idea, argument, or theory).
Respond	Often this verb means that you must evaluate or justify your response to whatever the question asks of you.
Synthesize	Bring together two or more ideas/subjects/ concepts that haven't been considered together and do more than simply summarize and compare them; explain why you have brought them together and what new understanding emerges from that.
Verbs of Explanation (Information)	**Required Action**
Define	Describe and give the meaning of the idea presented, using authoritative sources, comparing and contrasting it to other ideas that are related.
Enumerate	Present the steps, sequence, or events involved in a particular process in some detail.

(continued)

(continued)

Verbs of Explanation (Information)	Required Action
Trace	Like *enumerate*, trace asks you to describe a series of events, but in chronological order.
List	Like *enumerate*, this verb asks you to name several things that are connected to a main idea presented in the question.
Summarize	Present the main ideas of an argument or concept in an organized way.
Review	Quickly summarize something.
Illustrate	Describe specific examples of something and their relationship to each other and the larger subject given in the question.
Identify	Like *illustrate*, this verb asks you to describe something and show its relationship to a larger idea, but often it implies looking at just one or two things.
Discuss	At length and from different perspectives, describe and analyze the idea presented in the question, using specific examples and evaluating the strengths and weaknesses.
Research	Just as it implies, gather sources and analyze what you've found.

Verbs of Explanation (Relationships and Connections)	Required Action
Compare	Illustrate the similarities of two or more things.
Contrast	Illustrate the differences of two or more things.
Relate	Show the relationships among various things.
Cause	Illustrate how various events relate to each other and resulted in a particular effect.
Apply	Illustrate how a theory or concept works in another situation.
Construct	Sometimes asks you to create a model or diagram through which to present your ideas.

Noun Phrases. Now that you know you need to contrast two different ideas, you need to be sure you know what to contrast. Some essay questions are rather long, and it may be hard to decipher what, exactly, the subject of your answer should be. Usually the clues are in noun phrases ("parts of the cell," "factors that led to the Civil War," "three influences on Sylvia Plath's poetry"). If the question begins with a quotation, read the question carefully to see whether it's background information for the question or something you need to address in your answer. Underline all the key noun phrases that indicate the ideas/concepts you are expected to discuss.

Organizational Clues. Based on the subject and purpose of your answer, how might you best organize it? You may need to use a cause-effect, step-by-step, or thesis/support structure. Sometimes the question itself implies a structure. For example, if you are asked to analyze the cause and effect of the Great Depression, you'll use a cause-effect structure. If you are asked to identify three influences on Sylvia Plath's poetry and argue which is most significant, you'll name those three, then devote a separate paragraph for each one to discuss in more detail, ending with the one you believe is most significant. Before you begin writing, sketch an outline that seems appropriate for the question.

Planning and Drafting

Once you have analyzed the exam question and you have a good sense of what you are being asked to do, you need to draft an answer in a very short period of time. Before you begin writing your response, jot down a rough outline of what you'll say and the supporting details and examples you'll use. Put your points in the order of most to least important in case you run out of time. That way you know you've touched on the most important ideas before time is up. Then draft an introductory paragraph that summarizes your argument and gets right to your thesis statement at the end. Your lead doesn't need an attention grabber as much as it needs a clear direction for the essay and a clear statement of your answer in one or two sentences.

Focus your writing on the body of the essay, developing your points as fully as you can. Keep in mind what your instructor will value the most, and use the key terms that are used in the exam question to show how you are directly addressing it. Essay exams necessarily demand clear, simple, and direct writing. Leave some time at the end to reread your answer, editing it carefully and considering which sections need more information. Sometimes it helps to write on every other line of notebook or blue-book paper so you have space to write in when you revise. If you don't finish your answer in time, briefly describe for your instructor what you would do if you had more time. Write as legibly as you can, minimizing scratch-outs and keeping in mind how many exams your instructor will have to read.

When you analyzed the essay question, you paid some attention to the kind of structure the question was probably demanding. You may need to use a cause-effect pattern, a step-by-step pattern, or a thesis/support structure. Within the body of that structure, though, keep each paragraph to one main idea, using specific details to illustrate or support your main assertions. Then try to connect the idea in the paragraph back to your main thesis, explaining why it's important to what you are trying to say ("Another example of this phenomenon is _____" or "An additional factor that complicates this process is _____"). Your conclusion, then, will tie the essay together with a sentence or two restating your main claim and telling your instructor what all this information means.

Credits

Text

Page 42. From "Many Undergraduates Work Long Hours Balancing Jobs with Studies" from *The Chronicle of Higher Education Almanac 2011*. Copyright © 2011, The Chronicle of Higher Education. Reprinted with permission.

Page 53. "On Being a Cripple" from *Plaintext* by Nancy Mairs. © 1986 The Arizona Board of Regents. Reprinted by permission of the University of Arizona Press.

Page 58. "The Importance of Writing Badly" by Bruce Ballenger. Used by permission of the author.

Page 63. From "Are Reality TV Crime Shows Continuing to Perpetuate Crime Myths?" by Elizabeth Monk-Turner from *The Internet Journal of Criminology*, © 2007. Used by permission.

Page 64. Devold, Troy, *Reality TV: An Insider's Guide to TV's Hottest Market*. Studio City, CA: Michael Weise Productions, 2011, p. 22.

Page 77. "Every Morning for Five Years" by Laura Zazulak. Reprinted by permission of the author.

Page 80. "One More Lesson" is reprinted with permission from the publisher of *Silent Dancing: A Partial Remembrance of a Puerto Rican Childhood* by Judith Ortiz Cofer (© 1990 Arte Publico Press–University of Houston).

Page 86. "This I Believe," is a registered trademark of This I Believe, Inc. Used with permission.

Page 116. "Museum Missionary" by Bruce Ballenger. Used by permission of the author.

Page 119. "Passengers" by Ian Frazier. Copyright © Conde Nast. All rights reserved. Originally published in *The New Yorker*. Reprinted by permission.

Page 122. "Learning About Work from Joe Cool" by Gib Akin, *Journal of Management Inquiry*, March 2000 9:57-61. Copyright © 2000 by SAGE Publications. Reprinted by Permission of SAGE Publications.

Page 161. Amazon Kindle Fire Review from CNET. Reprinted by permission of The YGS Group on behalf of CNET.

Page 162. Taken from the ROGER EBERT column by Roger Ebert. © 2000 The Ebert Company. Dist. By UNIVERSAL UCLICK. Reprinted with permission. All rights reserved.

Page 166. "Nickelback's 'Here and Now'" by Melinda Newman. Reprinted by permission of HitFix, www.hitfix.com.

Page 169. "Grand Theft Auto Takes on New York" a review of the *Grand Theft Auto IV* video game by Seth B. Schiesel, *The New York Times*, April 28, 2008. Copyright © 2008 The New York Times. All rights reserved. Used by permission and protected by the Copyright Laws of the United States. The printing, copying, redistribution, or retransmission of the Material without express written permission is prohibited. www.nytimes.com. Reprinted by permission.

Page 200. "Why College Football Should Be Banned" by Buzz Bissinger, *The Wall Street Journal*, May 8, 2012. Reprinted by permission of The Wall Street Journal, Copyright © 2012 Dow Jones & Company, Inc. All Rights Reserved Worldwide. License number 2910390101644.

Page 203. Power Point presentation, "Green Dining." Used by permission of UC Santa Cruz Dining Services.

Page 206. "Why Bother" by Michael Pollan. originally appeared in *The New York Times*, April 20, 2008. Copyright © 2008 by Michael Pollan. Used by Permission. All rights reserved.

Page 250. "PowerPoint Is Evil" by Edward Tufte. Reprinted by permission, from Edward R. Tufte, *The Cognitive Style of PowerPoint* (Cheshire, Connecticut, Graphics Press, 2003), as appeared in Wired Magazine, September, 2003.

Page 257. "Is Humiliation an Ethically Appropriate Response to Plagiarism" by Loye Young, www.adjunctnation.com. Reprinted by permission of Adjunct Advocate/The Part-Time Press.

Page 289. "The Bluebird" from *The Last Night of the Earth Poems* by Charles Bukowski. Copyright © 1992 by Charles Bukowski. Reprinted by permission of HarperCollins Publishers.

Page 292. "Lullaby" from *Storyteller* by Leslie Marmon Silko, copyright © 1981 by Leslie Marmon Silko. Used by permission of Viking Penguin, a division of Penguin Group (USA), Inc.

Page 300. "Who's Irish?" by Gish Jen. Copyright © 1986 by Gish Jen. First published in *The New Yorker*. Reprinted with permission by Melanie Jackson Agency, LLC.

Page 311. "Our Zombies, Ourselves" by James Parker, *The Atlantic Monthly*, April 2011. Copyright 2011, The Atlantic Media Co. as published in The Atlantic Monthly. Distributed by Tribune Media Services. Used by permission.

Page 343. "The Myth of the Latin Woman: I Just Met A Girl Named Maria" from *The Latin Deli: Prose and Poetry* by Judith Ortiz Cofer, 1995. Reprinted by permission of The University of Georgia Press.

Page 348. From *My Freshman Year: What a Professor Learned by Becoming a Student,* by Rebekah Nathan. Copyright © 2005 by Rebekah Nathan. Used by permission of the publisher, Cornell University Press.

Page 390. "Bumble Bee Math," *National Geographic Magazine*, February 2012. Gretchen Parker/National Geographic Stock. Used by permission.

Page 392. "Facebook with Care: Social Networking Site Can Hurt Self-Esteem" by Stephanie Pappas, in *LiveScience*, February 6, 2012, www.livescience.com. Reprinted by permission of TechMediaNetwork, Inc.

Page 396. "The Impact of Social Media on Children, Adolescents, and Families" by Gwenn Schurgin O'Keeffe, et al. *Pediatrics*, April 1, 2011, Vol. 127, No. 4. Copyright © 2011 by the AAP. Reprinted by permission.

Page 405. "Pediatrics Gets It Wrong" by John Grohol, Psych Central. www.psychcentral.com. Used by permission.

Page 414. GOOGLE is a trademark of Google Inc.

Page 445. GOOGLE is a trademark of Google Inc.

Page 447. Courtesy of EBSCO.

Photo

Page 2. Radius/SuperStock

Page 9. Stanca Sanda/Alamy

Page 38. Stockbyte/Getty Images

Page 39 (l). Andrija Markovic/Can Stock Photo

Page 39 (m). Gillmar/Shutterstock

Page 39 (r). Andrija Markovic/Can Stock Photo

Page 49. Bruce Ballenger

Page 56. Image Courtesy of The Advertising Archives

Page 70. Bruce Ballenger

Page 76. Originally published in the *Unexpected World of Nature # 3* (Thirteen/WNET, 2008). Copyright © 2008 Josh Neufeld

Page 78. "Mable" Laura Zazulak

Page 84. Lauren Fleishman Photography

Page 89. Rottenman/Fotolia

Page 110. Jacques Jangoux/Photo Researchers, Inc.

Page 115. Infographic World, Inc.

Page 127. National Archives. ARC Identifier 518914

Page 154. Paramount Pictures/Everett Collection

Page 159 (bl). Dorothea Lange/Library of Congress, Prints & Photographs Division, FSA/OWI Collection, [LC-USF34-9095]

Page 159 (ml). Dorothea Lange/Library of Congress, Prints & Photographs Division, FSA/OWI Collection, [LC-USF34-9097-C]

Page 159 (tl). Dorothea Lange/Library of Congress, Prints & Photographs Division, FSA/OWI Collection, [LC-USZ62-58355]

Page 159 (mr). Dorothea Lange/Library of Congress, Prints & Photographs Division, FSA/OWI Collection, [LC-DIG-fsa-8b29516]

Page 159 (tr). Dorothea Lange/Library of Congress, Prints & Photographs Division, FSA/OWI Collection, [LC-USF34-9093-C]

Page 161. Amazon Kindle Fire Review from CNET. Reprinted by permission of The YGS Group on behalf of CNET.

Page 163. Everett Collection

Page 168. Rosie Greenway/Getty Images

Page 189. Paramount Pictures/Everett Collection

Page 190. Chris Pizzello/AP Images

Page 192. James Nesterwitz/Alamy

Page 199. Alexandra Muresan, www.ixycreativity.ro

Page 212 (l). Benjamin Damm

Page 212 (r). Benjamin Damm

Page 213 (bl). Benjamin Damm

Page 213 (br). Benjamin Damm

Page 213 (tl). Benjamin Damm

Page 213 (tr). Benjamin Damm

Page 219. Library of Congress, Prints & Photographs Division, FSA/OWI Collection, [LC-USF34-014113-D]

Page 234. Don Ryan/AP Images

Page 240. Photo B.D.V./Corbis

Page 249. Joe Heller/PoliticalCartoons.com

Page 251. AP Images

Page 284. Richard Megna/Fundamental Photographs, NYC

Page 290. Illustration by Monika Umba, www.umbastudio.com

Page 311. Sveinung Svendsen/IFC Films/Everett Collection

Page 315. *Young Ladies on the Banks of the Seine River* (1856), Gustave Courbet. Oil on canvas. Petit Palais, Musée Des Beaux-Arts De La Ville De Paris. The Bridgeman Art Library/Getty Images

Page 336. Adrian Sherratt/Alamy

Page 341. "Visual Ethnography of Jugglers" courtesy of Jill Blaeser, Emily Keenan and Caitlin Sidey

Page 342. Greg Smith/Corbis

Page 352. Eric O'Connell

Page 384. Blend Images/SuperStock

Page 390 (graphics). Lawson Parker/National Geographic Stock. Used by permission.

Page 390 (photo). Airborne Images/Alamy

Page 440. Moschen/Shutterstock

Page 458. Robert Bull

Page 461 (l). Brian Jackson/Fotolia

Page 461 (m). Tim/Fotolia

Page 461 (r). Xuejun li/Fotolia

Page 476. Andy Sotiriou/Photodisc/Getty Images

Page 532. Stockbyte/Getty Images.

Page 557 (b). Rafael Ben-Ari/Fotolia

Page 557 (m). DelMonaco/Shutterstock

Page 557 (t). Steven Russell Smith Photos/Shutterstock

Page 574. Goodluz/Shutterstock

Inquiring into the Details icon. Frederick Bass/Getty Images

One Student's Response icon. Purestock/Getty Images

Writing Beyond the Classroom icon. Fuse/Getty Images

Index